legal **skills**

Braboeuf Manor
Portsmouth Road
Guildford
Surrey GU3 1HA

legal skills

EMILY FINCH | STEFAN FAFINSKI

EIGHTH EDITION

The University of Law
Braboeuf Manor
Portsmouth Road, Guildford
Surrey GU3 1HA

OXFORD
UNIVERSITY PRESS

OXFORD

UNIVERSITY PRESS

Great Clarendon Street, Oxford, OX2 6DP,
United Kingdom

Oxford University Press is a department of the University of Oxford.
It furthers the University's objective of excellence in research, scholarship,
and education by publishing worldwide. Oxford is a registered trade mark of
Oxford University Press in the UK and in certain other countries

Fifth Edition 2015
Sixth Edition 2017
Seventh Edition 2019

Impression: 1

Public sector information reproduced under Open Government Licence v3.0
(http://www.nationalarchives.gov.uk/doc/open-government-licence/open-government-licence.htm)

Published in the United States of America by Oxford University Press
198 Madison Avenue, New York, NY 10016, United States of America

British Library Cataloguing in Publication Data
Data available

CIP data is on file at the Library of Congress

ISBN 978-0-19-289364-2

Printed in Italy by
L.E.G.O. S.p.A. Lavis (TN)

OUTLINE CONTENTS

DETAILED CONTENTS

ACKNOWLEDGEMENTS

We would like to thank everyone who has contributed to this edition, particularly our anonymous reviewers, our students, and the wonderful editorial team at OUP, especially Sarah Stephenson and Helen Swann, and the production team of Fiona Tatham and Brad Rau.

We'd also like to thank Matthew Walsh, a student at the University of Birmingham, for getting in touch and offering some very constructive and insightful suggestions for improvement which we have done our best to incorporate.

Em and Stef

GETTING THE MOST OUT OF *LEGAL SKILLS*

Legal Skills is a rich learning resource, enhanced with a range of features to help support a practical approach to learning. This guided tour shows you how to fully utilize the content and get the most out of your study of legal skills. Throughout the text you will find prompts to continue your development via the **online resources**.

www.oup.com/he/finch8e/

REINFORCE YOUR UNDERSTANDING through chapter summaries

The central points and concepts covered in each chapter are distilled into summaries providing a useful point for you to strengthen your learning.

READ & RESEARCH through further reading

Selected further reading is included at the end of chapters to provide a springboard for further study and to broaden your learning.

RECAP with self-test questions

Self-test questions in each chapter will help you assess your understanding of key skills, concepts, and your readiness to progress to the next topic. Answers are provided **online**, along with a commentary to help you understand how and why the correct answer was reached.

REVISE glossary terms

Key terms are highlighted in colour when they first appear and are clearly, concisely explained in definition boxes, and also collected in a glossary which can be found **online**.

APPLY YOUR SKILLS through practical exercises

Apply your understanding of the principles underpinning each skill, by practising them through the exercises provided throughout each chapter. You will find answers and further practical exercises online.

LAW UNIVERSITY LIFE demystified

Chapter 1 on 'Getting started' and chapter 10 on 'Study skills' help you develop a reflective approach to skills development and include new material on building good study habits, group working, and strategies for strengthening performance.

Lecture and tutorial videos provide insight into how to participate and best prepare to get the most out of your contact hours.

Screenshots from important electronic databases such as LexisLibrary and Westlaw Edge UK will help familiarize you with these vital online resources. There are also videos available demonstrating searches of the Westlaw Edge UK database.

Improve MOOTING SKILLS

Alongside chapter 19 on 'Mooting skills' you will find sample moots, including examples of mooting preparation plans, and skeleton arguments on the online resources.

Watch mooting in action with video clips of students demonstrating effective mooting strategies and illustrating the core skills of outlining submissions, dealing with judicial interventions, and handling case law.

Hone your ACADEMIC WRITING

Chapters on writing skills, referencing, essays, dissertations, and problem answers will help you develop and hone your writing skills, which you can take further with the **online resources** where you will find:

- Advice on good essay writing practice
- Videos on: how to research essays; how to approach and structure problem questions; and a video following one of the authors marking an essay and providing feedback
- Samples of good and bad answers to problem questions

Learn PRESENTATION and NEGOTIATION SKILLS

PRESENTATIONS

Alongside chapter 18 on 'Presentation skills', the **online resources** give a worked example of a presentation plan and examples of good practice in presentations.

There are also video clips of student performances demonstrating the desirable and undesirable characteristics of presentations, interspersed with comments from students on their own fears about delivering a presentation and their views on their own performances.

NEGOTIATION

To accompany chapter 20 on 'Negotiation skills' find hints and tips for undertaking negotiation and examples of scenarios for you to practise your negotiation skills on the **online resources**.

Also available are video clips of a negotiation interspersed with commentary on good and bad technique, bringing this activity to life and providing an engaging demonstration of different negotiation styles.

NEW TO THIS EDITION

- Fully reworked sections on the anatomy of an Act of Parliament and statutory instrument with up-to-date examples
- Fully reworked section on reading UK cases including a new section contrasting official judgments with law reports
- Further emphasis on the caveats on using the various rules of statutory interpretation and an illustration of the overlap between the mischief rule, the purposive approach, and the teleological approach
- Updated commentary on the likely impact of the Solicitors Qualifying Examination (SQE)
- Updated commentary on the progress of Brexit, the operation of the European Union (Withdrawal) Act 2018 (as amended), and the impact of the UK's withdrawal from the EU on the operation of the doctrine of precedent
- Updated examples and screenshots incorporated throughout chapters on finding legislation, finding cases, and finding secondary sources
- Expanded explanation of neutral citations and case referencing conventions
- New table of commonly encountered Latin and 'Law French' terms
- Expanded coverage of creating a bibliography in OSCOLA together with some practical tips on compiling the bibliography entries from footnote references
- Revised example moot problem, further guidance on courtroom etiquette, and forms of address
- Updated throughout to reflect the shift to hybrid and remote learning covering online and recorded lectures, online tutorials, study habits, group working
- Expanded coverage of reflective learning and self-evaluation together with more detail on understanding grade descriptors
- Completely rewritten chapter on revision and exams to reflect the increased use of take-home exams and multiple-choice tests.

INTRODUCTION

Every edition of *Legal Skills* has had some sort of lifebelt or buoyancy aid on the cover. Why do we have this strange obsession with floatation devices? Simply because the aim of *Legal Skills* has always been to provide you with a life-saving resource that will keep you afloat during your legal studies. The reason that we enjoy the images dates back to a question that someone asked us many years ago when we were putting together the very first edition: 'Why do you make such a fuss about skills? These students are at university. They ought to know how to study by now.' Our answer is that, yes, perhaps students *ought* to know how to write, reference, structure an argument, and do all the other things that are necessary to study the law effectively but if they don't know them it seems a bit unkind and unfair not to help them to develop the necessary skills. The swimming parallel that we make is that people *ought* to be able to swim but if they can't then it isn't really fair to push them overboard in the middle of the ocean. Why not? Because they are going to drown! Neither of us has ever been willing to stand by and watch students drown in front of us simply because they have never been taught the skills that are so necessary to engage in the study of the law. Of course this book covers a host of other skills as well.

The idea behind *Legal Skills* is that we thought there should be a book that you can consult to find out how to do the things that you need to be able to do in order to study the law, to perform effectively in assessment, to complete your law degree successfully, and either to prepare you for the professional stages of legal education and a career in the legal profession or an alternative career which makes the very best of the portfolio of skills you have developed throughout your legal studies. The skills that we cover in the book are important because it is not enough for you just to know the content of the law: to succeed, you must be able to find the law, explain it using appropriate language, criticize it and, most importantly, *think* about it. You should be able to find out what the law once was, evaluate whether you think it is currently effective and fair, and speculate about how it might develop in the future.

The first part of *Legal Skills* gets you started on your legal studies and then moves on to cover sources of law. This section of the book will enable you to understand where the law comes from, how to find it (in print and online), how to understand it, and how to use it. This focus means that there is some overlap in terms of content with textbooks on the English legal system. This overlap occurs because understanding matters such as hierarchy of the courts, the operation of precedent, and the way that judges interpret the law are essential both to learning about legal systems (hence their coverage in an English legal system textbook) and also to studying the law (which is why we cover them in *Legal Skills*). Our coverage of these issues is slanted towards a practical purpose: you need to know where the law comes from and how it is applied and interpreted in order to incorporate it into your coursework and exam answers. It is also the case that you will be expected to know these things by the time you enter into legal practice. As such, although there is this clear crossover with the academic study of how the legal system works, the ability to find and understand the law is an essential practical legal skill.

In the second part of the book, the focus shifts to academic legal skills. As you will see, the bulk of the chapters relate to improving your performance in assessment. This section of the book starts, however, with a consideration of study skills so the aim here is to help you to strengthen the way that you go about the everyday business of learning the law. Even if you are confident that you have already developed an effective approach to studying, it will be worth looking through this chapter as you may find some tips that will help you to study in an even more effective manner. This chapter also contains a section on reflective working, as well as guidance on the important skill of learning from feedback and using this to improve your performance and ultimately move your marks across grade boundaries. The chapter on writing skills is there since the ability to use language effectively is an essential skill for a lawyer. It is therefore of the utmost importance that you take time to learn how to construct a grammatical sentence now: not only will failure to use language correctly impact adversely on the marks that you receive in assessment, it is highly unlikely that prospective employers will bother to pursue an application that contains fundamental errors in the use of written language. There is a comprehensive chapter on referencing and avoiding plagiarism which reflects the concern that surrounds these issues: fear of being accused of plagiarism as a consequence of poor referencing is something that preoccupies many students. The chapter on legal reasoning and legal ethics is designed to help you engage with the law in more critical depth and to lead you to understand that judicial decision making is not just about the unthinking blind application of a set of rules. It also introduces you to the ethical principles to which all lawyers should subscribe and their fundamental importance in upholding public confidence in the administration of justice. The essay-writing chapter contains much advice on structuring an essay and putting together effective introductions and conclusions; areas which students have told us they find particularly troubling. The chapter on problem solving aims to provide a step-by-step guide to this important activity. We then have a chapter that focuses on revision and exams. Our experience in working with students towards exams suggests that a great many students approach revision without a clear idea of what they are trying to achieve other than simply to 'pass the exam'. We have sought to make a range of practical suggestions that will introduce variety into the revision process whilst ensuring that you will emerge at the end with a store of knowledge and a clear insight into how you might use this knowledge once the exam begins. The final chapter in the academic skills section of the book on dissertations acknowledges that the dissertation is more than a long essay: it is a challenging combination of research and writing skills that deserves separate focus over and above essay writing.

The final section of the book deals with the use of the law in three practical situations: presentations, mooting, and negotiation. The predominant means of assessment used at university is in written form but these activities are focused on your ability to present an oral argument. Presentation skills are important for everyone. It does not matter whether or not you intend to practise the sort of law that will involve appearances in court or, indeed, whether you intend to practise law at all: in most professions, the ability to deliver a clear and coherent presentation or simply to speak with confidence in front of others is highly valued. Mooting is also an important activity. Not only will it enhance your ability to research and analyse the law as well as developing your skills of oral presentation, it is also something that prospective employers are keen to see and there is a strong expectation that you should find opportunities to moot during your undergraduate studies. Despite the importance with which mooting is viewed, not all institutions teach students how to moot so we have aimed to create a guide that will take you through each of the stages involved in preparing for a moot and delivering your submissions. Negotiation is a core legal skill due to the ever-increasing importance of alternative dispute resolution. Although we argue that we are all instinctive negotiators, there is still much that we can do to develop this natural skill so the advice in the final chapter of the book is aimed at helping you to become more proficient in seeking creative ways to reach a solution that keeps all parties to the dispute happy and—if the negotiation concerns something contentious—out of the courtroom.

Throughout the book, we place a great deal of emphasis on practical activities. This is because we believe that people learn by doing things rather than by reading about doing things. After all, you wouldn't expect to be able to drive a car (safely) just because you had read a book that told you how to do it: you would expect to have to practise to build up the skills that you need. The same is true with your legal studies. The skills needed to find the law, extrapolate the key points, and craft them into a well-structured and focused essay or answer to a problem question are practical skills. The process of committing the law to memory, extracting it on demand, and using it to formulate a comprehensive and analytical essay under tight time constraints is a practical one. Most of the skills covered in this book are practical and require you to do something. For this reason, there is a range of practical activities for you to try out on the **online resources**.

As a closing point, we want to emphasize that our aim when we set out to write *Legal Skills* was to produce the sort of book that we would have wanted when we were undergraduate law students. Our aim is to create a book that answers every question that a law student could possibly want to ask about the business of studying the law, so we have tried to ensure that we have addressed as many of the points that students have asked us to explain to them over the years as we can—and to each of them, we are very grateful.

Enjoy the book: we really hope that you find it as useful as we want it to be.

Emily Finch
Stefan Fafinski

PART I

Getting started: Sources of law

This part of the book covers the skills that you will need to get started with your legal studies and to understand, use, and find various sources of law. The first chapter sets the scene for the rest of the book and deals with the common questions and concerns that students have when starting to study the law and beginning at university. The next three chapters cover the skills required to understand legislation as a source of law. This will include UK Acts of Parliament and delegated legislation as well as legislation that emanated from Europe. In chapter 2, the different types of legislation will be explained, and in chapter 3 you will learn the skills to find both the UK and European legislation discussed in the first chapter. chapter 4 will demonstrate how to use legislation, developing the skills you need to read and interpret legislation. The following three chapters will take a similar approach to building the skills required to deal with case law as a further source of law. Chapter 5 will explain the role of the common law, equity, and custom as case-based sources of law, as well as explaining the different courts that are involved in deciding cases. You will learn the skills to find cases from the UK, the European Courts, and the European Court of Human Rights in chapter 6. Chapter 7 will give you the skills to use cases, describing how legal principles can be extracted from a case and the extent to which those principles are binding on other courts in the future. Finally, in this part, chapter 8 will describe how books, journals, and official publications can be used as supplementary sources of law whilst chapter 9 will give you the skills you need to find these additional complementary resources.

Getting started

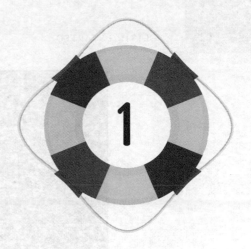

INTRODUCTION

The purpose of this chapter is to address some of the questions and concerns that students have about studying law and starting at university. In doing so, it serves as a starting point from which the skills discussed in the rest of the book can be understood. It will explain, therefore, something of the nature of the law and how it impacts on society before moving on to look at some of the practicalities involved in studying law as it considers how the degree is structured and how teaching and assessment will work. As you read through the chapter, you will see that there are references to other chapters in the book where you will find more detailed information about some of the subject matter.

In essence, this chapter will help students who have not yet started their degree or who are new to law to understand some of the key points about how the study of the law will operate. It has been written to address some of the common questions that students have when they embark on their degree. You should bear in mind, however, that each university has its own processes and terminology, so you might find that there are some differences to the way that things are described in the book. Nevertheless, this chapter will still serve as a useful guide to prepare you for the start of your studies.

1.1 THINKING ABOUT LAW

So you have decided to study law at university. This is an excellent choice. Law is a fascinating subject that has a real impact on society and everyone in it. It is also the gateway to a whole range of fulfilling and lucrative careers, not just in the legal profession but far beyond as the skills that you acquire on the law degree will be valued by employers across a broad spectrum of industries.

Before we get too far into this chapter, let's start with a question. Do you know who the man is in the photograph in Figure 1.1?

Take a close look . . . does he seem familiar at all? It is unlikely that you will recognize him but he is The Right Honourable The Lord Burnett of Maldon, and he was appointed Lord Chief Justice in October 2017. He and you have something in common. He studied law too. Like you, he started his degree not knowing very much about the law or how the legal system works. Furthermore, like you, he sat in a lecture theatre on the first day of his law degree and he did not know how to study the law or whether he would be any good at it. However, he learned, and he entered the legal profession, eventually being appointed to the most senior position in law in England and Wales.

Figure 1.1 Who is this man?
© Crown copyright, 2018

The point that we want you to appreciate here is that a whole world of possibility lies in front of you from this first step of starting a law degree. Everyone who has ever held the role of Lord Chief Justice, every senior judge, every barrister, and every solicitor started their study of the law in a lecture theatre at a university with all the doubts and questions that you have now. Your whole year group is made up of future lawyers and future judges as well as people who will excel in all sorts of other non-legal careers.

Everyone who sets out to study law does so without very much knowledge, without any in-depth appreciation of how the law works or what it does, and without knowing whether they will be any good at it at all. We all start from the same place and at times it will seem confusing or too difficult but your knowledge and skills will develop as your studies progress and you will start to gain a real understanding about how the law works. This book will help you with your studies. It covers a lot of the core information about the legal system and it explores all the key skills that you will need to study the law successfully.

1.2 WHAT IS LAW?

As you've decided to study law at university, it is likely that you already have some idea of what it involves but most students are still surprised when they realize just how great a role law plays in everyday life. Think about what you have done today since you woke up—you might have made a bowl of porridge, checked your emails, taken a bus journey, gone to the gym, bought a cup of coffee—all of these things are governed by the law. During the coronavirus pandemic, you may have had to wear a face mask to do some of those things, or some of them may have been prohibited entirely—by the operation of the law. If your porridge gives you food poisoning then you might turn to consumer law for compensation, the operation of email is governed by a complex set of laws that regulate the way that technology operates, the bus emissions are specified by environmental law and the driver has to abide by road traffic laws. You have a contract with the gym for your membership and with the coffee shop that sells you your cup of coffee. Law is all around us and it plays a role in virtually everything that we do, whether we realize that it is there or not.

The law plays a fundamental role in determining how society operates. It regulates where we can go, what we can do, and what we can say—in fact, it can be difficult to think of something that is not regulated by the law. Furthermore, it is not static. The law changes as society changes by responding to new problems that emerge and by adapting to new developments such those brought about by changes in technology. Think about how, for example, the law will need to alter in order to deal with artificial intelligence (AI). Could an AI algorithm commit a financial crime online? If so, who would be to blame? The law also creates change within society by establishing new rules that alter the way that people act and think: for example, the prohibition on smoking in public places both changed people's behaviour and resulted in a shift in attitudes towards smoking.

The law, therefore, seeks to regulate people's behaviour by establishing rules that determine how key aspects of everyday life function so that society will run smoothly. In this way, the law creates social order. For instance, just imagine the chaos that could ensue if we did not have road traffic laws. People would be able to drive on whichever side of the road they chose at whatever speed they wanted without having to stop at red lights or give way at junctions. Everything about the way that people use the roads is governed by the law and this reduces the danger involved in the use of cars and other forms of transport.

The law also regulates society at a higher level. The issues surrounding Brexit (which may or may not have been resolved by the time you read this book) concern the legal relationship between Britain and the European Union and is governed by the law. There are international laws that cover the way that different nations behave towards each other and that operate in relation to issues such as environmental protection and the use of military force. There are also laws that regulate the way that the Government behaves in relation to individuals, so that those in a position of authority do not exercise power in an arbitrary or abusive way. Criminal law sets the ever-changing boundaries of what conduct is prohibited and the punishments that different crimes attract. There are also laws that govern the way that organizations such as companies, factories, charities, places of worship, schools, and universities operate. There are laws that tell us where and at what time of day we can enter into marriage or civil partnership, limit what names we can give to our children, and determine what happens to our bodies after we die.

The law is everywhere.

Another characteristic of the law that makes it fascinating to study is that it does not cease to exist just because it is old or has not been used for a long time. Once a law has been created, it stays in force until it is repealed which can lead to some unusual situations. For example, a law created by Edward II in 1322 provides that all whales and sturgeon caught at sea must be offered to the monarch.[1] This law has never been repealed, and so it still applied in 2004 when a fisherman, Robert Davies, caught a 10-foot 264-pound sturgeon off the coast of Swansea. These valuable fish whose eggs are sold as caviar are usually only found in the Caspian Sea. Mr Davies duly contacted Buckingham Palace only to receive a reply advising him that the Queen did not want the sturgeon so he was free to dispose of it as he wished.

1.3 STUDYING LAW AT UNIVERSITY

Whether you came to university straight from school, or via college, or after a period away from study, it is likely that you will find it very different to your previous experiences of study. The emphasis at university is on independent study and equipping you with the skills you need to be able to operate as an autonomous learner after graduation: that is, someone with

---

1. Prerogative Regis of 1322, xiii.

the skills and confidence to learn new things for themselves without the need for instruction. The study of law at university also challenges you to be more evaluative and critical than you are likely to have needed to be in your previous studies. In other words, it will not be enough for you to learn simply what the law is on any particular subject; you will also need to be able to recognize its weaknesses, question its effectiveness, and suggest areas where it could be reformed. You will need to learn to look behind the law to the policy issues that led to its creation and to identify its purpose. These things can seem challenging to start with as they require so much more from you than simply learning a set of legal rules. You will also find that you have far more time for private study than you may have had in the past; typically, the approach at university shifts the emphasis to you to take responsibility for your own learning by building on the foundation of lectures and tutorials with your own reading and reflection far more than the earlier stages of your education did.

However, this does not mean that you are left without guidance or support. There will be plenty of people around you at university to make sure that you know what you are supposed to be doing and when you should be doing it:

- **Personal tutor/academic adviser.** The terminology varies between different universities but each student will be allocated a personal tutor or academic adviser who will meet with them soon after they arrive at university and at regular intervals throughout the year. Your personal tutor will be one of the lecturers in your school or department but they may never teach you because this is a pastoral role; in other words, this is a lecturer in your school or department who is there to ensure that you are navigating university life successfully. Their role is to help you to understand how university works, to discuss your progress with you, and to direct you to any other help that you need around the university. Ask them any questions at all—they are there to help you and they will point you towards the right person if they cannot answer the question themselves.

- **Module leader/convenor.** Every module has an academic in charge of it. They will usually be the person who delivers some or all of the lectures and who is responsible for disseminating information about the module, creating a module handbook, and updating the module area of the virtual learning environment with lecture slides. This is the person you should ask if you have any questions about a particular module.

- **Lecturers and tutors.** As the titles imply, a lecturer is someone who delivers lectures and a tutor is the person who conducts your tutorials. You should ask them any questions that you have about the specific sessions that they lead.

- **Law librarians.** Every library will have at least one specialist law librarian who will be able to help you to find the materials that you need to read for your classes and for your coursework. This includes online resources such as legal databases as well as finding cases, journals, and books in the library itself.

- **Administrators.** In addition to the academics who teach you, the university is staffed by a whole range of people in different administrative roles who support the academics in delivering your degree. These may be located within your law school or in the university more widely. It is well worth getting to know what the administrative support structure is at your university so that you know who you should approach if you have any questions about important things such as timetabling, finance, IT support, accommodation, and so on.

These are just some of the key people who you will encounter at university and remember that your institution may have slightly different roles. The important point to remember is that you should always ask for help if you are not sure about something. Far too many students do not feel comfortable approaching their lecturers, and this can mean that you are puzzling over something unnecessarily when there is someone who could easily and willingly answer your question.

As well as all these people, every university will have some sort of virtual learning environment that is a central source of information. This will usually have separate areas for each of the modules that you study where you will find materials such as module handbooks, tutorial questions, lecture slides and other online resources as well as details about your timetable and lecturer contact information. It is a really important source of information so make sure that you are clear about where to find it and how to use it from an early stage of your studies.

1.3.1 What about A level law?

One of the commonest questions that students ask at open day events is whether they need A level law and if it will help them to (a) get a place and (b) study law successfully at university.

There is no requirement for students to have A level law or any other prior legal study knowledge before starting a law degree. All law degree programmes are designed for people with no legal knowledge and will start from scratch to give you a foundation of understanding of what the law is and how the legal system works.

A level law may not be necessary, but is it helpful? Does the prior understanding of some areas of law plus the insight into how the legal system operates give students an advantage when they start a law degree? Unhelpfully, the answer to this question is both 'yes' and 'no'.

Let's start with the positives first. When you start a degree at university, there is a lot to learn and a lot of unfamiliar subject matter and terminology to master. Having a basis of understanding of the legal system and the language of the law will be reassuring and it will give you a little boost of confidence to find that some of the law that you are taught is already familiar. In that respect, therefore, an A level in law can get you off to a good start with your degree.

However, there is a downside to this. Students who have studied law at A level often struggle to adapt to the greater demands of undergraduate study, especially in the subjects that they have already studied at A level. It is surprising but true that students perform less well in modules where they have studied the subject matter as part of their A level. There seems to be two reasons for this: firstly, they feel that they have already mastered the content of the law and so they do not pay as much attention to it in their private study as they do to unfamiliar subjects and, secondly, they write about it in assessments in the same way that they were used to doing in their A level. Both of these things are understandable but they combine to create a situation in which previous study of law can be a disadvantage.

- **If you have A level law.** Treat it as a basis upon which to build but make sure that you do build on it rather than assume that what you know already will be enough. Always remember that your previous study of the law will have involved simplified versions of the concepts that you will encounter on your degree. Study every module as if the content was unfamiliar and, in particular, throw away your A level notes and make fresh ones as this will help you to engage at the right level of depth. When it comes to assessments, write essays and answer problem questions in line with the guidance you are given at university rather than sticking to the familiar techniques you used at A level as these will not be sufficient for the more rigorous demands of studying law at university level.

- **If you do not have A level law.** Don't worry, you don't need it. Students who have A level law have a slight head start in terms of terminology and some insight into the way that the law works but you will soon pick this up. It is important that you remember this, especially in the early weeks when you are starting to get to grips with new subject matter and terminology and particularly if you hear other students saying 'oh we did this at A level'. The degree is designed for people who have not studied law, so you will not be at a disadvantage and you will soon be equally familiar with the terminology and the operation of the legal system as those students who have studied some law previously.

1.4 WHAT LAW WILL I STUDY?

It is not possible for you to study all of the law that exists during the three or four years of your studies. Instead, the content of the law degree provides students with a grounding in basic principles of the law, an understanding of the operation of the legal system, and an ability to conduct legal research so that you have a foundation of knowledge upon which to build and the skills to find and understand other areas of law that you have not studied on the degree. In other words, the aim of the law degree is to equip you with an understanding of the building blocks of legal knowledge and the skills to supplement this by finding and understanding unfamiliar areas of law that are not taught as part of a degree programme.

For many years, this aim has been achieved by ensuring that all law students study the same 'foundations of legal knowledge' as a compulsory part of their degree, whatever university they attend. These subjects (also known as 'core subjects') were an essential ingredient of a 'qualifying law degree' (a law degree that enables you to pass on to the next stage of study that counts towards qualification as a solicitor or barrister). The core subjects were agreed to be an essential basis of legal knowledge and understanding by the two bodies that regulate the legal profession: the Bar Standards Board (BSB) and the Solicitors Regulation Authority (SRA). This meant that all law students at every university would study the same subjects which have to be passed with a mark of at least 40 per cent for a student to graduate with a qualifying law degree:

- Public law (including constitutional law, administrative law, and human rights)
- Criminal law
- The law of obligations (contract, tort, and restitution)
- Property law (also called land law)
- Equity and trusts
- Law of the European Union.

Every qualifying law degree will include these core subjects irrespective of which university you attend. Each university, however, will structure the law degree differently, so it is not possible to generalize about how these subjects will be spread out across the three or four years of your study. It is usual for the first year of the degree to be based upon some of these core subjects simply because they are such a good starting point for studying the law. You may also find that you have a module devoted to helping you understand the legal system and one in which legal skills are introduced; in fact, you may be reading this book as part of a legal skills module.

Aside from the core subjects, each law degree will also include a selection of other modules spanning a wide range of legal subject matter. Again, some universities offer a wider choice than others; it will depend on the expertise of the lecturers working in the law department. Common subjects include family law, medical law, company law, international law, the law of evidence, commercial law, environmental law, and intellectual property law, so there should be plenty of scope for you to choose subjects that are of interest to you. Many universities will also include the option for students to write a dissertation in their final year and this is an opportunity for you to select a topic for yourself and look at it in greater detail. You will find a whole chapter devoted to the process of researching and writing a dissertation later in this book (chapter 17).

This has been the basic structure for legal education for many years. However, legal education is undergoing reform as the way that people qualify as solicitors is scheduled to change from 1 September 2021 with the introduction of the Solicitors Qualifying Exam (SQE). The SQE is expected to comprise two stages that people wishing to practise as solicitors will need to pass. The first (SQE1) tests legal knowledge through multiple-choice questions. The second (SQE2) will assess legal skills and will have fifteen to eighteen exercises which cover a range of skills and practice areas including advocacy, negotiation, legal research, client interviewing, and legal drafting. You will find more information about the SQE and what, if any, impact it will have on you on the SRA website.[2]

Different universities have responded to these changes in different ways. Some universities intend to reformulate the structure and content of their law degree in response to the SQE whilst others take the view that their existing structure and content will, with a few amendments, be a really effective basis for students to tackle the SQE. After all, basis of legal knowledge remains unchanged: all that is different is that the SRA has changed the way that people qualify as a solicitor by removing the requirement of a law degree and replacing it with the requirement of legal knowledge and skills, howsoever acquired. This means that it is perfectly possible to take the SQE without ever having undertaken any formal study of law provided that sufficient knowledge and skills is acquired by some other means to pass the two stages of the SQE.

This change relates only to the route to qualification as a solicitor. The requirement of a law degree which covers the seven foundations of legal knowledge remains for those wishing to qualify as barristers.[3]

You will find more about the professional bodies' requirements for the academic stage of training on the relevant websites. It would be a good idea to familiarize yourself with these if you do aim to qualify as a solicitor or a barrister at the end of your studies. Irrespective of whether you take the solicitor or barrister route, or neither of them, the law degree will provide you with a strong foundation of knowledge of a range of law subjects along with a broad range of legal and transferable skills.

1.5 HOW WILL THE LAW BE TAUGHT?

Every university will have a slightly different way of structuring and teaching the law degree. A law degree is made up of 360 credits spread out over three years of study. Students taking a four-year sandwich degree will also study 360 credits over three years but with one year spent working in a professional setting or studying abroad. Each of the three years of study is further divided into modules. These are units of study on particular subjects within the law. This includes the seven core subjects discussed in the previous section plus a number of other modules often selected by the students from a range that are available. Each university makes its own decisions about which subjects are taught in which year and what subjects are offered to students outside of the core subjects. Each of these modules must be passed in order for the credits to be awarded and the pass mark for undergraduate study is 40 per cent. In other words, your law degree is divided up into a number of subject-specific modules, each of which must be passed, but the order of subjects and, to an extent, the choice of subject, will be different at different universities. For example, Student A at the University of A might study contract, crime, public law, and legal skills in their first year whilst Student B at the University of B might study English legal systems, contract, land, and tort. But whatever the method of organization within the degree, all students who qualify will have studied 360 credits from a range of compulsory and optional legal topics.

Law tends to be taught in quite a traditional manner at most universities, so you would normally expect that the majority of your teaching hours will be spent in large group teaching sessions (lectures) and small group classes (seminars, workshops, or tutorials). Many of these classes will take place in person but it is possible that you will also encounter online teaching,

2. <httpsı//www.sra.org.uk/students/sqe/> accessed 15 October 2020.

3. <https://www.barstandardsboard.org.uk/training-qualification/becoming-a-barrister.html> accessed 9 November 2020.

using video-conferencing platforms such as Zoom or Teams, or 'captured content' (recordings of lectures or other digital content that students can view in their own time). Whether these classes take place in-person, online or are pre-recorded, they will deliver the same content and it is important that you understand the different roles that lectures and small-group teaching sessions place in helping you to learn the law and to develop key legal skills.

1.5.1 Lectures

A lecture is a large group teaching session involving one lecturer who delivers a presentation for one or two hours with the help of some lecture slides to all of the students taking the module. The objective of a lecture is to communicate key pieces of information about a topic to the students to give them an overview of a particular area of law that they build upon in their private study time. It is important that you understand from the start that the lecture does not give you all the information that you need on a topic. It gives you an overview of a topic but you will need to add depth and detail to the information that has been provided. After the lecture, you will need to review your notes to fill in any gaps and then supplement the information that you have been given by reading the relevant chapter in the set textbook as well as any additional reading you have been given. You should read the section on making the most of lectures in chapter 10 for more information.

There are three main methods by which lectures can be delivered:

- The traditional approach is the in-person lecture which involves all the students sitting in a lecture theatre listening to a lecturer and taking notes. This is a timetabled event so everyone is present at the same time. The level of interaction will vary according to the lecturer's preferences. A more interactive lecture might involve the lecturer encouraging students to ask questions or setting activities for students to complete either on their own or in small groups whereas other lectures might offer no opportunity for interactions so your role as a student is to listen and take notes.

- Many universities use recorded lectures either as an alternative or in addition to in-person lectures. These tend not to be a timetabled event so offer students the flexibility to watch (and re-watch) at a time that suits them. The recording can be listened to in installments, paused to allow for notes to be taken and rewound so that points can be repeated. Some universities make recordings available for the duration of the module so that students can revisit them whenever they choose whilst other universities limit the availability of recordings to force students to study at a steady pace instead of watching all the recordings at the end of the module. As it is not a live event, there are no opportunities for interaction with the lecturer or discussion with other students. Some lecturers break the recording up into stages that are separated by activities that give students the opportunity to do something more active than just listening.

- An online lecture is a live event (although it may also be recorded for students to watch later) that takes place on one of the video-conferencing platforms. This is the virtual equivalent of a traditional lecture as all the students are present at the same time, listening to the lecturer and taking notes. Lecture slides can be used in the same way as they would in a live in-person lecture. The advantage that online lectures offer is that there is more opportunity for students to ask questions as these can be done by using a 'hands up' feature and speaking when invited to do so or by typing a question into the chat feature. This tends to be a less daunting prospect for many students than asking a question in a lecture theatre and it has the benefit of allowing you to clarify things that you do not understand at the time rather than having to remember to follow it up afterwards.

1.5.2 Tutorials, seminars, and workshops

Small-group teaching sessions are commonly used to help students deepen their understanding of topics covered in the lectures and are also used to give you the opportunity to practise and develop key skills such as analysing cases and answering problem questions. Terminology varies so these sessions may be called seminars, tutorials, or workshops at your university, but they are all essentially the same thing—smaller groups of students and a greater level of interaction than lectures.

The emphasis in these sessions is on preparation and participation. It is usual for students to be set a task to complete beforehand and for these to be discussed or developed in the session. Sometimes you might be asked to build on your preparatory work by completing a task in the tutorial, often by working with other students. The emphasis will be on collaborative learning, so you should attend these small-group sessions prepared to join in with the activities and discussions. This can be nerve-wracking and you will find some suggestions for overcoming your nerves and getting the most out of tutorials in chapter 10.

As small-group sessions are based upon activity and interaction, there is little scope for recorded alternatives but they have made the transition online with great success using video-conferencing technology. The lecturer can pose questions or discussion points and students can contribute their responses, or students can work together collaboratively in sub-groups whilst talking to each other through the computer and sharing their work on the screen. Online tutorials are a relatively new development, whereas online delivery of lectures has been around for longer, but many students who have made the shift to online tutorials have found it to be a positive experience (despite some initial reservations):

• I didn't like the idea of online tutorials because I couldn't see how the discussion would work and the idea of just listening to the lecturer go through the answers didn't appeal to me but they've actually been brilliant with just as much discussion as an ordinary tutorial. I really enjoy the breakout room activities and I feel like lecturers have been really creative in giving us tasks that work well in online discussion (Jasmine, final year).

• I'm quite a shy person and law is very new for me so I wouldn't dream of speaking out in a normal tutorial in front of everyone even though I often know the answers. I used to get quite frustrated with myself for being so self-conscious and not being able to answer questions in real tutorials but I've somehow found the confidence to speak up during the online tutorials. I was immediately comfortable at working in a pair with another student in the breakout rooms and then I thought that if I could do that then I could probably ask a question in the main group too so I made myself click on the 'hands up' symbol and then managed to speak when the lecturer called out my name. It was much easier than I thought and I join in regularly now so the online tutorials have really helped me find my voice (Lauren, first year).

• One of my lecturers asks us questions by name in online tutorials whereas he didn't do that before we went online. I suppose he can see our names on screen now. I was worried about being put on the spot because I know that there's always gaps in my tutorial preparation. I decided that I needed to prepare for the tutorial as if it was just me and the lecturer so that I'd have an answer for every question. It's made me work harder but I realized that I was quite lazy with my tutorial preparation before because I'd just leave out questions I couldn't answer and then write the answer in when someone else says it in class, whereas now I find that I actually can answer most of the questions if I put a bit more effort into my preparation. It's also improved my confidence to say 'I wasn't sure but this is what I thought' if I'm asked a question that I don't know the answer to and that's helped me a lot too because the lecturer helps you to puzzle out the answer (Harry, final year).

1.5.3 Remote learning

The previous section sets out the views of three students on their experiences of online tutorials. If you are new to remote learning, you might share some of the sorts of reservations that these students initially experienced: a concern about the effectiveness of the learning experience, a sense of awkwardness about the visibility that it entails in terms of joining a discussion and a concern about being singled out to answer questions. However, you will have also seen from their experiences that they either adapted their approach to learning or simply discovered that remote learning was not as daunting as they had initially feared. Nonetheless, any new experience is daunting at first so you might find the following suggestions helpful:

- Your university will have a remote learning policy that sets out what platform will be used (Zoom and Teams are popular but there are others) and what the expectation is of students in these sessions. Find the policy and familiarize yourself with it and have a trial run with the system that is being used if you have not encountered it before. Some systems require registration and you will want to do this in advance of the first session to make sure that you can join quickly and easily at the appointed time.

- Investigate whether your university or the lecturer taking the session have any stipulations about how students behave. For example, some universities have a 'cameras on' policy so that the lecturer can see the students and the students can see each other whereas others leave it as a matter of personal choice for the students. Similarly, there may be rules about the way that your name is displayed on the screen. If there is a policy, make sure that you adhere to it otherwise you may be asked to leave the session.

- If your university has a 'camera on' policy and you are not comfortable with that then give some thought to what it is that makes you uncomfortable so that you can find a way to address the problem. If it is the thought of other students seeing your surroundings then you can adjust your settings so that a different background appears so that you look as if you are sitting on a beach or in a library! Some systems allow you to blur the background so that it is indistinct. If it is the idea that you will be visible yourself, rather than your surroundings, then that is harder to address. The best advice is to make sure you are happy with how you look (no pyjamas!) and to remember that the other students will actually be concentrating on the lecturer and/or the slides that they are using or their own notes rather than looking at you. If you are really uncomfortable, try having a word with the lecturer to see if they will allow you to turn your camera off.

- Make sure you understand how to participate in the online learning sessions. Each system operates a little differently but all have the capacity to put your hand up if you want to ask a question or make a comment and there is a chat feature if you would rather type your question. Your lecturer will run through the rules of engagement at the start of each session.

- You will need to unmute your microphone to speak but otherwise keep your microphone on mute unless you are actually contributing to the discussion as the background noise will be a distraction for other students.

- Take care in using the chat feature. It is a good feature to enable you to ask questions or to otherwise contribute your thoughts to a discussion but try not to type too much or you will miss out on what's happening on the main screen. You should use the private message feature with caution as you could distract other students from the main discussion (some lecturers turn off the private chat feature for this reason). You will also want to take great care to ensure that you have selected the correct recipient for your messages: sending it to the wrong person or to the entire group, including the lecturer, could be embarrassing. The overall message here is that you should never really send messages that are not directly related to the session itself and the content should always be relevant, polite, and professional.

- Never leave your computer unattended during a remote learning session, not even for a few minutes to pop to the bathroom or to make drink. If your screen is unattended, a mischievous partner, friend, sibling, or passer-by (if you are in the in the library or other public area) could type a message that will appear to be from you.

Overall, then, the key point to bear in mind is to find out how the system works and how your university likes to use it and then find a way to use it to participate in remote learning that makes you comfortable. Bear in mind that you may be visible and that any unusual behaviour on the screen or background noise will distract other students as will messages that you send that are unrelated to the session that is taking place.

You may also find that these video-conferencing platforms are also very useful when it comes to working with other students, whether this is a requirement to complete a group project or activity or simply because you find working with others more enjoyable. The platforms allow you to discuss your ideas and understanding of the law, to share documents, to makes lists and diagrams using the whiteboard and the whole session can be recorded for future reference. They are excellent tools for collaborative working and developing the skills to use them proficiently and with confidence is something that will be useful in your studies and, looking beyond university, will prepare you for the remote working that is part and parcel of many professional environments.

1.6 HOW WILL I BE ASSESSED?

During the course of your studies, you will expect to encounter a series of assessments that are used to calculate the mark that you will receive for each module as well as your degree classification. You should expect to complete at least one assessment for every module that you study, with some modules having two or even three pieces of work for you to complete. In the sections that follow, you will find a description of the types of work that you are likely to encounter, a discussion of some issues related to coursework and exams at university level, and an explanation of the difference between formative and summative assessment. There is also an outline of the system of marking that is used at university.

1.6.1 Types of assessment

The most usual forms of assessment that you are likely to encounter on your law degree are essays and problem questions. Essays are more likely to be familiar to you from your previous study and are often used as a method of assessment because they test your understanding of the law and your ability to engage in legal analysis. Even though you may be familiar with writing essays, you might find that the standard, style, and approach of the essays that you need to write for your law degree are different from those that you have written previously. They will require a more critical approach and analytical reasoning that develops a clear line of argument that is supported by legal authority. They also require you to have a good standard of written English and an ability to structure an argument, both of which are crucial skills for a prospective lawyer to develop. You will find some guidance on writing skills (chapter 11) and essay writing (chapter 14) in the academic skills section of this book.

Most students embarking on a law degree will have written an essay at some point in their previous studies but far fewer have ever encountered a problem question before, so this is likely to be a new type of assessment for most students. It is a popular method of assessment in law because it is a way of helping students to develop the sorts of skills that are needed to give legal advice to clients. A problem question is based upon a short set of facts usually involving at least two people in which something happens that gives rise to a potential legal dispute. Your task is to work out what law applies to the situation and to puzzle out whether or not any of the people involved will be held liable for what has happened. This is essentially what happens in legal practice: a client tells you what has happened, you work out what law is relevant to their situation, and then you evaluate whether or not they are likely to be held liable if their case goes to court. Successful problem solving requires a particular type of methodical thinking and reasoning which is explained in detail in chapter 15.

There are other assessment tasks that you may encounter. Presentations are growing in popularity as universities seek to give students an opportunity to develop verbal communication skills. You will find plenty of tips and guidance on presentations in chapter 18. Another type of activity that is used to help you to develop verbal communication skills is a moot. A moot is a simulation of a court case at appeal level where students play the role of barristers arguing about points of law. It is a very skills-rich activity as it involves legal research and legal reasoning as well as good oral presentation skills and it provides a real sense of what it is like to practise law. For this reason, it is an activity that is prized by law employers, so it should certainly be on your 'to-do' list of things to try at university if it is not a compulsory activity as part of your assessment. There is a chapter on mooting in the practical skills section of the book (chapter 19).

You might also encounter multiple-choice questions in some modules, especially now these are to be used as the method of assessment in the SQE. It would be a mistake to think that this is an 'easy' type of assessment because the task that you are set is more straightforward than writing an essay or answering a problem question: multiple choice questions are knowledge intensive. This means that you have to know ever such a lot about the law in order to be able to answer them. In fact, lecturers use them to ensure that students have knowledge of the whole syllabus in their module. You may also find that the type of questions that are used are more complex than those that you have encountered previously. As with any type of assessment activity, make sure you find out what opportunities there are to practise this beforehand as it will be crucial that you are familiar with the style of questions that are asked in each module where this form of assessment is used. You will find more information on the types of multiple-choice questions that you are likely to encounter in chapter 16.

1.6.2 Formative and summative assessment

You will hear lecturers talk about formative and summative assessment, so it is important that you understand what is meant by these terms and how they work together. A formative assessment is a piece of work that is marked by one of your lecturers but the grade that it receives does not count towards your mark for the module. Therefore, it is a practice, a piece of work that allows you to test your knowledge and skills so that you can ascertain whether you need to change anything before completing the summative assessment where the mark awarded does contribute to your overall mark for the module and, in some instances, towards your degree classification.

Let's try and explain this more clearly by using an example. Imagine that you are a first-year student taking a criminal law module which includes one piece of coursework halfway through the module as well as an exam at the end. Before you submit the first piece of coursework—a problem question on liability for murder—you will need an opportunity to practise your problem-solving skills and find out whether you have understood the law correctly. You will therefore be given a piece of formative assessment which is also a problem question on murder albeit one involving different facts and different issues. This will be marked by your lecturer who will give it a grade and provide you with feedback that identifies what you have done well and highlights areas where improvement is necessary. The grade that you receive for this piece of work does not count towards your mark for the criminal law module, it simply gives you an indication of whether your work was good or not. In conjunction with the feedback that you have received, you should be able to work towards improving your performance when you complete the summative piece of coursework. The grade that you receive for your answer to the summative problem question will be combined with your mark in the end-of-module exam to give you an overall mark for criminal law.

However, because this module is a first-year module, the mark that you receive will not contribute towards the classification of degree that you receive. This is because only the marks that are awarded in the second and final years of your study are used to calculate your degree classification. You therefore have a whole year to get to grips with studying law and to develop your skills before your marks start to count towards your degree. This is a good situation, because most students improve by at least 10 per cent (a whole classification) during the course of their degree.

Formative grades, therefore, do not count towards your module mark or your degree classification. Summative grades always count towards the module mark but only count towards your degree classification in the second-year and final-year modules.

This leads some students to think that they can skip the formative assessment altogether because the grade that it receives does not count towards anything. This is a big mistake. A piece of work does not have to carry a mark in order to have value to you. The formative assessment is a risk-free opportunity to see if you have understood the law and if you are using it effectively in your essay or when you answer a problem question. If you do not know whether or not you can understand and use the law, how will you approach the summative assessment with confidence? Writing essays and answering problem questions are skills like any other—they get better the more you practise them. Why would you deprive yourself of the opportunity to practise and to receive feedback that will help you to do better next time?

Similarly, some students put minimal effort into their formative assessment and hand it to the lecturer saying 'I know it's not very good, I didn't have much time so I just spent an hour on it'. It is difficult to understand the logic here. Unless it represents your best effort, the feedback that you receive will not be very useful to you. Remember, formative assessment exists to help you achieve the best possible success in your summative assessment. However, you really will only get out of it what you put in, so make sure that you put aside sufficient time to produce a piece of work that is of the same quality that you would produce for a summative assessment.

1.6.3 Coursework and exams

Most students say that they either prefer exams to coursework or, more usually, that they prefer coursework to exams. Whichever your preference, you will encounter both on your law degree with some modules being assessed by a combination of coursework and exams and others being assessed solely by one method.

Coursework involves preparation of an answer to a question that has been publicized prior to the submission date. Students are therefore given time to prepare an answer and are able to access whatever material they choose to help them to do so. The key issue to bear in mind here concerns the use and acknowledgement of sources. It is very important that you acknowledge all the source material that you use in preparing your answer to coursework questions. If you use a source in your work and you do not acknowledge it, you will be vulnerable to accusations of plagiarism and this can have serious consequences. Not only can you be subject to disciplinary proceedings in your university, there is also an obligation to report academic dishonesty to the professional bodies, so it may impact on your ability to practise law in the future. You will find plenty of guidance on source material and how to use it in various chapters in this book and a whole chapter devoted to referencing and avoiding plagiarism (chapter 13).

If your module is assessed by an exam, it is worth making sure that you know as much as possible about what this involves. As a bare minimum, you need to know how long the exam lasts, how many questions are on the paper, and how many of these you have to answer. All of this information should be in your module handbook. You might also want to look at past exam papers in that module to get a feel for the sorts of questions that you might be asked. You will find all sorts of tips and advice on revision and exams in chapter 16.

One impact of the coronavirus pandemic has been the abandonment of exams in which everyone sits together in an exam room and has a strict time limit to produce handwritten answers to previously unseen questions. This traditional approach has given way to the take-home exam in which a question or set of questions is released to students online for them to answer within a specific time frame, often twenty-four hours. This takes away some of the pressure to commit the law to memory but the flipside of this is that less credit is available than would be the case in a traditional unseen exam for memorized content. The differences between the various types of exams, how to prepare for them, and how to perform well is covered in chapter 16.

1.6.4 The classification system

University degrees are awarded in classes. What this means is that the level of the degree that you receive when you graduate will fall into one of the classifications:

The percentage	The award	You say. . .
70% and above	A first class degree	'I got a first'
60–69%	An upper second class degree	'I got a two one'
50–59%	A lower second class degree	'I got a two two'
40–49%	A third class degree	'I got a third'
Less than 40%	This is a fail, so you would not receive a degree	

Each piece of work that you complete will also receive a mark that falls into one of these categories. If the grade is for a piece of summative assessment in a second- or final-year module then it will make a direct contribution to the final classification of your degree. In essence, every grade that you receive for a piece of summative assessment in your second and final year is combined together to calculate your degree classification. The method for calculating this will depend on a number of factors that are particular to each institution so it is not possible to explain them here, but it will be information that is provided to you in the programme handbook that accompanies your degree. If you are in any doubt, you can ask your personal tutor/academic adviser to explain it to you.

You will notice from this explanation that all work that receives a mark of 70 per cent or over falls into the first-class category. This may seem as if there are a lot of first-class marks available as there are 31 marks in this classification (70–100) by comparison with the 10 marks available in the other classifications (40–49, 50–59, and 60–69). The reality is that most universities do not use the full range of marks available, certainly not in subjects such as law. It is unusual for a law student to receive a mark over 75 per cent so you should certainly not be disheartened if you receive a mark of 71 per cent, thinking that it seems a long way short of 100 per cent, as any first-class mark means that you have done an excellent piece of work.

1.6.5 Understanding and using grade descriptors

The classification system is supplemented by the grade descriptors. Grade descriptors provide an explanation of what markers are looking for in a piece of work so are a way of telling you what you need to do to produce a piece of work that falls into each of the classifications. In essence, the grade descriptors list the attributes that students are expected to demonstrate in their work and then ranks the level of proficiency demonstrated by using a series of adjectives. So, for example, one of the attributes that students could be asked to demonstrate is 'referencing and citation practices' and the adjectives used to describe this might be:

- Excellent (in the 70+ classification)
- Good (60–69)
- Satisfactory (50–59)
- Basic with some errors or omissions (40–49)
- Poor (less than 40).

It is important that you find the grade descriptors used at your university and make sure that you understand what they are asking you to do because they are listing the things that your marker is looking for in your work. If you know what the marker is looking for in your work, you can use this as a checklist to make sure that you demonstrate these things. You can then review your work after it has been marked to see where improvements can be made so that you can continue to strengthen your performance each time. So if your referencing was described as satisfactory then you can see that this is an area to work on before you submit your next piece of work.

Some of the attributes listed in the grade descriptors might be easier to understand than others. For example, you will understand what 'referencing and citation practices' means even if you do not know how to reference well but the meaning of other attributes may be less obvious. Do you know, for instance, what 'synthesis of binding and non-binding authorities' means that you should be doing in your work? It can be a really effective technique to translate each of the attributes into a statement that makes sense to you. For example:

- Referencing and citation practices means that I have to acknowledge all my sources fully and in line with OSCOLA and use pinpoint references for every quotation and other specific points taken from source material.
- Synthesis of binding and non-binding authorities means that I have to use a range of different source material in my work—statute, case law, commentary—and show that I understand how they relate to each other, acknowledging the status of statute and binding case law and making persuasive arguments with other sources if I want to disagree with those sources.

You will find more discussion about grade descriptors and how to use them in chapter 10.

Watch a video of the authors talking about grade descriptors and how to use them on the online resources at www.oup.com/he/finch8e/.

1.6.6 First-year marks

In section 1.6.4, we mentioned that your final degree classification is based upon the marks that you receive for modules taken in your second and final year of study. The marks that you receive for first-year modules are not taken into account when calculating your final degree classification. This gives you a year to get to grips with studying law and to develop your skills before your marks start to count towards your degree. This is a good situation, since, as most students improve their marks during the course of their degree, any slip ups in the first year will not affect the overall degree result.

This does not mean that the first year does not matter. The first year is your opportunity to explore the most effective way for you to study so that you achieve the marks that you want to achieve. It is an opportunity to try different approaches to writing to see what you need to do to adjust to the greater demands of university study. You should still try to do as well as you possibly can. Also remember that if you are applying for a work placement after your first year, potential employers will want to know what your first-year marks were.

Every piece of work that you do—summative or formative, first year or otherwise—is important because it is an opportunity for you to develop and strengthen your skills of legal analysis and reasoning, your legal writing, and the application of the law.

1.7 AND FINALLY . . .

This is your degree and you want to do well but try not to forget that you should be enjoying the experience of learning about the law too. Try to develop a natural curiosity about the way that the law that you read in textbooks and hear about in lectures affects the world around you. Every time you learn a new piece of law, think about how that impacts on people and how they are able to behave as they go about their ordinary lives. Does it help them or constrain them? What is the purpose that the law is trying to achieve? Lawyers think about the law all the time and they see its influence everywhere. If you can start to see the world through the lens of the law then you will find it easier to start thinking like a lawyer and it will also help you to find the law truly interesting. This is important—it is far easier to study things that you find interesting—that little spark of enthusiasm for the law and what it does within society will help you to turn your attention to your books when you would rather do something else instead. A law degree involves many hours of study but this will seem less onerous if you can establish and maintain a genuine interest in the law. Finally, do not think that legal skills are just about getting you through a module or through your degree. The Lord Chief Justice—and everyone else in the legal profession—uses exactly the same skills that you are about to start developing for yourself. Never miss an opportunity to develop them further, no matter where you are in your studies or in your career afterwards. There is always more to learn about the law and always scope to strengthen your skills.

Legislation

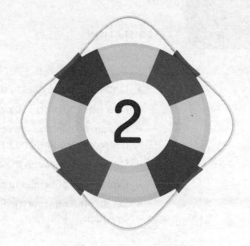

2

INTRODUCTION

This chapter deals with the first primary source of law that you will need to be able to find, understand, and use as part of your legal skills portfolio: legislation. It will begin by looking at the process by which an Act of Parliament comes into existence before turning to consider delegated legislation—that is, law that is made by other bodies under Parliament's authority. It will then move on to consider European Union legislation, which had an increasingly significant effect on the domestic law ever since the UK joined the European Economic Community in 1973. Although large areas of UK law remained unaffected by EU law, certain high-profile areas were significantly affected; these included employment law, commercial and consumer law, environmental law, intellectual property law, and the law relating to the free movement of goods and workers throughout Europe. However, following the June 2016 'Brexit' referendum, the UK left the EU on 31 January 2020. There was, however, a transitional period which ran until 11pm on 31 December 2020.

This chapter will, in any case, discuss the various institutions of the European Union and their role in the law-making process before looking at the different types of EU legislation in detail and explaining the circumstances in which individuals were able to use them in domestic courts. Finally, the chapter will discuss the impact of the European Convention on Human Rights and the Human Rights Act 1998.

Understanding legislation as a source of law is a fundamentally important legal skill. Every legal topic that you study will generally involve a mixture of legislation, delegated legislation, case law, and equitable principles. Therefore, a thorough understanding of how UK legislation works is essential. Furthermore, you must also understand the operation of EU legislation as it was a source of law that impacted many areas of the domestic law. Without understanding the effects of the EU sources on the domestic law, you will not be able to see the 'whole picture' of a particular area of legal study—especially in areas that have been highly influenced by the EU such as employment, commercial, environmental, and equality law.

 Learning outcomes

After studying this chapter, you will be able to:

- Explain the process by which Acts of Parliament come into being
- Describe various types of delegated legislation and their function

- Understand the roles of the various institutions of the European Union
- Describe the process by which European Union legislation comes into being
- Explain the differences between European Union treaty articles, regulations, directives, decisions, recommendations, and opinions
- Distinguish between the concepts of direct applicability and direct effect
- Explain the principles underlying the supremacy of European Union law
- Discuss the effect of the European Convention on Human Rights and the Human Rights Act 1998

2.1 DOMESTIC LEGISLATION

Legislation is a broad term which covers *statutes* (**Acts of Parliament**) and other types of legislation, such as **delegated** (or **subordinate**) legislation and **European Union** legislation.

2.1.1 Statute law

Parliament passes legislation in the form of statutes, or Acts of Parliament. On average, Parliament enacts around sixty or seventy statutes per session and, although this figure remains largely constant, the length of statutes seems to have expanded in recent years, hence increasing the overall volume of legislation.

An Act of Parliament will begin life as a Public Bill, Private Bill, or Hybrid Bill.

The procedure for enacting Private and Hybrid Bills is different to that for Public Bills. This chapter will concentrate on Public Bills and the resulting Public General Acts, although a brief overview of Private Bills, Hybrid Bills, and Private Members' Bills is included here for completeness.

2.1.1.1 Public Bills

Public Bills are introduced by the Government as part of its programme of legislation. Although many people think that most Public Bills arise from the commitments made by the Government as part of its election manifesto, in fact most Public Bills originate from Government departments, advisory committees, or as a political reaction to unforeseen events of public concern (such as the Dangerous Dogs Act 1991 in response to public and media outcry over a number of attacks by pit-bull terriers in which some unfortunate individuals were severely or disfiguringly injured).

If enacted, most Public Bills result in Public General Acts which, as their name suggests, affect the general public as a whole.

2.1.1.2 Private Bills

Private Bills are introduced for the benefit of particular individuals, groups of people, institutions, or a particular locality. They are promoted by organizations outside Parliament to obtain powers for themselves in excess of, or in conflict with, the general law. They often fail to become law due to insufficient time in a particular Parliamentary session. For example, before divorce became generally available under the public law, it was granted by Private Act of Parliament. Nowadays, personal Private Bills are extremely rare. There are now only a few Private Bills in each session. Private Bills tend to deal with nationalized industries, local authorities, companies, and educational institutions.

If enacted, Private Bills generally result in Private Acts (e.g. the most recent being the George Donald Evans and Deborah Jane Evans (Marriage Enabling) Act 1987), unless (as with Public Bills) they deal with local authorities, in which case the resulting legislation is known as a Local Act (the most recent examples being the University of London Act 2018 and the Middle Level Act 2018).

Take care not to confuse Private Bills with Private Members' Bills which are a type of Public Bill and are covered later in section 2.1.1.4.

2.1.1.3 Hybrid Bills

Hybrid Bills are a cross between Public Bills and Private Bills. According to the House of Commons Speaker, Hylton-Foster, they may be described as:

> A Public Bill which affects a particular private interest in a manner different from the private interests of other persons or bodies in the same category or class.

Bills which propose works of national importance that only affect a specific local area are generally Hybrid Bills; for instance the Bill passed that dealt with the building of the Channel Tunnel was a Hybrid Bill. The Public Bill Offices decide whether a Bill is Hybrid category. Both Houses debate Hybrid Bills and they go through a longer Parliamentary process than Public Bills. Opponents to Hybrid Bills may submit petitions and certain individuals and groups can state their case before a select committee. The most recent examples all deal with transport: the most recent is the High Speed Rail (West Midlands—Crewe) Bill 2017–19 which is still before Parliament at the time of writing. Each of these projects claim to benefit the country as a whole, although they clearly affect the private interests of those who are closest to the works more than those living a great distance from them.

2.1.1.4 Private Members' Bills

Private Members' Bills are non-Government Bills (Public, Private, or Hybrid) that are introduced by private Members of Parliament (MPs of any political party or members of the House of Lords who are not Government Ministers). They may be introduced in the Commons in a variety of ways: by ballot, under the 'ten minute rule', or by presentation. Private Members' Bills introduced in the House of Lords are treated in the same way as all other Public Bills. Relatively few Private Members' Bills end up as Acts of Parliament. Although they often deal with relatively narrow issues (such as mock auctions and drainage rates), they may also be used to draw attention to issues of concern that are not within the legislative agenda of Government. Significant pieces of legislation that have begun life as Private Members' Bills include the Abortion Act 1967 and the Hunting Act 2004, the most recent (at the time of writing) being the Assaults on Emergency Workers (Offences) Act 2018, sponsored by Chris Bryant and Baroness Donaghy which made certain offences aggravated (that is, more serious) when perpetrated against emergency workers in the exercise of their duties.

Be careful not to confuse Private Members' Bills with Private Bills.

2.1.1.5 Consolidating and codifying statutes

Statutes may also be passed to consolidate or codify the law.

Consolidating statutes

 A **consolidating statute** is one which re-enacts particular legal subject matter which was previously contained in several different statutes, which repeals obsolete law, or which gives effect to certain amendments.

According to the *Companion to the Standing Orders and Guide to Proceedings of the House of Lords*, the following types of Bill are classified as consolidation Bills:

- Bills, whether public or private, which are limited to re-enacting existing law
- Bills to consolidate any enactments with amendments to give effect to recommendations made by the Law Commissions
- Statute law repeals Bills, prepared by the Law Commissions to promote the reform of the statute law by the repeal of enactments which are no longer of practical utility
- Statute law revision Bills, which are limited to the repeal of obsolete, spent, unnecessary, or superseded enactments
- Bills prepared under the Consolidation of Enactments (Procedure) Act 1949, which include corrections and minor improvements to the existing law.

As Lord Simon stated in *Farrell v Alexander*:[1]

> All consolidation Acts are designed to bring together in a more convenient, lucid and economical form a number of enactments related in subject-matter [which were] previously scattered over the statute book.

Consolidation Bills are introduced in the House of Lords and are scrutinized by the Joint Committee on Consolidation Bills. Examples of such consolidation Acts include the Children Act 1989, the Companies Act 2006, and the Equality Act 2010.

Codifying statutes

 A **codifying statute** is one which restates legal subject matter previously contained in earlier statutes, the common law, and custom.

The meaning of 'common law' and 'custom' is considered in chapter 5.

Unlike consolidation, codification *may* change the law. Examples of codifying Acts are the Theft Act 1968, which attempted to frame the law of theft in 'ordinary language', and the Consumer Rights Act 2015 which brought together pre-existing consumer protection law that was previously spread across multiple statutes.

---

1. [1977] AC 59 (HL) 82 (Lord Simon of Glaisdale). This chapter, and the ones that follow, have several footnote references to different sources. You can find out more about how they work and how to use them in chapter 13.

2.1.1.6 The domestic law-making process

White Papers and Green Papers

Before a Bill is introduced into Parliament, it may be preceded by a White Paper or a Green Paper.

White Papers set out Government proposals on topics of current concern. They signify the Government's intention to enact new legislation and may set up a consultative process to consider the finer details of the proposal.

Green Papers are issued less frequently. They are introductory higher-level Government reports on a particular area put forward as tentative proposals for discussion without any guarantee of legislative action or consideration of the legislative detail.

Drafting the Bill

Proposed Government legislation is passed to the Parliamentary draftsmen (officially the 'Parliamentary Counsel to the Treasury') who draft the Bill acting on the instructions of the Government department responsible for the proposal. Oddly, it is conventional practice that the Ministers responsible for the Bill do not usually see the instructions sent from their departments.

Procedure for Public Bills

Once drafted, the Parliamentary procedure for Bills introduced in the House of Commons can be depicted as shown in Figure 2.1.

Bills introduced in the House of Lords

A Government Bill can be introduced into either the House of Commons or the House of Lords. Most Bills begin life in the House of Commons; particularly Bills which deal primarily with taxation or public expenditure. The House of Commons has priority in such matters by virtue of its financial privileges (see Parliament Acts 1911 and 1949). Conversely, Bills relating to the judicial system, Law Commission Bills, and consolidation Bills conventionally begin their passage in the House of Lords. A recent example of a House of Lords Bill which became law can be found in the Armed Forces (Flexible Working) Act 2018 which made provision for members of the regular forces to serve part-time or subject to geographic restrictions.

House of Commons—First Reading

The First Reading in the House of Commons is a formality. The Title of the Bill is read by the Clerk of the House and a date is fixed for the Second Reading. Conventionally, the Second Reading does not normally take place before two weekends have passed.

House of Commons—Second Reading

The Second Reading in the House of Commons involves the main debate on the principles of the Bill. For Government Bills, the debate is usually opened by the Minister responsible for the Bill and closed by a junior Minister. A vote is generally taken on the Bill as a whole at the end of the Second Reading. The Bill will then move to a Standing Committee (unless it is moved that the Bill be sent to a Committee of the whole House, a Select Committee, or a Special Standing Committee).

House of Commons—Standing Committee

Following the Second Reading in the House of Commons, most Bills are sent to a Standing Committee. The name 'Standing Committee' was coined from the time when Bills were sent

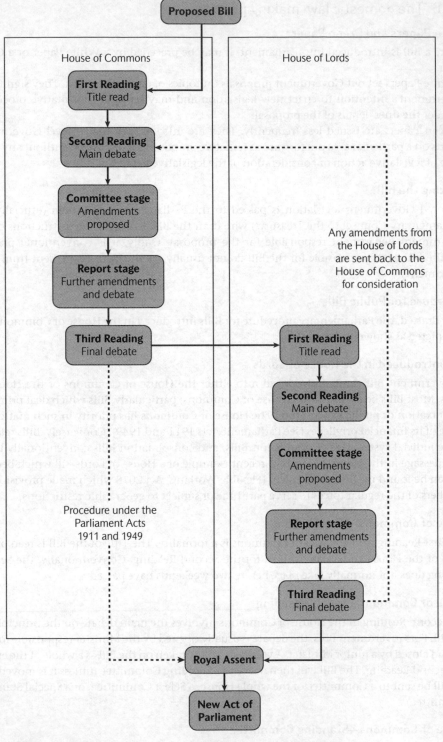

Figure 2.1 The Parliamentary procedure for Bills introduced in the House of Commons

to large, permanent committees which considered all Bills they received. The membership of the Standing Committee now varies for each Bill. Standing Committees can have as many as fifty members or as few as sixteen. The members are chosen by the Committee of Selection by virtue of their particular expertise or interest in the subject matter of the Bill and to ensure that the party political composition of the Committee is, so far as possible, representative of the overall party political composition of the House of Commons: in other words that the relative proportions of members of the various political parties are roughly the same in the Committee as in the House of Commons as a whole. The Chair of each Standing Committee is selected by the Speaker of the House of Commons from a panel of chairmen.

The Standing Committee examines the provisions of the Bill in detail and votes on whether each clause, as proposed, 'stands part of the Bill'. Amendments may be moved in Standing Committee. These amendments are also voted upon. The Bill (as amended in Standing Committee) then moves into a Report stage.

House of Commons—Report stage

Unless a Bill has been considered by a Committee of the whole House without amendment, the Committee stage is followed by a Report stage (sometimes referred to as a Consideration stage). Here, further amendments may be proposed and introduced, often in an attempt to undo the changes made in Committee. Once the Report stage is complete—which may take two or three days—the Bill finally proceeds to its Third Reading in the Commons.

House of Commons—Third Reading

In the Third Reading of the Bill, its contents are debated for a final time. It is unusual for any further amendments to be made at this stage. Indeed, unless six members table a motion that 'the Question be not put forthwith', the Third Reading does not have to involve any debate at all.

Once the Third Reading is over, the Bill is then tied up with a green ribbon and taken to the House of Lords by the Clerk of the House of Commons with a message kindly requesting the Lords' agreement to its content.

Procedure in the House of Lords

The procedure in the House of Lords mirrors that in the House of Commons. Bills have a formal First Reading, are debated on a Second Reading, proceed to consideration in Committee (although, unlike in the House of Commons, the Committee stage is almost invariably taken in the Committee of the whole House), are debated again on Report and then receive a final Third Reading. At the end of the Third Reading there is a formal motion 'that this Bill do now pass'.

Assuming that the Bill survives the motion at the end of the Third Reading in the House of Lords, it is returned to the House of Commons with the Lords' amendments which must be considered in the Commons. If the House of Commons does not agree with the Lords' amendments it can send it back with counter-amendments and its reasons for doing so. Therefore a Bill can go back and forth between the Houses several times until proceedings are terminated or the Parliamentary session runs out of time. However, in practice, the House of Lords often accepts the second offering from the House of Commons.

The Parliament Acts 1911 and 1949

These Acts provide a means by which the House of Commons can, under certain circumstances, bypass the House of Lords to present a Bill for Royal Assent without it having been passed by the House of Lords. The procedure under the Parliament Acts has historically been used infrequently.

The 1911 Act was used only three times: for the Welsh Church Act 1914, the Government of Ireland Act 1914, and the Parliament Act 1949, which amended the 1911 Act to reduce the power of the House of Lords further. Before 1997, the amended form of the 1911 Act had been used only once, in respect of the War Crimes Act 1991, but the 1997 Labour Government used the Parliament Acts to force through three Acts: the European Parliamentary Elections Act 1999, the Sexual Offences (Amendment) Act 2000, and the Hunting Act 2004. The Acts have not been used since.

The Parliament Acts do not apply to Bills which prolong the length of a Parliament beyond five years, Private Bills, Bills sent to the Lords less than a month before the end of the Parliamentary session, and Bills which are introduced in the Lords.

Royal Assent

Royal Assent is required before any Bill can become law. The monarch is not required by the constitution to assent to any Act passed by Parliament. However, assent is conventionally given by the monarch acting on ministerial advice. It has not been refused since Queen Anne refused to assent to the Scottish Militia Bill of 1707.

Indeed the Royal Assent Act 1967 has marginalized the personal involvement of the monarch to the extent that all that is now required for Royal Assent by Notification is a formal reading of the short title of the Act with a form of words signifying the fact of assent in both Houses of Parliament.

Without express provision to the contrary, an Act of Parliament is deemed to come into force on the day (and for the whole of the day)[2] that it receives Royal Assent. Otherwise it will come into force on a date specified within the Act itself, or via an 'appointed day' provision which allows the Act to be brought into force via a statutory instrument.

Statutory instruments are described in section 2.1.2.1.

Parts of the Act may be brought into force on different dates (e.g. some provisions of the Laser Misuse (Vehicles) Act 2018 came into force on the day it was passed, whereas others came into force in England, Wales, and Scotland two months later).

For more information on the coming into force of statutes, see chapter 4.

Territorial extent

There is a presumption in the absence of proof to the contrary that Acts of the UK Parliament enacted after 1707 apply to the whole of the UK. If such an Act, or any part of it, does not apply to Scotland, Wales or Northern Ireland, this will usually be expressly stated within the Act itself. In modern practice, an 'extent' provision setting out any limitations on the geographical application of the Act is usually found in one of the final sections of the Act. You will find more about this in section 4.1.8. Acts of the UK Parliament that apply only to particular regions are usually denoted by the inclusion of the name of the region in the short title of the Act, for example the Solicitors (Scotland) Act 1980.

Following the passing of the Scotland Act 1998 and the creation of the Scottish Parliament in 1999, statutes can be enacted by the Scottish Parliament provided that the subject matter of the Act is within its legislative competence. These Acts are given Royal Assent under Letters Patent (a published written order issued by the Crown). The UK Parliament retains the power to legislate for Scotland on all matters, including those matters that are now within the legislative competence of the Scottish Parliament. However, a convention has developed (the Sewel Convention)[3] that the UK Government will not normally introduce legislation dealing with matters that have been devolved to the Scottish Parliament, or the other devolved legislatures

---

2. *Tomlinson v Bullock* (1879) 4 QBD 230 (DC).
3. House of Commons, 'The "Sewel Convention"' (Library Standard Note) (25 November 2005) SN/PC/2084.

within the UK, without the agreement of the devolved legislature (which is given by their passing of a 'legislative consent motion').

In Wales, Measures of the National Assembly for Wales between 2006 and 2011 were given Royal Assent by means of an Order in Council. Following the extension of the Assembly's legislative powers after the 2011 referendum, Measures become known as Acts of the Assembly and are given Royal Assent via Letters Patent in the same way as Acts of the Scottish Parliament.

2.1.1.7 The impact of the Human Rights Act 1998

Section 19 of the Human Rights Act 1998 provides that the Minister in charge of each new Bill in either House of Parliament must, before the Second Reading of the Bill, either:

- Make a statement of compatibility—that is, state that the provisions of the Bill are compatible with the European Convention on Human Rights, or
- Make a statement acknowledging that it is not possible to make a statement of compatibility, but, despite this, the Government still wishes the House to proceed with the Bill.

The courts have no power to set aside any Act of Parliament that is incompatible with Convention rights; this is a function that is exercised by Parliament (which has a fast-track procedure under s 10 of the Act that it may use in such cases if it wishes to do so). The court may, however, make a 'statement of incompatibility' under s 4 of the Act if it is satisfied that the provision is incompatible with a Convention right. Such a statement does not affect the validity, continuing operation, or enforcement of the provision in respect of which it is given; and is not binding on the parties to the proceedings in which it is made.

2.1.2 Delegated legislation

Parliament has delegated legislative power to various other persons and bodies.

Delegated legislation is law made by persons or bodies with the delegated authority of Parliament. It is sometimes referred to as 'subordinate legislation'.

2.1.2.1 Statutory instruments

An Act of Parliament may grant the power to make statutory instruments, usually to a Minister of the Crown. The scope of this power can vary greatly, from the technical (e.g. varying the dates on which different provisions of an Act will come into force or changing the levels of fines or penalties for offences) to much wider powers such as filling out the broad provisions in Acts. Often, Acts only contain a broad framework and statutory instruments are used to provide the necessary detail that would be considered too complex to include in the body of an Act. Statutory instruments can also be used to amend, update, or enforce existing primary legislation. One Act of Parliament can spawn a large number of statutory instruments: for instance the Coronavirus Act 2020 has, at the time of writing, given rise to fifty statutory instruments covering matters from business tenancies and retention of fingerprint data to sick pay.

'Statutory instruments' is a general term that includes regulations, rules, and orders. A very common form of statutory instrument is a commencement order which brings all, or part, of an Act into force.

For examples of commencement orders, see chapter 4.

The procedure for introducing a statutory instrument is usually laid down partly in the enabling (parent) Act and partly in the Statutory Instruments Act 1946. The use of statutory instruments is becoming increasingly widespread as a means of introducing some flexibility into the legislative process as well as helping to contain the ever-increasing length and complexity of statutes. For instance Parliament passed thirty-one UK Public General Acts in 2019, but made 1,410 statutory instruments in the same year. While this may seem a lot, the most prolific year for statutory instruments was 2014 in which 3,481 were made—over one hundred times the number of Acts (thirty) passed in the same year.

Procedures for creating statutory instruments

The procedure for creating a statutory instrument is laid down in the parent Act. These procedures can be categorized as:

- Negative resolution
- Positive resolution
- No approval by Parliament.

Approximately two-thirds of all statutory instruments are made under the negative resolution procedure. It is named as such since it does not require Parliament to act unless it disapproves of the statutory instrument. It takes one of two forms depending on the state of the statutory instrument at the time that it is presented to ('laid before') Parliament. In the first form, the statutory instrument is laid before Parliament in draft and cannot be made if Parliament votes its disapproval within forty days. In the second form, the statutory instrument is actually made and laid before Parliament. If Parliament votes its disapproval within forty days, then the statutory instrument cannot remain in force.

A further 10 per cent of statutory instruments require positive resolution—in other words they require positive Parliamentary approval. This procedure takes one of three forms. The first of these requires the draft statutory instrument to be laid before Parliament. It can only come into force if approved by resolution of the House or Houses specified in its parent Act. The second form is similar, except that the statutory instrument is made before being laid before Parliament. However, it cannot come into force until approved by resolution as before. The final situation occurs where the statutory instrument has been made, comes into immediate effect, and is then laid before Parliament. It cannot continue beyond the period specified in the parent Act without positive resolution.

The final two-fifths of statutory instruments require no approval by Parliament. This either means that they do not need to be laid before Parliament at all, or that they do, but do not require any subsequent form of approval.

2.1.2.2 By-laws

By-laws are laws which are made by a local authority and only apply within a specific geographical area. By-laws are usually only created when there is no general legislation that deals with particular matters of concern to local people, such as waste collection and public park opening hours. By-laws are made under the Local Government Act 1972. However, by-laws can only come into force once they have been affirmed by the relevant Minister. By-laws come into force one month after affirmation unless a specific date is provided within the by-law itself.

2.1.2.3 The Rule Committees

The Rule Committees have delegated power to make procedural rules for the courts. These consist of the Civil Procedure Rule Committee (who are responsible for the Civil Procedure

Rules 1998 and their subsequent amendments), the Criminal Procedure Rule Committee, and the Family Procedure Rule Committee.

2.1.2.4 The Privy Council

The role of the Privy Council is described further in chapter 5.

The Privy Council may make Orders in Council, such as emergency regulations. These have the force of law. It may also implement resolutions of the United Nations Security Council.

2.1.2.5 Validity of delegated legislation

Unlike Acts of Parliament, delegated legislation may be challenged in the courts via the doctrine of *ultra vires*.

> *Ultra vires* is a Latin term meaning 'outside (their) powers'.

If a body acts beyond the powers that are delegated to it by the parent Act, then the delegated legislation can be declared void by the court. The body is said to have acted *ultra vires* by exceeding its powers. The delegated legislation may also be referred to as being *ultra vires*.[4]

Delegated legislation is also *ultra vires* if it conflicts with an earlier Act of Parliament or, prior to Brexit, European Union legislation under s 2(4) of the European Communities Act 1972.

Decisions which are made by the public bodies granted power by delegated legislation can also be challenged via judicial review. See section 5.3.4.2.

2.1.2.6 Advantages and disadvantages of delegated legislation

Advantages

The main advantage of delegated legislation is that detailed rules and regulations can be introduced relatively quickly without the need for full debate in Parliament that Acts would require. There is insufficient Parliamentary time available to debate all Bills in full and delegated legislation enables the most effective use of this limited time.

Moreover, Members of Parliament may not have the particular specialist knowledge to debate certain subject areas. It is therefore preferable to delegate authority to individuals or bodies with the requisite degree of specialist, technical, or local knowledge.

Disadvantages

Since delegated legislation is not debated before Parliament in the way that Acts are, the opportunity for public objection is minimized. Nor is delegated legislation publicized before and after implementation in the same way as some new Acts of Parliament. For instance, the Civil Partnership Act 2004 and the Identity Cards Act 2006 both received widespread media coverage, whereas a mass of delegated legislation was also introduced over the same period without any significant attention. While it could be argued that media attention derives from the very nature of primary legislation and its general public impact, it is also true that delegated

---

4. For examples of the ways in which the courts have approached the issue of *ultra vires*, see *Commissioners of Customs & Excise v Cure & Deeley Ltd* [1962] 1 QB 340 (DC) and *R v Secretary of State for Social Security, ex p Joint Council for the Welfare of Immigrants* [1997] 1 WLR 275 (CA).

legislation can have a significant public impact (e.g. the majority of the Identity Cards Act 2006 would have been brought into force by delegated legislation).[5]

Finally, the proliferation of delegated legislation means that in researching any area of law, it is important to be sure that your research is up to date.

2.2 EUROPEAN LEGISLATION

Since the UK joined what is now the European Union, an increasingly influential range of sources of law came from Europe. However, in the June 2016 referendum on the UK's continued membership of the EU—the so-called 'Brexit' vote—52 per cent voted to leave. After a considerable period of uncertainty, the UK finally left the EU on 31 January 2020, followed by a time-limited implementation period which lasted until 11.00pm on 31 December 2020. During the implementation period EU law continued to apply to the UK. Although the implementation period expiry date will have passed by the date of publication, it had not passed at the time of writing, so it will be important to make sure that you are up to date with any developments in this area throughout the lifetime of this edition.

With regard to human rights issues, individual citizens of the UK had the right to petition the European Court of Human Rights from 1966. Building on this, the Human Rights Act 1998 came into force in October 2000, allowing individuals to rely on (most) of the rights guaranteed by the European Convention on Human Rights directly in national courts as well as enabling courts to overrule earlier incompatible decisions. This section will consider European Union legislation in the form of treaty articles, regulations, and directives. It will also consider the European Convention on Human Rights as a further European source of law. However, it is important to remember throughout that the European Court of Human Rights is separate from the Court of Justice of the European Union and that the Brexit decision will have no impact on the UK's relationship with the European Court of Human Rights, its accession to the European Convention on Human Rights, or the operation of the Human Rights Act 1998. However, it is worth noting more generally that certain legislation that protects equality and human rights was led by EU law including the areas of data protection and privacy; human trafficking; workplace discrimination on the grounds of religion, belief, sexual orientation, and age; and equal pay for men and women.

2.2.1 European Union law

2.2.1.1 A brief history

The UK became a member of the European Communities on 1 January 1973 when the European Communities Act 1972 came into force.

At this time the 'European Communities' were the European Economic Community (the 'EEC'), established by the Treaty of Rome 1957, together with the European Coal and Steel Community,[6] and the European Atomic Energy Community ('Euratom'), with the EEC being the most significant.

The 1992 Treaty on European Union (also known as the Maastricht Treaty or TEU) renamed the EEC as the European Community (EC) and the geographical entity formed by the Member

---

5. Identity Cards Act 2006 s 44(3). The Identity Documents Act 2010 repealed the Identity Cards Act 2006 and requires the destruction of the information held on the National Identity Register.
6. Established by the Treaty of Paris 1951.

States became the European Union (EU) when it came into force on 1 November 1993. As such, the EU evolved from a trade body into an economic and political partnership.

The Maastricht Treaty is not the only treaty that you will encounter. The Single European Act 1986 (which is actually a treaty rather than an Act of Parliament—despite its name) initiated moves towards the harmonization of laws across the Member States. The 1997 Treaty of Amsterdam made further changes, not least of which was the renumbering of the pre-existing Treaty provisions.

The Maastricht Treaty established the three so-called 'pillars' of the European Union: the European Community, Common Foreign and Security Policy, and Police and Judicial Co-operation in Criminal Matters.

The 2001 Treaty of Nice effected further changes relating to the enlargement of the Community which allowed the addition of ten new Member States on 1 May 2004, and two more on 1 January 2007, increasing the membership from fifteen to twenty-eight by 1 July 2013 before reducing to twenty-seven following the UK's exit in 2020. The membership of the EU over time is illustrated in Table 2.1.

Table 2.1 The membership of the European Union

Year	Countries	Membership
1957	Belgium, France, Germany, Italy, Luxembourg, Netherlands	6
1973	United Kingdom, Denmark, Ireland	9
1981	Greece	10
1986	Portugal, Spain	12
1995	Austria, Finland, Sweden	15
2004	Cyprus, Czech Republic, Estonia, Hungary, Latvia, Lithuania, Malta, Poland, Slovakia, Slovenia	25
2007	Bulgaria, Romania	27
2013	Croatia	28
2020	United Kingdom withdrew from the EU	27
Candidate countries	Albania, Montenegro, Serbia, Republic of North Macedonia, Turkey	
Potential candidates	Bosnia and Herzegovina, Kosovo	

As the EU expanded to include more Member States, a new European Constitution was proposed which contained significant reforms to both the institutions of the EU and its operation. This proposed constitution was rejected by France and the Netherlands. Following this rejection, a new Reform Treaty was drawn up and was signed in Lisbon on 13 December 2007.[7] It was originally intended to have been ratified by all Member States by the end of 2008. However, following a referendum on 12 June 2008, the Irish electorate voted against its ratification by 53 to 47 per cent. This decision was reversed in a second referendum in 2009 after the Irish secured concessions on particular policies, including abortion, taxation, and military neutrality.

The Treaty of Lisbon was ratified by the UK on 19 June 2008 by the European Union (Amendment) Act 2008 and came into force on 1 December 2009.

7. Treaty of Lisbon amending the Treaty on European Union and the Treaty establishing the European Community (Treaty of Lisbon) [2007] OJ C306/1.

The Treaty of Lisbon amended the Treaty on European Union and the Treaty establishing the European Community (Treaty of Rome)—which was also renamed the Treaty on the Functioning of the European Union. Its most significant changes include:

- The creation of a long-term President of the European Council
- The elimination of the pillar system
- The division of European policy areas into three categories: exclusive competence, shared competence (with the Member States), and supporting competence (where the EU supports, coordinates, or supplements the actions of the Member States)
- More qualified majority voting in the Council of Ministers
- Increased involvement of the European Parliament in the legislative process
- The Charter of Fundamental Rights being given the status of a legally binding instrument.

Therefore, the two key treaties are the *Treaty on European Union* (TEU; Maastricht) and the *Treaty on the Functioning of the European Union* (TFEU; Treaty of Rome). The other treaties amended these as the scope of the EU changed over time.

2.2.1.2 The institutions of the European Union

It is important to be able to distinguish between the different institutions of the European Union and to understand their functions. These are set out in Article 13 TEU as:

- The European Commission
- The Council of Ministers/European Council
- The European Parliament
- The Court of Justice of the European Union
- The General Court
- The European Central Bank
- The Court of Auditors.

We will consider each of these in turn (with the exception of the European Central Bank and Court of Auditors which are less relevant to legal studies).

The European Commission

The **European Commission** represents the interests of the EU as a whole. It proposes new legislation to the European Parliament and the Council of the European Union, and it ensures that EU law is correctly applied by member countries.

The first main role of the European Commission lies in proposing new laws using its 'right of initiative' for the protection of the citizens and interests of the EU. It proposes such laws according to the principles of subsidiarity and proportionality: that is, it will only put forward proposals on issues that cannot be dealt with at national, regional, or local levels and then no more than necessary to achieve the agreed objectives. Legislative proposals are drafted by the Commission and, if approved by a minimum of fourteen of the (currently) twenty-eight Commissioners, are sent to the Council and the Parliament. Each EU Member State has one Commissioner, although the Commissioners are not representatives of their respective countries. Each Commissioner is responsible for one or more specific areas of policy. The appointments run for a term of five years and are subject to the approval of the European Parliament.

The second role of the Commission is in the enforcement of European law as 'guardian of the Treaties' together with the Court of Justice. It can take action, including the imposition of penalties, against an EU Member State that is allegedly in breach of its obligations under the Treaties (Article 258 TFEU) or for failure to implement a piece of EU legislation (Article 260 TFEU).

The Commission also has roles in managing the EU budget and allocating funding (with the Council and Parliament) and representing the EU on the world stage, negotiating agreements between the EU and other countries.

The Council of the European Union

The **Council of the European Union** represents the governments of the individual EU countries. It is one of the main law-making bodies of the EU, along with the European Parliament.

The Council of the European Union shares responsibility with the European Parliament for passing EU laws that are proposed by the Commission. It also coordinates the broad economic policies of the EU countries and develops the EU's foreign and defence policies. The Council also coordinates cooperation between the courts and police forces of EU countries to ensure equal access to justice for EU citizens throughout the Union and mutual recognition of court judgments. It is further concerned with policing the EU's borders and combating terrorism and organized crime. The EU budget is approved jointly between the Parliament and the Council. Finally, the Council can enter into international agreements on behalf of the EU on a range of diverse matters including: environment, trade, textiles, fisheries, science, technology, and transport.

The Council's members are politicians who are Ministers in their respective national Governments. Each Minister has the authority to commit its Government to a particular policy or decision. There are no fixed members: its membership fluctuates according to the subject matter under debate. For instance, if the debate concerned environmental issues, the UK would have been represented by the Secretary of State for Environment, Food and Rural Affairs. The presidency of the Council is held for six months by each EU Member State on a rotational basis.

The general voting method for the Council is qualified majority voting, except where the Treaties require a different procedure (e.g. a unanimous vote). This means that proposals require a majority of 55 per cent of the EU countries (so, a minimum of fifteen) but those members in favour must represent at least 65 per cent of the total EU population.

Take care not to confuse the Council of the European Union with the European Council or the Council of Europe. The Council of Europe is a separate body and has responsibility for the European Court of Human Rights.

The European Parliament

The **European Parliament** represents the people of the EU. It is one of the main EU law-making institutions, along with the Council of the European Union.

Members of the European Parliament (MEPs) are directly elected representatives of the people, with elections being held every five years. The first main role of the Parliament is debating and passing EU laws, together with the Council. The process by which this is done is known as the 'ordinary legislative procedure', set out by the Lisbon Treaty. In many areas (such as economic governance, immigration, energy, transport, consumer protection, and the environment) equal weight is given to the Parliament and the Council and most EU laws are adopted jointly between these two institutions. The steps in the ordinary legislative procedure are as follows:

- The Commission sends its proposal to Parliament and the Council.
- They consider it and discuss it on two successive occasions.
- After two readings, if they cannot agree, the proposal is brought before a Conciliation Committee made up of an equal number of representatives of the Council and Parliament.
- Representatives of the Commission also attend the meetings of the Conciliation Committee and contribute to the discussions.
- When the Committee has reached agreement, the agreed text is sent to Parliament and the Council for a third reading, so that they can finally adopt it as law. The final agreement of the two institutions is essential if the text is to be adopted as a law.
- Even if a joint text is agreed by the Conciliation Committee, Parliament can still reject the proposed law by a majority of the votes cast.

The number of MEPs for each EU Member State is broadly in proportion to its population, although, following the Lisbon Treaty, none may have fewer than six or more than ninety-six MEPs. Following the UK's withdrawal, the maximum number of members reduced from 751 (a maximum set by the Treaty) to 705. Twenty-seven of the UK's seventy-three seats were reallocated (to France, Spain, Italy, the Netherlands, Ireland, Sweden, Austria, Denmark, Finland, Slovakia, Croatia, Estonia, Poland, and Romania). The remaining forty-six seats were set aside for future allocations should new Member States join the EU.

The European Parliament also debates and adopts the EU budget with the Council. It also exercises democratic supervision of the other EU institutions: for instance, Parliament approves the nomination of the President of the Commission and the Commissioners (as a body)[8] and can censure the Commission, forcing its members to resign. It may also consider petitions from citizens and set up inquiry committees.

The Court of Justice of the European Union

The **Court of Justice of the European Union** (still often referred to by its former name as the **European Court of Justice** or **ECJ**) upholds the rule of EU law by ensuring consistency of application between EU countries, settling disputes between EU Governments and institutions, and hearing cases that are brought before it.

It is vitally important not to confuse the Court of Justice of the European Union (CJEU) (which sits in Luxembourg) with the European Court of Human Rights (which sits in Strasbourg). They are separate courts with separate jurisdictions.

The CJEU sits in Luxembourg and comprises one judge from each EU Member State. The judges sit in chambers of three or five as well as in plenary session (where all judges sit to hear

---

8. Art 17(7) TEU.

a case). They are assisted by eleven 'advocates general' whose role is to submit reasoned, public, and impartial opinions to the Court on the cases brought before it. Each judge and advocate general is appointed for a six-year term. The Court delivers a single judgment: separate concurring or dissenting judgments are not permitted.

The cases brought before the CJEU fall into certain types. The most common are:

- **Preliminary rulings.** National courts may make interim references directly to the Court if they need clarification on how a particular piece of European legislation should be interpreted. The need for such references will arise during the course of a national (domestic) action. In England and Wales this typically occurred in the Supreme Court (although it has been done directly from a magistrates' court).[9] In other words, if a national court cannot make a ruling because it is unsure how to interpret a piece of EU legislation, then it can effectively suspend the proceedings before it to ask the Court for its opinion. These references are made under Article 267 TFEU. The case will then proceed in the national court with the assistance of the European Court's ruling. It is the role of the national courts to give effect to and enforce the rulings of the CJEU.

- **Failure to fulfil an EU obligation.** The Court also hears actions for failure of an EU national Government to fulfil its obligations under EU law. Proceedings before the CJEU are preceded by an investigation conducted by the Commission, which gives the defendant EU Member State the opportunity to reply to the complaints made against it. If that procedure does not result in remedy of the failure by the defendant EU Member State, an action for breach of EU law may be brought before the CJEU. That action may be brought by the Commission[10]—as is practically always the case—or by another EU Member State.[11] If the CJEU finds that an obligation has not been fulfilled, the EU Member State concerned must remedy the breach without delay. If the Court later finds that the breach has not been remedied, it may, upon request of the Commission, impose a financial penalty.[12]

- **Actions for annulment.** The CJEU may also hear applications seeking the annulment of a regulation, directive, or decision. Such actions may be brought by a Member State, by the European Parliament, the Council of the European Union, or the European Commission, or by individuals to whom a measure is addressed or which is of direct and individual concern to them.

- **Actions for failure to act.** The CJEU may also review the legality of a failure to act on the part of an EU institution. Where the failure to act is held to be unlawful, it is for the institution concerned to put an end to the failure by appropriate measures.

- **Direct actions.** Any legal person can bring an action directly before the CJEU if they have suffered loss or damage as a result of the acts or omissions of the EU's institutions or its staff.

- **Appeals from the General Court.** Appeals on points of law only may be brought before the CJEU against judgments given by the General Court. If the appeal is admissible and well founded, the CJEU may set aside the judgment of the General Court. The CJEU may decide this itself or may refer the case back to the General Court, which is bound by the decision of the CJEU given on appeal.

---

9. Case C-145/88 *Torfaen Borough Council v B&Q plc* [1990] 2 QB 19 (CJEU) on application from Cwmbran Magistrates' Court regarding Sunday trading regulations.
10. Art 258 TFEU.
11. Art 259 TFEU.
12. Art 260 TFEU.

The General Court

The **General Court** has jurisdiction at first instance over all direct actions brought by individuals and EU countries, with the exception of those to be assigned to a 'judicial panel' and those reserved for the CJEU. It was formerly known (until 1 December 2010) as the **Court of First Instance**.

The Court of First Instance was established by the Single European Act of 1986 to ease some of the burden of cases on the Court of Justice. It was renamed as the General Court by the Treaty of Lisbon. It comprises up to two judges from each of the EU countries, but, unlike the CJEU, does not have permanent advocates general. It currently has fifty-four judges (some countries having not nominated their full quota of judges). Judges sit in chambers of three or five or, exceptionally, singly. For complex or important cases it may sit as a Grand Chamber of thirteen or as a full court. However, around 80 per cent of cases are heard by a chamber of three. It deals with:

- Direct actions against the institutions, bodies, offices, or agencies of the European Union
- Actions brought by the Member States against the Commission
- Actions brought by the Member States against the Council relating to acts adopted in the field of State aid, 'dumping', and acts by which it exercises implementing powers
- Actions seeking compensation for damage caused by the institutions of the European Union or their staff
- Actions based on contracts made by the European Union that expressly give jurisdiction to the General Court
- Actions relating to Community trade marks
- Appeals, limited to points of law, against the decisions of the European Union Civil Service Tribunal
- Actions brought against decisions of the Community Plant Variety Office or of the European Chemicals Agency.

There is a route of appeal to the CJEU within two months on points of law only.

As previously stated, it is vitally important not to confuse the Court of Justice of the European Union (CJEU) (which sits in Luxembourg) with the European Court of Human Rights (which sits in Strasbourg). They are separate courts with separate jurisdictions.

The European Council

The **European Council** is composed of the Heads of State or Government of the EU countries together with its President and the President of the Commission. It defines general political directions and priorities of the Union. It does not have any law-making function.

The European Council was introduced in 1974 in an attempt to deal with policy matters at the highest level, comprising the individual Heads of State or Governments of each of the Member States. It acquired a formal status in the Maastricht Treaty and became a formal institution of the Union following the Treaty of Lisbon.

The European Council defines the general political direction and priorities of the European Union, but does not exercise any legislative function. It meets twice every six months, convened by its President, but may convene specially if a specific situation requires it to do so. Decisions of the European Council are taken by consensus unless the Treaties require unanimity or qualified majority voting. The European Council elects its President by qualified majority. The President's term of office is two and a half years, renewable once.

Take care not to confuse the European Council with the Council of the European Union or the Council of Europe.

2.2.1.3 Sources of EU law

There are three sources of EU law:

- **Primary sources.** A number of primary sources of European law have already been mentioned. These are the founding Treaties: the Treaty on European Union and the Treaty on the Functioning of the EU. These Treaties provide the framework of competencies between the EU as a body and its member countries. They also set out the powers of the EU institutions. Therefore, they set out a broad legal framework within which the institutions implement EU policy. Other primary sources include the amending EU Treaties, the annexed protocols, and the accession Treaties for new EU countries.

- **Secondary sources.** Secondary sources supplement the primary sources by providing a more detailed treatment of the law in a given area and establishing how the principles and objectives identified in the primary sources are to be achieved. The secondary sources of European law comprise unilateral acts (regulations and directives, decisions, opinions, and recommendations) and conventions and agreements (international agreements between the EU and an external country or body and agreements between EU countries and between EU institutions).

- **Supplementary law.** This covers the case law of the CJEU, relevant international law, custom and usage, and general unwritten principles of law and justice.

The sources of EU law can be summarized as shown in Table 2.2.

Table 2.2 Sources of EU law

Primary sources of EU law	Secondary sources of EU law	Supplementary law
Treaty of Rome 1957	Regulations	Case law of the CJEU
Single European Act 1985	Directives	Principles of international law
Treaty on European Union (Maastricht Treaty) 1992	Decisions issued by the Commission	Unwritten principles of law and justice
Treaty of Amsterdam 1996	Opinions	
Treaty of Nice 2001	Recommendations	
Treaty of Lisbon 2009	Conventions and agreements	

The interrelationship between EU law and domestic law

This section remains current at the time of writing (October 2020).

The body of EU law became part of domestic law by virtue of the European Communities Act 1972. Section 2(1) of the Act provides that:

All such rights, powers, liabilities, obligations and restrictions from time to time created or arising by or under the Treaties, and all such remedies and procedures from time to time provided for by or under the Treaties, as in accordance with the Treaties are without further enactment to be given legal effect or used in the United Kingdom shall be recognised and available in law, and be enforced, allowed and followed accordingly; and the expression 'enforceable Community right' and similar expressions shall be read as referring to one to which this subsection applies.

This meant that all directly applicable EU law, regardless of whether it has already been made or is to be made in the future, became part of national law.

Before proceeding much further, we must cover some important terminology.

Direct applicability and direct effect

It is important that you understand the distinction between provisions of EU law which are directly applicable and provisions that are directly effective.

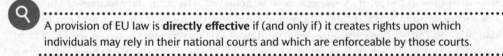

A provision of EU law is **directly applicable** if it automatically becomes part of the law of an EU Member State without the need for that EU Member State to enact any further legislation.

A provision of EU law is **directly effective** if (and only if) it creates rights upon which individuals may rely in their national courts and which are enforceable by those courts.

Thus, direct *applicability* is concerned with the incorporation of EU law into the legal system of an EU Member State, whereas direct *effect* is concerned with its enforceability.

Before considering which of the different types of EU law have direct effect (i.e. can be relied upon by individuals in national courts and are enforceable by those courts) it is necessary to understand the distinction between vertical direct effect and horizontal direct effect as illustrated in Figure 2.2.

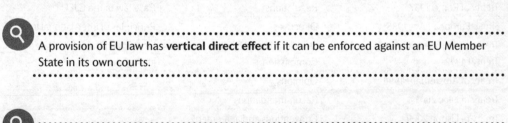

A provision of EU law has **vertical direct effect** if it can be enforced against an EU Member State in its own courts.

A provision of EU law has **horizontal direct effect** if it can be enforced against another individual in the courts of an EU Member State.

Therefore, provisions of EU law with vertical direct effect can be enforced against any EU Member State itself. Vertically directly effective provisions may also be enforced against so-called 'emanations of the state'—that is, bodies that provide a public service under the control

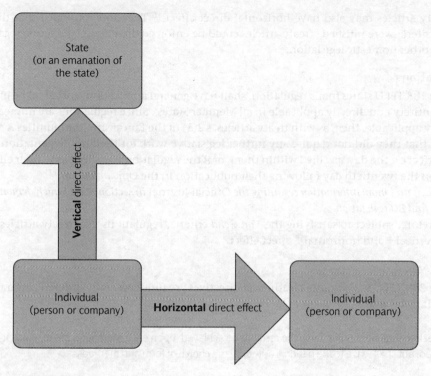

Figure 2.2 Horizontal and vertical direct effect

of government—such as local authorities and health authorities,[13] nationalized industries,[14] and public-sector employers.

You should take care when reading cases which consider the distinction between direct applicability and direct effect since the CJEU does not always distinguish between its use of the two terms.

We have looked at the different sources of EU law and the rules of direct applicability and direct effect which determine how those provisions operate within domestic law. To complete the puzzle, we finally have to establish the applicability and effect of each type of provision.

Treaty articles

Although it is for the CJEU to determine, treaty articles are normally held to be directly applicable. Therefore, following s 2(1) of the European Communities Act 1972, they required no further legislative action by the UK to take effect as law.

A treaty article will have vertical direct effect (it will create individual enforceable rights against the state) if its terms are 'clear, precise and unconditional' and its implementation required no further legislation in EU member countries (i.e. it was directly applicable).[15] These are often referred to as the *Van Gend* criteria from the case in which the matter was first considered. In other words, an Article has vertical direct effect if the EU countries had no discretion in the means of its implementation.

---

13. Case C-271/91 *Marshall v Southampton and South West Hampshire Area Health Authority (No 2)* [1993] ECR I-4367 (CJEU).
14. Case C-188/89 *Foster v British Gas plc* [1990] ECR I-3133 (CJEU).
15. Case 26/62 *Van Gend en Loos v Nederlandse Administratie der Belastingen* [1963] ECR 1 (CJEU).

Treaty articles may also have horizontal direct effect.[16] Therefore, provided that the *Van Gend* criteria were satisfied, Treaty articles could be enforced directly in UK courts, regardless of any other domestic legislation.

Regulations

Article 288 TFEU states that a regulation 'shall have general application' and 'shall be binding in its entirety and directly applicable in all Member States'. Since regulations are immediately directly applicable, then, as with treaty articles, s 2(1) of the European Communities Act 1972 meant that they did not require any further legislative work for their implementation. They took effect on the day specified within them, or if the regulation was silent as to their effective date, on the twentieth day following their publication in the *Official Journal*.[17]

You can find more information regarding the Official Journal *in section 3.2.1 which demonstrates how to find EU legislation.*

Therefore, subject to satisfying the *Van Gend* criteria, regulations, like treaty articles, have both vertical[18] and horizontal[19] direct effect.

Directives

Article 288 TFEU shows quite clearly that directives are fundamentally different from regulations. It states that:

> A directive shall be binding, as to the result to be achieved, upon each Member State to which it is addressed, but shall leave to the national authority the choice of form and methods.

In other words, directives tell the Member States of the EU what needs to be done, but leave each of the states to decide what provisions of domestic law to enact in order to implement that directive. There is always a specified period of time for the EU Member States to implement any given directive.

Directives often provide the fine detail on a given area; here, the EU recognizes that individual EU Member States may need to implement them in slightly different ways, to reflect their own national cultures or customs. Therefore, as long as the objective of the directive is met, the EU gives each EU Member State a measure of discretion as to its precise method of implementation in its domestic law. Many pieces of important and influential UK legislation arose from the implementation of EU directives, such as the Equal Pay Act 1970 and the Sex Discrimination Act 1975.

Since directives require domestic legislation for their implementation, they are not directly applicable forms of EU law. Moreover, if the directive has been properly implemented, an individual who wishes to bring an action based on that directive will use the national law rather than relying on the directive itself; therefore, in general, directives do not have horizontal direct effect.[20]

However, a directive will have vertical direct effect if it satisfies the *Van Gend* criteria and the time for implementation specified in the directive has passed.[21]

---

16. Case 43/75 *Defrenne v Sabena (No 2)* [1976] ECR 455 (CJEU).
17. Case 39/72 *Commission v Italy* [1973] ECR 101 (CJEU).
18. Case 93/71 *Leonesio v Italian Ministry of Agriculture* [1972] ECR 287 (CJEU).
19. Case C-253/00 *Antonio Munoz Cia SA v Frumar Ltd* [2002] ECR I-7289 (CJEU).
20. However, see Case C-1994/94 *CIA Security International SA v Signalson SA and Securitel SPRL* [1996] ECR I-2201 (CJEU) and Case C-443/98 *Unilever Italia v Central Food* [2000] ECR I-7535 (CJEU) where it appears that, in some instances, directives may be pleaded against an individual or non-state body.
21. Case 148/78 *Pubblico Ministero v Ratti* [1979] ECR 1629 (CJEU).

Directives may also be said to have indirect effect, since the CJEU also requires national law to be interpreted in accordance with directives.[22]

Finally, an EU Member State that has failed to implement a directive may be liable to compensate individuals who have suffered as a result.[23] In other words, if an individual has lost out because of defective implementation of a directive by an EU Member State, they may be able to sue that state for their losses provided that the breach was sufficiently serious (which will be so if the Member State 'manifestly and gravely disregard[ed]' its obligations).[24]

Decisions

The final secondary sources of European law are decisions. Article 288 TFEU provides that a decision 'shall be binding in its entirety upon those to whom it is addressed'. The addressees may be individuals, companies, or EU Member States. Thus, they are not directly applicable, but may be capable of having direct effect.

2.2.1.4 'Soft law'—recommendations and opinions

Recommendations

Recommendations are not legally binding. However, courts of EU Member States are required to interpret their own law in the light of recommendations.[25]

Opinions

In common with recommendations, opinions also have no legal authority. However, the opinion of the Commission may be a precursor to legal proceedings. If the Commission states an opinion that a Member State is in breach of an obligation, then it would be unwise for a Member State to ignore it.

Despite their persuasive nature, Article 288 TFEU states that 'Recommendations and opinions shall have no binding force'.

2.2.1.5 The supremacy of EU law

This section remains current at the time of writing (October 2020) but will change following the expiry of the implementation period on 31 December 2020.

From the point of view of the EU, where there is a conflict between EU law and the law of EU Member States, EU law prevails. This has been clear since *Van Gend en Loos* in 1963 where the European Court of Justice (as it then was) clearly stated that 'the Community constitutes a new legal order . . . for whose benefit the states have limited their sovereign rights'.[26]

In *Costa v ENEL*[27] the following year, the European Court of Justice made two important observations regarding the relationship between Community law (as it then was) and national law; first, that the Member States have definitively transferred sovereign rights to a Community created by them. They cannot reverse this process by means of subsequent unilateral measures which are inconsistent with the concept of the Community. In other words, the autonomy of the Member States to act as they wish has been limited by virtue of their membership of the Community.

---

22. Case 14/83 *Von Colson and Kamann v Land Nordheim-Westfalen* [1984] ECR 1891 (CJEU); Case C-106/89 *Marleasing SA v La Commercial Internacionale de Alimentacion SA* [1990] ECR I-4135 (CJEU).
23. Cases C-6/90 and C-9/90 *Francovich and Bonifaci v Italian Republic* [1991] ECR I-5357 (CJEU).
24. Cases C-178/94, etc *Dillenkofer and others v Germany* [1996] ECR I-4845 (CJEU).
25. Case 322/88 *Grimaldi v Fonds des Maladies Professionelles* [1989] ECR 4407 (CJEU).
26. Case 26/62 *Van Gend en Loos v Nederlandse Administratie der Belastingen* [1963] ECR 1 (CJEU).
27. Case 6/64 *Costa v ENEL* [1964] ECR 585 (CJEU).

Moreover, it is a principle of the founding Treaties that no Member State may call into question the status of Community law as a system uniformly and generally applicable throughout the Community. It follows that Community law, which was enacted in accordance with the Treaties, has priority over any conflicting law of the Member States. Therefore, in *Costa v ENEL*, the European Court of Justice emphatically established the primacy of Community law over national law. In *Simmenthal*, the Court further held that the principle of supremacy does not invalidate conflicting national law; but simply established that the national law was of no effect in the areas in which it conflicted. The Court also stated that national courts should apply European law in the case of a conflict without waiting for the setting aside of the conflicting national provision.[28]

This implies that the enactment of the European Communities Act 1972 prevented Parliament from introducing new statutes which conflicted with European law. This impacted upon the constitutional principle of Parliamentary sovereignty which, in essence, requires that Parliament has unlimited legislative competence (i.e. it may enact any law that it wishes) and that there is no competing legislative body (i.e. no body may challenge the validity of a properly enacted Act of Parliament). Initially, the UK courts view was that national law remained supreme. In *Felixstowe Dock & Railway Co v British Transport Docks Board*[29] Lord Denning stated *obiter*[30] that:

> It seems to me that once the Bill is passed by Parliament and becomes a Statute that will dispose of all discussion about the Treaty. These courts will have to abide by the Statute without regard to the Treaty.

However, in *Macarthys v Smith*[31] the Court of Appeal considered that national law *was* in fact subservient to Europe, although Lord Denning again considered that if Parliament deliberately and consistently breached European law, 'it would be the duty of our courts to follow the statute of our Parliament'.[32]

This situation was not tested in the domestic courts for some years. It was eventually considered in the *Factortame* cases.[33] Here, a conflict arose between certain provisions of the EC Treaty (as it was then) which prevented discrimination on the grounds of nationality and Part II of the Merchant Shipping Act 1988 which provided that fishing boats registered in the UK that were fishing for the quotas allocated to the UK by the EC must be owned and managed by UK citizens.

The House of Lords upheld the opinion of the European Court of Justice that it could grant an interim injunction against the Crown to prevent it enforcing an Act which contravened European law. The act of binding the Crown was previously constitutionally impossible. The House of Lords later held that parts of the Merchant Shipping Act 1988 were incompatible with the relevant provisions of the EC Treaty. This constitutional conundrum was cleverly and carefully reconciled by Lord Bridge.

He first considered s 2(4) of the European Communities Act 1972 which provided that:

> Any enactment passed or to be passed . . . shall be construed and have effect subject to the foregoing provisions of this section.

---

28. Case 106/77 *Amministrazione delle Finanze Dello Stato v Simmenthal* [1978] ECR 629 (CJEU).
29. [1976] 2 CMLR 655 (CA) 664 (Denning MR).
30. *Obiter* means that Lord Denning's statement was not an essential part of the judgment in this particular case: see section 7.3.
31. [1979] ICR 785 (CA).
32. ibid 789 (Denning MR).
33. *R v Secretary of State for Transport, ex p Factortame Ltd (No 2)* [1990] 2 AC 85 (HL).

In other words, any legislation passed or to be passed in the UK must be interpreted with applicable European law in mind.

Lord Bridge argued that, since s 2(4) of the European Communities Act 1972 states that any enactment must have regard to Community obligations, this effectively meant that Parliament's intention was that *all* future legislation would be EC-compliant and would contain a fictional 'invisible clause' to this effect, unless the incompatibility was so important that it needed to be explicitly stated in the new legislation. Lord Bridge said that:

> Whatever limitation of its sovereignty Parliament accepted when it enacted the European Communities Act 1972 it was entirely voluntary . . . when decisions of the Court of Justice have exposed areas of United Kingdom law which failed to implement Council Directives, Parliament has always loyally accepted the obligation to make appropriate and prompt amendments. Thus there is nothing in any way novel in according supremacy to rules of Community law.

Therefore the relevant provisions of the Merchant Shipping Act 1988 took effect subject to directly enforceable Community rights. In doing so, the House of Lords affirmed that, for all future cases, where a statute was silent on a matter covered by European law, it was presumed that it was intended to comply with European law.

The *Conservative–Liberal Democrat Coalition Agreement* published following the 2010 general election contained a promise to 'ensure that there is no further transfer of sovereignty or powers [to the EU] over the course of the next Parliament'; to 'amend the 1972 European Communities Act so that any proposed future treaty that transferred areas of power, or competences, would be subject to a referendum on that treaty'; and to 'examine the case for a United Kingdom Sovereignty Bill to make it clear that ultimate authority remains with Parliament'. The ensuing European Union Act 2011 contained a sovereignty clause in s 18 as follows:

> Directly applicable or directly effective EU law (that is, the rights, powers, liabilities, obligations, restrictions, remedies and procedures referred to in section 2(1) of the European Communities Act 1972) falls to be recognised and available in law in the United Kingdom only by virtue of that Act or where it is required to be recognised and available in law by virtue of any other Act.

Thus, s 18 demonstrated the clear intention of Parliament that if UK law clearly, deliberately, and explicitly stated that EU law was not to be followed then the courts should apply the domestic UK law. The associated Explanatory Note states that s 18 is 'declaratory' of the position at the time:

> This declaratory provision was included in the Act in order to address concerns that the doctrine of parliamentary sovereignty may in the future be eroded by decisions of the courts. By providing in statute that directly effective and directly applicable EU law only takes effect in the UK legal order through the will of Parliament and by virtue of the European Communities Act 1972 or where it is required to be recognised and available in law by virtue of any other Act, this will provide clear authority which can be relied upon to counter arguments that EU law constitutes a new higher autonomous legal order derived from the EU Treaties or international law and principles which has become an integral part of the UK's legal system independent of statute.

2.2.1.6 Brexit

Although the right to leave the EU has been a right under Article 50 of the Treaty on European Union since 2007, it had never been exercised by any Member State of the EU before the UK did so on 29 March 2017 following the Brexit referendum in 2016. This meant the UK was scheduled to withdraw from membership of the EU on 29 March 2019.

The day after triggering Article 50, the Government provided initial details of what was popularly known as the 'Great Repeal Bill' to ensure that EU law will no longer apply in the UK from 'exit day' (specifically 29 March 2019 at 11.00pm—which was midnight Brussels time). The European Union (Withdrawal) Act 2018 received Royal Assent on 26 June 2018. Its main provisions relating to EU legislation and its relationship to UK law are set out in Table 2.3.

Table 2.3 Main provisions of the European Union (Withdrawal) Act 2018

Section	Effect
1	Repeals the European Communities Act 1972 on exit day
2	EU-derived domestic legislation in effect before exit day continues to have effect on and after exit day
3	Direct EU legislation, so far as operative immediately before exit day, forms part of domestic law on and after exit day
4	Any rights, powers, liabilities, obligations, restrictions, remedies, and procedures which exist and are followed by virtue of s 2(1) of the European Communities Act 1972 immediately before exit day continue as such on, and after, exit day
5	The principle of supremacy of EU law does not apply to any enactment or rule of law passed or made on or after exit day
6	A court or tribunal is not bound by any decisions of the CJEC on or after exit day; neither can it refer any matter to the CJEC

According to the accompanying Explanatory Notes prepared by the Department for Exiting the European Union, the Act ends the supremacy of EU law in UK law, converts EU law as it stands at the moment of exit into domestic law, and preserves laws made in the UK to implement EU obligations. It also creates temporary powers to make secondary legislation to enable corrections to be made to the laws that would otherwise no longer operate appropriately once the UK has left, so that the domestic legal system would continue to function correctly outside the EU. The Act also enables domestic law to reflect the content of a withdrawal agreement under Article 50 of the Treaty on European Union once the UK leaves the EU, subject to the prior enactment of a statute by Parliament approving the final terms of withdrawal.

Of course, the UK did not leave the EU as originally planned. The European Union (Withdrawal) Act 2019 permitted the Prime Minister to seek an extension to the period set out in Article 50. The Prime Minister did so and asked to extend Article 50 to 30 June 2019. Following a European Council meeting the next day, the remaining EU leaders (the EU27) agreed to grant an extension comprising two possible dates: 22 May 2019, should the Withdrawal Agreement gain approval from MPs; or 12 April 2019, if it did not. On 2 April 2019, the Prime Minister announced she would seek a further extension to the Article 50 process and at a meeting of the European Council on 10 April 2019, the UK and EU27 agreed to extend Article 50 until 31 October 2019.

The European Union (Withdrawal) (No. 2) Act 2019, required the Prime Minister to seek a further extension to the 31 October 2019 date if the House of Commons did not give its consent to either a Withdrawal Agreement or leaving without a deal by 19 October 2019. The Act proposed a new withdrawal date of 31 January 2020 which was agreed by the EU.

The European Union (Withdrawal Agreement) Act 2020 received Royal Assent on 23 January 2020. It implemented the Withdrawal Agreement as agreed between the UK and the EU. This Act also set out that the UK and the EU agreed that the UK's exit on 31 January 2020 would be followed by a time-limited implementation period, which will last until 11.00pm on 31 December 2020. Section 33 of the Act also provides that the UK may not agree to an extension of the implementation period in the Joint Committee. During the implementation period, common rules will remain in place, with EU law continuing to apply to the UK under the terms set out in the Withdrawal Agreement.

The principal purpose of the European Union (Withdrawal) Act 2018 is to provide a functioning body of law when the implementation period expires.

As a general rule, the same rules and laws will apply on 1 January 2021 as they did the day before. It will then be for Parliament and, where appropriate, the devolved legislatures (Scotland and Wales) to make any future changes.

The Act performs four main functions. It:

- Repeals the European Communities Act 1972
- Converts EU law as it stands at the moment of exit into domestic law before the UK leaves the EU and preserves laws made in the UK to implement EU obligations
- Creates powers to make secondary legislation, including temporary powers to enable corrections to be made to the laws that would otherwise no longer operate appropriately once the UK has left the EU and to implement a withdrawal agreement (subject to the prior enactment of a statute by Parliament approving the final terms of withdrawal)
- Removes the existing restrictions on devolved competence in relation to acting incompatibly with EU law so that decision-making powers in areas currently governed by EU law will pass to the devolved institutions, except where specified in secondary legislation under this Act.

In essence, all existing EU law was 'copied across' to UK law on exit day to ensure a smooth legal transition, leaving Parliament to amend, repeal, and develop that body of law as it sees fit. However, the reality is that this will be far from straightforward: for instance, much EU-derived law refers to EU institutions. The Act gives power to create new law to deal with deficiencies to Ministers without full parliamentary scrutiny—including any provision that could be made by an Act of Parliament. The Government estimates that up to 1,000 statutory instruments may be required to make sure that the Brexit transition operates properly.

2.2.2 The European Convention on Human Rights

2.2.2.1 A brief history

The European Convention on Human Rights and Freedoms is a creation of the Council of Europe although it is, at least in part, based upon the 1948 United Nations Declaration of Human Rights. The Council of Europe was formed in 1949, shortly after the end of the Second World War, with the aim of international cooperation and the prevention of the kinds of widespread atrocious violations of human rights which had occurred during the war. The European Convention on Human Rights was signed in Rome in 1950, ratified by the UK a year later, and came into force in 1953.

2.2.2.2 Convention rights

The European Convention on Human Rights establishes a number of fundamental rights and freedoms (see Table 2.4). Some of the rights are absolute: this means that no interference with them is permitted. Others are limited: this means that no interference is permitted, but there may be limitations stated within the right itself. Finally, there are qualified rights: this means that exceptions (called 'derogations') or reservations are permitted, as long as the exception or reservation is proportionate (goes no further than it has to) in order to achieve a legitimate purpose.

Table 2.4 Convention rights by Article number

Article	Convention right	Type
1	Obligation to respect human rights	Absolute
2	Right to life	Absolute
3	Prohibition of torture, inhuman, or degrading treatment or punishment	Absolute
4	Prohibition of slavery and forced labour	Absolute
5	Right to liberty and security	Limited
6	Right to a fair hearing	Limited
7	No punishment without law	Absolute
8	Right to respect for private and family life	Qualified
9	Freedom of thought, conscience, and religion	Qualified
10	Freedom of expression	Qualified
11	Freedom of assembly and association	Qualified
12	Right to marry and found a family	Qualified
13	Right to an effective remedy	Qualified
14	Freedom from discrimination	Qualified

2.2.2.3 The European Court of Human Rights

The European Court of Human Rights was established in 1959 as a final avenue of complaint for claimants who had exhausted the remedies available to them in their domestic courts for alleged breaches of Convention rights. At the same time, the European Commission of Human Rights was also established. The Commission's role was to decrease the caseload of the European Court of Human Rights by filtering out some cases and attempting to resolve others by conciliation. The individual's right to petition the European Court of Human Rights became available to UK citizens in 1966.

The European Court of Human Rights and the European Commission of Human Rights were abolished on 31 October 1998 and replaced by a single Court of Human Rights. Questions of admissibility (formerly dealt with by the Commission) are now dealt with by its judges sitting in committee.

It is worth repeating the point that it is vitally important not to confuse the European Court of Human Rights (which sits in Strasbourg) with the Court of Justice of the European Union (which sits in Luxembourg). They are separate courts with separate jurisdictions.

 CHAPTER SUMMARY

Statute law

- Public Bills are introduced by the Government as part of its programme of legislation
- Private Bills are introduced for the benefit of particular individuals, groups of people, institutions, or a particular locality

- Hybrid Bills are a cross between Public and Private Bills
- Private Members' Bills are non-Government Bills that are introduced by private Members of Parliament
- Consolidating statutes re-enact a topic contained in several earlier statutes
- Codifying statutes restate a topic previously contained in statute, common law, and custom
- Government Bills can be introduced in the House of Commons or House of Lords
- The Parliament Acts 1911 and 1949 provide a means by which the House of Commons can (under certain circumstances) bypass the House of Lords to present a Bill for Royal Assent without it having been passed by the House of Lords
- Royal Assent is required before any Bill can become law; it is customarily given
- The Human Rights Act 1998 requires that new Bills must be accompanied by a statement of compatibility (or a declaration that a statement of compatibility is not possible)
- The courts may make a declaration of incompatibility for Acts of Parliament which are incompatible with the European Convention on Human Rights; this does not affect the validity of the Act
- Delegated legislation is made under powers delegated by Parliament
- Delegated legislation includes statutory instruments (rules, regulations, and orders) and by-laws

European institutions

- The European Commission represents the interests of the Union as a whole
- The Council of the European Union represents the governments of the individual member countries
- The European Parliament is directly elected by the citizens of the EU, which it represents
- The Court of Justice of the European Union (CJEU) interprets EU law to ensure uniform application and settles disputes
- The CJEU and the European Court of Human Rights are different
- The General Court deals with most European cases at first instance
- The European Council is composed of the Heads of State or Government of the EU Member States

Interrelationship between EU law and domestic law

- A provision of EU law is directly applicable if it becomes part of the law of a Member State without need for further legislation
- A provision of EU law is directly effective if it creates rights upon which individuals may rely in their national courts (and which are enforceable by those courts)
- A provision of EU law has vertical direct effect if it can be enforced against a Member State in its own courts
- A provision of EU law has horizontal direct effect if it can be enforced against another individual in the courts of a Member State
- Treaty articles and regulations have both vertical and horizontal direct effect if they satisfy the *Van Gend* criteria: that its terms are 'clear, precise and unconditional' and its implementation required no further legislation in Member States

- Directives do not have horizontal direct effect
- Directives may have vertical direct effect if they satisfy the *Van Gend* criteria and the time limit for their implementation has expired
- Prior to Brexit, where a statute was silent on a matter covered by EU law, it was presumed that it was intended to comply with European law—the UK's position was declared in s 18 of the European Union Act 2011

European Convention on Human Rights

- The European Convention on Human Rights establishes a number of fundamental rights and freedoms
- The European Court of Human Rights is a final avenue of complaint for individuals who have exhausted national remedies available for alleged breaches of Convention rights
- The European Court of Human Rights is not the same as the Court of Justice of the European Union

 FURTHER READING

- The law-making process is explained very clearly and with a good level of detail on the UK Parliament website at www.parliament.uk/about/how/laws/. In particular the site covers the reasons why new laws are needed and how they are developed, the use of draft Bills, the different types of Bill, the passage of Bills through Parliament, the nature of Acts of Parliament, the role of secondary legislation, and the use of the Parliament Acts.
- This chapter gives a very brief overview of the EU institutions and the sources of law which come from Europe. It does not attempt to cover the operation of the EU in its entirety. Further details can be found on the EU website at europa.eu/european-union/about-eu/institutions-bodies_ en. This site covers both the institutions introduced in this chapter as well as the law-making process.

Finding legislation

3

INTRODUCTION

The last chapter of this book described the various sources of legislation. This chapter will show you how to locate statutes, statutory instruments, and EU legislation. The methods you will use to search will depend on whether you know the name of the particular piece of legislation in question or whether you are looking for any legislation which covers a certain subject area. The chapter will then close by showing you where to find the European Convention on Human Rights.

The ability to find legislation is an important legal skill. Legislation is a primary source of law affecting virtually every area of legal study. Clearly, you will not be able to read, understand, and use legislation without being able to find it first.

Learning outcomes

After studying this chapter, you will be able to:

- Find Acts of Parliament and statutory instruments online
- Determine whether there is any statute law on a particular topic
- Work out whether a piece of legislation is in force
- Locate the official texts of EU treaty articles, regulations, and directives
- Source the official current text of the European Convention on Human Rights

Practical exercise

Although this chapter will use a number of examples of various materials to demonstrate the ways in which they can be used, these are no substitute for your own experience and practice. Spend as much time as you can getting familiar with the various online resources that are available to you. Even though you might think that everything you could possibly need to find is online, you should not overlook the usefulness of going to a physical law library and trying to find as many of these example resources as you can. Bear in mind that not all resources will be available in all law libraries. At the very least, you will become familiar with the contents and layout of your library, and you may get to know your librarian, which could save you a lot of searching time in the future.

3.1 FINDING DOMESTIC LEGISLATION

This section will describe the various ways in which statutes and statutory instruments can be located, both online and in a library. By way of example, we will use the Stalking Protection Act 2019, an Act which introduced a new stalking protection order (SPO). Throughout this section we will refer to s 1 of that Act: the provision that sets out the grounds on which an SPO may be sought.

3.1.1 Online

3.1.1.1 Legislation.gov.uk

UK legislation is published on the official legislation.gov.uk website, managed by the National Archives on behalf of the Government. It contains most types of UK legislation, from the Statute of Marlborough 1267 (relating to distress and waste), to the most recent (at the time of writing) The Health Protection (Coronavirus, International Travel) (Wales) (Amendment) (No. 15) Regulations 2020. It also carries draft legislation and UK impact assessments for all new legislation since 2008.

In addition, it links to the 'EU Exit Web Archive' (at webarchive.nationalarchives.gov.uk/eu-exit/) which carries a wide selection of documents including treaties, legislative documents, the Official Journal of the EU, case law and other supporting materials, and judgments of the Court of Justice of the EU (CJEU) in English, French, and German. This collection will continue to be updated up to the completion of the EU Withdrawal Implementation Period, on 31 December 2020. Once the Implementation Period has completed, it will provide a comprehensive and official UK reference point for EU law as it stood at IP Completion Day.

You can simply browse the legislation on the database, or search by title or keywords. Some revised legislation may also be viewed as a snapshot at a particular point in time. These options are found on the 'Advanced Search' page (see Figure 3.1).

Figure 3.1 Legislation.gov.uk screenshot

So, if you wanted to find the text of s 1 of the Stalking Protection Act 2019, you could simply enter the name of the Act in the search box, and browse to s 1 (Figure 3.2).

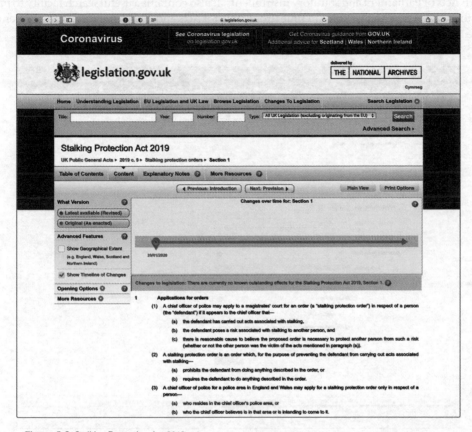

Figure 3.2 Stalking Protection Act 2019, s 1

You will also see that the site provides a graphical timeline of changes. This timeline shows the different points in time where a change occurred. The dates will coincide with the earliest date on which the change that was applied came into force. The first date in the timeline will usually be the earliest date when the provision came into force. In some instances, you will see the first date is 1 February 1991 (or, for Northern Ireland legislation, 1 January 2006). No versions before these dates are available.

However, you should take care when using the legislation.gov.uk website. Legislation carried on the site may not always be fully up to date. Therefore, it is always preferable wherever possible to find (or at least double check) legislative provisions using one of the commercially available databases which should be available to you and which also carry a lot of valuable additional information. For instance, you will have direct access to relevant case law and other resources once you have found the relevant legislation. Most institutions will subscribe to most of the main commercial databases that are covered in this book. You will probably be able to access these directly via your institutional login, but if you have difficulty, the best first point of enquiry will be your institution's library or learning resource centre.

3.1.1.2 Westlaw Edge UK

Westlaw Edge UK provides a range of browsing and searching facilities which can be used to find both Acts of Parliament and statutory instruments. It also contains a useful search facility to find historic law at a particular point in time (from 1991 for Acts and 1948 for statutory instruments) (see Figure 3.3).

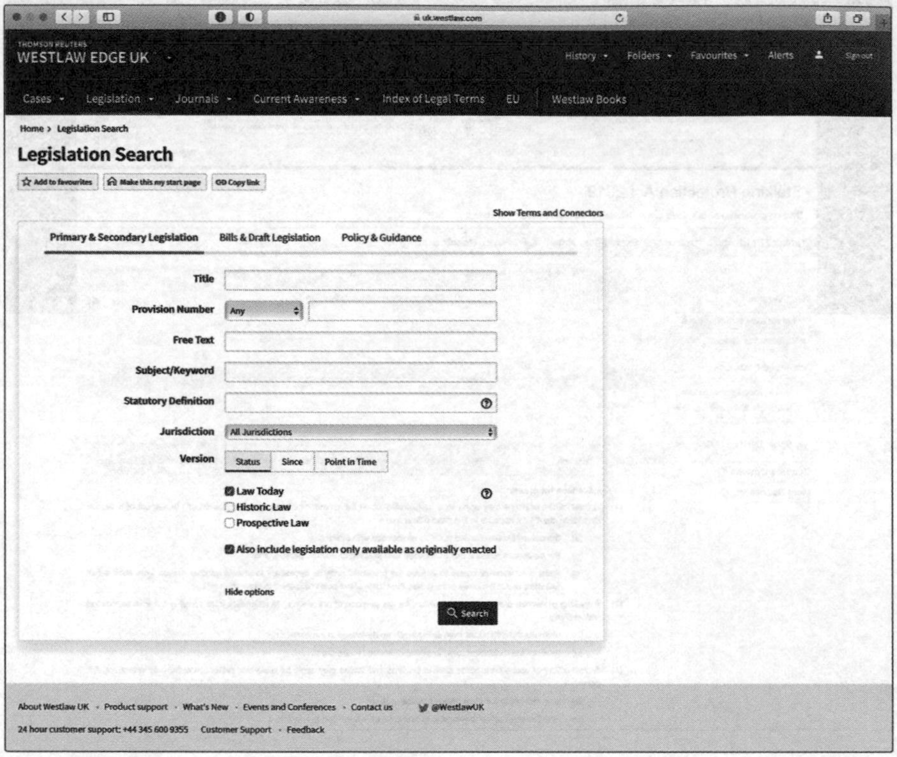

Figure 3.3 Westlaw Edge UK screenshot

So, if you use the browse or search facility to find s 1 you should also find some extra useful material (Figure 3.4).

First of all, you will see at the top of the bar to the right of the provision that it has the status of 'Law In Force'. In addition to the fact that s 1 is in force, you should also see the date on which it came into force, namely 20 January 2020, together with its broad subject area (criminal procedure) and some keywords describing it (application, chief police officers, conditions, stalking protection orders). Westlaw Edge UK also gives access to a great deal of further information about s 1 through the various options in the left-hand menu column. This includes a section on 'Statutory Annotations' including the relevant part of the Explanatory Note, notes on its passages through Parliament, sections of the Act where certain terms used in s 1 are defined (s 14), links to statutory guidance issued to the police, notes on key legal concepts associated with it, passages from key debates in Parliament which may assist with purposive construction or in cases of ambiguity. You can also find a table of amendments, details of the actual statutory instrument that brought the provision into force—in this case SU 2020/21 reg 2—with a link to the full Stalking Protection Act 2019 (Commencement) Regulations 2020/26, and its territorial extent, together with a list of other legislation that cites it, and links to any mentions in commentary or available topic overviews.

You will find more about the importance of commencement, extent, and interpretation in chapter 4.

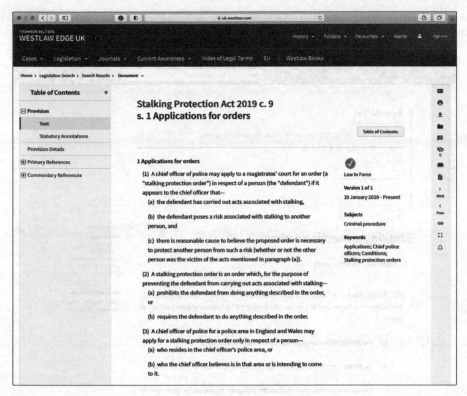

Figure 3.4 Westlaw Edge UK: Stalking Protection Act 2019, s 1

3.1.1.3 LexisLibrary

LexisLibrary provides searchable legislation and statutory instrument databases as well as cross-references to *Halsbury's Laws of England* (Figure 3.5). It has various online interactive tutorials.

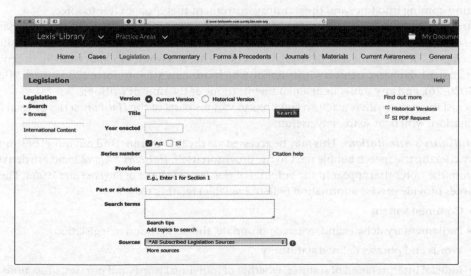

Figure 3.5 LexisLibrary screenshot
Reproduced with the kind permission of LexisNexis®

As with Westlaw Edge UK, LexisLibrary also offers browse and search facilities, as well as the ability to look for historic versions of legislation. Section 1 of the Act looks like this (Figure 3.6):

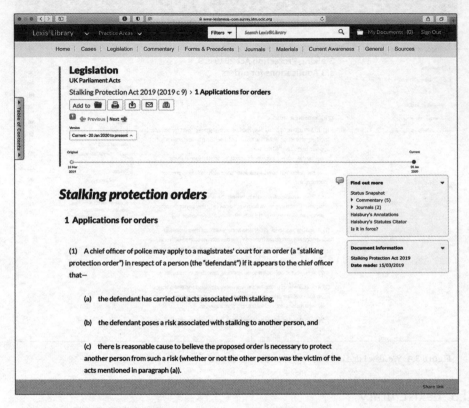

Figure 3.6 LexisLibrary: Stalking Protection Act, s 1
Reproduced with the kind permission of LexisNexis®

In the notes found by scrolling down to the bottom of the page, it also gives details of the section coming into force and the statutory instrument that brought it into force.

In addition, LexisLibrary also offers links (within the 'Find out more' box on the right-hand side of the page) to a number of other useful pieces of information. First, the 'Status Snapshot' which gives details of the date of Royal Assent of the Act as a whole (15 March 2019), the commencement date and statutory instrument which brought s 1 into force (20 January 2020; SI 2020/26), and any subsequent amendments (none at the time of writing).

LexisLibrary also offers (exclusively) links to various parts of the *Halsbury* series of legal information, which are extremely useful:

• **Halsbury's Annotations.** This may be accessed via the link within 'Find out more' or simply by clicking the speech bubble next to the provision itself. *Halsbury's Annotations* are derived from the notes that appear in the volumes of *Halsbury's Statutes of England and Wales*. These notes provide precise information (where available) relating to:

  • Commencement

  • Parliamentary debates and, where appropriate, the background to legislation

  • Words and phrases defined statutorily

  • Judicial interpretation of statutes, whether of individual words and phrases, or sections as a whole

- Cross-references to other provisions of the Act and to other relevant legislation
- Subordinate legislation
- The origin of consolidating legislation.

The annotations are updated weekly to reflect changes brought about by new cases and new legislation.

- *Halsbury's Statutes Citator.* This gives details of any amendments to the provision. *Halsbury's Statutes Citator* provides a comprehensive list of amendments to all statutes which have been considered in *Halsbury's Statutes* since 1929. Amendments are noted to provision level, with any general notes relating to the Act as a whole appearing as the first note.

- *Halsbury's Is it in Force?* This provides the information you need to establish the exact commencement dates of Acts passed since 1960. The short title and chapter number of every Public General Act is given, and the following details are generally provided:

  - The date on which the Act received Royal Assent
  - A list of provisions which deal with the commencement of the Act or any part thereof (including any commencement orders which have been made)
  - Any date or dates which have been appointed for the provisions of the Act to come into force
  - An indication where any provision is not in force.

Self-test questions

1. Which pieces of legislation amended s 39 of the Terrorism Act 2000 in 2007?
2. Which section was added to the Terrorism Act 2000 by s 117(2) of the Anti-terrorism, Crime and Security Act 2001?

Review the answers to the self-test questions to check your progress and watch the accompanying video explanations at ***www.oup.com/he/finch8e/.***

3.1.2 In a library

Although much legal research is now done online, the ability to use a law library is still a very useful legal skill. There are some suggestions for further reading which go into much greater depth than is possible in this book at the end of the chapter. More practically speaking, though, should you ever need to find legislation in the library (remember that online services can sometimes go offline; or, worse still, you find yourself without internet connection!), then you should first seek out your law librarian who will be able to assist.

Legislation is published in a range of print publications:

- *Public General Acts and Measures.* At the end of each year, the Public General Acts which have been enacted during the year are published together in the official series *Public General Acts and Measures.* This series includes an index to all Acts passed during the year in alphabetical order; a chronological index to all Acts passed during the year (by chapter number); the full text of all Public General Acts enacted during the year in chapter number (chronological) order; the full text of all the General Synod Measures of the Church of England passed in the year; and a list (but not the full text) of Local and Personal Acts enacted during the year.

- *Chronological Table of the Statutes.* The *Chronological Table of the Statutes* provides historical as well as current information. As its name suggests it lists all statutes enacted since 1235 (the Statute of Merton). It then shows, for each, whether it has been repealed or amended. The statutes are listed in year and chapter order.

- *Current Law Legislation Citator.* Since 1972 the *Current Law Legislation Citators* have provided an alphabetical list of statutes at the start of each volume. This can be useful if you know the name of the Act but are unsure of its year or chapter number.

- *Current Law Statutes Annotated.* *Current Law Statutes Annotated* provides the full text of all Public General Acts shortly after the official Act is published by the Queen's Printer (and will ultimately be bound into *Public General Acts and Measures*). They are supplied as individual booklets and filed in a loose-leaf service binder in chapter number order. The annotations generally provide a detailed account of the legislative history of the Act including references to the key debates in *Hansard*, provision by provision. Although these annotations carry no legal authority, they are extremely useful.

- *Halsbury's Statutes.* *Halsbury's Statutes of England* aims to provide current versions of all Public General Acts in force in England and Wales. As you would probably imagine, it is a mammoth undertaking which comprises a number of different volumes, all of which work together to keep the publication overall as up to date as possible. The information listed in the main volumes is brought up to date annually via the *Cumulative Supplement* with more recent (i.e. this year's) developments being available via the *Noter-Up Service*.

- *Halsbury's Is it in Force?* The quickest way to determine whether a particular statutory provision is in force is to use *Is it in Force?* which is part of the *Halsbury's Statutes* suite. However, it only covers statutes enacted since 1961. For older statutes, you should use the *Chronological Table of the Statutes*.

As you have already seen, the suite of *Halsbury* publications is available via LexisLibrary, where it is kept up to date.

3.2 FINDING EU LEGISLATION

3.2.1 The *Official Journal of the European Union*

The *Official Journal of the European Union* (generally referred to as the *Official Journal* or just the *OJ*) is the only official source of the officially adopted texts of the EU.

The *Official Journal* is published almost daily (usually around six times a week). It is vast—running to over 30,000 pages annually![1] It comprises several parts, as listed in Table 3.1.

---

1. The figure of 30,000 pages only refers to the *L series* and the *C series*. Adding the material that is only available online clearly expands the mass of information in the *Official Journal* even more.

Table 3.1 Parts of the *Official Journal*

Part	Contents
L series (Legislation)	The *L series* contains all EU legislation including: • Regulations • Directives • Decisions • Recommendations • Opinions The *Directory of Community Legislation in Force* is published as part of the *L series*. This lists references to the initial texts and to any subsequent amendments. It also includes references to agreements made and conventions signed by the European Union in the framework of external relations, binding acts under the EU Treaties, complementary acts, such as those of the Council of Ministers and Heads of State or Government, and other non-binding acts which are relevant for the institutions.
C series (Information and Notices)	The *C series* contains EU information and notices and includes: • Summaries of judgments of the Court of Justice and the General Court • Minutes of Parliamentary meetings • Reports of the Court of Auditors • Parliamentary written questions and answers from the Council or Commission • Statements from the European Economic and Social Committee and the Committee of the Regions • Competition notices for recruitment by the EU institutions (if you are interested only in these notices, there is a special subscription—see price list) • Calls for expressions of interest for EU programmes and projects • Other documents published pursuant to EU legislation • Public contracts for food aid • The table of contents of the *OJ CE series*
CE series	The *CE series* contains preparatory acts in the legislative process
S series (Supplemental)	The *S series* publishes details of public contracts which are open to competitive tender
Annex	The *Annex* contains full text transcripts of debates in the European Parliament
Special Edition	The *Special Edition* contains official English translations of all EC legislation in force as at 1 January 1973 when the UK joined the European Communities

Note that the *S series*[2] and the *Annex*[3] are only available online. The *S series* can be found in Tenders Electronic Daily (TED) at www.ted.europa.eu (Figure 3.7).

---

2. Since 1997,
3. Since 2000.

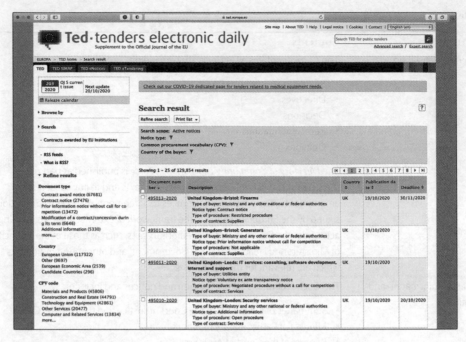

Figure 3.7 TED screenshot
© European Union, 1995–2019

Debates of the Parliament can be found at www.europarl.europa.eu/news/en/agenda (see Figure 3.8).

Figure 3.8 European Parliament screenshot
© European Union, 1995–2019

3.2.2 Finding treaty articles

As you will recall from chapter 2, the underlying source of EU law is found in the various treaties. The EU Treaty itself has been amended by the Single European Act and the Treaties of Maastricht, Amsterdam, Nice, and Lisbon.

3.2.2.1 Online

EU website

The text of the Treaties can be found online via the EU website at https://europa.eu/european-union/law/treaties_en (Figure 3.9).

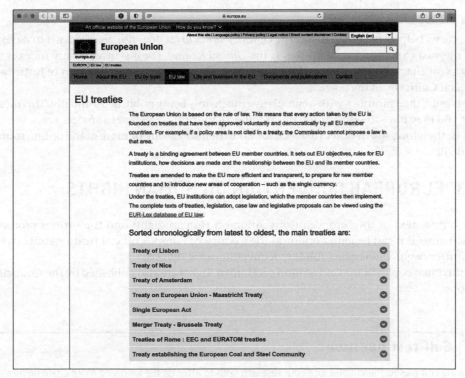

Figure 3.9 Europa screenshot: EU Treaties
© European Union, 1995–2019

3.2.2.2 In a library

The authoritative text for all EU legislation is the *Official Journal*.[4]

An unofficial, but nonetheless very useful, compilation of the unannotated texts of the main treaties can be found in N Foster, *Blackstone's EU Treaties and Legislation*, published and updated regularly by OUP.

---

4. For instance, the text of the Treaty of Nice was found in the *Official Journal C series* on 10 March 2001.

3.2.3 Finding EU secondary legislation

3.2.3.1 Online

EUROPA (www.europa.eu)

EUROPA is the main website of the European Union. It comprises over 1.5 million pages and contains a free searchable database of EU legislation and case law at www.europa.eu/eu-law/index_en.htm.

Other databases

LexisLibrary and Westlaw Edge UK also provide search facilities for EU legislation.

3.2.3.2 In a library

The *Official Journal Index*

Despite its helpful sounding name, the *Official Journal Index* does not greatly assist in navigating the vast expanse of material that is the *Official Journal*. For instance, it only indexes the *L series* (of enacted legislation) and the case lists and summaries (from the Court of Justice and General Court) from the *C series*.

It is published monthly, with a cumulative index only being published annually. This means that you may have to search through a number of monthly copies of the *Index*.

It is, therefore, much easier to search for EU materials via one or more of the online sources available.

3.3 EUROPEAN CONVENTION ON HUMAN RIGHTS

The official text of the European Convention on Human Rights and the various protocols which amend it can be found online at the Council of Europe's official treaty website (www.coe.int/en/web/conventions/full-list/-/conventions/treaty/005).

Individual copies of the Convention on Human Rights are also published by the Council of Europe.

Self-test questions

Having completed this chapter, use your research skills to attempt the following more challenging research questions involving legislation.

1. What is the *OJ* reference of the Preamble to the Accession Treaty of Austria, Finland, and Sweden to the European Union?

2. Which primary statutory provision concerns the use of poison against grey squirrels and coypus and what secondary legislation was made under it?

3. What legislation excepted the Brazilian wolf spider from the provisions of the Dangerous Wild Animals Act 1976?

4. Which private Act ensures that the flood arches at each end of Gunthorpe Bridge are at all times kept open and free for the passage of water?

5. What was the wording of s 15A of the Theft Act 1968 as at 20 January 1995?

Review the answers to the self-test questions to check your progress and watch the accompanying video explanations at www.oup.com/he/finch8e/.

CHAPTER SUMMARY

Domestic statutes

- The legislation.gov.uk website provides free links to the full text of all Public General Acts from 1988 and Local Acts from 1991

- Westlaw Edge UK and LexisLibrary all provide commercially available legislation search engines which are kept up to date and provide much additional valuable information

- *Halsbury's Statutes of England* provides current volumes of all Public General Acts, arranged by subject matter. It also contains a very useful *Is it in Force?* service

- *Public General Acts and Measures* contains the full text of all statutes

- The *Chronological Table of the Statutes* is useful for tracing very old statutes, but is of less use for modern statutes as it is often two or three years out of date

- The *Current Law Legislation Citator* lists all statutes and provides information as to where and how that legislation has been used

- *Current Law Statutes Annotated* provides the full text of all Public General Acts annotated with a detailed account of the history of the Act (including Parliamentary debate) and other useful notes and cross-references

EU law

- The *Official Journal of the European Union (OJ)* is the only official source of the officially adopted texts of the EU

- The *OJ* is vast and easier to navigate online

- The *CE series*, *S series*, and *Annex* to the *OJ* are only available online

- Compilations of EU legislation are widely available in student statute texts

- EU legislation can be found online for free via EUROPA

- Westlaw Edge UK and LexisLibrary all provide commercially available EU legislation search engines which are generally easier to use than EUROPA

- The European Convention on Human Rights and various protocols which amend it can be found on the Council of Europe official website

FURTHER READING

- Although almost all legal research is now done online, the ability to use a law library is still a very useful legal skill. Two books that go into greater depth than has been possible in this chapter are P Clinch, *Using a Law Library* (2nd edn, Blackstone Press 2001), and PA Thomas and J Knowles, *Dane and Thomas: How to Use a Law Library* (2nd edn, Sweet & Maxwell 2001).
  Despite being well over ten years old, the principles of library research remain the same, and these books will assist you in finding your way around the library at your own institution.

Using legislation

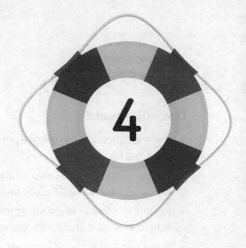

4

INTRODUCTION

The place of legislation within the range of sources of law was covered in chapter 2 while various means of finding legislation were considered in chapter 3. Having learnt where legislation fits into the structure of the legal system and how it can be found, this chapter will discuss how to use legislation. It will firstly look at the 'anatomy' of an Act of Parliament and describe each of its composite parts. It will then move on to consider the various means by which the courts can interpret the wording of statutory provisions, including a discussion of the impact of the European Communities Act 1972, the position following its repeal, and the Human Rights Act 1998.

Using legislation is an important legal skill. Legislation is a primary source of law and represents the will of Parliament as the legislature. Therefore it is essential that you are able to negotiate your way around a piece of legislation and understand how it all fits together. You will also need to be able to interpret potentially ambiguous legislative provisions to determine whether they will support your argument or whether an interpretation could be found that might go against your argument. Most importantly, using and understanding legislation is vital to the study of every area of law.

Learning outcomes

After studying this chapter, you will be able to:

- Navigate an Act of Parliament and a statutory instrument and distinguish its component parts
- Interpret the possible meanings of a legislative provision in the case of ambiguity
- Describe the impact that the European Communities Act 1972, the Human Rights Act 1998, and the European Union (Withdrawal) Act 2018 have had on the interpretation of legislation

4.1 ANATOMY OF AN ACT OF PARLIAMENT

In order to make any sense at all of a statute, you will need first to understand the way in which it is structured. We will use the Coronavirus Act 2020 as an example. Look at the extracts from the statute provided. You will see that a number of areas of the statute have been highlighted which we will cover in turn as we go through this section (see Figure 4.1).

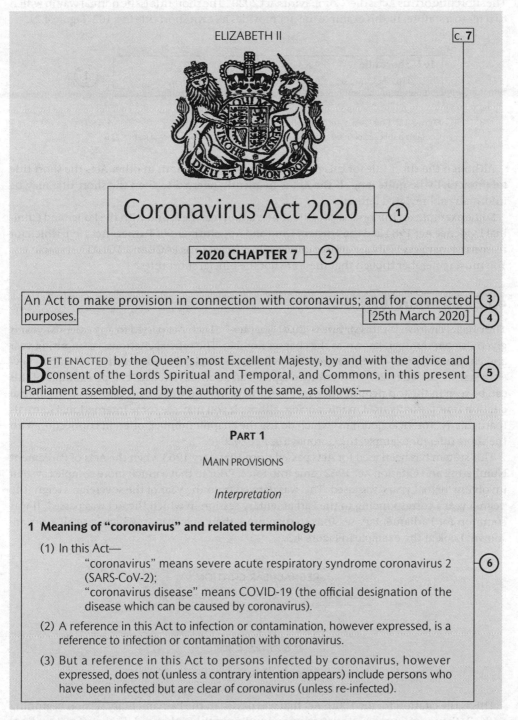

ELIZABETH II

c. 7

Coronavirus Act 2020 — ①

2020 CHAPTER 7 — ②

An Act to make provision in connection with coronavirus; and for connected — ③
purposes. [25th March 2020] — ④

BE IT ENACTED by the Queen's most Excellent Majesty, by and with the advice and consent of the Lords Spiritual and Temporal, and Commons, in this present — ⑤
Parliament assembled, and by the authority of the same, as follows:—

PART 1

MAIN PROVISIONS

Interpretation

1 Meaning of "coronavirus" and related terminology

(1) In this Act—

"coronavirus" means severe acute respiratory syndrome coronavirus 2 — ⑥
(SARS-CoV-2);
"coronavirus disease" means COVID-19 (the official designation of the disease which can be caused by coronavirus).

(2) A reference in this Act to infection or contamination, however expressed, is a reference to infection or contamination with coronavirus.

(3) But a reference in this Act to persons infected by coronavirus, however expressed, does not (unless a contrary intention appears) include persons who have been infected but are clear of coronavirus (unless re-infected).

Figure 4.1 Coronavirus Act 2020
Contains public sector information licensed under the Open Government Licence v3.0

4.1.1 Short title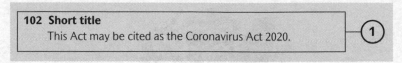

The short title of this Act is the 'Coronavirus Act 2020'. The short title is the normal way in which to refer to a statute. In this example the Act provides its own short title in s 102 (Figure 4.2).

102 Short title
This Act may be cited as the Coronavirus Act 2020.

Figure 4.2 Coronavirus Act 2020, s 102
Contains public sector information licensed under the Open Government Licence v3.0

Although the short title for this particular Act is actually short, in other Acts the short title might actually be quite long. If the Act is frequently referred to then the short title may be informally abbreviated further.

Some examples of informal short-title abbreviations can be found with the Police and Criminal Evidence Act 1984 and the Trusts of Land and Appointment of Trustees Act 1996 which for reasons of manageability are almost universally referred to as PACE and TOLATA respectively. You must remember though that these are not the official short titles.

4.1.2 Citation ②

The official citation for this statute is '2020 Chapter 7'. Each Act passed in any calendar year is given its own number, known as the chapter number. The official citations—comprising year and chapter number—are therefore unique. In our example, the Coronavirus Act was the seventh statute passed in 2020. The word 'chapter' can be abbreviated to 'c.'—an example of this can be seen in the top right-hand corner of the page. As you will see in chapter 13, the official citation is not usually used in referencing, although you may see some international journals (particularly American journals) which do use the chapter number, often in connection with the short title; for example, the Coronavirus Act 2020 (c. 7).

This system has been used for Acts passed since 1 January 1963 when the Acts of Parliament Numbering and Citation Act 1962 came into force. Prior to that a much more complex system involving 'regnal years' was used. This was derived from the year of the sovereign's reign (the 'regnal year') corresponding to the Parliamentary session in which the Act was passed. It was common for Parliamentary sessions to span more than one year, in which case all years are shown. Look at the example in Figure 4.3.

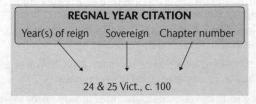

Figure 4.3 Regnal year citation

This is the citation for the 100th Act that was passed in the Parliamentary session beginning in the 24th year of Queen Victoria's reign and ending in the 25th year. Like the official citation, it tells us absolutely nothing about the purpose of the Act itself. This Victorian example is more commonly (and conveniently) known as the Offences against the Person Act 1861.

There is a very useful calendar year to regnal year conversion table covering 1235–1962 available on the JustCite website at www.justcite.com/kb/search-technology/regnal-years/.

4.1.3 Long title

The long title of this statute is 'An Act to make provision in connection with coronavirus and connected purposes'. Generally speaking, the long title of an Act gives an indication as to its purpose and content. While this Act is quite straightforward in its intentions, Acts may span many different areas and consequently have very lengthy long titles. For instance, the Criminal Justice and Courts Act 2015 has a 116-word long title to reflect its scope:

> An Act to make provision about how offenders are dealt with before and after conviction; to create offences involving ill-treatment or wilful neglect by a person providing health care or social care; to create an offence of the corrupt or other improper exercise of police powers and privileges; to make provision about offences committed by disqualified drivers; to create an offence of disclosing private sexual photographs or films with intent to cause distress; to amend the offence of meeting a child following sexual grooming; to amend the offence of possession of extreme pornographic images; to make provision about the proceedings and powers of courts and tribunals; to make provision about judicial review; and for connected purposes.

Many recent long titles end with the phrase 'and for connected purposes' as a catch-all for matters that are not specifically mentioned in the long title itself.

4.1.4 Date of Royal Assent ④

This Act received the Royal Assent on 25 March 2020. This is the date upon which the preceding Bill became law. The provisions of the Act come into force at the beginning of the day on which the Act receives the Royal Assent[1] unless the Act itself states otherwise in a commencement provision (see section 4.1.7). The year of the Act in its short title can sometimes be misleading if it differs from the year in which its provisions came into force. For example, the European Communities Act 1972 received the Royal Assent on 17 October 1972 but did not actually came into force until 1 January 1973.

4.1.5 Enacting formula ⑤

The enacting formula introduces the main provisions of the statute. It declares that the law derives its authority from having been properly passed by the legislature. The enacting formula is generally the same, namely:

> BE IT ENACTED by the Queen's most Excellent Majesty, by and with the advice and consent of the Lords Spiritual and Temporal, and Commons, in this present Parliament assembled, and by the authority of the same, as follows:

However, if the Parliament Acts 1911 and 1949 have been used to force legislation through Parliament against the wishes of the House of Lords, the enacting formula used is different:

> BE IT ENACTED by the Queen's most Excellent Majesty, by and with the advice and consent of the Commons in this present Parliament assembled, in accordance with the provisions of the Parliament Acts 1911 and 1949, and by the authority of the same, as follows:

---

1. Interpretation Act 1978 s 4.

This formula removes references to the 'advice and consent of the Lords Spiritual and Temporal'. *See chapter 2, section 2.1.1.6 for more information on the use of the Parliament Acts.*

4.1.6 Main body ⑥

The main body of this Act begins with section 1 which sets out some definitions: specifically the meaning of 'coronavirus' (and other related terms) for the purposes of the Act.

The main body of an Act is divided into sections, subsections, paragraphs, and subparagraphs.

You will see from Figure 4.1 that the section number is shown in **bold** next to a bold heading which gives an indication of the section's contents; in this instance 'Meaning of "coronavirus" and related terminology'. Underneath this you will see three subsections, each numbered in round brackets. So, for example, you would say that the definition of 'coronavirus disease' was found in section 1, subsection 1 of the Act. This is a bit cumbersome, so you could use section 1(1) instead. 'Section' is commonly abbreviated to 's'[2]—so it would be perfectly correct to write 'The definition of coronavirus disease is found in s 1(1) of the Coronavirus Act 2020'. An exception to the use of the abbreviation is that it is a matter of convention to write the word 'section' in full at the start of a sentence. Therefore, it would be generally preferable to say 'Section 1(1) of the Coronavirus Act 2020 defines coronavirus disease' rather than 'S 1(1) of the Coronavirus Act 2020 defines coronavirus disease'.

More complicated sections are broken down further beyond the subsection level into paragraphs and subparagraphs, in order to aid clarity. Figure 4.4 shows an extract from s 29 of the

---

29 Meaning of "food supply chain" and related expressions

(1) This section has effect for the purposes of sections 25 to 28.

(2) A "food supply chain" is a supply chain for providing individuals with items of food or drink for personal consumption, where the items consist of or include, or have been produced to any extent using—
  (a) anything grown or otherwise produced in carrying on agriculture, or
  (b) anything taken, grown or otherwise produced in carrying on fishing or aquaculture.

(3) The persons "in" a food supply chain are—
  (a) the persons carrying on the agriculture, fishing or aquaculture ("producers"), and
  (b) any persons in the supply chain between the producers and the individuals referred to in subsection (2) ("intermediaries").

(4) The persons "closely connected" with a food supply chain are—
  (a) persons supplying seeds, stock, equipment, feed, fertiliser, pesticides or similar items to producers for use in agriculture, fishing or aquaculture,
  (b) persons providing goods or services to producers or intermediaries, where the goods or services relate to—
    (i) the safety or quality of food or drink, or
    (ii) the welfare of animals, and ──────── ⑥
  (c) bodies representing persons in or closely connected with a food supply chain by virtue of the preceding provisions of this section.

Figure 4.4 Coronavirus Act 2020, s 29(4)(b)(ii)
Contains public sector information licensed under the Open Government Licence v3.0

---

2. Even though it might look unusual, OSCOLA referencing (see chapter 13) does not use a full stop after the 's' for 'section'.

Act which defines various terms relating to food supply chains. Section 29 is first divided into subsections. Subsection 29(4) defines persons who are 'closely connected' with a food supply chain. The first of these is in para 29(4)(a), namely persons supplying seeds, etc, for use in agriculture, fishing, or aquaculture. The second condition is in para 29(4)(b), which breaks down characteristics of certain goods or services into two subparagraphs, numbered (i) and (ii).

Particular paragraphs and subparagraphs can be precisely referenced in the same way as sections and subsections, by adding the extra levels of numbering; for example s 29(4)(b)(ii) includes the provision of goods or services relating to the welfare of animals as a close connection to the food supply chain for the purposes of the coronavirus legislation.

See chapter 11 for more discussion on written style.

4.1.6.1 Marginal notes

As you have already seen, the headings for each section give some indication of its content, but are not especially helpful in resolving matters of interpretation.

Many older statutes have marginal notes instead of headings. Look at the extract from the Misrepresentation Act 1967 in Figure 4.6. You will see an example of a marginal note highlighted.

Misrepresentation Act 1967

1967 CHAPTER 7

An Act to amend the law relating to innocent misrepresentation and to amend sections 11 and 35 of the Sale of Goods Act 1893.   [22nd March 1967]

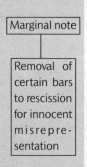

Marginal note

Removal of certain bars to rescission for innocent misrepresentation

B E IT ENACTED by the Queen's most Excellent Majesty, by and with the advice and consent of the Lords Spiritual and Temporal, and Commons, in this present Parliament assembled, and by the authority of the same, as follows:—

1. Where a person has entered into a contract after a misrepresentation has been made to him, and—

    (*a*) the misrepresentation has become a term of the contract;
      or
    (*b*) the contract has been performed;

or both, then, if otherwise he would be entitled to rescind the contract without alleging fraud, he shall be so entitled, subject to the provisions of this Act, notwithstanding the matters mentioned in paragraphs (*a*) and (*b*) of this section.

Figure 4.5 Misrepresentation Act 1967, marginal note
Contains public sector information licensed under the Open Government Licence v3.0

However, there is one key difference between marginal notes and headings. The headings are part of the Act (they are debated during the passage of the legislation) and marginal notes are not. This means that marginal notes have no direct legal effect. Despite this distinction, both marginal notes and headings are of limited use beyond being a useful means of navigating around the Act.

> ### Self-test questions
>
> **1.** When did the Misrepresentation Act 1967 receive Royal Assent?
>
> **2.** What is its long title?
>
> **3.** What is its citation?
>
> **4** What does '1967 Chapter 7' signify?
>
> *Answers to the self-test questions can be found at* **www.oup.com/he/finch8e/**.

4.1.7 Commencement and expiry ⑦

As we have already seen in section 4.1.4, the provisions of the Act come into force on the date of Royal Assent unless the Act itself states otherwise in a 'commencement provision'. The commencement provisions are normally found towards the end of the Act.

Look at Figure 4.6 which shows the start of the commencement provisions found in s 87 of the Coronavirus Act 2020.

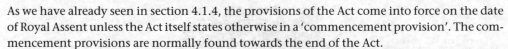

87 Commencement ⑦

(1) This Act comes into force on the day on which this Act is passed, subject to subsection (2).

(2) The following provisions of this Act come into force on such day as a Minister of the Crown may by regulations appoint, subject to subsections (3) to (9)—
   (a) section 8 (and Schedule 7);
   (b) section 9;
   (c) section 10 (and Schedules 8, 9, 10 and 11);
   (d) section 15 (and Schedule 12);
   (e) section 16;
   (f) section 17;
   (g) section 18 (and Schedule 13);
   (h) section 19;
   (i) section 21;
   (j) sections 25 to 29 (and Schedule 15).

(3) In the case of provision made by regulations under subsection (2) which could also be made by an authority under subsection (4), (6) or (8), a Minister of the Crown may not make the provision without the authority's consent.

Figure 4.6 Coronavirus Act 2020, s 87

You will see that s 87(1) sets out a default position that the Act comes into force on the day on which the Act is passed (that is, the day it received the Royal Assent, 25 March 2020). This default position is, however, subject to the restrictions set out in s 87(2) which provides that certain sections of the Act will only come into force as appointed by regulations of a Minister of the Crown. Therefore, Ministers have the power to decide when certain parts of the Act become law. Those parts of the Act will be brought into effect by a statutory instrument known as a commencement order.

Commencement provisions could also specify that certain sections come into force on a fixed date, or a date relative to the Act receiving Royal Assent.

Making certain sections subject to a commencement order might mean that they *never* come into force at all. For example, the Family Law Act 1996 was intended to revolutionize the divorce process. It received Royal Assent on 4 July 1996 but at the time it was not expected to be brought into effect until 2000. Section 67 of the Act gave the Lord Chancellor the power to bring parts of it into force by a commencement order. Unfortunately, the results from a pilot study established that the amendments that it proposed to bring into the divorce process were ineffective. This led to the Government abandoning the reforms altogether and consequently parts of the Act were never brought into force.

Acts do not take effect retrospectively unless expressly provided for within the Act. Examples of retrospective legislation are rare, but one example can be found in s 1 of the War Crimes Act 1991; an Act which confers jurisdiction on UK courts in respect of certain grave violations of the laws and customs of war committed in German-held territory during the Second World War.

Self-test questions

5. When did the Misrepresentation Act 1967 come into force?

Answers to the self-test questions can be found at www.oup.com/he/finch8e/.

Acts of Parliament normally remain in force until they are repealed by a later Act of Parliament. However, the Coronavirus Act 2020 is unusual in that it has an expiry provision as well. In Figure 4.7, you will see that s 89 provided that the Act will expire two years from the date that it was passed (subject to various conditions which it goes on to set out).

89 Expiry ⑦

(1) This Act expires at the end of the period of 2 years beginning with the day on which it is passed, subject to subsection (2) and section 90.

Figure 4.7 Coronavirus Act 2020, s 89

4.1.8 Extent ⑧

An 'extent' provision in the Act (or in a later commencement order made under the Act) might specify that certain provisions only come into force in particular areas. In the example shown in Figure 4.8, s 100(1) sets out provisions of the Coronavirus Act 2020 that apply to

England and Wales, Scotland, and Northern Ireland. Later subsections (not shown in the extract, but you can look them up online if you wish) set out different areas of territorial coverage for certain sections of the Act. For instance s 100(6) lists the sections that only apply to Northern Ireland.

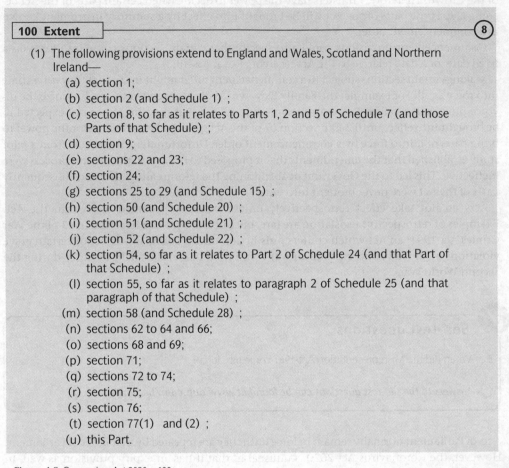

100 Extent   ⑧

(1) The following provisions extend to England and Wales, Scotland and Northern Ireland—
    (a) section 1;
    (b) section 2 (and Schedule 1) ;
    (c) section 8, so far as it relates to Parts 1, 2 and 5 of Schedule 7 (and those Parts of that Schedule) ;
    (d) section 9;
    (e) sections 22 and 23;
    (f) section 24;
    (g) sections 25 to 29 (and Schedule 15) ;
    (h) section 50 (and Schedule 20) ;
    (i) section 51 (and Schedule 21) ;
    (j) section 52 (and Schedule 22) ;
    (k) section 54, so far as it relates to Part 2 of Schedule 24 (and that Part of that Schedule) ;
    (l) section 55, so far as it relates to paragraph 2 of Schedule 25 (and that paragraph of that Schedule) ;
    (m) section 58 (and Schedule 28) ;
    (n) sections 62 to 64 and 66;
    (o) sections 68 and 69;
    (p) section 71;
    (q) sections 72 to 74;
    (r) section 75;
    (s) section 76;
    (t) section 77(1) and (2) ;
    (u) this Part.

Figure 4.8 Coronavirus Act 2020, s 100.

Be careful to check the extent provision in any Act that you are considering to ensure that it applies to the jurisdiction in which you are studying.

4.1.9 Schedules ⑨

Some statutes have one or more schedules at the end (see Figure 4.9).
    These may contain a number of different things, such as:

• Definitions of terms used in the Act (e.g. Schedule 1, Interpretation Act 1978)

• Detailed provisions which are referred to in the main Act (e.g. Schedule 1, Football (Disorder) Act 2000)

• Details of minor and consequential amendments to other legislation (e.g. Schedule 2, Football (Disorder) Act 2000)

• Repeals of pre-existing legislation (e.g. Schedule 3, Football (Disorder) Act 2000).

SCHEDULES

SCHEDULE 1   Section 2

EMERGENCY REGISTRATION OF NURSES AND OTHER HEALTH AND CARE PROFESSIONALS

Nursing and Midwifery Order 2001

1 (1) The Nursing and Midwifery Order 2001 (S.I. 2002/253) has effect as if it were subject to the following modifications.

(2) The Order has effect as if after article 9 there were inserted—

"9A Temporary registration in emergencies involving loss of human life or human illness etc

(1) The Registrar may register a person as a registered nurse, midwife or nursing associate, or the persons comprising a specified group of persons as registered nurses, midwives or nursing associates, if—

(a) the Secretary of State has advised the Registrar that an emergency has occurred, is occurring or is about to occur and that the Registrar should consider acting under this article, and

(b) the Registrar considers that the emergency registration requirement is met in relation to the person or group of persons.

Figure 4.9 Schedule 1—Emergency registration of nurses and other health and care professionals.
Contains public sector information licensed under the Open Government Licence v3.0

The Coronavirus Act 2020 contains no fewer than twenty-eight schedules. Schedule 1 provides various amendments to the Nursing and Midwifery Order 2001 (SI 2002/253) to permit emergency registration for nurses, midwives, and nursing associates. Those amendments have been set out in a separate schedule to enable easier navigation around the main body of the Act.

Schedules are divided into paragraphs and subparagraphs. 'Schedule' is often abbreviated to 'sch' and paragraph to 'para'. It is incorrect to refer to the divisions and subdivisions of a schedule as sections and subsections.

4.1.10 Preambles

Older statutes contain preambles, which describe the purpose of the Act in more detail than the long title. For example, the preamble to the Statute of Charitable Uses 1601 sets out a list of charitable purposes or activities.

The Statute of Charitable Uses (1601), 43 Elizabeth I c. 4
An Acte to redresse the Misemployment of Landes Goodes and Stockes of Money heretofore given to Charitable Uses

Whereas Landes Tenementes Rentes Annuities Profittes Hereditamentes, Goodes Chattels Money and Stockes of Money, have bene heretofore given limitted appointed and assigned, as well by the

Queenes most excellent Majestie and her moste noble Progenitors, as by sondrie other well disposed persons, some for Releife of aged impotent and poore people, some for Maintenance of sicke and maymed Souldiers and Marriners, Schooles of Learninge, Free Schooles and Schollers in Universities, some for Repaire of Bridges Portes Havens Causwaies Churches Seabankes and Highwaies, some for Educacion and prefermente of Orp hans, some for or towardes Reliefe Stocke or Maintenance of Howses of Correccion, some for Mariages of poore Maides, some for Supportacion Ayde and Helpe of younge tradesmen Handicraftesmen and persons decayed, and others for reliefe or redemption of Prisoners or Captives, and for aide or ease of any poore Inhabitantes concerninge paymente of Fifteenes, setting out of Souldiers and other Taxes; Whiche Landes Tenementes Rents Annuities Profitts Hereditaments Goodes Chattells Money and Stockes of Money nevertheles have not byn imployed accordinge to the charitable intente of the givers and founders thereof, by reason of Fraudes breaches of Truste and Negligence in those that shoulde pay delyver and imploy the same . . .

However, since the list was in the preamble, rather than in the main body of the Act, it did not form part of the statute. However, the list in the preamble to the 1601 statute has nevertheless formed the foundation of the modern definition of charitable purposes which can be found in s 2(1) of the Charities Act 2011: this requires a purpose which falls within the list of charitable purposes set out in s 3(1) and which is for the public benefit (s 4).

Preambles in older statutes are also useful if you need to evaluate whether an old piece of legislation has actually achieved what it set out to achieve. The purposes set out in the preamble can then be compared to the effect of the Act's application by the courts.

4.1.11 Explanatory Notes

Most recent Acts will carry accompanying Explanatory Notes. These are useful information but are not legally binding. The Office of Public Sector Information describes Explanatory Notes as follows:

The purpose of these Explanatory Notes is to make the Act of Parliament accessible to readers who are not legally qualified and who have no specialised knowledge of the matters dealt with. They are intended to allow the reader to grasp what the Act sets out to achieve and place its effect in context.

They can be extensive: the Explanatory Notes to the Coronavirus Act 2020 run to ninety-three pages. The Explanatory Notes can give an indication of the purpose of a particular statute which might be useful background when trying to establish the meaning behind any seemingly ambiguous provision. The Explanatory Notes to the European Union (Withdrawal) Act 2018 are also particularly extensive and very helpful.

See section 4.3 for a discussion of statutory interpretation.

4.2 ANATOMY OF A STATUTORY INSTRUMENT

Chapter 2 describes statutory instruments as sources of law.

Like Acts, statutory instruments are also built up from a number of standard components. In this section, we will examine parts of a statutory instrument (see Figure 4.10).

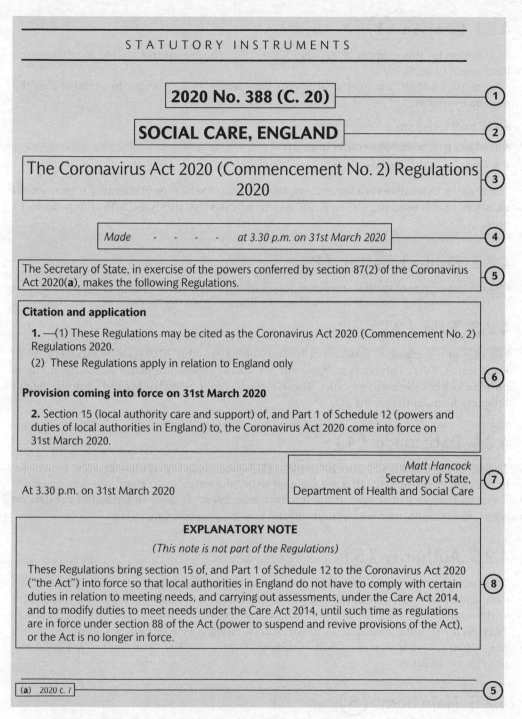

STATUTORY INSTRUMENTS

2020 No. 388 (C. 20) — (1)

SOCIAL CARE, ENGLAND — (2)

The Coronavirus Act 2020 (Commencement No. 2) Regulations 2020 — (3)

Made - - - - *at 3.30 p.m. on 31st March 2020* — (4)

The Secretary of State, in exercise of the powers conferred by section 87(2) of the Coronavirus Act 2020(**a**), makes the following Regulations. — (5)

Citation and application

1. —(1) These Regulations may be cited as the Coronavirus Act 2020 (Commencement No. 2) Regulations 2020.

(2) These Regulations apply in relation to England only

Provision coming into force on 31st March 2020

2. Section 15 (local authority care and support) of, and Part 1 of Schedule 12 (powers and duties of local authorities in England) to, the Coronavirus Act 2020 come into force on 31st March 2020. — (6)

At 3.30 p.m. on 31st March 2020

Matt Hancock
Secretary of State,
Department of Health and Social Care — (7)

EXPLANATORY NOTE

(*This note is not part of the Regulations*)

These Regulations bring section 15 of, and Part 1 of Schedule 12 to the Coronavirus Act 2020 ("the Act") into force so that local authorities in England do not have to comply with certain duties in relation to meeting needs, and carrying out assessments, under the Care Act 2014, and to modify duties to meet needs under the Care Act 2014, until such time as regulations are in force under section 88 of the Act (power to suspend and revive provisions of the Act), or the Act is no longer in force. — (8)

(a) 2020 c. 7 — (5)

Figure 4.10 The Coronavirus Act 2020 (Commencement No 2) Regulations 2020
Contains public sector information licensed under the Open Government Licence v3.0

4.2.1 Citation ①

The citation for this example is '2020 No 388 (C. 20)'. This means that it is the 388th statutory instrument of 2020.

Some (but not all) statutory instruments have letters and a number in brackets after the sequence number:

- C stands for commencement order
- L relates to fees and procedures in courts
- S relates to Scotland only

The number that follows is a sequence number relating to the type of statutory instrument in question. In this example, we see 'C. 20' which indicates that this is the 20th commencement order of 2020.

4.2.2 Subject matter ②

The subject matter of the statutory instrument in this case is social care in England.

4.2.3 Title ③

The title of the statutory instrument is 'The Coronavirus Act 2020 (Commencement No 2) Regulations 2020'. This refers to its parent Act, namely the Coronavirus Act 2020 and to its purpose as a commencement order. The 'No 2' refers to it being the second commencement order made under the parent Act.

4.2.4 Date made ④

The date shown in the statutory instrument (31 March 2020) is that on which it was made (or in the case of instruments that are required to be laid before Parliament, the date on which it was laid before Parliament). If the statutory instrument comes into force after the date on which it was made, then this section will also give its commencement date.

4.2.5 Authority ⑤

This section of the statutory instrument shows the authority by which it is made. In this case, the order was made under the power delegated to the Secretary of State (for Health and Social Care) by s 87(2) of the Coronavirus Act 2020—you can see this in Figure 4.6. There is a footnote reference (a) to the official citation (see section 4.1.2) of the parent Act—2020 c.7—which you should remember means that the Coronavirus Act 2020 was the 7th Act of 2020.

4.2.6 Main body ⑥

The main body of the statutory instrument contains paragraphs or articles if it is an order, regulations if it is a regulation, or rules if it is a set of rules. Regulations are often abbreviated to 'reg' and rules to 'r'. In this case, reg 2 brings s 15 and Part 1 of Schedule 12 of the Coronavirus Act 2020 into force on 31 March 2020 (which is less than a week after the parent Act received the Royal Assent).

4.2.7 Minister ⑦

This is the name of the Minister signing the order. In this case, Matt Hancock.

4.2.8 Explanatory Note ⑧

As with statutes, the Explanatory Note is not part of the statutory instrument. It generally either:

• Explains the purpose of the statutory instrument

• Details amendments or revocations of previous statutory instruments and/or

• Notes implementation of European legislation.

4.3 STATUTORY INTERPRETATION

Statutory provisions are, of course, made up of words and you will need to interpret those words in order to find the meaning of any particular piece of legislation. Language is an imperfect tool and consequently problems can arise when attempting to discern the meaning of and purpose behind the form of words used in the statute, particularly when provisions are phrased in highly technical language. A single form of words can often be interpreted in more than one way and competing interpretations are often the source of legal dispute.

While the words of an Act of Parliament are authoritative, it is the constitutional role of the judiciary in common law jurisdictions (such as ours) to apply the law. This is in contrast to civil law systems used in continental Europe where the statutory texts are applied more flexibly by the courts which may declare what the law should mean in a particular set of circumstances.

The Government (the executive) sets legislative priorities, Parliament (the legislature) creates the law, and the courts (the judiciary) apply the law. Because Parliament is supreme, the courts are obliged to apply the law irrespective of their agreement with it. As a consequence, historically, the courts were supposed to apply the law in the way that was meant by Parliament, rather than interpreting Parliament's words in a way that alters the operation of the law. Judges will seek the fairest outcome, sometimes in spite of the will of Parliament. It is often said that the role of the courts in statutory interpretation is to discern Parliament's intention from the words of the statute. However, it may be that the particular set of circumstances before the court were never actually foreseen or considered by Parliament (or that they had been considered and consciously left out), and therefore Parliament's intention could *never* be ascertained. In this case, it can be argued that the courts are trying to guess what Parliament *would have* meant had it directed its mind to the circumstances in question.[3] Put simply, when put to the test, the words in a statute mean what a court says that they mean.

Whatever the reasons for interpretation, the situation is straightforward. If the wording of the legislation is ambiguous or unclear, then its meaning will need to be interpreted. While the ordinary meaning of a word in the English language is a matter of fact, its legal meaning is, self-evidently, a matter of law. This can prove to be a great source of argument. Two examples of the distinction between everyday meanings and legal meanings are found in very ordinary foods: Jaffa Cakes and the bread used in a Subway sandwich. Both these items came before the courts in matters relating to taxation. In the UK, value added tax (VAT) is payable on chocolate biscuits but not chocolate cakes. United Biscuits, the manufacturer, argued that Jaffa Cakes

---

3. *Farrell v Alexander* [1977] AC 59 (HL) 95B (Lord Edmund-Davies).

were cakes for the purposes of VAT regulation, but Her Majesty's Customs and Excise argued that they were biscuits. In *Jaffa Cakes: United Biscuits* (LON/91/0160) a VAT Tribunal ruled that they were, in fact, cakes. While this might seem to be an obvious conclusion, the Irish Supreme Court[4] ruled that the bread used in Subway sandwiches had too high a sugar content to be categorized as bread for VAT purposes in Ireland. So, in the particular legal context of taxation, Jaffa Cakes are cakes, but Subway bread is not bread.

For that reason, an understanding of the approaches that can be used to interpret a statutory provision is vital. As Lord Steyn commented: 'The preponderance of enacted law over common law is increasing year by year . . . and the subject of interpretation has moved to the centre of the legal stage'.[5] In other words, the sheer volume of legislation and the pace with which it is introduced provides more opportunities for creative arguments before the courts. Knowledge of how to interpret a statutory provision in your favour—or know how it might be used against you—is therefore an extremely important practical legal skill.

4.3.1 How to interpret a statutory provision

Judges use a variety of different approaches when faced with an issue of statutory interpretation. These are generally referred to as the 'rules' or 'canons' of interpretation. They are sometimes referred to as the 'rules of construction'. The word 'construction' in this sense comes from the verb 'to construe', meaning 'to interpret'.

However, it is very important to remember that these are not rules set out by law. It is perhaps better to think of them as *approaches* to interpretation, rather than as hard-and-fast rules. Judges are not bound to follow one, or any, of them and do not (and in practice almost never actually do) state which 'rule' they have used. In actual fact, they may not consider the 'rules' at all, and it is left to us to try and work out how they went about making their decision by working backwards and looking at their reasoning. It is very important not to place too much emphasis on the rules in and of themselves, but to appreciate that there are a number of ways in which courts can go about discerning a particular meaning that best serves the interests of justice and fairness in the case before them.

The 'rules' we will first consider are:

- The literal rule
- The golden rule
- The mischief rule.

In addition to these 'classic' rules, there are two additional approaches: the purposive approach considers the wider purpose of the legislation and the teleological approach looking even more broadly at the spirit of the law is particularly important in the interpretation of European law. There are also various rules of language, presumptions, and extrinsic aids that can be used to help discover the meaning of a statute.

4.3.1.1 The literal rule

The **literal rule** says that words must be given their plain, ordinary, and literal meaning.

---

4. *Bookfinders Ltd v The Revenue Commissioners* (2020) S:AP:IE:2019:000131 (29 September).
5. Lord Steyn, '*Pepper v Hart*: a Re-examination' (2001) 21 OJLS 59.

The rationale behind the use of the literal rule is that if the words of the statute are clear they must be applied as they represent the intention of Parliament as expressed in the words used, even if the outcome is harsh or seems unfair, unjust, or undesirable.

The rule was set out clearly in the *Sussex Peerage Case*:[6]

> The only rule for construction of Acts of Parliament is that they should be construed according to the intent of the Parliament which passed the Act. If the words . . . are themselves precise and unambiguous, then no more can be necessary than to expound those words in that natural and ordinary sense.

An example of the use of the literal rule can be found in *Cutter v Eagle Star Insurance Co Ltd*.[7] The claimant was sitting in his friend's car in a car park and was injured when a can of lighter fuel exploded. The driver was insured, as required by the Road Traffic Act 1988, for injury caused while on a 'road'. Here the House of Lords ruled that a car park is not a 'road' for the purposes of the Road Traffic Act 1988, since the purpose of a road is a means for cars to move along it to a destination and the purpose of a car park is for cars to stand still. Parking a car on a road does not make it a car park. Driving a car across a car park does not make it a road as it is incidental to its main function.

In *Whiteley v Chappell*,[8] the defendant had impersonated a dead person and voted in an election in his name. The relevant statute provided that it was an offence to impersonate 'any person entitled to vote' at an election. Since the person impersonated was dead he was not entitled to vote, and thus Whiteley could not be convicted. Of course, this application of the literal rule went *against* Parliament's intention, which was to ensure that only those entitled to vote were able to do so, and then only to do so once at each election.

Although use of the literal rule gives utmost primacy to the precise words used by Parliament, emphasizing the literal meaning of statutory provisions can lead to 'unthinking' decisions where the meaning in the wider context is ignored or lost. It assumes perfection in Parliamentary draftsmen and ignores the natural limitations of language. However, there is still scope for judicial intervention: in deciding on the literal meaning of a word, the court may still refer to its own interpretation of the meaning of that word, or look to an extrinsic aid such as a dictionary to assist it in suggesting what the literal meaning of the particular word actually is.

4.3.1.2 The golden rule

The **golden rule** says that words must be given their plain, ordinary, and literal meaning as far as possible but not if the result is absurd (the 'narrow golden rule' approach) or against public policy (the 'wide golden rule' approach).

The golden rule is a modification of the literal rule. In terms of the relationship between the legislature and the judiciary, the golden rule may be used by the judiciary where the literal rule would produce a result that was actually contrary to the intention of Parliament. There is, however, a presumption that the literal rule should be used—in other words, that Parliament would not normally intend to legislate to produce absurdity or a result contrary to public policy. The failure of Parliament to consider a particular situation does not permit the courts

---

6. (1844) 1 Cl & Fin 85.
7. [1998] 1 WLR 1647 (HL).
8. (1868) LR 4 QB 147.

to depart from the literal rule if the words of the statute are clear and there is no absurdity created. In such an event, the court is limited to drawing the matter to Parliament's attention and urging the enactment of remedial legislation.

The rationale behind the golden rule is that it mitigates some of the potential harshness arising from use of the literal rule. An early reference to it can be found in *Grey v Pearson*:[9]

> The grammatical and ordinary sense of the words is to be adhered to unless that would lead to some absurdity or inconsistency with the rest of the instrument, in which case the grammatical and ordinary sense of the words may be modified so as to avoid that absurdity or inconsistency, but not farther.

In practice, the golden rule is not used that frequently.

Absurdity

R v Allen[10] concerned the application of s 57 of the Offences against the Person Act 1861. Allen had been charged with bigamy. The Act that set out the offence stated that 'whosoever being married shall marry any other person during the lifetime of his spouse' shall commit bigamy. If 'marry' had been interpreted literally the offence could never have been committed, since no one married could ever marry another. The court interpreted the words 'shall marry' as if they said 'shall go through the ceremony of marriage' and Allen was convicted.

Affront to public policy

A more unpleasant example of the rule is found in *Re Sigsworth*.[11] Under the Administration of Estates Act 1925 the estate of a person dying without leaving a will was to be divided among the 'issue'. Mrs Sigsworth was murdered by her son who stood to inherit her estate. Even though there was only one possible interpretation of the word 'issue' (meaning 'children' in this context) the court held that the son could not inherit the estate as it would be contrary to public policy for a murderer to benefit from his crime. Here the golden rule was applied in preference to the literal rule and the son did not inherit.

4.3.1.3 The mischief rule

The **mischief rule** (or the rule in ***Heydon's Case***)[12] involves an examination of the former law in an attempt to deduce Parliament's intention ('mischief' here means 'wrong' or 'harm').

The mischief rule applies only if the words used in the statute are ambiguous and the literal rule cannot be applied with certainty. It differs from the literal rule and the golden rule in that it places less emphasis on the words of the statute themselves, but instead seeks the reason for Parliament legislating in the first place. Once this is known, then it allows the courts to adopt an interpretation that fills the gap in the law that Parliament failed to address.

The mischief rule asks four questions, the answers to which provide some sort of structured evaluation of Parliament's intention in passing the Act in question:

1. What was the common law before the making of the Act?
2. What was the mischief and defect for which the common law did not provide?

---

9. (1857) 6 HL Cas 61.
10. (1872) LR 1 CCR 367.
11. [1935] Ch 89 (DC).
12. (1584) 3 Co Rep 7a.

3. What was the remedy proposed by Parliament to rectify the situation?

4. What was the true reason for that remedy?

In other words:

1. What did case law say before Parliament stepped in?

2. What was wrong with the case law? What situation did it not cover well enough that meant that Parliament decided to step in?

3. What did Parliament say should be done?

4. Why did they think that was what should be done?

The rule itself dates from a time when the law was primarily common (case) law and there was a relatively limited amount of statutes. Statutes were historically only enacted when Parliament wished to remedy what it considered to be a defect in the common law.

The rule was considered by Lord Diplock in *Jones v Wrotham Park Settled Estates*[13] where he identified three necessary conditions:

- It must be possible to determine precisely the mischief that the Act was drafted to remedy.

- It must be apparent that Parliament had failed to deal with the mischief.

- It must be possible to state the additional words that would have been inserted had the omission been drawn to Parliament's attention.

Corkery v Carpenter[14] concerned the interpretation of s 12 of the Licensing Act 1872. This provided that a person drunk in charge of a 'carriage' on the highway could be arrested without a warrant. The defendant was found drunk in charge of a bicycle. Although it was argued that a bicycle is not a carriage in the normal meaning of the word (the term generally refers to a vehicle of some kind), the Divisional Court held that a bicycle was a carriage for the purposes of the Act. The mischief here was the prevention of drunken persons from being on the highway in charge of some form of transportation and was addressed by the Act for the purposes of public order and safety.

Royal College of Nursing v DHSS[15] involved the wording of the Abortion Act 1963. This allows abortions by 'a registered medical practitioner'. The first part of the procedure was carried out by a doctor. The second part was performed by nurses but without a doctor being present. The House of Lords held by a 3–2 majority that this procedure *was* lawful because the mischief Parliament was trying to remedy was back street abortions performed by unqualified people.

In *Manchester City Council v McCann*,[16] the defendant had threatened a witness who had given evidence against his wife on his return home from court. Section 118(1)(a) of the County Courts Act 1984 provides that county courts may deal with anyone who 'wilfully insults the judge . . . or any juror or witness, or any officer of the court'. The Court of Appeal held that a threat was an insult for the purposes of the Act. The mischief here was protection of various participants in the civil process. Even though a threat is not necessarily an insult using the normal meanings of the words, the ability for the court to deal with insults but not threats was contrary to Parliament's intention. Of course, an Act may have more than one mischief, and this may affect the interpretation as a whole.[17]

---

13. [1980] AC 74 (HL).
14. [1951] 1 KB 102 (DC).
15. [1981] AC 800 (HL).
16. [1999] 2 QB 1214 (CA).
17. *R (Spath Holme Ltd) v Secretary of State for the Environment, Transport and the Regions* [2001] 2 AC 249 (HL).

4.3.1.4 The purposive approach

 The **purposive approach** involves seeking an interpretation of the law which gives effect to its general purpose. It is based upon the mischief rule.

The purposive approach is based upon the mischief rule. In this approach, the courts look beyond the wording of the legislation to find an interpretation which furthers its general purpose. In *Bulmer v Bollinger*,[18] Lord Denning stated:

> What are the English Courts to do when they are faced with a problem of interpretation? . . . No longer must they examine the words in meticulous detail. No longer must they argue about the precise grammatical sense. They must look to the purpose or intent . . . They must not confine themselves to the English text. . . . If they find a gap, they must fill it as best they can. They must do what the framers of the instrument would have done if they had thought about it. So we must do the same.

In that sense it is similar to the mischief rule, which attempts to deduce Parliament's intention (or purpose) in enacting a particular provision. It assumes that Parliament legislated intending to remedy some defect in the law and therefore that the courts should seek an interpretation of the legislation which gives effect to the purpose of legislating (which was to correct the defect).

The shift towards the use of the purposive approach was recognized by the House of Lords in *R (Quintavalle) v Secretary of State for Health*.[19] Here, the House of Lords endorsed the decision of the Court of Appeal who adopted a purposive approach to the interpretation of s 1(1) of the Human Fertilisation and Embryology Act 1990. Lord Steyn explained that:

> . . . the adoption of a purposive approach to construction of statutes generally, and the 1990 Act in particular, is amply justified on wider grounds. In Cabell v Markham (1945) 148 F 2d 737 Justice Learned Hand explained the merits of purposive interpretation, at 739:
>
> > Of course it is true that the words used, even in their literal sense, are the primary, and ordinarily the most reliable, source of interpreting the meaning of any writing: be it a statute, a contract, or anything else. But it is one of the surest indexes of a mature developed jurisprudence not to make a fortress out of the dictionary; but to remember that statutes always have some purpose or object to accomplish, whose sympathetic and imaginative discovery is the surest guide to their meaning.
>
> The pendulum has swung towards purposive methods of construction. This change was not initiated by the teleological approach of European Community jurisprudence, and the influence of European legal culture generally, but it has been accelerated by European ideas . . . In any event, nowadays the shift towards purposive interpretation is not in doubt. The qualification is that the degree of liberality permitted is influenced by the context, e.g. social welfare legislation and tax statutes may have to be approached somewhat differently.

A further example can be found in *Jones v Tower Boot Co Ltd*[20] which concerned a 16-year-old of dual ethnic heritage who worked at a shoe factory. During his employment he was

---

18. [1974] Ch 401 (CA).
19. [2003] 2 AC 687 (HL).
20. [1997] 2 All ER 406 (CA).

subjected to physical and verbal racial abuse from his work colleagues (including burning his arm with a hot screwdriver, throwing metal bolts at his head, and calling him racially abusive names including 'chimp', 'monkey', and 'baboon'). Jones sued the company for damages under s 32 of the Race Relations Act 1976 which said the employer shall be held liable for racial discrimination of its employees 'in the course of employment'. The company argued that the racial harassment was not done 'in the course of employment' because, according to the case law at the time, employees' conduct is only considered to be in the course of employment if it was directly authorized by the employer or closely connected to the job they were hired to do.

The Court of Appeal held that interpretation of the terms should not be restricted by the principles set out in the case law and that a broad interpretation had to be adopted. The court then looked at the purpose of the Act and held that the company was liable even though it had never authorized the racial abuse and the abuse had nothing to do with the abusers' job:

> A purposive construction accordingly requires section 32 of the Race Relations Act 1976 and the corresponding section 41 of the Sex Discrimination Act 1975 to be given a broad interpretation. It would be inconsistent with that requirement to allow the notion of the 'course of employment' to be construed in any sense more limited than the natural meaning of those everyday words would allow.

4.3.1.5 The teleological approach

The **teleological approach** requires that the spirit of the legislation, rather than merely its purpose, is considered. It is therefore much broader than the purposive approach.

The teleological approach is particularly important when considering EU law, since EU law is often drafted in terms of wide general principles and not in the detailed manner found in domestic legislation. It is the predominant approach used in civil law systems which tend to favour simplified drafting and a high degree of abstraction. It is also used by the Court of Justice of the European Union and was used by the UK courts when interpreting EU law.

You may wish to refer back to chapter 2 which considered the various types of EU legislation.

Pre-Brexit, s 2(4) of the European Communities Act 1972 provided that:

> . . . any enactment passed or to be passed . . . shall be construed and have effect subject to the foregoing provisions of this section.

The primary foregoing provision was s 2(1) of the Act which effectively incorporated all directly applicable EU law into the legal system.

> . . . all rights, powers, liabilities, obligations and restrictions from time to time created or arising by or under the Treaties, and all such remedies and procedures from time to time provided for by or under the Treaties, as in accordance with the Treaties are without further enactment to be given legal effect or used in the United Kingdom shall be recognised and available in law, and be enforced, allowed and followed accordingly.

In other words, when interpreting legislation which implemented EU law, the courts gave preference to an interpretation which gave effect to the general spirit of that legislation. This necessarily means that questions of wide economic or social policy were often considered by the courts.

In some circumstances this approach involved the courts reading certain words into legislation. This was a clear departure from using the literal words as chosen by Parliament. In *Pickstone v Freemans plc*,[21] the House of Lords held that it was proper to give a broad construction to the Equal Pay Act 1970, as amended by the Sex Discrimination Act 1975, so as to arrive at a result consistent with the UK's obligations under European law at that time.

A further example is provided by *Litster v Forth Dry Dock and Engineering Co Ltd*.[22] Here, employees were dismissed one hour before a business was transferred to a new owner. The employees claimed they were unfairly dismissed. The Transfer of Undertakings (Protection of Employment) Regulations 1981[23] ('TUPE') implemented a European directive designed to protect employees who were employed during the transfer of a business. However, taking a literal approach, the employees here were not actually employed at the moment of transfer, having been dismissed an hour previously, and therefore their situation seemed to fall outside the protection offered by TUPE. However, the House of Lords read in additional words such that the Regulations covered an individual who was employed 'or would have been so employed if he had not been unfairly dismissed as a reason connected with the transfer before the transfer'. In doing so, the spirit of the Directive, to protect the employees on the transfer of a business, was upheld.

You should now be able to see that there is an overlap, depicted in Figure 4.11 between the mischief rule, the purposive approach, and the teleological approach. All are concerned with determining the reason for the particular law's existence, but the range of considerations broadens.

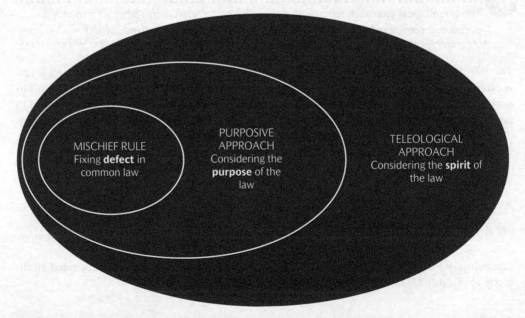

Figure 4.11 Overlapping approaches to interpretation

21. [1989] AC 66 (HL).
22. [1990] 1 AC 546 (HL).
23. SI 1794/1981.

4.3.1.6 Rules of language

In addition to the rules of construction, there are also rules of language which the courts may use. They are known by the following Latin terms:

- *Ejusdem generis*
- *Noscitur a sociis*
- *Expressio unius est exclusio alterius*

Ejusdem generis

Ejusdem generis means 'of the same type'.

In other words, if a word with general meaning follows a list of specific words, then the general word only applies to things of the same type as the specific words. The general words are interpreted as a continuation of the list of specific words. All the words must constitute the same 'type' of thing and that type must be construed as narrowly as possible. For example, a list stating 'hats, coats, scarves, gloves, and other articles' would imply that the list contained items of outdoor clothing and not all clothing (and certainly not all articles).

In *Powell v Kempton Park Racecourse*,[24] the defendant was operating an outdoor betting ring. It was an offence to use a 'house, office, room or other place for betting'. The court held that since the specific places listed are all indoors, an outdoor betting ring was not covered within the statute and the defendant was found not guilty.

Wood v Commissioner of Police of the Metropolis[25] considered whether a piece of (accidentally broken) glass was covered by 'any gun, pistol, hangar, cutlass, bludgeon or other offensive weapon'. It was held that the list contains items made or adapted for the purposes of causing harm. Therefore a piece of glass that had been broken accidentally was not included, although presumably it may well have been if it had been smashed in order to be used as a weapon.

Noscitur a sociis

Noscitur a sociis means that a word is 'known by the company it keeps'.

Words in a statute take their meaning from the words surrounding them. That is to say that a statutory provision should be read in the context of its neighbouring provisions. It is presumed that words have the same meaning throughout an Act—although this is not always the case. For instance, the word 'sexual' has a different meaning in s 71 of the Sexual Offences Act 2003 (sexual activity in a public lavatory) to that which it has in the rest of the Act. There is also a presumption that words in a list have related meanings and are to be interpreted in relation to each other.

---

24. [1899] AC 143 (HL).
25. [1986] 1 WLR 796 (DC).

In *Pengelley v Bell Punch Co Ltd*,[26] it was held that the word 'floors' in a statute requiring 'floors, steps, stairs, passages and gangways' to be kept clear did not include part of a factory floor used for storage, since the words listed related to passageways and not areas for static storage.

Muir v Keay[27] concerned a café owner. All houses kept open at night for 'public refreshment, resort and entertainment' had to be licensed. The defendant argued that his café did not need a licence because he did not provide (musical) entertainment. The court held that 'entertainment' did not mean musical entertainment but the reception and accommodation of people. Therefore the owner was required to have a licence by law.

Expressio unius est exclusio alterius

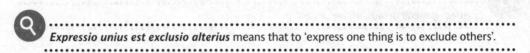

Expressio unius est exclusio alterius means that to 'express one thing is to exclude others'.

In other words, a list of a number of specific things may be interpreted as impliedly excluding others of the same type. If there are no general words, then the list is considered to be exhaustive. For example, in *R v Inhabitants of Sedgley*,[28] it was held that the poor rate levied on owners of 'lands, houses, tithes and coal mines' could not be levied on owners of limestone mines, as these were impliedly excluded by the specific mention of coal mines (but the outcome would probably have been different if the Act had just said 'lands, houses, tithes and mines').

4.3.1.7 Presumptions

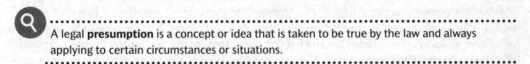

A legal **presumption** is a concept or idea that is taken to be true by the law and always applying to certain circumstances or situations.

In addition to the rules of construction and rules of language, there are also a number of presumptions which are made when interpreting legislation. These are generally expected to be taken 'as read' without the need for Parliament specifically to address them in the wording of a statute, since they deal with traditional ideas of natural justice and fairness or matters so uncontroversial that they would almost certainly represent the intention of Parliament. A number of these presumptions are as follows:

Against alteration of the common law

Although Parliament can change the existing common law, such an intention cannot be implied (e.g. *Beswick v Beswick*).[29]

Against retrospective operation of statute

It is presumed that statutes do not operate retrospectively—they cannot usually be 'backdated'. This is particularly important in Acts which create criminal offences, since backdating them could lead to criminal liability arising for things done before the Act was passed and which

---

26. [1964] 1 WLR 1055 (CA).
27. (1875) LR 10 QB 594.
28. (1831) 2 B & Ald 65.
29. [1968] AC 58 (HL).

were lawful when they were committed. This presumption can, however, be rebutted by express words by Parliament. For example, the War Crimes Act 1991 allows proceedings for murder, manslaughter, or culpable homicide to be brought if the offence was committed during the time of the Second World War in Germany (or a place occupied by Germany) and violated the 'laws and customs' of war.

Against deprivation of liberty

Parliament is presumed not to intend to deprive a person of his liberty; if it does, clear words must be used and will be construed so as to interfere with the subject's liberty as little as possible (e.g. *R (H) v London North and East Region Mental Health Review Tribunal*).[30]

Against deprivation of property and against interference with private rights

Parliament is presumed not to wish to interfere with a person's private rights or deprive him of his property without compensation (e.g. *Glassbrook Bros v Leyson*;[31] *Bowles v Bank of England*).[32]

Against binding the Crown

Parliament is presumed not to bind the Crown except expressly or by necessary implication of the statute (e.g. Equal Pay Act 1970; Sex Discrimination Act 1975).

Against ousting the jurisdiction of the courts

Even where clear ouster clauses (i.e. clauses which try to stop the judiciary reviewing them) have been used, the courts will try to construe them in a way which permits judicial review (e.g. *Anisminic Ltd v Foreign Compensation Commission*).[33]

Against criminal liability without *mens rea* (a guilty mind)

There is a presumption that, for statutory criminal offences, Parliament intended no liability without proof of *mens rea*—broadly speaking, criminal intent or state of mind (e.g. *R v K*).[34] This can be rebutted by express words or by implication in offences of strict liability (offences such as speeding for instance, when intention or otherwise makes no difference to criminal liability; just being over the speed limit is enough).

4.3.1.8 Intrinsic aids to interpretation

Intrinsic aids to interpretation are found within the statute itself.

Every statute must be read as a whole. That is to say that before looking outside the statute to seek its meaning, every word within the statute should be considered in the search for meaning. There are a number of areas within the statute which could potentially be used as an intrinsic aid to construction.

Look back at section 4.1 which describes the anatomy of an Act of Parliament.

---

30. [2001] 3 WLR 512 (CA).
31. [1933] 2 KB 91 (CA).
32. [1913] 1 Ch 57 (DC).
33. [1969] 2 AC 147 (CA).
34. [2001] 3 WLR 471 (HL).

Short title

This is usually descriptive only and therefore of limited value.

Long title

The long title may be considered but only where there is ambiguity within the body of the Act (e.g. *R (Quintavalle) v Secretary of State for Health*).[35]

Preamble

Preambles tend not to be found in recent statutes. Where preambles do exist, they may be considered for guidance purposes in cases of ambiguity.

Marginal notes

These are found in older Acts—they are not debated in Parliament and are not normally used in determining the precise scope of a provision (*DPP v Schildkamp*);[36] they can though give some general indication of the provision's purpose (*DPP v Johnson*).[37] They were, however, used relatively recently in *R v Montilla*.[38]

Punctuation

Old statutes did not use punctuation at all. Punctuation may be used as an aid to interpretation where there is ambiguity (*DPP v Schildkamp*).[39]

> *See chapter 11 for more information on punctuation.*

Examples

Statutes may provide examples to illustrate how the Act might work or how terminology within it might be used. These are part of the statute and carry great persuasive authority (see, e.g., s 44(6) of the Criminal Justice Act 2003 which gives three examples of situations which may show that there is a real and present danger that jury tampering had taken place).

Schedules

Some statutes may contain a schedule which includes an interpretation and definition section of terms used in the Act (e.g. Schedule 1, Interpretation Act 1978). These definitions are part of the statute and are strongly persuasive.

4.3.1.9 Extrinsic aids to interpretation

Extrinsic aids to interpretation are found outside the statute.

The Interpretation Act 1978 defines words that are commonly used within legislation. For example:

- In any Act, unless the contrary intention appears, words importing the masculine gender include the feminine and vice versa (s 6).

---

35. [2003] 2 AC 687 (HL).
36. [1971] AC 1 (HL).
37. [1995] 4 All ER 53 (DC).
38. [2004] UKHL 50; [2004] 1 WLR 3141.
39. [1971] AC 1 (HL).

- 'Land' includes buildings and other structures, land covered with water, and any estate, interest, easement, servitude, or right in or over land (sch 1).

- 'Writing' includes typing, printing, lithography, photography, and other modes of representing or reproducing words in a visible form, and expressions referring to writing are construed accordingly (sch 1).

Where a word has no specific legal meaning, dictionaries may be used,[40] although courts do not have to follow dictionary definitions of words. Courts may also consider the interpretation of the same words used in earlier or related statutes.

Historically, since the court was only allowed to interpret the words used, reference to preparatory works (known then as *travaux préparatoires*) was not permitted. Article 9 of the Bill of Rights 1689 provides:

> That the freedom of speech and debates or proceedings in Parliament ought not to be impeached or questioned in any court or place out of Parliament.

Therefore, members of the Houses of Parliament had the right to say whatever they wished and to discuss whatever they wished. Until 1993, the protection given by Article 9 was held to prevent the courts from using statements made in Parliament concerning the purpose of Bills as a guide to the interpretation of ambiguous statutory provisions. This meant that courts could not refer to records of Parliamentary debate on the statute in the official recorded transcript of the debate, known as *Hansard* (see section 8.3.4).

However, this rule was relaxed in 1993 following the House of Lords decision in *Pepper v Hart*.[41] Here the House of Lords held that the rule against the use of *Hansard* as an extrinsic aid to interpretation would be relaxed to permit reference to Parliamentary materials where:

- The legislation is ambiguous or obscure, or its literal meaning leads to an absurdity

- The material relied on consists of statements by a Minister or other promoter of the Bill together with such other Parliamentary material as is necessary to understand such statements and their effect, and

- The statements relied upon are clear.

The House of Lords held such use of statements did not infringe Article 9 because it did not amount to questioning a proceeding in Parliament. Indeed, they considered that far from questioning the independence of Parliament and its debates, the use of *Hansard* would allow the courts to give effect to what was said and done there.

Note that the use of *Hansard* is only permitted under the circumstances outlined in *Pepper v Hart*. It is a common mistake to state that reference to *Hansard* may always be made.

Although *Pepper v Hart* concerned the use of *Hansard*, its principles extend to the reports of recommendations made by the Law Commission and Government departmental committees. For example, in *R v Allen*,[42] the House of Lords considered the report of the Criminal Law Revision Committee when considering the meaning of s 3 of the Theft Act 1978. The Act was silent on the point in question—specifically, whether intent never to pay had to be proved as

---

40. See, e.g., *Cheeseman v DPP* [1992] QB 83 (DC) which concerned the interpretation of the word 'passengers' in relation to the users of a public lavatory.
41. [1993] AC 593 (HL).
42. [1985] AC 1029 (HL).

an element of the offence of making off without payment—but the committee report made it clear that such intention *did* have to be proved.

In practice, however, courts have demonstrated some reluctance to allow reference to *Hansard*.[43] In *Wilson v First County Trust Limited (No 2)*,[44] the House of Lords commented that:

> What is important is to recognise there are occasions when courts may properly have regard to ministerial and other statements made in Parliament without in any way 'questioning' what has been said in Parliament, without giving rise to difficulties inherent in treating such statements as indicative of the will of Parliament, and without in any other way encroaching upon parliamentary privilege by interfering in matters properly for consideration and regulation by Parliament alone. The use by courts of ministerial and other promoters' statements as part of the background of legislation, pursuant to *Pepper v Hart*, is one instance.[45]

In other words, the statement of a Minister does not necessarily reflect the intentions of Parliament as a whole. More recently, the House of Lords considered the use of *Pepper v Hart* in *R (Jackson) v Attorney General*,[46] in which Lord Nicholls of Birkenhead stated that it would be 'unfortunate' if the rule were sidelined. Lord Steyn, however, considered that 'trying to discover the intentions of the Government from Ministerial statements in Parliament is unacceptable'.[47]

The use of *Pepper v Hart* therefore remains the subject of judicial debate.

The courts may also refer to the Explanatory Notes which have accompanied all Acts since 1999. They do not form part of the Act and have not been debated by Parliament. They are there to assist in discerning Parliament's intention and have been referred to by the courts,[48] although it could be argued that the courts are giving them a status that they should not carry particularly since they have been drafted by the executive (the Government department supporting the original Bill) and not the legislature.

The courts may also sometimes refer to academic writing. For example, the court in *R v Dooley*[49] referred to *Smith and Hogan's Criminal Law*.

4.3.2 Interpretation, the European Communities Act 1972, and Brexit

Section 2(4) of the European Communities Act 1972 provided that:

> Any enactment passed or to be passed . . . shall be construed and have effect subject to the foregoing provisions of this section.

In other words, prior to Brexit, any legislation passed or to be passed in the United Kingdom had to be interpreted with applicable EU law in mind. There was therefore a strong presumption of compliance with EU law.

---

43. See, e.g., *Zafar v DPP* [2004] EWHC 2468 (Admin); *Hone v Going Places Travel Ltd* [2001] EWCA Civ 947; *Thet v DPP* [2001] 1 WLR 2022 (DC).
44. [2004] 1 AC 816 (HL).
45. [2004] 1 AC 841 (Lord Nicholls of Birkenhead).
46. [2006] 1 AC 262 (HL).
47. ibid [97] (Lord Steyn).
48. *Attorney General's Reference (No 5 of 2002)* [2005] 1 AC 167 (HL).
49. [2005] EWCA Crim 3093.

In *Garland v British Rail Engineering*,[50] Lord Diplock suggested that where words of domestic law were incompatible with the Community law in question, they should be construed so as to comply with it. This creative approach—not applying the plain meaning of words in a statute, if that meaning will conflict with EU law—was also taken by the House of Lords in *Pickstone v Freemans plc*.[51] The Court of Appeal had declared that the Equal Pay (Amendment) Regulations 1983 were inconsistent with Article 141 (ex 119) of the EC Treaty. However, the House of Lords ruled that the Regulations should in fact be interpreted in a manner compatible with the provisions of the Treaty.

The position for EU law retained after Brexit is set out in s 6(3) and s 6(4) of the European Union (Withdrawal) Act 2018. Any question as to the meaning of any retained EU law is to be decided in accordance with any retained case law and any retained general principles of EU law, but the Supreme Court will not be bound by any retained EU case law. According to the Explanatory Notes, this means, for example, taking a purposive approach to interpretation where the meaning of the legislation is unclear. It also means applying an interpretation that makes the provision of EU law compatible with the treaties and general principles of EU law. Non-binding instruments, such as recommendations and opinions, would still be available to a court to assist with interpretation of retained EU law after exit.

The supremacy of EU law and the impact of Brexit is considered in general in chapter 2.

4.3.3 Interpretation and the Human Rights Act 1998

The Human Rights Act 1998 has had an effect on the traditional role of the courts in the interpretation of statutes.

Section 3 of the Act provides that:

> **(1)** So far as it is possible to do so, primary legislation and subordinate legislation must be read and given effect in a way which is compatible with the Convention rights.
>
> **(2)** This section—
>
>   **(a)** applies to primary legislation and subordinate legislation whenever enacted;
>
>   **(b)** does not affect the validity, continuing operation or enforcement of any incompatible primary legislation; and
>
>   **(c)** does not affect the validity, continuing operation or enforcement of any incompatible subordinate legislation if (disregarding any possibility of revocation) primary legislation prevents removal of the incompatibility.

Section 3(1) imposes a duty upon the courts to try and discern a meaning *so far as it is possible to do so* with Convention rights. This is a weaker presumption of compliance than that which was in place concerning European law; s 2(4) of the European Communities Act 1972 used the imperative 'shall' rather than 'so far as it is possible'. If the courts are unable to find a Convention-compatible interpretation, then they may make a 'declaration of incompatibility' under s 4. The effect of such a declaration is that the law must then be changed to remove the incompatibility. Section 10(2) provides a fast-track route by which this may be done:

> If a Minister of the Crown considers that there are compelling reasons . . . he may by order make such amendments to the legislation as he considers necessary to remove the incompatibility.

---

50. [1983] 2 AC 751 (HL).
51. [1989] AC 66 (HL).

Here, 'by order', means by statutory instrument.

The s 3 power has been considered in a number of cases since the provision came into force on 2 October 2000.

R v A[52] concerned the interpretation of s 41 of the Youth Justice and Criminal Evidence Act 1999 which placed the court under a restriction that seriously limited the evidence that could be raised in cross-examination of a sexual relationship between an alleged rape victim and the accused. Section 41(1) provided that:

> If, at a trial, a person is charged with a sexual offence, then, except with the leave of the court—
>
> **(a)** no evidence may be adduced, and
> **(b)** no question may be asked in cross-examination, by or on behalf of any accused at the trial, about any sexual behaviour of the complainant.

This remained so even in a case where the defendant claimed that the complainant had consented. *A* argued that s 41 of the Act was incompatible with Article 6 of the Convention to the extent that it prevented him from putting forward a full and complete defence. The House of Lords held that s 3 required them to consider Article 6 and its concomitant right to a fair trial. This allowed them to read s 41 as permitting the admission of evidence or questioning relating to a relevant issue in the case where it was considered necessary by the trial judge to make the trial fair.

In reaching its decision, the House of Lords was well aware that its interpretation of s 41 went against its actual meaning, but it nonetheless (by a majority) felt it within its power to do so. As Lord Steyn stated:

> In my view s 3 of the 1998 Act requires the court to subordinate the niceties of the language of s 41(3)(c) of the 1999 Act, and in particular the touchstone of coincidence, to broader considerations of relevance judged by logical and commonsense criteria of time and circumstances. After all, it is realistic to proceed on the basis that the legislature would not, if alerted to the problem, have wished to deny the right to an accused to put forward a full and complete defence by advancing truly probative material. It is therefore possible under s 3 of the 1998 Act to read s 41 of the 1999 Act, and in particular s 41(3)(c), as subject to the implied provision that evidence or questioning which is required to ensure a fair trial under Art 6 of the convention should not be treated as inadmissible.[53]

Lord Hope (dissenting) felt that the courts were going too far towards legislating:

> The rule of construction which s 3 lays down is quite unlike any previous rule of statutory interpretation. There is no need to identify an ambiguity or absurdity. Compatibility with convention rights is the sole guiding principle. That is the paramount object which the rule seeks to achieve. But the rule is only a rule of interpretation. It does not entitle the judges to act as legislators.[54]

However, Parliament *did* seek to limit the rights of the defence to question alleged victims of rape. *R v A* could therefore be considered to be an act of quasi-legislation by the House of Lords.

---

52. [2002] 1 AC 45 (HL).
53. [2002] 1 AC 68 (HL).
54. [2002] 1 AC 87 (HL).

In *Re S (Care Order: Implementation of Care Plan)*[55] Lord Nicholls explained the operation of s 3 as follows:

> The Human Rights Act reserves the amendment of primary legislation to Parliament. By this means the Act seeks to preserve parliamentary sovereignty. The Act maintains the constitutional boundary. Interpretation of statutes is a matter for the courts; the enactment of statutes, and the amendment of statutes, are matters for Parliament.

In *Ghaidan v Godin-Mendoza*[56] the House of Lords significantly clarified the force to be given when construing legislation under s 3. Lord Nicholls stressed that the intention of Parliament in enacting s 3 was, to the extent bounded only by what is 'possible', to allow the court to modify the meaning and hence the effect of primary and secondary legislation,[57] pointing out that s 3 is the principal remedial measure and that declarations of incompatibility were a measure of last resort.[58]

He also rejected the literal approach to interpretation, emphasizing a broad approach, concentrating, amongst other things, in a purposive way on the importance of the fundamental right involved.[59] The practical effect of *Mendoza* is to establish a strong, but rebuttable, presumption in favour of an interpretation consistent with Convention rights.[60]

CHAPTER SUMMARY

Anatomy of an Act of Parliament

- The short title is the normal way in which to refer to a statute
- The chapter number of an Act (since 1963) is the sequence number of the Act in the particular calendar year
- The long title of an Act gives an indication of its purpose and content
- Royal Assent is needed before an Act can come into force
- The enacting formula declares that the law derives its authority from being properly passed by the legislature
- The main body of an Act is divided into sections, subsections, paragraphs, and subparagraphs
- Any commencement provisions are normally found towards the end of an Act
- Schedules may contain further information such as definitions, further detail, minor and consequential amendments to other legislation, or repeals of pre-existing legislation
- Older statutes may contain preambles which describe the purpose of the Act in more detail than the long title; these are not part of the Act itself
- Most recent Acts will carry accompanying Explanatory Notes which contain useful information but are not legally binding

---

55. [2002] UKHL 10; [2002] 2 AC 291.
56. [2004] UKHL 30; [2004] 2 AC 557.
57. [2004] UKHL 30; [2004] 2 AC 557, [33].
58. [2004] UKHL 30; [2004] 2 AC 557, [39].
59. [2004] UKHL 30; [2004] 2 AC 557, [42].
60. [2004] UKHL 30; [2004] 2 AC 557, [50].

Anatomy of a statutory instrument

- Statutory instruments show the authority by which they are made
- Orders are divided into paragraphs or articles

Statutory interpretation

- The literal rule provides that words must be given their plain, ordinary, and literal meaning
- The golden rule provides that words must be given their plain, ordinary, and literal meaning as far as possible but only to the extent that they do not produce absurdity (narrow approach) or an affront to public policy (wide approach); it is not used frequently
- The mischief rule (or the rule in *Heydon's Case*) involves an examination of the former law in an attempt to deduce Parliament's intention
- The purposive approach involves seeking an interpretation of the law which gives effect to its general purpose. It is based upon the mischief rule
- The teleological approach requires that the spirit of the legislation, rather than merely its purpose, is considered. It is therefore much broader than the purposive approach
- *Ejusdem generis* is a rule of language meaning 'of the same type'
- *Noscitur a sociis* is a rule of language meaning that a word is 'known by the company it keeps'
- *Expressio unius est exclusion alterius* is a rule of language meaning that to 'express one thing is to exclude others'
- A legal presumption is an inference established by the law as universally applicable to certain circumstances
- Intrinsic aids to interpretation are found within the statute itself
- Extrinsic aids to interpretation are found outside the statute
- *Pepper v Hart* allows courts to refer to clear statements made by a Minister or other promoter of a Bill in Hansard where the legislation is ambiguous or obscure or its literal meaning leads to absurdity
- Section 2(4) of the European Communities Act 1972 required that legislation must be interpreted with applicable EU law in mind. There was a strong presumption of compliance with EU law
- Section 3(1) of the Human Rights Act 1998 requires that legislation must be interpreted *so far as it is possible to do so* in a way that is compatible with Convention rights. Case law has established a strong, but nevertheless rebuttable, presumption of compliance with the European Convention on Human Rights.

 ## FURTHER READING

- An interesting article which considers the 'radical' approach to interpretation of s 41 of the Youth Justice and Criminal Evidence Act 1999 by the House of Lords in the light of s 3(1) of the Human Rights Act 1999 in *R v A (No 2)* [2002] 1 AC 45 is A Kavanagh, 'Unlocking the Human Rights Act: the Radical Approach to Section 3(1) Revisited' [2005] 3 EHRLR 259.
- A further discussion of the interpretative obligation arising from s 3(1) of the Human Rights Act 1999 and its impact on discerning the will of Parliament can be found in G Marshall, 'The Lynchpin of Parliamentary Intention: Lost, Stolen or Strained' [2003] Public Law 236.

- You can find a discussion on the differences between literal and purposive approaches to interpretation in I McLeod, 'Literal and Purposive Techniques of Legislative Interpretation: Some European Community and English Common Law Perspective' (2004) 29 Brooklyn Journal of International Law 1109.

- The use of the principle from *Pepper v Hart* is evaluated in A Kavanagh, '*Pepper v Hart* and Matters of Constitutional Principle' (2005) 121 LQR 98 and S Vogenauer, 'A Retreat from *Pepper v Hart*? A Reply to Lord Steyn' (2005) 25 OJLS 629.

- The use of dictionaries in legal cases and the problems that can arise from disputes over dictionary definitions is discussed in R Munday, 'The Bridge that Choked a Watercourse or Repetitive Dictionary Disorder' (2008) 1 Statute Law Review 26.

Case law

5

INTRODUCTION

This chapter will begin our investigation into case law as a source of law. Case law can be broken down into three main types: common law, equity, and custom. This chapter will begin with a discussion of common law and equity, including some brief legal history to help you understand how these sources came into being. We will then take a very quick look at custom as a further source of law. Since the common law comprises a great many cases decided by judges in different courts, this chapter will also include an introduction to the court system in the UK to help you understand how the various courts sit together in a hierarchy before closing with a discussion of the European Court of Human Rights and the impact of the Human Rights Act 1998 on case law.

Understanding the sources of case law is as fundamental a legal skill as understanding the role of legislation. Since all legal topics will generally include some case law, equitable principles, or both, you would not otherwise be able to understand how the particular area of law you are studying came into existence or has evolved over time. The law is constantly changing and takes its shape from a whole range of sources. You must therefore understand each of these different sources to understand the law and its development properly and thoroughly.

 Learning outcomes

After studying this chapter, you will be able to:

- Distinguish between the common law and equity as sources of law
- Chart the historical development of the common law and equity
- Appreciate the role of custom as a further source of law
- State the hierarchy of the courts and the types of case heard in the various courts
- Discuss the effect of the European Convention on Human Rights and the Human Rights Act 1998 on case law

5.1 COMMON LAW AND EQUITY

Having considered the role of legislation as a source of law in the last three chapters, the next sources of law to consider are the common law and equity. However, before looking at them in detail, it will be useful to provide a very brief legal history. This will help you to understand how the common law and equity developed as two separate, but important, sources of law and how they relate to each other today. It will also introduce some terminology which will be useful later as you move onwards.

5.1.1 A brief legal history

A timeline to give you an overview of the history that we are about to cover is provided in Figure 5.1.

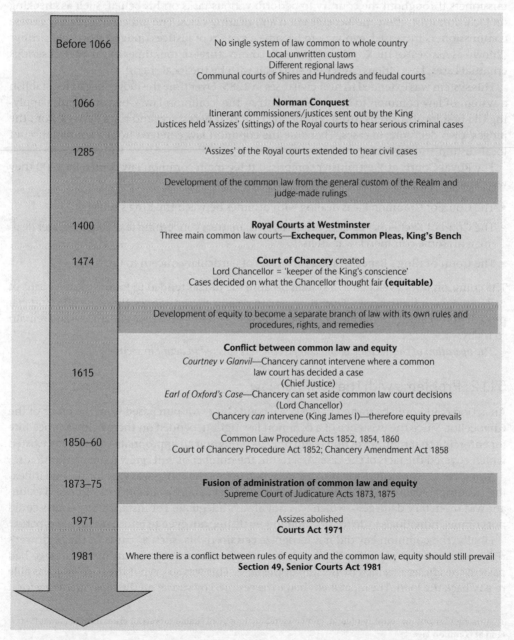

Figure 5.1 Timeline of legal developments

5.1.1.1 The emergence of the common law

Before the Norman Conquest in 1066 there was no single system of law common to the whole country. There was a range of local customs: these were unwritten and varied throughout the country, although the general effect of the local laws was similar in practice.

The use of custom as a source of law today is covered later in section 5.2.

Disputes according to these laws were judged by the local sheriffs sitting in the courts of the Shires and Hundreds (subdivisions of the Shires) and feudal courts held by landowners. In an attempt to create some level of uniformity and consistency in the law, the King sent commissioners throughout the country to perform various tasks on his behalf, such as checking on local administration and tax collection and hearing cases. The judicial functions of these commissioners increased, evolving to become a system of justices (judges) who held sittings (known as Assizes) of the Royal courts in each county, three or four times a year, to hear serious criminal cases. Less serious cases were still dealt with by the local sheriff.

This system was extended to hear civil cases in 1285. Over time the judges began to establish a system of law common to the whole country—the 'common law'—by consistently applying the best local customs (from outside the county if necessary) and rules derived from the judges' own decisions in cases. Therefore the common law emerged from a combination of local custom and case law.

The Royal Courts at Westminster comprised three main common law courts. By 1400 they were staffed by professional judges. The three courts were:

- The Court of Common Pleas dealing with disputes between the King's subjects
- The Court of Exchequer dealing primarily with matters concerning taxes but also later dealing with some common law matters
- The Court of King's Bench dealing with cases of particular concern to the King.

The common law developed as a system because the judges tended to follow the decisions of earlier judges in similar cases. Over time, and in certain circumstances, these so-called judicial precedents became binding rather than merely being useful persuasive guidance—and remain so today.

The operation of the doctrine of judicial precedent is covered in detail in section 7.3.

5.1.1.2 Problems with the common law

An action could only be started in the Royal courts by a writ purchased from the office of the Chancellor. Since the existence of a common law right depended on there being a procedure for enforcing that right, an action could only be brought if an appropriate writ already existed which covered the facts of the case. As a result, the number of writs grew to many hundreds.

Moreover, the procedure for bringing an action before the courts was very formal and inflexible, leading to delay and expense. The only remedy generally available to a successful claimant was monetary damages—which was not always adequate. For instance, the courts could not compel individuals to do (or stop doing) something; not even to return personal property.[1]

Finally, the common law did not recognize certain rights, such as trusts or the borrower's rights under a mortgage. At common law, once the date for repayment of a mortgage had passed, the lender regained ownership of the land. This was so even if the borrower was able to pay back the loan. The repayment had to be counted by sunset on the repayment day for it

---

1. Although actions for recovery of land, known as 'real actions', did enable successful claimants to recover their land at common law.

to be effective and prevent the lender from reclaiming the land. Many unscrupulous lenders mysteriously vanished on the repayment day, meaning that the borrowers lost the land.

5.1.1.3 The emergence of equity

The rigid nature of the common law, together with its associated expense and delay, led to an increasing number of unhappy citizens petitioning the King directly to exercise his Royal prerogative as the 'fountain of justice'. The King (in Council) originally heard these petitions, but as their number increased, this duty was delegated by the King to the Lord Chancellor, who, as a result, was known as the 'Keeper of the King's Conscience'.

In 1474, the Court of Chancery ('the Lord Chancellor's Court') was established, entirely separately from the King's common law courts. Proceedings in the Court of Chancery did not require a writ, and the Chancellor decided cases according to the rules of fairness and natural justice. In other words, he sought to achieve equity (here, equity means a situation in which everyone is treated fairly and equally). He was able to develop new equitable (fair) rights and remedies to take away some of the harsh or unfair results that the common law produced and he was not bound by the excessive procedural burden of the common law courts.

Although the Chancery was more concerned with equity in individual cases, general equitable principles which everyone accepted were just, fair, and reasonable (known as 'equitable maxims') developed along with a set of rules and procedures for their application.

Equitable maxims, rights, and remedies are covered later in section 5.1.3.

5.1.1.4 The conflict between common law and equity

In certain situations, the common law was directly challenged by equity. For instance, in the example given earlier regarding mortgages, equity deemed that it was unfair to the borrower to lose the right to redeem the mortgage even though the redemption date had passed. Therefore at common law, the borrower could not repay the mortgage after the redemption date, but in equity, this was permissible. This is known as the equity of redemption.

In 1615 the Chief Justice held that the Court of Chancery (i.e. equity) had no power to intervene where a common law court had decided a case[2] whereas the Lord Chancellor stated that the Court of Chancery could set aside the decision of the common law courts.[3] The matter was referred to King James I, who decreed that, even where a case had been decided at common law, the Court of Chancery could intervene. Therefore equity—and its ideas of fairness and justice—prevailed over the common law.

5.1.1.5 Reform and the present day

Over time, equity developed further and became more systematic. This led to a legal system with too many courts and too much jurisdictional overlap. As a result it was time-consuming, expensive, and difficult to resolve cases. Moreover, the disparate remedies meant that, in certain cases, a claimant would have to bring two actions arising from the same dispute: one in the common law courts for monetary damages and the other in the Court of Chancery for an equitable remedy.

The overhaul of this unsatisfactory system began in the 1850s with the Common Law Procedure Acts 1852, 1854, and 1860; the Court of Chancery Procedure Act 1852; and the Chancery

---

2. *Courtney v Glanvil* (1615) Croke Jac 343; 79 ER 294.
3. *Earl of Oxford's Case* (1615) 1 Rep Ch 1.

Amendment Act 1858. This enabled equitable remedies and defences to be available in the common law courts and allowed the Court of Chancery to make monetary awards of damages.

The Supreme Court of Judicature Acts 1873 and 1875 fused the administration of law and equity into a single court structure regulated by a single set of procedures. However, in cases of conflict (which are rare since equity evolved to supplement the common law), equitable principles still prevail.[4] In 1981, the Supreme Court of Judicature was renamed the Supreme Court of England and Wales.[5] This is not the Supreme Court as we know it today: at this time the 'Supreme Court' referred to the courts system, not the highest courts, which, at the time, was the House of Lords. The Constitutional Reform Act 2005 established a new Supreme Court of the United Kingdom from 1 October 2009, replacing the House of Lords. To avoid even more confusion, the Supreme Court Act 1981 was renamed the Senior Courts Act 1981, and all statutory references to the Supreme Court of England and Wales have been amended to refer to the Senior Courts of England and Wales: the Court of Appeal, the High Court, and the Crown Court.

An overview of the court structure and the jurisdictions and personnel of the courts is given in section 5.3.

5.1.2 The common law

With the brief history of the law in mind, you will have seen that, originally, the common law was the law that was decided by judges in particular cases and common to the whole of England. Although this is true, it is not nowadays the usual meaning of the phrase.

'The common law' today is usually taken to mean the law that is not the result of legislation; in other words the law which comes from cases decided by judges and the value of the judicial precedents that these decisions set. Case law is a major source of domestic law, since a great deal of law has not been enacted as legislation, and is therefore found in the results of decided cases.

The operation of the doctrine of judicial precedent is explained in section 7.3.

5.1.3 Equity

Equity is still a source of law. You may hear, or read, of the contrast between 'law' and 'equity'. However, in this case 'law' is an abbreviation for 'the common law'. Therefore equity *is* law in that it is part of the law of England and Wales. However, it is *not* part of the common law. Although the *administration* of common law and equity has been fused into the Senior Courts of England and Wales, the distinction between common law principles and equitable principles is still important. For instance, common law remedies are granted as of *right* whereas equitable remedies remain within the *discretion* of the court and are subject to equitable principles.

The brief history provided earlier referred to equitable maxims, rights, and remedies. These will be explained here in more detail.

5.1.3.1 Equitable maxims

Equitable maxims are sometimes referred to as 'equitable doctrines'.

---

4. Senior Courts Act 1981 s 49.
5. Supreme Court Act 1981 s 1(1) (as it was at the time; now the Senior Courts Act 1981).

There are a number of equitable maxims that have developed over the years. Table 5.1 sets out some of the more commonly encountered. Many of these will not make complete sense if you have not studied the specific areas of the law in which they feature yet, but you will encounter them throughout your studies.

Table 5.1 Some equitable maxims

Maxim	Meaning
He who comes to equity must come with clean hands	Equity will not be available to a party that has behaved unreasonably in relation to the disputed matter
Equity looks on that as done which ought to be done. Equity looks to intent rather than to form	Equity will enforce the intentions of the parties rather than enforcing the position reached by inflexible adherence to the common law
Delay defeats equity	Equity will not be available to someone who seeks it after an unreasonable delay
Equity is a shield not a sword	A party cannot bring a claim in equity (sword) but may rely on equity to protect their own position (shield)
Equity will not suffer a wrong to be without a remedy	Equity will allow a party that has been wronged the capacity to ask for a remedy
Equity follows the law	Equity will not allow a remedy that is contrary to law
Where there is equal equity, the law will prevail	Equity will not provide a remedy where the parties are equal, or where neither has been wronged
Equity will not assist a volunteer	Equity will not assist someone who has given no consideration for a promise
Equity will not allow a statute to be used as an instrument of fraud	Equity will not allow someone to rely upon an absence of a statutory formality if to do so would be unconscionable and unfair
Equity will not perfect an imperfect gift	In general, equity will not complete a gift where the formalities required at common law have not been effected (similar to equity will not assist a volunteer). However there is an exception in *Strong v Bird*:[6] where the donor appoints the intended donee as executor of their will, and the donor subsequently dies, equity will perfect the imperfect gift
Equity will not allow a trust to fail for want of a trustee	Where there is no trustee, whoever has title to the trust property will be considered the trustee, or the court may appoint a trustee
Equality is equity	If a trust does not specify how property is to be divided, then there is a presumption of equal shares

5.1.3.2 Equitable rights

Equity also evolved to recognize new rights that were not within the scope of the common law. These include the equity of redemption discussed earlier, which protects the rights of borrowers under a mortgage. A further example is that of the equitable rights of beneficiaries under a trust. Although the law of trusts (or, at the time, 'uses') developed in the 1200s as a means

---

6. (1874) LR 18 Eq 315.

of protecting the land of crusaders and land held for the benefit of religious orders, it is still relevant today in matters of, for example, co-ownership of property, wills, charity, pension funds, and taxation.

5.1.3.3 Equitable remedies

As mentioned in the brief history, the Court of Chancery developed a range of new equitable remedies. These still exist, but remember that they are only available at the discretion of the court. The most common equitable remedies sought are injunction, specific performance, and rescission.

Injunction

An **injunction** is a court order which compels a person or body to perform some action or to cease some action.

There are different types of injunction. Examples include:

- Mandatory injunctions compelling someone to perform an act
- Prohibitory injunctions restraining someone from committing some act
- Interim injunctions granted before trial to preserve the status quo until the case is decided.

Specific performance

An order of **specific performance** compels a person or body to perform their obligations under a contract or trust.

Specific performance is not generally available where damages (i.e. the common law remedy as of right) would provide an adequate remedy. It is therefore usually only relevant to special situations (such as a contract for the sale of land).

Rescission

An order of **rescission** sets aside a contract.

As well as being subject to the usual equitable principles, rescission is only generally available where it is possible to restore the parties to the contract to the positions that they were in before entering into the contract.

5.2 CUSTOM

In order to enforce a local custom as an exception to the common law, it is necessary to show that the custom meets seven main tests. These were introduced by judges as a means of giving them the power to disregard any local custom which they considered unsuitable for recognition as a legal right. As you will see, the tests are very difficult to establish:

- The custom must have existed from time immemorial. This was arbitrarily defined as meaning the year 1189 (or the start of the reign of Richard I). If it can be proved that the custom did not exist in 1189, then it will fail.
- It must have existed without interruption since 1189.
- It must have been enjoyed without force, stealth, or permission.
- It must have been observed because people felt that it was obligatory.
- It must be capable of being precisely defined.
- It must be reasonable. It must also have been reasonable throughout its entire period of use.
- It must be consistent with other local customs.

In practice, if the custom has been observed 'in living memory', this raises a presumption that it has been observed since 'time immemorial' unless evidence can be provided to rebut this presumption.

Custom is typically used in connection with land disputes, such as rights of way or access. However, as you might imagine, the difficulties involved in passing these tests mean that claims to local custom are nowadays extremely rare and success is rarer still. Despite the inherent difficulties in proving local custom, examples of successful claims include *Egerton v Harding*,[7] involving a customary duty to erect a fence to prevent cattle straying from the common, and *New Windsor Corporation v Mellor*,[8] in which the customary right of the mayor, bailiff, burgess, and others to indulge in lawful sports (including shooting) on land in a local borough was upheld.

5.3 THE COURTS, THEIR PERSONNEL, AND THEIR JURISDICTIONS

Without a set of institutions to enforce legal rules, there would be no legal system. A set of rules cannot usefully exist in isolation. There needs to be a system of courts to hear cases at first instance (for the first time), as well as higher courts which offer a way for individuals to bring appeals arising from the outcome of cases in lower courts.

As you will see when looking at the doctrine of judicial precedent in section 7.3, there are rules which determine whether or not a particular court will be bound by a decision of a higher court—generally meaning that it will have to follow the particular legal reasoning of that higher court.

Therefore, a thorough understanding of the institutions of the modern court system is vital to your study of law. This section will provide an overview of the various courts, the types of case which they hear, and the personnel who hear and decide those cases.

The domestic courts can be depicted as shown in Figure 5.2.

---

7. [1975] QB 62 (CA).
8. [1974] 1 WLR 1504 (DC).

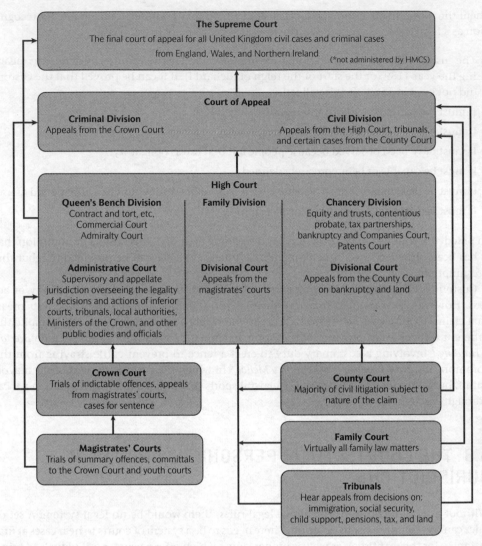

The Supreme Court
The final court of appeal for all United Kingdom civil cases and criminal cases
from England, Wales, and Northern Ireland
(*not administered by HMCS)

Court of Appeal

Criminal Division
Appeals from the Crown Court

Civil Division
Appeals from the High Court, tribunals,
and certain cases from the County Court

High Court

Queen's Bench Division
Contract and tort, etc,
Commercial Court
Admiralty Court

Family Division

Chancery Division
Equity and trusts, contentious
probate, tax partnerships,
bankruptcy and Companies Court,
Patents Court

Administrative Court
Supervisory and appellate
jurisdiction overseeing the legality
of decisions and actions of inferior
courts, tribunals, local authorities,
Ministers of the Crown, and other
public bodies and officials

Divisional Court
Appeals from the
magistrates' courts

Divisional Court
Appeals from the County Court
on bankruptcy and land

Crown Court
Trials of indictable offences, appeals
from magistrates' courts,
cases for sentence

County Court
Majority of civil litigation subject to
nature of the claim

Magistrates' Courts
Trials of summary offences, committals
to the Crown Court and youth courts

Family Court
Virtually all family law matters

Tribunals
Hear appeals from decisions on:
immigration, social security,
child support, pensions, tax, and land

Figure 5.2 The courts

5.3.1 Classification of the courts

Courts may be classified in two different ways:

- Criminal and civil courts
- Trial and appellate courts

5.3.1.1 Criminal and civil courts

🔍 **Criminal courts** determine the guilt or innocence of defendants according to the parameters of the criminal law and dispense punishment to convicted offenders.

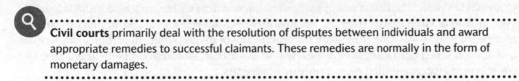

Civil courts primarily deal with the resolution of disputes between individuals and award appropriate remedies to successful claimants. These remedies are normally in the form of monetary damages.

You should note that a particular set of facts can give rise to proceedings in both the criminal and civil courts. For instance, if you were knocked down and injured by a reckless driver while walking down the street, this could lead to a case in the criminal courts (for, say, possible offences under the Road Traffic Act 1988) and in the civil courts (to seek compensation for your injuries in the tort of negligence).

The Crown Court deals almost exclusively with criminal matters. The County Court has only civil jurisdiction. However, all the other courts have both criminal and civil jurisdictions.

5.3.1.2 Trial and appellate courts

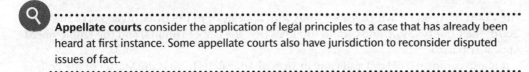

Trial courts hear cases 'at first instance'. This refers to the first time that a case is heard in court, before any appeals. They consider the matters of fact and law in the case and make an appropriate ruling.

Appellate courts consider the application of legal principles to a case that has already been heard at first instance. Some appellate courts also have jurisdiction to reconsider disputed issues of fact.

Trial and appellate functions are often combined within one court as you will see when considering the functions of each court in more detail.

5.3.2 Supreme Court of the United Kingdom

The Supreme Court was created on 1 October 2009 by s 23 of the Constitutional Reform Act 2005 and replaced the Appellate Committee of the House of Lords. The Supreme Court is the final court of appeal for all UK civil cases and criminal cases from England, Wales, and Northern Ireland and the Inner House of the Court of Session in Scotland.

The Supreme Court consists of twelve judges with a President and a Deputy President. The judges (other than the President and Deputy President) are styled 'Justices of the Supreme Court'. The Lords of Appeal in Ordinary became Justices of the Supreme Court; the senior Lord of Appeal in Ordinary became the President of the Court; and the second senior Lord of Appeal in Ordinary became the Deputy President of the Court.

The Supreme Court does not hear evidence from witnesses but instead considers legal argument and documentary evidence. It is located in Middlesex Guildhall on Parliament Square opposite the Houses of Parliament.

5.3.3 Court of Appeal

The Court of Appeal is the highest of the senior courts (which includes the High Court and the Crown Court). It is a single court which is split into two divisions—the Civil Division and the

Criminal Division. The Court of Appeal does not hear witnesses but instead considers legal argument and documentary evidence. The majority decision will prevail, so, in practice, an odd number of judges—usually three—sit. In certain cases of major public importance, sometimes five or even seven Lord Justices of Appeal will sit. Note that, although unlikely in practice, the court is properly constituted even if only one judge sits.

5.3.3.1 Court of Appeal (Criminal Division)

The Court of Appeal (Criminal Division), as its name suggests, has an entirely appellate jurisdiction. It mainly deals with appeals from the Crown Court against conviction, sentence, or a finding of fact; references made by the Attorney-General following an acquittal on indictment under s 36 of the Criminal Justice Act 1972 on a point of law (this is not an appeal by the prosecution as the Court of Appeal's findings will have no effect on the defendant who will remain acquitted whatever happens); references made by the Attorney General under s 36 of the Criminal Justice Act 1988 against an unduly lenient sentence; cases referred by the Criminal Cases Review Commission under s 9 of the Criminal Appeal Act 1995 where there has been a possible miscarriage of justice; and applications for leave (permission) to appeal to the Supreme Court.

It is comprised of Lord and Lady Justices of Appeal. Its head is the Lord Chief Justice.

5.3.3.2 Court of Appeal (Civil Division)

The Court of Appeal (Civil Division) deals with appeals from the three divisions of the High Court, the County Court, and certain tribunals (e.g. the Upper Tribunal and the Employment Appeal Tribunal).

It is also comprised of Lord and Lady Justices of Appeal. Its head is the Master of the Rolls.

5.3.4 High Court

The High Court is one court. However, it is divided into three 'divisions' for administrative purposes. These are the Queen's Bench Division, Chancery Division, and Family Division.

It is staffed by High Court judges (also known as *puisne* judges—from the Old French, pronounced 'puny' and meaning 'inferior in rank'). The head of the Queen's Bench Division is the Lord Chief Justice. The nominal head of the Chancery Division is the Lord Chancellor (who never actually sits in the Chancery Division); in effect it is headed by the Vice-Chancellor. The Family Division is headed by the President of the Family Division.

None of the Divisions has any practically significant criminal jurisdiction at first instance.

5.3.4.1 Queen's Bench Division

The Queen's Bench Division hears criminal appeals from magistrates' courts by way of case stated and from the Crown Court sitting without a jury (e.g. a Crown Court hearing an appeal from the magistrates' court). Its civil jurisdiction includes contractual disputes and actions in tort (with no upper limit on value) at first instance and appeals from the County Court. It also has notable specialist subdivisions: the Administrative Court (which deals with applications for judicial review); the Admiralty Court (dealing with shipping and aircraft); the Technology and Construction Court (which also deals with certain other types of complex civil litigation); the Election Court (which deals with disputed elections); and the Commercial Court (covering banking, insurance, and finance).

5.3.4.2 Judicial review

Judicial review is a procedure by which, on the application of an individual, the courts may determine whether a public body (or a private body exercising a public function) has acted lawfully. It is available to applicants with 'sufficient interest' in the matter to which the application relates.[9]

The most common classification of grounds of challenge in judicial review is that of Lord Diplock who defined three broad (and arbitrary) headings: illegality, irrationality, and procedural impropriety.[10] Illegality was defined as failure to recognize and give effect to the law which regulates a decision-making power: to determine whether a public body has acted *ultra vires* (i.e. outside its authority). Irrationality was described as a decision that was so outrageous in its defiance of logic or accepted moral standards that no reasonable decision-maker could have arrived at it. Procedural impropriety covers both any statutory procedural requirements and the common law rules of natural justice, namely bias and failure to give a fair hearing.

It is also unlawful for a public body to act in a way which is incompatible with the European Convention on Human Rights.[11] The victim of the breach of Convention rights relating to the actions of a public body (or a private body exercising a public function) may also challenge by judicial review. In reaching its decision, the court will consider:

- What Article was breached? How was it breached?
- Was the interference with the right prescribed by law?
- Was the interference necessary in a democratic society or in pursuit of a legitimate aim?
- Was the interference proportional?

5.3.4.3 Chancery Division

The Chancery Division deals with business and property-related disputes, competition, general Chancery claims, patents claims, intellectual property claims (patents, trade marks, and copyright), company law claims, insolvency claims, trust claims, probate claims, and appeals from the County Court on matters such as bankruptcy. It includes the Insolvency List, the Companies List, the Intellectual Property Enterprise Court, and the Patents Court.

5.3.4.4 Family Division

The Family Division has the inherent jurisdiction to deal with cases where a child who is the subject of legal proceedings must be protected. The most common type of case is where a child is made a 'ward of the court'. It also handles cases of international child abduction, forced marriage, female genital mutilation, and applications for financial relief where a divorce has taken place outside England and Wales.

5.3.5 Crown Court

The Crown Court deals with trials on indictment (by jury); cases where the magistrates have declined jurisdiction before trial; offences triable either way where the defendant has elected for trial by jury in the Crown Court; and referrals for sentence from the magistrates' court

---

9. Senior Courts Act 1981 s 31(3).
10. *Council for Civil Service Unions v Minister for Civil Service* [1985] 1 AC 374 (HL).
11. Human Rights Act 1998 s 6.

where the magistrates consider that their sentencing powers are inadequate for the case in question (by virtue of the statutory limit on sentences in magistrates' courts which are currently six months' imprisonment and/or a £5,000 fine).

The Crown Court hears appeals from defendants against conviction or sentence or both in the magistrates' court.

Its first instance civil jurisdiction is limited so much as to be practically insignificant. It is staffed by High Court judges, circuit judges, deputy circuit judges (part-time), recorders (part-time), assistant recorders (part-time), and a jury (for trials).

5.3.6 County Court

The County Court deals with all but the most complicated civil law matters, such as:

- Claims for repayment of debt
- Claims for compensation in personal injury cases
- Cases involving breach of contract concerning goods or property
- Administration of wills
- Bankruptcy proceedings
- Housing disputes, including mortgage and council rent arrears and repossessions.

Section 17(1) of the Crime and Courts Act 2013 removed the former geographical jurisdictional boundaries of county courts and established 'the County Court' with effect from 22 April 2014. The single County Court consists of an entirely civil jurisdiction: unlike its predecessor it does not have a family jurisdiction. Family proceedings are heard in the new Family Court, established by s 17(2) of the 2013 Act. The County Court has a national jurisdiction with unlimited financial jurisdiction and its business takes place at County Court hearing centres. These hearing centres correspond to the locations of the former 200+ county courts.

County Court proceedings can be submitted to the court in person, by post, or online (for some matters) through the County Court Bulk Centre. Cases are normally heard at the centre having jurisdiction over the area where the defendant lives.

The County Court Money Claims Centre (CCMCC) deals with claims for money only. If at any stage an oral hearing is required the claim will be sent to a local County Court hearing centre.

There are three 'tracks' which a case may take through the County Court. The small claims track (often referred to incorrectly as the 'small claims court') hears any claim which has a financial value of not more than £10,000 (except personal injury claims over £1,000, claims by residential tenants against landlords requiring repairs or other work with an estimated cost of over £1,000, or claims for a remedy for harassment or unlawful eviction relating to residential premises). The fast track hears claims which fall outside the scope of the small claims track, have a financial value of not more than £25,000, and which are likely to be tried in one day. Claims in the fast track also limit oral evidence at trial to two expert fields, with one expert per party in relation to each field. Finally, the multi-track hears any claim which falls outside the small claims track or the fast track. Therefore, the multi-track is generally used for higher value, more complex claims (with a value of over £25,000). Most commercial cases fall within the multi-track. The equitable jurisdiction of the court under s 23 of the County Court Act 1984 was increased from £30,000 to £350,000.

County Court staff comprise circuit judges, deputy circuit judges, district judges (formerly known as registrars), and deputy district judges (part-time).

5.3.7 Family Court

The single Family Court came into existence on 22 April 2014, created by s 17(2) of the Crime and Courts Act 2013. The Family Court has jurisdiction in all family proceedings (with some exceptions) and so there is no longer a separate family jurisdiction in the magistrates' courts or the County Court. The Family Court is a national court and can sit anywhere. In practice it generally sits at the same County Court hearing centres and magistrates' courts where family cases were formerly heard.

5.3.8 Magistrates' courts

All criminal proceedings begin in the magistrates' courts and well over 90 per cent end there. The main types of hearing are the trial of summary offences; applications for bail; issue of summonses and warrants for arrest or search; Youth Courts for defendants under the age of 18; plea before venue hearings; and committal proceedings for Crown Court trial or sentence.

Magistrates' courts also have an extensive civil jurisdiction, much of which concerns local Government matters. The main categories of civil hearing include: highways, public health, licensing, and recovery of civil debts such as National Insurance contributions and income tax.

Magistrates' court proceedings are either heard by Justices of the Peace (lay magistrates), usually sitting as a bench of three, or a single district judge (magistrates' courts) working on a full-time salaried basis.

5.3.9 The Judicial Committee of the Privy Council

The Judicial Committee of the Privy Council is the court of final appeal for UK overseas territories and Crown dependencies, and for Commonwealth countries that have retained the appeal to the Queen in Council or, in the case of Republics, to the Judicial Committee.

When we consider the doctrine of judicial precedent in section 7.3, you will see that decisions of the Privy Council are not binding on any domestic court, but are highly persuasive. This is a result of the high judicial standing of its members.

It comprises at least three, and usually five, of the following:

- Justices of the UK Supreme Court
- Other former Lords of Appeal in Ordinary (members of the former judicial committee of the House of Lords)
- Privy Councillors who are or were judges of the Court of Appeal
- Privy Councillors who are judges of certain superior courts in Commonwealth nations.

The Judicial Committee of the Privy Council hears appeals from many current and former Commonwealth countries, as well as the UK's overseas territories, Crown dependencies, and military sovereign base areas. It also hears very occasional appeals from a number of ancient and ecclesiastical courts. These include the Church Commissioners, the Arches Court of Canterbury, the Chancery Court of York, and the Court of Admiralty of the Cinque Ports.

5.3.10 Tribunals

It is usual to think of legal disputes being settled in the courts. However, there are other mechanisms for resolution, including tribunals. These are an alternative to using the 'traditional' courts and their use is, in fact, mandatory in certain types of dispute. Many disputes are dealt with in the network of administrative tribunals that has evolved throughout the twentieth century. Each tribunal dealt with a particular area of specialism such as employment, rent, immigration, and mental health.

Tribunals were seen as a more effective way of dealing with specialist disputes in such areas as they had particular expertise to deal with the intricacies of the law and a better understanding of the types of disputes that would come before them. They adopted less formal procedures to hear and decide cases more quickly: this, in turn, helped to minimize costs. The lack of formality also meant that, in theory at least, there would be less need for legal representation.

The function of tribunals was first reviewed in depth by the Franks Committee in 1957. It described them as:

> [Not] ordinary courts, but neither . . . appendages of Government Departments . . . Tribunals should properly be regarded as machinery provided by Parliament for adjudication rather than as part of the machinery of administration.

The Franks Committee Report made a number of recommendations for the reform of the tribunal system that would ensure that it had three key characteristics:

- Fairness
- Openness
- Impartiality.

It also listed the strengths of the tribunal system as cheapness, accessibility, freedom from technicality, expedition (being able to deal with cases relatively quickly, at least compared to the court system), and expert knowledge of their own area of jurisdiction.

Its recommendations were implemented by the Tribunals and Inquiries Act 1958. Later changes were also introduced by the Tribunals and Inquiries Act 1992.

The number of tribunals grew as new tribunals were introduced by legislation to deal with particular disputes. For example, the Mental Health Act 1983 created the Mental Health Review Tribunal, with responsibility for hearing applications from people who had been detained under the Act against their wishes. Each tribunal was operating under the rules stipulated by the particular piece of legislation that created it. For example, there were no uniform rules concerning the availability of appeals against tribunal decisions or the procedures by which an appeal could be brought.

These concerns of lack of consistency were addressed by Sir Andrew Leggatt who headed a review of the tribunal system. The brief of this review was to recommend a system that was 'coherent, professional, cost effective and user-friendly' and which would also be compatible with the Convention right to a fair trial under Article 6 ECHR. The resulting report *Tribunals for Users: One System, One Service* recommended that the tribunal system should be unified into a single administrative body.

The recommendations of the Leggatt Report were enacted by the Tribunals, Courts and Enforcement Act 2007.

The functions of the majority of existing tribunals have been transferred to the new First-tier Tribunal created by s 3 of the Act. This First-tier Tribunal is divided into a number of chambers, each of which has its own area of specialism as shown in Table 5.2.

Table 5.2 The Chambers of the First-tier Tribunal

General Regulatory Chamber	Charity
	Claims management services
	Consumer credit
	Environment
	Estate agents
	Gambling appeals
	Immigration services
	Information rights
	Transport
Social Entitlement Chamber	Asylum support
	Criminal injuries compensation
	Social security and child support
Health, Education, and Social Care Chamber	Care standards
	Mental health
	Special educational needs and disability
	Primary health lists
War Pensions and Armed Forces Compensation Chamber	War pensions and armed forces compensation
Tax Chamber	Tax
	MP expenses
Immigration and Asylum Chamber	Immigration
	Asylum
Property	Residential property
	Agricultural lands and drainage
	Land registration

It is envisaged that further tribunals will be added to the new structure as part of a phased implementation programme.

Section 11 of the Act creates an Upper Tribunal, which provides the normal route of appeal from decisions made by the First-tier Tribunal on a point of law. However, some decisions (such as decisions relating to asylum support and criminal injuries compensation) do not carry a right to appeal and can therefore only be challenged via judicial review. Some cases will commence directly in the Upper Tribunal.

The Upper Tribunal is divided into four chambers:

- Administrative Appeals Chamber
- Tax and Chancery Chamber
- Lands Chamber
- Immigration and Asylum Chamber.

Section 13 of the Act provides that a route of appeal lies from decisions of the Chambers of the Upper Tribunal to the Court of Appeal (Civil Division) on a point of law. See Figure 5.3 for an overview of the general structure.

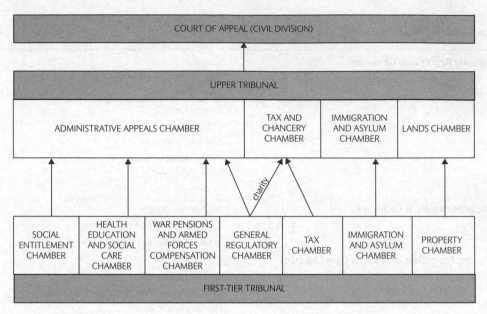

Figure 5.3 The structure of the tribunal system

Section 44 of the Tribunals, Courts and Enforcement Act 2007 created the Administrative Justice and Tribunals Council. This was a public body with responsibility for supervising and regulating the administrative justice system. In relation to the tribunal system, the Council had to review and report on the operation of the tribunals under its supervision and scrutinize legislation relating to tribunals. However, it was abolished in August 2013. Current oversight is provided by the Administrative Justice Council which is the only body with oversight of the whole of the administrative justice system in the UK, advising government, including the devolved governments, and the judiciary on the development of that system.

5.4 THE EUROPEAN COURT OF HUMAN RIGHTS

5.4.1 A brief history

The European Convention on Human Rights and Fundamental Freedoms is a creation of the Council of Europe although it is, at least in part, based upon the 1948 United Nations Declaration of Human Rights. The Council of Europe was formed in 1949, shortly after the end of the Second World War, with its aim of international cooperation and the prevention of the kinds of widespread atrocious violations of human rights which had occurred during the war. The European Convention on Human Rights was signed in Rome in 1950, ratified by the UK a year later, and came into force in 1953.

The European Court of Human Rights was established in 1959 as a final avenue of complaint for claimants who had exhausted the remedies available to them in their domestic courts for alleged breaches of Convention rights. At the same time, the European Commission of Human Rights was also established. The Commission's role was to decrease the caseload of the European Court of Human Rights by filtering out some cases and attempting to resolve others by conciliation. The individual's right to petition the European Court of Human Rights became available to UK citizens in 1966.

The European Court of Human Rights and the European Commission of Human Rights were abolished on 31 October 1998 and replaced by a single Court of Human Rights. Questions of admissibility (formerly dealt with by the Commission) are now dealt with by its judges sitting in committee. It is based in Strasbourg.

Remember that the Court of Justice and the European Court of Human Rights are different, as are the Council of the European Union and the Council of Europe.

5.4.2 The Human Rights Act 1998 and case law

The Convention is an international treaty that binds the states which sign it to certain standards of behaviour towards individuals. However, the Treaty was not enacted as part of the law of England and Wales until the Human Rights Act 1998 which received Royal Assent on 9 November 1998 and came into force on 2 October 2000. This means that individuals may rely on (most) Convention rights in domestic proceedings.

Section 2 of the Human Rights Act 1998 requires courts to take into account any previous decision of the European Court of Human Rights. This effectively allows the overruling of any previous English case authority that was in conflict with a previous decision of the European Court of Human Rights. This enables the courts to build a new body of case law where human rights issues are raised.

The impact of the Human Rights Act 1998 on the doctrine of judicial precedent is dealt with in section 7.4. Section 6.4 describes how to find decisions of the European Court of Human Rights.

 CHAPTER SUMMARY

Common law and equity

- The common law evolved following the Norman Conquest in 1066
- It emerged from a combination of local custom and case law
- The common law became very bureaucratic in operation, costly, and time-consuming
- The common law did not recognize certain rights
- Equitable rights and remedies became available from the Court of Chancery
- Where there was conflict between law and equity, equity prevailed
- The administration of common law and equity was fused by the Supreme Court of Judicature Acts 1873 and 1875
- Equity has its own system of equitable maxims (doctrines), rights, and remedies including injunctions, specific performance, and rescission

Custom

- Local customs can be enforced as exceptions to the common law
- In order to enforce a custom, it is necessary to show that it meets a very stringent set of conditions
- Custom is consequently very difficult to prove
- Custom is typically used in connection with disputes over land

The courts, their personnel, and their jurisdictions

- Criminal courts determine guilt or innocence of defendants and dispense punishment to convicted offenders
- Civil courts primarily deal with the resolution of disputes between individuals
- Trial courts hear cases at first instance—before any appeals
- Appellate courts consider the application of legal principles to cases that have already been heard at first instance
- The Supreme Court of the United Kingdom is the final court of appeal for all UK civil cases and criminal cases from England, Wales, and Northern Ireland
- The Court of Appeal is divided into Civil and Criminal Divisions
- The High Court is divided into three divisions for administrative purposes—the Queen's Bench, Family, and Chancery Divisions
- The Crown Court primarily deals with trial by jury in criminal cases
- The County Court deals with all but the most complicated civil law matters
- The Family Court deals with almost all family matters
- All criminal proceedings begin in the magistrates' court
- The Privy Council hears appeals from certain Commonwealth countries and UK overseas territories, appeals in professional disciplinary cases, and ecclesiastical appeals
- Tribunals are specialist bodies established with the aim of providing quicker, cheaper, and more accessible routes to justice

The European Court of Human Rights

- Not to be confused with the European Court of Justice
- The European Court of Human Rights is based in Strasbourg
- The European Convention on Human Rights was signed in Rome in 1950, ratified by the UK in 1951, and came into force in 1953
- The individual's right to petition the European Court of Human Rights became available to UK citizens in 1966
- The Human Rights Act 1998 came into force on 2 October 2000. This means that individuals may rely on (most) Convention rights in domestic proceedings
- Section 2 of the Human Rights Act 1998 requires courts to take into account any previous decision of the European Court of Human Rights
- This enables the courts to build a new body of case law where human rights issues are raised

FURTHER READING

- You can find a consideration of the creation of the UK Supreme Court in J Lennan, 'A Supreme Court for the United Kingdom: A Note on Early Days' (2010) 29(2) Civil Justice Quarterly 139.

- A brief discussion of the single Family Court can be found in H Johns, 'The New Family Court' (2014) Family Law 110.

- The discussion of custom as a source of law is covered very briefly in this chapter. If you would like to know more, then see EK Braybrooke, 'Custom as a Source of English Law' (1951) 50 Michigan Law Review 70.

Finding cases

6

INTRODUCTION

The previous chapter explained the role of case law as a source of law. This chapter will give you the skills to find cases. It will start by explaining the meanings of case citations before moving on to discuss how to locate domestic cases both in a law library and online via a number of the databases which are currently available. It will then explain how to find decisions of the Court of Justice of the European Union, the General Court, and the European Court of Human Rights.

The ability to locate case law is just as important as finding legislation. Without being able to find the primary sources of law you will struggle in every area of your legal study. You will need to be able to find the cases that you encounter during your studies in order to read and understand them. This is important both in terms of analysing the operation of particular areas of the law as well as more practically in constructing legal arguments based on the outcomes of previous cases.

 Learning outcomes

After studying this chapter, you will be able to:

- Understand the meaning of case citations
- Explain the use of the neutral citation system
- Distinguish between reported and unreported cases
- Find domestic and European cases in a law library and online

6.1 LAW REPORTING

Unless you are actually present in court at the time that the judgment in a particular case is made, you will have to rely on a report of the case to find out what happened. Clearly, then, accurate law reporting is extremely important and citations are the signposts you use for finding those reports.

6.1.1 Making sense of case citations

Case citations are an abbreviated form of reference to a particular report of a case. This section deals with the main citations for cases heard in England and Wales. For an explanation of citations used for EU cases, see 'Finding European case law' in section 6.3. By way of example, we will look at the case of *R v Copeland* which dealt with the availability of a defence to a charge of possessing explosives.

The citation for *R v Copeland* is [2020] UKSC 8; [2020] 2 WLR 681 and indicates where this particular reported case can be found. You will notice that this particular case has two citations: one *neutral citation* and one *law report citation* (see Figure 6.1).

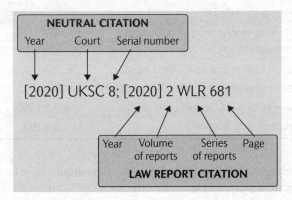

Figure 6.1 Case citations

6.1.1.1 Neutral citations

The neutral citation system was introduced to the Court of Appeal and the Administrative Court in 2001 and extended to all divisions of the High Court in 2002.

The main reason for the introduction of the neutral citation system was to facilitate the publication of judgments online and the access of judgments stored on online databases.

First, the *year* of the judgment is given in square brackets. This is followed by an *abbreviation for the court*, preceded by UK (for 'United Kingdom' in relation to the jurisdiction of the Supreme Court and its predecessor, the House of Lords) or EW (for 'England and Wales' in relation to the jurisdiction of the other courts). Finally, a unique *serial number* is given to each approved judgment.

The abbreviations used for each of the courts that use the neutral citation system (and the position of the serial number—denoted by #) are set out in Table 6.1:

Table 6.1 Abbreviations used in the neutral citation system

Court	Abbreviation and number placement
Supreme Court	UKSC #
House of Lords	UKHL #
Privy Council	UKPC #
Privy Council (devolution cases)	UKPC D #
Court of Appeal (Criminal Division)	EWCA Crim #
Court of Appeal (Civil Division)	EWCA Civ #
Family Court	EWFC #
Court of Protection	EWCOP #
High Court (Administrative Court)	EWHC # (Admin)

Court	Abbreviation and number placement
High Court (Chancery Division)	EWHC # (Ch)
High Court (Patents Court)	EWHC # (Pat)
High Court (Queen's Bench Division)	EWHC # (QB)
High Court (Commercial Court)	EWHC # (Comm)
High Court (Admiralty Court)	EWHC # (Admlty)
High Court (Technology and Construction Court)	EWHC # (TCC)
High Court (Family Division)	EWHC # (Fam)
Upper Tribunal (Administrative Appeals Chamber)	UKUT # (AAC)
Upper Tribunal (Immigration and Asylum Chamber)	UKUT # (IAC)
Upper Tribunal (Tax and Chancery Chamber)	UKUT # (TCC)
Upper Tribunal (Lands Chamber)	UKUT # (LC)

So, looking back at the neutral citation in Figure 6.1 you should now be able to see that *R v Copeland* was the eighth reported judgment of the Supreme Court of the United Kingdom in 2020.

The neutral citation *precedes* the citation for any law report in which the case has been published. If the report has not been published then the neutral citation stands alone. In summary:

- Pre-2001 cases give a law report citation only
- Post-2001 cases give the neutral citation *followed by* the law report citation if there is one available.

You may see cases given with a neutral citation which pre-dates 2001, particularly those retrieved from the BAILII database (see section 6.2.1.7). For example, *Carlill v Carbolic Smoke Ball Company* [1893] 1 QB 256 (CA) is shown on BAILII with a citation of [1892] EWCA Civ 1. These neutral citations are *not* official and must not be used in your written work. As the BAILII website itself states:

> Vendor and Media Neutral citations before 11 January 2001 are not authoritative and have been added by BAILII.[1]

6.1.1.2 Law report citations

The judgments of cases are also published in various series of law reports, the most authoritative of which are published by the Incorporated Council for Law Reporting. References to law reports follow a different convention to that used for neutral citations.

The first element of the citation is a *year*. This will almost always refer to the year in which the case was reported or, occasionally, to the year in which the judgment was given. These years are usually the same, since cases are most commonly reported in the same year as the

---

1. <https://www.bailii.org/ew/cases/EWCA/Civ/> accessed 19 October 2020.

judgment is given. There can, however, be situations where the reports are published in a different year:

- If the case was heard late in one year, but reported early in the next year. An example of this can be found in *R (Lancashire CC) v Secretary of State for the Environment, Food and Rural Affairs* [2019] UKSC 58; [2020] 2 WLR 1. The judgment in this case was handed down on 11 December 2019 but reported in the first issue (first page) of the second volume of the *Weekly Law Reports* of 2020.[2]

- If the importance of the case was not appreciated at the time of the judgment. For example, the judgment in *Mesher v Mesher* [1980] 1 All ER 126 which deals with the division of marital property on divorce, was reported in 1980 but delivered on 13 February 1973, some seven years previously.

The year is placed in brackets—these may be round or square—and there is a legal convention surrounding the use of round or square brackets around the year of the report.

First of all, for very old cases heard prior to 1890, the year is not part of the formal case citation. However, since knowing when a case was decided is always useful, the year is conventionally given for ease of reference, but is shown in (*round*) brackets to indicate that it is for information only. An example of this can be found in *R v Dudley and Stephens* (1884) 14 QBD 273, which considered the defence of necessity in relation to murder: specifically, the killing and cannibalization of a crewmember following a shipwreck.

From 1890 to the present day, the year of the case *is* part of the formal case citation, so it must always be provided. Whether it is put in (round) or [square] brackets depends on the way in which the individual report series is numbered.

In order to illustrate this, we will first look at a report in the European Human Rights Reports (EHRR). Volume 1 of the EHRR was published in 1979 and the most recent volume at the time of writing, covering 2020, is volume 71. Look at Figure 6.2 which shows how some of the reports might look on the library shelf.

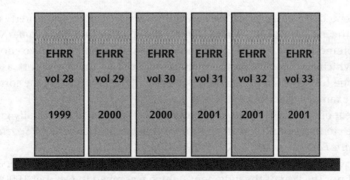

Figure 6.2 European Human Rights Reports (sequential volume numbers)

You will see from Figure 6.2 that there are more volumes than there are years between 1999 and 2001: this is because the reports for a single year often span more than one volume. The reports for 2000 are in two volumes and the reports for 2001 are in three. However, you should be able to see that the volume number alone (which is unique) will be enough to locate a particular report. For example, the report of *Riera Blume v Spain* begins on page 632 of volume 30.

---

2. You may wonder why a case reported so early in 2020 went into the second volume of the *Weekly Law Reports*. Cases of special importance are reported in volumes 2 or 3 (and then re-reported in the *Law Reports*—which is a more authoritative series). Cases in volume 1 are important enough to make it into the *Weekly Law Reports* but not important enough to merit re-reporting in the *Law Reports*.

You do not need to know the year to find the case as the volume numbers run sequentially and it would be easy for you to pick volume 30 off the shelf. Therefore, a citation of *Riera Blume v Spain* 30 EHRR 632 would be sufficient. Of course, it is very useful to know the year of the report as well, which, as you will see from Figure 6.2 is 2000. This is conventionally provided with the citation as well, but since it is not required uniquely to identify the report it is given in (round) brackets. The full citation of the case is therefore *Riera Blume v Spain* (2000) 30 EHRR 632. This case is another example in which the citation refers to the year of the report and not the year of the judgment (as the judgment in this case was given on 14 October 1999).

The year of the report is put in [square] brackets when you need to know the year of the case in order to find it. For example, the Appeal Cases reports do not have sequential volume numbers starting from 1. The reports are bound by year (and sometimes with multiple volumes within each year). Take a look at Figure 6.3 which shows some volumes of the Appeal Cases on our hypothetical library shelf.

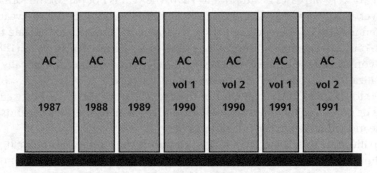

Figure 6.3 Appeal Cases Reports (non-sequential volume numbers)

In a series presented like the Appeal Cases, a volume number on its own is pretty useless. If you were told that the report of *R v Secretary of State for Transport, ex parte Factortame (No 2)* began on page 603 of volume 1 of the Appeal Cases Reports, you still would not have enough information to know which book to take off the shelf in order to find the case report, as there is more than one volume 1. You would need to know the year of the report to get the correct volume 1, which, in this example, was 1991.

When the year of the case is required in order to find it, it is conventionally given in square brackets in the citation, so the correct citation of this case is therefore *R v Secretary of State for Transport, ex parte Factortame (No 2)* [1991] 1 AC 603.

This case provides yet another example in which the year in the citation refers to the year of the report and not the year of the judgment (which was given in October 1990). Also, where there is only one volume for a year, as you will see was the situation in 1987, 1988, and 1989 for example, then the volume number 1 is omitted from the citation as providing it would not tell us anything that we did not already know: so *R v Gold* [1988] AC 1063 is correct (and *R v Gold* [1988] 1 AC 1063 is not, as it implies there are other volumes for 1988, which there are not).

Students are frequently confused on the conventional use of brackets and so this is an area of referencing that is often done badly. Practically speaking, you should just remember that the correct use of round and square brackets is important: all the legal databases use them correctly, and you should take care to be accurate when you are copying citations from materials that you find. If you are in any further doubt, Table 6.2 should guide you on the use of the convention for the most commonly encountered series of law reports.

To recap from the examples so far, then, the *volume number* of the law report series is given after the year, if the volume numbers run sequentially (as with the European Human Rights Reports), or if there is more than one volume of the reports for a particular year (as with the Appeal Cases Reports for 1990 and 1991). If neither of these situations apply, then no volume number is given.

Next comes an abbreviation for the *series of law reports* in which the case was reported. Some common series of law reports are listed in Table 6.2.

Table 6.2 Some common law report series

Abbreviation	Law report series	Year brackets
AC	Appeal Cases	Square
All ER	All England Law Reports	Square
All ER (EC)	All England Reports European Cases 1995–	Square
BCLC	Butterworths Company Law Reports 1983–	Square
Ch	Chancery	Square
CLR	Commonwealth Law Reports	Round
CMLR	Common Market Law Reports 1962–	Square
Cox CC	Cox's Criminal Law Cases	Round
Cr App R	Criminal Appeal Reports	Square
Cr App R (S)	Criminal Appeal Reports Sentencing	Square
Crim LR	Criminal Law Review	Square
ECHR	European Commission of Human Rights Decisions and Reports 1976–98	Square
ECR	European Court Reports 1954 (Court of Justice of the European Community)	Square
ECR I-	European Court of First Instance/General Court	Square
EHRR	European Human Rights Reports 1993–	Round
Fam	Family	Square
KB	King's Bench	Square
QB	Queen's Bench	Square
WLR	Weekly Law Reports 1957–	Square

The final part of the citation is the *page number* on which the report begins.

If there is no neutral citation, an abbreviation for the court in which the case was heard should follow the case citation in brackets: for example, *R v R* [1992] 1 AC 599 (HL) was heard in the House of Lords (and can be found on page 599 of volume 1 of the Appeal Cases Reports for 1992). You may see HL for House of Lords, CA for Court of Appeal, DC for Divisional Court, or PC for Privy Council. This designation is not required where the law report citation follows a neutral citation, since the court in which the case was heard is clear from the neutral citation itself.

6.1.1.3 Which citation?

The *Practice Direction: Citation of Authorities* [2012] 1 WLR 780 clarified the practice and procedure governing the citation of authorities and applies throughout the Senior Courts of England and Wales, including the Crown Court, the County Court, and in magistrates' courts. In summary:

- Where a judgment is reported in the official reports (AC, QB, Ch, Fam) it must be cited.
- If a judgment is not (or not yet) reported in the official reports, but is reported in the WLR or the All ER, then that should be cited. If it is reported in both the WLR or the All ER then either may be used.

- If a judgment is not in the official reports, the WLR, or the All ER, but is reported in any specialist reports which contain a headnote and are made by qualified practitioners in the senior courts, then the specialist reports may be cited.
- Failing all of the above, any other reports may be cited.
- For unreported cases, the official transcript may be used (available from BAILII):[3] however, unreported cases should not normally be used unless they contain a relevant statement of legal principle not found in reported authority.

This hierarchy of court reports is also important in mooting; see chapter 19.

6.1.2 Reported and unreported cases

Since only a relatively small proportion of cases end up being reported, it follows that there are a vast number of 'unreported' cases each year. There are an increasing number of these unreported cases available online. Since 1996, various unreported judgments have been freely available as courts have published verbatim transcripts online.

Practical exercise

Visit the free databases listed in this section. Have a look around each to get used to their layout and content. If you are using your own device, bookmark the sites for quick access later.

6.1.3 Case summaries

In addition to the full reports, there are a number of sources of case summaries and commentaries. For instance, the Criminal Law Review and the Journal of Criminal Law contain brief summaries of pertinent criminal cases. There are similar journals and digests for other areas of the law. The summaries tend to comprise a brief summary of the facts and the judgment accompanied by a pithy commentary.

However, you should remember that these summaries only provide indications of the law and pointers to the actual cases themselves. You should therefore use case summaries with caution—if you wish to rely on the opinion in a case summary, it would be wise to seek out the full transcript of the case to try and understand for yourself the reasoning used by the author of the summary.

6.2 FINDING DOMESTIC CASE LAW

6.2.1 Online

There are a number of freely available online resources for finding case law, as well as the subscription-only services which may or may not be available for you to use at your institution. The subscription services usually offer a selection of 'value-added' features that the free resources do not: these will be pointed out in the discussions of each. Remember that most institutions will provide a guide, or offer training (or both) to using each of the main databases and you should check with your law librarian for details. It may even be the case that you are required to do database training as part of your university induction, or as a component of a legal skills or legal systems

---

3. Note, however, the comment on BAILII's use of 'unofficial' neutral citations at the end of section 6.1.1.1.

module. LexisLibrary and Westlaw Edge UK often have student representatives at institutions who are another useful source of information. In any event, you will need to spend time finding cases throughout your studies, and there is no substitute for practical experience. You should therefore try to get familiar with the various searching tools at your disposal as soon as you can.

Practical exercise

Visit as many of the legal databases from this section as you can. Make a list of those to which you are allowed access. Take some time to click around them and perform a few practice searches.

6.2.1.1 Where to start?

So, let's imagine that you need to find the case report for *Donoghue v Stevenson*.[4] You could simply start by doing a Google search[5] which would turn up something like this (Figure 6.4):

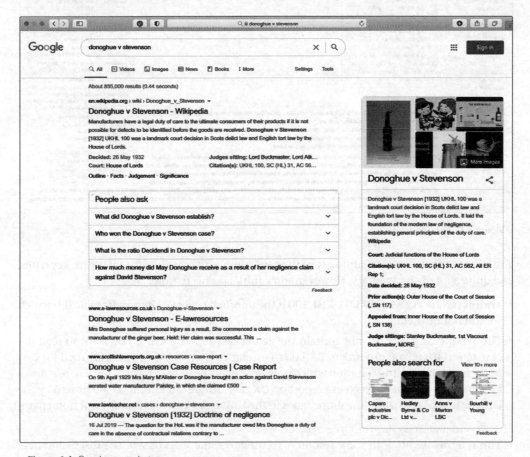

Figure 6.4 Google screenshot

4. This is a famous case from the 1930s which became the basis for the modern law of negligence today. If you have not come across it before, you will definitely do so quite soon.
5. Of course, other search engines are available.

The first four matches (of about 855,000!) are shown. The first of these is Wikipedia (Figure 6.5).[6]

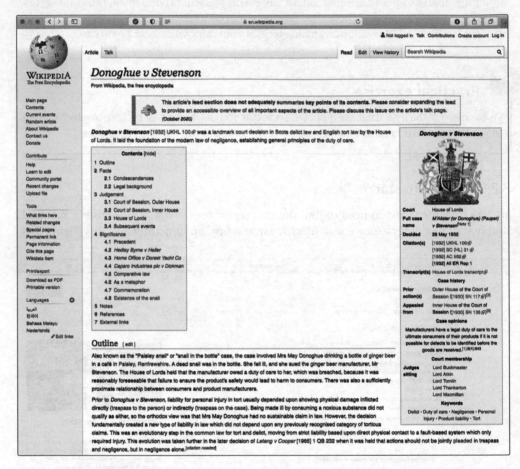

Figure 6.5 Wikipedia screenshot

You will see that this gives a summary of the case, some of the case history, citations, key dates, and quite a lot of commentary. However, some initial points to note:

• The first citation given [1932] UKHL 100 is the unofficial neutral citation from BAILII which should not be used.

• The Wikipedia page does not contain the actual case report itself. If you want to read the case report itself, you can link to BAILII (an unofficial site), or the Scottish Council for Law Reporting (via a Scottish citation which does give an authoritative transcript). There is also a broken link which used to go to a report on UK Law Online (an unofficial site hosted by the University of Leeds) but now simply goes to the University of Leeds Law School homepage.

The second match is e-lawresources.co.uk.

This is a private site with some resources relating to some areas of law. The discussion here is restricted to a short synopsis, rather than the official report and one brief quotation from the judgment itself. There are no links to actual reports, although the citation given is correct.

---

6. See section 14.3.4.5 on the general perils of using Wikipedia for legal research.

The third match goes straight to the Scottish Council of Law Reporting. This was also referenced from Wikipedia and has the benefit of being an accurate and authoritative transcript of the judgment itself. The fourth match is from www.lawteacher.net which gives a more detailed summary of the case, but no full case report. It also gives the unofficial BAILII neutral citation in its list of references, and the other citations given are not presented in a way that complies with the most common referencing system used in universities.[7]

As you can see, there is a wide variety of different sources available via a simple web search with varying degrees of completeness, accuracy, correctness, and legal authority. For that reason, it is preferable to use one (or more) of the recognized legal databases, all of which offer greater features and functionality, to find cases, rather than simply 'Googling about'. The question 'where to start?' then becomes 'which database to use?'.

However, although there are a number of different legal databases available online, not all databases contain all reports. Table 6.3 provides a summary of some of the more common report series and the database (or databases) in which they are covered.

Table 6.3 Law reports and online databases

Series	Citation	Database and dates
The Law Reports	AC, QB, Ch, Fam	Westlaw Edge UK (1865–)
		LexisLibrary (1865–)
		Justis One
Weekly Law Reports	WLR	Westlaw Edge UK
		LexisLibrary
		Justis One
All England Law Reports	All ER	LexisLibrary
English Reports	ER	Justis One
All England Law Reports European Cases	All ER (EC)	LexisLibrary (1995–)
Butterworths Company Law Cases	BCLC	LexisLibrary (1983–)
Butterworths Medico-Legal Reports	BMLR	LexisLibrary (1986–)
Common Market Law Reports	CMLR	Westlaw Edge UK (1962–)
Criminal Appeal Reports	Cr App R	Westlaw Edge UK (1990–)
European Commercial Cases	ECC	Westlaw Edge UK (1978–)
European Human Rights Reports	EHRR	Justis One, Westlaw Edge UK (1979/80–)
Family Court Reporter	FCR	LexisLibrary (1998–)
Human Rights Law Reports	HRLR	Westlaw Edge UK (2000–)
Industrial Cases Reports	ICR	Justis One, Westlaw Edge UK (1972–)
Industrial Relations Law Reports	IRLR	LexisLibrary (1972–)
Landlord & Tenant Reports	L&TR	Westlaw Edge UK (1998–)
Personal Injury & Quantum Reports	PIQR	Westlaw Edge UK (1992–)
Tax Cases	TC	LexisLibrary

6.2.1.2 How do the databases work?

A detailed description of the operation of each of the various databases is beyond the scope of this book.

---

7. This is called OSCOLA (the Oxford Standard for the Citation of Legal Authorities) and is covered in detail in chapter 13.

In general terms, the databases allow you to search by a name, citation, or keywords, or any combination of the above. The best strategy with all database searches is to try and keep it as simple as possible. For instance if you were searching for a case called *DPP v Majewski* it would be easiest to start by putting in the appellant's name. As it is an uncommon name, you would therefore not expect there to be too many cases involving a party called Majewski.

However, if the case was *R v Smith* and you did not know the year, you would need to try to find some appropriate subject matter keywords to narrow your search results; otherwise you would very likely end up with an unmanageable number of potential cases. The pictures that follow in this chapter show the options available on the main search screen of a range of different online resources.

6.2.1.3 Westlaw Edge UK

Westlaw Edge UK allows searching for cases by party name, citation, free text, keyword, or various other attributes (see Figure 6.6). Even if the case is not available in full text on Westlaw Edge UK, links will be given to the location of the report or transcript (if available). Westlaw Edge UK also contains transcripts of recent cases. However, Westlaw Edge UK does not contain all series of reports (see Table 6.3) and for this reason it is often best used together with another broad database such as LexisLibrary.

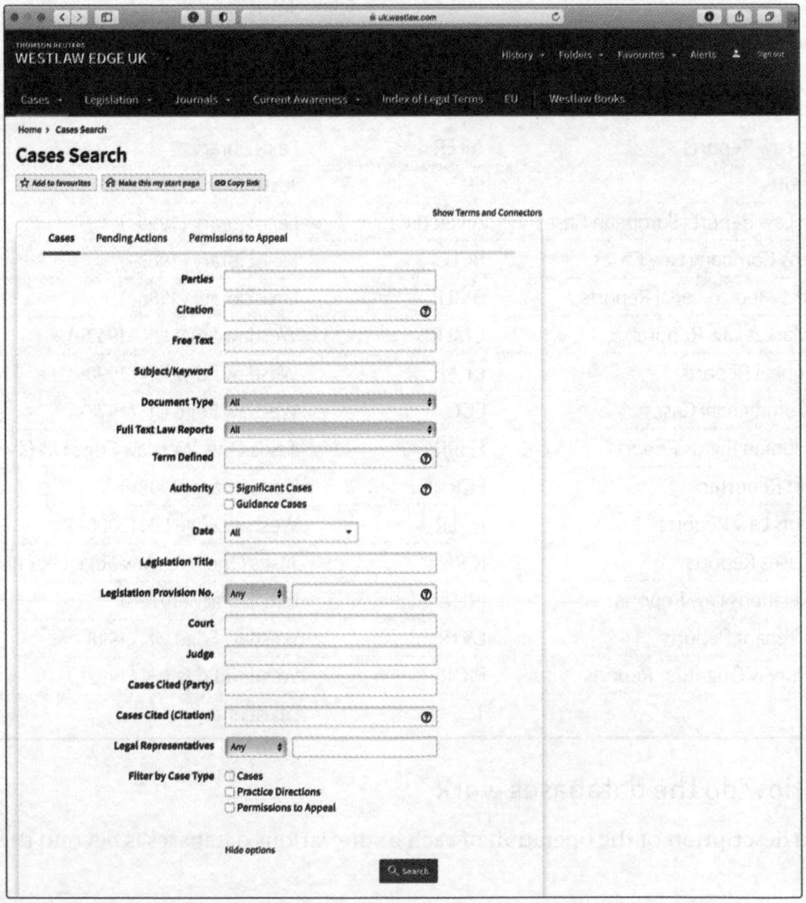

Figure 6.6 Westlaw Edge UK screenshot

6.2.1.4 LexisLibrary

Like Westlaw Edge UK, LexisLibrary is also a subscription service which contains a very broad selection of reports. As well as the standard search criteria it also allows searches by the judge (or judges) or searches for cases which refer to a particular statutory provision (see Figure 6.7). This can be useful if you need to research how a particular piece of legislation has been applied by the courts.

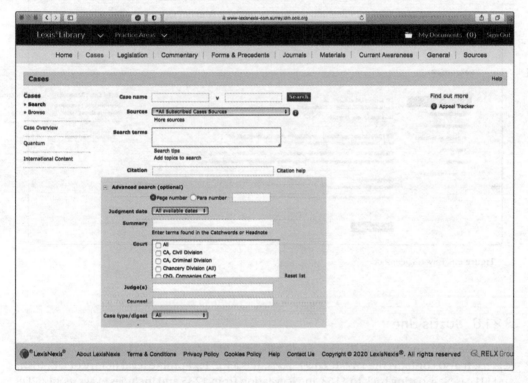

Figure 6.7 LexisLibrary screenshot
Reproduced with the kind permission of LexisNexis®

6.2.1.5 Lawtel

Lawtel is available via Westlaw Edge UK and is updated daily. It includes the following:

- A daily update
- Summaries of cases 1980–, with some links to full text from 1993–
- Personal injury quantum reports
- Practice directions 1980–

It contains summaries and transcripts only (see Figure 6.8). The summaries provide links to full reports. Lawtel covers an immense range of cases and often carries judgments which are not included in the other databases.

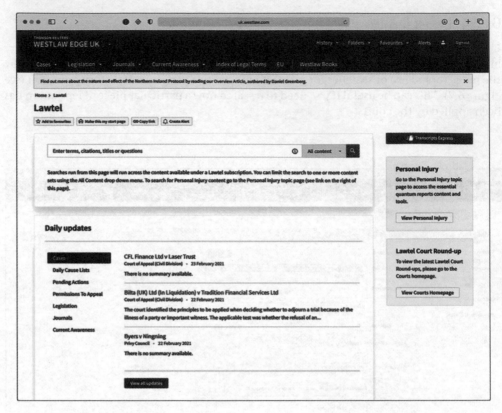

Figure 6.8 Lawtel screenshot

6.2.1.6 Justis One

Justis One contains the *Law Reports*, *English Reports*, *Industrial Cases Reports*, and *Family Law Reports*. It also contains the *Weekly Law Reports*. It is a full text online legal library of UK, Irish, and EU case law dating back to 1163 and legislation from 1235 and includes exact replica PDF files of reported cases.

6.2.1.7 BAILII

BAILII is a free service which contains judgments from a wide range of sources. It has an extremely comprehensive coverage of case law. BAILII's coverage extends beyond England and Wales to Scotland, Northern Ireland, and the European Union. It can be found at www.bailii.org. It allows searching by keyword and first named party (see Figure 6.9).

See the note on BAILII's use of unofficial neutral citations in section 6.1.1.1.

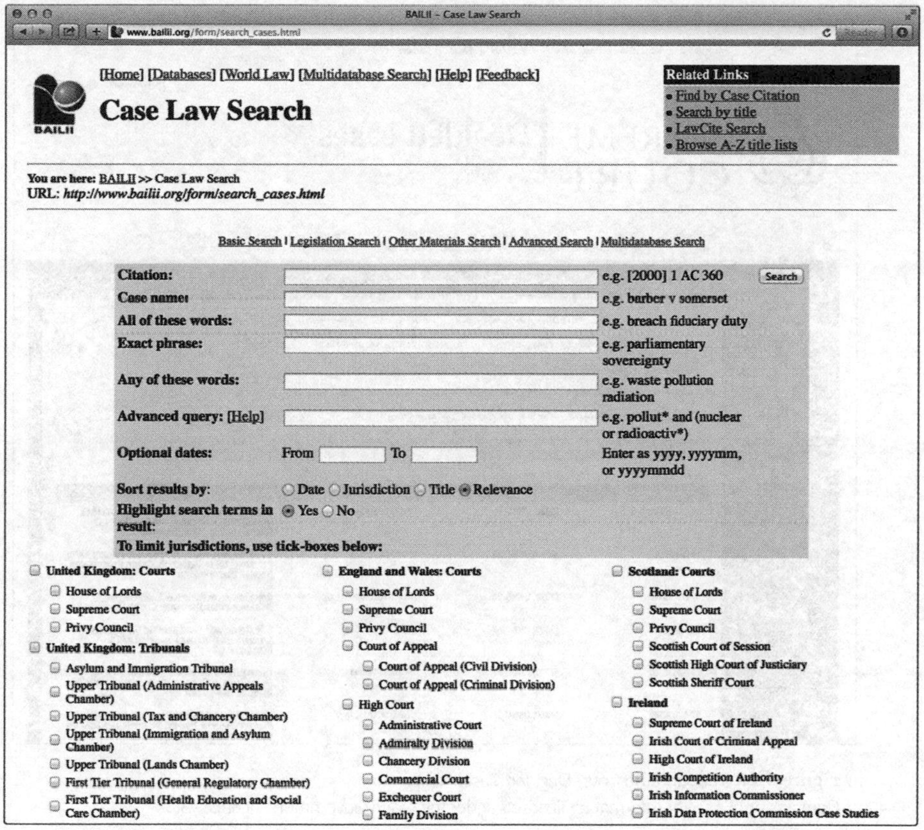

Figure 6.9 BAILII screenshot
www.bailii.org/

6.2.1.8 Supreme Court judgments

Decided cases from the Supreme Court are published on its website at www.supremecourt.uk/decided-cases/ (see Figure 6.10). It has fairly basic search facilities, but if you know the neutral citation it is easy to use. Each case also has a Press Summary which gives an outline of the case and the judgment. Be careful, though, to note the disclaimer on each:

> This summary is provided to assist in understanding the Court's decision. It does not form part of the reasons for the decision. The full judgment of the Court is the only authoritative document.

Therefore, when using extracts from the cases, ensure that you are looking at the full judgment and not the Press Summary (although the summaries are extremely useful to get a quick overview of the facts, the legal issue, and a basic understanding of the court's decision).

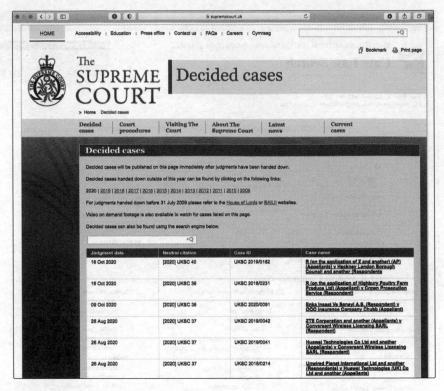

Figure 6.10 The Supreme Court Decided Cases screenshot
Contains public sector information licensed under the Open Government Licence v3.0

6.2.1.9 House of Lords judgments (1996–2009)

The UK Parliament website at www.publications.parliament.uk/pa/ld/ldjudgmt.htm contains html versions of all House of Lords judgments delivered from 14 November 1996 to its closure on 30 July 2009 with print-friendly versions of judgments since 2005 in PDF format (Figure 6.11).

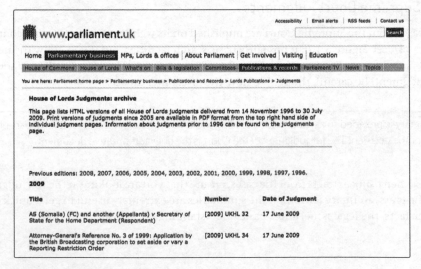

Figure 6.11 Parliament.uk screenshot
Contains Parliamentary information licensed under the Open Parliament Licence v3.0

6.2.1.10 Courts and Tribunals Judiciary

The Courts and Tribunals Judiciary website at www.judiciary.gov.uk/judgments/ carries certain judgments from 2012 from the Court of Appeal, High Court, Family Court, Crown Court, County Court, magistrates' court, Court of Protection, Military Court, and tribunals. It allows free text searches and filtering by court and/or jurisdiction, and date range (see Figure 6.12).

Judgments from 2009 are available via a link to the National Archives.

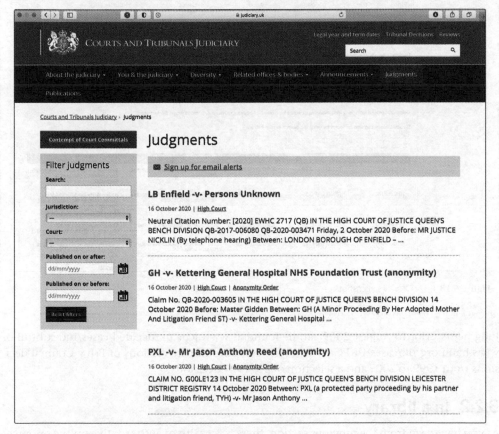

Figure 6.12 Courts and Tribunals screenshot
Contains Parliamentary information licensed under the Open Parliament Licence v3.0

6.2.1.11 Privy Council

Judgments of the Privy Council made after August 2009 are available on the Judicial Committee website at www.jcpc.uk/decided-cases/index.html (Figure 6.13).

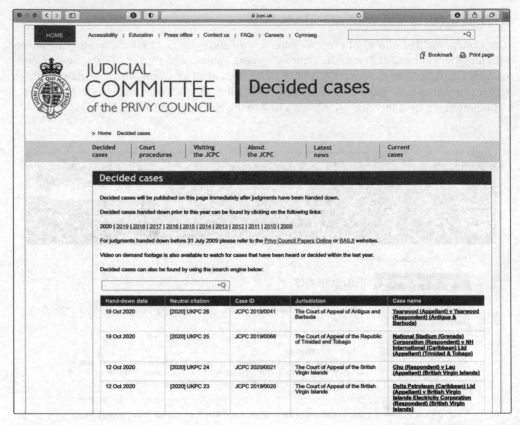

Figure 6.13 Privy Council screenshot

Judgments prior to August 2009 can be found at www.jcpc.uk/decided-cases/index.html or www.bailii.org/uk/cases/UKPC/. These sites contain full-text versions of Privy Council decisions from 1999 to 2009 and a selection of pre-1999 decisions.

6.2.2 In a library

As you have seen from the previous section, there is a wealth of authoritative online resources available for finding case law. The continuing increase in the availability of case law online and the power of online searches has, of course, impacted on the traditional methods of case law searching in a law library. Of course, there are a range of different paper resources that you can use to find case law in a library. It may also be the case that your institution requires you to demonstrate proficiency in library use. Even if it does not, you would be well advised to learn how to use paper resources. Online databases can (and do!) go down at the most inopportune times, so being able to use the library as a backup is essential. That said, virtually all case law research is now done online, and you should find that the cases you will need as an undergraduate exist on at least one of the databases somewhere. However, do not overlook the law librarian if you are stuck. Not only should they be able to help you with the legal databases, but also in the use of paper resources for any case rarities. Many libraries also offer 'Book a Librarian' service where students can book individual or group sessions with the librarian and get assistance with searching and locating resources, legal database training, search strategies, and referencing help. Some librarians are also involved in teaching legal research as part of the law programme but of course this varies between institutions. Many librarians create subject guides and online links to other resources that can support you in your studies. Your librarian is a very useful and skilled resource who often gets overlooked—remember that they are there to help. You will almost certainly meet your law librarian very early on in your time at university since most students attend a presentation given by their librarian and/or tour the law library in their first week.

6.3 FINDING EUROPEAN CASE LAW

Decisions of the European Court of Justice and the General Court/Court of First Instance also have a bearing on the law of England and Wales. It follows that you will need to know how to find EU case law.

For a reminder of the operation of the European institutions and courts, see section 5.4. The effect of European cases on the doctrine of judicial precedent is covered in section 7.5.

6.3.1 Making sense of European case citations

The official reports of cases are found in the *Reports of Cases before the Court*. These are more commonly referred to as the *European Court Reports*, abbreviated to ECR. The reports are structured differently from those of England and Wales. Their component parts are as shown in Table 6.4.

Table 6.4 Components of the European Court Reports

Reports before 1994	Reports since 1994
Report for the hearing	
Advocate General's opinion	Advocate General's opinion
Judgment of the court	Judgment of the court

The report for the hearing was included in reports before 1994. This is a summary of the facts and legal arguments prepared for the court by a 'reporting judge'. The Advocate General's opinion is precisely that—an opinion. Therefore, it is not binding (although in practice it is usually followed). It contains a detailed analysis of the facts and legal arguments. The judgment of the court is a single judgment, even though there are always at least three judges hearing the case. Unlike the courts of England and Wales, separate concurring or dissenting judgments are not permitted.

Since 1990 the *Reports* have been split into two parts. Part I covers reports of cases from the European Court of Justice and Part II contains cases from the General Court/Court of First Instance.

The main problem with the *European Court Reports* is the delay in publication. The courts can hear cases in any of the eleven official languages of the European Union, although they work in French. Judgments have to be translated into each of the official languages. This can take up to two years since the translations must be accurate and precise in each of the languages. Therefore, because of this delay, it is very difficult to use the *Reports* for relatively recent cases.

European cases are cited differently from those in England and Wales. We will use the following two cases by way of example.

- Case C-260/09 *Blizzard Germany GmbH v European Commission* [2011] ECR I-419
- Case T-465/08 *Czech Republic v European Commission* [2011] ECR II-1941

The elements of the citations are broken down in Figure 6.14.

Figure 6.14 Citing European cases

Looking at the elements of the citation, we can see that *Blizzard Germany GmbH v European Commission* was the 260th case (serial number) reported to the Court of Justice (serial number is prefixed by C and the report appears in Part I of the ECR) in 2009 (the year of application or reference is '09'). It was reported in Part I of the ECR for 2011 at page 419.

Similarly, you should be able to tell that *Czech Republic v European Commission* was heard in the General Court, since the case reference is prefixed by T (from the French *Tribunal*) and it is reported in Part II of the ECR for 2011 at page 1941. It was the 465th case heard by the General Court in 2008.

You will notice from both these examples that there is a lapse of time between the hearings (2009 and 2008 respectively) and the official reports (2011). This illustrates the delay in publication. Alternative (unofficial) reports of selected cases include the weekly *Common Market Law Reports* and the *All England Law Reports (European Cases)* published ten times a year.

For some European cases, you may also see a European Case Law Identifier (ECLI) which is a form of neutral citation for EU law. The ECLI is a uniform identifier that has the same recognizable format for all Member States and EU courts. It is composed of five, mandatory, elements:

- 'ECLI': to identify the identifier as being a European Case Law Identifier
- The country code
- The code of the court that rendered the judgment
- The year the judgment was rendered
- An ordinal number, up to twenty-five alphanumeric characters, in a format that is decided upon by each Member State. For instance, ECLI:NL:HR:2020:1254, would refer to decision 1254 of the Supreme Court ('HR') of the Netherlands ('NL') from the year 2020. The ECLI has not yet been formally incorporated into OSCOLA.

6.3.2 Online

There are various online resources for EU case law.

6.3.2.1 EUROPA/EUR-Lex

EUROPA is the main website of the European Union. It contains over 1.5 million pages and links to the European legal portal, EUR-Lex (https://eur-lex.europa.eu/homepage.html) (see Figure 6.15). This includes coverage of the judgments of the European Court of Justice and the General Court. It also includes opinions of the Advocates General as published in the *European Court Reports*. It is updated daily.

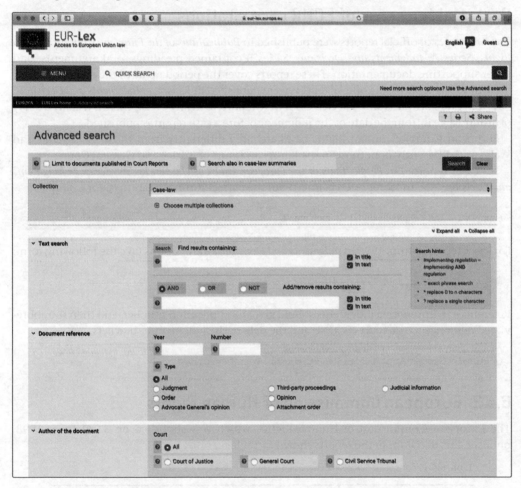

Figure 6.15 EUR-Lex screenshot
© European Union, 1995–2019

6.3.2.2 Other databases

LexisLibrary, Lawtel, and Westlaw Edge UK also provide search facilities for European cases (see section 6.2 for details).

Practical exercise

Access the European databases listed in this section. Try to find *Blizzard Germany GmbH v European Commission* and *Czech Republic v European Commission* in each of them.

6.4 FINDING DECISIONS OF THE EUROPEAN COURT OF HUMAN RIGHTS

The final cases that you will need to find are those decided in the European Court of Human Rights. *The operation of the European Court of Human Rights was dealt with in section 5.4.*

6.4.1 Making sense of ECHR case citations

The first series of official reports were published in *Publications of the European Court of Human Rights, Series A: Judgments and Decisions*. Series B contained pleadings, oral arguments, and other supporting documentation. These reports cover the period up until the end of 1995.

From 1996 onwards, the official reports were published in *Reports of Judgments and Decisions*, but from 2006 onwards only selected cases were reported. In any event, there is usually a delay of around a year from the date of the judgment before a case report is published.

European Court of Human Rights cases are cited differently from those in England and Wales and differently from those in the European Court of Justice and General Court.

For cases reported in *Publications of the European Court of Human Rights, Series A: Judgments and Decisions* (i.e. those reported before 1996) the correct form of citation is, for example:

Golder v United Kingdom (1975) Series A, no 18

For cases reported from 1996 in *Judgments and Decisions*, the citations take the following form:

Robins v United Kingdom [1997] ECHR 72

References to unreported judgments should give the application number, and then the abbreviated reference to the court (ECtHR) and the date of the judgment in brackets.

Goloshvili v Georgia App no 45566/08 (ECtHR, 20 November 2012)

6.4.2 European Commission of Human Rights

The European Commission of Human Rights, which was abolished on 31 October 1998, published its decisions in the reports shown in Table 6.5:

Table 6.5 Reports of the European Commission of Human Rights

1955–73	*Collection of Decisions of the European Commission of Human Rights* (vols 1–46)—cited as CD
1974–98	*Decisions and Reports* (vol 47 onwards)—cited as DR

These reports are cited following the usual citation system for law reports outlined in section 6.1. For example:

X v UK (1967) 25 CD 76
S v UK (1986) 47 DR 274

The Commission's role was to decrease the caseload of the European Court of Human Rights by filtering out some cases and attempting to resolve others by conciliation. Questions of admissibility are now dealt with by judges of the European Court of Human Rights sitting in committee.

6.4.3 European Human Rights Reports

The *European Human Rights Reports* are a commercially available series of reports, published monthly by Sweet & Maxwell. They contain the full judgments of all decisions of the European Court of Human Rights. They are commonly cited in courts in England and Wales and follow the normal citation system for law reports outlined in section 6.1, except that, from 2001, case numbers replaced page numbers.

You should cite either the official reports, that is the *Reports of Judgments and Decisions* or the *European Human Rights Reports* (EHRR), but be consistent in your practice.

For example:

Austin v United Kingdom (2012) 55 EHRR 32
Shannon v Latvia (2012) 55 EHRR 29

6.4.4 Online

HUDOC (www.echr.coe.int) is the official database of the European Court of Human Rights and contains all judgments.

Lawtel, Westlaw Edge UK, and Justis also provide search facilities for cases decided in the European Court of Human Rights.

Self-test questions

Having completed this chapter, use your finding skills to attempt the following research questions involving case law.

1. The Court of Appeal (Civil Division) heard a case in which a number 12 London Routemaster bus had seriously injured an 11-year-old boy. What was the name of the boy's litigation friend and their relationship to him?

2. Give the citation of a case in the House of Lords that involved a finger being mistaken for an imitation firearm.

3. Who represented the claimant found working in a halal butcher's shop in a 2010 judicial review case that considered the operation of s 94 of the Nationality, Immigration and Asylum Act 2000?

4. Which judges considered the appeal in a case involving covert police observation of indecent behaviour in a churchyard on 15 September 1989?

Review the answers to the self-test questions to check your progress and watch the accompanying video explanations at www.oup.com/he/finch8e/.

CHAPTER SUMMARY

Finding domestic case law

- Common case databases include Westlaw Edge UK, LexisLibrary, Lawtel, Justis One, BAILII, and JustCite

Finding European case law

- The official reports are found in the *European Court Reports*
- The *Common Market Law Reports* cover significant European cases from 1962
- The *All England Law Reports (European Cases)* have been published since 1995
- European cases may be found online via EUROPA, and EUR-Lex as well as via LexisLibrary, Lawtel, and Westlaw Edge UK

Finding decisions of the European Court of Human Rights

- The official reports are published in the *Reports of Judgments and Decisions* although there is often a delay of up to a year before publication
- The *European Human Rights Reports* contain full judgments of all decisions of the European Court of Human Rights and are published monthly
- European Court of Human Rights cases may also be found online via HUDOC as well as via Lawtel, Westlaw Edge UK, and Justis One

FURTHER READING

- You can find out more about the Incorporated Council of Law Reporting and the 2012 Practice Direction: Citation of Authorities at www.iclr.co.uk/about/.

- The Cardiff Index to Legal Abbreviations is an excellent free online resource which allows you to search for the meaning of a multitude of abbreviations for legal publications from over 295 jurisdictions. You can find it at www.legalabbrevs.cardiff.ac.uk/.

Using cases

7

INTRODUCTION

The two previous chapters described why case law is an important source of law and gave you the skills necessary to find it. This chapter will build on these skills by discussing how to use cases. It will firstly look at the 'anatomy' of a law report, before considering the means by which the key legal principles can be extracted from the case. Once the legal principles are known we will then consider the extent to which those principles are binding on other courts via the doctrine of judicial precedent. Finally, the chapter will consider the impact of the Human Rights Act 1998 and EU law (both before and after Brexit) on the operation of precedent.

The ability to use cases is a vital legal skill. You will come across a multitude of cases throughout your legal education, so you must be able to work with them effectively. Knowledge of the operation of precedent is also vital, since you will need to know whether the case which you hope to rely upon will have any legal force in the court where your case is being heard. Equally, when you chart the development of particular areas of law you must understand how the decisions given in cases have changed the law over time; this will also depend on the court in which they are heard. Therefore understanding cases is key to each and every area of law.

 Learning outcomes

After studying this chapter, you will be able to:

- Navigate a law report and identify its component parts
- Understand the meaning of case citations
- Explain the use of the neutral citation system
- Outline the operation of the doctrine of judicial precedent and explain whether a particular court will be bound by a particular decision
- Determine the *ratio decidendi* of a case and distinguish it from the *obiter dicta*
- Demonstrate how courts can avoid being bound by 'difficult' precedents
- Assess the impact of European law, Brexit, and the Human Rights Act 1998 on the system of precedent

7.1 READING CASES

Before you can start making effective use of cases, you will need to understand the layout of a reported case and the information that the reports provide. You will then be able to move onto analysing the information that you have been able to glean from the case before you. We will use a real example: *R v A*.[1] Part of this case, as it was reported in the *Weekly Law Reports*, is

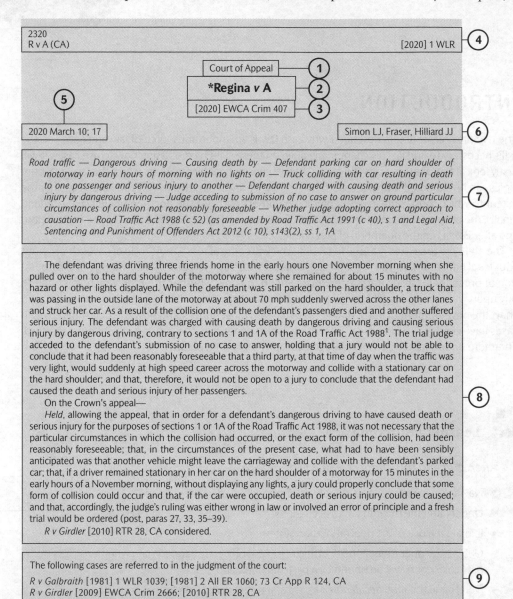

2320
R v A (CA)   [2020] 1 WLR   **4**

Court of Appeal   **1**

Regina v A   **2**

[2020] EWCA Crim 407   **3**

5

2020 March 10; 17   Simon LJ, Fraser, Hilliard JJ   **6**

Road traffic — Dangerous driving — Causing death by — Defendant parking car on hard shoulder of motorway in early hours of morning with no lights on — Truck colliding with car resulting in death to one passenger and serious injury to another — Defendant charged with causing death and serious injury by dangerous driving — Judge acceding to submission of no case to answer on ground particular circumstances of collision not reasonably foreseeable — Whether judge adopting correct approach to causation — Road Traffic Act 1988 (c 52) (as amended by Road Traffic Act 1991 (c 40), s 1 and Legal Aid, Sentencing and Punishment of Offenders Act 2012 (c 10), s143(2), ss 1, 1A   **7**

The defendant was driving three friends home in the early hours one November morning when she pulled over on to the hard shoulder of the motorway where she remained for about 15 minutes with no hazard or other lights displayed. While the defendant was still parked on the hard shoulder, a truck that was passing in the outside lane of the motorway at about 70 mph suddenly swerved across the other lanes and struck her car. As a result of the collision one of the defendant's passengers died and another suffered serious injury. The defendant was charged with causing death by dangerous driving and causing serious injury by dangerous driving, contrary to sections 1 and 1A of the Road Traffic Act 1988[1]. The trial judge acceded to the defendant's submission of no case to answer, holding that a jury would not be able to conclude that it had been reasonably foreseeable that a third party, at that time of day when the traffic was very light, would suddenly at high speed career across the motorway and collide with a stationary car on the hard shoulder; and that, therefore, it would not be open to a jury to conclude that the defendant had caused the death and serious injury of her passengers.

On the Crown's appeal—

Held, allowing the appeal, that in order for a defendant's dangerous driving to have caused death or serious injury for the purposes of sections 1 or 1A of the Road Traffic Act 1988, it was not necessary that the particular circumstances in which the collision had occurred, or the exact form of the collision, had been reasonably foreseeable; that, in the circumstances of the present case, what had to have been sensibly anticipated was that another vehicle might leave the carriageway and collide with the defendant's parked car; that, if a driver remained stationary in her car on the hard shoulder of a motorway for 15 minutes in the early hours of a November morning, without displaying any lights, a jury could properly conclude that some form of collision could occur and that, if the car were occupied, death or serious injury could be caused; and that, accordingly, the judge's ruling was either wrong in law or involved an error of principle and a fresh trial would be ordered (post, paras 27, 33, 35–39).   **8**

R v Girdler [2010] RTR 28, CA considered.

The following cases are referred to in the judgment of the court:

R v Galbraith [1981] 1 WLR 1039; [1981] 2 All ER 1060; 73 Cr App R 124, CA
R v Girdler [2009] EWCA Crim 2666; [2010] RTR 28, CA   **9**

[1]Road Traffic Act 1988, s 1, as substituted: "A person who causes the death of another person by driving a mechanically propelled vehicle dangerously on a road or other public place is guilty of an offence."
S 1A(1), as inserted: "A person who causes serious injury to another person by driving a mechanically propelled vehicle dangerously on a road or other public place is guilty of an offence."

Figure 7.1 *R v A: Weekly Law Reports* first page

1. [2020] EWCA Crim 407; [2020] 1 WLR 2320.

provided in Figures 7.1 and 7.2. We have also provided the official approved judgment as was handed down by the court in Figure 7.3. Each of the highlighted areas of the reports will be covered in turn. As we go through you will see that the report of the case in the *Weekly Law Reports* provides a lot more information, but keep in mind when comparing it to the approved judgment that the additional 'value-added' information has been written by the court reporter and is not part of the authoritative words of the Court of Appeal.

7.1.1 Court ①

The court is the court in which the case was heard; in this case, the Court of Appeal. It is important to know which court heard the case because of the doctrine of judicial precedent: generally speaking, the more senior the court, the more binding the legal principle.

7.1.2 Case name ②

The name of this case is *Regina v A*. This is a criminal case and, as such, one of the parties involved is the Crown, indicated by *Regina*. If the monarch at the time of the case were a King then the masculine form *Rex* would be used instead of *Regina*. *Regina* (or *Rex*) is often abbreviated to *R*, so the parties to this case could equally well be referred to as *R v A*. The person against whom a criminal case is brought is referred to as the 'defendant'. On appeal, the labels used for the parties change. The person bringing an appeal is the 'appellant' and the person against whom the appeal is brought is known as the 'respondent'. So in this case, it is the Crown that is bringing an appeal against the Crown Court. The fact that the case is an appeal from the Crown Court is made clear in the approved judgment but not in the reported version.

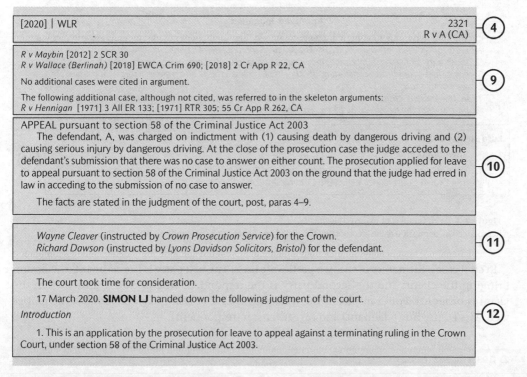

| [2020] 1 WLR | 2321 R v A (CA) | ④ |

R v Maybin [2012] 2 SCR 30
R v Wallace (Berlinah) [2018] EWCA Crim 690; [2018] 2 Cr App R 22, CA

No additional cases were cited in argument.

The following additional case, although not cited, was referred to in the skeleton arguments:
R v Hennigan [1971] 3 All ER 133; [1971] RTR 305; 55 Cr App R 262, CA ⑨

APPEAL pursuant to section 58 of the Criminal Justice Act 2003
    The defendant, A, was charged on indictment with (1) causing death by dangerous driving and (2) causing serious injury by dangerous driving. At the close of the prosecution case the judge acceded to the defendant's submission that there was no case to answer on either count. The prosecution applied for leave to appeal pursuant to section 58 of the Criminal Justice Act 2003 on the ground that the judge had erred in law in acceding to the submission of no case to answer. ⑩

    The facts are stated in the judgment of the court, post, paras 4–9.

Wayne Cleaver (instructed by *Crown Prosecution Service*) for the Crown.
Richard Dawson (instructed by *Lyons Davidson Solicitors, Bristol*) for the defendant. ⑪

The court took time for consideration.

17 March 2020. **SIMON LJ** handed down the following judgment of the court.
Introduction

    1. This is an application by the prosecution for leave to appeal against a terminating ruling in the Crown Court, under section 58 of the Criminal Justice Act 2003. ⑫

Figure 7.2 *R v A: Weekly Law Reports* second page

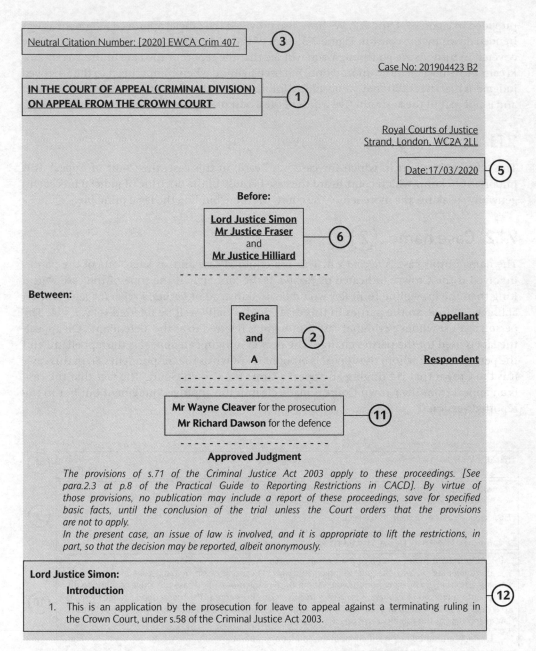

Figure 7.3 *R v A:* Opening of approved judgment
Reproduced by permission of the Incorporated Council of Law Reporting for England and Wales

In civil cases, the names of the two parties are used. The first party is the claimant (the person bringing the claim) and the second party is the respondent (the person against whom the claim is brought). For example, in the well-known case of *Donoghue v Stevenson*,[2] the parties were Mrs Donoghue (claimant) and Mr Stevenson (respondent).

2. [1932] AC 562 (HL).

You may also encounter the word 'plaintiff' which was historically used in civil proceedings instead of 'claimant', but 'claimant' has been the correct term for some considerable time.

There are other commonly encountered forms of case name as shown by the examples in Table 7.1:

Table 7.1 Case citations

R v Secretary of State for Foreign and Commonwealth Affairs, ex p World Development Movement Ltd[3]	Judicial review cases prior to 2001 are cited as the Crown against a particular public body *ex parte* (often abbreviated to *ex p*, meaning on behalf of) an applicant
R (Quintavalle) v Secretary of State for Health[4]	Judicial review cases after 2001 are cited with the applicant's name in brackets after the '*R*'. Such cases are read as '*the Crown on the application of Quintavalle against the Secretary of State for Health*'
R v R[5]	Family cases are usually kept anonymous. There is some scope for confusion here if one of the party's names begins with 'R'. It would not then be immediately apparent whether the case in question was a criminal matter or a civil matter. However, the facts of the particular case should make this clear very quickly. In our example the court has also chosen to protect the identity of the respondent, so their name is just given as 'A'.
Re W; Re: A; Re: B (Change of name)[6]	Cases in the family courts often have some explanatory subject matter text associated with them in order to aid identification and differentiation
In re Jones[7] (or *Re Jones*)	'In the matter of' Jones. This citation is often used in cases involving wills or probate where Jones is deceased, but what happens to their estate is contested or contentious
Liesbosch Dredger[8]	Shipping cases are conventionally referred to by the name of the vessel involved rather than their owners; in this example the *Liesbosch Dredger* was a ship

7.1.3 Neutral citation ③

The neutral citation of this case is '[2020] EWCA Crim 407'.
For information on the operation of the neutral citation system, see section 6.1.1.1.

7.1.4 Case citation—law report ④

The citation for this particular reported case is '[2020] 1 WLR 2320'. Of course, this citation is restricted to the *Weekly Law Reports* and is not provided in the approved judgment.
For a detailed description of case citations, see chapter 6.

3. [1995] 1 WLR 386 (DC).
4. [2003] 2 AC 687 (HL).
5. [1992] 1 AC 599 (HL).
6. [2001] Fam 1 (CA).
7. [1931] 1 Ch 375 (DC).
8. [1933] AC 449 (HL).

7.1.5 Date of the hearing and judgment ⑤

This case was heard on 10 March 2020 and the judgment was given on 17 March 2020. Remember from before that the year of the judgment might be different from the year of the report.

In a *reserved judgment* such as this one, the judges take time after the hearing to consider the issues and provide a written judgment at a later date. The date of the written judgment will be given before the judgment after the words 'The court took time for consideration'. In some older reports, you may see 'cur adv vult' used instead. This is short for *curia advisari vult* (literally 'the court wishes to be advised') and means the same in effect: there was a delay between the hearing and handing down the judgment.

7.1.6 Judges ⑥

In this case the Court of Appeal comprised Lord Justice Simon, Mr Justice Fraser, and Mr Justice Hilliard. It is sometimes useful to know the seniority or reputation of the judges involved in making a particular decision since this may affect the extent to which the judgment may be persuasive (if it is not automatically binding).

7.1.7 Subject matter ⑦

This section contains a series of catchwords which are provided by the editors of the law report. They do not appear in the approved judgment. The catchwords provides a brief list of the subject matter, main facts and key legal points of the case as well as any references to particular statutory provisions which the case considers (in this case, ss 1 and 1A of the Road Traffic Act 1988 (as amended). These points are also repeated in the summaries at the start of each volume of the reports.

7.1.8 Headnote ⑧

The headnote contains a summary of the case. However, the headnote carries no legal authority. When comparing Figures 7.1 and 7.3 you will see the headnote is prepared by the reporter and not by the judges. Although it usually carries an accurate summary of the case, it very occasionally does not. For instance, in *Young v Bristol Aeroplane Co*[9]—a case which we will return to later in this chapter when we consider the doctrine of judicial precedent—the headnote states that:

> (b) [The Court of Appeal] must refuse to follow a decision of its own which, though not expressly overruled, is inconsistent with a decision of the House of Lords.

whereas the actual text of the judgment says that:

> The third is where this court comes to the conclusion that a previous decision, although not expressly overruled, cannot stand with a *subsequent* [emphasis added] decision of the House of Lords.

---

9. [1944] KB 718 (CA).

Therefore the headnote of the case should always be used with some caution and you should read the whole judgment to develop your own understanding rather than relying on someone else's synopsis of what the judgment says.

The headnote may also usefully summarize the effect of the case on the existing case law, using the terms in Table 7.2.

The effect on the existing case law is explained in detail in section 7.6.

Table 7.2 Headnote terminology

Affirmed	The court in the present case agreed with the decision of a lower court on the same case
Applied	The court in this case considered itself to be bound by the precedent set by an earlier (and different) case and has therefore used the same legal reasoning in the present case
Approved	The court in the present case agreed with the decision of a lower court in a different case
Considered	The court discussed a different case. This is often a case that has been decided by a court at the same level in the hierarchy. (You will see in Figure 7.1 that the court in our example considered *R v Girdler* [2010] RTR 28, which was another decision of the Criminal Division of the Court of Appeal)
Distinguished	The court in the present case does not wish to (or cannot) overrule a previous decision and also does not wish to apply it. It has found sufficient differences between the cases to avoid being bound by the earlier case
Overruled	The court in the present case has overturned a decision in a different case, usually made in a lower court (although occasionally in a court of equal status)
Reversed	The court in the present case on appeal overturned the decision of a lower court in the same case
Semble	(A Law French term literally meaning 'it appears'). The court gives an opinion on a point that is not directly at issue in this case. (This is *obiter dictum*, which we will go on to explain in section 7.3.1)

7.1.9 List of cases

The report provides a list of cases in two sections. The first section contains four cases (*Galbraith, Girdler, Maybin,* and *Wallace (Berlinah)*) which were referred to by the judges in their judgment. The second section would contain a list of cases which counsel had also raised in argument but which were not referred to by the judges. These cases are of less importance as far as the judgment is concerned than those referred to directly by the judges. There were none of these in this example. Finally, the third section shows an additional case (*Hennigan*) that was not used at the hearing but had been referred to in the skeleton arguments. (Skeleton arguments are a written outline of the submissions provided to the court—and the other side—in advance. You will find out more about them in section 19.4.3.)

7.1.10 Details of the action (10)

This section is again also only available in the reported version. It provides a brief history of the case proceeding to date. In this example, the Court of Appeal (Criminal Division) is considering an appeal against a judge's decision to acquit a defendant who had been charged with causing death and serious injury by dangerous driving on the basis that the judge had 'erred in law'.

7.1.11 Counsel ⑪

The names of counsel who appeared for each party in the case are listed. These may be barristers or solicitor advocates. Senior barristers are known as 'Queen's Counsel' and will be designated by the letters QC after their name. The names of the barristers can be particularly useful to instructing solicitors. If a case with similar issues arises in the future, then solicitors may choose to instruct barristers who have had success or experience in such cases in the past.

This section may also inform us if any counsel were acting *'pro bono'*—that is, a Latin term meaning 'for good' or, in this context, without charging a fee.

7.1.12 Judgment ⑫

The judgment is the most important part of the report. Where there is more than one judge hearing a particular case, each judge may deliver his own judgment. Typically one judge—usually, but not always, the most senior—delivers the first judgment. The other judges may then (but do not have to) give their own judgments. These may be as brief as 'I agree' or given at length and dissenting (i.e. disagreeing with) from one or more of the other judgments. In this example, Lord Justice Simon delivers the judgment of the court in its entirely.

Judgments often (but not always) are broken down as follows:

• Summary of the material facts of the case
• Statement of the applicable law
• Legal reasoning
• Decision.

Some law reports also contain a summary of the arguments presented by counsel for each side. An example of this can be found in *R (Holding & Barnes plc) v Secretary of State for the Environment, Transport and the Regions.*[10]

Practical exercise

Look up the *Holding & Barnes plc* case referred to here and find the summary of counsels' arguments.

The judgment in *R v A* is divided up into numbered paragraphs. Pinpoint referencing provides a useful way of referencing particular quotations from a judgment in a piece of legal writing or to support an argument put forward in a moot. The reader (or judge) may then direct their attention easily to the precise wording to which you wish to draw reference.

For more information on pinpoint referencing, see chapter 13.

7.1.12.1 Latin and Law French

Although there has been a move away from the use of legal terms derived from Latin and French (known as 'Law French') in general, when reading a judgment—particularly an older one—you may encounter an unusual term. Table 7.3 sets out a number of such phrases and their meanings. Where the term is particularly associated with a specific area of law that is also shown.

---

10. [2003] 2 AC 295 (HL).

Table 7.3 Latin and Law French terms

Latin	Meaning
A priori	From earlier
Ab initio	From the beginning
Actus reus	Guilty act (criminal law)
Ad hoc	For this
Ante	Before
Bone fide	In good faith
Consensus ad idem	Agreement to the same (contract law)
Contra	Against
Contra proferentem	Against the one bringing the action (contract law)
De facto	In fact
De jure	In law
De novo	Anew
Dictum	(A thing which is) said
Doli incapax	Incapable of guilt (criminal law)
Ejusdem generis	Of the same kind (statutory interpretation)
Ergo	Therefore
Erratum	Made in error
Ex gratia	Done as a favour
Ex parte	Done for a party (judicial review)
Ex post facto	After the fact
Habeas corpus	'May you have the body': a writ to challenge unlawful detention
In camera	In private
Inter vivos	Between the living (trusts)
Ipso facto	In and of itself
Lacuna	Gap
Locus	Place
Locus standi	Right to bring a case
Mala in se	Wrong in itself
Mala prohibitum	Wrong because it has been prohibited
Mens rea	Guilty mind (criminal law)
Modus operandi	Way of doing things (usually used in relation to crime)
Non est factum	Not my deed
Novus actus interveniens	A new act intervenes (criminal law; tort law)
Noscitur a sociis	Known by the company it keeps (statutory interpretation)
Obiter dictum	Something said in passing (precedent)
Pari passu	Of equal rank
Per curiam	A decision of the whole court
Per incuriam	In neglect (precedent)
Prima facie	On the face of it

Latin	Meaning
Pro bono	Without charging a fee
Quantum	Amount
Ratio decidendi	Reason for the decision (precedent)
Res gestae	Things done
Res ipsa loquitur	The thing speaks for itself (tort law)
Stare decisis	To stand by things decided (precedent)
Ultra vires	Beyond its powers (judicial review)
Law French	**Meaning**
Chose	A thing (usually used in 'chose in action' or 'chose in possession')
Cy-près	'As near as possible' (trusts)
Laches	Delay
Semble	It appears to be
Voir dire	'To say the truth' (mostly used for decisions on admissibility of evidence)

7.1.13 Solicitors and reporter

The end of the *Weekly Law Reports* version is shown in Figure 7.4. It shows the outcome of the case. Sometimes this section gives details of the solicitors who represented each party and instructed counsel on their behalf. Finally, the name or initials of the law reporter are provided.

> 38. Accordingly, in the words of s.67 of the Criminal Justice Act 2003, the Judge's ruling was either wrong in law or involved an error of principle.
>
> 39. In these circumstances, and as provided by section 61(4)(b) of the Act, we will order a fresh trail of the defendant on count 1
>
> *Appeal allowed.*
> *Retrial ordered.*
>
> CLARE BARSBY, BARRISTER

Figure 7.4 *R v A*: final page
Reproduced by permission of the Incorporated Council of Law Reporting for England and Wales

7.1.14 Online reports

As well as paper law reports, most historic and all recent case reports are also available online. This section briefly considers the online versions of *R v A* that are available via LexisLibrary and Westlaw Edge UK which have been chosen to illustrate some of the distinctions between the online and paper presentations of the cases.

Practical exercise

Look up *R v A* on LexisLibrary and Westlaw Edge UK. Compare the online versions with the printed extracts from the *Weekly Law Reports*.

7.1.14.1 Alternative citations

You will see that the LexisLibrary report gives the neutral citation as well as [2020] 1 WLR 2320, together with an alternative report cited as [2020] All ER (D) 03 (Apr).

As well as these, Westlaw Edge UK also gives further report citations: [2020] 2 Cr App R 3, [2020] RTR 18 and [2020] Crim LR 838. It also gives [2020] 3 WLUK 580 which is its own internal Westlaw citation which is unofficial and should never be used. Nonetheless, the additional citations show that the case has been reported in multiple other publications as well as in the approved judgment and the *Weekly Law Reports*.

Self-test questions

1. What does [2020] 2 Cr App R 3 mean?

2. What does [2020] All ER (D) 03 (Apr) mean?

3. What does [2020] RTR 18 mean?

Answers to the self-test questions can be found at **www.oup.com/he/finch8e/**.

7.1.14.2 Content

You will see that both online databases provide additional information over and above the printed law report and the approved judgment in isolation, including further keywords, summaries, abstracts, and digests of the case. They also allow you to download PDF versions of the different case reports suggested that are identical in every respect to that which would be found in the printed volume in a law library.

Both reports contain paragraph numbers and show the corresponding page numbers from the bound version of the *Weekly Law Reports* inline in the text.

Therefore, if you need to refer to the page number of a particular part of an online transcript in a pinpoint reference, you must work backwards until you see a page number mark. The material you want to reference is on that page in the printed version.

However, the online versions also give direct links to academic and professional commentary on the case, as well as to cases which are referred to in the judgment and relevant passages of legislation considered so despite some differences from the paper reports, they are in almost every other respect a richer and easier to use resource than the paper reports in isolation.

7.2 READING EUROPEAN CASES

There are some differences in the ways that cases are presented in the official European Court reports, as you will see from Figure 7.5 which shows the start of the report of *Commission v Spain*.[11]

---

11. Case C-136/07 *Commission v Spain* [2008] ECR I-7793.

CASE C-136/07

Commission of the European Communities v Kingdom of Spain

(Failure of a Member State to fulfil obligations – Directives 89/48/EEC and 92/51/EEC – Recognition of diplomas and professional education and training – Profession of air traffic controller)

Summary of the Judgment

Where a Member State does not adopt a system for the recognition of the profession of air traffic controller, it fails to fulfil its obligations pursuant to Directive 89/48 on a general system for the recognition of higher-education diplomas awarded on completion of professional education and training of at least three years' duration and Directive 92/51 on a second general system for the recognition of professional education and training to supplement Directive 89/48.

Such a profession must be classified as a regulated profession within the meaning of those directives and thus falls within their scope where the pursuit of the activity of air traffic controller is effectively governed by legislative provisions creating a system under which that professional activity is expressly reserved to those who fulfil certain conditions and access to it is prohibited to those who do not fulfil them. That conclusion cannot be called into question by the fact that there is no training leading to a single diploma

which gives the right to pursue the profession in queation. As access to the profession of air traffic controller is subject to possession of a 'diploma' as defined by Directive 89/48, it follows that the Member State concerned must ensure provision for the recognition of diplomas which fall either within the definition contained in Directive 89/48, or within that contained in Directive 92/51. As the directives do not establish a system of automatic recognition, the specific or local character of certain ratings which a person wishing to pursue the profession of air traffic controller in the host Member State is required to have does not preclude the comparison of, first the skills attested to by the diplomas or the professional education and trainig acquired in a Member State other than the host Member State with the objective of pursuing that profession and, second, the knowledge and the ratings required for the pursuit of that profession in the Kingdom of Spain.

(see paras 38-40, 45, 47, 53, 55, 57 , operative part)

JUDGMENT OF THE COURT (Second Chamber)
16 October 2008

In Case C-136/07,

ACTION under Artical 226 EC for failure to fulfil obligations, brought on 7 March 2007,

Commission of the European Communities, represented by H. Støvlbæk and R. Vidal Puig, acting as Agents, with an address for service in Luxembourg,

V   applicant,

Kingdom of Spain, represented by M. Muñoz Pérez, acting as Agent, with an address for service in Luxembourg,

defendant,

THE COURT (Second Chamber),

composed of C.W.A. Timmermans President of the Chamber, L. Bay Larsen, K. Schiemamm (Rapporteur), P. Kūris and J.-C. Bonichot, Judges,

Advocate General: Y. Bot,

Registrar: R. Grass,

having regard to the written procedure,

having decied, after hearing the Advocate General, to proceed to judgment without an Opinion, gives the following

Judgment

By its action, the Commission of the European Communities asks the Court to find that, in failing to adopt, in connection with the profession of air traffic controller, the laws, regulations and administrative provisions necessary to comply with Council Directive 89/48/EEC.....

Figure 7.5 European Court Report
© European Union, 1995–2019

You will notice the following differences from a UK court report:

- **The court and chamber**. The report contains the name of the court and the chamber in which it was held. In this context, 'chamber' refers to a particular group of judges who are listed within the report. Here, the case was heard by the Court of Justice of the European Communities (now the CJEU) with the court comprising CWA Timmermans, L Bay Larsen, K Schiemann, P Kūris, and J-C Bonichot.

- **President, Rapporteur, Advocate General, and Registrar**. Each chamber has a president elected annually. In effect, each judge takes the presidency by rotation. Each case also has a rapporteur, who undertakes preparatory enquiries after an application has been received by the court. The rapporteur puts together a report for the court to decide on the procedure by which the case will be heard (including witnesses to be called and the number of judges that should sit). The Advocate General advises the court and gives a reasoned opinion to the court on the decision that, in their opinion, the court should reach. In this particular case, the court decided to proceed to give its judgment without the opinion of the Advocate General. The Registrar deals with procedural points and administration of the court itself.

- **Headnote**. Here the headnote gives only a few short phrases on the key points within the case itself.

- **Summary of the judgment**. Before the judgment is given in detail it is fully summarized as part of the official report.

- **Advocates**. Each party to the proceedings must usually be represented by an advocate.

- **Judgment**. Finally comes the judgment itself, which is given as a collegiate decision of the court as a whole. There are no opinions of individual judges, nor any dissenting judgments. Similarly, the language used may be more bland than the more creative and florid language often used by judges in England and Wales. The courts are also less inclined to speculate on alternative circumstances and this leads to judgments which are very focused on the particular matter in hand, but do not often consider the wider implications of the final ruling.

As you have seen in this case, the court decided to give its judgment without requiring an Advocate General's opinion. This is not always the case, and Advocate General's opinions may also be found, where available, via EUR-Lex. These look very similar to judgments of the CJEU themselves, and give a legally reasoned conclusion to the matter before the court, as you will see from the extract of the start and end of the opinion in Extract 7.1.

OPINION OF ADVOCATE GENERAL

BOT

delivered on 6 September 2012

Case C-456/11

Gothaer Allgemeine Versicherung AG,

ERGO Versicherung AG,

Versicherungskammer Bayern-Versicherungsanstalt des öffentlichen Rechts,

Nürnberger Allgemeine Versicherungs AG,

Krones AG

v

Samskip GmbH

(Reference for a preliminary ruling from the Landgericht Bremen (Germany))

(Judicial cooperation in civil matters—Recognition and enforcement of judgments—Regulation (EC) No 44/2001—Concept of "judgment"—Judgment of a court of a Member State declining jurisdiction—Judgment based on a finding as to the validity and scope of a term conferring jurisdiction on the Icelandic courts—Effect—Scope)

1. Does a judgment of a court of a Member State declaring, in the operative part, that it 'has no authority to hear and decide the case' after accepting, in the grounds of the judgment, the validity of a term conferring jurisdiction on the courts of a third State oblige the court of another Member State before which the same claim is brought also to decline jurisdiction?

2. That is in essence the question put by the Landgericht Bremen (Regional Court, Bremen, Germany) in connection with an action brought by Krones AG and its insurers against Samskip GmbH for compensation for damage allegedly caused during the transport of goods.

3. By that question the Court is asked to interpret Articles 32 and 33 of Council Regulation (EC) No 44/2001 of 22 December 2000 on jurisdiction and the recognition and enforcement of judgments in civil and commercial matters, (2) which deal respectively with the definition of the term 'judgment' within the meaning of Regulation No 44/2001 and the principle of automatic recognition of any 'judgment' given in a Member State.

...

99. In the light of the foregoing, I propose the following answer to the questions referred for a preliminary ruling by the Landgericht Bremen:

Articles 32 and 33 of Council Regulation (EC) No 44/2001 of 22 December 2000 on jurisdiction and the recognition and enforcement of judgments in civil and commercial matters must be interpreted as meaning that:

> a judgment by which a court of a Member State rules on its international jurisdiction, whether it accepts or declines jurisdiction, falls within the concept of 'judgment' within the meaning of Regulation No 44/2001, regardless of the fact that the judgment is classified as a 'procedural judgment' by the law of the Member State addressed; and

> where the court of the Member State of origin has declined jurisdiction after first ruling, in the grounds of its decision, on the validity and scope of an agreement on jurisdiction, the court of the Member State addressed is bound by that finding, regardless of whether it is regarded as *res judicata* by the law of the Member State of origin or the Member State addressed, except in the cases in which Article 35(3) of Regulation No 44/2001 authorises that court to review the jurisdiction of the court of the Member State of origin.

Extract 7.1 *Opinion of Advocate General Bot Case C-456/11*

7.3 JUDICIAL PRECEDENT

Having worked out how to navigate a law report, we must move on to consider how legal rules arise from these cases and how they might then be applied in later cases. The term 'judicial precedent' refers to the process by which judges follow the decisions of previously decided cases.

Before considering the doctrine of judicial precedent in more detail, it is important to recap on the way in which the courts are arranged in a hierarchy and to demonstrate the importance of the status of the courts in relation to the operation of judicial precedent.

7.3.1 Precedent and the hierarchy of the courts

The courts of the English legal system are arranged in a hierarchy which can be depicted as shown in Figure 7.6.

Since the courts at the top of the hierarchy are more 'important' than lower courts, their decisions carry a greater legal 'value' than the decisions of lower courts. It is the doctrine of judicial precedent, or *stare decisis*, that explains the way in which these decisions relate to each other.

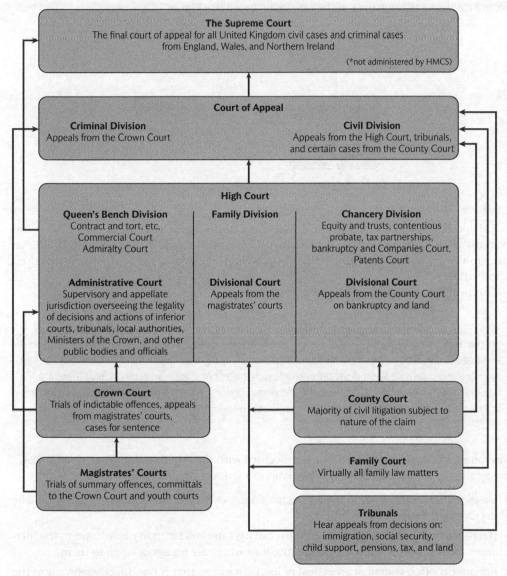

Figure 7.6 The hierarchy of the courts
Contains public sector information licensed under the Open Government Licence v3.0

Stare decisis is a Latin phrase which means 'let the decision stand'.

The doctrine of precedent is based on the principle that *like cases should be treated alike*. This means that once a decision has been reached in a particular case, it stands as good law and should be relied upon in other cases as an accurate statement of law. This is the essence of the doctrine of precedent.

For example, a case which is decided in the Court of Appeal could be relevant in three different directions: vertically up or down the hierarchy (Supreme Court and High Court respectively) and horizontally (other Court of Appeal cases). It is the doctrine of precedent that tells us in which of the courts such a Court of Appeal decision would be relevant and how it would influence the outcome of the case being heard (see Figure 7.7).

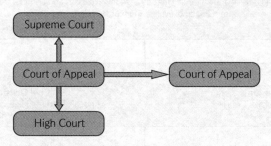

Figure 7.7 Possible directions in which a Court of Appeal case could be relevant

This preserves legal certainty and consistency in the application of the law. This is important to our ideas of justice and fairness. We would think it questionable if judicial decisions were contradictory or if there was no logical explanation to the pattern of their application.

This principle is encapsulated by Frankena:

> The paradigm case of injustice is that in which there are two similar individuals in similar circumstances and one of them is treated better or worse than the other. In this case, the cry of injustice rightly goes up against the responsible agent or group; and unless that agent or group can establish that there is some relevant dissimilarity after all between the individuals concerned and their circumstances, he or they will be guilty as charged (WK Frankena, *Ethics* (Prentice-Hall 1973) 49).

Therefore, the doctrine of precedent is concerned with the way that decisions in earlier cases are applied in subsequent cases. It is based upon a series of presumptions:

- Cases with the same or similar material facts (i.e. facts which are legally relevant) should be decided in the same way.
- Decisions made in the higher-level courts carry greater weight than those lower in the hierarchy, thus a court is normally bound by courts which are higher or equal to them.
- Judgments often contain a great deal of legal discussion that is not directly relevant to the issue at the heart of the case so a distinction should be made between the importance of those things that address the principle of law on which the decision is based (known as the *ratio decidendi*, 'the reason for the decision') and those which are peripheral to the outcome of the case (known as *obiter dicta*, 'things said in passing') and the weight given to these concepts in subsequent cases.

Ratio decidendi is a Latin phrase which means 'the reason for the decision' (plural *rationes decidendi*, although often simply stated as *ratios*). This is the (potentially) binding part of a judicial decision.

Obiter dictum is a Latin phrase meaning 'thing said in passing' (plural *obiter dicta*).

The first step in determining whether a precedent is binding or persuasive is to isolate the legally relevant facts and use them to distinguish between the *ratio* of the judgment and the *obiter dicta* as outlined earlier. Just because a statement is the *ratio* of an earlier case does not mean it is automatically binding in subsequent cases just as the fact that a statement is *obiter* does not mean that it has no precedent value—it all depends on the relationship between the court in which the original decision was made and the case in which the precedent is to be applied.

The general rule is that each court is bound by the decisions of those that are higher and of equivalent level in the hierarchy of the courts. For example, the Court of Appeal is normally bound by decisions of the Supreme Court (higher) and other Court of Appeal decisions (equivalent) (see Figures 7.8 and 7.9).

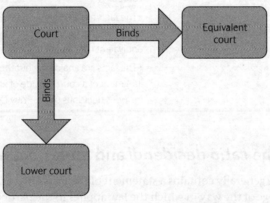

Figure 7.8 Courts binding equivalent and lower courts

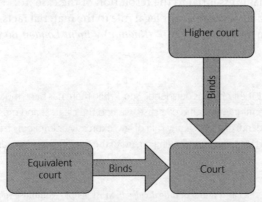

Figure 7.9 Courts being bound by equivalent and higher courts

7.3.2 Binding and persuasive precedents

A binding precedent is a decided case that *must* be applied in a later case—even if it is considered to have been wrongly decided. It exists when the material facts of a case are similar to those of an earlier decision in a higher or equivalent court in which the applicable statement of law was part of the *ratio* of the earlier decision.

A persuasive precedent is one which *may* be followed by a court (provided no binding precedent exists) but there is no compulsion on the courts to do so. See Table 7.4.

Table 7.4 Binding and persuasive precedents

Binding precedents	Persuasive precedent
• The facts in the decided case and the case before the courts must be sufficiently analogous to justify the imposition of the same legal principle/rule *and*	• The facts in the decided case and the case under consideration may have similar, but not directly analogous, facts *or*
• The decided case must have been heard in a court which is more senior in the hierarchy or at the same level as the court making the instant decision *and*	• The facts are analogous but the relevant legal rule is part of the *ratio* of a court that is lower in the hierarchy than the court making the decision *or*
• The part of the previous decision must be the *ratio decidendi* of the case rather than *obiter dicta*	• The facts are analogous but the legal rule was part of the *obiter dicta* of a case heard in a higher or equivalent court *or*
	• The facts are analogous but the legal rule is part of the dissenting judgment of a case heard in a higher or equivalent court *or*
	• The facts are analogous but the legal rule is part of a judgment of a court outside of England and Wales. This includes decisions of the Privy Council

7.3.3 Finding the *ratio decidendi* and *obiter dicta*

The judgment in a case generally contains a statement of the facts and the relevant law and an explanation by the judge of the way in which the law applies to the particular situation before him and his conclusion as to the outcome of the case. The *ratio* of the case is the legal rule and associated reasoning that is essential to the resolution of the case. It is the conclusion that is reached by the application of the relevant legal rule to the material facts.

This was summed up by Buxton LJ in *R (Kadhim) v Brent London Borough Council Housing Benefit Review Board*:[12]

> Cases as such do not bind: their rationes decidendi[13] do. While there has been much academic discussion of the proper way of determining the ratio of a case, we find the clearest and most persuasive guidance … to be … the ratio decidendi of a case is any rule of law, expressly or impliedly treated by the judge as a necessary step in reaching his conclusion, having regard to the line of reasoning adopted by him.

12. [2001] QB 955 (CA).
13. This is, strictly speaking, the Latin plural of *ratio decidendi*. Most people would use the English way of forming a plural and simply say *ratios*.

Therefore, in order to identify the *ratio* of a case, you must first isolate the material, or legally relevant, facts. Most judgments contain a wide general statement of the facts to establish the context in which the events occurred that gave rise to the case before the court. Many of these facts are not legally relevant—the outcome in the case would be the same even if these facts were different as they were not material to the legal question at the heart of the case.

In addition to isolating the material facts and determining what aspects of the reasoning are relevant to making a decision on the outcome of the case in order to identify the *ratio* of a judgment, the following are useful ways to identify *obiter*:

- The discussion, explanation, or reasoning of the judge is wider than that which is necessary to reach a decision on the facts of the case.

- The judge hypothesizes about the decision that he would have reached if the facts had been different.

- The judge explains what his decision would have been in this case if he had not been compelled to reach a different decision due to binding precedent.

- It is something said by a dissenting judge.

Identifying the *ratio* is often difficult as it can be difficult to separate it from the *obiter*. Judges do not specifically state the *ratio* of the case in their judgment and there is no straightforward set of rules to apply to a judgment to discern the *ratio* of that judgment.

This can be illustrated by way of example.

In *Donoghue v Stevenson*,[14] the claimant's friend purchased a bottle of ginger beer which was served in an opaque bottle. After drinking some of the ginger beer, the claimant discovered that the bottle contained the decomposing remains of a snail. The claimant was distressed as a result and suffered a period of gastric illness. There was no basis for a contractual claim as the claimant did not purchase the ginger beer and the friend could not claim as it was the claimant that suffered harm. The House of Lords held that the claimant could recover damages from the manufacturer due to its negligence, Lord Atkin stating that:

> … a manufacturer of products, which he sells in such a form as to show that he intends them to reach the ultimate consumer in the form in which they left him with no reasonable possibility of intermediate examination and with the knowledge that the absence of reasonable care in the preparation or putting up of the products will result in an injury to the consumer's life or property, owes a duty to the consumer to take that reasonable care.[15]

This case became the cornerstone of the duty of care in negligence and therefore guides the availability and operation of this tort. Each of the following could have been the *ratio* of this case:

- The manufacturer owes a duty to take reasonable care that the consumer is not injured as a result of a snail in a bottle of ginger beer.

- The manufacturer owes a duty to take reasonable care that the consumer is not injured by a foreign body in a container.

---

14. [1932] AC 562 (HL).
15. ibid 599 (Lord Atkin).

- The manufacturer owes a duty to take reasonable care that the consumer is not injured by defective products.
- A person owes a duty to take reasonable care that he does not commit any act which he could reasonably foresee as injuring another person.

The first option is too specific to the facts and would create an unrealistically narrow *ratio* that would be unlikely ever to be raised in later cases. The fact that it is a snail and a bottle of ginger beer is not material—the decision would have been no different if it had been a decomposed stag beetle in a chicken pie, for example. The second option is wider but it could still be questioned whether a *ratio* that limits the value of a case to foreign bodies in containers is desirable; would it really be sufficiently distinct if the snail had been in a sandwich? The third option seems reasonable; it is sufficiently general to create a legal principle that can be used in a range of situations thus not creating an undue restriction on its use in future cases. The fourth option may seem too wide; it moves beyond the particular relationship (manufacturers and consumers) and the particular negligent behaviour (failing to check the quality of products). However, it was this wide *ratio* that was followed in later cases and which is the basis for the law of negligence as it exists today. This *ratio* is so wide that it has been suggested that it was actually the third option that was the *ratio* and that the wider principle was merely *obiter* but obtained the status of binding precedent by its use in later cases. The *ratio* from *Donoghue v Stevenson* has been applied to products including lifts, chemicals, and motor cars, and manufacturers' liability extended to repairers and assemblers. Therefore it is perhaps more accurate to say that the *ratio decidendi* of a case is ultimately determined by its application by a court in a later case. The courts only need to interpret and determine the *ratio* of an earlier case when considering whether it applies to a new set of facts before them.

In a case with multiple judgments, the same overall decision may be reached for a variety of different reasons—so in a later case, the court will have to determine which of the possible *ratios*[16] it wishes to follow (or not).

You can find an example of this in section 12.5.

Isolating the material facts is not always straightforward. One test in deciding whether or not you think a particular fact is material to the outcome of the case is to ask yourself 'so what?' in relation to each one. If you think that changing a certain fact would have altered the legal reasoning such that the ultimate judgment was different, then it is likely that the particular fact was material to the case. If changing a fact would most likely have made no difference at all, then you should question whether it was a material fact.

7.3.4 The operation of judicial precedent in the courts

7.3.4.1 Court of Justice of the European Union

The CJEU is not bound by its own previous decisions, as it does not formally have the concept of *stare decisis*. This allows it to take future changes in European policy into account. However, it is strongly persuaded by its own previous decisions and rarely departs from them in practice in the interests of legal certainty. Prior to Brexit, UK courts were bound by the CJEU on matters of interpretation of EU Treaties themselves and on the interpretation and validity of EU regulations and directives.[17] However following s 6(1) of the European Union (Withdrawal) Act 2018, no UK court or tribunal will be bound by 'any principles laid down, or any decisions made, on or after exit day'[18] by the European Court and also cannot refer any matter to the

---

16. See footnote 13 if you need to be reminded that we are not showing off our prowess in Latin grammar here.
17. European Communities Act 1972, s 3(1).
18. Now after the end of the implementation period (31 December 2020).

European Court after exit day. That said, according to s 6(2), any court may still 'have regard' to anything done by the European Court afterwards, even though it is not bound by it. The extent to which courts will be persuaded by any such matter, of course remains to be seen. Section 6(4) of the Act clearly and unequivocally states that 'the Supreme Court is not bound by any EU retained case law'.

7.3.4.2 The Supreme Court

Until 1966 the House of Lords was bound by its own previous decisions. This was established in the mid-nineteenth century and became known as the *London Tramways* rule after the House of Lords affirmed the position in the 1898 case of *London Tramways Co Ltd v London County Council*.[19] Since the House of Lords was the highest appeal court in the hierarchy of the courts, it was considered to be in the public interest for its decisions to be final. The rule was intended to provide absolute certainty in the law and to cut down on cases being brought to court.

The rigidity of this rule was increasingly criticized throughout the twentieth century,[20] and the *London Tramways* rule was eventually abolished by the 1966 *Practice Statement (Judicial Precedent)*[21] made on behalf of himself and of the House of Lords by Lord Gardiner LC who stated:

> Their Lordships regard the use of precedent as an indispensable foundation upon which to decide what is the law and its application to individual cases. It provides at least some degree of certainty on which individuals can rely in the conduct of their affairs, as well as a basis for orderly development of legal rules.
>
> Their Lordships nevertheless recognise that too rigid adherence to precedent may lead to injustice in a particular case and unduly restrict the proper development of the law. They propose, therefore, to modify their present practice and *while treating former decisions of this House as normally binding, to depart from a previous decision where it appears right to do so.* [emphasis added].
>
> In this connection they will bear in mind the danger of disturbing retrospectively the basis upon which contracts, settlements of property and fiscal arrangements have been entered into and also the especial need for certainty in the criminal law.
>
> This announcement is not intended to affect the use of precedent elsewhere than in this House.

The impact of the *Practice Statement* gave the House of Lords sufficient flexibility to deal with novel situations and to ensure justice in each particular case. This flexibility meant that the law could develop in line with the changes in society and that judicial decisions would be in line with the morals and expectations of the community. While the *Practice Statement* was generally well received at the time, some considered that such a significant change in the judicial process should have been brought about via legislation rather than a 'mere' practice statement in which the House of Lords used its inherent jurisdiction to change its own practices. If an appellant or respondent in an appeal to the House of Lords intended to ask the House to depart from a previous decision, it had to draw specific attention to this in the appeal paperwork.[22]

---

19. [1898] AC 375 (HL).
20. See, e.g., *Midlands Silicones Ltd v Scruttons Ltd* [1962] AC 446 (HL) 475 (Lord Reid).
21. [1966] 1 WLR 1234 (HL).
22. *Practice Direction (House of Lords: Preparation of Case)* [1971] 1 WLR 534 (HL).

In *Austin v Southwark London Borough Council*,[23] the Supreme Court, for the first time, explicitly said that it considered that the *Practice Statement* applied to it in exactly the same way as it did to the House of Lords:

> The Supreme Court has not thought it necessary to reissue the Practice Statement as a fresh statement of practice in the court's own name. This is because it has as much effect in this court as it did before the Appellate Committee in the House of Lords. It was part of the established jurisprudence relating to the conduct of appeals in the House of Lords which was transferred to this court by section 40 of the Constitutional Reform Act 2005. So the question which we must consider is not whether the court has power to depart from the previous decisions of the House of Lords which have been referred to, but whether in the circumstances of this case it would be right for it to do so.

When will the Supreme Court depart from its own previous decisions?

The *Practice Statement* 'does not mean that whenever … a previous decision was wrong, we should reverse it' (*Miliangos v George Frank (Textiles) Ltd*).[24] This point of view might seem to contradict the *Practice Statement*; in fact it shows that the House of Lords was extremely reluctant to use it, as it was acutely aware of the need for certainty and the dangers attached to departing from its previous decisions (as stated in the *Practice Statement*). Thus, it required more than just a previous decision to be wrong; it would only be used where a previous decision caused injustice, uncertainty, or hindered the development of the law. It was not enough that the earlier decision caused grave concern or was passed by a narrow majority. Even if the *Practice Statement* might have applied, the House of Lords still considered whether legislation might provide a better solution than departing from its previous decisions.

In *R v Secretary of State for the Home Department, ex p Khawaja*,[25] it was held that, before departing from its own decisions, the House of Lords should be sure that continued adherence to precedent involves the risk of injustice and would obstruct the proper development of the law and departure from the precedent is the safe and appropriate way of remedying the injustice and developing the law.

Further evidence in support of the reluctance of the House of Lords to exercise its powers to bring about change to well-established law could be seen in the approach taken in *C v Director of Public Prosecutions*.[26] Here the House of Lords refused to abolish the presumption of *doli incapax* (the presumption that children under the age of 14 were incapable of criminal wrongdoing) despite finding it to be anomalous and absurd, preferring to call upon Parliament to remedy the situation. Lord Lowry stated the guidelines for judicial law-making which can be summarized as follows:

(a) judges should exercise caution before imposing a remedy where the solution to the problem is doubtful;

(b) they should be cautious about making changes if Parliament had rejected opportunities of dealing with a known problem or had legislated whilst leaving the problem untouched;

(c) they are more suited to dealing with purely legal problems than disputed matters of social policy;

(d) fundamental legal doctrines should not be lightly set aside; and

(e) judges should not change the law unless they can achieve finality and certainty.

23. [2010] UKSC 28, [25]; [2011] 1 AC 355 (Lord Hope of Craighead).
24. [1976] AC 433 (HL) 496 (Lord Cross).
25. [1984] AC 74 (HL).
26. [1996] AC 1 (HL).

Therefore, despite the freedom conferred by the *Practice Statement* to set aside its own decisions and exercise greater freedom in the development of the law, it is clear that the House of Lords was reluctant to exercise these powers.

However, there are examples of cases in which the House of Lords *did* depart from its previous decisions. The first example of this was in *Conway v Rimmer*,[27] where the House of Lords unanimously overruled its previous decision (made in wartime) in *Duncan v Cammel, Laird & Co*.[28] In *R v Shivpuri*,[29] the House of Lords overruled its decision in *Anderton v Ryan*[30] which it had made only one year previously, effectively admitting its error in the earlier case. As Lord Bridge commented: 'the Practice Statement is an effective abandonment of our pretension to infallibility'.[31]

In *R v Howe*,[32] the House of Lords took public and social policy factors into account in overruling its previous decision in *Director of Public Prosecutions for Northern Ireland v Lynch*[33] which involved the availability of the defence of duress to a person facing criminal liability for murder. More recently, in *Lagden v O'Connor*,[34] the House of Lords overruled its long-standing decision concerning the position of defendants who had no means to pay compensation that had earlier been established in the *Liesbosch Dredger*.[35]

It appears that Brexit will have no effect on the operation of precedent in the Supreme Court: s 6(5) of the European Union (Withdrawal) Act 2018 says that 'in deciding whether to depart from any retained EU case law, the Supreme Court ... must apply the same test as it would apply in deciding whether to depart from its own case law'.

7.3.4.3 The Court of Appeal

Civil Division

In *Young v Bristol Aeroplane Co Ltd*,[36] the Court of Appeal considered whether it is bound by its own decisions. It was held that it is normally bound, subject to three exceptions:

1. **Where its own previous decisions conflict**

   This may arise if the court in the later case was unaware of the decision of the earlier case; for instance, if the earlier case was very recent or unreported, or the second case might have distinguished the first, or one of the cases had been decided *per incuriam* (see definition later in this section). In such situations, the Court of Appeal must decide which of its previous decisions to follow and which to reject. Whilst this has obvious implications for the future precedent value of the decision which is not followed, its status is not technically affected by the fact that it has not been followed; it could still be adopted in subsequent cases. For example, in *National Westminster Bank plc v Powney*,[37] the Court of Appeal had to choose between its own previous judgments in *WT Lamb & Sons v Rider*[38] and *Lougher v Donovan*[39] which were irreconcilable.

---

27. [1968] AC 910 (HL).
28. [1942] AC 624 (HL).
29. [1987] AC 1 (HL).
30. [1985] AC 560 (HL).
31. [1987] AC 1 (HL) 23 (Lord Bridge).
32. [1987] 2 WLR 568 (HL).
33. [1975] AC 653 (HL).
34. [2003] 3 WLR 1571 (HL).
35. [1933] AC 449 (HL).
36. [1944] KB 718 (CA).
37. [1991] Ch 339 (CA).
38. [1948] 2 KB 331 (CA).
39. [1948] 2 All ER 11 (CA).

2. **Where its previous decision had been implicitly overruled by the House of Lords**

    This occurs when a previous Court of Appeal decision is inconsistent with a later decision of the House of Lords (and, now, a later decision of the Supreme Court). Therefore the Court of Appeal must refuse to follow a decision of its own which cannot stand with a decision of the House of Lords or the Supreme Court. For example in *Family Housing Association v Jones*,[40] the Court of Appeal refused to follow its own recent decisions which were inconsistent with the House of Lords' decision in *AG Securities Ltd v Vaughan*[41] and *Street v Mountford*,[42] even though the decisions of the Court of Appeal had not been expressly overruled by the House of Lords at that time.

    This situation does not apply where a Court of Appeal decision has been disapproved by the Privy Council. The Court of Appeal held this itself in *In Re Spectrum Plus*.[43] The House of Lords later agreed with this approach, although Baroness Hale considered that the question was open and that there was a possibility that an exception might be developed such that the Court of Appeal should refuse to follow a decision disapproved by the Privy Council.[44]

    An inconsistency can also arise where an appeal case has bypassed the Court of Appeal and gone straight to the Supreme Court via the so-called 'leapfrog' procedure.[45] Appeals direct from the High Court to the Supreme Court are very rare. An example can however be found in *Kleinwort Benson Ltd v Lincoln City Council*.[46]

3. **Where its previous decision was made *per incuriam***

    A decision made *per incuriam* is one made 'through carelessness' or without due regard to the relevant law. It should not be confused with the term *per curiam* which is a part of a judgment upon which all the judges are agreed.

Per incuriam is a Latin phrase meaning 'through carelessness'.

Examples of cases in which *per incuriam* decisions have been considered include *Morelle v Wakeling*[47] which provided a definition of *per incuriam* as 'decisions given in ignorance or forgetfulness of some inconsistent statutory provision or of some authority binding on the court concerned …'. In other words, where the decision was reached without due regard for the correct law. In *Duke v Reliance Systems Ltd*,[48] it was held that 'if the court has failed to consider the relevant law, the decision will be *per incuriam* if the court *must* inevitably have reached a different decision had it considered the correct law; it will not suffice that the court might have reached a different decision had it considered the correct law'. In *Williams*

---

40. [1990] 1 WLR 779 (CA).
41. [1990] AC 417 (HL).
42. [1985] AC 809 (HL).
43. [2004] 3 WLR 503 (CA).
44. [2005] 3 WLR 58 (HL).
45. Administration of Justice Act 1969 ss 12–15.
46. [1999] AC 358 (HL).
47. [1955] 2 QB 379 (CA).
48. [1988] QB 108 (CA).

v Fawcett,[49] the Court of Appeal declared several of its previous decisions *per incuriam* which had held that a person could not be committed to prison for breach of a non-molestation order unless the notice had been signed by the 'proper officer' of the court. Since this was not a requirement of the statute or of the procedural rules the decisions lacked a rational legal basis.

In *Cave v Robinson Jarvis & Rolf*,[50] the Court of Appeal stated that any departure from a previous decision is 'highly undesirable' and that the decision in question had to be 'manifestly' or 'incontestably' wrong before it could be declared *per incuriam*.

Criminal Division

All the exceptions from *Young v Bristol Aeroplane* that apply in the Civil Division also apply to the Criminal Division.[51] However, in practice, the Court of Appeal gives itself a wider discretion in criminal cases where the liberty of the individual is at stake. In *R v Gould*,[52] Lord Diplock stated:

> if upon due consideration we were to be of the opinion that the law had been either misapplied or misunderstood in an earlier decision … we should be entitled to depart from the view as to the law expressed in the earlier decision notwithstanding that the case could not be brought within any of the exceptions laid down in *Young v Bristol Aeroplane Co. Ltd.*

There has been no ruling on whether the Civil and Criminal Divisions are bound by each other. However, their predecessors (the Court of Appeal and the Court of Criminal Appeal) were not. It is also accepted that, when dealing with criminal appeals, a 'full' Court of Appeal (five judges) can depart from decisions made by three judges.[53] The rule in *Young v Bristol Aeroplane* gives the Court of Appeal some capacity to depart from its own decisions but only in narrowly defined circumstances. The Supreme Court has broad discretion to depart from its own decisions where it appears right to do so, but, in practice, this discretion is exercised sparingly.

7.3.4.4 The Divisional Courts and the High Court

The Divisional Courts (i.e. the Divisional Court of the appropriate Division of the High Court for the particular matter) are bound by their own decisions subject to the same exceptions as the Civil Division of the Court of Appeal, and, arguably, the Criminal Division (following the decision in *R v Greater Manchester Coroner, ex p Tal*).[54] Decisions of the Divisional Courts are binding on the High Court for that particular Division.

High Court decisions are not binding on the Divisional Courts (since the Divisional Courts operate at a higher level than the High Court by virtue of the nature of their jurisdiction, which is mostly appellate).

Decisions of individual High Court judges are binding on lower courts but not on other High Court judges. However, they are of strongly persuasive authority in the High Court and are

---

49. [1986] QB 604 (CA).
50. [2001] EWCA Civ 245.
51. *R v Spencer* [1985] 1 All ER 673 (CA).
52. [1968] 2 QB 65 (CA) 69 (Lord Diplock).
53. See, e.g., *R v Simpson* [2003] 3 WLR 337 (CA).
54. [1985] QB 67 (DC).

usually followed in practice. If they are not followed, then they are 'disapproved' rather than being formally overruled.

The structure of the High Court is complicated. You may wish to review the explanation of its organization which is provided in section 5.3.

7.3.4.5 The Crown Court, County Court, Family Court, and magistrates' courts

The Crown Court is not bound by its previous decisions but, in order to promote certainty in the criminal law, is strongly persuaded by them. Inconsistent Crown Court decisions are generally resolved by a higher appellate court as quickly as possible.

The County Court, Family Court, and the magistrates' courts are not bound by their own decisions and bind no other courts. The decisions made on points of law at this level are rarely of legal importance and are hardly ever formally reported in the law reports. However, their decisions can, of course, be considered on appeal in the higher courts in which case they will be reported, albeit indirectly.

In summary, the question 'who is bound by whom?' can be shown in a diagram as shown in Figure 7.10.

7.4 PRECEDENT AND THE HUMAN RIGHTS ACT 1998

Section 6(1) of the Human Rights Act 1998 provides that:

> **6.–(1)**   It is unlawful for a public authority to act in a way which is incompatible with a Convention right.

Section 6(3) of the Act makes it clear that 'public authority' includes a court or a tribunal. Therefore it is unlawful for courts to deliver a judgment which is incompatible with Convention rights.

Moreover, s 2(1) of the Human Rights Act 1998 provides that:

> **2.–(1)**   A court or tribunal determining a question which has arisen in connection with a Convention right must take into account any
>
> **(a)** judgment, decision, declaration or advisory opinion of the European Court of Human Rights,
> **(b)** opinion of the Commission given in a report adopted under Article 31 of the Convention,
> **(c)** decision of the Commission in connection with Article 26 or 27(2) of the Convention, or
> **(d)** decision of the Committee of Ministers taken under Article 46 of the Convention,
>
> whenever made or given, so far as, in the opinion of the court or tribunal, it is relevant to the proceedings in which that question has arisen.

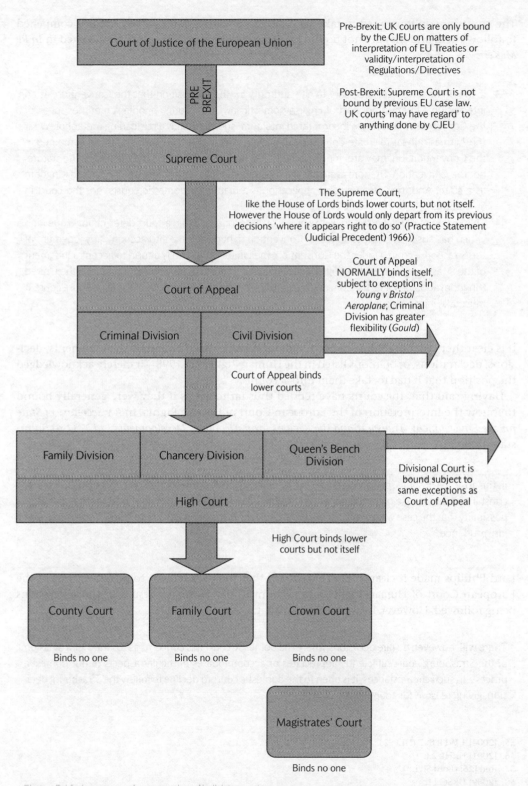

Pre-Brexit: UK courts are only bound by the CJEU on matters of interpretation of EU Treaties or validity/interpretation of Regulations/Directives

Post-Brexit: Supreme Court is not bound by previous EU case law. UK courts 'may have regard' to anything done by CJEU

The Supreme Court, like the House of Lords binds lower courts, but not itself. However the House of Lords would only depart from its previous decisions 'where it appears right to do so' (Practice Statement (Judicial Precedent) 1966))

Court of Appeal NORMALLY binds itself, subject to exceptions in *Young v Bristol Aeroplane*; Criminal Division has greater flexibility (*Gould*)

Court of Appeal binds lower courts

Divisional Court is bound subject to same exceptions as Court of Appeal

High Court binds lower courts but not itself

Figure 7.10 A summary of the operation of judicial precedent

The courts are only required to take such decisions 'into account'. They are not compelled to follow them and they are not bound by those decisions. As Lord Hoffmann stated in *In Re McKerr*:[55]

> 63   It should no longer be necessary to cite authority for the proposition that the Convention, as an international treaty, is not part of English domestic law … Although people sometimes speak of the Convention having been incorporated into domestic law, that is a misleading metaphor. What the Act has done is to create domestic rights expressed in the same terms as those contained in the Convention. But they are domestic rights, not international rights. Their source is the statute, not the Convention. They are available against specific public authorities, not the United Kingdom as a state. And their meaning and application is a matter for domestic courts, not the court in Strasbourg.
>
> 64   This last point is demonstrated by the provision in section 2(1) that a court determining a question which has arisen in connection with a Convention right must 'take into account' any judgment of the Strasbourg court. Under the Convention, the United Kingdom is bound to accept a judgment of the Strasbourg court as binding: article 46(1). But a court adjudicating in litigation in the United Kingdom about a domestic 'Convention right' is not bound by a decision of the Strasbourg court. It must take it into account.

It is clear then, that the House of Lords did not consider itself bound by the judgments, decisions, declarations, or opinions listed in the Human Rights Act 1998—it merely acknowledged the position that it had to 'take them into account'.

 Having said that, the courts have tended thus far to act as if they were generally bound to follow the interpretation of the European Court of Human Rights. In *R v Secretary of State for the Environment, Transport and the Regions, ex p Alconbury Developments Ltd*,[56] Lord Slynn stated that:

> In the absence of some special circumstances it seems to me that the court should follow any clear and constant jurisprudence of the European Court of Human Rights. If it does not do so there is at least a possibility that the case will go to that court which is likely in the ordinary case to follow its own constant jurisprudence.[57]

Lord Phillips made it clear in *R v Horncastle*[58] that the requirement to take decisions of the European Court of Human Rights into account would 'normally result' in those decisions being followed. However, he went on to say that:

> There will, however, be rare occasions where the domestic court has concerns as to whether a decision of the Strasbourg court sufficiently appreciates or accommodates particular aspects of our domestic process. In such circumstances, it is open to the domestic court to decline to follow the Strasbourg decision, giving reasons for adopting this course.[59]

---

55. [2004] 1 WLR 807 (HL) 825.
56. [2001] UKHL 23.
57. ibid [26] (Lord Slynn).
58. [2009] UKSC 14.
59. ibid [11] (Lord Phillips).

If a court decides that a previous decision by which it would otherwise be bound is incompatible with Convention rights (as determined by, for instance, a decision of the European Court of Human Rights) it is required by virtue of s 6(1) to give effect to any Convention-compatible decision from the European Court of Human Rights rather than the otherwise binding decision of the higher UK court. An example of this can be seen in *In Re Medicaments and Related Classes of Goods (No 2)*[60] where the Court of Appeal made a 'modest adjustment' to the House of Lords' decision in *R v Gough*[61] to make it compatible with the view of the European Court of Human Rights: although this 'modest adjustment' involved substituting an objective test to determine whether or not a tribunal was biased for the earlier subjective test. This fundamentally changed the decision of the House of Lords in *Gough*.[62]

7.5 PRECEDENT AND EU LAW

Prior to Brexit, s 3(1) of the European Communities Act 1972 (as amended by s 2 of the European Communities (Amendment) Act 1986) provided that:

> **3.–(1)** For the purposes of all legal proceedings any question as to the meaning or effect of any of the Treaties, or as to the validity, meaning or effect of any Community instrument, shall be treated as a question of law and, if not referred to the European Court, be for determination as such in accordance with the principles laid down by and any relevant decision of the European Court or any court attached thereto.
>
> **(2)** Judicial notice shall be taken of the Treaties, of the Official Journal of the European Communities and of any decision of, or expression or opinion by, the European Court or any court attached thereto, on any such question as aforesaid.

Under Article 267 TFEU, courts within Member States of the EU may if necessary (or in the case of the Supreme Court of any particular Member State, must) refer any question regarding the interpretation of EU legislation to the CJEU for a ruling:

> The Court of Justice shall have jurisdiction to give preliminary rulings concerning:
>
> **(a)** the interpretation of this Treaty;
> **(b)** the validity and interpretation of acts of the institutions of the Community and of the ECB;
> **(c)** the interpretation of the statutes of bodies established by an act of the Council, where those statutes so provide.
>
> Where such a question is raised before any court or tribunal of a Member State, that court or tribunal may, if it considers that a decision on the question is necessary to enable it to give judgment, request the Court of Justice to give a ruling thereon.
> Where any such question is raised in a case pending before a court or tribunal of a Member State against whose decisions there is no judicial remedy under national law, that court or tribunal shall bring the matter before the Court of Justice.

---

60. [2001] 1 WLR 700 (CA).
61. [1993] AC 646 (HL).
62. See also, e.g., *Price v Leeds City Council* [2005] EWCA Civ 289; [2005] 1 WLR 1825.

In *CILFIT Srl v Ministero della Sanita*,[63] the Court of Justice held that a reference is not necessary if:

(a) the question of Community law is irrelevant; or
(b) the provision has already been interpreted by the Court of Justice; or
(c) the correct application is obvious.

These are commonly referred to as the 'CILFIT criteria'.

The ruling of the CJEU given in response to a reference under Article 267 TFEU is then binding in that particular case. This means that domestic courts of EU Member States must follow decisions on European law made by the European Court of Justice in particular cases.[64] However, such decisions do not bind the UK courts in future cases. Since the CJEU is not bound by its previous decisions, the Supreme Court could refer the same point of law to the CJEU again in a later case if it considers that the earlier decision of the CJEU (by which the Supreme Court would have been bound in the particular case) was wrong, or merely if the Supreme Court considered it to be unsatisfactory.

This position changed after Brexit: s 6(1) of the European Union (Withdrawal) Act 2018 states that no UK court is bound by any CJEU decisions made on or after exit day[65] and removes the ability of UK courts to make reference to the CJEU at the same time.

7.6 AVOIDING DIFFICULT PRECEDENTS: DISTINGUISHING, REVERSING, AND OVERRULING

The 1966 *Practice Statement* and the rule in *Young v Bristol Aeroplane* give the Supreme Court (and its predecessor) and the Court of Appeal respectively the ability to avoid previous decisions of courts at the same level. In the case of the Court of Appeal, the circumstances in which the previous decisions of the Court of Appeal can be avoided are narrowly defined whereas the Supreme Court exercised its power with caution because of the wider implications of departing from its own decisions in terms of the legal principles that resulted.

Other than by the operation of these particular rules, there are several methods that a court (at any level) can use to avoid an otherwise binding precedent. The approach taken depends upon whether the court which is confronted with the precedent wishes merely to avoid the precedent but to allow it to continue to exist as legal authority or whether the court wishes to deprive the precedent of any future legal effect.

7.6.1 Distinguishing

As you have already seen, it is the *ratio decidendi* of a case that forms the binding part of the judgment and that *ratio decidendi* only applies to cases where the material facts are the same. In distinguishing a case, the court can decide that the case before it is materially different on the facts. By distinguishing in this way, the court is saying it will not be applying the *ratio* of the earlier case because it is not sufficiently similar to the case before it and that different reasoning must be used to reach its decision.

---

63. [1983] ECR 3415 (CJEU).
64. See, e.g., *Sharp v Caledonia Group Services Ltd* [2005] All ER (D) 09 (Nov) (EAT).
65. Now after the end of the implementation period (31 December 2020).

The courts will normally explain why an earlier case is being distinguished: of course, this new reasoning could be re-examined by a higher court in the event of an appeal. The appellate court could decide not to distinguish the case, reverse the decision of the court, and reapply the *ratio* of the case that the court sought to distinguish.

It has also been argued that distinguishing could be taken further to include not just material factual differences but also social changes that have taken place since the original precedent was decided. In this way, the courts would be free to develop the law in such a way that they could avoid being bound by precedents reflecting historic or outdated societal norms.

It could be said that the *ratio* of a case remains unclear until it is identified and applied by a later court. Accordingly, the operation of the doctrine of precedent is contingent not on the judgment at the time it is given but the way in which a case is used by later courts; a case does not necessarily have precedent value until it acquires precedent value by usage. Therefore, the decision as to whether a case has a wide or narrow *ratio* is one for the later courts. The court may also decide that an earlier case has no clear *ratio* at all and therefore cannot be binding. An example of such a case can be found in *Esso v Commissioners of Customs and Excise*[66] which has judicial conclusions on differing points of law, many *obiter* statements, and a dissenting judgment.

You will find a further detailed example of a case with multiple judgments in section 12.5.

7.6.2 Overruling and reversing

Overruling occurs when a court higher in the hierarchy overturns the decision of a lower court in a different case. This not only means that the higher court is not bound to follow the earlier decision but that it is negated of any legal force; indeed, it is regarded as never having been the law.

This is to be distinguished from reversing a decision whereby a court higher in the hierarchy overturns the decision (or part of the decision) of a lower court in the *same* case. For example, the House of Lords in *R v Woollin*[67] refused to follow the approach taken by the Court of Appeal in relation to oblique intention in the same case, upholding the defendant's appeal against his conviction for murder and reversing the decision of the Court of Appeal.

In both of these situations, the earlier decision (or part of it) is negated by the later decision of the higher court which forms the precedent for future cases.

 CHAPTER SUMMARY

Reading cases

- The party against whom a criminal case is brought is called the defendant
- The party bringing a civil claim is called the claimant
- The party against whom a civil claim is brought is called the respondent
- The party bringing an appeal is called the appellant
- The party against whom an appeal is brought is called the respondent
- The headnote of a case report is not part of the judgment

---

66. [1976] 1 WLR 1 (HL).
67. [1999] AC 82 (HL).

- The headnote may summarize the effect of the judgment on the existing case law
- Online reports may also provide links to related cases, relevant legislation, and useful academic and professional commentary on the case

Judicial precedent

- *Stare decisis* is a Latin phrase meaning 'let the decision stand'
- *Ratio decidendi* is a Latin phrase which means the 'reason for the decision'. This is the (potentially) binding part of a judicial decision
- *Obiter dicta* is a Latin phrase meaning 'things said in passing'
- Binding precedents must be applied in a later case
- Persuasive precedents may be followed in later cases, but there is no compulsion on the courts to do so
- The CJEU is not bound by its previous decisions
- Prior to Brexit, UK courts were bound by the CJEU on matters of interpretation of EU Treaties and the interpretation and validity of regulations and directives; post-Brexit, UK courts are not bound by new decisions of the CJEU
- The House of Lords was permitted to depart from its previous decisions where it appeared right to do so (*Practice Statement 1966*) although it was often reluctant to do so; the Supreme Court behaves in the same way
- The Court of Appeal (Civil Division) is normally bound by its previous decisions unless they conflict; its previous decision has been implicitly overruled by the Supreme Court, or; its previous decision was made *per incuriam* (*Young v Bristol Aeroplane*)
- *Per incuriam* is a Latin phrase meaning 'through carelessness'
- The Court of Appeal (Criminal Division) is also subject to the *Young v Bristol Aeroplane* exceptions, but does have greater discretion where the liberty of the individual is at stake (*Gould*)
- The Divisional Courts are bound by their own decisions subject to the *Young v Bristol Aeroplane* exceptions
- The High Court is bound by decisions of the Divisional Court
- Decisions of individual High Court judges are binding on lower courts, but not on individual High Court judges
- The Crown Court is strongly persuaded by its previous decisions
- The County Court, Family Court, and magistrates' courts do not bind themselves and bind no other courts
- The Supreme Court must take decisions of the European Court of Human Rights into account but is not bound by them (Human Rights Act 1998 s 2)
- However, courts must act in a way compatible with Convention rights (Human Rights Act 1998 s 6)
- Prior to Brexit, domestic courts had to follow decisions of the CJEU in matters of EU law in particular cases; post-Brexit, the courts are not bound by new decisions of the CJEU
- Difficult precedents may be avoided by distinguishing, reversing, or overruling
- Cases may be distinguished from one another if the material facts of the two cases are different

- Reversing occurs when a court higher in the hierarchy overturns the decision of a lower court in the same case
- Overruling occurs when a court higher in the hierarchy overturns the decision of a lower court in a different case

FURTHER READING

- Some of the issues that arise from using case law as a means of law-making are discussed in R Buxton, 'How the Common Law Gets Made' (2009) 125 LQR 60.
- A very comprehensive treatment of the use of precedent in English law set against the wider context of judicial reasoning and legal theory is provided in R Cross, *Precedent in English Law* (Clarendon Press 1991).
- The role of the courts of final appeal in doing justice in the particular appeal and in the setting of an improved precedent is discussed in BV Harris, 'Final Appellate Courts Overruling Their Own "Wrong" Precedents: The Ongoing Search for Principle' (2002) 118 LQR 408.
- Two contrasting articles on the meaning of *ratio decidendi* which illustrate the difficulties in defining it are JL Montrose, 'The *Ratio Decidendi* of a Case' (1957) 20 MLR 587 and AWB Simpson, 'The *Ratio Decidendi* of a Case' (1957) 20 MLR 413.
- The use of precedent in criminal appeal cases is considered in R Pattenden, 'The Power of the Criminal Division of the Court of Appeal to Depart from Its Own Precedents' [1984] Crim LR 592.

Books, journals, and official publications

8

INTRODUCTION

The earlier chapters in this part of the book have explored the primary domestic and European sources of law. As you will have seen, these sources derive either from legislation (an Act of Parliament, statutory instrument, EU treaty article, regulation, or directive) or from cases decided before the courts (common law, equity, or decision of the CJEU). However, in addition to these sources, there is a wide range of secondary sources of law. This chapter will complete your appreciation of the spectrum of legal sources by describing the role of books, journals, and official publications among the secondary sources that you might encounter during your legal studies.

Without a good grasp of secondary sources of law you will miss out on an entire range of legal knowledge and comment. Speaking more pragmatically, you will have to engage with secondary sources if you want to achieve higher marks: secondary sources are a vital resource for a fully rounded legal knowledge and will give you the means to start critically analysing the law as well as just reading and describing it. Successful essays and dissertations will require you to demonstrate understanding, analysis, and synthesis skills as well as merely demonstrating simple knowledge of a particular area of law: an appreciation of the range of sources which will help you to develop and demonstrate these skills is therefore essential.

Learning outcomes

After studying this chapter, you will be able to:

- Distinguish between textbooks, monographs, and practitioners' books
- Understand the role of legal encyclopedias and digests
- Appreciate the distinction between standard dictionaries, legal dictionaries, and specialist dictionaries
- Choose and use revision guides appropriately
- Understand the use of journals as important sources of information
- Describe the origins and sources of various official publications
- Express an awareness of newspapers, other reports, websites, and 'soft law' as other potential sources of law

8.1 BOOKS

8.1.1 Student textbooks

Student textbooks collect together, analyse, and criticize the law in particular areas. They traditionally deal with an individual area of legal study. There is a wide range of textbooks within each of the core subject areas:

- Constitutional and administrative law (or public law)
- Contract law
- Criminal law
- EU law
- English legal systems
- Equity and trusts
- Land law (or property law)
- Tort law.

as well as most of the popular optional subject areas such as family law, medical law, employment law, intellectual property law, and company law.

There are usually several textbooks available for each topic. You should be given guidance as to the preferred textbook for your particular course. However, textbooks are written in different styles and have widely varying degrees of difficulty. If you find that you are not getting on with your set text, you should ask your course leader whether there is a different text that might suit you better. For instance, if you find the set text hard to follow, then you might need a more basic book to give you a lower-level grounding in the material before building upon that with the set text. Equally, if you are fortunate enough to think that your textbook is too simple, then a higher-level text will allow you to deepen your understanding and build upon your skills of analysis and critical evaluation.

Textbooks do not generally carry any great legal authority although some established texts are occasionally cited in court. These include *Smith & Hogan: Criminal Law*, *Winfield and Jolowicz on Tort*, *Megarry & Wade: The Law of Real Property*, and *Treitel: The Law of Contract*. It is for this reason that textbooks—except perhaps for a handful of key authoritative works—should not be quoted as sources in coursework. They are useful as an introduction to topic areas or as a means of clarifying particular points, but you must use primary sources if you want to gain enough depth and understanding of the law to ensure success in coursework or dissertations.

Student textbooks undergo frequent revision to ensure that they stay current and relevant. You should always make sure that you are using the most recent edition of your particular textbook. For that reason, buying second-hand textbooks in student shops or online should be done with care, as you would not want to be working from a book which did not cover or explain more recent developments—unless you wanted to use one to research the state of the law at a particular point in time for some sort of comparative exercise. Generally speaking, though, if you use an old textbook, you run the risk of inaccuracy in your research for essays and problem answers. Even so, the lapse of time between manuscript submission and publication can mean that even new books can be out of date: for example, at the time of writing this edition, the implementation date for Brexit has not yet passed, but will have done by the time of publication. Moreover, each new edition has a lifespan of a few years: therefore, you must always supplement your reading with online research to look out for any contemporary developments during the text's lifetime.

8.1.2 Cases and materials books

Cases and materials books contain a collection of key cases, statutes, reports, articles, and book extracts arranged by topic area within a subject. These are sometimes stand-alone publications, although an increasing number of textbooks have accompanying books of cases and materials.

These are an extremely useful way of gathering together all the supplementary materials you need to support your studies. As with textbooks, they should be used with caution since they contain only extracts from the materials and those materials that the editor has considered appropriate. They are not a substitute for finding and reading the original and complete statutes, cases, and articles. Therefore, while very valuable as a starting point for research, a reliance upon cases and materials books alone can lead to lazy or unthinking research and, at worst, a blinkered view of the subject area. You must, of course, refer to the primary source materials in your assessed work and not to the cases and materials book in which they have been consolidated.

8.1.3 Monographs

Monographs are a detailed written study of a single specialized topic. They are usually more expensive than student textbooks and cover particular narrow subject areas in much greater depth (often considerably greater than that required for a first degree in law). For example, while you might think that your set criminal law textbook goes into more than enough detail, there are a large number of books which take particular topics and analyse them in very fine detail, such as:

- B Krebs (ed), *Accessorial Liability after 'Jogee'* (Hart 2020)
- D Ormerod and DH Williams, *Smith's Law of Theft* (9th edn, OUP 2007)
- I Kugler, *Direct and Oblique Intention in the Criminal Law* (Routledge 2003)
- E O'Moore, *Non-Fatal Offences Against the Person: Law and Practice* (Clarus Press 2017)

When you consider that many of these books are similar in size to an introductory-level student textbook designed to cover the whole of the criminal law, you should begin to appreciate the distinction between textbooks and monographs. The level and academic rigour of these books makes them entirely appropriate resources to use in your assessed work.

8.1.4 Practitioners' books

As distinct from textbooks, which are usually written by law lecturers for student use, practitioners' books are usually written by practising lawyers for practising lawyers (although some practitioners write student texts and academics sometimes write for the practitioner market). These are primarily reference works and often span several volumes. As a result, new editions appear much less frequently than for student textbooks and updates may be issued in the form of cumulative supplements. Some practitioner works are entirely loose-leaf, such as:

- *Chitty on Contracts*
- *Clerk and Lindsell on Torts*
- *Palmer's Company Law*
- *Woodfall: Landlord and Tenant*
- *Emmet & Farrand on Title*
- *Kemp & Kemp Personal Injury Law, Practice and Procedure*

They are also generally very expensive—the titles listed above range in price from around £200 to over £850. However, some of these (including *Chitty* and *Clerk and Lindsell*) are available on-line within Westlaw Books. These can be a useful pointer to primary sources and commentary for use in your assessments.

8.1.5 Legal encyclopedias and digests

There are various legal encyclopedias and digests which are extremely useful research tools.

8.1.5.1 *Halsbury's Laws of England*

Halsbury's Laws of England aims to provide a complete statement of English law, derived from all sources. As you can imagine, this is a massive work. It comprises sixty volumes in several parts. Using *Halsbury* in the library is quite an involved process. Should you wish to do so, then you should consult the law librarian at your institution. However, *Halsbury* is much easier to use in its online form available via LexisLibrary as a source under the 'Commentary' tab.

8.1.5.2 *Halsbury's Statutes of England and Wales*

Halsbury's Statutes of England and Wales aims to provide current versions of all Public General Acts in force in England and Wales. As with *Halsbury's Laws of England* these are arranged by subject area.

Each Act is fully annotated to provide precise information relating to Parliamentary debates, amendments and repeals, derivation notes in the case of consolidating legislation, commencement, cross-references to other provisions of the Act and to other relevant provisions in *Halsbury's Statutes*, cases, subordinate legislation, and references to words specifically defined in the Act.

8.1.5.3 *Halsbury's Statutory Instruments*

Halsbury's Statutory Instruments provides current information on all statutory instruments of general application to the whole of the England and Wales which are in force. Once again, these are arranged by topic.

8.1.5.4 *The Digest*

The Digest provides, in digested form, the whole case law of England and Wales, together with a considerable body of cases from the courts of Scotland, Ireland, Canada, Australia, New Zealand, and other countries of the Commonwealth. Cases dealing with EU law are also included. The case digests are printed with annotations listing the subsequent cases in which judicial opinions have been expressed in the English courts. *The Digest* contains summaries of hundreds of thousands of cases drawn from over a thousand different series of law reports.

8.1.5.5 *Current Law*

Current Law is published in several parts:

- *Current Law Yearbook*
- *Current Law Statutes Annotated*
- *Current Law Case Citator* 1947–76, 1977–88, and 1989–2002

- *Current Law Statute Citator* 1947–71
- *Current Law Legislation Citator* 1972–88, 1989–2002

Its component parts provide access to both legislation and case law along with commentary.

8.1.6 Dictionaries

8.1.6.1 Conventional and legal dictionaries

The *Shorter Oxford English Dictionary* is the conventional dictionary which is most frequently cited in court, followed by the *Oxford English Dictionary*.[1]

The *Oxford English Dictionary* is also available online at www.oed.com. This is not a publicly available resource, but many universities will have online access either direct or through a library portal.

As well as conventional dictionaries, there is a range of legal dictionaries available. If your course does not recommend a particular dictionary, it is a good idea to browse a few in the bookshop or the library. Legal dictionaries are very useful as a quick means of checking whether a word has a specific legal meaning as well as an everyday meaning. They can also be used when you encounter an unfamiliar term—which is likely, particularly if it is in Latin or Law French. Examples of legal dictionaries include:

- J Law (eds), *A Dictionary of Law* (9th edn, OUP 2018)
- M Woodley (ed), *Osborn's Concise Law Dictionary* (12th edn, Sweet & Maxwell 2013)

Finally, there are also a range of specialist dictionaries which cover definitions that are restricted to certain topics including employment law, company law, and commercial law. These will possibly be too detailed for the purposes of your course of study; therefore, one of the general legal dictionaries will probably be the more appropriate resource.

8.1.6.2 Judicial dictionaries

Judicial dictionaries contain details of the ways in which judges have interpreted particular words or phrases as well as definitions contained in statute. They are very expensive, so are best used as a library resource or online, for example via Westlaw's Index of Legal Terms.

Stroud's Judicial Dictionary of Words and Phrases includes definitions from English, Scottish, and Commonwealth sources. Judicial interpretations of words and phrases used in statutes which have been repealed or amended have been retained. It comprises six volumes and is updated annually.

Words and Phrases Legally Defined is similar to *Stroud's Judicial Dictionary* and is also updated via annual cumulative supplements.

Finally, *Halsbury's Laws of England* may also be used to find definitions of words and phrases via the index to the main volumes.

8.1.7 Revision guides

Many students rely upon revision guides as a safety net. Revision guides do exactly what their name suggests—they are guides to revision. They are not a substitute for attendance at lectures and seminars. Moreover, they do not provide an excuse not to read and follow your own

---

1. P Clinch, 'Systems of Reporting Judicial Decision Making' (PhD thesis, University of Sheffield 1989) 481.

course materials, textbooks, and primary sources and should definitely not cut down on the amount of reading and thinking that you have to do.

If you compare the size of most revision guides to that of your recommended textbook, it follows that a revision guide could never be expected to cover the subject in the depth required to succeed in coursework or examinations. However, they can serve a useful purpose in providing a concise overview of the key areas for revision—reminding you of the headline points to enable you to focus your revision and identify the key points you need to know. Some students also like to use revision guides at the start of a module to gain a quick overview of the subject. Even though we have written a few, never use them as sources in your coursework.

8.2 JOURNALS

Journals are also referred to as periodicals.

Journals are an important resource which can be used to keep up to date with latest developments in the law. They are also a key source of academic criticism and commentary upon the law which should be used in addition to textbooks, particularly when researching for a piece of written work, a seminar, or a moot. Books are always out of date to a greater or lesser extent. Even with a new book there is usually a delay of some months between the submission of the final manuscript by the author(s) and the book finally appearing on the shelves. New editions rarely come out more frequently than once every two years.

Journals contain a mixture of articles, news, notes, reviews, and digests. They are usually published as individual issues, which combine to make up volumes.

8.2.1 General journals

General journals tend to contain lengthy articles based on extensive academic research. Most include notes of recent cases, news of legal developments, and book reviews. The general journals most frequently encountered are the *Law Quarterly Review*, *Legal Studies*, the *Cambridge Law Journal*, the *Oxford Journal of Legal Studies*, and the *Modern Law Review*. They are published relatively infrequently; typically with four or six issues per year.

8.2.2 Specialist journals

Specialist journals are similar to the general journals in that they primarily provide academic commentary and news on the law. However, they focus on particular aspects of the law. Examples of these include the *Criminal Law Review*, *Family Law*, *Civil Justice Quarterly*, and the *Journal of Business Law*.

There are also shorter specialist bulletins and newsletters which are focused on the needs of practitioners, such as *Simon's Tax Intelligence*, *Property Law Bulletin*, and *Business Law Brief*. These are of less immediate importance to your core studies, although you should at least be aware of their existence.

8.2.3 Practitioner journals

Practitioner journals are usually published weekly or bi-weekly. These tend to contain shorter articles on a wide range of topics of interest to lawyers in practice as well as case notes, digests, and practice notes. The articles are not usually covered in as great a depth as the general or specialist journals and are often written by other practitioners rather than by academic lawyers. They still provide useful information and should not be overlooked, although they do carry less academic weight than the general and specialist academic journals. The journals in this category that you are most likely to encounter include the *New Law Journal*, *Solicitors' Journal*, the *Law Society Gazette*, *Counsel*, and *Justice of the Peace*.

8.2.4 Foreign journals

English-language journals, in particular those from other common law jurisdictions such as the United States, Canada, Australia, and New Zealand, can be useful when undertaking comparisons with the UK. Most libraries will carry a selection of foreign journals, such as the *Harvard Law Review*, the *Australian Law Journal*, and the *Canadian Bar Review*.

8.2.5 Some guidance on using journals

It is important to remember that academic journal articles are explanations, commentaries, criticisms, and analysis of specific aspects of the law and the significance or implications of the law—they are *not* the law itself. They are an opinion on the law and are therefore a useful *secondary* source which can be used in conjunction with *primary* legal sources (cases and legislation) to supplement the arguments which you are making. If you are talking about primary sources, you must reference them and not the article in which you have read about them.

While journal articles can certainly provide evidence of further research and reading, particularly in essay questions (see chapter 14) and dissertations (see chapter 17), you must still take care in selecting and using them. Ensure that the journals that you are using are appropriate. Academic journals are usually regarded as more authoritative than practitioner (or trade) journals. Although practitioner journals are useful for keeping you up to date with developments in the law since they are often published more frequently than the 'heavyweight' journals, you should try to avoid using them as serious academic authority. If you find an interesting article or case note in a practitioner journal, you should always try to see if you can find material on the same (or a similar) topic in a journal which carries greater academic authority. That is not to say that practitioner journals have no merit. They may carry the only commentary on a new development and, as such, can be used together with other journal articles within your essay. As long as you strike an appropriate balance between the two types of journal, you will demonstrate your ability to select and present commentary on the law.

You should also be careful to make sure that you understand the point which the article you wish to use is trying to make. Do not fall into the trap of using a quotation from an article 'just because it sounded clever' if you fail to realize the point that the author is trying to make. Your lecturer will understand the quotation and will also spot if you are misusing or misinterpreting it.

Ensure that you explain why the views you are including from journals are relevant to your essay and significant in terms of the argument you are putting forward. Well-used academic commentary should help you to support the points you are making. You can then give your own comment on the journal's perspective: do you agree or disagree with it? Explain why. This will demonstrate your ability to synthesize and analyse multiple sources.

Finally, be careful with articles which put forward extreme or sensationalist views. These will typically represent one side of an argument, and it is important to put forward a balanced view which evaluates and considers both sides.

8.3 OFFICIAL PUBLICATIONS

8.3.1 Command Papers

Command Papers derive their name from the fact that they are presented to Parliament 'by Command of Her Majesty'. In fact, they are generally presented by a Government Minister. Command Papers are papers of interest to Parliament where presentation to Parliament is not required by statute. The subjects may include:

• Major policy proposals (White Papers)

• Consultation documents (Green Papers)

• Diplomatic documents such as treaties

• Government responses to Select Committee reports

• Reports of major committees of inquiry

• Certain departmental reports or reviews.

8.3.2 Bills

As you will recall from section 2.1.1, Bills are draft Acts of Parliament, put forward for debate. They are particularly useful when used in conjunction with the reports of Parliamentary debate, as you will be able to follow the various amendments made between versions of the Bill and the final Act of Parliament alongside the debate in Parliament that drove those amendments.

8.3.3 Parliamentary papers

The papers of the House of Commons originate inside the House and are 'Ordered by the House of Commons to be printed ...'. They comprise the reports and evidence of Select Committees or the proceedings of Standing Committees considering legislation. Other House of Commons papers include:

• Reports of investigations of the National Audit Office

• Financial papers

• Annual reports of official bodies

• Accounts of official bodies

• Various administrative reports.

The House of Lords publishes substantially fewer papers than the Commons. Until the 1986/87 session both Bills and papers were numbered in one single sequence. From 1987/88 House of Lords papers and Bills are split into two separately numbered sequences.

8.3.4 Parliamentary debates (*Hansard* or the Official Report)

Parliament once prohibited all reporting and publishing of its proceedings, believing that it should deliberate in private. Indeed, it regarded any attempt to publicize its proceedings as a serious punishable offence. However, by the late 1700s, dissent both from the public and within Parliament persuaded Parliament to relax its stance. In 1803 the House of Commons allowed the press to enter the public gallery and William Cobbett, publisher of *Cobbett's Weekly Political Register*, added reprints of reports of speeches taken from other newspapers in a new supplement. In 1812 publication was taken over by Cobbett's assistant, Thomas Hansard, who in 1829 changed the title of the reports to *Hansard's Parliamentary Debates*.

By 1878 dissatisfaction with the accuracy of the report was being expressed, and Hansard received a special subsidy conditional upon his employing special Parliamentary reporters. In 1888 a Parliamentary Select Committee recommended that, rather than let Hansard publish the debates, an authorized version ought to be published. This version was published without using the name *Hansard*.

This authorized version was officially adopted by Parliament in 1907 as a 'full report, in the first person, of all speakers alike', with a full report being defined as:

> one which, though not strictly verbatim, is substantially the verbatim report, with repetitions and redundancies omitted and with obvious mistakes corrected, but which on the other hand leaves out nothing that adds to the meaning of the speech or illustrates the argument.

In 1943 it was decided to reintroduce the name *Hansard* because of its popular usage.

Therefore *Hansard* (the *Official Report*) is the edited verbatim report of proceedings in both the House of Commons and the House of Lords. Commons *Hansard* covers proceedings in the Commons Chamber, Westminster Hall, and Standing Committees. Lords *Hansard* covers proceedings in the Lords Chamber and its Grand Committees. Both contain Written Ministerial Statements and Written Answers.

8.3.5 Law Commission reports

The Law Commission was set up by the Law Commissions Act 1965 for the purpose of promoting reform of the law. Its key aims are:

- To ensure that the law is as fair, modern, simple, and as cost-effective as possible.

- To conduct research and consultations in order to make systematic recommendations for consideration by Parliament.

- To codify the law, eliminate anomalies, repeal obsolete and unnecessary enactments, and reduce the number of separate statutes.

Law Commission reports provide a useful insight into reasons behind law reforms and more than two-thirds of the Commission's law reform recommendations have been implemented. There are also recommendations that are waiting for the Government's decision, or Parliamentary time for debate. Recent examples of legislation that have followed, in whole or in part, from Commission reports include the Mental Capacity (Amendment) Act 2019 and Part 6 of the Policing and Crime Act 2017. Even recommendations that have not been implemented will give an overview of the problems that were perceived in the law and may prove useful in essays that require a critical discussion of the topic.

The Law Commission Act 2009 was implemented to improve the rate at which the Commission's recommendations for reform of the law are implemented by Government. It requires the Lord Chancellor to report annually to Parliament on the extent to which Government has implemented Law Commission recommendations.

Many Law Commission reports are published as Command Papers or Parliamentary Papers. You can find a useful table on reports and their implementation status on the Law Commission website at www.lawcom.gov.uk/our-work/implementation/table/.

8.4 OTHER SECONDARY SOURCES

8.4.1 Websites

Although there is a vast amount of material available online, you need to exercise care to ensure that material you find is reliable, valuable, and credible. This can be a difficult task, although the following pointers should be borne in mind:

- Does the material give an author's name? If so, is the author a reputable academic or practitioner? Can you find any biographical information which will enable you to determine the academic value of the material?
- Is the information in a reputable online publication?
- Does the article carry a bibliography? Is it adequately referenced (either using footnotes, endnotes, or *Harvard* referencing)?
- Is the material on an official website or a personal website? The latter should be used with caution since anyone can set up a personal site.
- Has the material been evaluated independently before publication?

There is more in-depth guidance on evaluating the provenance of online and other resources in chapter 14.

8.4.2 Newspapers

In addition to law reports, newspapers often contain comment and analysis on recent legal developments and interesting background material on topical issues. *The Times* in particular carries a law supplement on Thursdays.

8.4.3 Think-tanks

Think-tanks are typically research institutes or other organizations who provide specialist advice and ideas on national problems, such as the Centre for Policy Studies, the Commonwealth Policy Studies Institute, or the Institute for Public Policy Research. While their reports are not official, they can sometimes be influential in driving legislative policy.

8.4.4 'Soft law'

Soft law is sometimes referred to as *quasi-legislation*—or 'law-which-is-not-law'.

There are a number of sources of 'soft law'. Soft law is typically administrative in nature and is probably best explained by way of examples (see Table 8.1).

Table 8.1 Some examples of 'soft law'

Category	Examples
Prescriptive rules	• Codes of Practice issued under the Police and Criminal Evidence Act 1984 • Highway Code • ACAS (Advisory Conciliation and Arbitration Service) codes relating to employment disputes
Procedural rules	• Practice Directions • Prison rules • Gaming Board rules for application for gaming licences • Codes of Practice issued under the Police and Criminal Evidence Act 1984
Instructions	• Home Office circulars to magistrates' courts • Home Office circulars to chief constables • Prison department circulars, orders, and regulations
Guides to interpretation	• Official statements explaining how terms or rules will be interpreted
Recommendations	• Specimen directions to juries formulated by the Judicial Studies Board • Guidance notes issued by the Health and Safety Executive
Rules of practice	• Tax concessions made by the Commissioners for the Inland Revenue outside those permitted by statute
Voluntary codes	• Broadcasting Complaints Authority • Press Complaints Commission • City Code on takeovers and mergers

The legal effect of these various sources is not certain until they have been tested in court. Sometimes they are given legal effect, sometimes not, and in some instances, inconsistently. The House of Lords[2] has expressed concern regarding the uncertain legal consequences of non-compliance and the Cabinet Office has provided some 'Guidance on Codes of Practice and Legislation' in its *Guide to Making Legislation*.[3]

 CHAPTER SUMMARY

Books

- Student textbooks collect together, analyse, and criticize the law in particular areas; they do not generally carry any great authority
- Cases and materials books provide a useful starting point for research, but are not a substitute for finding and reading original materials

---

2. HL Deb 15 January 1986, vol 469, cols 1075–1105.
3. Cabinet Office, *Guide to Making Legislation* (July 2017) Appendix D <https://assets.publishing.service.gov.uk/government/uploads/system/uploads/attachment_data/file/645652/Guide_to_Making_Legislation_Jul_2017.pdf> accessed 22 October 2020.

- Monographs are a detailed written study of a single specialized topic; they cover particular narrow subject areas in much greater depth than student textbooks
- Practitioners' books are primarily reference works for practising lawyers
- Legal encyclopedias and digests such as *Halsbury's Laws of England, Halsbury's Statutes*, and *The Digest* are extremely useful and comprehensive research tools
- Legal dictionaries exist alongside conventional dictionaries; some specialize in a particular topic
- Judicial dictionaries are large reference works which provide detailed commentary on judicial interpretation of words and phrases
- Revision guides can serve a useful purpose, but are not a substitute for attendance at lectures or seminars or a shortcut for reading and thinking

Journals

- Journals are an important resource which can be used to keep up to date with the latest developments in the law
- General journals contain articles based on extensive academic research
- Specialist journals also contain academic articles but with a focus on a particular area of the law
- Practitioner journals carry less academic weight but are published more frequently; they tend to contain shorter articles
- Foreign journals from other common law jurisdictions can be a useful resource when undertaking comparative research

Official publications

- Command Papers contain matters of interest to Parliament
- Bills are draft Acts of Parliament put forward for debate
- Papers of the House of Commons primarily comprise reports and evidence of select committees or the proceedings of standing committees
- The House of Lords publishes substantially fewer papers than the Commons
- *Hansard* (the *Official Report*) is the edited verbatim report of proceedings in both the House of Commons and the House of Lords
- Law Commission reports give insight into areas of the law requiring reform; over two-thirds of its recommendations are implemented

Other secondary sources

- Online material can be useful but should be used with caution
- Newspapers often contain comment and analysis on recent legal developments
- Think-tank reports can be influential in driving legislative policy
- 'Soft law' comprises rules, guidelines, codes, and recommendations which may be given legal effect when tested in court

FURTHER READING

- An interesting historical legal perspective on the emergence of quasi-legislation is given in RE Megarry, 'Administrative Quasi-legislation' (1944) 60 LQR 125.
- The varieties of quasi-legislative rule, the means by which the courts have dealt with them, and how they may best be accommodated within the UK constitutional framework is discussed in R Baldwin and J Houghton, 'Circular Arguments: The Status and Legitimacy of Administrative Rules' [1986] PL 239.

Finding books, journals, and official publications

9

INTRODUCTION

Chapters 3 and 6 covered the ways in which you can locate legislation and case law. However, as you will appreciate from the explanation provided in chapter 8, there are a range of important sources of law beyond legislation and case law. These are materials that provide information on the content, meaning, and operation of the law and which will assist you in your quest to understand the law. This chapter will complete your portfolio of 'finding' skills by explaining how to find these important supplementary resources, both in the library and online. It will cover books, journals, official publications, Bills, and *Hansard*.

The ability to find supplementary legal resources will give you a fully rounded set of skills by which you can find the most useful sources of law. The use of supplementary resources will give you a much greater depth of knowledge than can easily be acquired from statutes and cases alone. There is a wealth of legal literature available, so without the ability to find it you will find yourself unable to benefit from the learned commentary of others—all of whom will (usually) have much more legal experience than you.

 Learning outcomes

After studying this chapter, you will be able to:

- Use online library catalogues and legal bibliographies to find books on a particular topic
- Understand journal citations
- Recognize the more common journal abbreviations
- Find journals in a library and online
- Distinguish between the various series of Command Papers
- Locate official publications in both paper and online
- Find Parliamentary Bills
- Use *Hansard* to find and follow debates in the House of Commons and House of Lords

9.1 FINDING BOOKS

The ability to find books, either a specific title or a range of books on a particular topic, is important. Even if you purchase the set textbook for each of your subjects, there will still come a time when you need to find out what other books are available. You might, for instance, find that the set text is too complex, in which case you will want to find a more straightforward alternative. Conversely, if you are researching for a tutorial, a moot, or a piece of coursework, you may want to find books that go into more detail than the textbook that you have purchased.

9.1.1 Library catalogues

The first place to start looking for books on a particular topic is in your own library's catalogue as this will enable you to find which books are held at your own institution. However, there are also catalogues that provide information about the holdings of other libraries. This will be useful information if you want to know whether the university near your home town has sufficient books for your purposes during the vacation, for example, or it can enable you to locate a particular book that you need and order it from another library.

It is clearly impossible to provide details of how the catalogue works at every library. You should take time to familiarize yourself with the catalogue at your own institution. Your library will have instructions on how to use its catalogue. However, the experience of trial and error is also useful. Pick an area of law and try a few searches.

9.1.1.1 Library Hub Discover (discover.libraryhub.jisc.ac.uk)

The Library Hub Discover library catalogue (formerly known as Copac) gives free access to the merged online catalogues of 169 major university, specialist, and national libraries in the UK and Ireland, including the British Library (see Figure 9.1).

It is a great resource for tracking down less common materials, such as specialist monographs or theses, that may not be available in your local library. It can also be used for searching across a subject, checking document details, and downloading records to create a bibliography.

Figure 9.1 Library Hub Discover

9.1.2 Legal bibliographies

Whilst the ability to locate books using the library catalogue and the internet are useful skills, you should not overlook the importance of 'paper-based' research skills. It may be, for example, that you are using a library that does not have computer terminals in the area that you are using and you want to be able to locate material without constantly trotting backwards and forwards between the library catalogue and the area where the books are shelved. Equally, it can be very frustrating to have to wait in a queue to use a catalogue or online search facility when you are in a hurry and want to find a book. At such times, the ability to locate materials using an alternative method may be invaluable.

9.1.2.1 *Current Law Monthly Digest*

The *Current Law Monthly Digest* contains a list of new books published during the month. At the end of the year these lists are reprinted in the *Current Law Year Book*.

This is useful to check for current books which might have been published in a particular area very recently, although it can be cumbersome to use when looking for books over more than one or two years, since the list is not cumulative and the subject headings used are quite broad.

9.1.2.2 Specialist legal bibliographies

As well as *Current Law* there are a number of other legal bibliographies which provide listings of books for particular areas of law. These are too numerous to list here; you should check with your law librarian which ones are available.

9.1.2.3 References in textbooks

Never underestimate the value of simple strategies for locating secondary sources. All good-quality textbooks contain references to further secondary sources such as books and articles, either in the footnotes, additional reading sections, or in the bibliography. Not only do these provide the bibliographic details of books but also may give you an indication of *why* they are valuable sources. For example, if your textbook touches on a particular topic but not in any great detail—perhaps the point is too marginal for any great coverage in a textbook—it may provide a pointer to the leading work(s) on that topic.

9.2 FINDING JOURNALS

It is inevitable that you will need to locate journal articles at some point during your studies. Your tutorial reading is likely to contain references to publications in journals and, of course, you will want to demonstrate your research skills in your coursework essays by making reference to relevant journal articles.

See chapter 11 (writing skills) and chapter 14 (essay writing) for a more detailed discussion of the value of journal articles in coursework.

The approach that is needed to locate journal articles will depend upon whether you are looking for a particular article that you know exists or whether you are having a speculative search to determine whether there are any articles on a particular topic.

9.2.1 Making sense of journal references

Journal references are used as a convenient shorthand means of pinpointing the location of a particular article. In other words, if you want to find a particular journal, its reference is the 'address' you need to track it down.

Journal references are covered in section 13.3.6.1.

For example, if you wish to find the article cited as:

> H Stalford and K Hollingsworth, '"This case is about you and your future": Towards Judgments for Children' (2020) 83 MLR 1030.

you need to extract the key elements from the citation, so that you may find it easily in a library or online (see Figure 9.2).

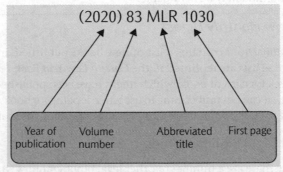

Figure 9.2 Journal citation

The year of publication and first page number are self-explanatory. However, unlike the various series of law reports, there is unfortunately no single standard way of abbreviating journal titles. There are sometimes a couple of options for each journal.

Sometimes journal titles are written out in full rather than being abbreviated which makes the task of finding them much easier.

A useful free online guide to deciphering the multitude of journal (and law report) abbreviations is the *Cardiff Index to Legal Abbreviations* available online at www.legalabbrevs.cardiff. ac.uk. It can be searched either from abbreviation to title or from title to abbreviation. It is also possible to search from abbreviation to title using only a part of an abbreviation, and from title to abbreviation using any words (not just the first word) which appear in the title.

There may or may not be a volume number. Some journal series are just referenced by their year of publication (and do not have consecutive volume numbers). Other references might provide an issue number as well as a volume number, given in brackets after the volume number.

Breaking down the elements of the citation, you should see that it refers to:

- An article by H Stalford and K Hollingsworth
- In volume 83
- Of the *Modern Law Review*
- Which was published in 2020
- Called 'This case is about you and your future': Towards Judgments for Children
- Starting on page 1030

This should be all the information you need to find the article, either online or in the library.

9.2.2 Online

There are a number of online databases devoted to legal publications that you will find useful when searching for journal articles. You should, however, be aware that each database will only list articles in journals that are published by an organization that licences its content to that particular database. This means that you may find that the results of your search in any one database will not necessarily give you information about all the articles that have been published on a particular topic, only the articles that have been published in journals that have paid to be listed in that database. Therefore, you may need to make reference to more than one database in order to find the article that you want or to obtain a complete list of all available articles.

By way of example, a search for articles using the search term 'intoxicated consent in rape' conducted in 2020 found 106 matches in Westlaw Edge UK and 7 in LexisLibrary.

9.2.2.1 Westlaw Edge UK

Westlaw Edge UK lists all articles that appear in its publisher's own journals as well as a selection of those owned by other publishers such as Oxford University Press. You can find the full list under 'Publications' from the 'Journals' menu. It is updated daily, so it is a good way of locating articles that have just been published. It has the advantage of being a full-text database in relation to many of its journals which means that it not only finds the article but also provides it in full for you to read on screen or print out.

Westlaw Edge UK has a 'quick search' page which enables you to get straight on with a search of journals, case law, or legislation as well as more detailed search facilities (see Figure 9.3). If you are looking for an article that you know exists, it is likely that you will have sufficient information to find it without a great deal of difficulty by using the title of the article or the name of the author in combination with a keyword as the basis of the search.

However, it will often be the case that you are looking for articles on a topic and are not sure whether any have been written. Here, you will need to use keyword searching and it may take a fair amount of experimentation with search terms to find material that is useful to you.

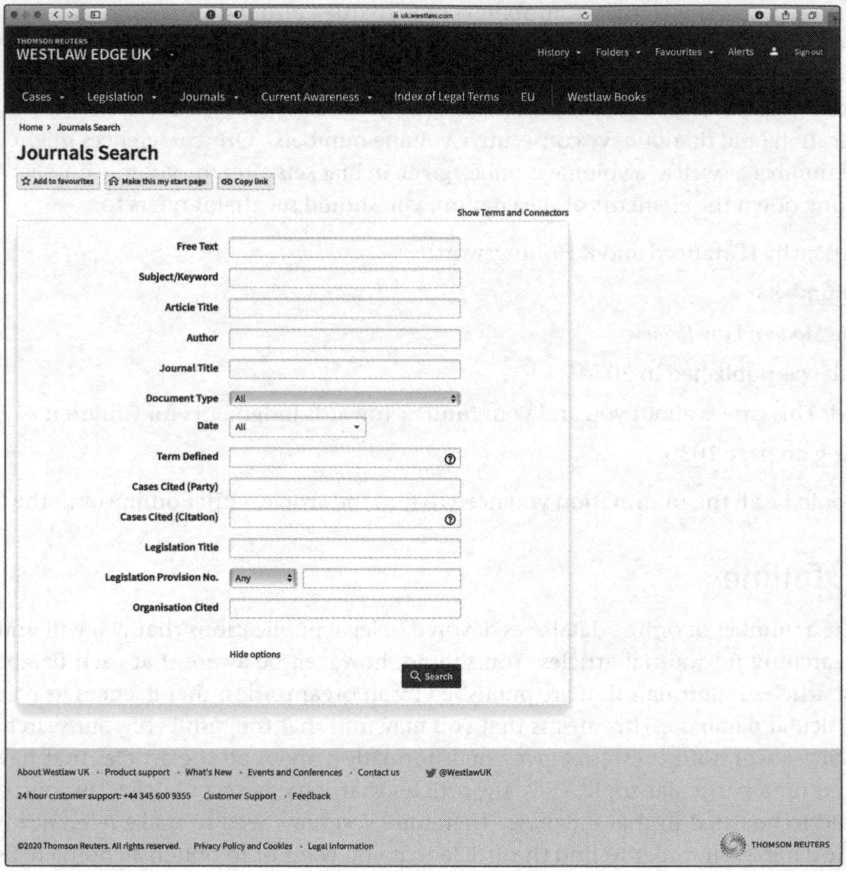

Figure 9.3 Westlaw Edge UK

9.2.2.2 Lawtel

Lawtel also provides a search facility for many different UK legal publications (see Figure 9.4). It is now part of Westlaw Edge UK. Lawtel also includes a number of practitioner-focused journals such as the *Solicitors Journal* and *Counsel* as well as more academic titles. Practitioner journals can be particularly useful as they are published far more frequently than academic journals—the *Solicitors Journal*, for example, is a weekly publication—so it often has comment on recent cases and events. Lawtel also provides access to newspaper law reports from *The Times*, *The Independent,* and *The Guardian*.

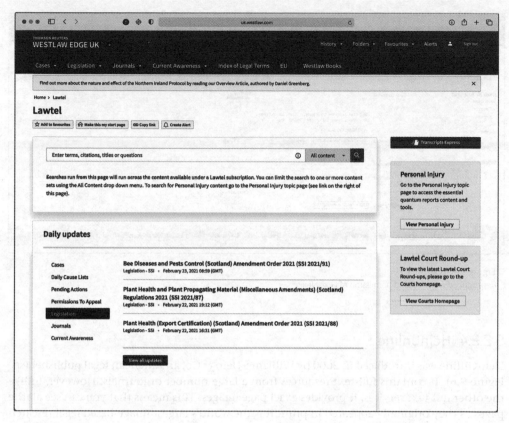

Figure 9.4 Lawtel

9.2.2.3 LexisLibrary

LexisLibrary contains the full text of articles published in around eighty-five journals and summaries of the articles found in many more journals. It is also updated regularly. In addition to academic journals, LexisLibrary covers a range of practitioner titles such as the *New Law Journal*.

As with Westlaw Edge UK and Lawtel, it provides the ability to search by title, author, or general search terms but it has the additional benefit of providing a drop-down list of the journals covered which can facilitate a more focused search of a particular publication (see Figure 9.5). For example, if you were looking for articles on a topic within criminal law and did not want to trawl through a long list of results, you could search exclusively within the *Journal of Criminal Law*. This can be useful in speeding up your search and eliminating unwanted materials from the outset. You should be wary, however, of being overly selective in your searching as general journals, such as the *Oxford Journal of Legal Studies*, cover articles on any topic within the law, so searching in a particular specialist journal would automatically exclude relevant articles published in general journals.

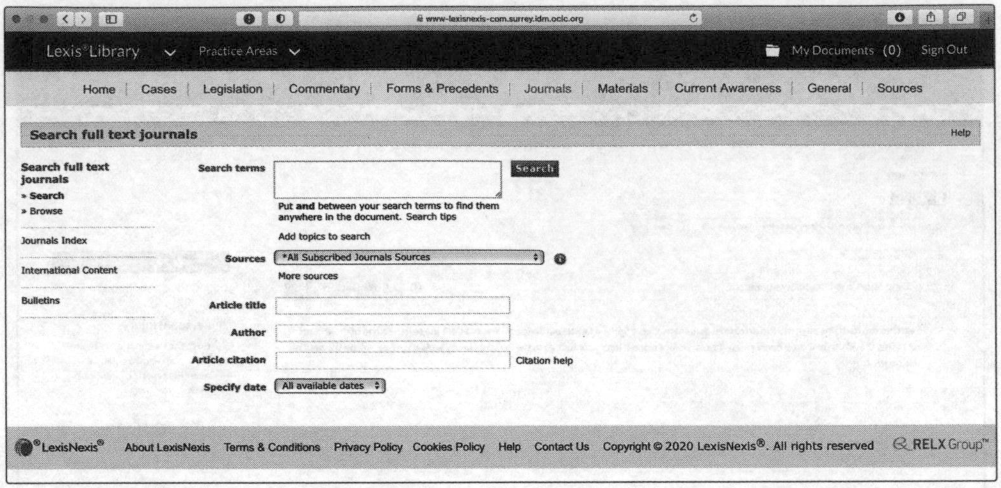

Figure 9.5 LexisLibrary
Reproduced with the kind permission of LexisNexis®

9.2.2.4 HeinOnline

HeinOnline was introduced in 2000 by William S Hein & Co, an American legal publisher (see Figure 9.6). It contains full-text resources from a large number of journals. However, unlike the other full-text services, it provides exact page images. This means that you can see all the pages as they originally appeared in print. It is the world's largest image-based legal research database. However, as you might expect from an American service, the journal coverage is predominantly American, although it does cover certain volumes of a number of the major UK journals. It also carries *Statutes of the Realm* (1235–1713) and a full reprint of volumes 1–176 of the *English Reports* (1694–1867).

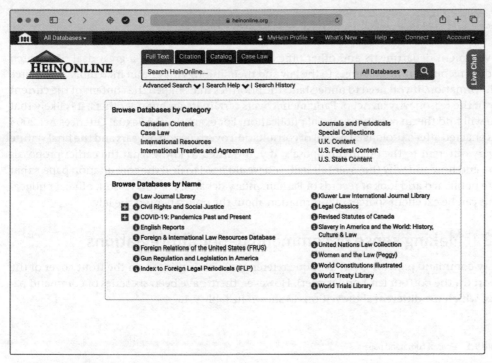

Figure 9.6 HeinOnline
Used with permission of William S Hein & Co, Inc

9.2.3 In a library

If you have the citation of the article, it should be a relatively straightforward task to find it in your library. Check the library catalogue or ask your librarian to make sure that the library carries the particular series of journals covering the date and/or volume that you need. Not all libraries carry all journals. To make matters even more complicated, even if your library *does* carry the series you need, there is no guarantee that it will have the particular volume you want. The library may have begun its subscription after the date you are looking for or cancelled its subscription before the date you require.

Practical exercise

Try to find the following articles either online or in the library:

1 C Walker, 'The Governance of Emergency Arrangements' (2014) 18 International Journal of Human Rights 211.
2 C Piper, 'Neglect Neglected in the Crime and Courts Act' (2013) 43 Family Law 722.
3 R Pattenden, 'Machinespeak: Section 129 of Criminal Justice Act 2003' [2010] Crim LR 623.

9.3 FINDING OFFICIAL PUBLICATIONS

Government departments and other official organizations conduct a great deal of research prior to recommending changes to the law and their findings may be an incredibly rich source of information. If you need to understand the priorities that shaped the content of the current law or the reason why an Act of Parliament covers certain issues but not others, it is likely that you will find the answer in an official publication. For example, the Sexual Offences Act 2003 was enacted after a prolonged period of consultation over a period of years and the final statute is very different to the original proposals. If you wanted to know what the earlier proposals were and how and why they were altered, you would need to find the consultation papers that were published and look at records of Parliamentary debates. For this reason, official publications can be excellent sources of information about the policy behind the law.

9.3.1 Making sense of command paper abbreviations

Every command paper is given a unique reference which is printed on the front cover of the report (in the bottom left-hand corner). However, there have been six series of command papers, which use different abbreviations as shown in Table 9.1.

Table 9.1 Series of command papers

Series	Dates	Abbreviation
1	1833–69	[1]–[4222]
2	1870–99	[C 1]–[C 9550]
3	1900–18	[Cd 1]–[Cd 9329]
4	1919–56	[Cmd 1]–Cmd 9889 (the use of square brackets was discontinued in 1922)
5	1956–86	Cmnd 1–Cmnd 9927
6	1986–2018	Cm 1–Cm 9756
7	2019–	CP 1– (up to CP310 at the time of writing)

It is important to look at the style of abbreviation. This will give you an indication of the date of the command paper—remember that there is a thirty-seven-year gap between Cmd 1 and Cmnd 1 for example.

9.3.2 Online

9.3.2.1 gov.uk publications

The gov.uk website contains an extensive search facility for official documents available at www.gov.uk/government/publications (see Figure 9.7). It allows searching by topic, Government department, geographical location, and official document type as well as filtering by date range.

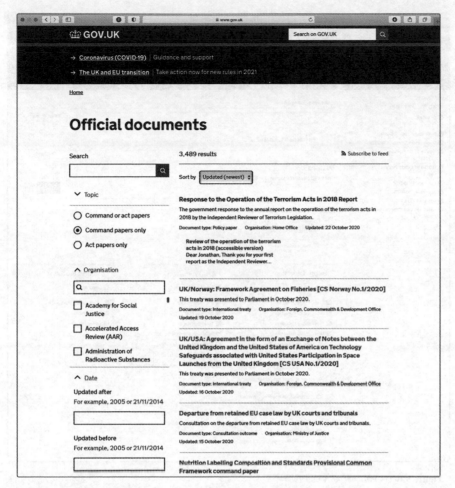

Figure 9.7 gov.uk publications
© Crown copyright

9.3.2.2 *UK Parliamentary Papers*

UK Parliamentary Papers is a commercially available service (https://parlipapers.proquest.com/parlipapers) (see Figure 9.8). It provides a searchable full-text facility as well as a detailed index. It includes over 200,000 House of Commons Sessional Papers from 1715 to the present with supplementary materials from 1689.

Figure 9.8 *UK Parliamentary Papers*
The screenshot is published with permission of ProQuest LL. Further reproduction is prohibited without permission. www.proquest.com

9.3.3 In a library

Most libraries will contain a collection of Command Papers. These may be arranged by series and number, in which case it is a very straightforward task to find the paper you want. However, some libraries organize their Parliamentary materials in *sessional sets*: in other words, they are bound together in volumes for a particular session of Parliament. These will therefore be organized by year. If your library organizes its Command Papers in this way, you will need to have some idea of the year of the paper as well as its abbreviated reference.

9.4 FINDING BILLS

9.4.1 Making sense of Bill citations

The role of Bills in the Parliamentary process is covered in chapter 2.

Public Bills carry a serial number in the bottom left-hand corner of the first page of the Bill. For example, the 2019– 21 Vagrancy (Repeal) Bill is Bill 118.

A
BILL
TO

Make provision about slavery, servitude and forced or compulsory labour; to make provision about human trafficking; to make provision for an Antislavery Commissioner; and for connected purposes.

Be it enacted by the Queen's most Excellent Majesty, by and with the advice and consent of the Lords Spiritual and Temporal, and Commons, in this present Parliament assembled, and by the authority of the same, as follows:—

PART 1

Offences

Offences

1 Slavery, servitude and forced or compulsory labour

(1) A person commits an offence if—

    (a) the person holds another person in slavery or servitude and the circumstances are such that the person knows or ought to know that the other person is held in slavery or servitude, or

    (b) the person requires another person to perform forced or compulsory labour and the circumstances are such that the person knows or ought to know that the other person is being required to perform forced or compulsory labour.

(2) In subsection (1) the references to holding a person in slavery or servitude or requiring a person to perform forced or compulsory labour are to be construed in accordance with Article 4 of the Human Rights Convention.

(3) In determining whether a person is being held in slavery or servitude or required to perform forced or compulsory labour regard may be had to all the circumstances.

(4) For example, regard may be had to any of the person's personal circumstances (such as their age, family relationships, and any mental or physical illness) which may make the person more vulnerable than other persons.

Bill 8

Extract 9.1 2019–21 Vagrancy (Repeal) Bill

This Bill would be cited as shown in Figure 9.9.

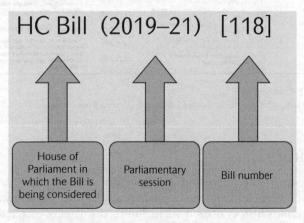

Figure 9.9 Bill citation

The convention for citing Bills therefore begins with HC (for House of Commons) or HL (for House of Lords). Since Bill numbering restarts at 1 with every new Parliamentary session, the dates of that session must be given to identify the Bill precisely. Finally, the citation provides the number of the Bill.

Traditionally, Bills in the House of Commons had a number in square brackets, and Bills in the House of Lords had a number in round brackets. You will still see the square bracket convention used in relation to Commons Bills, but Lords Bill numbers have now lost their brackets.

9.4.2 Online

Details of the Bills before Parliament in the current session can be found on the UK Parliament website: https://services.parliament.uk/bills (see Figure 9.10).

Figure 9.10 Parliament Bills
Contains Parliamentary information licensed under the Open Parliament Licence v3.0

9.4.3 In a library

The *House of Commons Weekly Information Bulletin* gives details of Bills that are before Parliament in the current session. Bills are listed alphabetically by title. The *Bulletin* also provides details of the Parliamentary history of each Bill including the dates of each reading in the House of Commons and House of Lords and any proceedings in Standing Committee.

9.5 FINDING PARLIAMENTARY DEBATES

Remember that the Official Reports of Parliamentary Debates are generally referred to as Hansard. *See chapter 4.*

9.5.1 Online

Hansard is available free of charge online on the UK Parliament website at https://hansard. parliament.uk (see Figure 9.11).

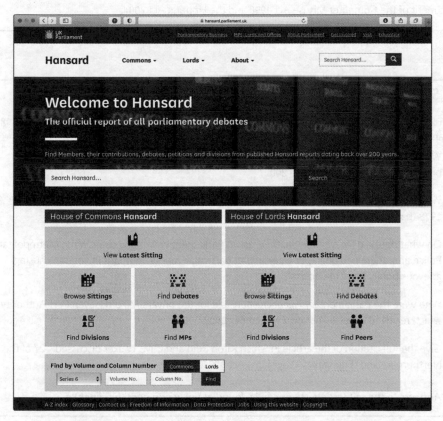

Figure 9.11 *Hansard*
Contains Parliamentary information licensed under the Open Parliament Licence v3.0

Hansard online describes itself as an ongoing project involving the Commons and Lords *Hansards* and the Parliamentary Digital Service. When the site was first launched, it offered content from 2010 to the present day. It has now added the historical archive to the site, meaning that you can access records of debates from as far back as the early nineteenth century.

9.5.2 In a library

Hansard is published daily and reprinted each week as *Weekly Hansard*. An index to the debates is also published every two weeks.

At the end of each Parliamentary session *Hansard* is republished as a set of bound volumes with a corresponding index. These volumes are numbered sequentially—there are approaching 600 of them. *Hansard* is printed in a two-column format, and references to *Hansard* quote column numbers rather than page numbers. If you have a volume and column number, it is a simple task to find the extract you require in the printed volume.

Practical exercise

Try to find the debates in both the House of Commons and the House of Lords leading to the enactment of the Computer Misuse Act 1990 and the Hunting Act 2004.

Self-test questions

Having completed this chapter, use your research skills to attempt the following more challenging research questions involving books, journals, and official publications.

1. What is the Command Paper reference for the Annual Report by the Wales Office that was presented to Parliament in June 2005?

2. Who was the author of an article on the meaning of 'charity' under the Bermuda's Charities Act 1978 that was published in *Trusts & Trustees?*

3. On what date did Sir Waldron Smithers ask in Parliament how many cases in the Metropolitan Police area there had been per week in that particular year of 'footpads in London causing grievous bodily harm to citizens'?

4. Who were the Parliamentary Agents responsible for the private Milford Haven Port Authority Bill which received Royal Assent on 7 November 2002?

5. Give the full citation of the article in which Kiron Reid and Clive Walker discussed s 27 of the Northern Ireland (Emergency Provisions) Act 1991.

 Answers to the self-test questions can be found at **www.oup.com/he/finch8e/**.

CHAPTER SUMMARY

Books

*   Your own library's catalogue is the first place to start looking for books
*   The Library Hub Discover library catalogue (formerly known as Copac) is a free consolidated online catalogue covering the libraries of 169 institutions
*   The *Current Law Monthly Digest* and *Current Law Year Book* provide lists of new books published during a specific month or year, although they can be difficult to use

Journals

- The *Cardiff Index to Legal Abbreviations* is a useful free online resource to help you decipher unfamiliar journal abbreviations
- Westlaw Edge UK, Lawtel and LexisLibrary index a broad spectrum of UK journals
- HeinOnline is an American database, with sporadic coverage of major UK journals. It has a good selection of historical material and provides page images of the journals. It also carries *Statutes of the Realm* and the *English Reports*

Official publications

- Most libraries carry a range of official publications in print
- The website gov.uk is the official free online reference facility for Command Papers, containing a selection from 1994–2005 and all from 2005/06 onwards
- *House of Commons Parliamentary Papers* is a commercial service with searchable full text and an index for papers since 1801

Bills

- Details of Bills can be found either in the *House of Commons Weekly Information Bulletin* or online via the UK Parliament website

Hansard

- *Hansard* provides a verbatim transcript of all Parliamentary debates
- It is freely available online on the UK Parliament website which also provides comprehensive search facilities

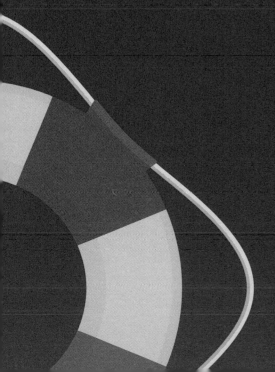

PART II
Academic legal skills

This section of the book covers the many different skills that you need in order to get to grips with the academic requirements of legal study. The starting point is a chapter on study skills that will help you to develop effective study habits and this is followed by a chapter that focuses on written communication skills. You will then find a chapter that introduces you to the idea of legal reasoning; that is, it will help you to understand how judges decide cases and give you the skills that you need to analyse case law. There is also an important chapter that discusses the risk of inadvertent plagiarism and provides clear information about when and how to reference a range of legal sources. The chapters that follow focus on how you will use these skills to write essays and answer problem questions. There are also chapters on writing a dissertation and on preparing for exams. Overall, these chapters will equip you to study law effectively and to perform to the best of your ability in assessments.

Study skills

INTRODUCTION

This part of the book starts with a focus on study skills. 'Study skills' is an umbrella terms that includes a wide range of skills that make the business of being a student and studying law generally easier and more manageable. The chapter is structured around the main activities that make up your law degree: attending lectures and tutorials, engaging in private study, and preparing for assessment as well as a section on improving your performance. You will find that some topics are repeated or, rather, the topic is divided and covered in the sections where it is most relevant. For example, there is a discussion on note-taking in lectures and another exploration of note-taking strategies in the section on private study. Some of the topics that are covered in these sections, such as working with others, could be seen as personal skills rather than study skills but the approach taken in this chapter is to outline ways in which these personal skills contribute to more productive study habits. For example, the chapter will explain how strong time-management skills can contribute to the development of a more effective approach to tackling assessments and how being able to work with others can deepen your own understanding of the law. The overall aim of this chapter is to help you to develop effective study habits so that you become a confident and independent learner with an ability to reflect on your own performance.

Resist any temptation to dismiss study skills as unimportant or to assume that they are something that you must already possess as you have enjoyed sufficient success in your studies to take you to university. Study skills are important as they underpin the whole process of learning a new subject and acquiring knowledge. If you think that you are already good at this, perhaps you are but why would you not want to improve and to find ways to make study an even smoother process? Moreover, study at degree level is bound to be different and require more from you than your previous studies so it is important to adapt and develop your existing skills to ensure that you are able to work successfully at this higher level. Finally, study skills should be seen as something that evolves and matures all the time that you study. Hopefully, you will complete your degree not only with a comprehensive mastery of the law but also with an increased confidence in your ability to engage in self-supported independent study.

 Learning outcomes

After studying this chapter, you will be able to:

- Appreciate the contribution made by personal skills of communication and organization to the evolution of effective study habits and practices
- Recognize the way in which lectures and seminars/tutorials contribute to learning and find ways to gain maximum benefit by preparing for participating in these activities

- Develop efficient study habits and find effective techniques for taking and organizing notes
- Reflect on the way that you organize your studies and adopt some useful strategies to help you to manage your study time more effectively
- Review your approach to learning from feedback and develop skills of self-reflection so that you can improve your performance in assessments
- Evaluate your proficiency in various key skills and identify a strategy for filling in any gaps in your skills especially those that are attractive to potential employers

10.1 STUDYING THE LAW

As you will have read in chapter 1, each university is different in the way that a law degree is structured and organized. Despite this, there are some core characteristics that are common to almost all university law programmes so it is likely that your degree will be delivered using a combination of lectures and small-group teaching sessions in conjunction with an expectation that you will undertake a significant amount of private study as you work towards an assessment. Each of these activities contributes to the way that you will learn the law and you will need to develop effective study skills to make the most of each of these learning experiences.

10.2 LECTURES

A lecture is an overview of key information on each topic by the lecturer to all the students taking the module. Traditionally, this sort of teaching session has taken place in a lecture theatre and involves the lecturer speaking, usually whilst showing lecture slides, and students listening and making notes of what is said. In recent years, even before the coronavirus epidemic, many universities were either shifting away from in-person lectures in favour of online alternatives or supplementing traditional live lectures with recordings of the session that students could consult after the session. The onset of lockdown led to the replacement of in-person lectures with online or recorded alternatives but the basic premise of the lecture as a means of imparting information about a topic from the lecturer to the student remains unaltered whether lectures are in-person, online, or recorded.

Whatever format it takes, a lecture may seem like a straightforward and rather passive way of learning. Even lectures that incorporate activities or use some form of voting system to increase engagement are still largely focused on the communication of information on the topic from the lecturer to the students. The onus on participation and contribution that characterizes a tutorial is absent and may create the impression that little more is required of students than that they attend, listen, and make notes. However, it is important that you remember that the creation of a set of notes is not an objective in itself. The purpose of a lecture is not to provide you with a set of notes, it is to teach you about a topic so that you go away with an understanding of the subject matter. A set of notes is not an end in themselves but a means to an end. In other words, there is no point in notes if they are not useful in helping you to capture the points that you want to remember. For this reason, it is important to develop an effective approach to taking notes in lectures.

10.2.1 Effective note-making in lectures

You will take a lot of notes during your time as a student—notes for tutorials, revision notes, notes as part of your preparation for coursework. You will want to make sure that all these notes are clear, comprehensive, and well organized and you will find some detailed advice on how to achieve this later in this chapter.

For now, though, the focus is on taking notes in lectures. This type of note-taking differs from others because you cannot work at your own pace if the lecture is live, either in-person or online, so you will always be trying to do several things at once: you will be trying to listen to the lecturer, understand what they are saying, and work out which parts of it are important as well as trying to create a set of notes. With all this going on at once, it is hardly surprising that a significant number of students say that the notes that they make in lectures are so unhelpful that they never read them again. Other students say that their lecture notes are so untidy and haphazard that they spend several hours after the lecture writing them out again so that they make better sense. Another common observation that students make about lecture notes is that they are so focused on writing down as much as possible that the lecturer says that they do not really listen to what is being said. All of these factors limit the effectiveness of the notes that are taken.

Practical exercise

Take a moment to reflect on the usefulness of your lecture notes. Find some that you made recently and take an objective look at them. Do they seem to be well organized so that you can find all the information that you need easily? Are they complete or are there gaps where you missed key points? Do you feel that they are useful notes that capture your understanding of the subject matter or are they just words on screen or paper? If you are not happy that you have created a useful set of notes, try to pinpoint what is wrong with them as this will help you to make changes to strengthen your note-taking strategy with the help of the suggestions set out in this chapter.

As noted above, note-taking in lectures is different to note-taking in other situations as you are always trying to keep pace with the lecturer. There are a number of different ways to take notes. The majority of students either make handwritten notes during a lecture or type notes on a laptop or tablet. Some students prefer to make an audio recording of the lecture (with permission of course—not all lecturers will agree to being recorded) and a small minority of students prefer to sit and listen without making any notes at all. Each approach offers its own benefits:

- **Typing notes** tends to be quicker than writing by hand and it avoids any problems with legibility. The notes can be reordered after the lecture and further information added without disrupting the structure of the notes.

- **Handwritten notes** can take the form of words but can easily incorporate charts and diagrams. They need not be linear so can include techniques such as flow charts and mind maps to capture relationships between concepts. Some students say that writing by hand helps to fix information in their memory more effectively than typing.

- **Recording notes** creates an accurate record of what was said and ensures that no key information is missed. Many students who use this method report, however, that they rarely listen to the recordings after the lecture because they do not find them useful. Some even say that they spend several hours listening to the recordings and typing them up because it is more useful to them to have written notes.

- **Making no notes** at all may seem like a dangerous strategy—you might question how you will remember all the information if you do not write it down. However, students who prefer not to make notes during a lecture say that it allows them to concentrate fully and really think about what the lecturer is saying which enables them to recall a lot of information afterwards.

There is no single right way to make notes—it is very much a matter of personal preference so you should adopt whatever approach works for you. As it is commonplace for lecturers to release presentation slides prior to the lecture, there is also always the option of annotating these instead of starting your own set of notes from scratch. It is also the case that many universities are using lecture-capture software which records the lecturer's words over the lecture slides so that these can be viewed afterwards by students. Of course, any recording of a lecture also gives you the ability to pause to make notes and rewind if you have missed information. Be careful that you do not let this ability tempt you into making a transcript of the lecture though: as will be discussed later in this chapter, note-taking needs to be selective and purposeful in order to be useful.

Practical exercise

Why not experiment with different approaches to note-taking?

 Watch a video of a typical lecture at **www.oup.com/he/finch8e/**.

While watching the lecture take notes using your usual method and then watch it again trying a different approach: if you usually write by hand, try typing and vice versa. You might even like to try listening without making notes and seeing how much information you can retain afterwards. Have a look at the different sets of notes you have created and compare your notes online with some example notes from the authors. Can you see much difference in them and, if so, which do you think is the most effective?

10.2.2 Reviewing your understanding

When the lecture is over, what do you do with the notes you have made? One common mistake that students make, especially at the beginning of their studies, is to assume that the lecture provides all the necessary information about a topic. This means they tend to assume that they have acquired all the information that they need on a topic by attending the lecture and making notes.

This is a mistake as very few, if any, lecturers set out to tell you everything that you need to know about a topic in a lecture. There would not be enough time to cover all the material in sufficient detail and, in any case, the objective is for you to learn how to find out about the law for yourself so there is an expectation that you will supplement your lecture notes with several hours of private study. This means that it is important you view your lecture notes as a starting point rather than treating them as a comprehensive account of the topic. The question is, however, what reading should you do after the lecture? The answer will depend upon what the lecturer set out to achieve in the lecture so you need to know what the purpose of the lecture was in order to understand what you need to do to complete your understanding of the topic (see Table 10.1).

Table 10.1 Suggestions on what to read after a lecture

Purpose of the lecture	What this gives you	What you need to do
To outline the basic aspects of a whole topic in order to provide students with a framework upon which to build	An overview of the topic but without exploring all/any of the issues in sufficient depth and detail	Your aim is to find out more about the points that were covered in the lecture. Read about the key cases and the difficulties of a topic
To get students started on a topic by covering some of the initial issues in an engaging manner to capture the interest of students	The first part of the story of a topic in detail but leaves you to complete the story yourself after the lecture	You will need to build on what was covered in the lecture to complete your study of the topic in the same level of detail
To build upon basic knowledge acquired through private study undertaken prior to the lecture by explaining more complex concepts	Here the lecturer expects students to come to the lecture with a basic understanding of the topic so that they can devote the lecture to dealing with more complex issues	You will need to do some work in getting to grips with a topic before the lecture and then review your understanding afterwards in light of the new information provided

You can see that whatever approach your lecturer takes there will always be an expectation that you do something after the lecture to consolidate your learning and build on the information that you have been given. However, students can feel a bit lost about what reading to do especially as not all lecturers specify what they want you to read.

- **Review your notes.** How much of the topic do you feel that you understand? Highlight any gaps in your notes where you might have missed some information or where you feel that you did not really grasp what the lecturer was telling you.

- **Start by reading the relevant chapter in the set textbook.** Add new information to your notes, paying particular attention to areas where you noticed that there were gaps or lack of clarity.

- **Review your notes again and ask the same question**—'how well do I understand the topic now?'. Hopefully your understanding has improved and the gaps in your notes have been filled.

- **Find an alternative textbook in the library that explains the same points in a different way** if you are really struggling with some (or all) of the subject matter. This can be really helpful. All textbooks have their own style even though they cover the same material and you may find one that you understand better. If you are still struggling, think about where else you can find help.

- **Think about doing some additional reading** if you feel you have gained a solid understanding of the topic. You could read one of the leading cases or find an article that deals with the subject matter. This will help you to really develop and deepen your understanding.

10.2.3 Asking questions in lectures

Should you ask questions in lectures? The key point to remember is that lectures exist to help you to understand something about the law. If you feel that you have not understood something then you may want to ask a question. Bear in mind, though, that the lecturer has a set amount of material that they will need to cover and they may not be keen to take up too much time answering questions. In fact, some lecturers have a 'no questions in lectures' policy and will simply tell you to raise your question in the seminar or tutorial instead. Others, however, may be perfectly happy to take questions and, in fact, may welcome questions to keep the lecture interactive and to ensure that points that are not clear are explored in more detail. Therefore, it is fine to ask a question in the lecture if you have one but always be aware that the lecturer may not want to disrupt the flow of the lecture by taking questions so you may have to find an alternative way of getting the answer.

Asking questions in a lecture may be far easier with the advent of live online lectures as most video-conferencing systems that are used for online lectures have a chat mechanism where you can type your question and many have a 'hands up' feature that you can use to indicate to the lecturer that you have a question. However, just because it is easier to ask a question, it may still be that your lecturer does not welcome questions as it can really disrupt the flow of the lecture, especially if the question is not directly relevant to the point that they are making at the time. Recorded lectures offer no scope for asking questions at the time so you will need to make a note of your question and find the answer after you have finished watching the recording.

There are a number of different options for finding the answer if it is not possible to ask a question during the lecture and, of course, you may prefer these anyway as many students do not feel comfortable interrupting the lecturer and asking a question in front of a large group of other students. Instead, you could email the lecturer after the class has finished or talk to them in person at the end of the lecture (some lecturers really like it when students stop to chat). You might want to make a note of the question and ask it in the tutorial or seminar instead. You could try to find the answer for yourself as part of your post-lecture study as this is a good way to become a more self-sufficient learner but be sure to check with the lecturer if you are still not sure that you have the right answer.

Do whatever feels most comfortable to you as long as you do something—gaps in your knowledge need to be filled so make sure you find the answer to your question, one way or another.

10.2.4 Getting the most out of lectures

Before we move on to look at other types of learning activities, Table 10.2 provides a summary of some of the key points to ensure that you get the most value from your lectures:

Table 10.2 Tips for getting value from lectures

Do	Don't
Listen and think about what the lecturer is saying. It is more important to understand what is said than it is to capture every word in note form.	Write everything that is said without thought. Try to be selective and note only key points. This will make your notes more manageable.
Make use of recordings of lectures to create complete notes by pausing and rewinding to ensure you capture key information.	Assume that because a recording exists, you will not need to make notes. It will be time-consuming to watch it again so make notes in the same way that you would if it were a live lecture.
Review your notes after the lecture. Make a note of anything that you do not understand and follow up any points that are not clear to you by using a good textbook and supplement your notes with independent reading.	Rely on the lecture to give you all the information that you need about a subject. A lecture gives you a framework of information and you should supplement this with your own reading to build a more complete picture of the subject.
Reflect on your approach to note-taking to see if you can become more efficient at recording information. You will find some more tips on note-taking in section 10.5.	Spend hours after the lecture rewriting the same notes to make them tidier. Many students waste a lot of time doing this. Notes need to be useful not tidy!
Ensure that you find answers to any questions raised by the lecture whether that is by asking a question at the time or some other method.	Arrive late, leave early, or talk to other students during the lecture. These things are very disruptive for the lecturer and other students.

10.3 SEMINARS AND TUTORIALS

Seminars and tutorials are both terms used to describe small-group teaching sessions. These may take place in person or online using video-conferencing systems. They are opportunities for students to explore some issues related to a topic in more detail and they usually require students to complete a task in advance that will be discussed during the session. This may involve answering a series of set questions, reading a case or article, writing an answer to a problem question, or preparing a short presentation to give to other students. Whatever the task that has been set, make sure you do it otherwise you will not get the most benefit from the session. Likewise, seminars and tutorials focus on group discussion so you should be prepared to join in with whatever activities are happening during the session. In essence, preparation and participation are the key to ensuring you gain the most value from small-group teaching sessions.

10.3.1 Preparation

Preparation for a seminar or tutorial is essential. The whole session revolves around the tasks that have been set so it stands to reason that you will get very little out of it if you have not completed the required preparation. This can be daunting, particularly at the early stages of your studies, because you may not feel that you have been able to complete the task that you have been set very well—perhaps you could not find all the answers to the question or you did not understand the case you were asked to read. Try not to let that bother you. The whole point of the tutorial is to give you an opportunity to see what you have learned and to help to develop your understanding further. Trying to answer the questions and finding out which ones were right and which ones were wrong will therefore help you to learn so much more effectively than by going along with a blank sheet of paper and waiting to be told the answers.

One technique that some students have found especially useful is to divide their paper into two columns, writing their answer on the left-hand side in advance of the tutorial. As the questions are explored in the tutorial, you can either put a tick in the right-hand column against parts of the answer that you got right or makes notes next to the points where you were not correct. By using this technique, you will have tackled everything and you will be able to see at a glance which points you had answered correctly. It can be very encouraging to see a line of ticks against points that you felt may have been wrong.

Your tutorial preparation should also help you to identify aspects of the topic that you find difficult. Make sure you make a note of these things so that you can use the tutorial to find answers. That does not mean that you have to ask all your questions during the session—it is likely that some of the answers will emerge naturally as the session progresses or other students ask questions. Nevertheless, it is really important that you use the tutorial to get answers to the questions that you have as well as preparing answers to the questions that you were asked because the tutorial is your main opportunity to clarify things that you have not understood. It can also be good to have some questions to ask because this will help you to get used to speaking out in these small-group sessions.

10.3.2 Participation

Tutorials and seminars are centred around student participation. The objective of small-group teaching is for students to explore and deepen their understanding of the law and this can only really happen if you are prepared to join in and contribute to the discussion. It is quite usual for students to feel nervous about speaking out in tutorial discussion, especially in the early stages of their studies, and this can lead to a reluctance to make a contribution. The main reasons for this tend to relate to lack of confidence: either a general lack of confidence about speaking in front of others or a lack of confidence in the accuracy of their legal knowledge (see Table 10.3).

Table 10.3 Common fears concerning participation in seminars

I'm not confident that I know the right answer	Some people find that starting your answer by saying 'I'm not sure about this but I thought . . .' takes some of the awkwardness out of getting the wrong answer. It's also likely that there are other people in the group who thought the same as you. At least once the wrong answer is out of the way, you will be closer to finding out what the right answer is. Also, the tutor will give you some feedback on why your answer was wrong so it will help you to learn.
I don't understand the question so how can I give an answer?	You can't answer a question if you don't understand what it is asking but you can (and should) tell the lecturer that you don't understand the question so that he can explain it to you in a different way. Once you do understand the question, you may realize that you know the answer after all.
I don't like speaking out in front of others in the group	This is generally linked to a fear of giving the wrong answer but it can be a more general anxiety about speaking in front of others. Why not set yourself a challenge to speak out once in every tutorial and see if it gets easier as your confidence builds. You might find that it is easier to ask a question rather than to volunteer an answer or to add something to another student's answer. You could also tell the tutor before the tutorial that answering questions is a problem for you and discuss how they can bring you into the discussion without you feeling 'put on the spot'.
I've got a question but I don't want to ask it in case I look stupid	If you don't ask your question, you will never know the answer. In any case, it is extremely likely that other students in the group are stuck on exactly the same point but won't ask for exactly the same reason. Try to be supportive; if someone else asks a question, say 'yes, I was wondering that too' and even that will help you to feel that you've played an active part in the tutorial.
There are some really talkative people in my group and I'm not sure how to involve myself in the discussion	It can be a problem if a couple of confident students make a great deal of voluntary contribution to discussion which causes less confident students to feel as if they cannot chip in too. Try not to let that stop you making a comment or asking/answering a question because it is your tutorial too and you need to make sure that it serves its purpose of strengthening your grasp of the topic. It can be useful to wait for a gap in the discussion to interject or to raise your hand slightly and make eye contact with your lecturer, who will then spot this and draw you into the discussion. If you feel that it is a major problem, raise this with your tutor, in person or by email, so that they are aware that you want to speak but are a little shy; once they are aware of this, they will be able to ensure that you have a chance to contribute.

These concerns are perfectly natural—many people are reluctant to put themselves in a position where they might get something wrong in front of other people. Try to find your voice in tutorials though. By answering questions and making a contribution to the discussion, you will be able to learn more from the session. Also, and just as important, it can be a valuable step towards helping you to develop those all-important verbal communication skills that are valued by potential employers.

It has been interesting to find that many students have reported that they feel more confident contributing to discussions in online seminars and tutorials (see chapter 1).

There seems to be two main reasons for this. Firstly, there is a sense that the ground rules for participation are clearer because lecturers often set them out at the beginning of an online session in a way that rarely happens at the start of an in-person teaching session. Secondly, many students have said that they feel less self-conscious because they are sitting in their own room with their computer rather than in a teaching room surrounded by other students who can see them. This combination of knowing the ground rules and feeling less visible online seems to have helped many students to find their voice to ask and answer questions in online tutorials.

Practical exercise

Think about your feelings about participation in tutorial discussion. Do you take part enough (or at all)? Can you pinpoint what it is that is making you reluctant to speak? Are you more likely to answer questions in some tutorials than others and, if so, what is it that makes a difference for you: is it the lecturer, the subject, your confidence in your understanding of the subject, the other students in the group, or even the layout of the room? Reflect upon these questions and try to identify three things that would make you feel able to make more contribution to tutorial discussion. You could discuss these with your personal tutor if you think it would help you to build your confidence to participate.

Overall, the message with small-group teaching sessions is that you will learn so much more from them if you prepare thoroughly and try to join in with the discussion. Try not to worry if you find speaking out in front of the group a bit daunting. Hopefully your confidence will grow as you become more comfortable in the group and tutorials often involve activities undertaken in pairs and small groups where you would be able to join in without speaking in front of the whole group. Remember though, it is your tutorial and is being run to help you to learn so try to make the most of it by taking part as much as possible.

10.3.3 Getting the most out of seminars and tutorials

Tutorials and seminars provide a really important learning opportunity for students as they are the place that your understanding of the law gets challenged and your ability to use the law is explored. Here is a summary of some key ways in which you can get the most value out of your small-group teaching sessions:

- Find out what preparation is needed and give yourself plenty of time to complete the tasks thoroughly.

- Answer all the questions even the ones where you are not confident about the answer. Getting things wrong and receiving feedback is one of the best ways to learn.

- Make sure you take all the things that you need with you. This should include the questions you have been set, your answers to them, the textbook, and copies of any materials that you were asked to read.

- Try to participate in all the activities as much as possible, whether that involves working on a task with other students or answering questions posed by the tutor.

- If you lack confidence at speaking in front of others, tutorials are a real opportunity for you to try to improve your verbal communication skills. Ask the tutor for support with this if it is a struggle for you.

- Remember that this is a group activity and that you are learning group-working skills. These include listening to other people and encouraging other group members as well as speaking out yourself. Try to notice students in your group who do not seem confident and try to support them—just saying 'that's what I thought too' when they answer a question will make them feel so much better if they get the answer wrong.

- Do not be discouraged if the tutor appears to disagree with your contribution to discussion— tutors will often play devil's advocate to encourage you to develop your ability to defend your argument or to open up the debate.

- Remember that these small-group sessions are an opportunity to engage in discussion with the tutor and other students to help you to deepen your understanding of the law. As such, you should go along expecting to speak and listen rather than to write notes. Of course, there will be points that you want to note during the discussion but try not to scribble all the time at the cost of joining in with the discussion.

10.4 PRIVATE STUDY

A significant proportion of your time as a student should be spent in private study; that is, time away from the classroom where you are working to strengthen and expand your understanding of the law. This is largely unstructured time as you will have to make decisions for yourself about what you do, how much you do, and how and when you do it. For some students, this level of freedom can be confusing and the question 'what am I supposed to be doing?' is a common one. This section of the chapter will help you to answer this question and give you some guidance on how to develop effective study habits that will enable you to work productively in your private study time.

10.4.1 What should I be doing?

This is not an easy question for anyone else to answer for you but it is possible to identify a series of considerations that will help you to answer the question for yourself. The objective of private study is to give you a firm foundation of understanding of the law that you are studying and to prepare you to perform effectively in tutorials and assessments. One way to work out what you need to do is to think about the tasks that you have in each module:

- Supplement your lecture notes with your own reading, starting by reading the relevant chapter in the set textbook or any other reading that your lecturer has indicated.

- Assess how well you have understood the week's topic and fill in any gaps in your knowledge.

- Prepare for the tutorial by reading the suggested materials and completing any tasks that have been set for you.

- Keep an eye on any formative or summative assessments that are coming up and start to read up on the subject matter.

Do not fall into the trap of assuming that you do not need to do anything other than attend lectures and prepare for tutorials just because nobody has told you what to do. Not all lecturers will specify what reading you should do simply because they believe that this will vary enormously between different students and that allowing you to make your own choice is the best way to encourage you to develop into independent learners. If you find it difficult to work out what reading you should be doing in your private study time then you should ask the lecturer responsible for each of your modules for some guidance or talk to your personal tutor who will help you to create a study plan.

10.4.2 Building good study habits

Think for a moment about how you like to study, reflecting on the following questions:

- Do you like to make an early start or do you find that you work better in the afternoon?

- Do you have a regular place to study with all your things around you or do you prefer to vary your work environment, perhaps switching between your room, the library, and a coffee shop with your laptop?

- Do you work for long periods of time or do you find that you need regular breaks or you lose concentration?

- Do you like to read up on a topic straight after the lecture or do you like to take a break to digest the subject matter before doing your follow-up reading?

- Do you create a study timetable that gives you a set pattern of working that is built around your lecture and tutorial commitments or do you work on whatever you feel like doing at the time?

There are no right answers to these questions; it is all a matter of personal preference. We all have our own ways of working so if you have a system that works for you then it does not matter if it is different to your friends or flies in the face of conventional study advice.

As with everything you do as part of your degree, it is important to reflect upon your private study habits periodically to determine if you could improve your working practices. For example, if you are doing three hours of private study a day but are not managing to get your tutorial preparation done and feel that you are falling behind with your studies then you need to make a change, either to work more hours or to work more efficiently in the time that you have set aside for private study. Time management and the ability to organize a pattern of work to ensure that you meet all your goals are important skills that you will need in the workplace as well as during your studies. These skills are even more important whilst more teaching is being provided remotely as it offers a sense of structure to your day and purpose to your study. There is a more detailed discussion of the demands of remote learning in chapter 1.

If you do feel that you need to make a change to improve your study habits, here are suggestions of things that some students find useful:

- **Create a daily study routine** broken down into periods of study interspersed by breaks. Be clear about what you want to achieve in each period of time, writing it down as a visual reminder of the task at hand. This way, you are working with a purpose and to a set time frame. If you do not achieve that task in the set period of time, try to identify what stopped you from doing so. If the task is too big for the time available then you need to set yourself more realistic goals otherwise you will soon become demotivated. However, if something interrupted your study time then think about removing distractions from your work environment.

- **Create a weekly study plan** that takes into account your lectures and tutorials as well as private study time and periods for other non-study activities. A weekly plan is preferable to a term-long study timetable because you can adjust it each week as you learn how long it takes you to do things. You can also adapt it to accommodate things that do not occur every week like formative assessments or to take account of periods of illness where you cannot work as much as usual.

- **Establish a study zone** with space for all the things that you need to do your work: laptop, paper and pens, books, and so on. Make sure the room is well lit and that it is not too hot or cold. Try and make it free of distractions (how many times do you check your phone when you're studying?) and do not be afraid to ask people not to disturb you when you are studying. You might like some water and snacks to hand and perhaps some background music playing but try not to make it anything that will break your concentration.

- **Build variety into the tasks** that you set yourself as you will quickly become bored if all you do is sit for hours on end copying chunks out of a textbook. Try to find ways to keep your mind engaged with what you are doing. This could involve switching between different modules, interspersing note-taking with writing answers to tutorial questions, creating a case bank, drawing concept maps, or researching the law online.

- **Create a study group** with some friends so that you can share the workload and learn from each other. Never underestimate how much you will learn from talking to other people about the law or how helpful you will find it to be able to puzzle things out together. You will find a discussion about the benefits of working with others later in this chapter (section 10.7.4).

10.5 TAKING NOTES

Reading and taking notes is a significant part of studying the law. We have discussed the importance of taking notes in lectures, consolidating them after lectures, and making notes to prepare for tutorials and as part of your private study. You will also want to make revision notes. This part of the study skills chapter looks at different techniques for effective note-taking as well as the importance of establishing a clear system for organizing your notes. Before we look at these issues, however, we will address a question that is the key to effective note-taking: why are you taking notes?

10.5.1 Why are you taking notes?

The most important point to remember about note-taking is that you should consider before you write a single word what it is that you are trying to achieve: what is your goal in taking notes? It may sound as if the answer is obvious—'to record the important pieces of information in this lecture, book, article, or case'—but so many students say that they find themselves unthinkingly copying large chunks of material out of books without any real thought of why they are doing it. If you give yourself a specific goal then you will be taking notes with a purpose and this should mean that you are able to work more quickly and effectively.

Consider the difference between reading a chapter of a textbook to supplement your lecture notes and reading the same chapter to find answers to a tutorial question. In both instances, you will want to read the entire chapter but the information that you record in your notes should differ: your notes on the topic will be more extensive than the selective approach that you would take to record specific points that are relevant to your answer to the tutorial questions. This latter approach is an example of focused note-taking as you are reading the whole chapter but with the purpose of extracting specific information that is relevant to you.

Focused note-taking can work particularly well when you are reading articles and cases as these sources often have a lot of information that is not directly relevant to you. Despite this, many students say that their notes on cases and articles tend to be a slightly shorter version of the original. This suggests that they may be writing too much detail in their notes, much of which is not relevant to them.

To understand this point better, imagine that three students are reading the same case but for different reasons—one has a general interest in the case as it is a new development in the law, the second is looking for arguments to use in an essay, and the third student wants to know how the case changed the law in order to answer a tutorial question. The three students each have a different purpose in reading the case so you would expect their notes to be different. If you are clear, therefore, about what you want from the material that you are reading, you should find it easier to make focused notes that are more useful to you.

Practical exercise

Have a look at the article about criminal liability for injuries caused during sports that you will find at www.oup.com/he/finch8e/.

Read through it and make notes imagining that you have one of the following aims in reading the article:

1. To identify key cases for an essay about criminal liability for injuries sustained in the course of sports.

2. To find out the author's views about the relationship between criminal and civil law in relation to sporting injuries for your dissertation.

3. To prepare for a seminar question that asks 'Professor Davies was playing in a staff-against-students football game. James, a final year student, was mocking Professor Davies' performance, calling out "come on grandpa, try and get the ball". Professor Davies tries to tackle James but by the time he made contact the ball had been passed to another player. James fell awkwardly and broke his leg. Professor Davies wants to know whether he may be criminally liable for causing the injury to James'.

Once you have prepared your notes, have a look at the commentary at www.oup.com/he/finch8e/.

10.5.2 Linear notes

Many law students take linear notes. This is the traditional approach to note-taking using blocks of text, often separated by bullet points or headings with key points underlined or highlighted. It is a useful form of note-taking for a word-focused subject like law but, as we have already said, try to avoid an approach in which you capture every word from a lecture or written source or you will create a dense set of notes that are not very useful to you. Have a look at the two examples of note-taking in Figure 10.1 and Figure 10.2. They are notes of the same evidence lecture which discussed s 80 of the Police and Criminal Evidence Act 1984 (PACE) and both use a linear approach to note-taking, but they are very different.

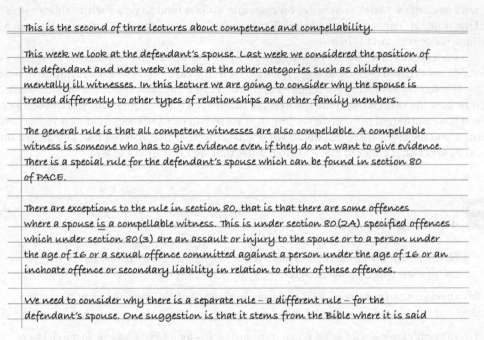

This is the second of three lectures about competence and compellability.

This week we look at the defendant's spouse. Last week we considered the position of the defendant and next week we look at the other categories such as children and mentally ill witnesses. In this lecture we are going to consider why the spouse is treated differently to other types of relationships and other family members.

The general rule is that all competent witnesses are also compellable. A compellable witness is someone who has to give evidence even if they do not want to give evidence. There is a special rule for the defendant's spouse which can be found in section 80 of PACE.

There are exceptions to the rule in section 80, that is that there are some offences where a spouse is a compellable witness. This is under section 80(2A) specified offences which under section 80(3) are an assault or injury to the spouse or to a person under the age of 16 or a sexual offence committed against a person under the age of 16 or an inchoate offence or secondary liability in relation to either of these offences.

We need to consider why there is a separate rule – a different rule – for the defendant's spouse. One suggestion is that it stems from the Bible where it is said

Figure 10.1 Evidence lecture notes

Can you see that the first set of notes contains far more words but that both contain largely the same information? Which set do you find easier to use? Looking at both sets of notes, try and find the exceptions to s 80. It is likely that you found the information more quickly in the second set of notes because the information was not hidden in amongst a mass of words. It is not just the spacing of words that makes the second example a better set of notes: have a look for some of these features and think about how you can use them to improve your approach to note-taking.

- **Labelling.** The second set of notes is dated and labelled with the number of the lecture. The title of the lecture is included and the pages are numbered. It only takes seconds to incorporate these features into your notes and they are valuable ways to ensure that your notes are well organized so that you are not confused by them at a later date.

- **Spacing**. There are plenty of gaps on the page where additional information could be added after the lecture. For example, some information was missed in the lecture about which statute amended s 80 of PACE. After the lecture, this information can be found and added to the notes. Well-spaced notes are also easier to navigate so that information can be located easily.

- **Abbreviations and symbols.** It is sensible to use abbreviations in your notes: think how much time is saved by writing 'D' rather than 'the defendant'. The second set of notes uses 'SP' for 'spouse', 's' for 'section', and 'H/W' for 'husband and wife'. Work out a system of abbreviations to use in your notes, making sure that you can remember what each abbreviation means and never use the same letter or symbol to mean more than one thing. Can you imagine the confusion caused by a student who used the letter 'T' to stand for trust, trustee, and testator in a single set of notes? You can use symbols as well as letters: see how the second set of notes uses an outline of a key to symbolize an important (key) case.

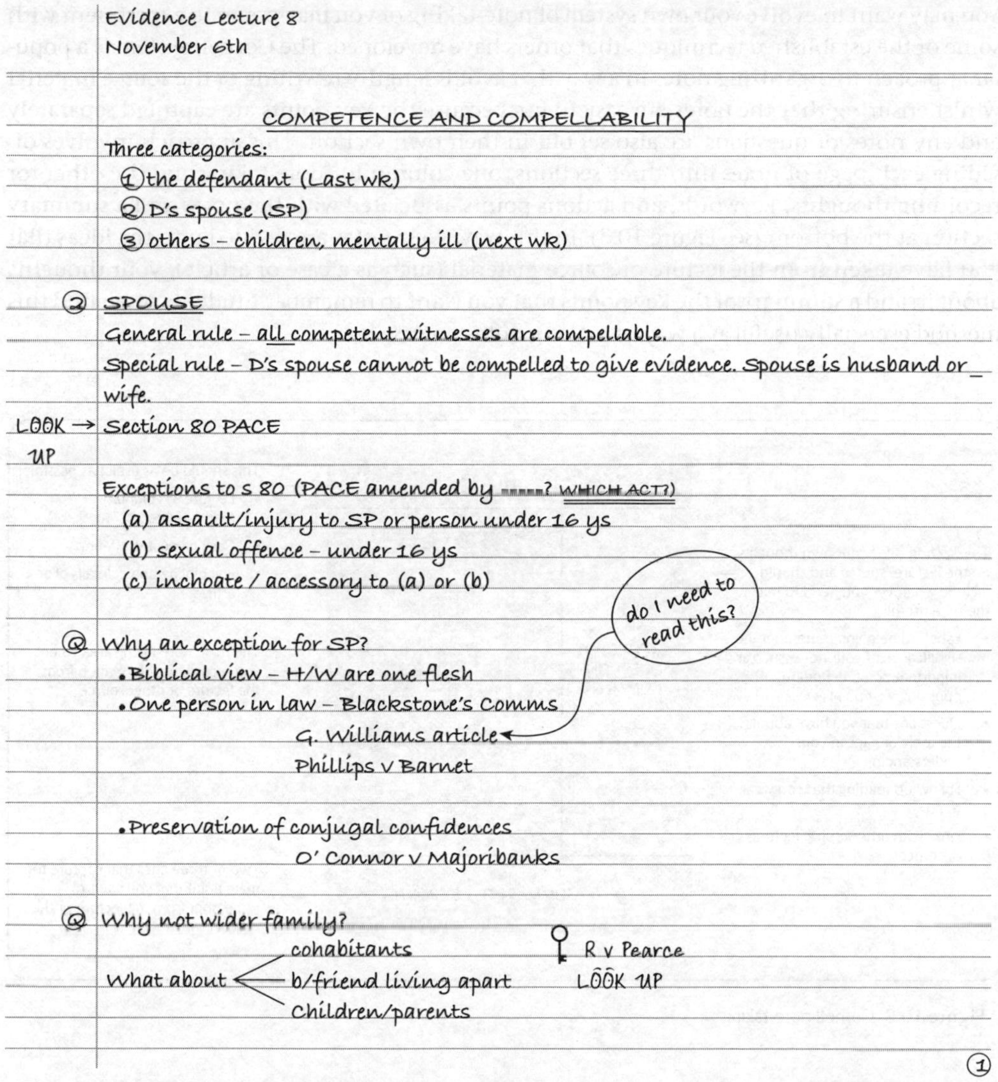

Evidence Lecture 8
November 6th

COMPETENCE AND COMPELLABILITY

Three categories:
   ① the defendant (Last wk)
   ② D's spouse (SP)
   ③ others – children, mentally ill (next wk)

② SPOUSE

General rule – <u>all</u> competent witnesses are compellable.

Special rule – D's spouse cannot be compelled to give evidence. Spouse is husband or wife.

LOOK → Section 80 PACE
UP

Exceptions to s 80 (PACE amended by _____? WHICH ACT?)
   (a) assault/injury to SP or person under 16 ys
   (b) sexual offence – under 16 ys
   (c) inchoate / accessory to (a) or (b)

@ Why an exception for SP?
   • Biblical view – H/W are one flesh
   • One person in law – Blackstone's Comms
               G. Williams article ←
               Phillips v Barnet

   • Preservation of conjugal confidences
               O' Connor v Majoribanks

@ Why not wider family?
                  cohabitants   ⚲ R v Pearce
   What about ← b/friend living apart   LOOK UP
                  children/parents

do I need to read this?

①

Figure 10.2 Alternative evidence lecture notes

- **Annotation.** It can be a good idea to add notes to remind yourself of points that occurred to you when you were writing your notes. This might be a reminder to look up the wording of a statutory provision or to read a case that seemed to be particularly important. You might want to highlight any points that you did not understand so that you can remember to pay particular attention to these when reading your textbook to supplement your lecture notes. Questions might occur to you that you want to remember to follow up in seminars or you might notice points that seem particularly relevant to coursework. Equally, the lecturer might say something like 'this is just the sort of issue that might come up in the exam' in which case this is certainly something that you would want to remember. Some students use colour coding rather than annotation which can also be effective but make sure that you can remember what each colour represents as it would be unfortunate if you were reading your notes after the lecture and could not remember whether purple highlighting meant 'important point for coursework essay' or 'don't understand this point'.

You may want to evolve your own system of note-taking or you may prefer to experiment with some of the established techniques that others have developed. The Cornell system is a popular approach to organizing notes in a way that avoids lengthy rewriting of the source material whilst ensuring that the notes are easy to use because the key points are captured separately and any notes or questions are also set out in their own section. This approach involves dividing each page of notes into three sections, one column for note-taking and the other for recording thoughts, keywords, and actions points associated with the notes and a summary section at the bottom (see Figure 10.3). In this way, your notes are divided into the ideas that you have taken from the lecture or source material (such as a case or article), your thoughts about it, and a summary of the key points that you want to remember. Students often find this method especially useful as a way of making notes on case law.

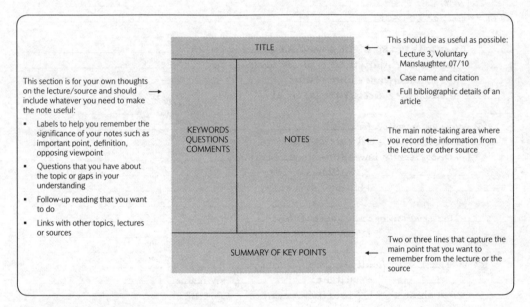

Figure 10.3 Cornell note-taking

10.5.3 Alternatives to linear notes

There are alternatives to linear notes that you could consider. Flow diagrams are a way of organizing information so that it is easy to see at a glance how the points relate to each other. You will see an example in Figure 10.4 that shows the elements of an offence. Flow diagrams tend to be easier to produce when you have all the information in front of you so it is probably not a method you could use effectively for taking notes in a lecture but, of course, you could produce a flow chart from your lecture notes as part of the review process.

Mind maps (also called concept maps or spider diagrams) are another way of recording the relationships between concepts and ideas but in a way that is more personal and less rigid than flow diagrams. What this means is that if ten students created a flow chart of an offence, you would expect them to all look the same but you would see a lot of differences if they each created a mind map because it will be based upon the way that each of them conceptualizes the subject matter and the links between the different concepts. This is because a mind map reflects the way that its creator's mind works and how it makes associations between different

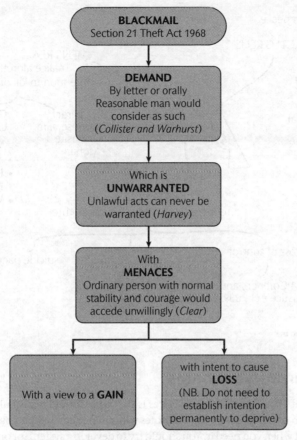

Figure 10.4 Flow diagram

pieces of information stored in your memory. Students who try mind-mapping often find them to be an excellent revision tool (see chapter 16) because they can visualize the shape of their mind map and that helps them to recall the information recorded on it. They are also a great tool to brainstorm ideas for an essay and to show the relationships between them which will help you to plan a structure (see chapter 14).

There is software available that will help you to produce mind maps but it is very simple to do using a pen and paper. Simply draw a shape in the centre of a piece of paper and write the name of the topic in it. Many students use a rectangle or circle as their central shape but some students like to use shapes that reflect the nature of the topic: in the example in Figure 10.5, you will see that a gun has been used as the topic is murder. As each major theme emerges, draw a line that runs from the central shape and write the name of the theme at the end of the line. Repeat this for other major themes: in Figure 10.5, you will see that the three 'big' ideas are *actus reus*, *mens rea*, and defences. More lines run from these ideas to create links to particular aspects of this idea: for example, defences divides into three topics: loss of control, diminished responsibility, and suicide pacts. If any of these topics have their own separate mind map, a box has been drawn around them to indicate this as you will see in relation to causation and oblique intention. You can use images, symbols, or colours to help points to stand out and stick in your mind. For example, you will see simple drawings accompany the case names listed under oblique intention.

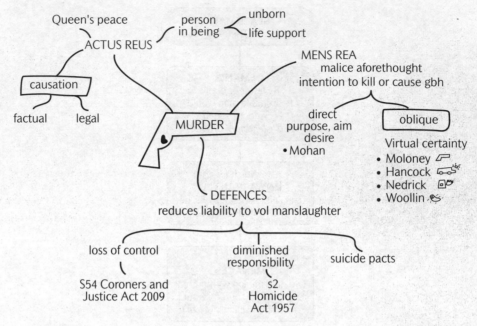

Figure 10.5 Mind map

10.5.4 Organizing your notes

The most important characteristic of your notes is that they should be useful. However, you can have the best system of note-taking but your notes will still not be useful if you cannot find the information you want when you need it. You should try to develop a system for organizing your notes that will ensure that you are not left with random files on your computer or an ever-increasing pile of papers in which everything is 'in there somewhere'. This will make your life much easier when you want to find information in them, especially at revision time when you have too much to do to spend hours trying to create order in the chaos of a semester's worth of random notes.

An obvious system of organization is to break your notes down by module then by topic and then to separate this into lecture notes, seminar notes, and notes from your private study. That is not the only method so experiment a little and see what system seems logical to you. Whatever system you decide, try and stick to it as consistency is the secret of good organization.

If you make your notes on a laptop or tablet, you can always search by keyword if you are looking for a set of notes on a particular topic but this is not possible with handwritten notes so it is useful to create an index instead to help you to navigate your way through the many pages that you will generate in the course of your studies. Numbering pages is also a good idea: not only will this be invaluable if you knock a big pile of written notes off the desk, it will also enable you to create a way of finding the information that you need if you are making a plan of where to find information in your notes when it comes to assessment (see section 10.7).

10.6 STUDY GROUPS

Working with other students can be an excellent way to add variety and interest to your private study. It also offers a great deal of value in terms of skills development because working in a group will give you an insight into other people's study habits and practices as well as offering you an opportunity to deepen your understanding of the law by discussing it with others. It is often the case that we do not realize how much (or little!) we have understood a concept until we try to explain it to someone else. It is also inevitable that other people in the group will have different opinions on some of the law to you and you will build your legal reasoning skills by defending your views and explaining your reasoning.

You may also find that working in a study group helps you to work more effectively. You can divide tasks up between you, perhaps agreeing that everyone will read one case and report back to the group on it, which will reduce your workload and you may work more effectively with the deadline of the next group meeting looming. You could also agree that you will all complete the same task such as reading an especially tricky case and then compare notes of what you have understood from it. Shared knowledge is never a bad thing and the ability to work effectively with other people is a really important transferable skill.

Just as some of your teaching may take place online using video-conferencing packages, there is no reason why study groups cannot make the shift online too: in fact, it is a good way to make sure you get the opportunity to share your ideas and understanding of the law with other students if there are currently fewer or no ways for you to do this in person.

Another benefit of group working is that it is reassuring to know that other people get stuck sometimes; otherwise you can become anxious that you are the only person who is struggling to understand all the law that you study. Of course, you will also have the opportunity to get help from the other group members with areas of law that you are struggling to understand or you can try, as a group, to puzzle out a particular area of law that you are all finding difficult. Collectively you may be able to find a solution that none of you would have discovered as individuals. It is also the case that many people find it hard to ask lecturers for help as they do not like to stand out as a person who has not understood something whereas you may feel less exposed if you ask for help for your study group.

As you can see, there are many benefits to forming a study group and it can be a really enjoyable way to study as well as improving your group work skills. However, there is a risk that study groups can lose focus and become unproductive so it is always worth trying to ensure that each meeting has a purpose.

You will find further discussion of group working in the next section on assessment where we look at the challenges involved with group assessment especially when you have no choice over group composition.

10.7 ASSESSMENT

There is a detailed discussion of essay writing and problem solving in chapters 14 and 15. The purpose of this section is not to replicate that discussion but to look at some of the core study skills that will help you perform to your best in your assessments so the focus is on planning and avoiding procrastination. This section will also discuss the benefits and pitfalls of working in a group for assessments purposes.

10.7.1 Planning

Planning is important to ensure that all your work gets completed before the deadline so that you can submit it on time knowing that you have had time to do your very best work. That last-minute rush to meet the submission deadline is stressful and unpleasant and can leave you with a sense that you would have done a much better piece of work if only you had a little more time.

It goes without saying that the earlier you start your coursework, the more time you will have to complete it. You should put your assessment dates in your calendar as soon as you have them and start to build time into your weekly study plan to work steadily towards these deadlines. How long will it take you to complete your essay on public law or a problem question on contract? Try to answer this question in the number of hours rather than in elapsed time, that is, 'it will take me fifteen hours' rather than 'it will take me a week'.

By specifying a number of hours, you can work backwards from the submission deadline and create a plan that will help you to work steadily towards your goal. It is fine to make guesses about how long it will take you to complete a piece of work—after all, you will not know at first how long it will take you to complete your assessment. It will help you, however, to make an estimate for planning purposes and then you can check afterwards whether or not you were correct—you may have budgeted fifteen hours and actually only needed ten. By measuring the time that the work took you against your prediction of how long you thought it would take, you will be able to make a more accurate estimate next time.

 Practical exercise

You might find it interesting to see how long it does take you to do the various things that you need to do as part of writing an assignment: how long do you think it will take you to do the following things?

- Complete a search for secondary literature on your essay topic
- Read one article and make notes on it
- Create a footnote for a case reference that includes a pinpoint reference
- Proofread the first draft of your essay

The next time you complete each of these activities, set a timer and find out how much time they actually take. Were you quicker or slower than your estimate?

Or turn this around and see how much work you get done in a particular period of time. Set a timer for one hour and make a list at the end of that time of how much work you got done and how much time you spent on each activity.

By understanding how much time it takes you to work, you can improve your planning by making more realistic plans that give you enough time to do all that you need to do for each assignment.

It will also be important to build time for thinking into your study plans. Producing a good piece of coursework takes a lot of thought so be sure that you leave yourself enough time to read source material and think about what it means and how you will use it in your work. You should always plan to give yourself plenty of breaks. You will work much more effectively if you break your study time into chunks and give your brain time to relax. Finally, try to trick yourself into finishing before the deadline by planning your time so that your work is complete at least twenty-four hours before it is due to be submitted. This will give you a little bit of breathing space if your work takes you longer than you expected and make sure that you have time to proofread your work thoroughly before submission. It will also give you some flexibility to deal with unforeseen last-minute catastrophes like computer problems.

10.7.2 Procrastination

Research indicates that up to 40 per cent of university students view procrastination (constantly putting work off until later) as a problem[1] so if you procrastinate then you are not alone. It is hardly surprising that students procrastinate as you are expected to meet deadlines for coursework and exams in an environment that is full of other events and activities that are competing for your attention, most of which will be far more enjoyable and less stressful than getting on with your work.

Procrastination is a natural response to stressful activities and students often spend more time on tasks that they feel are manageable than those where they think that they will struggle. It is for this reason that some students keep on researching and finding material to put in their essay rather than making a start on writing it. The problem with this is that the difficult task does not go away, you just end up with less time to do it which actually makes it even more stressful as, of course, you end up with insufficient time.

Practical exercise

Sometimes people deal with feelings of being overwhelmed by the amount of work that they have to do by making a 'to-do' list. This can be helpful in identifying everything that needs to be done but it can be your enemy if you are prone to procrastination because it gives you options of different things to do. This means you can feel as if you are working productively by doing things on your 'to-do' list while avoiding the core task that needs to be done. In other words, a 'to-do' list can actually encourage procrastination.

As an alternative to a 'to-do' list, try making a 'one item' list. This involves writing your 'to-do' list on a piece of paper and then taking one item from it—the most urgent or most daunting task—and writing this on a separate blank piece of paper and then working on it until it is done. This will help you to focus on the task at hand without offering you the distraction of easier or more enjoyable items on your 'to-do' list.

Even if you do have a one-task list, it can still be difficult to start working. Try to identify what it is that is making it difficult for you. It is often a fear that you will not be able to do the task or the sense that it is too hard for you that is the barrier to getting the task done. It can be really frustrating to be desperate to write a good essay but feel that you do not know how to do it and to see time ticking away as the deadline draws ever closer.

- **Break the task down into the smallest possible chunks.** What things do you need to do to write your essay? Make a list of things that you can do in ten minutes: read one page of a textbook, make a list of cases that you want to read later, search on Westlaw Edge UK for those cases and print them out, write a description of a key concept that you want to include in your essay, update your bibliography. It does not matter what it is as long as it (a) takes you a step further along with your essay and (b) is a short and self-contained task.

- **Do one of those tasks.** It does not matter which one—pick whatever seems most appealing and set a timer so that you only spend ten minutes on it. At the end of that time, give yourself

1. WK O'Brien, 'Applying the Transtheoretical Model to Academic Procrastination' (2002) 62(11-B) Dissertation Abstracts International, Section B: The Sciences and Engineering 5359.

a reward. It can be anything you like but make sure you have it—a cup of tea and a biscuit, a twenty-minute run, an episode of your favourite show, ten minutes listening to music.

- **Repeat the process again and again.** Keep breaking your work down into the smallest possible tasks and giving yourself a reward each time you have completed one. Hopefully you will get to a point where you think 'I don't need to stop now, this is going fine so I'm going to keep working on it'. There you have it—you've stopped procrastinating. Do not think, however, that you have stopped forever—you are bound to start again but now you have a technique for breaking the deadlock.

One final thought before we move on—if you know that you procrastinate, be kind to yourself about it. People who procrastinate tend to be very self-critical and that creates a cycle of destructive thoughts that actually makes you more likely to procrastinate in the future because you are shaking your own confidence with negative thinking. Instead, tell yourself a different story (Table 10.4):

Table 10.4 Different thoughts about procrastination

Negative thoughts	Positive (and more accurate) alternative
I'm procrastinating because I can't do this essay. I'm not clever enough to do it.	I'm procrastinating because I care so much about my studies that I want to write an excellent essay.
I only did ten minutes work today. That's just not enough—I'll never get this essay done at this rate and I bet I get stuck again tomorrow.	I broke my procrastination habit today and managed to do ten minutes towards my essay. I'll build on that tomorrow now I know that I can.
I'm not going to get this essay done in time and I'm going to fail.	I've always met every coursework deadline so I know that I can beat procrastination.

10.7.3 Asking for help

Students are often strangely reluctant to ask for help. Perhaps there is a sense that you do not want to tell the lecturer that you cannot understand something or perhaps it is uncertainty about whether you should be asking for help, especially with coursework. However, if you are stuck on any aspect of your studies, including coursework, and it is upsetting you then there is no shame at all in asking for help. Your lecturers are there to help you and they want to help you but they cannot do that unless they know that you need help. You will need to take the first step and tell someone that you are struggling so that they can help you. If it feels more comfortable, you could approach your personal tutor rather than the lecturer responsible for the subject that you are finding difficult. Remember, though, that they will not think that you are asking for the answer: they will understand that you are asking for help to be able to find the answer for yourself. Those are two very different things.

10.7.4 Working with others

Sometimes you can break a tendency to procrastinate by working with other students. We discussed the benefits of having a study group earlier in this chapter and it is something that people can find particularly useful at assessment time. It is often the case that students can find it hard to get started on their coursework because they are not sure what the question means or they are not sure they understand the subject matter. Group work can help here.

A brainstorming session that analyses an essay title or unpicks the facts of a problem question can give you confidence to tackle the question and you might find that you are really motivated to make progress with your work if you have agreed with the other members of your group that you will complete a certain amount of work before your next meeting. Be sure that you do not take collaboration too far though; preliminary discussion is fine but you must produce your answer independently or there is a risk that you will be vulnerable to accusations of plagiarism.

You will find more detailed discussion of plagiarism in chapter 13.

You may also find that you have to work with other students on a group assessment, perhaps creating a report, giving a presentation, or taking part in a moot. Group assessments are increasingly common as universities seek to ensure that students have opportunities to develop group-working skills during their degree as these skills are highly valued by employers.

However, although this sort of activity is excellent in terms of skills development, it can create problems if the group does not work effectively together. The key issues that students report from group working are to do with conflict resolution when group members cannot agree on a direction for the assessment and issues to do with people who do not engage or pull their weight in the group. The latter is especially problematic if your work is going to be given a single mark—it seems unsatisfactory that students who do not contribute to a group project get a mark based on the rest of the group's hard work—and many institutions are moving towards individual marks for group projects for this very reason.

One way to resolve conflict within a group is to set out ground rules for working from the outset. At a first meeting, give everybody a chance to contribute their views about how the group should work and use this to draw up a set of rules. Here are some of the key issues that might need to be addressed:

- **Is someone going to be in charge of the group?** People have differing views about whether a group needs a leader and it can actually cause problems if group members simply refuse to do what the leader requests. An alternative approach can be to have a rotating group leader so that every group member is in charge for one meeting. Another way of approaching this is to give everyone responsibility for something: one person can deal with communications, another with arranging the date for the next meeting, someone else can take notes at the meetings and so on.

- **How will you resolve disputes?** Imagine you are working in a group of six and you cannot agree on the topic of your presentation. What will you do? It is usual to think at the beginning about what you will do to resolve disagreements so that you have a process to follow if a dispute arises. A simple agreement that the majority rules will suffice but it is better to agree this in advance so that nobody can quibble with it as a solution after an argument has happened.

- **What will you do if someone's work is substandard?** As a group, you are collectively responsible for the quality of the work that you produce so are you going to check each other's work or just leave it as a matter of trust that each person will produce a good contribution. Some groups agree that every task will be done twice by two different people to ensure that there is some check on quality.

- **What will you do if someone does not join in with the group?** This is a difficult issue as you cannot compel other students to work with you. This can be a particular problem if you are allocated to groups by the lecturer as you lose the sense of accountability that you have when you form a group with your friends. All that you can do is make repeated attempts to contact your missing group member, keeping a record of what you have done, and ask the lecturer responsible for the module to intervene.

10.8 IMPROVING PERFORMANCE

There are two aspects to your performance as a student: firstly, there are the marks that you get for your work and, secondly, there is how hard you have to work to get those marks. Most of us will always be striving to improve our performance—we will either want to achieve better results or, if we are happy with the results that we are achieving, we will want to use up less time and/or effort to get the same marks. This final section of the chapter focuses on different sources of guidance and support that you can use to try to improve your performance.

10.8.1 Learning from feedback

The first thing that most students do when they receive their marked coursework is to look at the mark, and about a third of students admit that they rarely read the feedback comments, especially if they are pleased with their mark. Does that sound like you? If so, you are missing a really valuable opportunity to improve your work in the future because feedback is there to identify strengths (on which you can build further) and weaknesses (which you can address). Even if you are pleased with your mark—perhaps it is the best mark that you have ever received—the feedback will be useful to you so that you can see what it was that you did that earned you that mark. Once you know this, you can make sure that you do it again next time.

If you receive a mark that is less good than you expected or hoped then you might feel frustrated, upset, or angry but try not to let these perfectly understandable emotions stop you engaging with the feedback that has been provided by the lecturer marking your work. Perhaps you will need to leave it a couple of hours or even a couple of days until you feel ready to read the feedback objectively but try to make sure that you do read it. After all, the best way to avoid another disappointing mark in the future is to ensure that you do not make the same mistakes again and you have no way of knowing what mistakes you made unless you read the feedback.

10.8.2 Finding support and guidance

It can be really difficult to understand why your work was given a particular mark, especially if you know that you worked hard but your mark is disappointing. However, it is crucial to your future marks that you understand why you got this one. Therefore, if you feel that you do not understand the feedback and you cannot, on reflection, recognize what the weakness was in your work, you should ask the lecturer who marked your work to help you understand their perspective on it. It is important that you approach a discussion with the marker in the spirit of wanting their help to understand what went wrong and how to put it right. This can be a challenge if your mark was disappointing as a natural defensiveness can creep in and make us reluctant to accept the validity of criticism. Do not waste time trying to convince your lecturer that the work was better than they considered it to be as they are not going to change their view or the mark that was awarded, so use the time productively to understand how to strengthen your next piece of work.

You may want to seek guidance from other sources. You could talk to your personal tutor about your work and they can help you to understand the feedback comments and signpost you to resources to help you to improve your writing skills or referencing skills if these things were a problem in your work. There is also likely to be a study support centre at your university, often located in the library, where students can make appointments with study-skills advisers who will review your work with you and discuss how it can be improved.

10.8.3 Evaluating your own work

When marked formative or summative work is returned to you, take time to reflect on your performance and to read your feedback carefully as this will help you to see the strengths and weaknesses in your work. You should do this after every piece of feedback, however good or bad the mark you received, because you may be able to spot themes in your work: perhaps you are always told that your essays are too descriptive or that you do not use the facts well when answering problem questions. Maybe you will see inconsistencies; you may have demonstrated a good approach to problem-solving in one piece of work but been told that your approach was not effective in a different piece of work. The solution then is to study both pieces of work to see if you can work out what you did differently. Try to be really dispassionate, perhaps trying to imagine that you are reading someone else's work rather than your own—this skill of self-evaluation is a really crucial one that will help you to learn from your mistakes and produce better work in the future.

10.8.4 Using the grade descriptors

You can also use the grade descriptors to help you to understand your mark and to identify areas where future work can be strengthened. As you will have read in chapter 1, every university has its own grade descriptors and they will be worded in slightly different ways but they all list the characteristics that the university expects to see from work that falls into a particular band of marks. So each band of marks is described using a list of attributes that work is expected to demonstrate and a series of adjectives to indicate the level of proficiency that the student has achieved in their work. In essence, then, the grade descriptors identify the characteristics of an essay or answer to a problem question and the mark that you receive for your work is a reflection of how well you have demonstrated these characteristics. As such, the grade descriptors can be incredibly useful to you in identifying ways to improve your work because they tell you what your markers are looking for in your work.

Not only do the grade descriptors give you an indication of the attributes that you need to demonstrate, they also describe those attributes using adjectives that give an indication of the level of proficiency that is expected in each classification. For example, as you will see in Figure 10.6, one of the attributes that determines how good an essay is will be the extent to which it answers the question and there are different adjectives to describe how well this needs to be done in order to fall into one of the four main bands of marks.

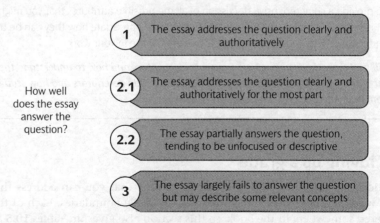

Figure 10.6 Extract from a set of grade descriptors

Once you understand the grade descriptors, you can use them as a checklist when you create your coursework to make sure that you are demonstrating each of the attributes. You can also use them to evaluate your work after it has been marked: understanding why one piece of work received the mark that it did is the first step towards ensuring that the next piece of work that you produce will be better as you can replicate the things that you did well and improve on the areas that were less good.

Practical exercise

Try this exercise to help you gain familiarity with the grade descriptors and to give you an insight into the strengths and weaknesses of your own work.

1. Find your university's grade descriptors. These may be generic or tailored to law.

2. Print a piece of your previous work to evaluate.

3. Create a table with two columns in a word document or using a pen and paper.

4. Write the first characteristic listed in the grade descriptors in the first column.

5. Read through your work looking for evidence that this characteristic has been demonstrated in your work.

6. Make a note of where this occurs in the second column and make an honest evaluation of how well you think that you have done it, looking at the adjectives used to describe the characteristic.

7. Repeat this for all of the characteristics listed in the grade descriptors.

8. Be sure to ask the person who marked your work for help with this if you are struggling to understand how to match what you have written with the grade descriptors.

It is well worth taking time to complete this exercise. The more familiar you are with the grade descriptors, the better you will be able to tailor the way that you write essays and answer problem questions to ensure that their characteristics are demonstrated. You will also find it easier to understand how to improve your work once you can see which of the characteristics you do well and which ones need a bit of polish. This will be particularly helpful if you are trying to move your marks up into the next classification.

If you find that you are struggling to translate the grade descriptors, make sure that you seek some help with this from your personal tutor or module leader because it really is essential that you understand them. Each university will have its own grade descriptors so it is beyond the scope of this book to provide a comprehensive discussion of all the possible attributes that you might find on them. What is important is that you know that they exist and appreciate how they can be used to help you understand what knowledge and skills to demonstrate in your work.

You will find more detailed discussion of grade descriptors and how to understand them in chapter 1 and you can see the authors talking about grade descriptors and how students can use them in a video at www.oup.com/he/finch8e/.

10.8.5 Moving up a grade

In this section, we will summarize some of the points that you can address that will improve your work and raise your standard across the grade boundaries. Each of these points will be covered somewhere in the book, so this section also gives (in Tables 10.5 and 10.6) a cross-reference to the section or sections where you can find out more. It might be helpful for you to find a copy of your course grade descriptors or assessment criteria to have to hand as you work through this part.

Table 10.5 Finding out more: 2.2 to 2.1

Issue	Where to look
Poor technical execution	Referencing—section 13.3
	Use of language—section 11.2
	Grammar and punctuation—section 11.3
	Paragraphs—section 11.4
	Using quotations—section 11.5
	Word limits—section 11.6
	Presentation—section 11.7
Too much description	Description versus analysis—section 14.4.5
Not answering the question	Focus on the question(s)—section 14.3.1
Insufficient research	Preparation: research and planning—section 14.3
Inclusion of irrelevant content	Organizing your research—section 14.3.6
	Relevance—section 14.3.5.2

Table 10.6 Finding out more: 2.1 to First

Issue	Where to look
Perfect referencing	Referencing—section 13.3
Sophisticated use of language	Use of language—section 11.2
Engagement with theory: essays	Legal reasoning—chapter 12
Wide-ranging research: essays	Preparation: research and planning—section 14.3
Finding a different angle: essays	Academic commentary—section 14.3.4.4
Clever use of facts: problems	Application and evaluation—section 15.5

10.8.6 Moving from a 2.2 to a 2.1

The most common characteristics of a lower second class piece of work are:

- **Poor technical execution.** Technical issues can make a difference to the overall impression of your essay. In particular a lack of care with typos and incomplete or inconsistent referencing can hold back an otherwise reasonable piece of work.

- **Too much descriptive detail.** Weaker work tends to contain far too much description. This, in turn, takes up words that would have been much better used in analysis.

- **Not answering the question.** Many weaker pieces of work talk about the subject matter in general terms but do not do enough to actually answer the question in the sense of providing a specific answer to the particular question asked. This weakens the focus of the work and limits its success.

- **Insufficient research.** Markers are looking for evidence that students have gone beyond (a) the textbook and (b) the cases and articles that have been discussed in lectures and tutorials.

- **Inclusion of irrelevant content.** This is another way in which the focus of the work can be weakened. Make sure that every point serves a purpose in the work and has direct relevance to the question that has been asked.

10.8.7 Moving from a 2.1 to a First

Some of the characteristics of a first class piece of work are:

- **Perfect referencing.** Your technical execution must be flawless so be sure that references are provided wherever needed, that they are complete, and in the correct format including pinpoint references wherever necessary.

- **Sophisticated use of language.** Take great care to express your ideas with precision and accuracy but also aim to try and develop eloquence in your written expression that makes your essay pleasing to read. Think carefully about every word and try to develop your vocabulary.

- **Engagement with theoretical concepts: essays.** Remember that an essay should not just consider *what* the law is, it should also engage—where appropriate—with *why* it is as it is. Thoughtful discussion of theoretical legal concepts and reasoning demonstrates a more sophisticated level of understanding than might be expected of an upper second class essay.

- **Wide-ranging research: essays.** Strong essays will contain a great breadth and depth of research. You should incorporate your findings and commentary in your essay, but remember that research should be used to support, and not to displace, analysis.

- **A different angle: essays.** If you are looking for ways in which to set your essay apart, then see if you can find a different angle for discussion, such as proposals for legal reform, or a comparative slant drawing on treatments of the legal issue in other jurisdictions (but choose your comparators wisely).

- **Clever use of facts: problems.** The heart of good legal problem solving is creative and thoughtful application of the law to the facts. See if you can find a way to use the facts to demonstrate that the requirements of the law are—or are not, depending on the circumstances—satisfied.

It may be that you feel that you are already working to a high standard and are struggling to see what else you could do to move your work from a high 2.1 to a First. Sometimes the solution is to be found in polishing everything that you are already doing rather than making significant changes. Motivational writer James Clear calls this the 'aggregation of marginal gains':[2] in other words, a series of small changes can have a big impact. So be prepared to dissect your work and think about small changes that will make the good things that you are already doing even better.

10.9 REFLECTING ON YOUR SKILLS

The emphasis in this chapter has been on the skills that you will need to study the law effectively. All the skills that we have discussed will help you to work to the best of your ability to understand the law and achieve good marks. However, that is not the only purpose of many of the skills that we have discussed—these 'general', 'transferable', or 'soft' skills have a relevance and value beyond the world of university as they are also skills that are important in the workplace, whatever profession you enter. It is therefore worth spending a little time reflecting upon what skills you have gained from your studies and how you could evidence these to prospective employers.

It is never too early to start thinking in terms of how you can market your skills and experience to enhance your employment prospects. Even if the end of your degree feels like it is a

---

2. J Clear, *Atomic Habits* (Random House Business 2018) 13.

long way into the future, it will come round quickly enough and, in the meantime, there are work experience, mini pupillages, and placements to apply for that will require you to show what skills you have that will be useful in a work environment.

10.9.1 Personal development planning (PDP)

Your university may run a formal personal development planning (PDP) scheme as the Dearing Report[3] into higher education recommended that there should be 'a means by which students can monitor, build and reflect upon their personal development'. This recognized the views of some employers that they needed more information to differentiate between growing numbers of graduates over and above basic degree classification and transcript information. PDP was defined by the Quality Assurance Agency for Higher Education (QAA)[4] as: 'a structured and supported process undertaken by an individual to reflect upon their own learning and to plan for their personal, educational and career development'.[5]

The key points within this definition are those of *planning*, *structure*, and *support*.

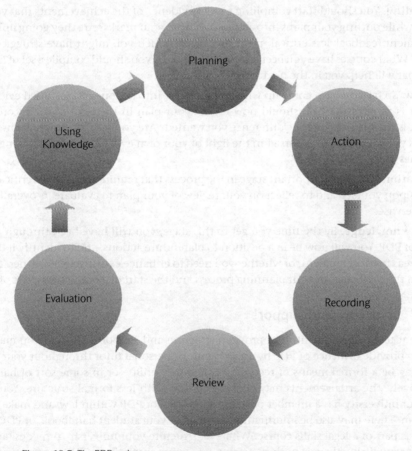

Figure 10.7 The PDP cycle

3. The Dearing Report is actually a series of reports commissioned by the UK government into higher education in the UK. It is available online at <http://www.leeds.ac.uk/educol/ncihe/> accessed 5 February 2019.
4. The body which checks standards in UK higher education institutions.
5. QAA, *Personal Development Planning: guidance for institutional policy and practice in higher education* (QAA 2009) <https://www.qaa.ac.uk/docs/qaas/enhancement-and-development/pdp-guidance-for-institutional-policy-and-practice.pdf?sfvrsn=4145f581_8> accessed 5 February 2019.

10.9.1.1 Planning, action, review, and reflection: the PDP cycle

Effective PDP will involve you in a continuous cycle of activity, which can be depicted as shown in Figure 10.7.

As you can see, there are several stages in the process:

- **Planning.** Planning for PDP purposes requires you to set a list of targets and to work out how you can best achieve them. While this might sound straightforward, you will need to consider your skills and abilities and think about which facets of your legal studies you are good at, why you are good at them, and whether there are any particular areas that you need to develop. Once you have identified areas for development, think about how you can go about improving them. Do you need more feedback? Are there any training opportunities that your university offers that could be of use to you?

- **Action.** Having identified areas for development, you now need to engage in the process necessary to reach the planned targets. Start taking the steps that you considered useful in the planning stage.

- **Recording.** You should start compiling a set of evidence of the achievements that you have made while putting your plans into action. What are your marks? Are they going up? Is your assessment feedback less critical in the areas with which you might have struggled previously? What courses have you been on? In other words, you should compile a set of information that will help you in the next stage of the process.

- **Review.** So far you have come up with a plan, put it into action, and recorded evidence of how it is progressing. You should now review your plan in the light of the recorded evidence. Is the plan making the difference you wanted? Are you making progress towards the targets you identified for yourself in the light of your own evaluation of your strengths and weaknesses?

- **Evaluation.** This is an important stage in the process that requires you to pass critical judgement upon yourself and to reflect on your review of your plan to evaluate its overall success or otherwise.

- **Using knowledge.** By the time you get to this stage, you will have been through a whole cycle of PDP. You will now be in a position to plan future actions, and to identify if there are new areas for development, or whether you need to enhance existing areas further. This will inform the next stage of your planning process and the start of a brand new cycle of PDP.

10.9.1.2 Structure and support

The extent to which an institution provides structure and support will vary. You may be required to provide evidence of PDP by an academic or personal tutor throughout your studies. There may be a formal means of recording PDP either online or in some sort of handbook. Alternatively, the arrangements may be more ad hoc, with less formal structure. You should see if your university has a member of staff responsible for PDP within law, and make contact with them. There may also be information provided in your student handbook, or PDP may be covered as part of a legal skills course. Whatever structure your university provides (and even if there is very little), there is nothing to stop you going through the PDP process yourself, or within a group of friends, or suggesting that a more formal arrangement might be of benefit to students. All that is required is a desire to improve, self-reliance to take action for your own learning, and the maturity to reflect critically on your own abilities. Practically speaking, evidence of PDP and the ability to describe your own PDP experience is something that may well be of use to you in moving on to the next stage of your legal career, be it vocational or academic.

10.9.2 Skills beyond your studies

One of the objectives of your studies will be that you emerge with a good degree that will help you to enter the world of employment, whether this is within the legal profession or elsewhere. Remember, however, that potential employers are not interested just in your degree classification but the skills that you acquired along the way that will give them an insight into whether or not you will be able to perform effectively in the workplace.

With this in mind, it is a good idea to reflect not only on how the skills that you are developing on your degree will transfer to the workplace (as you will do as part of the PDP process) but also to give some thought to the sort of skills that an employer will value that you may have less (or no) opportunity to develop on your degree. Can you identify a 'skills gap' between the skills you have and the skills that a potential employer will want based upon your research into what skills are valued in your chosen profession? And how do you think that you will find opportunities to develop those skills, especially if they are not ones that are likely to be part of your law degree? The careers service at your university should be able to help you to identify core skills that are relevant to particular professions and advise on how you might develop them.

10.9.2.1 Commercial awareness

Whatever profession you are planning to enter, you will find that prospective employers are looking for evidence of commercial awareness; that is, your knowledge and understanding of the industry and how it operates in a way that enables it to achieve its objectives in a professional and profitable manner. For example, if your aim is to practise law, you will need to understand how the legal profession operates in general with particular emphasis on the type of practice that is of interest to you.

Of course, one way to develop this understanding is to undertake as much work experience as possible within the legal profession. Try to make sure that there is variety within this; try to ensure you have experience in different sized law firms and in different areas of practice. You should also try to expand your knowledge of the working of the law—have you been on a court visit? Or perhaps you could apply to your local court for marshalling work or to shadow a judge for the day. Take every possible opportunity to see the law in action.

Beyond this, you should ensure that you spend time keeping yourself abreast of what is happening in the legal profession. This could involve subscribing to a politics podcast that will keep you updated about changes in government policy or legislation or doing your own research online by visiting the websites of law firms or law blogs. You should also take a look at the excellent commercial awareness resources on the Practical Law website provided for free by Thomson Reuters (https://uk.practicallaw.thomsonreuters.com). This will give you some comprehensive guidance on how to develop your commercial awareness and help you to understand how law firms operate as businesses including the key factors, such as developments in technology and politics, that affect them.

 CHAPTER SUMMARY

Lectures

- Lectures give a framework of information which should be supplemented by your own reading
- Try to listen and think about what is being said in lectures as well as taking notes

- Reflect on the content of the lecture and review your notes soon afterwards to identify what you have understood and which aspects of it need to be followed up in your private study time
- Be aware that different lecture formats—live in-person, online, and recorded—make different demands on students in terms of engagement and note-taking and be sure to adapt accordingly

Seminars and tutorials

- Prepare thoroughly for seminars and tutorials, attempting all tasks and questions even if you are unsure about them
- Make the tutorial useful for you by taking a list of questions or points of uncertainty so that you can update your notes as they are addressed
- Play an active role in all tutorial activities and join in with the discussion. If you find speaking out in class difficult, try to develop your confidence and verbal communication skills by resolving to make at least one contribution each session
- Many students find participation in online tutorial discussion to be less daunting than speaking out in front of a classful of other students so try to take advantage of any online teaching to take a more active role in tutorials

Private study

- Organize your study time every week and establish a suitable study environment
- Get into the habit of creating a study plan each week so that you can organize your time effectively to complete all your tasks
- Think about the benefits of working with other students and consider joining a study group to give yourself opportunities to discuss the law

Taking notes

- Devise a system for organizing your notes so that you can find things quickly and easily
- Remember that notes should be useful so experiment with different styles of note-taking to see what works best for you
- Avoid the temptation to write very detailed notes, especially if this means copying large chunks of text from a book, case, or article, or transcribing a recording of a lecture
- Devise a system of abbreviations to make your approach to note-taking more efficient

Study groups

- Study groups help to clarify your ideas and understanding
- Make sure that every study group meeting has a purpose
- Working with others is an important transferable skill and can make your studies more enjoyable
- Consider forming an online study group if it is not possible or practical to meet in person

Assessment

- Find out what formative and summative assignments you have each semester and incorporate these into your study plans so that you make steady progress towards them rather than being rushed at the last minute

- Identify your assessment dates and create a realistic plan to help you manage your time effectively as you work towards the deadlines
- Recognize and address procrastination, remembering to break your work up into the smallest possible chunks to give you an achievable target if you are struggling to get started
- Adjust your study plans continuously as you learn by experience how long it takes you to complete the tasks involved in completing your assignments
- Try working with other students to help you understand the law and how to tackle each assignment but remember that the final piece of work must be your own to avoid problems with plagiarism
- If you are completing a group assessment, consider establishing ground rules from the start so that you have a system in place for dealing with any difficulties that may arise

Improving your performance

- Make sure that you take every opportunity to engage with feedback that is provided to you
- Take time to understand the strengths and weaknesses in your work: develop strategies to build on the former and improve on the latter
- Find the grade descriptors and take time to think about what they mean as these can help you to improve your performance in assessments
- Be aware of sources of support and guidance in your university and do not be afraid to ask for help if you need it

Reflecting on your skills

- It is important to have a clear idea of what skills you have and where you need to work on developing and strengthening skills
- Take part in a PDP scheme if there is one at your university or develop your own system for reviewing your skills
- Think about the skills that are valued by potential employers and seek opportunities to develop these whether this is within your studies, through work experience, or by other means

Writing skills

11

INTRODUCTION

This chapter will outline the elements of good written English with particular emphasis on the way that language is used in academic legal writing. It does not aim to be a complete guide to English usage but a reflection of the issues that students tend to find difficult. You will find sections on language, grammar, and punctuation as well as practical guidance on matters such as selecting quotations and writing in a concise manner so as to keep within the word limit. The material covered in this chapter should be seen as the foundation upon which good essays are built and should be read in conjunction with the guidance provided on writing essays (chapter 14) and answering problem questions (chapter 15). Some of the issues covered will also be useful in terms of examinations but a more complete guide on writing answers in examinations can be found in chapter 16.

The ability to use language, orally and in writing, is one of the key 'tools of the trade' for a lawyer, so it is essential that you are able to use language correctly and prepare precise and accurate written documents. Many cases turn on the interpretation of a particular word or phrase so it is essential that you have the skills to appreciate the implications of the choice of particular words and that you are able to communicate the precise meaning of the law. On a more pragmatic level, you need good writing skills to demonstrate your understanding of the law to your lecturers in your coursework and examinations. This requires that you adopt the styles and conventions of language used in the law. It is a mistake to think that an essay that is accurate in terms of its legal content will succeed irrespective of the language used to express the arguments or the way in which the essay is structured. Content is important but the way that a piece of writing is organized and expressed can be equally fundamental to its success or failure. You would not like this book if it were written in ungrammatical language so that you could not readily make sense of it or if it were so poorly structured that you could not locate the information that you needed. This means that you recognize the value of good writing skills so you should strive to ensure that your own work reaches the standards that you expect in the work of others.

Learning outcomes

After studying this chapter, you will be able to:

- Make reasoned choices about the language and written style that you use in the preparation of coursework
- Construct a grammatical sentence that uses words correctly and which communicates your meaning to the marker

- Produce a polished piece of work that is free of common grammatical errors and which uses punctuation correctly
- Create paragraphs that keep a strong focus on the question and which link to each other to produce a flowing line of argument
- Select appropriate quotations to support your argument and integrate these effectively into your essay
- Write within the word limit and produce a piece of work with flawless presentation

11.1 WHY ARE WRITING SKILLS IMPORTANT?

In August 2008, a judge criticized the CPS solicitor who produced an indictment in a criminal case that was 'littered with errors' including five misspellings of the word 'grievous' and a reference to an offensive weapon 'namely axe' (rather than 'namely an axe').[1] Judge David Paget threw the indictment down, saying:

It's quite disgraceful. This is supposed to be a centre of excellence. To have an indictment drawn up by some illiterate idiot is just not good enough.

If you think about it, a piece of writing that does not comply with the expected standards and conventions of correct written English suggests one of only two possibilities:

1. The writer cannot use the rules of language, grammar, and punctuation correctly (in which case, they lack sufficient ability in something that is fundamental to the study and practice of the law) or

2. The writer cannot be bothered to correct the mistakes that they have made in their first draft (in which case, they lack the attention to detail and the awareness of the importance of language).

Neither of these is the impression that you want to give to lecturers who are marking your work, to potential employers considering your application, and to members of the profession if you enter into legal practice. As John Redwood MP commented on his blog:[2]

Many of the [people who have sent CVs for a job] have degrees. They send in CVs which start with similar paragraphs that they have been taught to write. They usually claim to be . . . brilliant communicators . . . The rest of the CV sometimes belies the standard phrases of the opening. Some are unable to write a sentence. There are usually spelling and typing errors – understandable in the rush of everyday communication but glaring in a considered and formal document like a CV. One example produced the following second sentence to the application: 'I fill the experience I have gained in past employment will put me in good persian for this role'.

Unfortunately, some students seem to have gained the erroneous impression that it does not matter how language is used in their coursework (or applications for work placements and training contracts) provided the content is correct. This is not a position that is acceptable in

---

1. '"Illiterate" worker angers judge' *BBC News Online* (12 August 2008) <http://news.bbc.co.uk/1/hi/england/london/7554857.stm> accessed 20 January 2019.
2. Statement by J Redwood MP (Personal blog entry 12 June 2010) <http://www.johnredwoodsdiary.com/?p=6410> accessed 20 January 2019.

the law because ability to use language correctly and to express shades of meaning is vitally important, as the following example demonstrates.

A contractual dispute in Canada hinged on the presence of a single comma in one of the clauses.[3] Rogers Communications entered into a contract with Aliant Inc involving the installation of cable onto utility poles across Canada. It was intended that the contract would run for an initial five-year period and thereafter for renewable periods of five years. This meant that, at the very least, the contract would run for five years. However, the contract contained a clause which stipulated that the agreement:

> shall continue in force for a period of five years from the date it is made, and thereafter for successive five-year terms, unless and until terminated by one year prior notice in writing by either party.

The problem lies in the positioning of the second comma (after the words 'successive five-year terms') as this means that the entire contract can be cancelled with one year's notice. If you remove the comma and read the clause again, you will see that it then only gives the parties the right to cancel the contract with one year's notice *after* the original five years has expired. This error in punctuation cost Rogers Communications $2.13m.

As this example illustrates, precision in the use of language and the ability to use grammar and punctuation correctly is important as incorrect usage can alter the meaning of the words that you have used. Remember, it is not enough to write in a way that makes sense to you: what is more important is that your writing makes sense and communicates your precise meaning to the person reading it.

In pragmatic terms, during the course of your studies, you will find that students who can write in a way that fits with the expectations and requirements of the lecturers will achieve greater success in their coursework. This is because you are assessed not solely on your legal knowledge but on your ability to write in a way that is in keeping with the formality and precision of language use within the legal profession.

11.2 LANGUAGE

Practical exercise

Look at the following two paragraphs which were written by the same student. Which one of these was (a) the introductory paragraph to an essay about the independence of the judiciary and (b) was a section from an email to his mother about his essay?

EXAMPLE A	EXAMPLE B
I have to write this essay about the judiciary – you know, judges and the courts and all that. Basically, it is about whether the judiciary is independent enough. Why is it important that they are independent? Yeah, I don't know but I guess that I will do by the end of the essay!	Many commentators state that the independence of the judiciary is a fundamental safeguard against injustice within the legal system. The reasons given for the independence of the judiciary will be explored and a conclusion reached about whether the judiciary can be said to be truly independent.

Figure 11.1 Comparison of writing styles

3. 'The case of the million-dollar comma' *OUT-LAW News* (26 October 2006) <http://www.out-law.com/page-7426> accessed 20 January 2019.

> Hopefully, you will have identified that Example A is the email and Example B is the introduction to the essay. Consider, though, what it was about the way that language is used that enabled you to reach this conclusion: after all, neither of the examples makes explicit reference to an essay or an email and both make largely the same points. If your answer is, as it should be, that Example A uses the informal language of conversation or email whereas Example B uses the more formal legalistic style of writing that is characteristic of an essay then you are already recognizing a very important point: there is a style of writing that is appropriate to an essay and other styles of writing which have their own roles but which should not be used in an essay.
>
> *Have a look online at **www.oup.com/he/finch8e/** where you will find two further samples of writing. Consider whether you think that they are written in a style that is appropriate for a piece of law coursework. If you think that there are problems, make some suggestions for amending the style so that it is more appropriate and compare your answers with those provided.*

It is important that you adopt an appropriate level of formality in your written style. The best way to gauge the appropriate level is to read a good-quality textbook that is written in language that you understand and to emulate that style.

11.2.1 Too formal or too informal?

Some students err on the side of excessive formality, believing this to be appropriate to legal writing, peppering their writing with words such as 'hereinafter' and 'henceforth'. Whilst there is nothing wrong with this as such, there is an increasing move towards the use of plain English within the legal profession, so it can be preferable to use words which are more readily understood. Moreover, using unfamiliar words raises the possibility that they will be misused, which will detract from the polished and professional impression that you are striving to present with your writing.

More frequently, students adopt an informal approach that is conversational in nature and more suited to a diary or an email to friends than a piece of academic writing. For example, there is nothing wrong in grammatical terms with sentences such as '[h]aving talked about the meaning of x, we now need to take a look at y', but it is nonetheless rather chatty and informal for a piece of coursework.

In essence, the language that is appropriate in informal communications between friends is not the sort of language that should be used in legal writing.

11.2.2 Appropriate legal writing style

As the examples in Figure 11.1 make clear, there is not a constant 'correct' style that can be applied to all forms of written communication. In essence, 'correct' means 'appropriate' so you should strive to develop a written style that is appropriate for communication in academic law, one that is relatively formal and which uses language in an accurate and precise manner. There are a few other matters that require particular consideration before the discussion of language is concluded.

11.2.2.1 Use of the first person

The grammatical first person is a way of referring to the participant role of the speaker or the writer. Accordingly, when a person writes as 'I', they are writing in the first person. This is entirely appropriate in informal communications and in other situations in which it is necessary to express a personal viewpoint but it is not appropriate in objective academic writing and tends not to be welcomed by lecturers (although there are a range of views on this so check with your lecturer to determine their preferences before starting to write your coursework). Some students, lacking a grasp of the complexities of English grammar, try to get around this prohibition on writing in the first person by switching to 'we' (first person plural), 'you' (second person singular or plural), or 'one' (third person neutral), not realizing that they are equally unacceptable.

In addition to being an informal writing style, the first person also situates the writer as an authority within the piece of writing: in other words, it makes you the narrator of the essay so that you are expressing your own perspective and views when it would be more appropriate to present the views of writers, judges, and other experts. If you accept that it is never appropriate to write 'I think' or 'I would argue' in your essay, then you will never be tempted to express your own opinion on the state of the law and you will have to resort to repeating the views of more experienced writers and commentators.

If you are accustomed to writing in the first person and struggle to find a form of words to use, then Table 11.1 should give you some ideas for alternative phraseology to get you started.

Table 11.1 First person writing and objective alternatives

First person	Objective alternative
In this essay, I am going to outline the elements necessary to establish that a defendant is liable for negligence	This essay will outline the elements necessary to establish that a defendant is liable for negligence
Alternatively, one could argue that . . .	Alternatively, it could be argued that . . .
In conclusion, I do not see any need for reform in this area	In conclusion, the majority of writers do not see a need for reform in this area

Practical exercise

This is an aspect of academic writing that a great many students find difficult, especially if they have an educational background where informal writing was encouraged. Have a look at the following sentences and think about how you would reword them to create a more formal style of writing:

1. We have seen that the postal rule has been criticized by many academic commentators and that there is little judicial support for its continued use. I think that this indicates that the rule has no value in modern contract law and should be dismissed as an anachronism.

2. As the defendant did not suffer a loss of control that came from one of the qualifying triggers, I would conclude that he cannot rely on the defence of loss of control in the Coroners and Justice Act.

3. You could argue that the law in this area is outdated and should not be applied but one must appreciate that an old law is not necessarily a bad law.

You will find suggested answers at www.oup.com/he/finch8e/ together with an explanation of how the answers were reached.

11.2.2.2 Gender-neutral language

It is accepted convention in legal writing to use the masculine word forms to encompass the feminine: Interpretation Act 1978 s 6. In other words, 'he' means 'he or she' and 'his' means 'his or hers'. Some academics frown upon this approach, believing that the prevalence of male-orientated references is exclusionary and inappropriate. This is a matter of personal preference but do be aware of the need not to cause offence in your choice of language whilst balancing this against the pragmatic challenge of writing to a word limit (writing 'he or she' is three words when just 'he' would reduce your word count by two words each time) . It would be worth checking if your institution, department, or lecturer has any strong views on the subject and adapting your use of language accordingly.

11.2.2.3 Latin and Law French

There are many legal terms derived from Latin and French (known as 'Law French'). However, in recent years, there has been a move away from the use of Latin and Law French words and phrases within the legal profession. Certain Latin legal terms have been renamed, for example, an order of *certiorari* is now known as a quashing order whilst an *ex parte* application has been renamed an application without notice.

However, there are areas of law in which the continued use of Latin and Law French is accepted; the conduct element of a crime is still known as the *actus reus*, for example, whilst it is accepted that phrases such as *res ipsa loquitur* and *cy-près* are terms of art with an express legal meaning.

Be aware of the decline in the use of Latin and Law French and be sure to check both your textbooks and course materials for the appropriate approach to terminology. If you do have cause to use Latin and Law French words or phrases in your writing, there is a long-standing legal convention that they should always be italicized. However, according to the OSCOLA referencing system (see chapter 13 for more details) words that are in common usage in legal English are not italicized. OSCOLA gives a list of examples, such as ultra vires, stare decisis, obiter dicta, and ratio decidendi. There is no single correct approach here; check with your lecturers to see if they have a particular preference.

For explanations of some Latin and Law French terms you may nevertheless encounter, see section 7.1.12.1

11.2.2.4 Legal words

As you will become increasingly aware as your studies progress, many words in everyday usage also have particular legal meanings that differ significantly from their ordinary dictionary definitions: intention, consideration, assault, nuisance, appropriation, land, property, consent, and negligence, for example. As these words hold a particular legal significance, you should avoid using them in their ordinary sense within the subject area where they have a specialist meaning.

For example, if you write that 'the defendant's assault caused the victim's death', this could be confusing as it will not be clear to your lecturer whether you are using the word in the legal sense or whether you intend the word to have its everyday meaning (Figure 11.2).

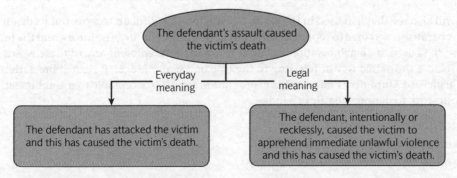

Figure 11.2 Everyday and legal meanings

To avoid any confusion, especially when it carries the risk that your lecturer will think that you misunderstand the law, it is advisable to find a synonym to use in place of any word that has a clear legal meaning.

11.2.2.5 Abbreviations

Some students are very keen to use abbreviations as a means of reducing the overall word count of their coursework but this can be a problem. Not only does the excessive use of abbreviations make a piece of work read more like a set of notes than an essay, it can also be confusing if non-standard abbreviations are used. Look at the following example:

Practical exercise

Read the following extract of text from an essay and see if you can decipher its meaning despite the overuse of abbreviations.

> One of the main factors thought to contribute to the tendency of J to return NG verdicts in RTiC is that both D and V are presenting very similar versions of the facts to J. The evidence of D and V may differ only in the smallest details so it becomes difficult for J, even with the guidance of J, to determine which version of the facts is the truth. In such situations, the correct course of action is for J to return a NG verdict as they are not sure of D's guilt BRD but this nonetheless impedes the SOA from achieving its purpose of improving conviction rates in RTiC.

Were you able to work out the subject matter of this writing? Which, if any, abbreviations did you recognize as standard ones used in law? Did you think it was appropriate to use these abbreviations in an essay? The meaning of the abbreviations is noted in the discussion that follows, which will also explain which sorts of abbreviations it is acceptable to use in a piece of coursework.

Some of the abbreviations in the extract are commonly used in law. It is usual for lecturers to refer to the defendant as 'D' and the victim as 'V' in handouts and on lecture slides. However, while such abbreviations will save you time when you are making notes, this does not mean that they should be used in an essay. Remember that your coursework will generally require a more formal written style so it may be sensible to write these words out in full. There are other commonly used abbreviations that you might find useful when taking notes but which should not really find their way into your essay:

- G and NG = guilty and not guilty
- DC, CA, HL, and SC = Divisional Court, Court of Appeal, House of Lords, Supreme Court

You will also see that 'J' is used in the extract. If you found it difficult to work out its meaning, this is because it was used to represent three different things: the jury, the jurors, and the judge. When 'J' is used as an abbreviation in law, it is not used to represent any of these words but is instead a shortened way of referring to the title of a senior judge: 'J' is an abbreviation for 'Mr Justice' so Mummery J refers to Mr Justice Mummery. It is acceptable to use abbreviations in your work to denote the title of a judge:

- Denning J = Mr Justice Denning
- Denning LJ = Lord Justice Denning
- Denning CJ = Lord Chief Justice Denning
- Denning MR = Lord Denning, Master of the Rolls

It is also common practice to abbreviate the names of some statutes. In the extract, the Sexual Offences Act 2003 was written as 'SOA'. It is acceptable to abbreviate statute names in this way provided that the statute is written in full the first time it is mentioned and the abbreviation noted in brackets, for example the Police and Criminal Evidence Act 1984 (PACE). It is also acceptable to abbreviate certain other things in this way, for example:

- Crown Prosecution Service (CPS)
- Director of Public Prosecutions (DPP)
- Attorney-General (A-G)
- Anti-social Behaviour Orders (ASBOs)

The earlier extract also uses some non-standard abbreviations. These are essentially abbreviations that the writer has invented in order to reduce the word count of their essay rather than established acronyms used in law. In the example, 'RTiC' is used in place of 'rape trials involving consent' and 'BRD' replaces 'beyond reasonable doubt'. Inventing abbreviations in this way makes life more difficult for your marker, who has to puzzle out what you mean, and may lead to a deduction in marks for poor written style.

   The guiding principle is that if the abbreviation is used in spoken language (such as GBH) then it can be used when you are writing but if it is not used in speech then it should not be used in formal writing. Think about the sentence 'the D had the AR of s18 so is liable for causing GBH'. In speech, this would be 'the defendant had the *actus reus* of section 18 and so is liable for causing GBH' which shows you that GBH is an acceptable written abbreviation whereas D and AR are not acceptable in writing. The exception that you see here is 'section' which can be written as the abbreviation 's' even though this would always be spoken as 'section'. This is because it is a legal convention which makes it an acceptable abbreviation.

11.3 GRAMMAR AND PUNCTUATION

Good writing is about more than just words on paper: the words need to be arranged in such a way that they make proper sense to the reader. It is grammar and punctuation that transform a collection of words into meaningful sentences that can be understood by the reader. This is a particularly important factor in legal education as the ability to communicate precise and accurate meaning is crucial, and correct grammar and punctuation are central to this. Without grammatical expression and grammatical accuracy, the meaning of words can change as the following two sentences demonstrate:

> The panda eats, shoots and leaves (he has his dinner, kills another panda with his shotgun and moves on to a new territory); or,
>   The panda eats shoots and leaves (the diet of the panda is shoots and leaves).[4]

If this seems like a trivial example, remember that the interpretation of statutory provisions can hinge on the meaning of one word or even on the positioning of punctuation; it is often said that Roger Casement was 'hanged on a comma', meaning that his execution was inevitable if he was convicted of the offence of which he was charged. His liability for this offence hinged upon the interpretation of the statute which was, in turn, contingent on the positioning of the comma. The importance of positioning of punctuation has already been seen in the Canadian contract example in section 11.1.

---

4. L Truss, *Eats, Shoots and Leaves: the Zero Tolerance Approach to Punctuation* (Profile Books Ltd 2003).

Unfortunately, not all students are able to construct a grammatical and well-punctuated essay by the time they arrive at university. This problem is compounded by the fact that many of these students will be unaware that there is any problem with their grammar and punctuation. You will find that the extent to which lecturers will (a) draw attention to grammatical deficiencies and (b) offer guidance on improvement varies enormously and the approach that they take will determine the response that is needed from the student:

- Lecturer A will not mention problems with writing at all, merely deducting marks for lack of clarity of expression without giving any indication that there is a problem with written style, grammar, or punctuation. This can be unhelpful because it fails to alert students to the existence of a problem that needs to be addressed, but if your work is not getting the marks that you feel that you deserve then you will need to take proactive steps to obtain some feedback on the accuracy of your written style, either from one of your lecturers or from the study skills centre.

- Lecturer B will comment that the grammar and/or punctuation in the essay was weak or could be strengthened but will not actually correct any inaccuracies. This alerts you to the problem and places the responsibility on you to make the necessary changes. Again, the lecturer themself, your personal tutor, or the study skills centre will be good sources of guidance.

- Lecturer C will identify each problem the first time that it occurs in your work and tell you how to correct it. This alerts you to the problems and shows you the solution but leaves the responsibility with you to identify further instances in your work and correct them yourself as a way of ensuring that the problems do not occur in subsequent pieces of work.

- Lecturer D will correct every inaccuracy in your work and may include explanations of the why there is a problem and how to correct it. This is a lecturer who is trying to be helpful but it can be very dispiriting for students to see their work littered with critical comment and it can give the impression that the content has been ignored in favour of a focus on what may seem like the minutiae of rules of grammar. Try to avoid a defensive response and remember that your harshest critic can be your greatest ally when it comes to improving your work. Step back from your disappointment and try to learn from the feedback that you have been given, seeking further guidance if you are struggling to understand how to correct your work.

11.3.1 Spotting the problem

As discussed earlier, not all lecturers will point out the problem so you will need to be alert for the signs that there may be a problem with your grammar and/or punctuation.

Poor grades provide a good indication that *something* is wrong. If you are receiving marks that are lower than you would hope or expect (remembering to be realistic), then it may be that you are not expressing yourself with sufficient clarity or precision. Poor grammar and punctuation frequently result in a lack of clarity as the words that you have written simply do not do the job that you want them to do.

If your marks are less than you hoped, have a close look at the feedback that has been provided, both on the feedback sheet and the script itself. Are there any comments, however vague, about the quality of your written style? Comments on the script such as 'lacks clarity', 'poorly expressed', 'what does this mean?', or 'vague' can also indicate that the problem is not with your understanding of the law but with the way that it is expressed. Some lecturers will simply underline phrases that they cannot understand and put a question mark in the margin whilst others will correct errors so do keep a look out for changes that have been made on your essay by your lecturer.

Some feedback sheets have categories of skills that the lecturers can tick to indicate your level of competence. The categories used will obviously vary between institutions but there will usually be some that refer to the technical aspects of the construction of the essay as well as to the use of the law itself. Have a look at the feedback form when you receive it. Do any of the categories refer to written style generally or to grammar or punctuation in particular? Anything less than 'good' could indicate a problem, as 'satisfactory' is another way of saying 'could be improved'.

11.3.2 Getting help

Once you are aware that there is a problem, finding sources of assistance with strengthening your grammar and punctuation should be straightforward. Even if they cannot help you themselves, your lecturer or your personal tutor will be able to point you towards sources of assistance, whether this is a specialist skills adviser in your department or a study skills or student support service elsewhere in the university. You should not hesitate to seek help if you (or the person marking your work) feel that it is necessary; many writing problems result from a lack of understanding of the correct way to go about things and these can be corrected very easily with a little specialist assistance. Although the rules of grammar may seem complex and impenetrable, once they have been explained to you clearly and you have examples of correct usage, you will probably find that it is not difficult to adjust your written style to take these rules into account.

An alternative source of assistance is one of the many works on correct English usage. These can be found in the library and are increasingly available online. You could, of course, purchase a concise guide to English grammar and make reference to it as you write an essay.

A final, and frequently overlooked, source of guidance is the written work of others. Whether this is the work of your fellow students or the work of experienced academics in articles and textbooks, you should scrutinize the way that others write in order to gain experience of good writing practice. It is often the case that students who read a great deal have a better grasp of grammar and punctuation as they acquire an appreciation of the rules by virtue of encountering them more frequently in the writing of others. Ideally, you should aim to improve your written style on each piece of work that you submit and one really effective way of doing this is to evaluate the way that others write with a view to adopting examples of good practice that you encounter.

11.3.3 Varying approaches to grammar

One of the difficulties with choosing an appropriate approach to language is that there is a difference of opinion regarding the application of the rules. Some academics consider that particular rules of grammar are outdated or overly pedantic whilst others fear that failure to adhere to these rules is part of a larger picture of declining standards of literacy. This book does not intend to engage in that debate but rather to offer students advice on how to avoid falling foul of the debate.

It seems that those with a preference for traditional approaches to grammar are likely to take issue with its absence whereas it is unlikely that a lecturer with a more relaxed attitude is going to correct your work with a comment 'this is not incorrect but a little bit out-of-date'! For example, the paragraph below would offend a lecturer with traditional views about grammatical written English:

> There may be a difference of opinion as to the relevance of certain rules of grammar in today's society. But, in order to ensure that nobody is offended by your writing, it is a sensible idea to adhere to the correct approach wherever possible.

However, if this paragraph was presented as a single sentence (using 'but' in the traditionally correct manner), it is unlikely that anybody would object. Lecturers who take a more progressive approach to grammar tend to believe that certain of the rules of grammar are unnecessary but they do not tend to intervene if students use them. This is because the modern view is not that the traditional approach is incorrect, just that it is outdated. This is contrary to the traditional viewpoint, which holds that the modern stance is inaccurate, hence should be corrected.

It is for this reason that it is advisable to take a formal approach to grammar wherever possible in order to avoid any question of incorrect usage. It is also the case that the law tends to be rather traditional in its approach to writing so if you are not sure how to phrase your work, err on the side of formality.

11.3.4 Foundations of grammatical writing

Although there is not scope to provide a detailed explanation of the rules of grammar in this book, the following is a summary of some of the basic principles that you need to be able to put into practice if you want to produce a competent piece of writing in law.

11.3.4.1 Basic word types

It is a good idea to ensure that you are familiar with the terminology used to describe the construction of a grammatical sentence and that you understand what each of the words and phrases that you have written contributes to the final sentence (see Table 11.2).

Table 11.2 Basic word types

Term	Explanation	Example
Noun	A word which names a person, thing, or object. It is usually preceded by 'a', 'an', or 'the'. Proper nouns describe actual names of people and places. Only proper nouns start with capital letters irrespective of where they appear in the sentence.	The *trial* took place before a *judge* and a *jury*. The *appeal* was heard by *Lord Justice Beard* in the *High Court*.
Pronoun	A word that is used in place of a noun to avoid repetition: he, she, it, him, her, it, we, they, them	The defendant entered a plea when *he* appeared in court. The jury did not look at *him* when *they* entered the court.
Adjective	A word that describes a noun	The *serious* case was heard by a *lenient* judge.
Verb	A word that describes an action (doing something) or a state (being something). It changes tense to indicate when things happened.	The jury *believed* the defendant's version of events. The judge *frowns* at the jury as he *thinks* that the defendant *had lied*.
Adverb	A word that describes how an action is done. It describes how the action (verb) is carried out. Adverbs also explain when or where something happened.	The client listened *carefully* to the solicitor's advice when they met *yesterday*.
Conjunction	A word that joins two parts of a sentence together: because, and, but, so, or, when	The solicitor hurried to court *because* he was running late. The judge frowned at the solicitor *when* he arrived.
Preposition	A word that links a noun, pronoun, or noun phrase to the rest of the sentence, usually in terms of space or time: to, with, in, through, by, under, at, for, from, of, under, over	The defendant read a book *during* the trial. The jury searched *for* the truth *of* the matter.
Article	A word that introduces the noun. It can be a definite article (*the* judge) or an indefinite article (*a* judge).	*The* defendant wanted to hit *a* policeman (indefinite: he wants to hit any policeman) or *the* defendant wanted to hit *the* policeman after he was arrested (definite: he wants to hit a particular policeman).

Practical exercise

It will help you to construct more grammatical sentences if you become familiar with the types of words that comprise a sentence and how they relate to each other. Have a look at the following examples and use the explanations provided to identify what type of word has been italicized in each sentence.

1. The *definition* of rape was expanded by the Sexual Offences Act 2003.

2. *Special* measures have been introduced to *protect* vulnerable witnesses.

3. *The* law was changed by statute in 1990 *but* these changes have not yet been implemented.

You will find answers to these questions and many more exercises that will help you to test your ability to identify these different parts of a sentence at www.oup.com/he/finch8e/.

11.3.4.2 Constructing a (grammatical) sentence

One lecturer recently told the story of how he wrote 'not a sentence' in several places on a student's essay to draw attention to the ungrammatical use of language. The student returned the essay to him with a request that he reconsider the grade as the criticisms were not justified because 'they were sentences. They started with capital letters and ended with full stops'. The lecturer amended his comments to read 'not a grammatical sentence' and returned the essay to the student with the grade unchanged.

This anecdote illustrates that there is much more to building a sentence than adhering to the conventions for starting (capital letter) and ending it (full stop): the words and punctuation that go in between are also vitally important.

A grammatical sentence can vary in length from a single word ('Guilty!' is a complete grammatical sentence) to thousands of words (there is a 4,391-word sentence in *Ulysses* by James Joyce).

Simple sentences have a subject (the defendant) and a verb (sobbed) or a subject (the defendant), a verb (sobbed), and an object (in court). An essay comprised solely of such short simple sentences has a rather bumpy and disjointed feel to it:

> Murder is a common law offence. It is the most serious form of homicide. It carries a mandatory life sentence. The judge has no discretion in sentencing. Loss of control and diminished responsibility are defences to murder. They reduce murder to voluntary manslaughter. Any sentence can be imposed for voluntary manslaughter. The penalties range from an absolute discharge to life imprisonment.

There are two ways to create longer sentences from these short sentences.

1. **Compound sentences** join two simple sentences together using a conjunction such as 'and' or 'but'. For example, 'It is the most serious form of homicide *and* it carries a mandatory life sentence'.

2. **Complex sentences** formed of an independent and a subordinate clause. An independent clause is one that can stand alone as a simple sentence whilst a subordinate clause is one that does not make sense alone and needs to be joined to another sentence. The subordinate clause can precede the independent clause ('as the most serious form of homicide [subordinate clause], it carries a mandatory life sentence [independent clause]') or it can follow the independent clause ('loss of control and diminished responsibility are defences to murder [independent clause]), which reduce liability to voluntary manslaughter [subordinate clause]'.

Using these techniques, you can reformulate the eight simple sentences into a combination of compound and complex sentences to create a more flowing and mature piece of writing:

> Murder is a common law offence. As the most serious form of homicide, it carries a mandatory life sentence thus the judge has no discretion in sentencing. Loss of control and diminished responsibility are defences to murder which reduce liability to voluntary manslaughter and can attract any sentence from an absolute discharge to life imprisonment.

You will notice that the rewritten form preserves the first simple sentence—'murder is a common law offence'. Simple sentences can have more impact than longer sentences simply because they are short and therefore sometimes seem to 'speak more loudly' to the reader. A combination of short and simple sentences with longer compound and complex sentences creates a more lively piece of writing that is more interesting for the reader.

11.3.4.3 Avoiding common errors

The following are common problems with sentence construction that can be easily resolved. They are a good place to start if you want to strengthen your written style.

- **Do not start a sentence with a conjunction.** The role of conjunctions such as 'and', 'but', and 'or' is to join two clauses together into a compound sentence. This means that these should never be used to start a sentence. A good way to avoid problems is to make a list of conjunctions and check your work to make sure that you never use one at the beginning of a sentence.

- **Do not end a sentence with a preposition.** Try to remember that good spoken English and good written English are two different species of the same language. When speaking, you might say 'I was told to find a case that I'd never heard of' but it is not something that you should write. Try correcting this by rephrasing the sentence: 'I had never heard of the case that I was told to find'.

- **Do not omit articles to defeat the word limit.** There are always some students who try to get around the word limit by taking every instance of 'the' out of their essay. This does reduce the word count but the ungrammatical essay that results will lose marks because it does not make sense. Never sacrifice the proper use of language in the interests of the word limit: rewrite sentences in a more concise manner.

- **Avoid illogical predication errors.** The word 'when' describes the time at which something happened and 'where' describes a location. However, students often use these words to introduce a definition or explanation: for example, 'a fixed trust is *where* the beneficiaries and their interests are stipulated by the settlor' or 'a fixed trust is *when* the trustee has no discretion as to the extent of the beneficial interest or the identity of the beneficiaries'. This is known as an illogical predication error or a faulty equation and it can be corrected by rewording the sentence: 'a fixed trust is *one in which* the beneficiaries and their interests are stipulated by the settlor'.

- **Avoid run-on sentences (also known as the comma splice).** This is a sentence made up of separate grammatical clauses that become ungrammatical due to the overuse of commas. For example, 'Serious cases are sent to Crown Court for trial, they are heard by a jury, composed of twelve ordinary people, selected at random from the public, who do not have legal training'. Check any long sentences that contain commas to make sure that you avoid this problem. Correct it by rewording the sentence. This example uses italics to emphasize the changes that have been made: 'Serious cases are sent to Crown Court for trial. They are heard by a jury, *which is* composed of twelve ordinary people *who are* selected at random from the public *and* who do not have legal training'.

- **Be careful with 'who' and 'whom'.** 'Who' usually takes the place of a subject, and 'whom' generally replaces the direct object: 'the judge who delivered the verdict' and 'the defendant to whom the verdict was delivered'.

- **Look out for sentence fragments.** These are sentences that do not work as complete grammatical sentences because some essential component of the sentence is missing. They tend to start with words such as who, which or where, or with words ending in -ing. For example, 'the defendant's privilege against self-incrimination includes the right to silence. Which was modified by section 34 of the Criminal Justice and Public Order Act 1994'. This can be corrected in four ways as illustrated in Figure 11.3.

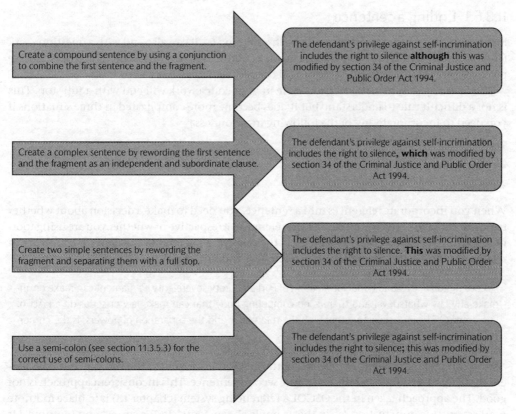

Figure 11.3 Sentence fragments

11.3.5 Punctuation

When people speak to each other, they use a range of devices to ensure that the intended meaning of the words is communicated to the listener. Think about the different meanings that you can convey in the single word 'hello': it can be spoken in a friendly tone as a greeting, shouted as a means of attracting attention, stated in a tone that conveys surprise or shock, or in a flat tone that indicates that the recipient is not liked or welcome, or it can carry an implied 'what do you want?' if it is said in a questioning tone of voice. In written language, it is not possible to convey different meanings by using tone, stress, or volume but punctuation, used correctly, can encode particular meaning into words to help the reader to extract the intended message.

Every written sentence is a combination of words and punctuation. The words and punctuation marks are selected by the writer as the best way to communicate the thoughts that are in the writer's head. In other words, when you write your coursework, you aim to capture your understanding of the law on paper using appropriate words and punctuation. If you want your meaning to be clear to the reader, you must use punctuation in the same way that they do or there is a risk that your meaning will be lost.

Even experienced writers struggle with the complexities of some rules of punctuation and there are areas of disagreement amongst experts about usage of punctuation in certain situations but this does not mean that you can disregard certain basic rules. Your lecturers will expect you to attain a certain level of communicative competence that includes the ability to use punctuation correctly.

11.3.5.1 Ending a sentence

Most people know that a sentence ends with a full stop (.). It can also end with a question mark (?) or an exclamation mark (!). There is no other correct way to end a sentence so one of these pieces of punctuation should be at the end of every sentence that you produce.

The majority of sentences that you write in your coursework will end with a full stop. This is not a difficult rule to understand but it does become more complicated in three situations if you need to incorporate any of the following into your essay:

• References

• Quotations

• Questions.

When you incorporate references into a sentence, you need to make a decision about whether to position the full stop before or after the reference, irrespective of whether you are using footnotes or in-text referencing. Have a look at the following paragraph. Can you see a problem in relation to the positioning of footnote references and full stops?

> According to Dicey's traditional formulation of Parliamentary sovereignty, Parliament can make or unmake any law whatsoever and there is no competing body that can make law or set aside an Act of Parliament.[1] This principle, together with the rule of law and the separation of powers, is the cornerstone of the UK's unwritten constitution[2].

As you can see, the reference at the end of the first sentence follows the full stop but the reference is before the full stop at the end of the second sentence. This inconsistent approach is not good. The approach taken in the OSCOLA referencing system (chapter 13) is to place footnote markers outside punctuation (so in the example above, footnote 1 is correct and footnote 2 is incorrect according to OSCOLA).

The position regarding quotations and full stops is also not complicated if you stop to think about the sentence as a whole. If the quotation is incorporated into one of your own sentences (as in the following example) then the full stop must appear outside the quotation marks to denote that the sentence in its entirety is at an end.

> However, Ainsworth suggests that 'the traditional stance on sovereignty has not stood the test of time and the Dicean view cannot, in the face of the demands of Europe and the gentle erosion of the Human Rights Act 1998, be said to be correct in today's society'.[3]

If, however, the quotation is used alone without any of your words to introduce it then it is a complete sentence in its own right and the full stop should be inside the quotation marks as the example below demonstrates. You should, however, avoid using quotations as stand-alone sentences (as demonstrated in the following extract) unless you are using them as block quotations (see section 11.5.1) in which case you do not need quotation marks so the issue of positioning the full stop will not arise.

> However, some academic commentators believe that this view of sovereignty is no longer an accurate description of the position within the UK. 'The traditional stance on sovereignty has not stood the test of time and the Dicean view cannot, in the face of the demands of Europe and the gentle erosion of the Human Rights Act 1998, be said to be correct in today's society.'[3]

The key to success when asking a question and selecting the correct punctuation is to determine whether the question is a direct question or an indirect question:

- A direct question is one that is asked as if it were being spoken directly to someone: should the UK adopt the Euro as its currency? If a direct question is included in your essay, it does require a question mark at the end of the sentence.

- An indirect question is a statement that a particular question needs to be asked: it is necessary to consider whether the UK should adopt the Euro as its currency. In this case, the sentence should end with a full stop, not a question mark. This is because you are not actually asking a question but merely identifying a question that needs to be asked.

11.3.5.2 Commas

Of all the punctuation marks, the comma is probably the most frequently misused. The *Penguin Guide to Punctuation* suggests that this is because children are taught to use a comma in written language whenever they would pause when speaking, which is very misleading advice and tends to lead to commas being put into all sorts of unusual places in a sentence. There are actually only four uses for the comma (see Table 11.3):

Table 11.3 Uses for the comma

Use	Explanation	Example
Listing items	The comma is used to separate words in a list so replaces the words 'and' or 'or' so that the sentence is less cumbersome.	1. 'The defendant was charged with theft and burglary and arson and resisting arrest' becomes 'The defendant was charged with theft, burglary, arson, and resisting arrest'. 2. 'The defendant could be charged under section 18 or section 20 or section 47 depending on the seriousness of the victim's injuries' becomes 'The defendant could be charged under section 18, section 20, or section 47 depending on the seriousness of the victim's injuries'.
Joining two sentences together	The comma links two separate sentences into a single sentence. It can only be used in this way if it is followed by a word that connects the two sentences together: but, and, or, while, yet. Other connecting words cannot be used after a comma so it is incorrect to join two sentences together with a comma if it is followed by any of these words: however, thus, therefore, hence, consequently, nevertheless.	Correct: 'The terms of the offer were unclear, and the claimant sought to argue that he was not bound by the contract'. Incorrect: 'The terms of the offer were unclear, therefore the claimant sought to argue that he was not bound by the contract'.

(Cont)

Table 11.3 *(Cont)*

Use	Explanation	Example
To allow words to be omitted from a sentence	A comma can be used to show that words have been left out of a sentence if the missing words would be a direct repetition of words already used earlier in the sentence.	'Some members of the jury wanted to convict the defendant; others, to acquit him'. The use of the comma makes it unnecessary to repeat the words 'members of the jury wanted' a second time.
To mark the insertion of additional detail in a sentence that interrupts the main point	The comma is used here to separate the additional comment from the main sentence. In this role, the comma is sometimes called a bracketing comma or an isolating comma to indicate its purpose in separating a minor part of the sentence from the major part. Check to see if you have used commas correctly for this purpose by removing the bracketed phrase: the sentence should still make grammatical sense without it. The minor part of the sentence can appear at the beginning, middle, or end of the sentence.	Beginning 'Having discussed the jury selection process, it is necessary to move to consider the role of the jury in a criminal trial.' Middle 'The jury, composed of twelve ordinary men and women, are not equipped to hear complex fraud trials.' End 'Complex fraud trials usually last at least eight months, which places a great burden on the jury.' *Do you see that the main sentence still makes sense without the words separated by the comma or commas?*

11.3.5.3 Colons and semi-colons

There is often great confusion between these two types of punctuation. Both colons and semi-colons appear in the middle of sentences and they are similar in appearance so many students tend to use them interchangeably. This is a mistake because they have different roles to play in a sentence as Figure 11.4 and Figure 11.5 demonstrate.

The colon is used to divide a sentence into a statement followed by elaboration on that statement. The part of the sentence that precedes the colon should be a complete sentence but that part that follows the colon need not be a complete sentence: it could be a single word and often takes the form of a list.

FOR EXAMPLE

There are three key constitutional principles that underpin the unwritten constitution: Parliamentary sovereignty, the separation of powers, and the rule of law.

Can you see that the words after the colon elaborate on the statement prior to the colon by identifying the relevant principles?

Figure 11.4 Role of the colon

> **;** The semi-colon is used to divide a sentence into two separate statements, each of which is a complete sentence in its own right and which could be separated with a full stop or joined with a conjunction. The reason that the two sentences are joined with a semi-colon is to demonstrate the close link between them.
>
> **FOR EXAMPLE**
>
> Most countries have a written constitution which outlines the rights and responsibilities of the State and its citizens; the constitution of the UK is unwritten.
>
> Can you see that the sentence could be divided into two using a full stop in place of the semi-colon or the two parts could be joined by inserting the word 'but' in place of the semi-colon?

Figure 11.5 Role of the semi-colon

It might help you to ensure that you have a good grasp of the difference between colons and semi-colons and the job that they do in a sentence if you compare their operation with that of the full stop in three sentences which are identical except for the differences in punctuation (see Table 11.4).

Table 11.4 Full stops, colons, and semi-colons

Punctuation	Example	Explanation
Full stop	The judge directed the jury to find the defendant 'not guilty'. One of the jurors admitted to using a Ouija board in the jury room in an attempt to contact the dead victim during the murder trial to find out the identity of the murderer.	This is two separate sentences that make two separate statements of fact. By separating the sentences with a full stop, you are suggesting that there is no relationship between them: they are just facts about the trial.
Semi-colon	The judge directed the jury to find the defendant 'not guilty'; one of the jurors admitted to using a Ouija board in the jury room in an attempt to contact the dead victim during the murder trial to find out the identity of the murderer.	The use of a semi-colon here suggests that the two statements are related in some way: perhaps the lack of evidence against the defendant caused the judge to direct to acquit and frustrated the juror so that he tried to find an alternative (spectral) source of evidence.
Colon	The judge directed the jury to find the defendant 'not guilty': one of the jurors admitted to using a Ouija board in the jury room in an attempt to contact the dead victim during the murder trial to find out the identity of the murderer.	The use of the colon indicates a causal relationship between the two sentences. Remember that the statement after the colon explains the statement that precedes the colon. Here, then, the judge has ordered that the defendant should be acquitted because of the use of the Ouija board by the juror.

11.3.5.4 Apostrophes

One of the problems with the apostrophe is that it is so widely misused that it is easy to see all sorts of examples of its incorrect use: menus offer 'free pizza's for the under 12's' (two instances of incorrect use), shops advertise 'ladie's shoe's' (another two examples of misuse), and even museums have signs that state that the exhibit 'was used in the 1920's'. With all this misuse of the apostrophe in evidence, it is hardly surprising that students struggle to master the correct usage of this form of punctuation.

There are two situations in which you are likely to want to use an apostrophe:

- **Contractions.** An apostrophe is used to indicate that a word or words have been shortened by the omission of letters: shouldn't (should not), can't (cannot), he'll (he will), I've (I have), o'clock (of the clock).

- **Possession.** The apostrophe is used to indicate possession: the victim's injury, the judge's summing-up, the UK's role in the European Union.

One very easy way to reduce the problems posed by apostrophe use in your coursework is to make sure that you do not use contractions at all. These are informal forms of expression so should never be used in academic writing. Do not make the mistake of thinking that contractions are an easy way to cut back on words and fit your essay into the word limit: the marks that you will lose for poor written style will be more than those you will gain in the few extra words that you save by using contractions.

Once you have ruled out the possibility of using contractions, the apostrophe should only make an appearance if you are using it to indicate possession. The secret of success here is to distinguish between possession and pluralization. Both of these involve the use of the letter 's' but only the former requires an apostrophe.

- **Possessive not plural:** the claimant's claim in negligence was dismissed by the court (there is one claimant and it is his claim so an apostrophe is needed).

- **Plural not possessive:** the claimants claimed damages in negligence (there are several claimants so the letter 's' is added to the word but the sentence refers to their actions rather than to possession so no apostrophe is needed).

- **Plural and possessive:** the claimants' claim was unsuccessful (there are several claimants so the 's' is added to change the word 'claimant' into its plural form. These claimants have a claim so an apostrophe is added after the plural 's' to indicate possession).

If you can get to grips with the distinction between plural and possessive word forms, you will be well on your way to mastering the use of the apostrophe. Take particular care when making reference to a period of years: many people write 'in the 1990's' as if it were possessive whereas it is actually a way of describing a collection of years so it is plural and should be expressed without the apostrophe as 'in the 1990s'.

One final problem concerns the word 'its' (in the possessive sense rather than as a contraction of 'it is'): the court delivered its judgment, Parliament determines its own procedural rules. Students often use an apostrophe here, writing 'its' as 'it's' to denote possession. However, this is not correct: 'its' is the abstract equivalent of 'his' or 'hers' and you would not consider using an apostrophe with those words. The simple way to avoid problems is to make sure that 'it's' (with an apostrophe) never appears in your academic writing: if you are using the apostrophe correctly then you are using the contraction for 'it is' and contractions are too informal for inclusion in academic writing but if you are using 'it's' as a possessive form then it is incorrect use of an apostrophe so the word should be corrected so that it appears without punctuation.

Practical exercise

Have a look at the following passage of text and see if you can spot and correct the incorrect use of apostrophes.

In the 1980's, there was an increase of case law that examined the role of the trust in relation to domestic property ownership. It's role was of particular importance in relation to spouse's who had not made a direct contribution to the properties purchase price. This was criticised as unduly harsh on spouses who's financial contribution has facilitated the property's purchase as it's too generous to husband's and wife's who had not paid towards the price of the property. Many argue that it isn't fair to give a beneficial share in property to a non-contributing spouse.

 *You will find the answers and an explanation of them at **www.oup.com/he/finch8e/** where you will also find other examples for you to use to improve your understanding of the correct use of the apostrophe.*

11.4 PARAGRAPHS

Paragraphs exist for the convenience of the reader. It is far easier to follow your argument if it is broken up into a series of separate points using paragraphs. Each paragraph should contain a separate idea which should flow from the paragraph before it and lead into the paragraph that follows after it.

Unlike sentences, there are no hard and fast rules about paragraph construction but it can be useful to use the following technique in helping you construct useful paragraphs that flow into each other and which link back to the question.

- **Topic.** The topic sentence announces the main focus of the paragraph.

- **Expansion.** The sentences that follow should explain the topic or elaborate upon it. There should be at least one sentence that elaborates on the topic and there is no maximum number although it is important that paragraphs do not become long and unwieldy: for instance, 700-word paragraphs are undesirable (especially in an essay with a 1,500-word limit). You should aim to have at least two paragraphs on a single side of A4 if you are using double-line spacing. Paragraphs should also not be too short, otherwise you could end up with an essay that reads more like a set of notes or bullet points.

- **Illustration.** You will usually want to provide an example to support the point that you have made or to demonstrate how a particular principle operates. Case law will often be a source of illustrations but there are a range of alternatives including hypothetical examples and points taken from articles, government reports, or newspapers.

- **Link.** The paragraph should end either by leading into the paragraph that follows or by relating the content of the paragraph directly back to the question by, for example, explaining how the point made in the paragraph addresses the point raised by the question.

You will see in the example in Figure 11.6 that there is an extra line space to separate the paragraphs. This makes it clear to the reader where one paragraph ends and the next paragraph begins. The alternative approach is to indent the first line of the new paragraph. Either approach is acceptable. Remember that the aim is to make the essay clear and easy for the marker to follow.

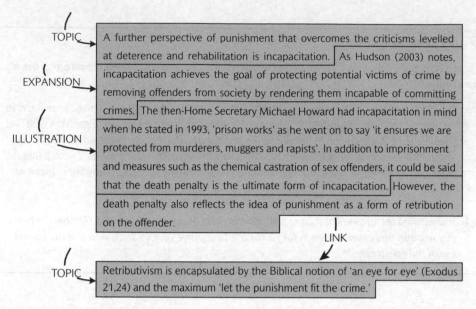

TOPIC

EXPANSION

ILLUSTRATION

A further perspective of punishment that overcomes the criticisms levelled at deterence and rehabilitation is incapacitation. As Hudson (2003) notes, incapacitation achieves the goal of protecting potential victims of crime by removing offenders from society by rendering them incapable of committing crimes. The then-Home Secretary Michael Howard had incapacitation in mind when he stated in 1993, 'prison works' as he went on to say 'it ensures we are protected from murderers, muggers and rapists'. In addition to imprisonment and measures such as the chemical castration of sex offenders, it could be said that the death penalty is the ultimate form of incapacitation. However, the death penalty also reflects the idea of punishment as a form of retribution on the offender.

LINK

TOPIC

Retributivism is encapsulated by the Biblical notion of 'an eye for eye' (Exodus 21,24) and the maximum 'let the punishment fit the crime.'

Figure 11.6 Paragraph construction

A final point to note is that there has been a recent proliferation of the idea of primary and secondary paragraphing to denote the strength of the relationship between a paragraph and the one that follows it by varying the size of the gap between the paragraphs. This is nonsense and not something that would be acceptable in writing at university level. There are sentences and there are paragraphs. If a sentence is closely related to the previous sentence, it belongs in the same paragraph; if it is not closely related, it belongs in the following paragraph.

*You will find further examples of these rules and their application at **www.oup.com/he/finch8e/**.*

11.5 USING QUOTATIONS

Quotations can add authority to your work as you are, in effect, using the words of someone with far more legal expertise than yourself to support your argument. They can also give you a form of words to describe something in a way that is far better than you would be able to explain it yourself.

Although the judicious use of quotations can strengthen your argument and provide evidence of the breadth of your research, they it can have a negative impact on your work if the quotations are not used with care. Have a look at the extract taken from an essay on the role of equitable maxims in trusts as it demonstrates two of the most common problems that arise in relation to quotations in student essays.

A maxim is defined in the Oxford English Dictionary as a 'general truth or a rule of conduct expressed in a sentence' thus an equitable maxim is 'a general truth or rule of conduct about the operation of equity'.[1] 'The maxims are not rules to be construed like statutes, but rather a general basis around which much of equity formed'[2] and they can be said to be 'an attempt to formulate in short pithy phrases the key principles which underline the exercise of equitable jurisdiction'.[3]

[1] R Clements and A Abass, *Equity and Trusts: Text, Cases and Materials* (OUP 2008) 34.
[2] S Wilson, *Textbook on Trusts* (OUP 2005) 9.
[3] R Pearce and J Stevens, *The Law of Trusts and Equitable Obligations* (3rd edn, Butterworths 2002).

There is heavy reliance on quotations in the extract: sixty-two out of the eighty-five words (about 73 per cent) were not written by the student and the overall impression given is that this is an essay that is made up of a series of joined together quotations. The problem that this raises can be seen clearly if you read the same extract with the quotations taken out.

> A maxim is defined in the Oxford English Dictionary as a . . . thus an equitable maxim is . . . and they can be said to be . . .

As you can see, once the quotations are omitted, there is nothing in the words remaining that demonstrates the student's knowledge of the subject matter. As such, it would be difficult for the marker to award marks for the student's understanding of equitable maxims. Remember that you should use your own words to explain key concepts to show the marker that you understand them or, alternatively, use a quotation and follow this with an explanation of your own.

The second problem with the extract is that it uses textbooks as a source of its quotations. Try to remember that textbook writers have gathered together all the relevant statutes, case law, academic commentary, and other source material and distilled it into a condensed and accessible explanation of the law to help students. As such, textbooks are explaining the law that can be found elsewhere or comments made about the law by experts. Ideally, you should use the textbook to give you an overview of the topic and then follow up the references or conduct your own research to find the law and comment upon it to use as the source material for your essays rather than relying on the explanations provided in textbooks. By quoting from cases and articles, you are demonstrating your research as well as supporting your work with authority so try to ensure you quote from these sources rather than textbooks wherever possible.

11.5.1 Presentation of quotations

The way to present a quotation within your work depends on the length of the quotation. Anything from a single word to a fragment of a sentence of about a line-and-a-half of text can be incorporated as part of your sentence whilst longer quotations and those that are complete sentences in their own right should be presented as block quotations.

> An equitable maxim is a statement that sums up 'in short pithy phrases'[1] the principles and operation of equity.

In this example, a short quotation that captures part of the nature of an equitable maxim has been incorporated into the sentence. Note that the quotation appears within quotation marks and is accompanied by a reference that indicates the source of the material; both of these features are essential in order to ensure your work is referenced properly and to avoid any suspicion of plagiarism (see chapter 13 for more detail on these issues).

By contrast, a longer quotation is set apart from the main body of your essay and quotation marks should not be used: they are not needed as the indentation of the quotation separates it from your own work and indicates to the marker that it is a quotation (see Figure 11.7). A reference must still be provided that acknowledge the source of the words.

This example also illustrates the practice of using single line spacing to present quotations as a further way of differentiating the words of others from the main text of the essay. This is a matter of preference: it is perfectly permissible to use the same spacing for quotations as you have used for the rest of the text.

See further section 11.7.1 on formatting.

An equitable maxim is a concise statement that captures one of the principles of equity. These maxims are not rules with the capacity to bind in future cases like principles of common law but are more like general guidelines that capture the central sentiments of equity. As Marshall explains:

> Equitable maxims do not bind or control but guide and inform. They are a gentle reminder of the principles of fairness that permeate the system of equity. If they were to be harsh and unyielding, they would not serve the purpose that equity exists to achieve.[1]

This reference to equitable maxims as a 'gentle reminder' highlights the relationship between equity and the 'harsh and unyielding' common law as equity originally operated as a separate system of law administered by a different court in order to counteract any unfairness that arose due to the strict application of the common law.

Figure 11.7 Using quotations in an essay

11.5.2 Effective use of quotations

There is quite a skill to using quotations effectively. Too many students fail to realize this and, as a result, the quotations that are included in their essay serve to highlight this lack of skill so that the quotations actually weaken rather than strengthen their work. The following guidelines should help you to use quotations to good effect in your writing.

- **Introduce your quotations.** Irrespective of whether you are using a few words or several sentences of quoted material, you must blend it into your essay with words of introduction. This could be a simple identification of the author such as 'As Jones argues "the remedial constructive trust offers little of value to the modern law of trusts"' or a more detailed approach that introduces the topic as well as its source: for example, 'Jones argues that the constructive trust has little role to play in modern trust law, suggesting that "it is an exhausted anachronism that should be laid to rest and never revived"'. It is very poor practice to have a quotation as a stand-alone sentence with no words of your own to introduce it.

- **Use an appropriate verb to situate the quotation.** You could introduce every quotation with the words 'Keller says the postal rule is outdated' or 'Keller states the postal rule is outdated' but 'says' and 'states' are neutral verbs that do not give the reader any clues as to how the quotation that follows fits into the rest of your essay. Think about the difference that it would make to introduce a quotation with the words 'Keller alleges that the postal rule is outdated'. This implies that you will be disagreeing with this view in your essay; you would expect the quotation to be followed by 'but' and an argument in favour of the postal rule. Compare this with the impression given by the statement 'Keller notes that the postal rule is outdated'. Take time to think about the role of the quotation in your essay and select a verb that is appropriate to that role. The following are some of the verbs that you could use.

says	observes	alleges	argues	thinks
states	notes	claims	asserts	remarks
comments	explains	suggests	affirms	adds

- **Discuss the quotation.** Remember that the purpose of a quotation is to support your own words, not to replace them. This means that you should make the quotation work for you by explaining its meaning or relevance rather than leaving it to speak for itself. If you look back at Figure 11.7, you will see that a good example of how Marshall's quotation is discussed and key terms from it are used to develop the writer's own argument. Whether you are using a quotation to illustrate a point or support your argument, it will only do this if you make it clear to the reader what its purpose is and how the quotation is relevant to your essay.

- **Avoid lengthy quotations.** Quotations are not a substitute for your own words. You should look for short phrases or a few sentences that make a point that you could not make in your own words or that is better expressed in the words of the original author. Try to capture a particular idea with a quotation but to explain its detail, significance, or operation in your own words. Markers will not be impressed to read long quotations when what they want to read is your own explanation, interpretation, and evaluation of the law.

- **Incorporate quotations so that they make sense.** Used properly, quotations should blend in with your own words. This means that if you have a sentence that is part quotation and part your own words, the two should combine to make a complete grammatical sentence. You can take words out of a quotation to help with this provided you indicate that words are omitted by the use of ellipses (. . .) and you can add words that are not in the original quotation using square brackets. Square brackets can also be used to indicate a change from upper to lower case (or vice versa). For example, if you wish to take a fragment of a quotation and use it as a complete sentence, you will need to change the initial letter of the first word from lower to upper case as demonstrated in Figure 11.8.

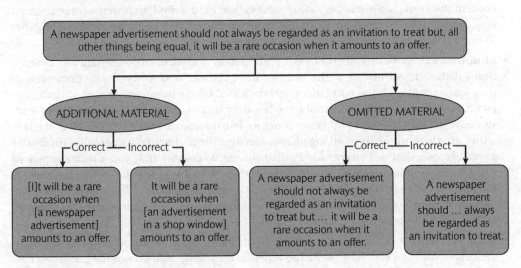

Figure 11.8 Adding and deleting words from quotations

11.6 WORD LIMITS

It is likely that most, if not all, of the coursework that you complete during your studies will have a word limit. It is usual for the word limit to be absolute—that is, it is the maximum number of words that can be used and this cannot be exceeded by even one word—but some universities operate a ranged approach to the word limit which means that it can be exceeded by a certain number of words. You must check what the policy is at your own university and be sure to stick to it as there is usually a penalty for exceeding the word limit which means that your mark will be reduced.

Students tend to dislike word limits. They see them as an unnecessary restriction that means that they cannot write all that they want to write. However, assessments are written carefully by lecturers to ensure that they can be answered fully and to a very good standard within the word limit. It is harder, though, to write within the word limit as it forces you to really think about how much relevance each point has to the question and how much detail you need to include as well as requiring you to work on your written style so that it is sufficiently concise.

11.6.1 Tips for meeting the word limit

When trying to write within the word limit, try to take these three points into account as you write:

- **Test all material for relevance.** Make sure that you have understood the question and that you are responding to what it asks rather than simply writing about the topic it identifies (see chapter 14 on essay writing for further discussion of this point). Evaluate each point that you plan to include and assess its match to the question. Check to make sure that you have not gone off at a tangent: sometimes you can move away from the question without realizing it. Are you determined to include a particular point in your essay because it was something that you struggled to understand, or it involves a source that was hard to find, or you are proud of the way that you have written it? This can happen but remember that content does not gain marks because it is clever, was hard to find, or is well written unless it is also relevant to the question. Relevance has to be the touchstone for determining whether or not a point has a place in your answer.

- **Eliminate excessive descriptive detail.** A good essay is a balanced combination of description (of the subject matter at the heart of the question) and analysis (the discussion of that subject matter in the particular context created by the question). It is an unfortunate fact that it is much easier to describe the law than it is to analyse it. This sometimes leads students to fill their essays and answers to problem questions with descriptions of the law, either omitting any analysis all together or leaving it until the final paragraph. This creates a weak answer that will enjoy only limited success. Make sure that you allocate sufficient words to allow you to engage in in-depth analysis by describing only that which is necessary for the analysis to be understood. In other words, descriptive content should only be there because it supports the analysis and helps it to make sense: only describe things that you really need to describe.

- **Aim to develop a concise written style.** Written style is a contentious topic as some students take the view that they 'write the way that they write' and do not have a willingness to change or adapt their written style. However, law is a very precise and concise discipline. This means that you need to be able to use words accurately to capture the specific meaning of the law and that you need to do so in a way that is not excessively wordy. It is also often the case that a concise written style is one that uses language in a more sophisticated way. A good way to learn this is to read articles in academic journals and try to emulate the way that authors write. You can also use the written style of judges in appeal cases as a source of inspiration to help you to develop an appropriate legalistic writing style.

If you try to bear these points in mind as you write, you should end up with a piece of work that is close to the word limit and will only need a little refining to reduce it further. However, creating a concise, analytical, and focused piece of work takes practice so you should not be too dismayed if you still end up with a first draft of your work that is quite a way over the word limit. Resist the temptation to cut whole paragraphs out of your work: students sometimes do this as a desperate word-reduction measure and then end up with work that (a) omits an important point and (b) does not flow properly as the missing paragraph contained a link to the material before and after it. It is far better to follow the four steps shown in Table 11.5 to try and reduce the word count of your work in a more measured way that should hopefully strengthen as well as shorten it.

Table 11.5 Techniques for reducing word count

Remove	Cut out any material that is unnecessary or irrelevant. When writing an essay, this means taking another look at the question and being sure that each point that you include makes a contribution to answering it rather than simply being something about the topic more generally. When answering a problem question, be sure that you have not included discussion that is not required such as advising additional parties. Be cautious when removing material though: if you thought it was relevant and necessary when you created your first draft, be sure that you understand why you have changed your view on this as this will help you ensure that you are not just culling material out of a desperate desire to meet the word limit.
Reduce	You can reduce the bulk of your essay by ensuring that there is a lack of repetition in your answer. For example, you should never use two authorities to support a single point of law and you should not repeat explanations of the law that have already been set out earlier in your work. When answering a problem question, check to ensure that it is strictly necessary if you find yourself using the same facts more than once.
Rephrase	Once you have removed unnecessary material and reduced your work then you are left working with the content that you want to appear in the final version of your coursework. So now you have to find a way to make this shorter without removing any further substance from your work. This means that you need to reword your essay so that it has fewer words without losing any of the meaning. One of the best ways to do this is to work through your essay methodically from the beginning with the aim of removing at least one word from each sentence. Of course, you may need to rewrite the whole sentence rather than simply deleting a single word or perhaps you will find a way to lose words by combining two sentences into one.
Reference	Effective referencing and cross-referencing can be invaluable when it comes to cutting words. You will find a detailed discussion of this in chapter 13.

Practical exercise

Have a look at the paragraph below. It is the second paragraph of an essay that considers whether it is true that the law does not allow a trust to be established to benefit a purpose rather than an individual. Work through the paragraph and try to (1) remove any irrelevant material, (2) remove excessive descriptive detail, and (3) reword it so that it is more concise without losing its main points.

There are quite a lot of situations that are exceptions to the rule against purpose trusts. Two situations in which a purpose trust can exist even though there are no identifiable human beneficiaries are the establishment of a purpose trust for the care of animals and a purpose trust that is dedicated to the erection and upkeep and maintenance of a monument. This use of a purpose trust to care for animals is illustrated in the case of *Pettingall v Pettingall*. In this case, the testator left the sum of £50 a year to the upkeep of his favourite black mare. This was held to be valid. In *Re Dean*, a trust was upheld to maintain a horse and some hounds for fifty years provided that the animals lived that long. These cases demonstrate that purpose trusts can be valid if they are aimed at caring for particular animals. An illustration of a valid trust to maintain a monument can be seen in the case of *Mussett v Bingle* where the testator left a sum of money to erect a monument in memory of his first wife. Also in the case of *Pirbright v Salway*, the court upheld a trust to maintain a family burial enclosure and in *Re Hooper* the court upheld a trust to ensure that a vault was maintained in good condition. However, in the case of *Re Endacott*, the settlor left his residuary estate to his local parish council for a particular purpose which was to provide a useful monument to him but this was held to be void because the court felt that the line of case law involving specific graves and monuments should not be extended. Although this case does demonstrate that not all trusts established to achieve a particular purpose will be valid, there is a fairly sizeable body of case law that does recognise that there can be a trust for a purpose if that purpose is to erect a specific monument or maintain a particular burial plot. These examples demonstrate that there are some exceptions to the more general rule that a trust cannot exist for a purpose but only for human beneficiaries.

> *You will find a rewritten version of this paragraph at* **www.oup.com/he/finch8e/** *with an explanation of the way that it was reduced from 362 to 120 words: cut by two-thirds but still making essentially the same points.*

Alternatively, it may be that you find that you have said everything that you want to say but have not yet reached the word limit. Whether or not this is a problem depends upon how many words you are short of the limit. If you are ten words under, it may well be the case that you have an admirably concise written style and have included only relevant material. However, if you are significantly short of the word limit then it is likely to mean that your work has one (or both) of the following problems:

- **Omission of relevant material.** If you are more than one hundred words below the word limit then it is likely that you have left something out that needed to be included. Go back to the question and review your reading to see if there is anything that you may have overlooked that needs to be included.
- **Lack of necessary detail.** It may be that you have gone too far in your effort to be concise and perhaps have left out some of the description that was needed to support your analysis. Alternatively, perhaps you have neglected to develop your arguments sufficiently or you have misjudged the complexity of a particular issue and failed to explore it in sufficient detail.

Essentially, if you have produced a first draft of your essay that is significantly short of the word limit, this should ring alarm bells and indicate that there is still much work to be done.

You will find more detailed advice on interpreting questions, selecting relevant material, and keeping a strong focus on the question in chapter 14.

11.6.2 Why stick to the word limit?

It is essential that you do adhere to the word limit, however challenging that may seem, as most institutions impose a penalty for failure to do so. This may be a deduction of marks or a refusal to read any words that go over the specified limit. Either type of penalty will reduce the mark that your work receives. In some institutions that have a cumulative deduction policy, that is, a deduction of two marks for every ten words over the limit, an essay which was too far over the limit could end up with a mark that was lower than the pass mark once all the deductions have been taken into account.

Do not make the mistake of misstating the word limit—quoting that you have used 1,495 words in a 1,500-word limit when you have really used 1,743—as this generally attracts an even more severe penalty, sometimes zero and a requirement that the coursework be repeated.

11.6.3 What counts towards the word limit?

Always check your department's regulations to determine how the word count is calculated. Some institutions exclude references to statute and case law from the word count, for example, so all statutory references and case citations can be deducted from the overall limit. This is likely to apply only to actual references rather than all discussion of case or statute law, so make sure that you make an accurate deduction. Equally, some departments will state that all references are included in the word count (which makes checking that you have made an accurate declaration of the word limit easier) whereas others exclude footnotes from the word count but specify that they must only be used to reference and not to introduce any additional text. There are many other potential policies on counting words that may arise at different institutions. This chapter does not aim to outline all the possibilities, rather just to orientate you to the existence of the different methods of counting words. It highlights the need to check the rules in order to ensure that you are adhering to the requirements of the word limit in force at your institution.

11.7 PRESENTATION

Presentation of coursework, or how it looks on the page, is important. If you look at several pieces of work with identical content, you will probably find that you make instinctive evaluations about their quality on the basis of their visual appearance. A well-presented piece of work that complies with any institutional requirements with regard to font choice or formatting, for example, will create a good first impression with the marker. Whilst this may not necessarily contribute to the grade that the essay receives (unless your department awards marks for presentation), it cannot do any harm to ensure that the person marking your work feels favourably disposed towards it from the outset.

11.7.1 Formatting

If there is a house style with regard to presentation, use it even if you do not like the style chosen. Most people have a font style or pattern of layout that they favour but that is no reason not to adhere to the specifications that you have been given. Some departments even impose an automatic deduction of marks for failure to comply with the presentation requirements of assessed coursework, so it is always advisable to find out what the requirements are and follow them to the letter. In the absence of any specifications as to style, you may like to bear the following in mind when choosing how to present your work:

- **Font and font size:** choose a relatively straightforward font that is easy for the marker to read. It would generally be unnecessary to have a font size larger than 12-point in the main body of your text.

- **Line spacing:** double or one-and-a-half line spacing is advisable as it is easier to read in large quantities than single-spaced text. Moreover, wider line spacing ensures that your work covers more pages and gives the marker more space to write comments in the margin.
- **Margins:** as with line spacing, wide margins allow the marker space to write comments. The default settings should give sufficient space.
- **Paragraphing:** using a double space between paragraphs creates more 'white space' that makes the page easier on the marker's eye and gives additional space for comment.

Overall, these guidelines are aimed at ensuring that the page is not too crowded so that the words look squashed onto the page.

11.7.2 Statutes and cases

It is usual to use different formatting to ensure that statutory references and case names stand out from the bulk of the text. Your institution may have particular requirements in this respect but, if not, choose a style and stick to it throughout your essay. As with so many aspects of presentation, consistency is the key to success.

It is conventional to italicize case names but not the full citation.

For further information on referencing, see chapter 13.

11.7.3 Headings

This section addresses issues of the presentation of headings rather than their use in essays (which can be found in chapter 14). If you are using headings in your work, make sure that you use an appropriate and consistent approach to formatting them. For example, if you use two levels of heading (main headings and subheadings), make sure that the style you use for the main heading is more prominent than that of the subheading and that you use the same style throughout your work. Finally, do make sure that something follows the heading; leaving a heading 'hanging' as the final words on the bottom of the page whilst the text follows on the next is not an effective approach to the use of headings.

11.7.4 Page numbers

It is useful to ensure that the pages of your work are numbered. If your marker drops your essay, it might be difficult to reorder them if they are not numbered. Equally, if you staple the pages in the incorrect order (it happens!) and they are not numbered, your lecturer may not realize that the pages are not in order and merely assume that the flow of your argument is not logical.

11.7.5 Capital letters

There is an unfortunate tendency amongst students to capitalize every word that seems significant, such as Judge, Court, Case, and Law, or any phrases that seem sufficiently important, for example, Rule of Law, *Actus Reus*, or Invitation to Treat. This is incorrect and should be avoided. The use of capital letters should be reserved for the word at the start of a sentence and proper nouns only.

11.7.6 Checking for errors

Although the aim is to allow the marker plenty of space to write comments, you really want to attract feedback about the content of your legal argument rather than technicalities of presentation, so do ensure that the spelling, grammar, and punctuation are correct. There are few things more disheartening for a student than the return of an essay that is covered in corrections, so avoid this by ensuring that you do not give the marker a great deal to correct. It should go without saying that the work should be meticulously checked for basic errors prior to submission, but far too many students submit work that looks suspiciously like a first draft in that it is peppered with the sorts of error that should have been corrected prior to submission.

The solution is to leave sufficient time prior to submission to check your essay thoroughly for accuracy. Use the spell check, making sure that it is set to UK English rather than US English (the spelling differs between the two) but remember that it cannot check for context. Accept that the spell check is not infallible (for instance, it will not catch errors such as statue/statute, trail/trial, electoral role/electoral roll) and proofread your essay yourself or, as it is often difficult to spot your own errors as you tend to read what you meant to write rather than what you have actually written, get a friend to check it for you.

One technique that can be particularly useful, even after you have strengthened your writing skills through years of study, is to compose a personalized checklist of potential problems. Everyone has some weakness in their writing style and it is easy to be blind to your own errors, so finding a way to remind yourself to take particular care over certain issues can be an excellent way of ensuring that you produce a polished and accurate piece of work. You could start with quite a general checklist in the early stages of your studies that reminds you to check such basics as spelling or the technicalities of presenting case names and citations correctly. As your written style strengthens, some of the basics will become second nature whilst other more specific problems will inevitably emerge. For example, perhaps you find the distinction between plural and possessive 'its' confusing or you are unclear about the difference between 'affect' and 'effect'. Irrespective of the nature of your problem, your checklist can evolve to reflect this as you progress.

One example of the sorts of points that you could include on your checklist is given in Figure 11.9.

Check spelling and grammar	☐	Are footnotes on the right page?	☐
Check 'its' and 'it's'	☐	References: complete and correct?	☐
Does it look right on paper?	☐	Italics for case names	☐
Any hanging headings?	☐	Does it make sense?	☐
Check use of capitals	☐		

Figure 11.9 Checklist

🕒 *You will find further details on checking for errors, both in style and presentation and a suggested error-checking template to get you started at* **www.oup.com/he/finch8e/**.

CHAPTER SUMMARY

Language

- Strive for an appropriate level of formality in your written style; the approach used in good textbooks and articles will provide a useful example
- Avoid casual language such as text speak and the use of the first person
- Be alert for the conventions relating to gender-neutral language and the use of Latin
- Be aware that words that have legal and non-legal meanings, such as assault, can confuse the reader

Grammar and punctuation

- Take care to ensure that your work is grammatical as this contributes towards accuracy and precision
- Look for evidence that would suggest that there is a problem with your grammar and punctuation and ensure you seek appropriate assistance if it appears necessary
- Take note of the common problems that arise and strive to eliminate them from your writing

Quotations

- Incorporating quotations into your work can add strength to your arguments but you must ensure that you do not use a quotation out of context or misrepresent its meaning
- If you add or remove words or emphasis, this must be noted in the quotation or its reference as appropriate. Ensure that any changes do not alter the meaning of the quotation
- Do not overuse quotations. The bulk of your essay should be expressed in your words as opposed to merely joining together a string of quotations. Equally, do not use quotations, particularly from textbooks, to express concepts that could be expressed in your own words; your ability to explain legal concepts will attract more credit than your ability to select an appropriate quotation

Presentation

- Discover whether there are any mandatory requirements for the presentation of coursework and, if so, ensure that you adhere to them
- Ensure that you leave sufficient time prior to the deadline for submission to check your work thoroughly for presentational errors

 FURTHER READING

- If you require greater guidance on the essential matters of grammar, spelling, and punctuation than it has been possible to provide in this chapter, see J Peck and M Coyle, *The Student's Guide to Writing: Grammar, Punctuation and Spelling* (Palgrave 1999).
- A good source of grammar tips can be found online at www.grammar.quickanddirtytips.com.
- Clear definitions and guidance of each type of punctuation are given in RL Trask, *The Penguin Guide to Punctuation* (Penguin 1997).

Legal reasoning and ethics

INTRODUCTION

This chapter provides an introduction to legal reasoning. In the first part of the book, you will have begun building the skills that you need to find and read the law and have also been introduced to the idea of judicial precedent and statutory interpretation. You will understand, then, that the law develops as a result of decisions made by the courts as well as new legislation that comes from Parliament or the European Union. This chapter will start giving you the skills to analyse the way in which judges decide cases. There are various points of view that judges can (and do) take in deciding the outcomes of cases, so this chapter will introduce some of the theory behind judicial reasoning before moving on to show how judges reason in practice. It should be read in conjunction with chapter 4, which focuses on using legislation and chapter 7, on using case law.

The ability to appreciate and understand legal reasoning is an important academic legal skill, although it also has some practical advantages. One of the keys to academic legal success is the ability to engage critically with the law and so it is important that you begin to build your skills in analysis by seeking out the reasons that underlie particular decisions. Students often make the mistake of thinking that applying the law is simple, but this is not the case: there are many other factors which can be taken into account when deciding what the outcome of a case should be. This context provides a backdrop for the historical development of the law, an appreciation of which will enable you to develop and demonstrate your critical thinking skills.

Learning outcomes

After studying this chapter, you will be able to:

- Understand the processes involved in logical legal reasoning
- Explain how legal reasoning is more than just the mechanical application of law to facts
- Distinguish between natural law, legal positivism, and legal realism
- Be able to read a judgment and analyse the factors taken into account by judges
- Appreciate the practical benefit of understanding legal reasoning

12.1 REASONING

The *Oxford English Dictionary* defines the verb 'to reason' as:

> To think something through, work out in a logical manner

and 'reasoning' as:

> The action of reason; especially the process by which one judgement is deduced from another or others which are given.

You can see, then, that 'reasoning' (in the general sense) is working something out logically in a process of deduction. Before we move on to see what this means for legal reasoning, we must first take a brief look at some theory of logic.

12.1.1 Logic

One key form of logical argument is the *logical syllogism* which dates back to the time of the ancient Greeks (in particular Aristotle and Zeno of Citium in the third century BC). In syllogistic reasoning, one proposition is deduced from two or more others. The proposition that is deduced is the *conclusion* and the two or more statements from which it is inferred are called *premises*.

Practical exercise

You have probably encountered syllogistic reasoning without actually having realized so. Many logic puzzles are based upon the syllogism. For instance:

- *Premise 1*: All dogs are mammals
- *Premise 2*: All mammals are animals
- *Conclusion*: All dogs are animals

Have a look at the following logic puzzles and decide whether or not the conclusion is valid or invalid: in other words, whether it follows logically from the two premises without the need for any further information.

1. If today is Tuesday, then I have a criminal law seminar. If I have a criminal law seminar, then I will pack *Smith and Hogan* in my bag. Therefore, if today is Tuesday, I will pack *Smith and Hogan* in my bag.

2. All mice in England eat sunflower seeds. Some rodents eat sunflower seeds. Therefore, some rodents are mice in England.

3. All lawyers are highly intelligent. Some lawyers are not polite. Therefore, no polite people are highly intelligent.

You will find answers to these puzzles and an explanation of how they were reached at **www.oup.com/he/finch8e/**.

So, a syllogism consists of two premises and a conclusion. For a syllogism to be valid, it must be logically impossible for its premises to be true and for its conclusion to be false. You will have seen from the practical exercise that it is not sufficient that both premises are true for the conclusion also to be true. Look at this example:

- All dogs are mammals.
- Some mammals can fly.
- Therefore some dogs can fly.

The first two premises are certainly true: dogs are mammals and some mammals (including bats and flying squirrels) can fly. However, outside the realms of mythology, there are no flying dogs. The fact that dogs are mammals and that some mammals can fly does not prove anything about the airborne capabilities of dogs. So, in this example, since it is logically possible for the premises to be true *and* the conclusion to be false, then the argument is not logically valid.

In legal arguments, the parts of the local argument take certain forms. The first premise (known in logic as the *major premise*) is generally a statement of law. This is an abstract statement of a legal rule. The second premise (known as the *minor premise*) is usually a statement of fact; a statement which concerns a specific person, thing, or state of affairs. The conclusion draws together the general statement of law with the particular statement of fact and therefore explains how the general rule applies to the particular facts. In the legal context, this is *applying the law to the facts* and is the simplest form of legal analysis or reasoning.

12.1.2 Simple legal reasoning

Legal reasoning is founded on the basic syllogistic framework. The steps in the process are as shown in Figure 12.1.

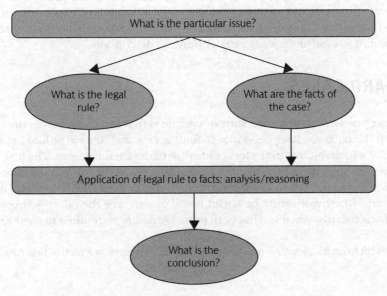

Figure 12.1 The process of legal reasoning

The steps in this process can be illustrated with a simple example:

- The *issue* in this particular case is whether Oz is criminally liable for the murder of Kalvinder.
- The *facts of the case* are that Oz knocked on Kalvinder's front door. When Kalvinder answered the door, Oz said 'I hate you and I want you to die'. She then shot Kalvinder in the head, killing her instantly. Oz was not insane.
- The *legal rule* is the definition of murder: where a person of sound mind and discretion unlawfully kills any reasonable creature in being (i.e. a human being) under the Queen's Peace (i.e. not in wartime) with intent to kill or cause grievous bodily (really serious) harm.

The *application of the law to the facts* is straightforward:

- Sound mind? We are told that Oz was not insane, so she was of sound mind at the time of the killing.
- Unlawful killing. There is nothing to suggest that Oz was acting in self-defence, was of diminished responsibility, had lost control, or was killing in pursuit of a suicide pact. Oz killed Kalvinder by shooting her in the head. The killing is therefore unlawful.
- Reasonable creature in being. Kalvinder is (was) a human being.
- Queen's Peace. There is nothing to suggest that this happened during wartime.
- Intention to kill/cause grievous bodily harm (GBH). Oz's intention is demonstrated by her words and actions. At the very least, shooting someone in the head would cause really serious harm.

Therefore, given that all the elements of the offence are made out, then Oz is criminally liable for the murder of Kalvinder.

If only it was always that straightforward! Many law students—particularly those new to the study of law—assume that legal reasoning simply involves a mechanical application of the rules to the facts. This is not so. There are many other issues that courts take into account when deciding how the law should apply to particular cases. While it is true that many simple cases do involve the application of rules, there are also many hard cases that come before the courts which do not neatly fall under such a straightforward description.

12.2 HARD CASES

The next exercise will illustrate the sorts of dilemmas that can come before the courts, and will also test the skills you have developed in finding case law. You will be looking at two hard cases, both of which resulted in the loss of life in extreme circumstances. The first, *R v Dudley and Stephens*, involves the cannibalism of a cabin boy following a shipwreck in order to save the lives of the remaining crew. The second, *Re A (Children)*, concerned conjoined twins, Jodie and Mary, and whether it would be lawful to kill one to save the other, acting against the wishes of their parents, when leaving both joined would have resulted in their joint premature death.

You may wish to revisit chapter 6 to refresh your memory on ways in which to find case law.

> ## Practical exercise
>
> Using the database of your choice, find the following cases:
>
> > *R v Dudley and Stephens* (1884) 14 QBD 273
> >
> > *Re A (Children)* [2001] Fam 147 (CA)
>
> and answer the following questions for each case:
>
> 1. What was the legal issue in the case?
> 2. What was the legal rule that applied in this case?
> 3. What were the particular facts of this case?
> 4. What made this case a hard case?
> 5. Do you agree with the decision of the court?
>
> *You will find some comments on each of these questions at **www.oup.com/he/finch8e/**.*

You should have seen by studying the two cases *Re A (Children)* and *Dudley and Stephens* that the courts sometimes have to deal with very sensitive and delicate issues. You may also have heard in the news about one or more of the 'right-to-die' cases: Tony Nicklinson, who had been paralysed from the neck down since suffering a stroke in 2005, died in August 2012 after failing in a legal bid to end his life with the help of a doctor. This case ultimately ended in the Supreme Court which rejected the 'right-to-die' argument but the Supreme Court said that there is a 'real prospect' a future human rights challenge would succeed if Parliament did not reconsider the current ban. You can find the full judgment at *R (Nicklinson and another) v Ministry of Justice* [2014] UKSC 38, introduced by Lord Neuberger (President) who said:

> These appeals arise out of tragic facts and raise difficult and significant issues, namely whether the present state of the law of England and Wales relating to assisting suicide infringes the European Convention on Human Rights, and whether the code published by the Director of Public Prosecutions ('the DPP') relating to prosecutions of those who are alleged to have assisted a suicide is lawful.

So, judges have to deal with legal, ethical, and moral questions when making their decisions. Balancing these issues requires analysis of the relationship between law and morality and the role of the judiciary in making law and setting precedent. These are more abstract theoretical issues in law than you may have encountered so far in your legal studies, but it is worth persevering even if the immediate relevance of legal theory might not seem clear to you. The next section will introduce you to three different schools of legal thought before moving on to look at a classic example of different judicial approaches to the same difficult legal problem.

12.3 AN INTRODUCTION TO LEGAL THEORY

The philosophical consideration of law is commonly referred to as jurisprudence. While jurisprudence is not a compulsory topic in a qualifying law degree, some institutions require students to take a jurisprudence module at some stage in their legal studies as even a basic understanding of why the law is as it is assists in understanding the law in a deeper way and can have practical application in the real-world practice of law.

Within this section, we will introduce three key areas of legal theory:

- Natural law
- Legal positivism
- Legal realism.

12.3.1 Natural law

Proponents of natural law consider it to be a system of law based on the laws of nature and which is, therefore, universal in application. It considers that law and morality are connected and that it is a higher system of law than any legal system constructed by man. It upholds certain rights or values that are inherent in human reason and human nature.

Natural law has been considered by philosophers over many centuries. Cicero commented in *De republica* ('on the commonwealth') that:

> True law is right reason in agreement with nature; it is of universal application, unchanging and everlasting; it summons to duty by its commands, and averts from wrongdoing by its prohibitions . . . We cannot be freed from its obligations by Senate or People, and we need not look outside ourselves for an expounder of interpreter of it. And there will not be different laws at Rome and at Athens, or different laws now and in the future, but one eternal and unchangeable law will be valid for all nations and for all times . . .

The basic principle of natural law is that, as a higher law, any law made by man must accord with its principles in order to be valid. If law is not moral, then it is not law and has no authority.

Practical exercise

Consider your viewpoint on the following issues:

1. Is it natural to be racially or religiously prejudiced?
2. Is it natural to die by taking your own life?
3. It is natural to be monogamous?
4. Is it natural to use contraception?

These questions are up for debate and there are not necessarily 'right' answers to them, although you will find some comments on each of them at www.oup.com/he/finch8e/.

So, natural lawyers will always seek to reason for an outcome that upholds morality. St Thomas Aquinas (1225–1274), the Christian philosopher and theologian, called law without moral content a 'perversion' of law since 'good is to be done and promoted, and evil is to be avoided'.

The difficult question then becomes what is moral, or good, or evil and do the morals of the judiciary necessarily accord with the morals of the public?

A good example of a case that raised difficult moral issues was that of *Gillick v West Norfolk and Wisbech Area Health Authority* [1986] AC 112 (HL). This case followed the publication of guidance by the Department of Health and Social Security to area health authorities on family planning services which contained a section dealing with contraceptive advice and treatment for young people. It stated that clinic sessions should be available for people of all ages and that, in exceptional circumstances, a doctor could exercise his clinical judgement to prescribe contraception to children under 16 without parental consent. Mrs Gillick, a Roman Catholic, sought an assurance from her local health authority that no contraceptive advice would be given to any of her daughters while they were under 16 without her knowledge and consent. The conflicting arguments were:

- If parental consent was necessary, levels of teenage pregnancy would increase.

- If parental consent was not necessary, the courts would be encouraging underage sex.

Practical exercise

Gillick was determined by a 3–2 majority in the House of Lords. Using your research skills, find the case and read the judgment. Then answer the following questions:

1. What was the outcome?
2. What were the arguments put forward by the majority?
3. What did the dissenting judgments say?
4. Do you agree with the outcome?

You will find some commentary on these questions at www.oup.com/he/finch8e/.

12.3.2 Legal positivism

In contrast to natural law, legal positivism holds law and morality to be separate issues. Man-made law is stated (or 'posited'; hence 'positivism') by the legislature, and, provided that it has been properly enacted, it is legally valid, regardless of its moral content (or lack thereof). Put another way, whereas natural law is considered valid by virtue of its content (and thus invalid due to a lack of moral content), positive law is considered valid by virtue of its source only (and thus would be valid despite a lack of moral content). Legal positivism considers that law is a human construct and does not recognize a higher natural law.

Thus, for the legal positivists, law is a clearly defined set of rules that is established by the state for the benefit of the state as a whole. It has no moral purpose other than to ensure the survival of the state. The theory of natural law was put forward from the sixteenth century. Thomas Hobbes in *Leviathan* considered that without a man-made state, the natural law would result in a 'war of all against all' and, in the absence of a sovereign power controlling (amongst other things) executive, legislative, and judicial power would result in this:

In such condition, there is no place for industry; because the fruit thereof is uncertain: and consequently no culture of the earth; no navigation, nor use of the commodities that may be imported by sea; no commodious building; no instruments of moving, and removing, such things as require much force; no knowledge of the face of the earth; no account of time; no arts; no letters; no society; and which is worst of all, continual fear, and danger of violent death; and the life of man, solitary, poor, nasty, brutish, and short.

Following on from Hobbes, Jeremy Bentham proposed the utilitarian principle of positive law, which evaluates actions based on their consequences: for Bentham, the law should create the greatest happiness for the greatest number. Bentham was not a fan of natural law, calling it 'nonsense upon stilts'. John Austin was greatly influenced by Bentham whose theory of law also separated moral concerns by saying that law is the command issued by a sovereign, backed by threat of sanction:

> The existence of law is one thing; its merit or demerit is another. Whether it be or be not is one enquiry; whether it be or be not conformable to an assumed standard, is a different enquiry. A law, which actually exists, is a law, though we happen to dislike it.

The focus of legal positivism shifted during the mid-twentieth century from the role of the legislative institutions to the role of the courts. Hans Kelsen proposed a pure theory of law which also rejected the necessity of a connection between law and morality, stating that laws did not require additional moral content for their legitimacy. More recently, HLA Hart in *The Concept of Law* developed the theory of legal positivism which has been continued by Joseph Raz.

Practical exercise

Look up the case of *Knuller v DPP* [1973] AC 435 (HL). This case involved a magazine which contained advertisements from adult males seeking replies from other adult males who were prepared to consent to engage in homosexual activity in private. The appellants were convicted on counts of conspiracy to corrupt public morals and conspiracy to outrage public decency.

1. What was the outcome in the case?
2. Do you think that gay dating advertisements are immoral?
3. To what extent have attitudes to gay dating changed since 1973?
4. How do you think this case would be/should be decided today?

You will find some commentary on these questions at www.oup.com/he/finch8e/.

12.3.3 The Hart–Devlin debate

The contrast between the natural law and positivist positions was set out in a series of articles between Hart and Devlin following the consideration of the issue of legalizing homosexuality and prostitution by the Wolfenden Committee (1957). The Wolfenden Report claimed that it is not the duty of the law to concern itself with immorality.

Devlin's position on the function of morality within the law was as follows:

> Without shared ideas on politics, morals and ethics, no society can exist . . . If men and women try to create a society in which there is no fundamental agreement about good and evil, they will fail; if having based it on common agreement, the agreement goes, the society will disintegrate. For society is not something that is kept together physically; it is held by the invisible bonds of common thought. If the bonds were too far relaxed, the members would drift apart. A common morality is part of the bondage. The bondage is the price of society; and mankind, which needs society must pay its price.[1]

1. P Devlin, *The Enforcement of Morals* (OUP 1965) 26.

So, Devlin considered that there is a common public morality that must be protected by the law and that to remove the regulation of morality by law would inevitably lead to the spread of immoral behaviour and the disintegration of society. It followed, for Devlin, that conduct which was viewed as immoral by the majority at the time, which it was argued included homosexuality, needed to be suppressed in the interests of society.

Devlin's position was criticized by Hart.[2] Hart disagreed with Devlin over the existence of a common morality, preferring instead the idea of a 'number of mutually tolerant moralities'[3] and that the use of law to reflect a snapshot of the dominant morality of the time was potentially harmful. Hart believed that the prohibition of conduct on the basis of a moral consensus was an unjustifiable interference with the rights of the individual to do as they wished. Therefore, legislation designed to enforce moral standards could be flawed due to the difficulties of defining morality and deciding between what is immoral and what is not. However, Hart did concede a role for the law in the *maintenance* of morality, but only where necessary to protect those who would engage in such immoral activities. Hart's reluctance to treat law as a moral issue was later criticized by Dworkin who considered that law could never be entirely divorced from morality.[4]

12.3.4 Legal realism

Legal realism takes a different view to that of natural law or legal positivism. Legal realists are less concerned with what the law should be, or its precise wording in statute, instead holding the view that the law should be understood in the context of how it is used in practice. In other words, this position is more 'real-worldly' in that the law is reflected in the decisions of judges. Legal realists simply look to describe what the law *is*, rather than what it *ought* to be. The leading proponent of legal realism was an American jurist, Oliver Wendell Holmes, who considered that if law just required the mechanical application of rules, then there would be no need for adversarial proceedings: courts would just apply the law. However, realistically speaking, judges do have discretion in how they decide cases and their individual political views,[5] social class, temperaments, and philosophies will all have a bearing on their reasoning and the ultimate outcome of the case before them.

12.3.5 Summary

This section has set out to introduce some of the main areas of legal theory and its key commentators. It is necessarily brief, but should have led you to realize that there are different schools of thought that can be applied to complex legal issues. These are summarized in Table 12.1.

Table 12.1 Key points in legal theory

Natural law	Legal positivism	Legal realism
Laws of nature are superior to any laws made by man	There is no superior 'higher law' than that made by man	Law is reflected in and explained by the decisions of the courts
Law and morality are inextricably linked	It is not necessary for law and morality to be linked	
Immoral laws are not valid	Laws lacking in moral content are still valid provided that they have been enacted in the proper way	

2. HLA Hart, *Law, Liberty and Morality* (OUP 1963).

3. ibid 62–3.

4. R Dworkin, *Law's Empire* (Belknap Press 1986).

5. For more on this point, see JAG Griffith, *The Politics of the Judiciary* (Manchester University Press 1977).

You may well be wondering what the real-world application of these theoretical perspectives are—after all, this is a book on legal skills and not on jurisprudence. However, an appreciation of the rudiments of legal theory can greatly assist you in understanding the principle and policy decisions behind judicial decision making and legal reasoning which can, in turn, enable you to demonstrate a greater level of critical engagement with case law when using it, particularly in essays or dissertations, in preparation for tutorials, or in the exam room. The next section will look in detail at an example which will further emphasize the point that there is no single correct answer available in relation to legal reasoning.

12.4 ONE CASE, MULTIPLE APPROACHES

This section is based around a famous hypothetical case known as 'the Case of the Speluncean Explorers' written by Lon Fuller and published in the *Harvard Law Review* in 1948. It is similar in some respects to the real case of *R v Dudley and Stephens* which you encountered earlier in the chapter. It is set in the fictional land of Newgarth and the case is being heard in its Supreme Court.

In summary, five cave explorers (spelunkers) were caught underground after a tunnel collapsed. They learned through radio contact that rescue was at least ten days away, and that they could not survive that long without food. They also learned that they could survive if they were to eat one of their number. They radioed to the outside to ask whether it would be legally and/or morally permissible to kill one among them to sustain the others, but no one above ground would answer the question.

One of the explorers, Whetmore, suggested that they throw dice to determine who should be eaten, and they all agreed. Just before the dice were thrown, Whetmore suggested that they wait until they were closer to death before proceeding; but he was outvoted, and a die was cast on his behalf. Everyone, including Whetmore, agreed that the dice were thrown fairly. Whetmore lost. When the rescuers finally reached the explorers, they found that Whetmore had been killed and eaten.

The remaining explorers were put on trial for murder under the statute which stated 'Whoever shall willfully take the life of another shall be punished by death' to which there was no exception applicable to this case. They were found guilty and sentenced to be hanged.

The case is now on appeal to the Supreme Court comprising five Justices: Truepenny CJ, Foster J, Tatting J, Keen J, and Handy J.

Practical exercise

 Download the case of the Speluncean Explorers which you will find at **www.oup.com/he/ finch8e/**. *Read the full judgment carefully.*

In order to analyse the reasoning of each Justice, we can start by listing whether or not they would have affirmed the conviction and sentence of the Court of General Instances as shown in Table 12.2.

Table 12.2 Verdicts of the Justices in the Case of the Speluncean Explorers

Justice	Opinion
Truepenny CJ	Affirmed conviction and sentence
Foster J	Reversed conviction
Tatting J	Withdrew from decision
Keen J	Affirmed conviction and sentence
Handy J	Reversed conviction

Overall, with the Supreme Court being evenly divided, the conviction and sentence of the Court of General Instances was affirmed, and the Public Executioner was directed to hang each of the defendants by the neck until they were dead.

You should already be able to see that, even on one set of facts, the Justices came to divergent opinions—two to convict, two to acquit, and one abstention. The next part of the exercise involves a more detailed reading of each Justice's opinion in order to determine their reasoning. We will use the opinion of Truepenny CJ as an example. He states (at page 619):

> It seems to me that in dealing with this extraordinary case the jury and the trial judge followed a course that was not only fair and wise, but the only course that was open to them under the law. The language of our statute is well known: 'Whoever shall willfully take the life of another shall be punished by death.' N. C. S. A. (N. S.) § 12-A. This statute permits of no exception applicable to this case, however our sympathies may incline us to make allowance for the tragic situation in which these men found themselves.
>
> In a case like this the principle of executive clemency seems admirably suited to mitigate the rigors of the law, and I propose to my colleagues that we follow the example of the jury and the trial judge by joining in the communications they have addressed to the Chief Executive. There is every reason to believe that these requests for clemency will be heeded, coming as they do from those who have studied the case and had an opportunity to become thoroughly acquainted with all its circumstances. It is highly improbable that the Chief Executive would deny these requests unless he were himself to hold hearings at least as extensive as those involved in the trial below, which lasted for three months. The holding of such hearings (which would virtually amount to a retrial of the case) would scarcely be compatible with the function of the Executive as it is usually conceived. I think we may therefore assume that some form of clemency will be extended to these defendants. If this is done, then justice will be accomplished without impairing either the letter or spirit of our statutes and without offering any encouragement for the disregard of law.

Therefore, for Truepenny CJ, the law is clear. The statute clearly applies to the conduct of the defendants: they wilfully took the life of another by putting Whetmore to death before eating him. For Truepenny CJ, it is not open to the court to ignore the clearly drafted words of the legislature. He recognizes that the Executive may provide clemency (i.e. moderate the severity of the punishment) and comments that it is not the role of the Executive to hold a hearing to judge the merits of the case: this would be encroaching too far on the role of the judiciary. Truepenny CJ concludes that justice would be done, with the defendants escaping death as the sanction for their actions via executive clemency, while leaving the integrity of the legal rule intact. Truepenny CJ does not use any arguments based on moral values in reaching his judicial decision. For him, the law is the law and the courts apply it. It is for the Executive to dispense justice in these particularly extreme circumstances. As his reasoning divorces law and morality, you should be able to see that he is approaching the issue from a legal positivist standpoint.

You may be interested to note that in the real-life case of *Dudley and Stephens* which you encountered earlier in the chapter, the court sentenced the defendants to the statutory death penalty with a recommendation for mercy. Their sentences were ultimately commuted to six months' imprisonment by the Home Secretary (exercising executive power).

Practical exercise

Reread the judgments of each of the other Justices in the Case of the Speluncean Explorers carefully. For each of the Justices, consider the following questions:

1. What were the facts or issues that concerned them most in reaching their decision?

2. What theoretical position do they most closely seem to represent?

3. What do they think their role as a judge demands?

4. What do they consider to be the correct outcome?

Once you have analysed each opinion:

5. Which of the Justices do you agree with most closely, and why?

6. Which of the Justices (whose opinion you ultimately disagree with) do you find most persuasive, and why?

You will find some commentary on these questions at www.oup.com/he/finch8e/.

The purpose of this exercise is to demonstrate how the different theoretical perspectives introduced in section 12.3 are reflected in practice, and to underline the point that legal reasoning can be much more than the simple application of rules to a set of facts. Moreover, you should have grasped by now that, since the law of England and Wales is based on an adversarial system, that law is all about argument and, therefore, there is no single 'right' answer in legal reasoning.

In practical terms, barristers get to 'know their judges' and understand the types of argument that will stand the strongest chances of being persuasive. For example, if you were defending the Speluncean Explorers in front of Truepenny CJ, and knew that he was, in essence, a positivist that holds to the letter of the law, you would not succeed if you ran a defence that said that the laws of society did not apply to the defendants once they were cut off from society, or that the purpose of the law of murder would not be fulfilled if it were applied to the men who acted in a way to provide the greatest chance of preserving the most life. However, if you used the same defence in front of Foster J, you would stand a much greater chance of winning your case.

12.5 MULTIPLE APPROACHES IN REAL LIFE

In this section, we will consider a case which involved multiple judgments and examine the different reasoning used by the judges in what was a 3–2 split decision. The case is

Gregg v Scott[6] which concerned the question of whether someone can claim financial damages in respect of a 'lost chance'. Here are the facts:

> The claimant, Mr Gregg, went to see his GP, Dr Scott. Gregg had just moved into the area and this was his first visit. While he was there (for sinusitis), he also mentioned a painless lump under his arm. Dr Scott described the lump as benign fatty tissue. In fact, a malignant tumour was developing. Nine months later, Gregg had moved house again and went to his new GP about the lump. The new GP also though that the lump was benign but, as a matter of caution referred Gregg on a routine basis to a surgeon. The surgeon thought something more ominous was occurring and ordered further tests, after which the cancer was discovered and treatment commenced.
>
> At the time of the initial misdiagnosis, the claimant's chance of surviving for ten years was 42 per cent; at the time that treatment commenced it was 25 per cent. At neither time was survival for over ten years probable (on the balance of probabilities).

The trial judge in *Gregg v Scott* considered himself bound by a previous House of Lords authority[7] which said that, if, on the balance of probabilities, even correct diagnosis and treatment would not have prevented an injury from occurring, it followed that the claimant failed to establish that the misdiagnosis was the case of their injury. The Court of Appeal also dismissed the appeal by a majority. The claimant appealed further to the House of Lords.

Practical exercise

Based on the facts that you know, and ignoring the operation of precedent:

1. What do you think the outcome should be?
2. Should Mr Gregg be allowed to claim damages because his statistical chance of survival had been adversely affected by the delay in treatment caused by Dr Gregg's misdiagnosis?

The House of Lords eventually dismissed the appeal by 3–2, but each judge employed different reasoning as summarized in Figure 12.2.

Practical exercise

1. Look at the summaries of each judge's position in Figure 12.2.
2. Which of these, if any, is closest to your own position?
3. Do you think the House of Lords, as a whole, reached the right outcome?

You should see that there are a number of different ways in which you can think about the facts and the implications of a decision. There is no single reason that the House of Lords used in order to dismiss the appeal, but a simple 3–2 vote based on divergent sets of reasons. You should also appreciate that this situation has implications for the operation of the doctrine of precedent (sections 7.3.3 and 7.6) as there is no single *ratio decidendi* that can be distinguished in this judgment. Therefore, a later Supreme Court hearing could choose to follow any one of

---

6. [2005] UKHL 2; [2005] 2 AC 176.
7. *Hotson v East Berkshire Area Health Authority* [1987] AC 750 (HL).

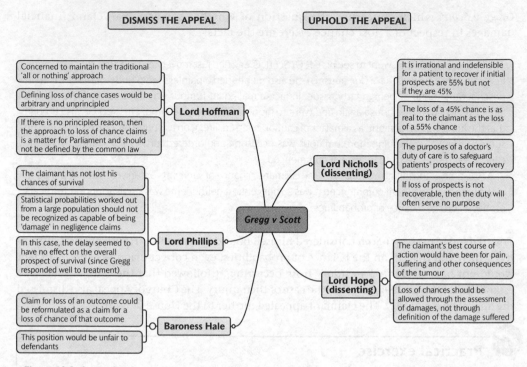

Figure 12.2 *Gregg v Scott*

these sets of reasons (or more than one, or indeed none at all). *Gregg v Scott* illustrates the point that, in practice, judges can reach decisions based on their own reasoning and consideration of the issues that they feel are most important to them and to their personal understanding, and corresponding obligations, relating to their role as a member of the judiciary.

Practical exercise

Find the full judgment of *Gregg v Scott* online and read it in detail.

1. Have you changed your mind after having examined the full reasons behind each judge's reasoning?

12.6 LEGAL ETHICS

Earlier in this chapter, we considered ideas of morality insofar as they related to legal reasoning. In this section we will introduce the closely related idea of ethical behaviour and its importance in legal practice.

Before considering this topic in more detail though, think about the following questions which begin to explore the similarities and differences between lawful behaviour and ethical behaviour:

• Is acting ethically the same as acting legally?

• If something is unethical, does that make it illegal?

• Does the illegality of an act automatically make it unethical?

• What should you do if something is illegal, but you think that it is ethical?

Very broadly speaking, acts can be categorized into one of four contexts as shown in Figure 12.3.

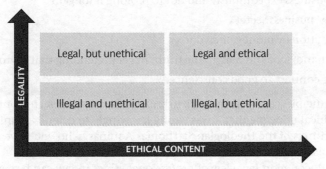

Figure 12.3 Legality and ethics

Two of these categories present no problem. Clearly we should do things that are legal and ethical and not do things that are illegal and unethical. The issues lie in the other two categories. If you have ever downloaded music, television programmes, or films from the internet then this probably constitutes illegal copyright infringement: but you may think that there is nothing unethical in doing so. You may think, for example, that musicians, actors, and film-makers get enough money as it is, so depriving them of some extra royalties is not that big a deal. Does the same logic apply to the authors of textbooks who may find their work available as a free PDF on a torrent site? As authors, we would hope not, but of course we recognize that there are pirate copies of this textbook in circulation which deprive us of the royalty payment that we get each time a copy is sold. What about the situation in which drivers flash their lights at oncoming traffic to warn them about a police speed trap? This may be illegal, but could it be argued to be ethically justifiable?[8] These acts create ethical dilemmas and ultimately an individual's actions in such situations reflect their own personal system of values. Similarly, it is perfectly lawful to break a promise (unless it has the surrounding circumstances to make it a legally binding contract) but is widely thought of as unethical. If your parents told you that they would buy you a car if you got a first in your law degree, you would probably think it was unethical (amongst other things) if they told you after the graduation ceremony in which you picked up your first class law degree that they had actually changed their minds.

The role of ethics within the legal profession is tied up with the idea of professional misconduct. There have been principles of ethical behaviour applied to the legal profession for centuries: the Statute of Westminster I (1275) prohibited 'deceit or collusion' by lawyers. Professional misconduct was simply described in 1889 as something which is 'dishonourable to him as a man and dishonourable in his profession',[9] and the earliest formulation of a code of professional conduct dates from the times of Henry VII:

- To assist the poor and oppressed without reward
- To give counsel to anyone who should seek it

8. Although prosecutions have been brought in such cases for obstructing the police in the course of their duty, the High Court ruled in *DPP v Glendinning* [2005] EWHC 2333 (Admin) that flashing vehicles will not obstruct officers in the exercise of their duty unless there were vehicles that could have been affected by the signals that were actually speeding or were likely to speed.

9. *Re G Mayor* (1889) 5 TLR 407. As well as encapsulating the idea of professional legal misconduct, the use of the male gender in this quote clearly shows it to be a creature of its time.

- To dissuade clients from pursuing unjust causes and to advise them to abandon causes if it appeared that they were in the wrong

- To deal with business expeditiously and not to prolong it for gain

- To keep clients' business secret

- To avoid corruption by money or favour

- To 'stick with hand, foot and nail' to the truth, never pretending that a wrong is right

- To do nothing contrary to good conscience.[10]

Some of these principles can be linked back to broader theories of legal reasoning, for instance, the medieval ethical principle that it was wrong knowingly to defend an unjust cause can be traced to the writings of the theologian St Thomas Aquinas, who you have already encountered in the discussion of natural law in section 12.3.1.

The traditional, common law view of professional ethics in law can be summed up in the idea of 'responsible lawyering' which includes the lawyer's responsibility to the court and to the processes of justice as well as to their client. In *Giannarelli v Wraith*,[11] Mason CJ encapsulated it like this:

> The advocate is as essential a participant in our system of justice as are the judge, the jury and the witness and his freedom of judgment must be protected . . . The performance by counsel of his paramount duty to the Court will require him to act in a variety of ways to the possible disadvantage of his client. Counsel must not mislead the court, cast unjustifiable aspersions on any party or witness or withhold documents and authorities which distract from his client's case. And, if he notes an irregularity in the conduct of a criminal trial, he must take the point so that it can be remedied, instead of keeping the point up his sleeve and using it as a ground of appeal.
>
> It is not that a barrister's duty to the Court creates such a conflict with his duty to his client that the dividing line between the two is unclear. The duty to the Court is paramount and must be performed, even if the client gives instructions to the contrary. Rather it is that a barrister's duty to the Court epitomises the fact that the course of litigation depends on the exercise by counsel of an independent discretion or judgment in the conduct and management of a case in which he has an eye, not only to his client's success, but also the speedy and efficient administration of justice.

Although the courts still have the right to regulate the conduct of lawyers, the governing bodies of the profession—the Solicitors Regulation Authority (SRA) and the Bar Standards Board—generally set and administer the codes of professional behaviour. Additionally, the Legal Ombudsman for England and Wales was set up by the Office for Legal Complaints under the Legal Services Act 2007 as a free scheme to resolve legal service disputes.

The right to a fair trial, as set out in Article 6 of the European Convention on Human Rights, means that the parties to a dispute, whether civil or criminal, are entitled to rely on the proceedings being conducted in line with recognized ethical principles. The mandatory principles set out by the SRA require solicitors to:

- Uphold the rule of law and the proper administration of justice

- Act with integrity

---

10. Mark Humphreys, 'Legal Ethics, Past and Present' *Law Society Gazette* (30 November 2009).
11. (1988) 165 CLR 543.

- Not allow their independence to be compromised
- Act in the best interests of each client
- Provide a proper standard of service to their clients
- Behave in a way that maintains the trust the public places in them and in the provision of legal services
- Comply with their legal and regulatory obligations and deal with their regulators and ombudsmen in an open, timely, and cooperative manner
- Run their business or carry out their role in the business effectively and in accordance with proper governance and sound financial and risk-management principles
- Run their business or carry out their role in the business in a way that encourages equality of opportunity and respect for diversity, and
- Protect client money and assets.

If you compare these to the Henry VII principles we covered earlier, you will see that such principles have subsisted for many years and work to uphold public interest in the legal system and to ensure that the system is just and fair.

CHAPTER SUMMARY

Logic and simple legal reasoning

- The logical syllogism involves forming a conclusion from two premises
- In legal reasoning, the major premise is a statement of law; the minor premise is the statement of fact. Forming the conclusion is referred to as applying the law to the facts
- There are many cases which come before the courts that do not neatly fall within the construct of simple legal reasoning

Hard cases

- Hard cases involve legal, ethical, and moral questions
- Determining hard cases requires an understanding of the relationship between law and morality and the constitutional role of the judiciary

Legal theory

- Natural law theory considers that the laws of nature are superior to the laws of man; that law and morality are inextricably linked; and that immoral laws lack legitimacy
- Legal positivism holds that there is no superior higher law than that made by man; that there is no link necessary between law and morality; and that 'immoral' laws are still valid provided that they have been enacted properly
- The relationship between law and morality was considered at length in the Hart–Devlin debate
- The legal realist position is that law is reflected in, and explained by, the decisions of the courts

Reasoning in practice

- The adversarial system in England and Wales is based upon argument and therefore there is no single 'right' answer in legal reasoning
- 'Knowing your judge' can assist in formulating arguments that stand a greater chance of success
- Decided cases can involve multiple sets of reasons from different judges with the simple majority deciding the overall outcome

Legal ethics

- Ethical principles of justness and fairness have existed for centuries and aim to underpin a just and fair legal system for all

Referencing and avoiding plagiarism

INTRODUCTION

This chapter deals with referencing and avoiding plagiarism. These skills are of critical importance to your studies since your academic work will inevitably require you to read, critically consider, and evaluate the work of others. However, you must ensure that you carefully and meticulously distinguish between your own work, ideas, and arguments and those of the authors or judges that you have encountered during your research. This is done by providing thorough references to the sources that you have used in your work. Failing to do so may leave you vulnerable to accusations that you have presented the work of others as your own—that is, plagiarism. This chapter will explain what is meant by plagiarism in more detail and introduce you to the most widely used system of referencing in academic law which will help you to avoid inadvertent plagiarism: footnote referencing (specifically, the Oxford University Standard for Citation of Legal Authorities, invariably abbreviated to OSCOLA). We will then show you how to reference the most commonly encountered sources using OSCOLA. This chapter should be read in conjunction with the chapters on writing essays (chapter 14), answering problem questions (chapter 15), and writing dissertations (chapter 17) which follow.

The ability to reference thoroughly, properly, and consistently should become second nature to you as you progress through your legal studies. Plagiarism is invariably treated very seriously by institutions and any suspected cases are investigated thoroughly. If a case of suspected plagiarism is upheld, then it is likely that some adverse penalty will be applied which could seriously limit your prospects of success in your course overall. Worse still, plagiarism could be considered to be evidence against good character by the Law Society and the Bar Standards Board which would mean that even if you successfully complete the academic stage of legal training, you may be unable to proceed to the Legal Practice Course or the Bar Professional Training Course. There is too much at stake to risk deliberate plagiarism or ignoring the requirements of good referencing needed to avoid inadvertent plagiarism.

Learning outcomes

After studying this chapter, you will be able to:

- Define what is meant by plagiarism
- Know when to provide references and avoid inadvertent plagiarism
- Understand the risks associated with deliberate plagiarism
- Reference your sources consistently and thoroughly using OSCOLA

13.1 PLAGIARISM

It is commonplace to think of plagiarism as a deliberate copying from an unacknowledged source with the intention to deceive, but this is not the case. Plagiarism covers *all* instances in which the work of another is used without sufficient acknowledgement.

 The *Oxford English Dictionary* defines **plagiarism** as 'the action or practice of taking someone else's work, idea, etc., and passing it off as one's own; literary theft'.

Universities may have their own definitions within their regulations on academic conduct. By way of example, the University of Leeds defines plagiarism as follows:

> Plagiarism is defined as presenting someone else's work, in whole or in part, as your own. Work means any intellectual output and typically includes text, data, images, sound or performance.[1]

As you see from these definitions, the essence of plagiarism is the failure to give an indication of the source of material upon which reliance has been placed in a piece of work. This may be deliberate, such as in situations where a student copies material from the internet (or a fellow student) and passes it off as their own or buys an essay from an internet essay bank or essay-writing service, but it is more often inadvertent, arising as a consequence of poor or lazy referencing or from a lack of understanding about the need to provide a reference. Plagiarism does not require a deliberate attempt to cheat.

13.1.1 Inadvertent plagiarism

The most effective means of avoiding inadvertent plagiarism is to ensure that every piece of work that you produce is thoroughly and correctly referenced. This raises two issues: *when* to reference and *how* to reference. The latter issue will be addressed in the referencing section later in the chapter whilst the remainder of this section will deal with the question of when a reference must be provided.

13.1.1.1 When to reference

Certain situations are straightforward. Most students would appreciate that a reference to the source of the following should be provided:

- **Statements of law** should be attributed to the relevant case or statutory provision.
- **Direct quotations** should be attributed to their source in a book, article, case, or other material.
- **Factual material** such as statistics or the findings of a research study should be attributed to their source, whether this is an official report or an academic or commercial study.
- **Definitions** of legal concepts or any other matter should be attributed to the appropriate source in a dictionary, case law, statute, article, or other material.

1. University of Leeds Office of Academic Appeals & Regulation, 'Cheating, plagiarism, fraudulent or fabricated coursework and malpractice in University examinations' <http://www.leeds.ac.uk/secretariat/documents/cpffm_procedure.pdf> accessed 20 January 2019.

An essay is an accumulation of a number of different things. It is composed largely of the writer's own words and thoughts, which need no reference, but may be interspersed with other material from the four categories outlined above that add the weight of authority to these words and thoughts. Definitions and quotations are the direct use of another's words, and must therefore be acknowledged as such, whilst factual material and statements of law need to be referenced to their source in order to substantiate and evidence their authoritative status.

There are three main ways in which you might incorporate the work of another author in your legal writing:

- **Summarizing**—where the author's original words are rewritten in a shortened form but which captures the key points which the author made.

- **Paraphrasing**—where the author's original words are rewritten, but the original meaning is retained.

- **Direct quotation**—where the author's original words are reproduced exactly.

Take a look at the following piece of source material and the examples of each form of use which follow:

Source:

The ability of networked technologies to disseminate, share, or trade informational (intellectual) property in the form of text, images, music, film and TV through information services has been one of the more significant developments of the internet. This property is informational, networked and also globalized, and its authors, or their licensees, have a right of ownership or control over it, including the right to receive payment for access to the content. Both the means of access to the services and also their informational property content have a market value which simultaneously creates opportunities and motivations for what has become known as cyber-piracy.

(DS Wall, *Cybercrime* (Polity Press 2007) 94)

Summarized version:

Cyber-piracy has arisen as a result of the internet's capability to deliver content (for which the intellectual property owner may have a right to be paid) globally.[1]

....

[1] DS Wall, *Cybercrime* (Polity Press 2007) 94.

Paraphrased version:

Networked technologies have enabled intellectual property such as words, pictures, sound and video (TV or film) to be distributed, broadcast or dealt through online mechanisms. This is one of the most important advances that the internet has made. The property in this information is available globally via the network and the owners or licensees of this property have the right to deal with this property in accordance with their own wishes. This includes the ability to charge for allowing the content to be viewed or downloaded. Therefore, the way in which the information is accessed and the proprietary nature of the material has some economic worth which then gives rise to the prospects and incentives for so-called cyber-piracy.[1]

....

[1] DS Wall, *Cybercrime* (Polity Press 2007) 94.

Direct quotation:

Cyber-piracy has arisen because 'the means of access to the services and also their informational property content have a market value which simultaneously creates opportunities and motivations'.[1]

---

[1] DS Wall, *Cybercrime* (Polity Press 2007) 94.

While it might seem obvious that direct quotations need a reference, paraphrased and summarized sections of another's work must also be referenced in full. Paraphrasing someone else's work without reference is still using their work as your own even though very few of the words between the source and the paraphrase match. What you are doing here is putting together the same core idea in a different way and using different words to convey an identical meaning. As such, a paraphrase can *never* be the product of your own academic reasoning or argument. Similarly, a summary is a condensed version of another's work, not your own.

Another instance where inadvertent plagiarism may arise is in the case of an article, say, that gives a commentary or analysis of another piece of work:

Sources:

In this case [*Re A (Conjoined Twins)* [2001] 1 FLR 1 (CA)], one can say that the judges first reject, then accept, the existence of a contextual moral threshold concerning how intention is to be judged. They alternate their definition of intention to achieve the desired moral result, that the doctors can operate to save Jodie. The underlying problem is that the legal concept of intention is really out of phase with the intuited moral result. One might say here, rephrasing the old saw, that truly the road to legal hell is paved with good intentions.

  (A Norrie, 'From Criminal to Legal Theory: The Mysterious Case of the Reasonable Glue Sniffer' (2002) 65 MLR 538)

As Norrie explains, the Court of Appeal's approach offers a good example of orthodox subjectivism being manipulated to satisfy the moral context of the case.

  (N Lacey, C Wells, and O Quick, *Reconstructing Criminal Law* (3rd edn, LexisNexis Butterworths 2003) 752)

Here, a student might have read the secondary source (Lacey, Wells, and Quick), but not the primary source (Norrie). In this instance it would be plagiarism to include material from the secondary source while only providing a reference to the primary source:

For Norrie, the Court of Appeal in *Re A (Conjoined Twins)*[1] exemplified the manipulation of orthodox subjectivism to satisfy the moral circumstances of the case.[2]

---

[1] [2001] 1 FLR 1 (CA).
[2] A Norrie, 'From Criminal to Legal Theory: The Mysterious Case of the Reasonable Glue Sniffer' (2002) 65 MLR 538.

This would be plagiarism as it relies heavily on the analysis of Norrie's article by Lacey, Wells, and Quick, but does not acknowledge the source of that analysis. In essence, it is passing off the work of Lacey, Wells, and Quick as the student's own without attribution, while also conveying the (false) impression that the student has read the primary source

(Norrie's article in the *Modern Law Review*). This could be avoided by providing a full reference as follows:

> For Norrie, the Court of Appeal in *Re A (Conjoined Twins)*[1] exemplified the manipulation of orthodox subjectivism to satisfy the moral circumstances of the case.[2]
>
> ---
>
> [1] [2001] 1 FLR 1 (CA).
> [2] A Norrie, 'From Criminal to Legal Theory: The Mysterious Case of the Reasonable Glue Sniffer' (2002) 65 MLR 538 in N Lacey, C Wells, and O Quick, *Reconstructing Criminal Law* (3rd edn, LexisNexis Butterworths 2003) 752.

A more difficult situation exists in relation to material that has been read during the production of an essay but which is not referred to specifically within the text. This includes materials such as books and articles that have influenced your thinking about the topic or which have shaped the points that you have raised in your essay. It is in relation to this that the greatest uncertainty about whether to reference exists. There are two general rules that can be used as guidance:

1. If you are using your own words to express an idea that is specific to a particular writer, for example something that a judge has stated in a case or the views of the author of an article, then a reference to the source of the idea should be provided even though you have used your own words to explain that idea. If, however, you have read several textbooks to gain an overview of a topic and the same issue is expressed in each book, then you are free to use your own words without providing a reference. This is because the mention of the idea in several places demonstrates that it is a general issue of common knowledge, so it does not need to be attributed to a particular source.

2. If in doubt, reference. It is preferable to provide too many references in your essay rather than to face an accusation of plagiarism or receive a deduction of marks for providing insufficient references. If you receive a comment from a lecturer that a piece of work contained too many unnecessary references, you should make a point of asking them to point out to you which references were unnecessary and why this was the case so that you can make adjustments in subsequent pieces of work.

13.1.1.2 Common knowledge

Material that is 'common knowledge' generally does not need to be referenced. While this might seem obvious and straightforward, it is unfortunately complicated by the fact that there is no consensus as to what falls within common knowledge. Experts on plagiarism and academic malpractice disagree on what counts as common knowledge. Some only consider factual material such as current and historical events potentially to be common knowledge (for instance, 'Adolf Hitler was the leader of the German Nazi Party during the Second World War while Winston Churchill was Prime Minister of Great Britain throughout most of the conflict'). Others consider common knowledge to be that which is commonly known within the particular broad subject area (for instance, 'the UK has an unwritten constitution').

To complicate matters further, as you become more expert in your study of the law, what counts as common knowledge becomes even harder to define. Should common knowledge be defined in terms of reasonably educated people in general or reasonably educated law students? Within law (as with every other discipline) there is a body of common knowledge which even an educated outsider might not know.

Two tests which are often used in helping to decide whether or not a piece of information is common knowledge are:

• **Quantity**—can the information be found in numerous places?

• **Ubiquity**—is the information known by many people?

Of course, the problem with this is how many places are needed to consider that the information can be found in 'numerous' places. As a rough rule of thumb, many guidelines consider 'numerous' to mean 'five or more', but again, you must remember that this is not a hard and fast rule. If the information crops up in all your textbooks on the subject without further attribution, it is likely to be ubiquitous enough to be 'common knowledge'. If you are still in doubt, you could seek guidance from your lecturer. Otherwise, point 2 made earlier still applies—if in doubt, reference.

You should always keep the notes you have made in preparation for your work (see chapter 10 on note-taking). You may be asked to provide your notes and draft work to your institution in case there is an allegation of academic misconduct. By doing this, you will at least be able to provide some evidence that you have done the necessary research and read the materials—and therefore that your plagiarism might actually be as a result of poor referencing rather than a deliberate attempt to cheat.

> *You will find more examples and guidance relating to inadvertent plagiarism at **www.oup.com/he/finch8e/**.*

13.1.2 Deliberate plagiarism

If inadvertent plagiarism arises from lack of clarity about referencing requirements, deliberate plagiarism arises when students make a deliberate decision to try and pass off the work of others as their own. Deliberate plagiarism is almost never successful, so why do students try to plagiarize and what are the reasons that such behaviour is unwise?

13.1.2.1 Why do students plagiarize?

There are many reasons why students may make a conscious decision to take words from a source and seek to pass it off as their own work. Plagiarism can arise from a failure to understand what the coursework requires, a desperate desire to obtain a good mark, an unwillingness to interfere with the way that an idea has been expressed, or simply from the pressure of time as a deadline is looming. Ultimately, these are all manifestations of a lack of confidence in one's own ability to provide an answer to the question. Alternatively, students may resort to plagiarism because they cannot be bothered to produce their own work or because they feel that their course was badly taught and therefore does not deserve the effort that it would take to write an original piece of work.

Another reason often given by students is that they believe that everyone else is doing it and that they will not get caught. It was reported in October 2008 that almost half of students admitted to plagiarism in a poll carried out by a students' newspaper at the University of Cambridge and that only one in twenty students had been caught.[2] In October 2009, *The Times* reported that 300 students per year are caught cheating.[3] Many students who plagiarize

---

2. M Stothard, '"1 in 2" admit to plagiarism' *Varsity* (Cambridge, 30 October 2008) <http://www.varsity.co.uk/news/1058> accessed 20 January 2019.

3. G Slapper, 'Plagiarism can have serious consequences for law students' *The Times* (London, 15 October 2009).

often think that because they have not been caught then they have 'got away with it'. However, this is not always the case. For some lecturers, the additional effort required to research and prosecute a potential case of plagiarism might be too great. Instead, they may penalize the student heavily for producing a piece of work which is overly derivative or poorly referenced.

In any event, there is no justification for plagiarism and, certainly, none of the possible 'excuses' given here will provide a defence when plagiarism is detected and you are called to account by your institution.

13.1.2.2 Turnitin

Turnitin is a web-based plagiarism detection system which is in use in most UK universities. It is usually accessed through the university's own online learning environment. Students upload their work to the system which is then analysed and compared against multiple sources, including websites, books, journals, and other student assignments that have previously been submitted to Turnitin—not just from their own university, but from all universities accessing the Turnitin databases. Once work is submitted to Turnitin, it is usually stored within the Turnitin student assignment database so that it can be cross-checked against future submissions from other UK universities.[4]

Turnitin provides the following for each piece of submitted work:

- **Similarity index.** This indicates (as a percentage score) the proportion of the submitted work that Turnitin identifies as matching other sources in its database.
- **Originality report.** This report shows each of the matches in more detail, including the precise location of the duplicate content within each source.

While this might sound alarming, you should remember that Turnitin does not directly identify plagiarism: it provides information that shows where plagiarism *may* have occurred. An accusation of potential academic misconduct could only be made once the Turnitin report has been reviewed by your lecturer in detail and in the light of their academic experience, expertise, and judgement. For example, a 20 per cent match could comprise a number of short phrases, case names, or statute names spread throughout the work, which should not be an issue. However, the 20 per cent could equally represent a few whole paragraphs that are copied.

Turnitin absolutely does not replace academic judgement: however, it can reduce the time spent by lecturers investigating possible cases of plagiarism and it does reduce the prevalence of plagiarism in institutions where it is used. Moreover, if you have the opportunity to run your work through Turnitin before submission, it can also help with the recognition of potential plagiarism by flagging up areas that could possibly be of concern.

13.1.2.3 Reasons to avoid plagiarism

As well as the automated plagiarism detection provided by Turnitin, many experienced lecturers have also developed an instinctive 'nose' for suspected plagiarism which often proves to be correct. Overall, it is virtually impossible to copy from a source of material that cannot be detected, therefore resorting to plagiarism in an attempt to acquire a good mark will ultimately be unsuccessful. Such is the battle against plagiarism that many institutions annotate

---

4. A common concern raised by students is that of copyright: students retain the copyright and all other intellectual property rights in the work they submit. The developers of Turnitin work closely with the UK Information Commissioner's Office to ensure that student work is used fairly and legally.

degree transcripts to include an explanation that a mark in the relevant subject was amended following a finding of plagiarism; something which is hardly going to impress future employers. Moreover, the Law Society and the Bar Standards Board require universities to notify them of proven cases of plagiarism: since plagiarism involves dishonest academic practice, a proven finding against a student suggests that they are not of good character for the purposes of a career in the legal profession. This is particularly so if, as is increasingly common, you are required to sign some sort of statement that all due credit has been given to the work of others as part of your submission rules. Dishonestly signing a false declaration would not be received well by your university or the professional bodies.

More than this, plagiarism is actually counterproductive as it deprives the student of the opportunity to test what they do know and how well they are able to express this. In other words, the learning opportunity provided by the coursework is wholly negated and the student learns nothing as a result. You will never improve your legal skills if you are not prepared to try and receive feedback on your ability. There is nowhere else in the progression of becoming a lawyer that you will be able to learn these skills and the later stages of qualification as a lawyer will expect that you are able to identify, explain, and analyse the law, so you need to acquire these skills now by a process of trial and error.

Finally, there is no guarantee that the source that you plagiarize will be good. This is particularly true of material taken from the internet. Anyone can post anything on the internet; there is no quality control or mechanism of checking, amending, or removing inaccurate material. Essay banks are equally unreliable and cost vast sums of money. Think about the rationale behind it. Students sell essays that they have written to an essay bank who may have no expertise in the subject at all. Essays with higher marks sell for a higher price, so students are likely to exaggerate the mark in order to gain maximum profit, so there is nothing to say that the essay that you buy as a first did not actually receive a lower second-class mark. Irrespective of this, that essay may be on the same subject matter but it does not answer the same question as that set as your coursework, so there is no point in submitting it. All you are doing is paying a vast amount of money for a piece of work of questionable quality that does not answer the question that you have been set and which is likely to be detected. Essays from essay-writing services often contain extensive material from online sources as well as content from essay banks that have been recycled many times over. If you buy a 'custom-written' essay, it is still likely to be flagged by Turnitin. And if it is not, then you will have to live with the knowledge that you did not earn or deserve your law degree: that is your choice.

Ultimately, plagiarism achieves nothing and will cause you untold grief when it is detected. Do not do it.

13.2 REFERENCING STYLES

On a practical point, it is essential that your written work is fully and correctly referenced otherwise you will lose marks. Not only are these relatively simple marks to gain, but poor referencing also detracts from the overall quality of your work and can leave a negative impression in the mind of your marker. In the worst case scenario, failure to reference your sources may leave you vulnerable to accusations of plagiarism and all the consequences that follow on from this. The previous section discussed the situations in which referencing should be provided whilst this section gives an overview of the most commonly encountered referencing system which we will go on to cover in more detail later in this chapter. Before introducing this system, though, we must first consider 'house style'.

13.2.1 House style

'House style' is any official guidance that you have been given by your institution about how to provide references within your work. It should therefore be the starting point for deciding how to reference. If you have not yet found any guidance, make sure that you investigate further as you will need to consult it in order to ensure that your work is correctly referenced. The level of guidance varies between institutions so you may find that you are provided with detailed instructions with examples, given direction to use one of the standard referencing schemes (if so, this is most likely to be OSCOLA) or, merely told that 'footnotes must be used' or 'your work must be fully referenced'.

If you have been given instructions as to what style to use, it is imperative that you use this and not some other style of your own making or that you have used previously.

If you have not been given any detailed guidelines, the remainder of this chapter looks at OSCOLA which is the most commonly encountered system in academic law today. Note that while the detailed guidance covers the most common materials that you will need to reference, it is impossible to cover all the possible sources within the scope of this book. There are some excellent online resources, which are highlighted in the Further Reading section at the end of this chapter. Remember that if there is a particular source which you are unsure how to reference, check your house style first (if you have one) or, failing that, ask your lecturer who should be willing to help.

13.2.2 Footnotes and OSCOLA

Most legal writing uses footnotes (sometimes called Roman, Oxford, or numerical referencing). This is a system of referencing in which the reference details are provided at the bottom of the same page and their position in the text is denoted by a small raised (superscript) number. In longer works (or where required in your assessment guidelines) a bibliography is then provided at the end of the work, which details all secondary sources (so, excluding legislation and case law) that you have cited within it. In other words, the bibliography contains everything that you have referenced in your footnotes other than primary materials (these can, of course, be provided in separate tables of cases and legislation).

A **bibliography** is a list of all secondary materials that have been cited within your work.

OSCOLA stands for the 'Oxford University Standard for the Citation of Legal Authorities' and is a footnote-based system that is becoming widely adopted as standard in other universities.[5] The most recent (fourth) edition of OSCOLA was released in November 2010.

13.2.3 Never mix different referencing styles

As a final word of caution, you must *never* mix different referencing styles together in the same piece of work. This mixing of styles can sometimes happen accidentally especially if you copy directly from source material that uses different styles. Remember that journals, books, and materials that you may find in online databases could have their own house style: OSCOLA is

---

5. We use OSCOLA in this book.

not universally adopted. For example, if you were writing an essay on *R v Barnes*,[6] you could find a source which simply said in the main body of the text:

> Fafinski (2005) considered the role of consent in establishing criminal liability for sporting injuries.

You might just pick up the reference to Fafinski (2005) and write something in your work that looked like this:

> Fafinski (2005) discussed the implications of *R v Barnes*[1] in relation to the role of consent in establishing criminal liability for sporting injuries.
>
> ---
> [1] [2004] EWCA Crim 3246; [2005] 1 WLR 910.

In this example there is an in-text reference to the article by Fafinski published in 2005 and a footnote reference giving the citation for *Barnes*: part of this complies with OSCOLA and part does not. This should be corrected by consistent use of footnotes, like this:

> Fafinski[1] discussed the implications of *R v Barnes*[2] in relation to the role of consent in establishing criminal liability for sporting injuries.
>
> ---
> [1] Stefan Fafinski, 'Consent and the Rules of the Game: The Interplay of Criminal and Civil Liability for Sporting Injuries' (2005) 69 JCL 414.
> [2] [2004] EWCA Crim 3246.

The key message here is to be careful to ensure that you are consistent in your use of referencing styles and *always check and reformat references if necessary* to suit your chosen style.

13.2.4 Conventions used in this chapter

The remainder of this chapter will show how to reference the most common sources using OSCOLA. The discussion of each source begins with a schematic showing the elements of the citation. Using case law by way of example, a typical schematic will look like this:

> *First party* | **v** | *Second party* | **(**year**)**/**[**year**]** | report abbreviation | page number | **(**court**)**

The conventions used in all these schematics are as follows:

- **Vertical lines** (|) are used to delineate elements of the citation. These are simply used to assist clarity and are *not* used in the actual reference itself.
- **Bold type** is used to denote text or punctuation that appears in the final reference: in the above example, the *v* between the parties, the round or square brackets around the year of the case report, and the round brackets around the court are always provided. It is shown in bold for emphasis only: it is not bold in the actual reference.
- **Italic type** is used to denote elements of the reference that appear in italics in the final reference itself. Here, names of the parties to the case are shown in italics.
- **Regular type** is used to describe each element of the citation.
- **Slashes** are used to denote alternatives: here the year of report would either be in round or square brackets depending on the numbering of the particular report series being referenced.

---

6. [2004] EWCA Crim 3246; [2005] 1 WLR 910.

13.3 HOW TO REFERENCE USING FOOTNOTES/OSCOLA

Referencing with footnotes is a three-stage process:

1. Positioning the footnote marker in the text
2. Providing the content of the footnote itself at the foot of the page; the precise way in which this is done will depend on the nature of the source itself (case, book, article, etc)
3. Compiling a bibliography

This section will walk through each of those stages in turn.

     *You will find videos showing how to reference cases, legislation, articles, and books using OSCOLA at **www.oup.com/he/finch8e/**.*

13.3.1 Positioning the footnote marker in the text

Footnote markers appear *outside* any punctuation (i.e. *after* a punctuation mark and not before):

> The positioning of footnotes is discussed by Finch and Fafinski in *Legal Skills*.[1] Note that the footnote marker (superscript number 1) appears after the closing full stop in the last sentence.
>
> ---
> [1] Emily Finch and Stefan Fafinski, *Legal Skills* (8th edn, OUP 2021) 295.

The footnote marker usually appears at the end of a sentence, although it is perfectly permissible to include a footnote marker within a sentence at the point where the material to which the reference refers appears for the sake of clarity, as these two examples illustrate:

> As Finch and Fafinski note, it is common practice to provide a footnote reference to material at the end of the sentence in which it is mentioned.[1]
>
> ---
> [1] Emily Finch and Stefan Fafinski, *Legal Skills* (8th edn, OUP 2021) 295.

> As Finch and Fafinski[1] explain, it is perfectly permissible for the sake of clarity to provide a reference for a particular book or journal at the point at which the name of the author or the title of the work is mentioned.
>
> ---
> [1] Emily Finch and Stefan Fafinski, *Legal Skills* (8th edn, OUP 2021) 295.

Providing footnote markers within a sentence can also be useful if more than one source needs referencing in the same sentence. For example:

> As Fafinski comments,[1] the Court of Appeal's judgment in *Barnes*[2] meant that conduct in sport that was outside the rules of the game and led to injury still might not result in criminal liability.
>
> ---
> [1] Stefan Fafinski, 'Consent and the Rules of the Game: The Interplay of Criminal and Civil Liability for Sporting Injuries' (2005) 69 JCL 414.
> [2] *R v Barnes* [2004] EWCA Crim 3246.

13.3.1.1 A note on quotations

You have already seen that direct quotations require a footnote and a reference. OSCOLA has specific rules on how quotations should be presented. Shorter quotations (of three lines in length or fewer) are incorporated in the text within single quotation marks. For instance:

> As Walker commented, fairness 'cannot readily be measured in a quantum of hours or conversant relatives'.[1]
>
> [1] Clive Walker, 'The Threat of Terrorism and the Fate of Control Orders' [2010] PL 4, 5.

(Note that the footnote here contains a pinpoint reference—see section 13.3.6.1—to show that the quotation is found on page 5 of the article. The article itself begins on page 4 of the *Public Law* journal.)

If you need to provide a longer quotation, it should be introduced with a colon and presented in an indented block paragraph, like so:

> **As Walker commented:**
>
> There have been squeals of anguish along the way from Home Secretaries, bemoaning that control orders 'have got holes all through them' or that adverse court decisions are 'extremely disappointing'. Yet, the Home Office has not issued a prospectus for replacement and has contrarily shown a liking for the flexibility of the case law.[1]
>
> [1] Clive Walker, 'The Threat of Terrorism and the Fate of Control Orders' [2010] PL 4, 5.

Finally, if you miss out a part of a quotation, then you should use an ellipsis (three full stops. . .) to indicate that some of the original text is missing. For instance, if you left out part of the quotation in the previous example, you could have:

> **As Walker commented:**
>
> There have been squeals of anguish along the way from Home Secretaries . . . Yet, the Home Office has not issued a prospectus for replacement and has contrarily shown a liking for the flexibility of the case law.[1]
>
> [1] Clive Walker, 'The Threat of Terrorism and the Fate of Control Orders' [2010] PL 4, 5.

You should always consider the use of the ellipsis if there are parts of a lengthy quote that are straying away from the main points that you are trying to convey—the judicious omission of material can demonstrate greater understanding of your source and precision in its use than simply cutting and pasting a whole chunk of it into your work. It also helps you keep to the word count.

13.3.2 Providing the content of the footnote

The sections that follow demonstrate how to reference different sources using OSCOLA. Before getting into the details, it is important to cover some general points on content that apply to all footnotes and to explain the conventions used in the remainder of this section.

13.3.2.1 Additional material in footnotes

As well as the basic references themselves, it is sometimes acceptable to include a *short* note in a footnote if this relates to something explanatory that would interest the reader or assist their understanding but which would break the flow of the argument if included in the main body of the text.

For example, if your essay discusses a particular line of authority, you may want to add some interesting information about it or draw attention to an article that takes a critical approach to the law that you are outlining. This draws the reader's attention to it at the appropriate point of the essay but ensures that the flow of your argument is not broken. In many respects, notes provided in footnotes can be regarded as interesting asides:

> The House of Lords affirmed the current 'virtual certainty' test for oblique intention in *R v Woollin*.[1]
>
> ---
>
> [1] [1999] 1 AC 82 (HL). The line of authority that led to this point is complex: *Hyam v DPP* [1975] AC 55 (HL); *R v Moloney* [1985] AC 905 (HL); *R v Hancock and Shankland* [1986] AC 455 (HL); *R v Nedrick* [1986] 1 WLR 1025 (CA).

You should, however, exercise caution when including anything other than a reference in your footnotes (particularly if your word limit *excludes* words that are in footnotes) as this is sometimes viewed with suspicion by lecturers, who recognize that it is an attempt to circumvent the word limit by including material in the footnotes that should rightly be in the body of the essay:

> The House of Lords affirmed the current test for oblique intention in *R v Woollin*.[1]
>
> ---
>
> [1] [1999] 1 AC 82 (HL). The facts of *Woollin* are as follows: The defendant violently shook his 3-month-old baby and then threw him across the room. The baby died. The defendant accepted that there was a risk of injury and admitted that the baby had hit the floor hard, but he did not think that it would kill him. The trial judge told the jury that they might infer intention if the defendant appreciated a 'substantial risk' of serious harm. The Court of Appeal held that although the words 'virtually certain' as in *Nedrick* were preferable, the jury was not misdirected if it was clear that the decision was theirs. The House of Lords held that the judge had confused the jury and since it was impossible to know which of the two statements the jury had followed this must be a material misdirection. The 'virtual certainty' test from *Nedrick* was affirmed with the modification that the jury may 'find' rather than 'infer' the requisite intention.

Avoid doing this; not only is it poor academic practice, it may result in losing marks for poor referencing. As always, it is advisable to check the rules of your institution to determine whether there are any rules as to what can and cannot be included in a footnote.

You do not have to write 'See . . .' in a footnote (e.g. 'See *R v Moloney* [1985] AC 905 (HL)') unless you actually want the reader to go off and look at the source that you have indicated.

13.3.2.2 Punctuation in footnotes

As you will see in the examples that follow, OSCOLA referencing uses minimal punctuation. Each section will explain precisely what is required, but you will note that footnote text in OSCOLA is always closed with a full stop, question mark, or exclamation mark and is never left 'hanging'.

13.3.2.3 Cross-referencing between footnotes

If you have already referenced a source in full in a footnote, but need to refer to it again in a later note, you can simply provide an abbreviated identification to the full source and a cross-reference in brackets to the footnote in which the full citation is found—unless it is the immediately preceding footnote, in which case you should use ibid (see section 13.3.2.4). This is a useful technique to use for brevity, especially if your word count rules include material and references provided in footnotes. However, it is also perfectly acceptable to give the full citation every time a source is cited (and some law schools may prefer this to the use of short forms, so do check before you abbreviate).

For instance, if you needed to cite this book in two places you could do it like this:

> [1] Emily Finch and Stefan Fafinski, *Legal Skills* (8th edn, OUP 2021) 102.
>
> . . .
>
> [29] Finch and Fafinski (n 1) 320.

So footnote 1 gives a full reference to the book with a pinpoint to page 102, whereas footnote 1 just refers to the authors' surnames and a cross-reference to note 1, together with a pinpoint to page 320.

Be careful if you use the cross-reference method though, as footnote numbers can change if you add new ones as you write—you must check them thoroughly once you have finished. For this reason, especially if word count is not an issue, it can be safer and actually less time-consuming simply to provide full citations each time (with the notable exception of ibid situations—see section 13.3.2.4).

13.3.2.4 Latin abbreviations in footnotes

You may see all sorts of Latin referencing abbreviations for referring to material that has already been referenced elsewhere such as *op cit*, *loc cit*, *ante*, *id*, *supra*, and *infra*. OSCOLA does not use these. OSCOLA recognizes two Latin 'gadgets' (as it calls them), namely 'ibid' and 'cf'.

'Ibid' is short for *ibidem* which means 'in the same place'. This is used to refer to the immediately preceding footnote provided that it is identical in every respect, that is 'in the *very* same place'. If you want to refer to a different page in the work cited in the immediately preceding footnote, you could say 'ibid 123' which means 'in the same work referred to in the previous footnote, but at page 123'.

'Cf' is an abbreviation for the Latin *confer*, which means 'compare' or 'consult'. You could therefore say 'cf Finch and Fafinski (n 12)' which means 'Compare this with whatever Finch and Fafinski say in whatever is referred to by footnote 12'.

Within OSCOLA, 'ibid' and 'cf' are always written in regular type (not italics) with no punctuation and never capitalized, even if they are at the start of the footnote text.

13.3.3 Referencing cases using OSCOLA

13.3.3.1 UK cases (non-judicial review)

The elements of a typical case citation in OSCOLA are as follows. First where there is a neutral citation:

> *First party* | v | *Second party* | [year] | court | number | (year)/[year] | report abbreviation | first page

and secondly where there is no neutral citation:

> *First party* | v | *Second party* | (year)/[year] | report abbreviation | first page | (court)

The party names are given in italics. OSCOLA separates them with a lower case unpunctuated italic *v*. Other sources you see might present the 'v' in different ways. Therefore you might see, for example:

- *Entores v Miles Far East Corporation* [1955] 2 QB 327 (CA)
- *Entores v. Miles Far East Corporation* [1955] 2 QB 327 (CA)
- *Entores* v. *Miles Far East Corporation* [1955] 2 QB 327 (CA)

Only the first of these is OSCOLA-compliant—so do not copy blindly from other sources without thinking to check formatting and amend if necessary. The year of the report is put in [square] brackets when the volume of the report series in question is identified by the year itself. For report series in which the volume numbers run sequentially, then the year that the case was heard is given in (round) brackets.

For more information on case citations including the use of neutral citations and different bracket conventions see section 6.1.1.

OSCOLA also uses no punctuation in abbreviations for law reports—so, in the earlier examples you will see 'QB' for the Queen's Bench report rather than 'Q.B.'. Again, remember to check this and amend if necessary if you are copying from another source (Westlaw Edge UK, for instance, punctuates law report abbreviations). For cases after 1865 and where there is no neutral citation, the court is also given in brackets at the end of the citation. If a case has a neutral citation, this should be given before any reference to a report of the case and separated from it by a semi-colon. There is no need to identify the court at the end if there is a neutral citation, since the court is identified within the neutral citation itself. Here is a House of Lords case which has both a neutral citation and a reference to the Appeal Cases reports:

- *R v G* [2003] UKHL 50; [2004] 1 AC 1034

When referring to a case name itself in the main body of the text, the case citation is given in the footnote and not in the text. The text itself only contains the names of the parties to the case, like this:

Astill J's dicta were disapproved by the House of Lords in *R v Bow Street Metropolitan Stipendiary Magistrate and Allison, ex p Government of the United States of America*.[1] This case involved the attempted extradition from England to the United States of an individual who had allegedly obtained 189 sets of credit card account information.

[1] [2000] 2 AC 216 (HL).

OSCOLA referencing does not require the case name to be repeated in the footnote, unless the text itself does not mention the parties by name, in which instance the full citation (including the parties) *must* be given in the footnote, as shown:

The offence created by section 3 of the Computer Misuse Act 1990 was designed to encompass activities involving computer viruses, 'Trojan horses' and worms as well as interference with websites[1] or accessing subscription cable television channels without paying the subscription.[2]

[1] *R v Lindesay* [2002] 1 Cr App R (S) 370 (CA).
[2] *R v Parr-Moore* [2003] 1 Cr App R (S) 425 (CA).

13.3.3.2 Pinpoint referencing of cases

The page number given in a case citation denotes the page in the law report on which the case report begins. If a case is used as an authority for a specific point of law or to demonstrate the application of the law in a particular factual scenario, then a general reference to the case using just this opening page number will suffice:

> Outside the established duty situations, the existence of a duty of care between claimant and defendant is determined on the basis of individual circumstances.[1]
>
> ---
> [1] *Donoghue v Stevenson* [1932] AC 562 (HL).

However, case reports can be very lengthy and often cover a considerable number of pages. If you need to refer the reader to a particular page in the case report, then you need to provide a *pinpoint reference*. This is usually required when you want to draw attention to a particular argument or if you provide a quotation from the case. You should include a page reference/ paragraph number and state the name of the judge concerned at the end of the citation in the footnote.

> The existence of a duty of care between claimant and defendant is determined on the basis of the 'neighbour principle' formulated by Lord Atkin in *Donoghue v Stevenson* who stated:
>
> > You must take reasonable care to avoid acts or omissions which you can reasonably foresee would be likely to injure your neighbour . . . persons who are so closely and directly affected by my act that I ought reasonably to have them in my contemplation as being so affected when I am directing my mind to the acts or omissions which are called in question.[1]
>
> ---
> [1] [1932] AC 562 (HL) 580 (Lord Atkin).

If the reference is to be attributed to a specific judge, then the judge's name is added in round brackets at the end of the citation. You may see attribution to judges shown as '*per* Lord Atkin' in other sources, but the Latin '*per*' attribution is not used in OSCOLA.

Any pinpoint reference to a particular page is given *after* the designation of the court except when a case has both a neutral citation and a law report citation. As the court is not identified at the end of the citation any pinpoint page references to the law report are delineated by a comma, like this:

- *R v G* [2003] UKHL 50; [2004] 1 AC 1034, 1037

If the judgment uses paragraph numbers, as is invariably the case with neutrally cited cases, it is perfectly acceptable to use a paragraph number as a pinpoint (and essential if it is not published elsewhere, as pure neutral citation reports are not paginated). OSCOLA uses square brackets to denote paragraph numbers and to differentiate them from page numbers:

> The House of Lords held that it was 'not addressing the meaning of "reckless" in any other statutory or common law context'.[1]
>
> ---
> [1] *R v G* [2003] UKHL 50 [28] (Lord Bingham).

In this example, Lord Bingham's quote can be found in paragraph 28 of the judgment.

Note that the conventions on pinpoint referencing explained here apply equally to the other types of case report covered in the remainder of this section.

13.3.3.3 Judicial review cases post-2001

Judicial review cases are cited differently. In judicial review, the courts supervise the exercise of public power on the application of an individual, and there are therefore three parties involved:

- The public authority called in question (the respondent)
- The applicant
- The Crown (notionally representing the interests of the applicant against the public authority).

Judicial review cases post-2001 are cited in OSCOLA as follows:

R | (Applicant) | v | Respondent | (year)/[year] | report abbreviation | first page | (court)

For example:

- *R (Lichniak) v Secretary of State for the Home Department* [2003] 1 AC 903 (HL)

You may also see such cases cited using the phrase 'on the application of' which may make it clearer that it involves judicial review, although this approach is not OSCOLA-compliant:

- *R (on the application of Lichniak) v Secretary of State for the Home Department* [2003] 1 AC 903 (HL)

As ever, check for non-compliance with OSCOLA and reformat as necessary.
Neutral citations must precede the law report citation where available.

13.3.3.4 Judicial review cases prior to 2001

Judicial review cases prior to 2001 (when Order 53 of the Rules of the Supreme Court, which contained the rules of procedure for judicial review, was replaced by Part 54 of the Civil Procedure Rules) are cited slightly differently again:

R | v | Respondent | ex p | Applicant | (year)/[year] | report abbreviation | first page | (court)

For example:

- *R v Secretary of State for Transport ex p Factortame Ltd (No 2)* [1991] 1 AC 603 (HL)
- *R v Secretary of State for the Home Department ex p Bentley* [1994] QB 349 (DC)

Here *ex p* is short for *ex parte* which means 'by or for one party'. You may also see judicial review cases cited using *ex parte* in full in place of the abbreviated *ex p* used within OSCOLA, like this:

- *R v Secretary of State for Transport ex parte Factortame Ltd (No 2)* [1991] 1 AC 603 (HL)

Although the meaning is the same, you should abbreviate *ex parte* to *ex p* to be OSCOLA- compliant.
Neutral citations must precede the law report citation where available.

13.3.3.5 Court of Justice of the European Union/General Court cases

Cases in the Court of Justice of the EU and the General Court also require the case number:

Case number | First party | v | Second party | [year] | report abbreviation | first page

Where possible, you should cite the reference from the official report: that is, the *European Court Reports* (ECR). CJEU cases are reported in volume 'ECR I' and General Court cases are reported in volume 'ECR II'. Note here that the volume numbers are given in Roman numerals using the letters 'I'/'II' and *not* the numbers '1'/'11'. The volume number and page number are joined with a dash. Since 1989 case numbers in the ECJ have been prefixed with 'C-' and cases in the Court of First Instance with 'T-'.

For example:

- Case C-176/03 *Commission v Council* [2005] ECR I-7879
- Case T-201/04 *Microsoft v Commission* [2004] ECR II-4463

Case numbers before 1989 carry no prefix:

- Case 203/80 *Re Casati* [1981] ECR 2595

If there is no official report available, you should cite the *Common Market Law Reports* (CMLR) in the same way as for any other series of law reports, such as:

- Case C-440/05 *Commission v Council* [2008] 1 CMLR 22

If there is no report available, you should just provide the case number and party names with the court and date in round brackets like this:

- Case C-444/02 *Fixtures Marketing Ltd v OPAP* (ECJ 9 November 2004)

The current edition of OSCOLA does not cover the use of the ECLI, but it is suggested that if you want to use it, then you should treat it like a UK neutral citation and place it after the case name but before the report citation:

- Case C-176/03 *Commission v Council* EU:C:2005:542, [2005] ECR I-7879

13.3.3.6 European Court of Human Rights cases

Decisions of the European Court of Human Rights up to 1 November 1998 are cited in the following way:

| *First party* | *v* | *Second party* | (App no | application number) | (year) | Series A | no | case number |

For example:

- *Golder v UK* (App no 4451/70) (1975) Series A no 19

From 1 November 1998 the official reports were renamed Reports of Judgments and Decisions and are cited as 'ECHR' with the appropriate case number as follows:

| *First party* | *v* | *Second party* | (App no | application number) | [year] | ECHR | case number |

For instance:

- *Janowski v Poland* (App no 25716/94) [1999] ECHR 3
- *Spyropoulos v Greece* (App no 5081/03) [2005] ECHR 569

13.3.4 Referencing legislation using OSCOLA

13.3.4.1 UK legislation

Acts of Parliament are referenced by their short title and year (in that order). There is no comma before the year. For instance:

- Theft Act 1968
- Gender Recognition Act 2004
- Education Act 1996

Note that when you are mentioning an Act of Parliament within a piece of work, you should *never* capitalize 'the' before the short title like this:

> The law of theft was greatly simplified by The Theft Act 1968.

Parts of an Act are cited differently depending on their position in the sentence. If you are starting a sentence with a reference to a statutory provision, you should spell out 'section' in full:

> Section 3 of the Theft Act 1968 defines appropriation.

However, if you are referring to a particular provision later in the sentence, you may (if you wish) use an abbreviated form, like this:

> Appropriation is defined in s 3 of the Theft Act 1968.

Note that there is no full stop after the 's'.

However, when referring to a statutory provision in a footnote, the name of the Act comes first, followed by a comma and the provision number, but with no other punctuation other than the closing full stop:

> The *actus reus* of theft is comprised of three elements each of which is further defined in statute, namely, the appropriation[1] of property[2] belonging to another.[3]
>
> ---
> [1] Theft Act 1968, s 3.
> [2] Theft Act 1968, s 4.
> [3] Theft Act 1968, s 5.

In this example, you could also use ibid (but without a comma following):

> The *actus reus* of theft is comprised of three elements each of which is further defined in statute, namely, the appropriation[1] of property[2] belonging to another.[3]
>
> ---
> [1] Theft Act 1968, s 3.
> [2] ibid s 4.
> [3] ibid s 5.

Statutory instruments are cited by name, year, and serial number, where available. For example:

- Data Protection Act 1998 (Commencement No 2) Order 2008 SI 1592/2007
- Equality Act (Sexual Orientation) Regulations 2007 SI 1063/2007

13.3.4.2 European legislation

European legislation (Regulations and Directives) are cited as follows:

> Legislation type | Legislation number | Full title | [year] | OJ L | Issue number | / | Page number

The full title is found in the *Official Journal of the European Communities*. For instance:

- Council Directive (EC) 80/181/EEC of 20 December 1979 on the approximation of the laws of the Member States relating to units of measurement and on the repeal of Directive 71/354/EEC [1980] OJ L 39/40

- Council Regulation (EC) 460/2004 of 10 March 2004 establishing the European Network and Information Security Agency [2004] OJ L 77/1

13.3.5 Referencing books and edited collections using OSCOLA

13.3.5.1 Books

The basic elements of a book reference within a footnote are as follows:

> Author | *Title* | (series title | edition | publisher | date) | pinpoint page reference

Author's names are given exactly as they appear in the publication (which may include first names) with the first name or initial first in the footnote. However, in the bibliography they are presented surname first, then initial(s) only (see section 13.3.9).

If a book has up to three authors, then all are listed. If a book has more than three authors, then give the name of the first author only followed by 'and others'. You may also see et al used in some books. This is short for *et alii* meaning 'and others' in Latin but this is not OSCOLA-compliant. The author's name (or authors' names) are followed by a comma. There is no comma before the 'and' at the end of the list.

The title of the book is then given in *italics*. It is not enclosed in any form of single or double quotation marks.

After the title of the book, publication information is provided in round brackets. First, if the book is in a series, then the series title is provided and followed by a comma, otherwise this part of the reference is omitted. Similarly, if the book is not a first edition, the edition number is given, followed by 'edn' with a trailing comma. The name of the publisher is always given followed by the year of publication.

Here are some examples of citations as they would be shown in footnotes (authors would be surname first and initials only in the bibliography):

- David Ormerod and Karl Laird, *Smith and Hogan Criminal Law* (14th edn, OUP 2015)
- Stefan Fafinski, *Computer Misuse: Response, Regulation and the Law* (Routledge 2009)
- Lucia Zedner, *Criminal Justice* (Clarendon Law Series, OUP 2004)
- Yaman Akdeniz, Clive Walker and David Wall, *The Internet, Law and Society* (Pearson 2000)
- Roy Goode and others, *Transnational Commercial Law: International Instruments and Commentary* (OUP 2004)

13.3.5.2 Edited collections

If the book is an edited collection, then the same rules apply as for books above, except that (ed) is put after the editor's name (or (eds) if there are multiple editors). Note that no full stops are used in these abbreviations:

- Yvonne Jewkes (ed), *Crime Online* (Willan 2007)
- Chris Hale and others (eds), *Criminology* (3rd edn, OUP 2013)
- Roger Brownsword and Karen Yeung (eds), *Regulating Technologies* (Hart Publishing 2008)
- Mike Maguire, Rod Morgan and Robert Reiner (eds), *The Oxford Handbook of Criminology* (5th edn, OUP 2012)

13.3.5.3 Pinpoint referencing of books

When using footnotes, you should always provide a complete reference. This should include pinpoint references:

- For a direct quotation from a certain page of a book (or article—see section 13.3.6).
- If the reference is for an idea that is located on a particular page (or pages) rather than in the book (or article) in general.

Here is an example of a general reference where the sentence in the text refers to the overall theme of the book rather than a particular page or section. In this case, the footnote reference need not specify a chapter or page number:

> Finch and Fafinski emphasize the importance of the ability to identify, locate, and understand the law as well as the ability to use this effectively within written work.[1]
>
> [1] Emily Finch and Stefan Fafinski, *Legal Skills* (8th edn, OUP 2021).

Where the sentence in the text concerns a specific issue, reference is needed to the particular page (or pages) of the book that address that issue:

> It is essential that precise and detailed references are provided for all materials that are used in the construction of an essay.[1]
>
> [1] Emily Finch and Stefan Fafinski, *Legal Skills* (8th edn, OUP 2021) 305.

Any pinpoint page references are always given after the closing bracket in the reference.

13.3.6 Referencing journal articles and chapters in edited collections using OSCOLA

13.3.6.1 Journal articles

The basic form of an article reference within a footnote is as follows:

Author | 'Title' | date | volume number | journal title | start page | pinpoint page reference

Author name(s) are provided in the same style as for books. The title of the article is then given in Roman (regular) type (rather than *italics* as used for book titles) and is enclosed in single inverted commas.

The year of publication is provided next. The same convention here is used as in case reporting where the publication year is given in square brackets if it identifies the volume, and in round brackets where the journal volumes are numbered consecutively (and thus the year of publication is not required in order to locate the volume).

Any volume number is given next, followed by the title of the journal (or abbreviated title of the journal) in Roman (regular) type and the number of the page on which the article starts. If you need to add a pinpoint reference to a particular page (see section 13.3.5.3) then add a comma after the reference to the start page, followed by the particular page you wish to reference.

Here are some examples of journal articles correctly referenced using OSCOLA:

- Robert Baldwin, 'The New Punitive Regulation' (2004) 67 MLR 351
- Antonia Cretney and Gwynn Davis, 'Prosecuting "Domestic" Assault' [1996] Crim LR 162

13.3.6.2 Edited collections

Another source commonly encountered is a chapter in an edited collection: that is, a contribution by a particular author to a book edited by someone else. The format of this reference is as shown here:

> Author of chapter | 'Chapter Title' | in Editor (ed/eds) | *Title of Edited Collection* | (series title | edition | publisher | date)

It is not necessary to give the page number of the contribution.

Here are some examples of chapters from edited collections:

- Emily Finch, 'The Problem of Stolen Identity and the Internet' in Yvonne Jewkes (ed), *Crime Online* (Willan 2006)
- Mike Levi and Andrew Pithouse, 'Victims of Fraud' in David Downes (ed), *Unravelling Criminal Justice* (Macmillan 1992)

13.3.7 Referencing internet sources using OSCOLA

A high proportion of plagiarism cases seem to involve material taken from the internet that is not acknowledged as such. It is possible that at least some of these cases arise from a lack of understanding as to how to reference such material or, indeed, a lack of awareness that material derived from the internet requires a reference.

A distinction can be made between material that is published solely on the internet and that which is available in hard copy elsewhere and has simply been accessed online in the interests of convenience. In the case of the former, as it is only available on the internet, it is essential that adequate information is provided to enable the reader to locate the same material.

As such, websites are generally referenced like this:

> Author | 'Title' | (Type of resource | date) | accessed date of access

For web resources where the author is not known, you should use two conjoined 'em-dashes'. These are dashes which are longer than the hyphens commonly produced in word processing software and look like this:—. The precise way in which you insert them will depend on your word processing software. In Microsoft Word (Windows and Mac), they are found under Insert > Symbol > Special characters.

The title of the document is given in single inverted commas, followed by the type and/or date of the document in round brackets if this information is available. This is followed by the URL, or web address, in angled brackets < >. It is essential that you are accurate in recording the URL as this enables the reader to find the material. You can increase accuracy by using the 'cut and paste' option from the address bar of your browser to your document. This will eliminate the possibility of typing errors and can be particularly useful in relation to long and complex URLs. It is important to remember, however, to ensure that the pasted URL matches the format of the rest of your text: coloured hyperlinks (usually either blue or purple) in the midst of your essay give a very poor impression of the care you have taken with presentation, particularly if you print your work on a colour printer before handing it in. If you right-click on a hyperlink in Microsoft Word, you should see a 'Remove Hyperlink' option (on Windows) or a 'Hyperlink . . .' menu (on Mac).

Finally the date of access should be provided. It is important to include the date that the material was accessed as internet content is frequently changed and updated, so there may be no permanent record of the material that you have referenced, unlike the situation in relation to printed material. It is for this reason that it can be useful to print out material found online that is not available elsewhere to ensure that you do have a permanent record that you can produce if the integrity or accuracy of your research is ever questioned.

For example:

- Council of Europe, 'Countries worldwide turn to Council of Europe Cybercrime Convention' (Press Release 413(2007) Strasbourg 13 June 2007) <https://wcd.coe.int/ViewDoc.jsp?id=1,150,107> accessed 21 October 2018
- RA Duff, 'Theories of Criminal Law' (Stanford Encyclopaedia of Philosophy, 2002) <http://plato.stanford.edu/entries/criminal-law/> accessed 21 October 2018
- ——, 'Avoiding plagiarism' <https://ilrb.cf.ac.uk/plagiarism/tutorial/index.html> accessed 21 October 2018

Although OSCOLA (4th edition) does not specifically mention podcasts or YouTube, it is reasonable to adopt the same approach for these as for other online resources:

- J Rozenberg, 'Reinventing the law' (BBC Radio 4 'Law in Action' Podcast, 18 June 2020) <https://www.bbc.co.uk/programmes/m000k2m4> accessed 27 October 2020
- Lord Burnett of Maldon, Untitled (15 October 2019) <https://www.youtube.com/watch?v=LanhJXj5EeY> accessed 27 October 2020

In relation to material that is accessed online but is available elsewhere, such as a Home Office report, some might say that there is no need to include any mention of the internet as the report can be referenced without it in a way that enables the reader to identify the source material and locate it themselves should they wish to do so. From this perspective, the fact that the report was found online is irrelevant, so to include the URL upon which the report can be found would be the equivalent of adding 'as read in the university library on 20 January 2019' in the footnote in relation to a hard copy.

Whilst there is some sense in this view, it can never hurt to note the use of the internet in relation to such material just to indicate that you have not actually read the report in the printed original. Strictly speaking, you should only do this if you have used an online version because the hard copy was not available to you.

One exception here is that you do *not* need to give details of websites on which you found cases or statutes. This is quite a common error. It is not necessary to give URLs to LexisLibrary, Westlaw Edge UK, or the Statute Law Database if you have been looking up cases or legislation: your references should never look like this:

> The interpretation of s 192 of the Road Traffic Act 1988[1] was considered in *Cutter v Eagle Star Insurance Co Ltd*[2]
>
> ---
>
> [1] <http://login.westlaw.co.uk/maf/wluk/app/document?&srguid=i0ad69f8e000001589c3e7cff3ed56556&docgu id=I5FFAEF41E42311DAA7CF8F68F6EE57AB&hitguid=I5FFAEF41E42311DAA7CF8F68F6EE57AB&rank=1&spos= 1&epos=1&td=12&crumb-action=append&context=19&resolvein=true> accessed 20 January 2019.
> [2] [1997] 1 WLR 1082 (CA) <http://login.westlaw.co.uk/maf/wluk/app/document?&suppsrguid=i0ad62903000001589c3 f6debd3162bf3&docguid=I9374E520E42711DA8FC2A0F0355337E9&hitguid=I9374BE10E42711DA8FC2A0F0355337E9&r ank=3&spos=3&epos=3&td=3&crumb-action=append&context=29&resolvein=true> accessed 20 January 2019.

The following, also commonly encountered, is also incorrect:

> The interpretation of s 192 of the Road Traffic Act 1988[1] was considered in *Cutter v Eagle Star Insurance Co Ltd*[2]
>
> ---
>
> [1] Accessed on Westlaw Edge UK on 20 January 2019.
> [2] [1997] 1 WLR 1082 (CA) accessed on Westlaw Edge UK on 20 January 2019.

It should simply look like this, regardless of where you found the information:

> The interpretation of s 192 of the Road Traffic Act 1988 was considered in *Cutter v Eagle Star Insurance Co Ltd*.[1]
>
> ---
>
> [1] [1997] 1 WLR 1082 (CA).

However, commentary on legal databases that is not published in hard copy, such as Westlaw's Insight, should be cited as such:

> Gillian Geddes, 'Human Trafficking' (*Insight*, 22 January 2015) <Westlaw> accessed 30 March 2015.

13.3.8 Referencing other sources using OSCOLA

13.3.8.1 Law Commission reports

Law Commission reports should be referenced as follows:

> Law Commission | 'Title of Report' | (Law Com number | Command Paper number | year) | pinpoint page/paragraph reference

For example:

- Law Commission, 'Criminal Law—Computer Misuse' (Law Com No 186 Cm 819, 1989)
- Law Commission, 'Intoxication and Criminal Liability' (Law Com No 314 Cm 7526, 2009)

13.3.8.2 Command papers

Command papers should be referenced as follows:

> Author | 'Title of Command Paper' | (command paper number | year)

For example:

- HM Treasury, 'Investing in Britain's Potential: Building our Long-term Future' (Cm 6984, 2006)
- Secretary of State for Work and Pensions, 'Ready for Work: Full Employment in our Generation' (Cm 7290, 2007)

See section 9.3.1 for information on command paper abbreviations.

13.3.8.3 Parliamentary reports

Parliamentary reports should be referenced as follows:

> Committee Name | 'Title of Report' | HL/HC | (year of Parliamentary session) | report serial number | pinpoint page/paragraph reference

HL is used for House of Lords reports and HC for House of Commons. The report serial number can generally be found on the bottom of the report's title page. Joint Committee reports will have both a HL and a HC serial number, separated by a semi-colon. For example:

- European Union Committee, 'The Criminal Law Competence of the European Community: Report with Evidence' HL (2005–06) 227
- Joint Committee on Human Rights, 'The Council of Europe Convention on the Prevention of Terrorism' HL (2006–07) 26; HC (2006–07) 247

13.3.8.4 Parliamentary debates (*Hansard* or the *Official Report*)

Hansard debates are generally referenced as follows:

> Hansard | HL/HC | volume number | column number(s) | (date)

For instance:

- Hansard HC vol 166 col 1135 (9 February 1990)
- Hansard HL vol 684 cols 604–606 (11 July 2006)

There have been six series of *Hansard*:

- Series 1 1803–20
- Series 2 1820–30
- Series 3 1830–91
- Series 4 1892–1908
- Series 5 1909–1981
- Series 6 1981–

The first four series have reports from the House of Lords and House of Commons bound together and are known as Parliamentary Debates. In the fifth and subsequent series the reports of the two Houses are bound into separate volumes (HL and HC). Reports prior to 1909 are referenced like this:

Hansard Parl Debs | (series number) | volume number | column number(s) | (date)

For instance:

- Hansard Parl Debs (series 3) vol 33 cols 121–2 (22 April 1836)

However, there are a couple of complications in respect of written answers to questions. For written answers after 2001, you should put 'WA' *before* the column number for House of Lords Hansard, and put 'W' *after* the column number for House of Commons Hansard, like this:

- Hansard HL vol 673 col WA261 (21 July 2005)
- Hansard HC vol 449 col 1199W (25 July 2006)

For written answers before 2001 put 'WA' in parentheses after the date, regardless of whether you are considering the House of Lords or the House of Commons, like this:

- Hansard HC vol 357 cols 234–45 (7 February 1940 WA)

13.3.8.5 Newspapers

Articles from newspapers are referenced like this:

Author | 'Title' | *Newspaper* | (Place of publication | full date) | page

Articles from online newspapers are referenced similarly, but with the URL and date of access also provided:

Author | 'Title' | *Newspaper* | (Place of publication | full date) | | accessed date of access

As with websites (see section 13.3.7), if the author is unknown, use two conjoined em-dashes (these are the longer dashes that look like this:——), unless the source is an unnamed editorial piece, in which case you should cite the author as 'Editorial'. URLs should be given in angled brackets as for general internet sources. For example:

- ——, 'Ombudsman denies Law Society bias' *The Times* (London, 9 January 1984) 2
- Editorial, 'The cost of free speech: England's libel laws are still rotten' *The Guardian* (London, 13 April 2000) 23

- A Cramb, 'Eurasian beavers to be given formal protection and allowed to remain in Scottish countryside' *The Telegraph* (24 November 2016) <http://www.telegraph.co.uk/news/2016/11/24/eurasian-beavers-given-formalprotection-allowed-remain-inscottish/> accessed 20 January 2019

13.3.9 Compiling a bibliography using OSCOLA

The final stage in footnote referencing is compiling your bibliography. You may also be required to list a table of cases and a table of legislation at the end of your work. This is good practice in any event. Remember that a bibliography contains all the secondary sources that have been explicitly referenced in footnotes. You may wish to compile your bibliography as you go, rather than doing it all at the end. If you do not, remember to allow enough time to do this thoroughly, particularly if you are working to a tight deadline.

The bibliography should list all sources, in alphabetical order by author surname. It should not contain any pinpoint references or full stops at the end of each item. The key difference, however, between bibliography entries and footnote entries, is that in bibliographies the surname comes *first* followed by initial(s) only. There should be no comma between surname and initials, but there should be a comma after the final initial.

Students often ask why OSCOLA imposes this seemingly arbitrary change of formatting. The OSCOLA guide does not explain specifically, but our best guess at the rationale is this:

- **Why no pinpoints?** A pinpoint reference is essential in the text as the reader may wish to go to your source at the point they are reading your work. As the bibliography is a list of sources at the end of the work, then the pinpoint references are not needed there. Bibliography references are not tied to any specific part of the text in the same way as footnotes.

- **Why no full stops?** Full stops in a long list would just look a bit odd. Footnotes, though, would look incomplete and 'hanging' without them.

- **Why list surname first?** For ease of reference. If we simply replicated the format of the footnote, then it would be very hard to find a particular source in a bibliography as the entries would generally be listed in first name order: for example, Lucia Zedner would come before Ryan Abbott in the list.

- **So why do footnotes not just have surname first then?** The only explanation we can come up with is that the footnote remains absolutely true to the presentation of the author's (or authors') name(s) on the publication itself.

In terms of the mechanics of putting a bibliography together, you will need to find an approach that works for you. We will set out one way of doing it, using many of the examples from this chapter.

Step 1. Compile your list of sources

It is best to do this as you write. When you put a new footnote reference in your work, copy that footnote into a separate document. Keep the document up to date as you go. You may want to combine this with Step 2 but you do not have to worry about any of the formatting changes or order at this stage. Figure 13.1 shows an example list of raw footnote sources.

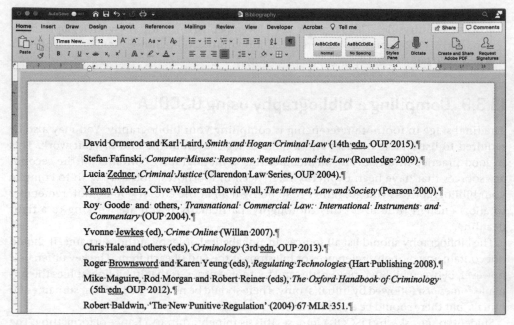

Figure 13.1 List of raw footnote sources

Step 2.   Turn the footnotes into bibliography format

Next, if you have not done so as part of Step 1, you will have to go through the document and apply the necessary changes (rearranging names and removing pinpoints and full stops). The downside of leaving it until the end is that you can be faced with a boring, fiddly, and repetitive task just when you feel like you have finished your work, so some feel it is better to spread the pain by reformatting the bibliography document as you go. Either way, you should end up with something like Figure 13.2.

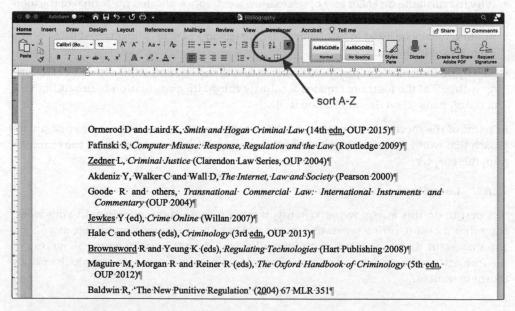

Figure 13.2 List of footnote sources turned into bibliography format

Step 3.   Sort by surname

You can either sort the paragraphs manually, by dragging and dropping them, or selecting the whole list and clicking the 'sort A-Z' button (shown highlighted in Figure 13.2). This should give you the option of sorting automatically by 'Paragraphs' type 'Text' 'Ascending'. This should give you your final bibliography as seen in Figure 13.3, ready to cut and paste across into your work.

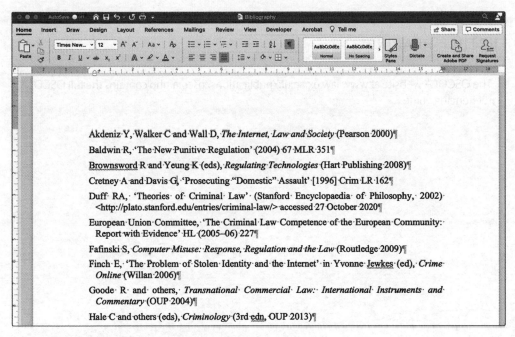

Figure 13.3 Bibliography sorted by surname.

13.3.10 Automated referencing tools

There are an increasing number of online automated referencing tools available (such as citethisforme.com). These will certainly take much of the hard work (and sometimes tedious reformatting) out of producing OSCOLA references, but, as with any automated tool, do not rely on such apps blindly. At the very least make sure that you sanity-check the output in line with the OSCOLA principles that have been covered in this chapter, just in case there is an issue.

CHAPTER SUMMARY

- Plagiarism is a form of academic dishonesty that is readily detected and attracts negative consequences both within your institution and in the professional world

- Bear in mind that a thorough and precise approach to references will avoid accusations of inadvertent plagiarism; if in doubt, reference

- Note the situations outlined in this chapter in which a reference should be provided, taking particular care to ensure that ideas are attributed to their source

- Find out whether your institution or department has a 'house style' and, if so, ensure that you follow it
- Never combine footnotes and in-text references
- Familiarize yourself with the conventions for referencing and cross-referencing
- Take particular care with internet sources
- Always provide a complete bibliography

FURTHER READING

- The OSCOLA website at www.law.ox.ac.uk/publications/oscola.php contains the full OSCOLA referencing guide.

Essay writing

14

INTRODUCTION

The focus of this chapter is essay writing. Earlier sections of this book have outlined techniques for locating and understanding primary and secondary legal sources. This chapter builds on those skills by exploring the ways that this source material can be used in your coursework. It will also guide you through the stages of planning, research, and construction of an essay with practical advice on interpreting the question and producing a structured response that demonstrates the required skills and knowledge. It should be read in conjunction with chapter 11, which focuses on writing skills and chapter 13, for information on referencing. Doing so will ensure that you produce a polished piece of work that is well expressed and fully referenced in an appropriate style.

The essay is a popular method tool of assessment in law, and essay questions make frequent appearances on exam papers across a range of modules as well as featuring heavily in coursework assessment. Given the prevalence of this method of assessment, it is important that you ensure that your essay-writing craftsmanship is of the highest level. Students often make the mistake of thinking that an essay is marked on its content alone but this is not the case: a good essay is a combination of knowledge and skills. In fact, there are a whole package of skills involved in essay writing, all of which need to be demonstrated if your work is to achieve good marks. This chapter will introduce these skills and explain what you need to do to demonstrate them to the marker who is reading your mark.

Learning outcomes

After studying this chapter, you will be able to:

- Appreciate the combination of knowledge and skills required to produce a successful piece of written work
- Be able to 'unpick' the question to ensure that you have a clear grasp of its requirements
- Conduct effective research and extract relevant information to enable you to produce a focused and well-supported essay
- Create an effective introduction and conclusion to your essay and structure a cohesive line of argument
- Evaluate the essay that you have written to ensure that it demonstrates the relevant skills and knowledge and that it adheres to the necessary style and referencing requirements

14.1 WHAT MAKES A GOOD ESSAY?

This is an important question as you cannot be expected to produce a good essay until you know what features combine together to create a good essay. In essence, a good essay is one that answers the question and, in doing so, demonstrates a range of written and analytical skills. It is important to emphasize that a good essay requires as much thought to be given to the way that the essay is constructed as is given to its content. In other words, it is not enough that you know the relevant law and commentary, you must also know what to do with it in order to write an effective essay. A good essay should demonstrate the following:

- A foundation of accurate and relevant knowledge about the legal topic that is the subject of the question
- Wide-ranging research that identifies a variety of relevant source material appropriate to the subject matter
- Effective use of source material so that it is integrated into the essay and used to strengthen your arguments in a way that demonstrates your understanding of the material and its role in your work
- The ability to filter out irrelevant or peripheral points and to maintain a firm and consistent focus on the central issue raised by the question
- A flowing line of argument set in a clear structure with an effective introduction and conclusion
- An appropriate balance between description and analysis
- Good written communication skills in producing a coherent and eloquent piece of work
- A thorough approach to referencing that ensures that all source material is acknowledged in a complete and appropriate style.

This mix of knowledge and skills can be further illustrated if the process of creating an essay is broken down into stages as illustrated in Figure 14.1.

This chapter will provide a detailed account of the requirements of each of these stages in order to assist you with the production of an essay that answers the question set, demonstrates appropriate skills, and which meets with the approval of your marker. Remember, though, that it may be necessary to move backwards and forwards through the stages: you may, for example, find that you need to do more research once you have moved into the writing stage or that you need to reconsider what the essay means during the research stage, but that is not a problem. This chapter does not intend to suggest that there is a rigid progression through the stages but to ensure that each stage is given adequate attention to help you with the production of your essays.

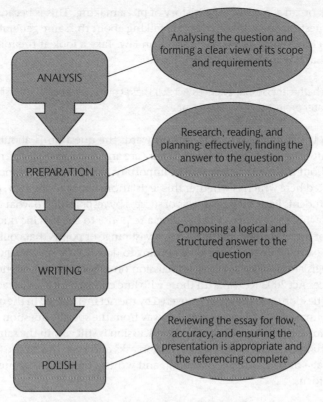

Figure 14.1 The four stages of essay writing

14.2 ANALYSING THE QUESTION

It is important to take time to analyse the question in order to work out what it requires. This is a fundamental first step although it may have to be combined with some initial research to help you understand the precise requirements of the question. For example, you may be able to identify the subject matter of the question on the basis of its wording and your existing knowledge but a little preliminary investigation in your textbook might be necessary to help you understand the question more fully. However, try to pinpoint the precise requirements of the question as early as possible as this will add focus to your research and enable you to identify relevant material more effectively.

14.2.1 What does the question ask?

It is essential to the effectiveness of every stage of the essay-writing process as well as to the overall success of the essay, in terms of the mark that it is awarded, that you focus on what the essay *asks* rather than what the essay is *about* in broader terms. Responding to what the question asks involves creating a line of argument whereas an essay that responds to the general topic will tend to be descriptive and unfocused.

For example, if you asked someone how to make pizza, you would be annoyed if they responded by telling you where to buy pizza or how many calories there are in the average pizza or if they embark on an account of the history of pizza making. This is because they have not answered your question even though they are talking about the same general topic.

The same principle applies to essay questions in law. Take a look at the following question and decide (a) what it is about and (b) what it asks:

> Critically assess whether the Sexual Offences Act 2003 has achieved its objectives of simplifying the law and affording greater protection to victims of rape.

The answer to the first question is straightforward: the question is about sexual offences legislation and the offence of rape. However, there are any number of different questions that could be asked about this topic so it would be important that your answer focused on the specific question asked here which is whether this legislation achieved the two stated objectives.

Far too many students limit their prospects of success by responding to what the essay is about rather than narrowing their focus and providing a response to the specific question. This leads to the inclusion of irrelevant material as there is a vast range of points that could be made about the general topic (sexual offences) that have nothing to do with the specific question (the effectiveness of the legislation). For example, a discussion on grooming—an offence introduced by the Sexual Offences Act 2003 to deal with those who lure children into sexual activity—has little relevance to the question even though it is covered by the Act mentioned in the question. In other words, you do not have to take too many steps away from the specific question asked in order to stray into the realms of irrelevancy, even if your discussion is still within the same broad topic.

It is essential that you identify what the question asks and keep this to the forefront of your mind at every stage of the research, planning, and writing process to ensure that your essay does not lose its focus:

- Make sure that you isolate the specific question asked about the topic and write this in a prominent place so that it acts as a reminder whilst you are working on your essay.

- Check every point that you find during your research for its relevance to the question (not the topic). You might want to develop a simple ranking system to help you with this.

- Points that do not have immediate relevance can be made relevant if you slant them towards the question. For example, you could include a discussion of grooming in the earlier example if you used it to illustrate how it criminalizes conduct that might precede a rape.

- When you are drafting your essay, make sure that each paragraph touches base with the specific question. You can use signposting to do this (this is discussed in section 14.4.4 later in this chapter).

14.2.2 Rewording the question

One of the most effective ways to work out what the question asks is to rewrite it in your own words with the aim of discovering one or two clear questions that you understand. For example, the following two questions simplify the sexual offences question and make it far easier to keep its core issues in mind when researching and writing the essay:

- Is the offence of rape easier to understand than it was prior to the introduction of the Sexual Offences Act 2003?

- Has the Sexual Offences Act 2003 improved the protection available for victims of rape?

This approach will enable you to establish and retain a focus on the question posed by the essay and it also offers a starting point for structuring the essay as it is clear that there are two separate issues that need to be addressed.

It can also be helpful to reword an essay question if it is phrased in a way that does not give you much by way of clues as to what is expected. A question that is made up of a quotation followed by the instruction to 'discuss' is an example of this as it puts the onus on the student to work out what it is that needs to be discussed. The way to deal with this is to reword the question yourself using alternative words so that you make a distinction from the start about what aspect of the question needs to be described and what it is that needs to be analysed.

You will find an explanation of how so-called 'process words'—such as 'discuss'—are used in the construction of essay questions and how these can help you to understand what the question requires of you in section 14.4.5 later in this chapter.

Practical exercise

It is a good idea to practise analysing essay titles by rewording them as this will give you the confidence to do it with your own coursework questions. There is an example below followed by some questions for you to try yourself:

The problems concerning the separation of powers have been resolved by the Constitutional Reform Act 2005. Discuss.

This can be reworded using process words to indicate what needs to be described in the question and what part of it should be the focus of analysis:

Outline the changes made to the separation of powers that were introduced by the Constitutional Reform Act 2005. Assess whether these changes have resolved all the problems associated with the separation of powers.

This can be made clearer still by breaking this down into a series of questions that need to be answered:

- *What is meant by the separation of powers?*
- *What was the position prior to 2005?*
- *What changes were introduced by the Constitutional Reform Act 2005?*
- *Why were these changes made? What problems were they trying to address?*
- *What is the current situation?*
- *Do the previously identified problems still remain?*
- *Are there new problems?*

So—have the problems concerning the separation of powers been resolved by the Constitutional Reform Act 2005?

Try to identify the questions that are asked by the following essay titles. You should be able to make an attempt at this even if you have little prior knowledge of the subject matter.

1. The postal rule is outdated and has little place in modern contract law. Discuss.

2. If the United Kingdom has a constitution at all, its central pillar is Parliamentary sovereignty. Evaluate this statement with particular reference to the European Union.

3. Outline the approaches that a judge may take to statutory interpretation and consider their relevance following the enactment of the Human Rights Act 1998.

You will find answers to these questions and an explanation of how they were reached at www.oup.com/he/finch8e/.

Remember that you are rewording the question to enhance your understanding of what it requires. You must take the utmost care to ensure that you are not rewording it in a way that changes its sense or meaning. When your essay is marked, it will only attract credit for material that is relevant to the question that was asked and not for other points, however interesting or clever, that are not pertinent.

14.3 PREPARATION: RESEARCH AND PLANNING

The preparatory stages of research and planning should take at least as much time as the actual writing of the essay. During this stage you will find different points of interest leading towards a draft conclusion, select material for inclusion in your essay, and engage in some preliminary planning of the structure of your argument. Taking care with these preparatory stages does make the writing of the essay less troublesome, as many of the difficult issues will have already been resolved.

14.3.1 Focus on the question(s)

The aim of the last section was to emphasize the importance of working out the requirements of the question before starting the process of research, planning, and writing that will produce the essay. This is because you cannot answer a question effectively unless you know what it is asking. Students sometimes think that research is the first stage, but you will be so much more effective in your research if you start with a clear idea of what you are trying to find out.

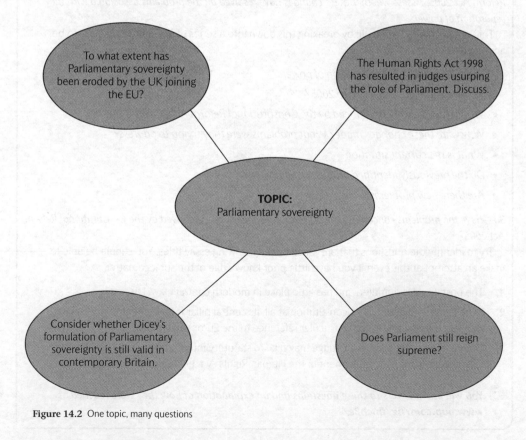

To what extent has Parliamentary sovereignty been eroded by the UK joining the EU?

The Human Rights Act 1998 has resulted in judges usurping the role of Parliament. Discuss.

TOPIC:
Parliamentary sovereignty

Consider whether Dicey's formulation of Parliamentary sovereignty is still valid in contemporary Britain.

Does Parliament still reign supreme?

Figure 14.2 One topic, many questions

Try to remember that you do not need to know the answer in order to conduct research: after all, that is what research is all about—finding answers. Of course, you are likely to discover information during your research that assists you to reach a more closely informed understanding of the question.

You should be able to identify the general topic from the wording of the question itself and this will enable you to start your research. Remember that each topic has a number of different questions that can be asked about it (see Figure 14.2) and your initial job is to sift through the information on the topic and identify material that is pertinent to the particular question that you have been asked.

14.3.2 Brainstorming

One method of exploring what you already know about a topic is brainstorming. This involves writing down everything that you can think of about a topic in the order it comes into your mind. This technique is useful in essay writing as a way to establish a list of potential topics for inclusion in your essay so that you can make some preliminary decisions about relevance and thus direct the focus of your research and reading.

Practical exercise

Brainstorming can be a good way of getting all your possible points about a topic down on paper so that you can look at them and assess their relevance to your essay. You might find it useful to work with a friend as you can share ideas and discuss the relevance of the different points that you generate.

1. Write the topic at the top of a piece of paper and divide the paper into two columns.

2. Give yourself a set period of time—two minutes should be ample—to make a list of all the points that spring into your mind about that topic. Do not worry about their relevance at this stage—just get all your ideas down on paper.

3. When your time is up, review the points that you have listed and think about their relevance to the particular question that is asked in your essay. Use a ranking system in which 1 = highly relevant, 2 = some relevance, and 3 = irrelevant. You can also add notes that reflect your thoughts about the role of each point that is relevant in your essay.

4. Reorder your points according to their relevance. Alternatively, you might want to start grouping similar points together to create a draft structure for your essay.

This approach may not capture all of the points that you want to include in your essay as you are likely to find new material as your research progresses but it will help to give some direction to your research by identifying potential lines of investigation.

🌐 *You will find an example of a brainstorming exercise at **www.oup.com/he/finch8e/**.*

14.3.3 Getting started

It can be extremely difficult to make a start on the research and planning of an essay just because it all seems such an immense task, particularly if you feel that you are overwhelmed from the start because you are faced with a topic that you do not understand. This section outlines some of the early steps that can be taken that will help you to make a start on your preparation.

Earlier chapters in this book have provided in-depth coverage of a range of sources, how to find them, and how to make effective use of them. This chapter will not repeat that information but will merely highlight a few key points of particular relevance to conducting research for an essay. You will probably find that you need to make reference to earlier chapters to help you with the research process.

The most sensible starting point for your research is the relevant chapter(s) in a textbook. This is because textbooks are designed to provide exactly what you need at this point in time: a clear and relatively comprehensive explanation of areas of law. It is important that you use textbooks in an appropriate way when conducting research for your coursework. This means that you must use them in a way that is (a) useful to you and (b) acceptable to your lecturers.

- **Start with the set textbook.** Even if you do not like the book and have found an alternative, it would be a mistake not to read it in case you miss out on information that the lecturer expects you to know and that other students on your module will have read.

- **Make sure that you understand the basics of the topic.** If the set textbook does not give you a clear understanding of the important points, make a note of them and find a simpler explanation in an alternative book. You may need to try several textbooks before you find one that explains the issues in a way that makes sense to you but you must persevere with this as it is crucial that you have a grasp of the basics from a source aimed at students before you start to explore the issues in greater depth.

- **Use a range of textbooks.** Each author will explain the key points in the legal subject matter in their own way and will use different examples to illustrate their points so you can gain a broader perspective on the topic by using several different textbooks.

- **Do not make too many notes at this stage.** You are reading textbooks to gain an overview of the topic and to identify useful source material and lines of investigation relevant to your essay. It is not a good use of your time to copy large chunks out of the textbook so try to use a condensed approach to note-taking in which you describe the points that you want to find again and note the page on which it occurs. For example, you might write 'p. 174 talks about the "red hand" rule and p. 178 refers to a useful article by Macdonald in *Legal Studies*'.

- **Move on to consult a wide range of sources.** Remember that textbooks are written for students. They do all the hard work for you by summarizing the information that you need to understand legal topics. You are expected to use this as a starting point to enable you to identify source material such as case law, relevant journal articles, and official reports that you will then read yourself and use as authority in your essay.

14.3.4 Gathering supporting materials

Once you have an idea of the basic points that you want to raise in your essay, you will need to turn your attention to the selection of supporting material. In other words, you will want to provide authority to substantiate your arguments. In particular, you should ensure that all statements of law are attributed to a particular source, whether this is case law or statute. It also adds strength to your arguments about the interpretation or application of the law if you can make reference to material which backs up your position.

14.3.4.1 Textbooks

As a general rule, you should only use textbooks to support your argument if you have quoted directly from them and you should only quote directly from them if there is no other source available and you feel that you cannot express the idea in your own words. Textbooks exist to give you an accessible summary of the law and the central debates surrounding the law; basically, they are the starting point upon which you should build your legal understanding. As such, you will be expected to demonstrate that you have read a variety of sources in the preparation of your essay rather than simply relying on textbooks.

Of course, some textbooks have an excellent reputation for their analysis of the law, in which case you may find that there are ideas expressed in there that you would like to incorporate into your essay. If this is the case, it may be a good idea to find out if the author of the textbook has elaborated on this point in an article or monograph and, if so, to rely on this to support your argument instead. Overall, it is advisable to be sparing in your reliance on textbooks in your essay.

14.3.4.2 Statutory provisions

The position regarding statutory provisions is straightforward. If you are referring to a particular piece of legislation, you should always indicate the name of the statute and, if appropriate, the section or subsection number. This does not necessarily mean that you should quote the full wording of the section itself; it will often be more appropriate to paraphrase the statutory provision or to select a segment of the section.

14.3.4.3 Case law

There are four main ways in which you might want to use case law in your essay to support your answer.

- **The source of a legal principle.** If a legal rule, definition, or test has evolved in case law, you should attribute it to its source in the same way that you would if the area of law was governed by statute. For example, in criminal law, the test for oblique intention was formulated by the House of Lords in *R v Woollin* [1999] 1 AC 82 (HL).

- **An elaboration on the meaning of a word or phrase.** Case law is a major source of interpretation of the meaning and application of words and phrases used in law. For example, the phrase 'ethnic origin' as found in the Race Relations Act 1976 was subjected to in-depth interpretation in *Mandla v Lee* [1983] 2 AC 548 (HL).

- **The operation of the law.** If you want to ascertain the scope of the law and how it applies in particular situations, you can look at how it has taken effect in case law. For example, if you were addressing the tort of defamation in relation to media coverage of the private lives of celebrities, you could use the cases involving the right to freedom of expression to determine the scope of the law. You can also use case law to demonstrate the impact of changes in the law as you can show how the outcome of a decided case would differ; this can be an especially powerful way to support your arguments for or against a particular interpretation of the law. For example, in relation to the sample essay, you could use cases decided under the old law and, in order to demonstrate its impact, explain how they would have a different outcome under the new law.

- **Judicial consideration of issues relevant to your essay.** Case law contains some fascinating in-depth evaluations of how the law is and how it could be as well as the implications of different interpretations of the law. Do not overlook dissenting judgments as these are often a great source of inspiration for opposing arguments.

14.3.4.4 Academic commentary

Sources such as journal articles and monographs can provide valuable support for the arguments made in your essay. It is suggested that you should also strive to include at the very least two, preferably opposing or contradictory, academic viewpoints within your essay to demonstrate the different perspectives that exist in relation to the issue under consideration.

This approach is much stronger than merely asserting your own opinion of the law, although it is perfectly permissible to produce academic arguments that concur with your own preferences. Remember, though, that there is a need for balance and objectivity; whatever your preferred view, you should ensure that an alternative stance is at least acknowledged in your essay. From a pragmatic point of view, identifying two different standpoints is likely to attract greater credit from the marker than reliance on a single view, plus you are also demonstrating your research skills in identifying more than one opinion on the same issue, thus showing evidence of wide reading.

You will find a video screencast on different ways of incorporating academic authority into your essay at **www.oup.com/he/finch8e/**.

14.3.4.5 Online sources

Students like using online searches as part of their research because they are quick and easy type in a word or phrase and you will be presented with a whole host of results within a split second. However, traditional legal resources are reliable and accurate whereas the quality of material found online cannot be guaranteed because anyone can publish anything online. It is acceptable to use the internet to access official publications, such as those found on the Ministry of Justice website, but you should use material of uncertain origin with great caution.

In particular, you should avoid websites that provide a potted summary of the law, especially those aimed at A level students because these will be simplistic and are not appropriate sources for undergraduate writing. There is a great temptation to rely on websites that make the law sound so straightforward but it is not a good idea: it is the online equivalent of relying on the simplest textbook on the topic. You do not demonstrate understanding of your topic if you rely on these sorts of web sources as the message that it gives to your marker is 'I used Google to find some websites that make the law really easy and here is my rewording of their analysis of the law'. This is not the message you want to give as it conveys a poor impression of (a) your research skills and (b) your level of comprehension of the topic.

If you need any further persuasion that many internet sources are not the most suitable authority to cite in an essay, look no further than Wikipedia itself. Wikipedia reminds users that encyclopedias (hard copy or online) are not viewed as good academic sources:

> Most educators and professionals do not consider it appropriate to use tertiary sources such as encyclopedias as a sole source for any information—citing an encyclopedia as an important reference in footnotes or bibliographies may result in censure or a failing grade. Wikipedia articles should be used for background information, as a reference for correct terminology and search terms, and as a starting point for further research.
>
> As with any community-built reference, there is a possibility for error in Wikipedia's content—please check your facts against multiple sources and read our disclaimers for more information.[1]

---

1. <http://en.wikipedia.org/w/index.php?title=Special:Cite&page=Law&id=387,799,726> accessed 20 January 2019.

If even Wikipedia itself suggests that you should not rely upon its content without checking it thoroughly, this should give you a very good reason indeed to avoid using it as a source. When selecting supporting material, bear in mind the following guidelines:

- Statements of law need to be supported by reference to their source in either statute or case law.

- Factual statements should be attributed to their source, for example a statement that 'over 5,000 women are killed by their partners each year in England and Wales' must provide a reference to the source of the statistic.

- Analysis, discussion, and speculation about the law are strengthened by reference to supporting material so look for articles, official reports, and commentary in good textbooks.

- A balanced argument is more effective than a one-sided stance, so select supporting material that takes into account a range of perspectives on the issue under consideration.

- Be cautious in your use of textbooks, using them only if you can find no other supporting material for a particular argument, example, or opinion and never as a reference point for a statement of law that is contained in a case or statute.

Remember that all supporting material must be fully and appropriately referenced in your essay. Failure to do so carries a risk that you will be accused of plagiarism. You will find detailed information on correct approaches to referencing in chapter 13.

14.3.5 Assessing the quality of source material

There are various means of evaluating the relevance and value of source material. One that you may find useful was developed by the Open Library (the library service of the Open University) that uses the mnemonic PROMPT as shown in Figure 14.3.

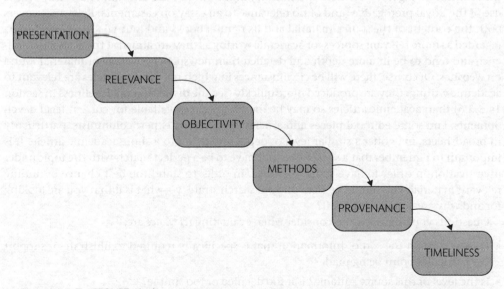

Figure 14.3 The PROMPT criteria

Each of the parts of this mnemonic will be explained in the sections that follow. Remember that you should carry out a PROMPT analysis in the context of a particular piece of work or a specific topic, as an assessment of relevance needs a point of reference: a meaningful PROMPT analysis cannot really be done in the abstract.

14.3.5.1 Presentation

Presentation refers to the appearance of the source material. For example, an academic article is characterized by dense text, mature use of language, and the inclusion of specialist terminology thus indicating that it is aimed at an expert audience, whereas a newspaper article will use more straightforward language and a more accessible layout to suit the general reader. Remember that the level of information aimed at the general reader might be too simplistic for your purposes (see the discussion on relevance in section 14.3.5.2).

The balance between text and illustrations can also give insight into the intended readership. Websites tend to vary in their presentation according to their target reader/user. Other aspects of presentation may be related to the credibility of the source: academic articles include institutional affiliations whilst websites might contain the logo of reputable organizations to add weight to their content.

Questions you might wish to consider when evaluating *presentation* are:

- Is the information communicated clearly?
- Are there errors of spelling, grammar, or presentation?
- What does the writing style suggest about the author or the audience?

14.3.5.2 Relevance

Relevance is closely associated with the purpose for which the source will be used. For example, a newspaper article covering proposed anti-terrorism legislation would be relevant to an essay that considered legal responses to extremism, but it would be less relevant to an essay on the use of the Royal prerogative[2] and of no relevance to an essay on easements. Relevance covers both the content of the source material and its nature: books and journal articles tend to be regarded as more relevant sources for academic writing as they are aimed at the academic audience and tend to be in more depth and detailed than newspaper coverage or material found on websites. Of course, there will be circumstances in which newspaper articles are relevant to academic writing: they are produced more quickly (see the discussion on timeliness in section 14.3.5.6) than academic articles so may be the only source available for current legal developments, and some editorial pieces and articles produced by expert columnists, particularly in broadsheets, may offer a similar level of depth and detail to a short academic article. It is important to remember that a source does not have to be a perfect match with the topic under investigation in order to have some relevance. In order to stand the best chance of finding relevant material, you should be clear on your search strategy—what is it that you are looking for and why are you looking for it?

Questions you might wish to consider when evaluating *relevance* are:

- Does it contain the sort of information that is specifically required to illustrate or support the particular point being made?
- Is the level of this source suitable? Is it too detailed or too simple?
- Does it relate to a country or jurisdiction that is not under consideration?

---

2. Although there is a power under the Royal prerogative to refuse or withdraw passports from British nationals who 'may seek to harm the UK' by travelling on a British passport to take part in terrorist-related activity.

14.3.5.3 Objectivity

Objectivity refers to the extent to which the source material takes a neutral stance or presents a balanced argument rather than arguing from one particular perspective. Journal articles tend to be more objective than media or online sources although this varies according to the nature of the source material. Academic writers tend to explore issues rather than to seek to promote a specific viewpoint, and even those which seek to persuade the reader that a particular approach is preferable tend to include and dissect contrary viewpoints. Newspaper articles may promote a single viewpoint or present more than one view but give primacy to one over the others; a good way to check for balance is to count the number of words that a newspaper article gives to each stance and to consider the relative positioning in the article of the viewpoints (early viewpoints tend to be more dominant). Web sources often have a single viewpoint to promote so care needs to be taken when relying upon them and consideration given to the interests of the individual writer or the organization in control of the publication. You will need to develop the skill of recognizing the perspective put forward by an author—biased opinion is fine, as long as you are able to recognize it as such.

Questions you might wish to consider when evaluating objectivity are:

- Do the writers state their position on the issue?
- Does the source use an emotive, sensational, or journalistic tone?
- Are there any hidden or vested commercial, political, or media interests? (See discussion on provenance in section 14.3.5.5.)
- Is the source a mask for advertising a particular product, service, or organization?
- Is the information fact or opinion?
- Is the source complete, or does it just consider one point of view?
- What are the goals or objectives of the source?

14.3.5.4 Methods

Searching for an understanding of the methods used to produce the information within the source may be a useful indicator of its quality. While the idea of methods applies most commonly to socio-legal empirical research, you should consider where the information contained in the source document came from and whether or not it is reliable. For instance, an article might carry a review of the available literature together with some indication as to how that literature was selected for comment.

Questions you might wish to consider when evaluating *method* are:

- Are clear details provided within the document about its sources?
- Is the material simply an opinion or does it carry supporting evidence (documentary, case law, legislation, or otherwise)?
- Are vague terms such as 'sources/commentators suggest' used?
- If a newspaper article has used quotations, are these from experts?

14.3.5.5 Provenance

Provenance concerns the origins of the material—who produced it and where it came from—and can also give useful insight into its quality. However, each source should be judged on its merits. Some academic work is considered to be of great importance just because it is published in a prestigious journal, yet equally valuable work can readily be found in journals that are considered 'lesser' in some way. That said, provenance is an indirect indicator of quality and reliability—but remember that you should also consider the other areas of enquiry in the PROMPT criteria as well. In the context of your coursework, provenance is also important for your marker to be confident that you are using appropriate sources.

Knowledge of the author is helpful, as it enables you to see if they are acknowledged as an expert in a particular area (although remember that everyone has a first article—so the absence of a body of literature from the same person does not necessarily devalue their early work). It also helps you to see if their work has been referenced in other literature on the topic, or to see if they are well known for espousing a particular viewpoint or court controversy. Similarly, if the material was sponsored by a particular association, you will want to consider the purpose of that organization, to determine whether it is likely to have a particular agenda that would lead to a subjective viewpoint being expressed.

With regard to articles in newspapers, you should remember that the purpose of these articles is to sell newspapers—this can lead to the omission of detail or the sensationalism of the facts, or reporting the story in such a way as to suit the political leanings of the newspaper (see the discussion on objectivity in section 14.3.5.3). Consider also the distinction between broadsheets and tabloid newspapers.

Finally, as you have already seen in this chapter, remember that anyone can publish on the web or post to a discussion forum: this is where the author's credentials are a useful indicator of quality. There is, however, a distinction between material that is *published* on the web and that which is *available* on the web: an article from the *Criminal Law Review*, for example, that is viewed online will be identical to that which first appeared in print and will have been subject to the same review processes. Most (but not all) academic journals are peer-reviewed: articles that are submitted will be evaluated by at least two independent experts and revisions may well be required before an article is accepted for publication. By contrast, not all electronic journals operate a peer review process—check to see if there are any statements on editorial policy.

Questions you might wish to consider when evaluating *provenance* are:

- Who wrote the material? Is there an institutional affiliation? Have they provided a contact email address?

- Is the author a well-known authority in the field? Are they trustworthy?

- If the material is supported by an organization, what are their interests? Who is paying for the material?

- Where is the information published? Has it been edited or reviewed prior to publication?

14.3.5.6 Timeliness

Timeliness relates to the currency of the information contained in the source material. This is particularly important in law where material—especially case law—can date very rapidly. That is not to say that there is no value in older source material: for example, in *De l'esprit des lois* (1748), Montesquieu described the separation of powers between the legislature, the executive, and the judiciary. Just because this view is over 250 years old does not make it invalid today. Older material can be informative in setting out the evolution of a certain theory or society's view of a particular issue at a certain point in time, or it may simply relate to a relatively static area of law. That said, you must remember to take the date of publication into account when assessing the source, but also remember that whether or not material is out of date depends on the purpose for which you want that material. Consider whether new research has been published since the source material that supersedes it or casts new light onto its findings.

Questions you might wish to consider when evaluating *timeliness* are:

- Do you know when the material was produced?

- Does the date of the material fit your needs?

- Is the information obsolete or superseded?

Finally, remember that the PROMPT criteria may not contain all of the factors that you want to take into account when assessing the value of a piece of source material. Any analysis undertaken using these criteria may also quite validly contain a critique of PROMPT as a method of assessing the usefulness of sources.

14.3.6 Organizing your research

During the course of your research, you will use a variety of sources and you will want to keep a record of the relevant information that you have found. There are two aspects to this: first, recording the points from the sources that you want to include in your essay and, secondly, ensuring that you keep a full record of the bibliographic details of each source so that you can reference it appropriately in your work.

The most popular method of recording information is, unfortunately, the least effective as it involves rewriting every textbook, article, and case in a more condensed form. This is labour-intensive and does not produce a very useful set of notes. A less time-consuming alternative is described earlier in this chapter. This involves making a note of the value of the point that you have found rather than writing out the point itself.

Although this method is quicker than writing full notes, it still results in a set of notes that is organized on a source-by-source basis. In other words, you have a set of condensed notes of each article as you read them. There is an alternative approach to organization that will make your notes easier to use when it comes to working out how they fit into your essay which is issue-by-issue.

This approach uses the points that you identified during your analysis of the question and your brainstorming as the basis for arranging your notes.

- Identify key words and phrases from your analysis of the question and brainstorming session and write each of these at the top of a separate sheet of paper (or create a document for each if working on a computer).

- Select a piece of source material and read it carefully, looking out for any points that are relevant to the issues that you have identified. If you are working from a copy, you could highlight these points or annotate the page to indicate that they are important points.

- Make a descriptive note of the point such as 'discusses the validity of consent procured by fraud' under the relevant heading. Be sure to include something that identifies the source such as the name of the author or the article and the page on which the point appears.

- Review your headings from time to time. It may be that certain issues need to be amalgamated or a discrete issue may emerge under one of your headings that you decide to treat separately. You may find material during your research that identifies a new issue that you had not originally thought of but which you discover has a place in your essay.

These points will be the building blocks of your essay so it will be useful to have your notes arranged in this way. You will see an example of notes organized by issue in Figure 14.4. It shows sub-divisions within the page of notes on the left-hand side which have allocated space to note questions that have arisen during the research process and further avenues of investigation to be pursued. These separate sections within each page or document will serve as a useful reminder of thoughts that occurred to you as you were reading and will act as a prompt when you are deciding what further research needs to be undertaken.

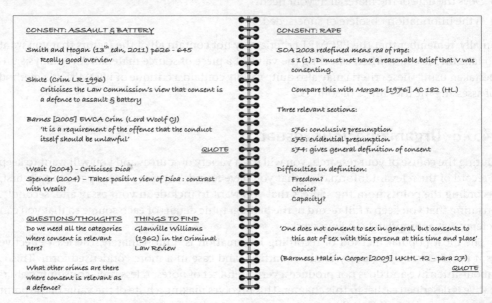

Figure 14.4 Notes organized by issue

You may also have noticed that some points in the example are written in full and that the word QUOTE appears in capital letters beside them. You might think that this is unnecessary as the words appear inside quotation marks but it very good practice to do everything possible to draw your attention to the fact that these words are not yours and must be attributed to their source if used in your essay. It is very easy to forget to add quotation marks or overlook them when reading your notes some time after they were written and think 'what a good point. I've expressed that really well' and include it in your essay without realizing that it was a quotation. As you will see from the discussion in chapter 13, even unintentional replication of the work of others without acknowledgement will contravene the plagiarism/unfair practice rules at your university so it is worth taking extra effort to ensure that you do not make a mistake when using your notes to create your essay.

Whichever approach you use to record and organize your material, it is important to remember that you must ensure that you keep full bibliographic details of all your source material. There is nothing more frustrating than having the feeling of success and relief that accompanies finishing your essay replaced by the realization that you still need to track down references for your source material. One useful approach is to start a separate document entitled 'references' as soon as you start working on your essay and add each source to it as you read it. You might also find it useful to keep a separate list of literature that you want to read but have not yet found, just as a reminder.

You will find some information on effective note-taking techniques in chapter 10.

14.3.7 Planning a structure

The structure of the essay is important as it is this that determines the coherence of your argument. Determining the best structure involves deciding which points should be grouped together into a paragraph and the order of these paragraphs in relation to each other. In other words, you need to decide on the content of each paragraph and then fit these paragraphs together so that they present a logical line of argument. It is useful to give at least some thought to this during the research stage so that you have an idea of how your points fit together before you start to write.

As your research progresses and you gather a detailed set of notes, you should develop some idea of the points that you want to make in your essay. If you organized your research by issue as illustrated in Figure 14.4, you should find that your notes are already arranged into categories that can help you to determine the content of each paragraph. This is just a starting point so be prepared to make some adjustments when dividing your points into paragraphs when you come to write your essay.

There is a more detailed discussion on creating structure within a paragraph in section 14.4.3

It is a good idea to create a working structure for your essay as you are conducting research as it will give you an idea of how all your ideas fit together and help you to identify any gaps in

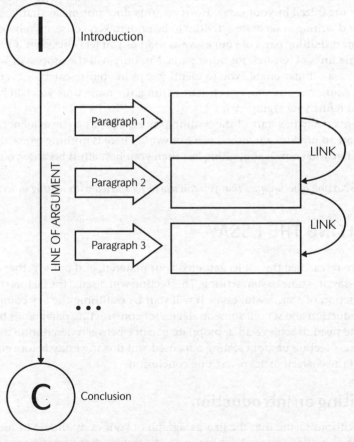

Figure 14.5 Structuring an essay

your argument that can be filled with further research. It will also reduce the amount of work that you have to do at the writing stage as you will have a preliminary structure in mind from the outset. Of course, it is often the case that your structure will change as you write but it is still a good idea to have a tentative idea of the shape of your essay before you start to write. One way to do this is to create a structure using the ideas for each paragraph as illustrated in Figure 14.5.

This structure reminds you that your essay must have an introduction, a conclusion, and a line of argument that runs through it whilst giving you space to label each paragraph according to its content or purpose. You can then use each label as a heading on a separate sheet of paper and make a list of the points that you plan to include in that paragraph. Alternatively, you might want to start by making a list of all the points that you want to include in your essay and then group them into paragraphs before deciding on a label for the paragraph and putting the paragraphs in order. The presence of the arrows acts as a reminder that each paragraph must be linked to the next and/or back to the question. You might find it helpful to add a few words to your plan to capture the nature of the link.

There is a discussion on the use of signposting words and phrases to create links between paragraphs and between your essay and the question in section 14.4.4.

14.3.8 Planning and drafting

Activities that you undertake during the preparation stage should make writing a draft of your essay much easier as you will have your source material to hand and a good idea of how your points will be organized in your essay. However, this does not mean that you should treat preparation and writing as separate activities to be undertaken consecutively—it is actually a good idea to start drafting parts of your essay as soon as you feel able even if you are still following up some lines of research for other parts. Not only will the process of writing help to develop your ideas, it may enable you to identify gaps in your research or even new lines of investigation. Moreover, the sooner you start writing, the more time you will have to redraft your essay and refine your arguments.

Some students delay the start of the writing process and, as a consequence, are left with insufficient time to produce a polished piece of work. There is nothing worse than having to submit work that you know is something less than your best effort because you have run out of time.

There is a discussion of techniques that you can use to get started with writing in section 14.4.2.

14.4 WRITING THE ESSAY

Once you have researched the topic, gathered your material, and put together a preliminary plan of your essay, it is time to start writing. This section will discuss the factors that contribute to the construction of a successful essay. It will start by outlining the key components of an effective introduction and set out some strategies for constructing paragraphs before moving to consider the need to achieve an appropriate balance between description and analysis. It will then address techniques for creating a focused and flowing essay before ending with an exploration of the characteristics of a strong conclusion.

14.4.1 Writing an introduction

It should go without saying that the first paragraph of your essay should be an introduction that unpicks the question and explains how it will be tackled, but a great many undergraduate essays simply launch straight into the first substantive point without any attempt at an introduction. This may be an accidental omission by students who do not understand how to create an introduction and who believe that their first paragraph is actually fulfilling the role of an introduction. Alternatively, it may be a deliberate omission by students who have sacrificed the introduction in order to meet the word limit in the belief that it makes no difference to the essay whether or not it has an introduction. This is a mistake. The introduction has a number of functions to fulfil, all of which are important to the overall success of the essay:

- It identifies the central subject matter of the essay.

- It unpicks the question thus demonstrating to the marker that you have understood the requirements of the essay.

- It sets out the issues that will be addressed in the essay in order to answer the question which gives the marker an idea of what to expect in the essay.

- It may give an indication as to the conclusion that is reached in the essay (although opinion is divided on this point).

In essence, then, the introduction gives the marker an instant impression of whether you have understood what the question requires and an indication of the points that you have included in your essay. This is why, from a pragmatic point of view, it is important for you to provide an introduction and to make sure that it is a good one: first impressions count so make sure that the first impression that your marker has of your essay is one that shows you are going to discuss appropriate subject matter in an organized manner. You will find an explanation of how to do this in Table 14.1 in response to the question:

> Discuss the extent to which the legitimacy of judicial review depends more on advancing constitutional values than accountability to the political process.

Table 14.1 Structuring an introduction

Line	Role	Example
Your first sentence should grab the marker's attention.	Your marker has to read your essay but you should strive to make him want to do so by making your first sentence one that identifies the theme of the question in an interesting way or that shows you are engaging directly with the question. Under no circumstances should your essay start with the words 'this essay': it is very dull!	The legitimacy of judicial review depends more on advancing fundamental and enduring constitutional values than in accountability to the political process.
The next sentence establishes the specific focus of the essay question.	This sentence can start with 'this essay' as its role is to explain to the marker the objective of your essay.	This essay will consider this position and question how the courts in judicial review cases give effect to the constitutional values on which it is based.

(Cont)

Table 14.1 (*Cont*)

Line	Role	Example
The next sentences should set out how the objective of the essay will be established.	This gives the marker an indication of the content of your essay and the structure that it will take. In essence, this aspect of the introduction tells the marker what to expect in your essay.	In order to do so, it will first analyse the constitutional values of doctrine of separation of powers, the rule of law, and Parliamentary sovereignty as they are affected by judicial review. It will examine the nature of judicial review in the context of political accountability and the relationship between Parliament, the executive, and the judiciary. Finally, the relative strengths of these sources of legitimacy will be considered in the light of the proposition along with any arguments to the contrary.
Some lecturers like the final sentence of the introduction to give an indication of the conclusion. Be aware that some lecturers really dislike this, believing that the conclusion belongs at the end of the essay only. It would be worth checking with each lecturer to see if they have any strong preferences.	This ensures that the introduction provides a complete snapshot of the essay by giving the marker an insight into your conclusion right from the start.	Although there are contrary perspectives, it will be argued that judicial review upholds the rule of law, the separation of powers, and Parliamentary sovereignty protecting, in turn, the fundamental values of legitimacy, justice, and fairness which are the primary sources of the legitimacy of judicial review.

Many students prefer to write the introduction to the essay at the end of the writing process so that they can reflect what is actually in it. This can be a useful approach because the eventual content of your essay may be different to your planned essay as your ideas evolve once you start writing. However, there is no harm in writing a draft of an introduction at the beginning so that it is always taken into account in the overall word limit. You can always amend it once the essay is finished. More than this, though, writing an introduction at the start will help you to focus on your line of argument. This needs to be at the forefront of your mind as you are writing otherwise your essay may lose its sense of purpose.

14.4.2 Start writing

It is very frustrating to be in a situation in which you know that your essay deadline is approaching but you feel unable to start writing. There can be a number of reasons for this:

- **I don't know enough about the subject matter to start writing.** Be realistic. If you have done a lot of research, you should have sufficient source material to start to write even if there are still a few elusive sources that you have not been able to track down. You cannot expect to find everything that has been written on the subject matter so you may have to start writing on the basis of what you have been able to find. Of course, if you have only read a couple of sources, it is likely that you are right and you are not yet ready to start writing so keep going with your research until you feel better prepared.

- **I don't know where to start.** This is quite common and can be very frustrating. You have done all your research, it is organized into issues, and you have broken it down into paragraphs but still the words will not come. One way around this is to write something that you know will have a place in your essay: it might be a definition of a key concept, a summary of the views of a particular theorist, or an outline of a relevant criminal offence. In other words, write content without context, that is, without knowing where your words will fit in the essay, just so that you get over the block of staring at a blank sheet of paper or empty computer screen.

- **I can't write because I don't understand it.** Obviously it is not a good idea to start writing an essay if you have not yet understood the subject matter. Try to find a really simple explanation in a basic textbook, perhaps even using one that is not intended to be used at degree level. Once you have got the basic idea, you can revisit the section in your set textbook and see if it makes sense. Alternatively, you may have to ask a lecturer for help but remember that this may not be forthcoming in relation to assessed coursework. You could also try to write the parts of the essay that you do understand—it is sometimes the case that this will make things click in your mind and it will all become clear.

- **I just can't write.** Sometimes, the requirement to write in quite formal language can be off-putting so try writing in a way that is easier for you just to get your ideas flowing. One way of doing this is with free-flow writing.

You may find the following suggested approach to be useful in overcoming writer's block.

- Get a blank sheet of paper or open a fresh document on your computer.
- Write a trigger word or phrase at the top of the paper or document. This can either be a key term relevant to the essay or some idea that you want to put in it such as:
  - The aim of my essay is to . . .
  - In the first paragraph, I am going to explain . . .
  - The main argument that I want to make is . . .
  - What is it that I'm trying to say?
- Set yourself a short period of time—one or two minutes is plenty—and start writing. Do not worry about how you express your ideas or the order in which you make them. Just get your thoughts down on paper so you can see them.
- Make sure that you keep writing for at least the period of time that you have set yourself even if you feel as if you are writing nonsense. However, if you find that you still have points to make when the time is up then be sure to keep writing until you have exhausted your ideas.
- When you are finished, review what you have written. You should have produced something that captures your ideas in ordinary language but you can easily reword them into a more appropriate written style. You will probably need to reorganize your ideas too. This is fine. At least you are writing and getting your ideas down on the page.

14.4.3 Creating paragraphs

Paragraphs are the building blocks of your essay. They divide your essay into smaller, easily digestible chunks with each one containing a separate idea or argument. Each paragraph should follow on logically from its predecessor and lead into the paragraph that follows it.

In other words, there should be a sense of logical progression to your essay as your paragraphs are organized in such a way that each one contributes to the construction of a flowing line of argument.

This idea that each paragraph should contain a separate idea or argument does not really give a clear idea of how much detail should be in each paragraph. In fact, one of the commonest questions asked by students on this topic concerns the ideal length of a paragraph. This is a difficult question to answer. On the one hand, a paragraph should be as long as it needs to be in order to explain its argument but, on the other hand, it can be really hard work for the marker to read paragraphs that are pages long. Many markers would say that there should be at least two paragraphs on every page of your essay. One technique that is quite widely used to determine the content of a paragraph is the PEE technique (point, elaboration, example) which has been modified here by the addition of a fourth characteristic (link) to create the PEEL technique:

- **Point.** A paragraph should start by outlining its central point.
- **Elaboration.** The sentences that follow should expand on this point to explain it in greater detail.
- **Example.** This provides support for the argument that you are presenting to make it more convincing.
- **Link.** The final sentence should either relate to the point made, back to the question, or provide a link to the next paragraph.

You will find a more detailed discussion of paragraphing in section 11.4.

14.4.4 Signposting

Signposting is the process of making your essay clear to the reader. It refers to the words and phrases in your essay that explain the significance of your points. In essence, signposting words and phrases creates focus (by linking your points to the question) and flow (by explaining how each paragraph relates to the next).

One way in which signposting is useful to the reader is in indicating the big ideas and themes in your essay. This is the equivalent of this book stating 'this chapter will deal with coursework' or 'this section explores issues associated with planning your essay'. This sort of signposting involves phrases that give the reader an insight into the overall focus of the whole essay or the next significant section of your essay and creates a strong structure for your work:

- The central focus of this essay is . . .
- The main theoretical perspectives examined in this essay are . . .
- The first section of this essay will be a review of the literature that examines . . .
- Having discussed [insert topic], it is now necessary to consider . . .
- The main argument that emerges from the case law is . . .

Signposting is also commonly used to communicate the relationship between different points and ideas to the reader. You might think that this is unnecessary and that the links are obvious but remember that you see your own work with full knowledge of the thinking behind it which gives you an advantage over your reader who has only the words on paper to rely upon. What seems obvious to you is therefore far less obvious to the reader so it is a good idea to add signposting to your essay so that your meaning is clear to the reader. The importance of signposting to indicate the relationship between points raised in your essay is demonstrated in the following example:

- Croall[3] states that technological change affects opportunities for crime, the forms of crime that are prevalent, and patterns of crime. Heidensohn comments that criminality takes novel forms from time to time.

What is the relationship between these sentences? Do Croall and Heidensohn agree or disagree with each other? Is the essay presenting two opposing views or is it using two viewpoints in conjunction with each other to strengthen the argument? These questions can be answered without difficulty with the insertion of a single word.

- Croall states that technological change affects opportunities for crime, the forms of crime that are prevalent, and patterns of crime. Moreover, Heidensohn comments that criminality takes novel forms from time to time.

- Croall states that technological change affects opportunities for crime, the forms of crime that are prevalent, and patterns of crime. However, Heidensohn comments that criminality takes novel forms from time to time.[4]

The use of the word 'moreover' indicates that the points are to be read in conjunction with each other with Heidensohn's point adding support to Croall's view whereas the use of the word 'however' indicates that the two views are incompatible with each other.

As this example illustrates, a single word can add a great deal of clarity to your writing. Table 14.2 sets out the different roles played by signposting words and phrases in signalling the relationship between the points made in your essay.

Table 14.2 Signposting words and phrases

Agreement or similarity	moreover, also, similarly, in addition, furthermore, additionally, as well as, what is more, in the same way, likewise
Disagreement or contrast	however, nevertheless, on the other hand, conversely, by contrast, but, yet, by comparison, although, alternatively
Providing exemplification or explanation	because, due to, as a result, owing to, by virtue of, as a consequence of, therefore, thus, particularly, hence, by way of illustration, including, especially
Reformulating or reiterating an idea	in other words, in essence, that is, in simple terms, to clarify, rather, to paraphrase, to reiterate
Enumerating and sequencing	there are a number of considerations, firstly, secondly, finally, subsequently, consequently, before, eventually, first and foremost
Providing examples	to illustrate this point, for example, for instance, this can be demonstrated, such as
Summarizing	in conclusion, in summary, finally, hence, as an overview

---

3. H Croall, *Crime and Society in Britain* (Longman 1998).
4. F Heidensohn, *Crime and Society* (Macmillan 1989).

14.4.5 Description versus analysis

Earlier in this chapter, it was said that a successful essay is one that answers the specific question asked rather than discussing the topic in general terms. In order to answer the question, your essay must be analytical rather than merely descriptive. A descriptive essay is one that explains the key concepts whereas an analytical essay moves beyond this to investigate how those concepts operate or relate to each other, depending on the requirements of the question. For instance, if you were answering the question about judicial review that was used as an example in Table 14.1, a descriptive approach would explain what is meant by judicial review, Parliamentary sovereignty, the rule of law, and the separation of powers, but would not do enough to discuss how judicial review gains its legitimacy from furthering those constitutional values.

It is understandable that students often produce very descriptive essays, especially in the early stages of their legal studies, because it is far easier to describe than it is to analyse. Every textbook in law will provide its own descriptions of core concepts so all that is required is that these descriptions are read and reworded in your essay. Textbooks are far less likely to provide inspiration for the analysis part of an essay because the question will have been set by your lecturer to test your powers of reasoning and your ability to criticize and appraise issues in law. Many students lack the confidence to do this, particularly if they cannot find any source material to rely upon, and so fill their essay with description, often only trying to explain how this answers the question in the final paragraph.

Descriptive essays are limited in the success that they will achieve. It is essential that you create an essay that is a combination of description and analysis. You will be better able to do this once you have a good understanding of the clues provided by the wording of the question that will indicate what concepts need to be described and what direction the analysis should take. You can do this by using the 'do what to what?' technique. This asks 'what does this essay require me to do (skill) with what concept in law (description)?' as is illustrated in Figure 14.6.

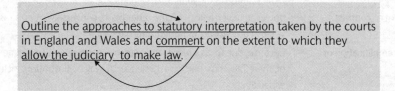

Outline the approaches to statutory interpretation taken by the courts in England and Wales and comment on the extent to which they allow the judiciary to make law.

Figure 14.6 'Do what to what'?

This will give you a clear idea as to what needs to be described and what needs to be analysed:

- Do what? Outline
- To what? Approaches to statutory interpretation in England and Wales
- Do what? Comment
- To what? The extent to which they allow judicial law-making

Of course, the success of this method rests on your ability to recognize what the words used in the question require you to do in your essay. The words which give you instructions are called process words and these are best understood by considering the work of educational psychologist, Benjamin Bloom. He conducted research into the skills demonstrated by students in their essays, divided them into six categories, and arranged them in a hierarchy to demonstrate their importance and complexity as illustrated in Figure 14.7.

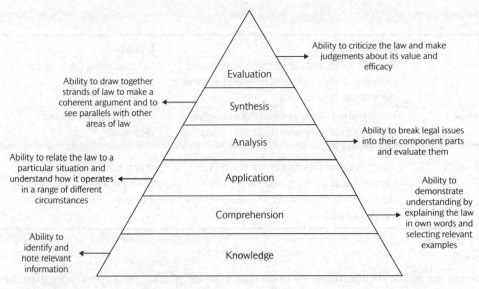

Ability to criticize the law and make judgements about its value and efficacy

Evaluation

Ability to draw together strands of law to make a coherent argument and to see parallels with other areas of law

Synthesis

Analysis

Ability to break legal issues into their component parts and evaluate them

Ability to relate the law to a particular situation and understand how it operates in a range of different circumstances

Application

Ability to demonstrate understanding by explaining the law in own words and selecting relevant examples

Comprehension

Ability to identify and note relevant information

Knowledge

Figure 14.7 Bloom's taxonomy

Bloom described knowledge and comprehension—the two categories of skills at the bottom of the hierarchy—as lower-order skills because they are easier to demonstrate. By contrast, the higher-order skills of application, analysis, synthesis, and evaluation are harder to master and provide evidence that the student is able to *use* knowledge rather than simply to acquire and repeat it.

To take a very basic example, if you needed to drive to a new area that you had not visited before, you would be able to demonstrate *knowledge* by finding a map of the area and *understanding* by explaining the route to another person, but application would be demonstrated by actually reaching your destination. Once there, you might want to *analyse* how useful the route was and, ultimately, decide whether to use it again or to find an alternative.

You can identify the skills that are important within an essay by the process words that are used in the question. Table 14.3 identifies some of the process words commonly associated with each of the categories of skills and provides some elaboration on what each of these requires from the writer of the essay.

Table 14.3 Skills and process words

Skill	Indicated by . . .	Example
Knowledge	Words that invite a factual or descriptive response or a straightforward statement	describe, define, outline, state, identify, list, what, how, when, which
Comprehension	Words that require an explanation, interpretation, or the ability to extrapolate key information	explain, use examples, summarize, paraphrase, interpret
Application	Words that suggest the need to apply theory to different circumstances or to predict how such theories would react to a new situation	apply, demonstrate, advise, predict

(*Cont*)

Table 14.3 (*Cont*)

Skill	Indicated by . . .	Example
Analysis	Words that indicate that a legal principle should be broken down into their component parts and subjected to close scrutiny	analyse, assess, consider, measure, quantify, how far
Synthesis	Words that indicate the ability to draw together strands of an argument and to identify similarities and differences	justify, compare, contrast, distinguish
Evaluation	Words that indicate whether a response to a particular issue is effective, consistent, moral, desirable, better than before, or a useful solution to a particular problem	appraise, criticize, evaluate, comment, reflect, discuss, how effective

Bloom's taxonomy demonstrates the point that a successful essay rests upon more than mere identification and explanation of the relevant theory or literature relating to a particular topic. The lower-order skills are considered to be more straightforward and easier to demonstrate, so an essay which moves beyond knowledge and comprehension to demonstrate higher-order skills is likely to be more successful. That does not mean that the lower-order skills are unimportant or should be omitted, merely that they should be considered the foundation upon which a demonstration of higher-order skills is based. In other words, you need to be able to describe the state of the law in order to analyse it.

It is essential that you remember that a successful essay requires an appropriate balance between description and analysis. An essay that is heavily descriptive does not demonstrate sufficient higher-order skills to achieve a high mark whilst an essay which contains insufficient description will also struggle because analysis needs to be based upon a foundation of description in order to make sense. For example, you could not comment on the accuracy of measurement of recorded crime without first describing the methods by which crimes are recorded.

Achieving the right balance between the two is a difficult task as there is no magic formula that sets out the appropriate contribution of each to an essay as this will vary according to the question. The most effective rule to apply is to include sufficient description to support the analysis; in other words, describe things that need to be understood so that the discussion will make sense to the reader.

14.4.6 Writing a conclusion

As with the introduction, the conclusion plays a crucial role in your essay and yet it is often absent thus leaving the marker with the distinct feeling that the student just stopped writing when they ran out of time, inspiration, or words.

Remember, the conclusion is the last thing that your marker reads before he starts deciding what grade to award. Make sure that they are left with a good impression of your work by ensuring that it has a strong conclusion that ties together the strands of the argument that you have outlined in your essay to create a direct response to the question. This should include the following:

- A statement of the aim of the essay
- A brief reminder of the arguments that you have presented

- An evaluation of which of any opposing views is to be preferred

- A direct answer to the question.

Your conclusion should not, as a general rule, introduce any new material that has not been discussed in the body of your essay, although it can make reference to a point that has not been discussed if it is simply there to emphasize your conclusion.

14.4.7 Remember your assessment criteria

Assessment criteria have an obvious importance to your essay as they are the criteria against which it will be marked. You should therefore make sure that you understand how essays are marked at your institution and what is expected of you. Assessment criteria tend to be agreed on a department-wide basis and identify the factors that your marker will be looking for in your essay. You will find a short screencast of a marker's thoughts as they are marking an essay that will give you an insight into the way that your work is viewed by the marker on the online resources that accompany this book. You may find these on an assessment feedback form that may be attached to your work when it is returned to you. It is often the case that the relevant criteria are listed and accompanied by a series of tick boxes in which the marker can indicate your level of achievement in each area (see Figure 14.8).

	Weak	Below Average	Satisfactory	Good	Excellent
Critical analysis	☐	☐	☐	☐	☐
Research	☐	☐	☐	☐	☐
Referencing	☐	☐	☐	☐	☐
Written style, grammar, and punctuation	☐	☐	☐	☐	☐

Figure 14.8 Sample assessment criteria

By looking at the categories that are listed on the form, you can identify what skills are being evaluated in your work and try to ensure that these are demonstrated. Another approach that is used to communicate the assessment criteria to students is to categorize the level of skills that are expected in work that falls within a particular classification. This is demonstrated in the example that follows.

There are, therefore, various methods that can be used to ascertain what skills and competences you need to demonstrate to impress your lecturers with the quality of your essay. For some reason, students often fail to take these matters into account and continue to produce essays that comply with their own personal view of a good essay. This can be extremely costly in terms of lost marks if their view does not coincide with what the lecturer considers to be a good essay. Lecturers are looking for a combination of legal knowledge and an ability to use it and thus are likely to consider the following factors to be important:

- The relevance of the material included and the arguments put forward to the question

- Evidence of comprehension and an ability to analyse the law

- A strong structure and clear and logical organization of material
- Evidence of research and incorporation of wider reading into the essay
- An appropriate written style with good grammar and punctuation
- Full and accurate referencing including a bibliography
- Good presentation.

Example assessment criteria by classification

FAIL: Less than 40%

A weak answer that fails to address the questions posed and which shows inadequate understanding of the subject area. Little or no evidence of reading or research and reference to irrelevant materials. Significant weakness in presentation and organization as well as numerous errors of grammar and punctuation.

PASS, THIRD CLASS: 40–49%

A fair answer that provides some material of relevance to the question posed and which shows some limited understanding of the subject area. There may be some reference to supporting materials but little, if any, attempt at analysis; a highly descriptive answer with some errors and omissions. Presentation and organization are likely to be poor and there may be significant errors of grammar and punctuation.

LOWER SECOND CLASS: 50–59%

A satisfactory answer that covers a fair degree of the material of relevance to the question albeit in largely descriptive detail. There may be an attempt at analysis that is either ineffective or fails to get to grips with the issue at the heart of the question. There should be evidence of a reasonable level of understanding and an ability to incorporate some supporting materials into the answer. There may be some grammatical and presentational errors but these should not be widespread.

14.5 POLISH

It is a mistake to think that your essay is finished as soon as you have written the final word: this is just a first draft and there is still work to do to ensure that the work is ready for submission. This section covers a range of activities that should be done at the final stage of the essay-writing process to ensure that you produce a piece of work that is expressed with clarity, that develops a logical line of argument, and that has had sufficient attention paid to all aspects of its presentation. You should allow yourself plenty of time to do these things so do not leave it until an hour before the submission deadline.

14.5.1 Structure, flow, and focus

Remember that your essay must present a flowing argument that develops in a logical way and which answers the question. This means that you need a strong structure, clear links to be made between each paragraph, and frequent references back to the question. Check that your essay has structure, flow, and focus using the following steps:

- **Structure.** Read each paragraph and describe its content in a few words. Look at the list that this produces and see if it tells a story in a logical order. Compare your list with the plan of your essay that you created before you started writing (see Figure 14.5). Departure from this plan is not necessarily a problem as your essay may not have fitted together as you expected before you started writing but it will be a useful reference point if you find that your essay does not seem to have a logical structure.

- **Flow.** Check that the relationship between the end of one chapter and the beginning of the next is clear. If not, add signposting words and phrases to clarify the connections between your ideas as this will ensure that there is a logical development to your essay. If you find a point or a paragraph that cannot be linked to the ideas around it using signposting then it does not belong in that part of your essay and must be moved. If you cannot find a new place where it fits then it is likely that it does not belong in your essay at all.

- **Focus.** Does every paragraph make a contribution to the development of an argument that actually answers the question rather than simply being about the relevant topic? You might find that you need to 'touch base' with the question explicitly to strengthen your focus. You can do this by repeating key words from the question or by relating the point that you have made in your paragraph back to the question.

14.5.2 Proofreading

It is tempting to heave a sigh of relief when the final word of your essay is written and think 'that's it done' but you should really not assume that you got everything right in your essay in the first draft. Neither should you rely on the spelling and grammar checking tools on your computer to pick up all your mistakes—there are plenty of common typing errors that the computer will miss.

Practical exercise

Proofreading is an essential part of the process of ensuring that your work is fit for submission. Careless errors suggest lack of care and this is not the impression that you want your marker to have of your work. Many lecturers will deduct marks from work that is strewn with errors so it is worth taking great care to ensure that this does not happen to your essay.

1. Print a copy of your essay. It is much easier to read what you have actually written on paper than it is to spot errors on a computer screen.

2. Read it very carefully and slowly. Remember, you are not reading to find out what you have written but to spot mistakes and that requires you to pay close attention to every word. Some people find that reading out loud helps with this.

3. Circle every error and make a note in the margin as to what is wrong. You might also like to note how you intend to correct the error.

4. Pay particular attention to punctuation. If you are unsure as to whether you have used, say, a semi-colon correctly, reword your sentence so that it does not need one.

5. Use a thesaurus to check the meaning of any words if you are not confident that you have used them correctly.

6. Once you have been through the entire document, make all the necessary changes. Cross each circle made on your printed version so that you have a record of which problems have been addressed.

Ideally, you should carry out this process once again after the errors have been corrected just to be sure that no mistakes remain. Leave it overnight if possible or at least have a break of a few hours and start again with a clean printed copy of your work.

 *There is an essay online at **www.oup.com/he/finch8e/** for you to proofread along with an annotated version for you to compare your work with.*

It is often easier to spot mistakes in the work of others because you will read it with fresher eyes. When you read your own work, there is a tendency to skim it because you are so familiar with its content whereas proofreading requires far more detailed attention. As such, you might find it useful to see if someone else will proofread your essay for you. Remember, though, that you must correct any errors that they spot yourself.

14.5.3　Referencing

You should have been adding references to your work as you wrote it so use this final stage of the essay-writing process to check that all the necessary references are present, both in the text and in the bibliography. You should also ensure that your references are complete. This means that the reference in the text to specific points and quotations should include a page reference and full bibliographic information in your list of references is provided.

 *You will find detailed guidance on when and how to reference in chapter 13. You will find a video online at **www.oup.com/he/finch8e/** which gives a spoken commentary about an example essay. This illustrates many of the points made in this chapter and gives an insight into the sorts of thoughts a marker might have when assessing your work.*

 CHAPTER SUMMARY

Preliminary analysis

- Make sure that you take time at the outset to analyse the question rather than starting research or, worse still, writing without having identified the focus of the essay
- Rewrite the question(s) at the heart of the essay in your own words to make sure that you have a simple and clear grasp of what is required, taking care not to change the meaning of the question

Research and planning

- Start by consulting a textbook to ensure that you have a clear understanding of the topic area but make sure that you move on to consider other materials such as monographs and articles; an essay written solely on the basis of textbook research will probably lack depth of analysis and certainly will not demonstrate impressive research skills or width of reading
- Keep careful note of the sources used in your research but try to avoid excessive note-taking that can degenerate into compulsive writing that is not accompanied by sufficient thought. Remember, you are looking for answers to a particular question, not producing a summary of all the material that you locate

- Plan a working structure for your essay that can be used as a framework for your writing. Make sure that you think about the way that your arguments will flow and never forget the importance of keeping a firm focus on the central issue of the question
- Give careful consideration to the selection of supporting materials, remembering that it is important to present a balanced argument that acknowledges different perspectives on the issue at hand

Writing the essay

- Make sure that you give yourself sufficient time to write the essay and bear in mind that the structure you have planned may not work in practice, in which case you may need to start from scratch and reorganize your arguments
- Take care to ensure that every paragraph does something to further your argument and give thought to the balance between description and analysis in your essay
- Keep a firm focus on the question; if you cannot see how a point relates to the question, it may be that it has no place in your essay. Remember, you are answering a specific question rather than merely writing about a particular topic
- The purpose of an essay is to test knowledge and understanding of the topic but also to assess the level of skill that you have in using your sources appropriately. Ensure that your essay strikes an appropriate balance between description and analysis
- Write an effective introduction and conclusion. The introduction is the first impression that your marker receives of the quality of your work whilst the conclusion is the last thing that they read, so either or both may stick in their mind as indicative of the overall quality of your essay whilst they are marking

Polish and presentation

- Allow plenty of time to check your essay for coherence, accuracy, and consistency
- Find out what the requirements are for the presentation of essays and ensure that you adhere to these requirements to the letter. Easy marks can be lost for failing to do so and it gives the marker a poor impression of your essay if you have not troubled to follow the rules regarding the submission of coursework
- Check the presentation of your essay and, in particular, check that the referencing and bibliography are immaculate

Answering problem questions

15

INTRODUCTION

This chapter builds on the earlier sections in the book that outlined how to locate and understand the law by explaining how to use your legal knowledge. Chapter 14 provided guidance on how to use this knowledge to construct a focused and analytical essay whereas this chapter will concentrate on the very different set of skills that are needed to use the law to answer a problem question. It will guide you through the process of analysing a scenario in order to identify the relevant issues to ensure that your answer is comprehensive and does not miss any important points. It will outline strategies to use to ensure that the law is applied effectively and that good use is made of supporting authorities. This chapter should be read in conjunction with chapter 11 which covers writing skills, and chapter 13 on referencing as this will ensure that your problem answer is well-written, presented in an appropriate manner, and is thoroughly referenced.

The ability to use the law to determine the outcome of a dispute is one of the most important skills that a lawyer must develop. An abstract understanding of the law based upon how it has been used in decided cases is not enough; you must be able to apply the principles of the law to new and unusual factual situations. Remember, a client who comes to you for advice does not want an explanation of how the law has been used in other cases; he wants to know how it applies to his situation. It is also an important skill because problem questions are a popular means of assessing knowledge and skills in both coursework and examinations but, unfortunately, many students limit their success because they have not developed an effective problem-solving technique. This step-by-step guide to problem solving aims to help with this by explaining how to tackle problem questions and by demonstrating the steps with examples to ensure that you have a clear picture of what is required.

 Learning outcomes

After studying this chapter, you will be able to:

- Differentiate between the skills needed to answer a problem question and those required for the construction of an effective essay
- Analyse a problem question in order to identify the legal issues that need to be resolved
- Prepare to answer the question by engaging in effective research and planning
- Structure the answer in a logical and organized manner

- Provide concise and well-supported statements of law that are applied to the facts of the question in an effective manner
- Evaluate the answer that you have written to ensure that it demonstrates the relevant skills and knowledge and that it adheres to the necessary style and referencing requirements

15.1 ALL ABOUT PROBLEM QUESTIONS

Before launching into an explanation of how to deal with problem questions, it seems sensible to take a little time to describe what problem questions are and what they seek to achieve for students who are new to studying law. If you appreciate what it is that they aim to assess, this will help you to understand how to set about dealing with them in a way that is likely to meet with the approval of your lecturers.

15.1.1 What is a problem question?

A problem question involves a set of hypothetical facts that raises at least one question, usually more, that needs to be answered by reference to the law.

In other words, it is a short story about events that give rise to potential legal responsibility about which you are expected to offer advice to one or more of the parties or otherwise to comment on the legal position that arises from the facts. This is sometimes called a fact pattern or scenario question. The reason that this is used as a method of assessment in law is that it replicates what is happening when you give legal advice to a client.

When you are writing your answer, try to imagine that you are telling someone how the law applies to their situation. That should help you to appreciate the basic technique involved in problem solving.

Problem questions tend to end with a question or instruction that reflects this idea of giving advice to someone involved in the scenario:

- Does Gurprit have a claim in negligence?
- Can the contract be enforced?
- Advise Dawn as to the extent of her liability for property offences.
- Do Ashley's actions amount to a breach of Article 11 of the European Convention on Human Rights?

The facts of the problem will be constructed with care so that the answer to the question is not clear but needs to be puzzled out. You are unlikely to encounter a problem question (other than the example in chapter 12) that begins:

> Peter hates Tony so he shoots him in the head at point-blank range shouting 'I want you to die'.

This is because there is no complexity to the issue: both elements of the offence of murder are so readily established that the question could be answered in a few lines.

This demonstrates a major characteristic of problem questions: they are designed to raise issues that do not have an obvious and straightforward answer so that you have to explore the intricacies of the law and speculate a little in order to reach a conclusion.

You will find an example of a problem question in section 15.3. This will be used in this chapter to demonstrate the process of building an answer that demonstrates both a good grasp of the relevant law and of the legal skills that are being assessed.

15.1.2 It is not an essay!

It is essential that you appreciate that the distinction between an essay and a problem question is not solely one of presentation; they each require something qualitatively different from the student in terms of the skills used and the nature of the answer produced.

In general terms, an essay involves an exploration and analysis of a particular topic, whilst a problem question requires the student to apply the law to a set of facts and reach a conclusion about the legal responsibility of the parties involved.

If you take the same approach to answering a problem question that you do to writing an essay, your problem answers will be weak and will not achieve high marks.

15.1.3 What skills are required?

There are a range of skills involved in dissecting and answering a problem question. As you will see, although legal knowledge is important, you will need to be able to do more than merely outline the relevant law; you must also be able to use it to reach a conclusion about the legal liability of the parties. This involves:

- The ability to sift through the mass of facts to identify those that are relevant, those that set the scene, and to oust any potential red herrings.
- Sufficient knowledge of the area of law to be able to identify a potential basis for legal action, to establish a starting point for research, and to be able to understand the law that is uncovered during the research process.
- Research skills that enable you to investigate the area of law and to locate statutory provisions and cases that are relevant to the facts of the problem.
- Writing skills that enable you to structure an answer, to organize its content in a clear and logical manner, and to incorporate authority into your answer.
- The ability to apply the law to the facts of the question in order to determine the extent of the parties' legal liability.

Although all of these skills are important and play a role in constructing an effective answer to a problem question, it is the last of these—application of the law to the facts—that is crucial to the success of your answer.

In chapter 14, you will find a section which examines Bloom's taxonomy of skills and discusses these in the context of legal writing (see section 14.4.5). The higher-order skills of application and analysis are particularly important to problem solving.

15.2 PROBLEM-SOLVING TECHNIQUE

The key to success in problem solving is to develop an effective technique. This is something that will be invaluable in both coursework and examinations and which is transferable between the different topics that you study; in other words, a good problem-solving technique is equally applicable to criminal law, equity and trusts, employment law, or any of the other subjects on the law curriculum that use problem solving as a means of assessment.

Your own university may provide guidelines on problem solving. If this is the case, you should study these carefully and take note of the information provided. Alternatively, there are well-publicized techniques that you may find useful; these have different names but share a common basis in their approach to breaking down the tasks involved in problem solving (see Figure 15.1).

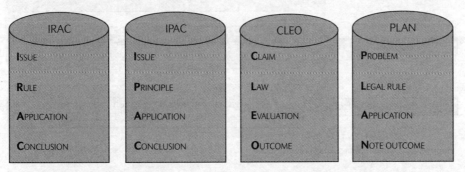

Figure 15.1 Some mnemonics for problem solving

Despite the difference of terminology, each of the four stages used in each method is the same:

1. Identify the question that needs to be answered.
2. State the law that enables the question to be answered.
3. Work out how the law would operate in relation to the question identified.
4. Reach a conclusion that answers the question.

You might find it easier to understand this process in relation to a non-law example.

> Imagine that your university has a policy regarding the late submission of coursework that states that the penalty for submission up to one day after the deadline without good cause or prior permission attracts a deduction of ten marks. Furthermore, work that is submitted more than one day late but within a week of the deadline attracts a deduction of twenty-five marks and work that is submitted more than one week late receives a mark of zero. The essays are stamped with the time and date of submission upon receipt in the general office. The submission deadline for your essay is 4pm on Friday. Your essay is submitted at 4.02pm.

This is a very simple example but it demonstrates the process that is involved in problem solving (see Figure 15.2).

It is ironic that the method involved in problem solving causes so many headaches for students but, in reality and stripped of its legal content, the process of identifying a question to be answered, the applicable rule, and combining the two to reach a conclusion is one that we all do, all of the time, as part of everyday life: eligibility for a discount, complying with a shop's refund policy, nightclub opening hours, and even reading a train timetable all involve a similar process of the identification and application of a general rule to a particular factual situation.

Of course, your concern is to take this technique and apply it to legal problems. There are also other factors to take into account such as the level of detail needed, the correct approach to incorporating case law, and the difficulties of a factual situation that does not have

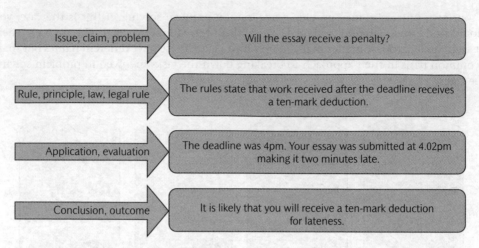

Figure 15.2 The problem-solving process

a determinative answer, and all of these points will be addressed in the course of this chapter. However, quite apart from these complexities that are particular to law, it is reassuring to know that the technique that is the cornerstone of effective problem solving is one that is familiar.

With this in mind, why not try the technique outlined earlier in relation to the following non-law examples:

Practical exercise

These examples are designed to help you develop a methodical approach to problem solving. As such, they are very simple so you could reach a conclusion without going through the steps outlined earlier but that would defeat the purpose of the exercise. Try to follow the four-stage procedure with these simple facts to build up your confidence and expertise ready for solving more complex problems as the chapter progresses.

1. The Post Office has introduced a system of calculating the cost of postage based upon weight and size. A letter is one which weighs less than 100g, has maximum dimensions of 240mm x 165mm, and is no thicker than 5mm. This costs 60p postage. A large letter can have maximum dimensions of 353mm x 250mm, weigh up to 750g, and be up to 25mm in thickness and costs 90p postage if it weighs 100g or less, £1.20 between 101g and 250g, £1.60 between 251g and 500g, or £2.30 between 501g and 750g. You wish to post a package that weighs 90g and is 4mm thick, 240mm long, and 170mm wide. How much will this cost?

2. Your grandmother offers you a cash incentive to encourage you to study for your exams. She agrees to pay you £10 for every exam that you pass and £50 extra if you pass all five exams. You pass four exams. How much money can you expect to receive?

3. You notice an advertisement for an essay-writing competition on the law school noticeboard. The first prize is £500 so you would like to enter. The competition rules state that the essay must be written by an undergraduate student under the age of 21 at the closing date (next 31 March) who has not yet studied tort law. Do you qualify to enter the competition (based on your own circumstances)?

You will find suggested answers to these questions at **www.oup.com/he/finch8e/** *where there is also an explanation of how the answers were reached.*

You probably found it easy to work through these exercises and you should take heart from this because it means that you have already grasped the essential skills that you need to succeed in answering problem questions in law. These skills will need to be honed and developed and you will find help and guidance on this in the remainder of this chapter. The following sections explore each aspect of problem solving in greater depth in order to help you develop your understanding of what is required.

15.2.1 Warning

It is of fundamental importance that you separate the question into a series of issues and deal with each of these separately. The IRAC, IPAC, CLEO, and PLAN techniques will not work if you try and apply them to the question as a whole. It is a common mistake for students who first encounter this technique to use it as a means of splitting their answer into four sections and dividing the content as follows:

1. Issues: all the issues from the question as a whole are identified and listed
2. Rules: an abstract discussion of all the law that is raised by the issues, all amalgamated together
3. Application: a short section that is usually extremely weak because it is detached from the law and it does not break the question down into sufficiently small issues
4. Conclusion: a short factual paragraph that summarizes the findings.

If you make the mistake of dividing the whole answer into sections as explained above, rather than slicing it up into a series of issues and sub-issues as explained in the following section, it is extremely likely that your answer will fail as you will not have demonstrated an effective problem-solving technique to the marker.

🕤 *You will find an example of how not to use IRAC together with a short video screencast explaining how to use IRAC effectively on the online resources at www.oup.com/he/finch8e/.*

15.3 ISSUES, CLAIMS, AND PROBLEMS

The first stage in the problem-solving process is to identify the question that needs to be answered. In the earlier example about late submission of coursework, this was quite simple: will the essay receive a penalty? However, it is not always a straightforward matter to identify the issue within a problem question; indeed, it is likely that there will be multiple issues within a single question that need to be extrapolated from the mass of detail. This is an important stage in the process as if you do not isolate the correct question to ask, you cannot hope to reach the right conclusion.

This is an example of a typical problem question that you might encounter. As you see, it involves a series of events that involve several different parties. This tort problem about injuries sustained by visitors to a farmyard activity centre will be used throughout this chapter to demonstrate the process of building up an answer to a problem question.

> Brian runs a small farmyard activity centre in West Yorkshire. Gladys and her granddaughter, Camilla (7) visit the centre. They go into the stableyard where there are large signs that read 'horses may bite, so mind your fingers' and 'please do not feed the horses—they may think you're offering them an apple and gnaw your hand instead'. Gladys sees the signs but has left her glasses in the car so cannot read what they say. She feeds slices of apple that she has brought with her to several horses and receives a nasty

bite from Clopper, the centre's temperamental stallion. There used to be a sign on his door that warned that stallions can behave unpredictably but it had fallen off the previous day and not yet been replaced. Upset by her experience, Gladys goes into the cafeteria. She tells Camilla not to wander off but Camilla ignores Gladys and goes into Brian's exhibition of farm equipment. Two of the rarest machines are roped off to protect them from the public (and the public from them). Camilla climbs over the ropes and starts to climb on one of the machines but receives a deep laceration from one of the exposed cutting blades. In the cafeteria, employee Betty is making a pot of tea for Gladys. The cafeteria is newly refurbished. The work was done by local handyman, Andy, who is an excellent carpenter but who lacks expertise in electrical fitting. As a result, some of the wiring is incorrect and this causes a massive power surge during which the tea urn explodes, showering Betty with boiling water and causing her to suffer serious burns.

Advise Brian as to the extent of his liability, considering occupiers' liability only and not considering any potential claims in negligence.

15.3.1 Analysing the question

The most effective means of identifying the issues in a problem question is to analyse the facts that you have been given and take a note of relevant facts relating to the two key variables: parties and events. This will help you to address the key question: who has done what to whom?

15.3.1.1 Parties

There will be at least one party in the problem, probably more in many subject areas. You may encounter a single party in problem questions on public law topics, such as constitutional and administrative law and criminal law, as these areas of law involve the liability of an individual in relation to the state. Of course, it is possible for public law topics nonetheless to involve other parties; there may be multiple applicants in a judicial review problem, for example, or several defendants or a range of victims in a criminal law problem. Problem questions in areas of private law, such as contract and tort, will involve at least one party making a claim against another, so it is important that you identify both the claimant(s) and the defendant(s) (see Table 15.1).

Table 15.1 Parties in the problem question

Claimant	Defendant	Other parties
Gladys	Brian	
Camilla	Brian	Gladys (child's grandmother)
Betty	Brian	Andy (the handyman)

Make a list of the people in the question and determine whether they are parties who have a claim or parties who face liability. It may be that there are other people in the question who fall into neither of these categories. If this is the case, do not simply ignore them but consider why they have been included. It is likely that they are there for a reason.

The instructions that accompany the problem facts are often an excellent source of information that will assist you in the identification of the roles of the various parties. In the example given in this chapter, you are told to advise Brian about the strength of the claims against him, so it is a straightforward matter to identify him as the defendant.

15.3.1.2 Events

It is also important to work out what has happened to the parties as this provides the necessary information to ascertain what area of law is relevant to the topic. It is extremely useful to
establish these facts at the outset as this will act as a reminder that precise reference needs to
be made to them at some point in your answer. As you will see in the discussion of application
later in the chapter, one of the more common weaknesses in a problem answer is the failure
to make reference to precise facts, therefore having a list to hand from the outset may help to
overcome this problem (see Figure 15.3).

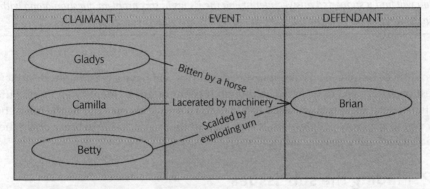

Figure 15.3 Claimants, events, and defendants

This diagram depicts the answer to the 'who did what to whom' question in the sample question and this gives three potential situations in which Brian may be liable. In a question
involving several parties, the obvious structure for your answer is to consider each party in
turn, particularly if the basis for liability is the same for each of them as it is here (the issue is
occupiers' liability in each case).

It is important to be methodical and thorough. Start at the beginning of the question and
work through each sentence in turn, making a note of potentially relevant information. It may
not be clear at this stage how each piece of information is relevant but this should become
apparent as you become more familiar with the legal issues raised by the question during the
course of your research.

It is important to devote time and attention to this early stage of the problem-solving process as it is the cornerstone of the success of your answer. If you fail to identify issues at this
stage or omit relevant facts, it is inevitable that the remainder of your answer will have gaps.
You should bear in mind that it is not always straightforward to identify the issues in a problem
question.

Practical exercise

Use the techniques outlined earlier to identify the issues in this problem question. Do not worry if
you cannot make an exact identification of the relevant offences; focus on framing the issues at this
stage. It is perfectly permissible to identify a range of potential offences, that is, burglary/theft, or to
go for a general topic, that is, one of the non-fatal offences against the person, at this stage as the
research that you go on to conduct will help you to narrow down the possibilities.

Matt is short of money and hopes to borrow £500 from his brother, Luke. In order to get into Luke's good books, Matt decides to take him a bottle of whisky that he plans to steal from the local supermarket. Once inside the supermarket, Matt loses his nerve and leaves without going near the alcohol aisle. Instead, he goes into a department store and uses his credit card to buy Luke an expensive sweater, knowing that he is over his credit limit. Luke is thrilled with the sweater but refuses to lend Matt any money. Matt punches Luke in the face causing a cut which requires stitches. Luke sets fire to the sweater and leaves it burning on Matt's doorstep the following day.

Discuss the criminal liability of the parties.

🕮 *You will find a suggested answer, identifying the issues in this problem question along with an explanation of how the answer was reached at* **www.oup.com/he/finch8e/**.

Once you have completed a preliminary analysis, you will have a reasonably clear picture of the questions that need to be asked. Although it is important to identify and frame the 'big' issues that raise questions about the liability of the parties, this may not be the most effective way for you to structure your answer. It is important that you are able to break down the topic into smaller and more manageable sub-issues.

15.3.2 Finding the sub-issues

At this stage of the analysis of the sample problem, we have three 'big' issues which were identified by concentrating on the parties and the events:

1. Can Gladys hold Brian liable for her injuries after she was bitten by a horse?
2. Can Camilla hold Brian liable for the lacerations caused by his machinery?
3. Can Betty hold Brian liable for the burns she received when the urn exploded?

In order to break this down into more manageable sub-issues, more information is needed about the basis upon which Brian may be liable. In this particular example, the instructions that accompany the facts make it clear that the relevant area of law is occupiers' liability. This makes it an extremely straightforward matter to break each of the big issues down into sub-issues on the basis of the elements that have to be established in order to establish occupiers' liability (see Figure 15.4).

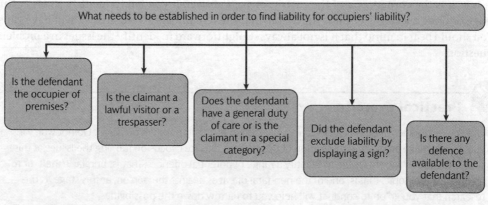

Figure 15.4 Sub-issues

By exploring the sub-issues within the big issue, you are effectively breaking the answer down into a series of mini problem questions, so the techniques outlined earlier can be used in relation to each sub-issue. As such, it will be a succession of IRACs (or whichever of the acronyms you prefer).

By taking each sub-issue in turn and subjecting it to a methodical analysis, you will give the answer a strong structure and it should help to ensure that you are thorough and do not omit any important points from consideration.

ISSUE 1: Is Brian liable under Occupiers' Liability for the injury sustained by Gladys when she is bitten by his horse?

- **Sub-issue 1.1** Is Brian an occupier of premises?
  - State the law
  - Apply it to the facts
  - Conclusion
- **Sub-issue 1.2** Is Gladys a lawful visitor or a trespasser?
  - State the law
  - Apply it to the facts
  - Conclusion
- **Sub-issue 1.3** Is there a general duty of care or does Gladys fall into a special category?
  - State the law
  - Apply it to the facts
  - Conclusion
- **Sub-issue 1.4** Has Brian excluded his liability by displaying a sign?
  - State the law
  - Apply it to the facts
  - Conclusion
- **Sub-issue 1.5** Is there any defence available to Brian?
  - State the law
  - Apply it to the facts
  - Conclusion

Conclusion on the big issue by drawing together the strands of argument presented in the sub-issues.

You would then repeat this technique with the next two big issues and this would provide a structure for your answer.

15.3.2.1 Identifying the correct area of law

However, if the problem question does not specify the particular basis of liability, you will have to identify this from the nature of the question. Imagine that the sample question merely asked 'Advise Brian of the extent of his tortious liability'. This would require you to identify the relevant basis of liability and this makes the problem question more challenging as inaccuracy here can put the entire answer off course.

There are various steps that you can take to help you identify the relevant topic(s):

1. Look at your syllabus and eliminate all topics that you will not have covered by the time that the coursework is due for submission.

2. Make a list of topics covered on your course so far and summarize them in a few words that capture their essential nature. If you do that with topics which are likely to be found

on a tort course, you will see that some of the topics covered have no relevance at all to the sample problem. For example, if you used this technique on the sample question, you would soon conclude that only negligence, occupiers' liability, and employers' liability (in relation to Betty) could possibly have any relevance to the question:

- Negligence: breach of duty of care leading to harm
- Special duties: particular type of negligence
- Nuisance: interference with quiet enjoyment of one's property
- Employers' liability: duty towards employees
- Occupiers' liability: duty of landowner to visitors and trespassers
- Defamation: harm to person's reputation.

3. If all else fails, ask for guidance. You can share information with other students (remembering not to take this too far for fear of contravening plagiarism regulations: see chapter 13) but you could also check with your lecturer. They will not be prepared to give you too much specific guidance but a quick (and polite: see chapter 10 for guidance on how to get help from lecturers) email saying 'I was planning to cover negligence, employers' liability, and occupiers' liability, in my answer but am concerned that this may be too broad and perhaps I should focus exclusively on occupiers' liability' could elicit a helpful response.

15.3.2.2 Multiple areas of law

Many problem questions will involve several different legal topics within a problem question. One of the reasons for this is that it enables the lecturer to assess your knowledge of more than one topic but, more importantly, it tests your ability to differentiate between different topics.

This is an important facet of learning a topic. It is a relatively straightforward matter to look up the relevant law and apply it to the facts if you are told what topic needs to be considered, but it is far more difficult to work out from the facts what the relevant topic is in the first place. Imagine how much harder the question about Brian and his farmyard activity centre would have been if it had not been specified that the relevant area of law was occupiers' liability and not negligence.

If you are confident that a particular issue raises potential liability in more than one area of law, you will need to discuss both and this will require some careful thought in terms of the structure of the answer. You will, however, be able to gain additional credit by evaluating which area is the most suitable basis for liability.

15.4 RULES, PRINCIPLES, AND LAW

The first stage of the problem-solving process is to identify the question that needs to be answered. Once that is identified, the next stage is to provide a statement of law that will enable that question to be answered.

15.4.1 Researching the law

In order to identify and state the law as part of your answer to the problem question, you will need to undertake research to ensure that you have a good understanding of the relevant law. The following suggestions should help you to carry out effective research:

- Start with a textbook and read the entire chapter or section of the chapter that is relevant to your legal issue. This will give you a solid overview of the topic.

- Once you have a grasp of the topic, you should have a clearer appreciation of how accurate you have been in framing your issues and sub-issues. Review these now and make any changes that are necessary in light of your initial research.

- Take each sub-issue individually, using a separate sheet of paper for each if this helps you to organize your thoughts. Make a note of any material in the textbook that seems pertinent to each issue, paying particular attention to statutory provisions and case law.

- If you feel that you are struggling to understand the law, try consulting a different textbook to see if that makes the issues clearer. Different authors explain the same concepts in different ways so you may be more able to follow the explanations in an alternative textbook.

- Make sure that you are precise in noting the wording of statutory provisions and in recording full case citations; you will need these when you come to write your answer.

- Be prepared to follow up references contained in the footnotes of your textbook. For example, if a case is cited in the footnote in relation to the definition of an occupier but there is nothing in the text that elaborates upon this, you will need to find the case to discover whether it says anything that is relevant to your question.

- Remember that a problem question is concerned with the current law and its interpretation. Concentrate on finding this and do not be distracted by discussion of how the law used to be or how it came to be as it is today. This sort of historical background is relevant to an essay question and to your broader understanding of the topic but it has no place in an answer to a problem question.

- Bear in mind that problem questions are designed to assess your ability to apply the law to new and novel situations, so do not expect to find an exact answer to all the issues raised in your question in the textbook. It is likely that some of the issues are framed so that you have to look at what law there is and speculate upon how that might apply. With this in mind, try to find cases that state general principles that can be applied to your issue or which deal with similar, although not identical, situations.

Taking these points into account, you should aim to have a series of notes that gives you the basis to make statements of law in relation to each of the issues raised on the facts of the problem. You might want to note your thoughts about the way that the issue is likely to be decided as you go, as this will make the job of applying the law to the facts much easier (see Figure 15.5).

DEFINITION OF OCCUPIER

No statutory definition although Occupiers' Liabilty Acts 1957 (visitors) and 1984 (trespassers) deal with liability in general.

Defined in *Wheat v E Lacon & Co Ltd* [1966] AC 552 (seems to be leading case) as person who exercises an element of control over premises.

This includes physical control of premises and legal control of premises—*Harris v Birkenhead Corporation* [1976] 1 WLR 279

THOUGHTS: seems straightforward as Q says that Brian runs the farmyard activity centre so presumably has physical control of the centre even if he is not the legal owner.

Figure 15.5 Thoughtful research with notes organized by issue

15.4.2 Stating the law

This is a crucial part of the problem-solving process and what is required is an initial abstract statement of a legal principle (from statute or case law) and, if necessary in relation to the issue at hand, some further elaboration on aspects of that principle.

This can be quite difficult to understand so the first sub-issue from the sample question will be used to demonstrate this technique in practice:

ISSUE 1: Is Brian liable under Occupiers' Liability for the injury sustained by Gladys when she is bitten by his horse?

> • Sub-issue 1.1 Is Brian an occupier of premises?
>   • **State the law**: There is no statutory definition of 'occupier' under the Occupiers' Liability Acts 1957 and 1984 but an occupier is defined in *Wheat v E Lacon & Co Ltd* [1966] AC 552 (HL) as a person who exercises an element of control over premises.
>   • **Apply it to the facts**
>   • Conclusion

This demonstrates an initial statement of a relevant legal principle which could be applied to the facts as they stand. However, it might be useful to elaborate on this by reference to case law that provides further clarification of the meaning of this definition, as this will facilitate more precise application:

> • Sub-issue 1.1 Is Brian an occupier of premises?
>   • **State the law:** There is no statutory definition of 'occupier' under the Occupiers' Liability Acts 1957 and 1984 but an occupier is defined in *Wheat v E Lacon & Co Ltd* [1966] AC 552 (HL) as a person who exercises an element of control over premises. In *Harris v Birkenhead Corporation* [1976] 1 WLR 279 (CA), it was held that this meant physical control over the premises as well as legal control.
>   • **Apply it to the facts**
>   • Conclusion

It is always a question of judgement as to how much law to state in relation to any particular point. In the sample problem, the issue of occupier of premises is not particularly complicated but needs to be established with sufficient clarity because it is the foundation of Brian's liability in this area of tort law. There are other issues in the problem that will require more detailed exploration with reference being made to different statements of law.

As a general rule, the more uncertain the area of law and the more complicated the issue, the more legal principles you will need to include within your answer.

15.4.3 Common problems

This stage of the problem-solving process is relatively straightforward and does not pose as great a challenge for the student as breaking the problem question down into appropriate issues and the application of the law. However, there are problems that do arise with a fair degree of frequency in relation to this stage of the process that are worthy of mention.

15.4.3.1 Law in large chunks

Success in problem solving is dependent on breaking the law down into small chunks and dealing with each chunk individually. Therefore, an answer which deals with a clump of legal issues together is going to be weaker than one that separates them out for individual attention. It is essential to remember that once you have sliced up each issue into a series of sub-issues, each one of these should have some statement of law, however brief.

> Three certainties are required for the existence of a valid trust. There must be certainty of intention, certainty of subject matter and certainty of objects. Certainty of intention requires . . . Certainty of subject matter requires . . . Certainty of objects requires . . . The first of these is satisfied by . . .

This example starts well by identifying the main issue and breaking it down into three sub-issues, but then it provides a statement of law for each of these without any application. This provides a block of legal statements pertaining to three separate sub-issues. A preferable approach would be to complete the discussion of each sub-issue by providing a statement of law, applying it to the facts, and reaching a conclusion before moving on to state the law relevant to the next sub-issue, as the following example illustrates:

> Three certainties are required for the existence of a valid trust. There must be certainty of intention, certainty of subject matter and certainty of objects. Certainty of intention requires that there is evidence that the testator intended to create a trust rather than disposing of his property as an outright gift. The testator has (application and conclusion). Certainty of subject matter requires . . . This is established by . . .

15.4.3.2 No abstract statement of the law

This stage of the problem-solving process is concerned with providing an accurate and concise statement of the current law. It does not require that this law is explained in the context of the particular facts of the problem; that is an issue of application which is important at the next stage of the process.

  If you combine the statement of law and its application, you are failing to demonstrate an appropriate problem-solving technique *and* omitting to demonstrate your knowledge of the law. However, it is common for students to provide an explanation of the law in the context of the facts. If you do not understand what is meant by this, the examples shown in Table 15.2 should demonstrate the point:

Table 15.2 Examples of abstract statements of law

Explanation of law in context of the facts	Abstract statement of the law
The *actus reus* of theft is putting the cuff-links in his pocket	The *actus reus* of theft is the appropriation of property belonging to another
The relevant standard of care is that of a qualified and experienced doctor	The relevant standard of care is that of the reasonably competent professional
The applicant will have standing to bring a claim for judicial review because the grant of planning permission will have an effect on his everyday life	The applicant will have standing to bring a claim for judicial review if he has sufficient interest in the issue

The statements in the first column are *not* accurate statements of the law; they are explanations of how the requirements of the law are satisfied in relation to a particular set of facts. As such, they are *applying* the law rather than *stating* it.

Students sometimes take the combined approach as a deliberate ploy to conserve words. This is a mistake: it may save words but it loses marks.

15.4.3.3 Too much detail

A further factor that can weaken a problem answer is the inclusion of an excessive level of detail when providing a statement of law. This tends to take two forms:

- Too much descriptive detail, for example the detailed facts of a case
- Inclusion of irrelevant material, for example issues not raised by the facts.

Both of these problems can be addressed by use of the 'so what?' test. This involves asking 'so what does this contribute to my answer?' in relation to each sentence included in your answer. If the answer is 'nothing', the sentence should be removed. It is seeking to identify material that is not directly relevant to the issue at hand.

Practical exercise

Use the 'so what?' technique to eliminate the unnecessary material from these sample answers based upon examples used earlier in the chapter.

Sample 1. Sheena has submitted her essay at 9.15am the day after the deadline for submission. The rules state that there is a ten-mark penalty for submission up to one day after the deadline. *An essay which is more than one day late will receive a twenty-five-mark penalty if it is within one week of the deadline but after that it will receive zero.* It is likely that Sheena will receive a ten-mark penalty unless she can establish that she had good cause for late submission.

Sample 2. Steve has punched Adam in the face causing a cut which required stitches so may be liable under s 20 of the Offences against the Person Act 1861. The *actus reus* requires a wound or the infliction of grievous bodily harm. Grievous bodily harm is defined as 'really serious harm' and according to the CPS Charging Standards includes serious injuries such as broken limbs. *Moreover, it has been held by the House of Lords that psychological injury can amount to grievous bodily harm if it is sufficiently serious and is established as a matter of expert evidence. It does not include mere emotions such as distress or fear but requires an established psychiatric injury.* A wound is defined as a break in the continuity of the skin and will be satisfied as a cut that requires stitches must have broken Adam's skin.

These are quite straightforward examples to demonstrate the point, but you will find suggested answers identifying the unnecessary material along with an additional exercise at www.oup. com/he/finch8e/ that you may find useful in helping you to eliminate irrelevant details from your answers.

15.5 APPLICATION AND EVALUATION

It is this stage of the process that is at the heart of problem solving. The first stage enabled you to identify the questions that needed to be answered; the second stage involved identification of the law needed to answer these questions, but it is this third stage that involves combining the issue and the law and actually answering the question.

This is the aspect of problem solving with which students struggle the most and yet it is quite straightforward, as the following example demonstrates:

- Sub-issue 1.1 Is Brian an occupier of premises?
  - **State the law:** There is no statutory definition of 'occupier' under the Occupiers' Liability Acts 1957 and 1984 but an occupier is defined in *Wheat v E Lacon & Co Ltd* [1966] AC 552 (HL) as a person who exercises an element of control over premises. In *Harris v Birkenhead Corporation* [1976] 1 WLR 279 (CA), it was held that this meant physical control over the premises as well as legal control.
  - **Apply it to the facts:** As Brian is described as the person who runs the farmyard activity centre, this implies that he has physical control over the premises even if he is not the legal owner of the centre.
- Conclusion

As you see in this example, the essence of application/evaluation is to draw upon the facts provided to demonstrate how the requirements of law are satisfied.

Here, the law defines an occupier as a person who exercises a degree of control over the property so the application/evaluation stage of problem solving picks up on evidence from the scenario which demonstrates that Brian exercises control over the farmyard activity centre.

The application stage is sometimes said to require the greatest level of skill and understanding of the law as it requires the student to look at the facts and select the ones that fulfil the requirements of the law. This is not something that can be cribbed from a textbook, remembered from a lecture, or looked up on the internet; it requires actual understanding of the requirements of the law and an ability to recognize them amongst a mass of facts.

Practical exercise

It is a good idea to practise with some simple examples to gain confidence in identifying the relevant facts. Have a look back at the farmyard activity centre scenario and pick out the facts that satisfy the following requirements:

1. If the definition of 'premises' includes land and buildings, what facts suggest that the injuries sustained by Gladys, Camilla, and Betty occurred on the premises?

2. To fall within the provisions of the Occupiers' Liability Act 1957, the person who is harmed must be a lawful visitor to the premises, that is, someone with express or implied permission from the occupier to be on the premises or whose presence is known to the occupier. What facts suggest that Gladys, Camilla, and Betty are visitors?

3. An occupier will not be liable for a visitor's injury if he has given sufficient warning to enable the visitor to be reasonably safe. Are there any facts that suggest that any of those who have been injured have been given a warning and, if so, was it sufficient to enable them to be reasonably safe?

4. An occupier may have to take additional measures to protect children from harm, especially if there are allurements on the premises, but the law strives to seek a balance between the duty of an occupier and the responsibility of parents for the safety of their children. In this scenario, what might act as an allurement to a child, what measures has Brian taken to protect against this, and what factors might suggest some element of parental responsibility?

🌐 *Answers to the questions can be found at www.oup.com/he/finch8e/ along with an explanation of how the answers were reached. You will also find a further example which will test your ability to identify relevant facts from the question that will demonstrate that the requirements of law are satisfied. This is an important area, so it will be worth taking some time to ensure that you are able to apply the law effectively to the facts.*

15.5.1 Common problems

This stage of application/evaluation does hold a range of pitfalls that can lead students astray. The following is an outline of some of the problems that seem to arise frequently, with some suggestions for their avoidance.

15.5.1.1 Lazy application

This is a phrase that can be used to describe situations when students have made some mention of the facts but in such a general way that it is not really application at all as it does nothing to resolve the issue at hand. Examples include phrases such as 'this requirement is satisfied on the facts' or 'it is clear from the facts that this is satisfied'. This may well be so, but there is no credit available for application that does not refer to *specific* facts from the problem to establish that the requirements of the law are satisfied.

It also describes the situation when the student abdicates responsibility for application by delegating it to someone else, usually 'the court' or 'the jury'. Here, the student is acknowledging that a decision will have to be made about whether the requirements of the law are satisfied but strives to find a way to avoid doing this themselves. To be clear, even if the issue is one of fact that will be decided in court by the jury, that is not a useful stance to take in a problem question. Imagine if a client says to you 'am I going to be convicted of murder?'. He will not be in the least impressed if your advice is that this will be a question of fact for the jury! Accordingly, you must extrapolate evidence from the facts that give an indication of how the issue is likely to be decided. You might find that speculative application (see section 15.5.2.1) helps to overcome this problem.

The example shown in Figure 15.6 demonstrates both of these flawed approaches to application as well as some illustrations of a more effective approach.

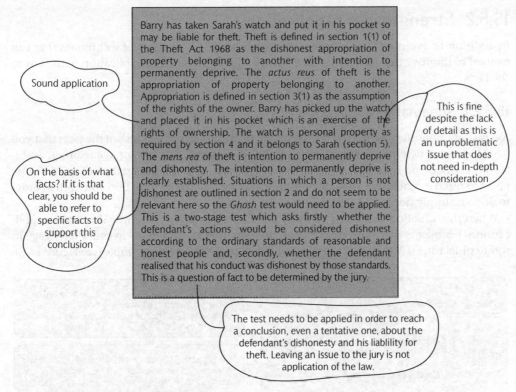

Figure 15.6 Lazy and effective application

15.5.1.2 Essays in disguise

Another weakness which limits the success of many answers is a greater resemblance to an essay than to a problem question. This arises when students engage in detailed discussion of the law raised by the question that strays further and further away from the issue at hand.

Try to remember that essays and problem questions have very different requirements. A problem question requires a concise and focused statement of the relevant law. Exploration of how the law used to be, how it might be in the future, or what it is in other jurisdictions are only rarely relevant in a problem question.

Students also have a tendency to include far too much descriptive detail of the law and this gives their answer the feel of an essay (see section 15.4.3.3). Try not to test relevance by asking 'is this point relevant?' as this question will be answered in relation to the topic in general. 'Is this point necessary to establish this part of the law?' is a far better question and one that will keep your answer focused and prevent it from turning into an essay on the general issue.

Another useful way of keeping the answer to the point is to ensure that every paragraph includes a mention of the name of one of the parties and at least some mention of specific facts from the problem. By doing this, you will force yourself to link up with the question and this should stop you from straying too far into abstract discussion.

15.5.2 Strengthening application

In addition to avoiding these common problems, there are a variety of techniques that can be used to improve the quality of your answer by strengthening the application of the law to the facts.

15.5.2.1 Speculative application

As you have doubtless realized by now, problem questions do not provide all the facts that you need to reach a determinative answer to all the issues raised. You will often encounter a situation in which you have worked through the sub-issues and need to establish just one more point to reach a conclusion about liability, only to find that the information you need in order to do so is simply not included in the question.

When this situation arises, it is perfectly permissible to engage in a little speculative application. This means that you can explore some hypothetical situations in order to engage in some conjecture: if *X* then *Y*. This is demonstrated in the following example (see Figure 15.7).

Huw has submitted his essay after the 4pm deadline. The rules state that essays submitted after the deadline that are up to one day late will receive a 10-mark penalty.	Application of the general rule could be followed by a conclusion that Huw will receive a penalty but there are exceptions to the rule so it is reasonable to speculate about whether Huw might fall within them.
There are some exceptions to this noted in the rules. For example, if Huw had been granted an extension by a lecturer, there would be no penalty. There is nothing in the facts to suggest that this is the case.	This is a straightforward situation to discuss as Huw either has an extension or he does not so there is little more to be said on this point.
Equally, the rule states that a person who has good cause for late submission will not be penalised. If Huw was late because his printer broke, this is unlikely to be regarded as a good reason as it is such a commonplace occurrence that he should have contemplated that it could happen and have planned for it. However, if Huw was late because he was knocked off his bicycle on the way to submit his essay and delayed by the need to seek medical treatment, this is likely to be regarded as a good cause for lateness.	This situation can involve more detailed speculation as it revolves around interpretation of 'good cause'. Inclusion of hypothetical possibilities to illustrate understanding of the scope of the exception add further strength to the answer. This approach can be used when case law has considered the interpretation of a particular word or phrase.
There is no evidence to suggest that Huw has received an extension or has good cause to submit his essay late; thus, in the absence of such circumstances, it seems likely that Huw will receive a 10-mark deduction for late submission.	The conclusion that follows speculative application should always draw reference to its contingent nature by noting that it is the best conclusion possible on the known facts but may alter if further facts come to light or a particular interpretation is preferred and applied.

Figure 15.7 Speculative application

15.5.2.2 Taking a balanced approach

The central premise of the legal system is that claims are tested against each other in order to establish which of the opposing arguments between private parties (in civil cases) or between the state and an individual (in criminal law) is the stronger. As such, it is important that you demonstrate this objectivity in your answers by considering both sides to the argument when exploring liability. Moreover, from a pragmatic perspective, if you present one argument, you will get credit for that but if you provide a second argument to counter that initial point, there is additional credit available.

Therefore, it is important to scrutinize every issue to determine whether there is a viable counter-argument that needs to be considered. There will not always be a counter-argument;

in the scenario involving the theft of Sarah's watch (see Figure 15.6), it is a straightforward matter to determine that the watch is personal property, so there is no counter-argument to consider. However, moving on to consider the issue of intention to deprive permanently, although it is reasonable to assume that this is Barry's intention as he has surreptitiously placed the watch in his pocket, it may be that he only wants to borrow it because, moving on to consider the issue of dishonesty, he wants to have it cleaned and repaired as a surprise for Sarah. If the facts are silent on an issue, it may be necessary to engage in speculative application in order to explore both sides of the argument (see section 15.5.2.1).

Equally, if the issue involves interpretation of a particular word or phrase, do not be content with finding one case on the issue and assuming that this provides the answer. You should research the issue and see if there is any conflicting authority that suggests an alternative outcome is possible.

15.5.2.3 Supporting authority

The inclusion of authority to support your application of the law is a real strength but it is also something that is not always done very effectively by students. All too often, an argument is raised that requires support which is either not provided at all, or the relevant case is added on in brackets at the end of the sentence or in a footnote reference with no indication of how it supports the proposition asserted.

> Although Camilla is a lawful visitor to the farmyard activity centre, she may have become a trespasser by climbing on the roped-off machinery (*The Calgarth* [1927] P 93).
>
> Although Camilla is a lawful visitor to the farmyard activity centre, she may have become a trespasser by climbing on the machinery as it was roped off to prevent the public approaching it. This issue was discussed in *The Calgarth* [1927] P 93.

Neither of these examples makes effective use of the authority; in fact, the second is misleading as it could be read as meaning that the issue of moving into a roped-off area was discussed in *The Calgarth*. A better approach is one that explains the principle from the case:

> Although Camilla is a lawful visitor to the centre, she may have become a trespasser by entering the roped-off area. It was said in *The Calgarth* [1927] P 93 that a person who is given permission to enter a house is not necessarily given permission to slide down the banisters, so it may be that Camilla has exceeded the permission given to her by entering the roped-off area.

One way to ensure that you use authority effectively is to make sure that you have linked the case to the facts in some way. This requires you to explain how it is relevant and consider how it might impact on the outcome of the case.

15.6 CONCLUSION AND OUTCOME

The final stage of the process involves reaching a conclusion on the basis of the preceding application of the law as is demonstrated by reference to the sample question:

> • Sub-issue 1.1 Is Brian an occupier of premises?
>   • **State the law:** There is no statutory definition of 'occupier' under the Occupiers' Liability Acts 1957 and 1984 but an occupier is defined in *Wheat v E Lacon & Co Ltd* [1966] AC 552 (HL) as a

person who exercises an element of control over premises. In *Harris v Birkenhead Corporation* [1976] 1 WLR 279 (CA), it was held that this meant physical control over the premises as well as legal control.

- **Apply it to the facts:** As Brian is described as the person who runs the farmyard activity centre, this implies that he has physical control over the premises even if he is not the legal owner of the centre.
- **Conclusion:** Therefore, Brian will be regarded as the occupier of the farmyard activity centre for the purposes of establishing occupiers' liability.

You will need to reach a conclusion for each sub-issue and then draw these together to reach a conclusion for the main issue. If you consider the issue of Brian's liability for the injury sustained by Gladys, you will see that it contained a series of sub-issues that combine to provide an answer to that main issue. Each of these—whether Brian is an occupier, whether the stable yard is premises, whether Gladys is a visitor, and so on—will be considered and a conclusion reached and these can then be considered cumulatively to reach a conclusion on liability.

Of course, it may be that it is not possible to reach a definite conclusion. It is a mistake to think that there is always an answer in law: it is not usually a case of right and wrong but of strong and weak arguments, so you should remember that you are not looking for the 'right' answer but for the conclusion that is likely to be reached based upon which argument is the strongest.

Take the following factors into account when reaching a conclusion:

- **There are three different levels of conclusion:** (a) a conclusion for each sub-issue; (b) a cumulative conclusion that draws upon each of these to reach a conclusion for each issue; and (c) an overall conclusion to the problem question. This should outline the liability of the party or parties for each issue that was raised by the question. In essence, the end conclusion is a summary of your findings.

- **Make sure that your final conclusion is consistent with your earlier discussion.** It would be unfortunate if, in the early stages of the essay, you concluded that Brian had given sufficient warning of the dangers posed by feeding the horses only to state in your final conclusion that he was liable for the injury sustained by Gladys. Thorough checking once the answer is complete should help you to spot any inconsistencies.

- **Do not be afraid to reach an 'it depends' conclusion.** As stated earlier, it is not always a case of finding the right answer but of exploring the possibility of liability, so it is perfectly acceptable to reach a conclusion that says 'it seems that Brian may be liable for the injury sustained by Gladys but this depends upon whether his notices are regarded as adequate warning of the dangers inherent in feeding the horses'. Making a note of the contingencies will strengthen your answer.

- **Provide an overall conclusion.** Given the constraints of the word limit, students are sometimes tempted to stop writing after dealing with the final issue and leave the marker to pick out the conclusions for each issue that are distributed throughout the answer. This is poor practice and will weaken your answer. The question will require that you discuss someone's liability and your conclusion should always provide a concise and focused answer to the question posed, so it is important that you draw together all the strands of your argument here.

15.7 TIPS FOR SUCCESS IN PROBLEM QUESTIONS

There are a range of points to bear in mind that will help you to strengthen your problem-solving technique.

15.7.1 Follow the instructions

This is an obvious but frequently overlooked point. If the instructions tell you to discuss the liability of a particular party and to consider liability in a particular area of law, this is all that you should cover in your answer. There is no credit available for discussing other issues that are raised on the facts but which are excluded by the instructions.

For example, if a problem stated that Tom had smashed his way into David's house and injected him forcibly with a lethal dose of heroin and you were asked to discuss Tom's liability for homicide offences, there would be no point whatsoever in establishing that Tom is liable for criminal damage to David's door, or considering whether the injection constituted a battery or assault occasioning actual bodily harm—David is dead, so there is no point in discussing non-fatal offences against the person!

Consideration of irrelevant issues will not give you any marks and it will weaken the quality of your answer because it will either cost you words that could be used to discuss a relevant issue (in a piece of coursework) or time that could be devoted to a relevant issue (in an examination).

Students sometimes think that discussing points that are outside the scope of the instructions will attract additional credit from the marker, particularly if this means covering an area of law that is not covered on the course syllabus, because this will demonstrate their research skills. This is generally not the case, so avoid the temptation to do this and concentrate on the instructions that you have been given and the areas of law covered on your syllabus.

Similarly, if a question is broken down into parts and subparts such as (a), (b)(i), (b)(ii), etc, then you must make sure that you answer the question in the same order and label the parts of your answer accordingly. Do not make up and impose your own structure. This will make your marker's life difficult, since marking schemes may give a total number of marks for each part answer and presume that the structure set out in the question will be followed. Your aim is to make your marker's task as easy as possible, so, quite simply, if there is a structure in the question, then you should follow it.

15.7.2 Get to the point

Be careful not to write lengthy introductions to problem questions that simply restate the facts given. For instance, look at the following introduction:

> The following is an essay that uses three statutes: the Offences against the Person Act 1861, the Theft Act 1968 and the Criminal Attempts Act 1981, to interpret criminal liability for the fictional characters involved in a hypothetical scenario. The scenario involves a young man (Adrian) taking his Uncle Dave's sports car to drive to his mother in the hospital, and having a road accident on the way. The accident is witnessed by a bystander—Claire—who invites Adrian into her cottage, where he attempts to steal two of her Japanese miniatures. Meanwhile, a local gang-member—Den—attempts to break into Dave's house . . .

As you can see, this sets out some relevant law and then recites the facts of the question. It also uses 102 words. There is very little credit to be gained in restating material from the scenario without application of the relevant law: it is also a waste of words which could be better used in application and analysis.

15.7.3 Methodical approach

If you follow the guidance given in this chapter, you should be able to work through each of the issues in turn in a methodical manner. This should ensure that you do not miss any important issues and that your answer is thorough and systematic. These are essential features of a strong answer. Students are often tempted to 'jump in' and deal with the most obvious issue first—usually something that they can recall discussing in a seminar or which bears a strong resemblance to a decided case—but this makes the answer weak because you are failing to deal with the other issues that are also raised by the question but may be less obvious, and you are also not demonstrating a thorough and methodical approach to problem solving.

15.7.4 Embrace uncertainty

There are always gaps and ambiguities in the facts of problem questions. These are there deliberately to give students an opportunity to demonstrate some of the more sophisticated problem-solving skills. If there is a gap in the facts, rather than ignoring it or stating that there is insufficient information to reach a conclusion, you could instead speculate about what the facts might be and discuss how these alternatives would make a difference to your conclusions about liability. In other words, you are filling in the gap in the facts with a little bit of guesswork (based upon the surrounding information) about what the facts might be and demonstrating your understanding of the law by explaining what the conclusion would be if either of the guesses that you have made about the facts were correct. Similarly, if the facts are ambiguous, rather than picking one interpretation and assuming it to be correct, acknowledge that there is ambiguity and create alternative arguments based upon the two different interpretations. The ability to deal with gaps in the facts and ambiguities are more advanced problem-solving skills. You should keep a lookout for an opportunity to try out these skills as it is only by doing so that you will get better at problem solving and, in any case, even if you do not it very effectively on the first occasion that you try, your marker will see that you have made an attempt and give credit for it plus they will give you some feedback that will help you to improve the next time.

15.7.5 Check and polish the final answer

You should never submit the first draft of your answer. It is important that you take the time to check every aspect of the answer prior to submission: the formatting, spelling, and grammar, the referencing, and, of course, the accuracy of the content. Try to leave sufficient time before submission to have a break from the answer and come back to read it with fresh eyes otherwise it is all too easy to read what you think you have written rather than what you have actually written, so mistakes could be overlooked. It might help to read your answer on paper rather than on the computer screen as mistakes can seem more visible in print.

You will find more detailed guidance on writing skills in chapter 11 and referencing in chapter 13 that will help you to ensure that you submit a well-written and thoroughly referenced piece of work.

Practical exercise

Reflect upon the guidance provided in this chapter and use it to evaluate an answer to a problem question that you have written either as part of your coursework or in preparation for a seminar. Make a list of its strengths and weaknesses to identify areas where improvement can be made in subsequent pieces of work. As the chapter on study skills suggests, reflecting on your own work can be an excellent way to improve your performance.

 However, if you would like to use the points raised in this chapter to evaluate answers written by others, have a look at www.oup.com/he/finch8e/ where there is a practical evaluation and marking exercise that you might find useful.

 CHAPTER SUMMARY

Finding the issues

- Take time to analyse the facts of the problem question in terms of the parties and events so that you know 'who has done what to whom' as this provides a good basis for structuring your answer

- Break an issue down into a series of sub-issues so that each can be considered in turn. It is essential that the issues are sliced up into manageable chunks, so that the law can be stated and applied to the facts

Stating the law

- Start by consulting a textbook to ensure that you have a clear understanding of the area of law but make sure that you move on to consider case law as this will ensure that your answer has sufficient depth of understanding

- Provide concise and abstract statements of the law that can be applied to the facts. Avoid reams of descriptive detail such as lengthy explanations of the facts of cases

- Make sure that there is some supporting authority—either statute or case law—for each statement of law that is made

- Remember to look at both sides of the argument for complicated issues. It may be necessary to search for cases that give alternative outcomes or different definitions of key words or phrases

- Keep careful notes to record your research. It is very frustrating to arrive at the writing stage and not be able to find details of a case you need because you thought you would remember. A systematic approach to note-keeping is a real asset and can save a great deal of time

Application of the law

- Look at the facts and extrapolate specific information that demonstrates that the requirements of the law are satisfied

- Never rely on lazy application such as 'this is clearly established on the facts'. If the facts are that clear, it should be easy for you to identify them and include them in your answer! Equally, never abdicate responsibility for application of the law to the fictitious jury

- Speculative application that considers hypothetical situations can be a useful way of increasing the depth of analysis in your answer and demonstrating your understanding of the law, but do not stray too far away from the facts provided in the answer
- Support your application with case law wherever possible but make sure that this is done effectively by stating the principle and incorporating it into your answer. Case names tacked onto the end of a sentence add nothing to the quality of your answer
- Present a balanced and objective answer by looking at both sides of the argument

Conclusion

- Reach a conclusion on each sub-issue, issue, and the overall liability of the parties and make sure that there is consistency between these different levels of conclusion
- Do not be afraid to reach a conclusion that is not determinative. Problem questions are written to raise difficult issues, so it may be that the best answer is one that says 'it depends' and then notes the contingent factor(s)
- Make sure that the final conclusion draws together all the strands of your answer and provides a concise summary of your findings as to the liability of the parties
- Do not be tempted to omit the final conclusion in the interests of the word limit

Revision and examination skills

16

INTRODUCTION

The earlier chapters in this part of the book have been aimed at helping you to develop the skills that you need to succeed as your course progresses. Chapter 10 outlined a range of study skills whilst chapter 11 provided a detailed examination of writing skills and chapters 14 and 15 contained detailed guidelines on writing essays and answering problem questions. This chapter focuses on the skills that you need to ensure that you are able to perform well in a range of non-coursework assessments, whether these are traditional unseen examinations, take-home or online exams, or multiple-choice tests. The chapter will discuss the types of challenges presented by each of these forms of assessment and provide guidance on how to formulate a revision strategy that will enable you to approach them with confidence.

Revision strategies and exam skills are really important as they have a direct bearing on how well students prepare for and perform in assessments but these topics are not always covered in study skills sessions or resources. This may be due to an assumption that students who have worked steadily all term will inevitably be equipped with all that they need to succeed in the exams without any additional guidance or it could be a reflection of the belief that each student prepares for exams in a way that suits them best based upon their previous experiences. These are unfortunate assumptions because it is often the case that students are not sure how to prepare for exams and tend to fall back on rereading and rewriting their notes, which is not the most effective approach to preparation. This chapter offers students a range of different approaches to revision and explores how they can be adapted to the three different types of assessment. The overall aim is to provide students with ways that revision can be made more variable, more engaging, and more effective.

 Learning outcomes

After studying this chapter, you will be able to:

- Appreciate the differences between unseen and take-home exams both in terms of the practicalities of the assessment and the skills required from students
- Recognize the range of challenges presented by multiple-choice tests according to whether the question tests knowledge, understanding, or reasoning
- Formulate an appropriate revision strategy for each type of assessment
- Create a realistic and effective revision plan

- Identify appropriate topics for revision
- Use a range of strategies to engage in active revision
- Acknowledge the value of practice answers and incorporate these into your revision strategy
- Plan and produce focused and successful answers to exam questions
- Avoid the common problems that limit exam success

16.1 TYPES OF ASSESSMENT

For many years, the usual approach to assessment in a law degree has involved a combination of coursework and unseen examinations with both of these forms of assessment featuring a mixture of essays and problem questions. More recent times have seen a diversification of approaches to assessment that has led to greater creativity in the way that legal knowledge and legal skills have been assessed. It is not unusual for students to find an assessment moot or presentation cropping up somewhere in their degree as universities seek to provide opportunities for students to demonstrate oral presentation skills, and assessed group tasks are also becoming more common to reflect the desirability of collaboration skills in the workplace. These skills are covered elsewhere in the book but the focus in this chapter is on preparing for, and performing well in, traditional unseen examinations as well as two other forms of assessment that have gained popularity in recent years: take-home exams and multiple-choice tests.

16.1.1 Unseen exams

An unseen exam is the traditional type of examination in which students sit together in an exam hall in the presence of an invigilator to answer questions in time-limited conditions, usually between one and three hours. The exam paper will contain questions that students have not seen prior to the exam. There may be one or more compulsory questions or students may have free choice to select from the range of questions. Some exam papers will be divided into separate parts with a requirement to answer one question from each part: for example, a paper could be divided into an essay section and a problem question section with the instruction to answer one question from each section. Unseen examinations will either be 'closed book' in which case no materials can be taken into the exam room or 'open book' in which case one or more books can be used for reference purposes during the examination. Open book exams may stipulate which book can be used—typically the set textbook or a statute book—or students may be permitted to take the book of their choice. A variation on an open book exam is one in which students are permitted to take their own notes in to the exam with them, sometimes within specific limitations such as a single sheet of A4.

As you can see, then, there is a lot of variation as to what a student might encounter with an unseen exam in terms of the number of questions, how much freedom there is to choose which questions to answer, and whether materials can be taken into the exam room. The only consistent characteristic is that the student will not have seen the questions that they have to answer in advance. The rationale for this type of exam as a means of testing knowledge is that students do not know what questions they will be asked and so they have to learn everything about the subject matter in order to be prepared for whatever questions they encounter. From a preparation perspective, this places a lot of emphasis on ensuring that information is committed to memory and so this becomes a key part of revision strategy as you will see later in this chapter.

16.1.2 Take-home exams

The take-home exam has existed as an alternative to the unseen exam for many years but was not greatly used as an assessment in law until the rapid expansion of online teaching and assessment necessitated by the coronavirus pandemic of 2020. It is called an exam but it is really a hybrid of an exam and coursework, sharing some characteristics with each of these methods of assessment. Like an unseen exam, there are a series of questions set out in an exam paper that have to be answered within time constraints and these have not been seen by the students prior to the start of the examination period. However, the time frame of the exam is longer than the usual one–three hours of an unseen exam and as it is not completed in 'exam conditions' there is the opportunity to carry out research and to consult whatever notes and books seem appropriate. For this reason, it can seem that it is more like a piece of coursework but one which has to be completed in a much shorter period of time: usually either a working day (questions realized at 9am and answers to be submitted by 5pm) or a calendar day (answers to be submitted within twenty-four hours of the release of the questions). This longer time frame tends to create an expectation that answers will be more structured and polished than would be the case with handwritten answers produced within tight time constraints in an unseen exam. Another key difference with take-home exams is that the ability to consult materials whilst writing answers takes away the emphasis on memorization of information that tends to characterize revision for an unseen exam sat in traditional exam conditions.

16.1.3 Multiple-choice tests

A multiple-choice test presents students with a series of questions and each question is accompanied by a choice of possible answers. The task of the student is to select the correct answer from this list. This often seems like an easier option from the student's perspective than asking them the same question and requiring them to answer it from their own thoughts, knowledge, and understanding. For example, the question 'what is the *actus reus* of theft?' requires you to remember the complete answer yourself whereas asking that question with a range of possible answers (as shown in Figure 16.1) gives you some clue that might jog your memory as to what the answer is plus there is always the possibility of a lucky guess if you have no idea about the correct answer.

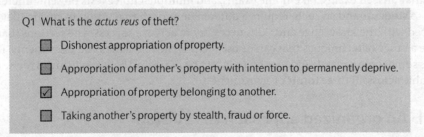

Figure 16.1. A criminal law multiple-choice question

On this basis, it might be tempting to assume that a multiple-choice test requires little or no preparation. This is a mistake. Multiple-choice tests tend to contain a lot of questions and so cover a great breadth of the syllabus. In fact, they are often used by lecturers to force students to study all of the subject matter in a module rather than engaging in selective learning as can be the case with a single piece of coursework for assessment or 'question spotting' leading to targeted exam revision. In essence, a multiple-choice test requires you to have a good level of understanding of everything that has been covered in a module and will often test very precise details by presenting possible answers that are very close to each other in their wording. It is also the case that multiple-choice exams offer no scope for discretion: an answer is either right or wrong whereas there is scope for shades of meaning in, for example, an essay written for coursework or in an exam or an answer to a problem question in which you might get credit for your reasoning process even if your conclusion is incorrect.

It is also important to remember that not all multiple-choice questions have straightforward factual answers. Multiple-choice questions can be used in a variety of ways to create really challenging tasks to test understanding as well as recall. For example, you could be presented with a principle from a case and asked to select which of a range of scenarios best reflects that legal principle in operation, you might be asked a question about a line of reasoning developed by a particular judge in a case, or you could encounter a series of multiple-choice questions asked about a problem scenario. There are lots of possibilities beyond straightforward recall of factual information.

Multiple-choice tests are likely to feature more frequently in undergraduate assessment in law now that they are being used as part of the SQE in the two functioning legal knowledge (FLK) tests that make up SQE1. Each of these tests has 180 multiple-choice questions, each of which has five possible answers. The tests are divided according to subject matter as follows, with questions about ethics and professional conduct being woven into both of the tests:

1. Business law and practice, dispute resolution, contract, tort, legal system of England and Wales, constitutional and administrative Law, EU law, legal services.

2. Property practice, wills and administration of estates, solicitors accounts, land law, trusts, criminal law and practice.

It would be a good idea to familiarize yourself with the style of questions by looking at sample papers provided by the Solicitors Regulation Authority (SRA) if you are planning to qualify as a solicitor after the SQE is introduced on 1 September 2021.[1]

16.2 REVISION STRATEGIES

It should be clear, just from this brief outline of the characteristics of the three types of assessment, that unseen exams, take-home exams, and multiple-choice tests present different challenges to students and, as such, require a different approach to revision to ensure that you are equipped with the knowledge and skills necessary to achieve success. The sections that follow outline a range of techniques that can be used to prepare for each of the assessments. But first, there is some more general guidance on points to bear in mind before starting to revise that are applicable across all three forms of assessment.

16.2.1 An organized approach to revision

Planning and preparation are the keys to successful revision. Too many students dive straight into the revision process without any clear idea of what they are trying to achieve. This unstructured approach can lead to revision time being used in an inefficient way which can

---

1. SQE1 Functioning Legal Knowledge Sample Questions, 14 April 2020
<https://www.sra.org.uk/globalassets/documents/sra/sqe1-functioning-legal-knowledge-sample-questions.pdf?version=4af5a6> accessed 25 January 2021.

lead to panicky last-minute cramming as students realize that they have not covered all the topics that they wanted to during the revision period. Taking a little time to organize your thoughts at the outset and devising a workable and effective revision strategy can be a really good investment of time that will actually help you to use the revision period in a more productive and effective way.

In order to plan your revision, it is essential that you have a clear picture of the task ahead of you. A vague knowledge that you have to sit five papers in five weeks' time is not sufficient information upon which to base an effective revision strategy. Try to ensure that you can answer the following questions as your first step in the revision process:

- **When do your exams start?** This question is important because it dictates how much time you have available for revision. Count how many days, including weekends, there are from the first day of your revision to the first day of the exam period. If you divide each day into two study periods, you can give yourself half-day breaks to give yourself some relief from studying. Once you have divided your days into study periods, you can start to allocate topics to them.

- **How much time is there between exams?** You may be fortunate and find that your exams are spaced out across the exam period giving you time to revise between exams or you might be unlucky and find that you have four exams in five days. Whatever the spacing between your exams, try to start out with an objective to have your revision complete by the date of the first exam and use the time between exams to refresh your memory and practise answering questions. If you work on the assumption that the four-day gap between two exams will be sufficient for you to revise for the second exam then you will be in difficulty if you are ill and do not feel able to revise.

- **How many exams are you sitting?** Your revision time should be split fairly evenly across the number of modules you are taking even if they have different credit weighting. For example, if you have one 30-credit module and two 15-credit modules with exams then you may well want to treat them all as equal in terms of allocating revision time even though two of the exams carry less weight than the other.

Once you have these details, you can get a good idea of how many days you have available to revise each module. For example, if you have fifteen days until the first exam, this gives you thirty half-day study periods to allocate to revising for your four exams. If you take some half days out to give yourself a break from revision, you might be left with twenty-four study periods to use for revision. Rather than dividing this by four, you may want to take other factors into account when deciding how much revision time to allocate to each module. For example, you may have found some modules more difficult than others (you could rank them on a 1–5 scale where 1 is the most difficult) or perhaps some modules are assessed solely by exams so that there is more at stake than there is in modules where 50 per cent of your mark has already been gained by coursework (see Table 16.1).

Table 16.1 Allocating revision time

Subject	Percentage of exam	Difficulty	Number of sessions
Family	50	5	3
Medical	25	4	3
Company	25	1	6
International	100	1	12

Once you know how many study sessions to allocate to each module, the final decision is whether to cluster your revision for each module (for example, the first three study sessions are devoted to family law before you move on to medical law for the next three sessions) or whether you alternate between different topics. The first method allows a concentrated focus on one module whereas the second can make revision more enjoyable as you switch between modules each session but it can lead to a lack of continuity of thought. There is no right way to do this—it is a matter of personal preference and trial and error as you discover what works best for you.

Once you have divided your revision time between the modules, it can help to keep you on track if you create a visual reminder by drawing up a revision calendar or using a wall calendar so that you can see very easily where you are in the revision process. It is also very satisfying to be able to cross out completed tasks, giving a real feeling of progress.

16.2.2 The timing of revision

Obviously, it is up to you to decide how to divide up your time during the revision period but it seems wise to add a note of caution at this point about devoting the majority of the revision period to modules with unseen exams. Students often think that unseen exams need more time devoted to revision than multiple-choice tests (where it is assumed that the answers will jog your memory) or take-home exams (where there is the opportunity to consult materials) but, in actual fact, all exams and text require an equal amount of preparation but the sort of preparation involved differs between the three types of assessment. It is true that unseen exams seem to require that material is condensed and committed to memory which is very time-consuming but there is an equal amount of work to be done for multiple-choice tests and take-home exams.

It is worth taking a little time at the outset to think about the different types of assessment that you are facing and to work out what sort of revision they require so that you can decide how much time to allocate to revision in each module and, crucially, when this revision should start.

The previous section focuses on a revision period which is assumed to run from the time that teaching finishes to the date of the first exam. This makes sense to a degree because the revision period is a time to consolidate your understanding of the material covered in the module once it has all been covered. But there is work that can be done prior to the start of the revision period that will reduce your workload during this time and make the task of revising a more manageable one. The nature of the task will depend on the sort of assessment:

- **Unseen exams.** Much of the focus in preparation for unseen exams is on your ability to remember information. Notes should always be made with a purpose so it would be helpful if you made notes with revision in mind. Students often talk about turning their lecture notes into revision notes when they are revising which seems to mean identifying the most important points and condensing them down in a way that makes them easier to memorize. This is something that could be done each week during the teaching period rather than left until teaching is complete. If you get into the habit of creating a set of revision notes after each lecture then you have saved yourself a lot of time when the revision period starts as your materials will be ready. It is also a lot easier to identify key points when the lecture is fresh in your mind rather than trying to remember them weeks or months after the lecture took place when you come to the end of the module. There is guidance on making effective notes in chapter 10.

- **Take-home exams.** Perhaps the greatest obstacle that students face when it comes to take-home exams is that they do not require revision at all because there is a period of time after the questions are released in which materials can be consulted and gaps in legal knowledge can be filled. This really is not a good strategy because it uses up the time that you could be planning and writing your answers with tasks that could easily have been done in advance. The day of the take-home exam is not the time to be learning a topic for the first time or realizing that you had never quite understood a particular topic the first time around! The revision period should be used to refamiliarize yourself with the content of the module and to consolidate your understanding of the subject matter covered in the same way that you would if you were preparing for an unseen exam. Prior to the revision period, you can collect materials to use in your preparation. Take-home exams place far greater emphasis on the ability to use materials than unseen exams so it is a good idea to collect and collate cases and articles during the teaching period that are relevant to each topic and make notes that will help you once the revision period arrives.

- **Build up a store of multiple-choice questions.** Multiple-choice tests tend to cover the entire syllabus so it makes sense to work steadily throughout the module to accumulate the knowledge and understanding that you will need to do well. Find out what type of questions you will encounter as early as possible, asking the lecturer to show you some examples, and then look at each topic as you study to anticipate that sorts of questions that you might be asked. Make lists of key concepts, cases, and definitions on each topic. If you know that the questions will cover particular cases or set reading, make sure you go through these carefully and note the sort of points that could pop up as questions. You could write your own multiple-choice questions at the end of every lecture and then use these during the revision period to see how much you have remembered and to test your own understanding.

The overall message here is that revision does not have to be confined to the revision period but is something that can usually be done all the way through the module. Think about the materials that you need to start revision and make sure that you create these during the teaching period. Not only will this relieve some of the pressure during the revision period by reducing the amount of work to be done but the tasks that you complete during the teaching period will actually help to consolidate your understanding of the law as you go thus ensuring that you have a strong basis of knowledge already at the start of the revision period.

16.2.3 Choosing revision topics

One of the first things that you will want to do at the start of the revision period is to look at the syllabus of each module that you have studied and decide which topics to revise. In a perfect world, you would revise every topic that you have been taught so that you have a comprehensive understanding of the module in its entirety but the world is not perfect and revision time is limited. And, of course, there may be really good reasons why you decide not to revise a particular topic: if you did not understand a topic at all at the time it was taught, it is probably a good idea to eliminate it from your list of revision topics rather than burn up your valuable time trying to master it during the revision period. The exception to this advice would be if it is the topic of a compulsory question in which case you are going to have to devote time to trying to understand it.

Start by studying the syllabus to make a list of all the topics that you have covered, making a note of any that were especially significant or that you particularly enjoyed as well as noting any 'clues' that the lecturer gave you about the likelihood of a topic being examined. Lecturers vary enormously in their willingness to give an indication of what topics are likely to appear on an exam paper with some refusing to comment at all and others giving a list of examinable topics so keep your ears open for any guidance that is available. You might also want to be sure that you can answer the following questions as these will help you to decide how many and which topics to revise:

- **How many questions do you have to answer?** The more questions you have to answer, the more topics you will need to revise.

- **Are there any compulsory questions?** This is crucial information because failing to cover the topic of a compulsory question will have an obvious adverse impact on your ability to answer that question. Sometimes you will be given some information about the topic and/or format of the compulsory question which will help to focus your revision.

- **Does each topic have a separate question or are they merged so that one question covers several topics?** If you know that each topic has a separate question, it is easier to work out how many topics to revise but a paper that merges topics could combine them in a number of ways so it is prudent to revise more topics to increase the likelihood that you can tackle all parts of the question.

- **Do you have free choice of what questions to answer?** Some exam papers give students an entirely free choice of questions but others will be divided into parts with a requirement that one question is answered from each part. This division might be on the basis of question type (one part being essays and the other being problem questions) or subject matter. For example, a tort module might have one section devoted to questions on negligence (as it is such a significant topic) and one section containing questions on the other torts. A question paper divided into parts can be an indication that you need to revise more topics: if your module covered six topics and there are three questions in each part, you would need to revise four topics to be sure that you could answer one question from each part.

- **How prominent was each topic?** The emphasis given to a topic by your lecturers can give some insight into its overall importance to the subject, hence the likelihood that it will feature in the exam. For example, if five out of the twelve weeks in tort were given to the study of negligence, it does not make sense to disregard it as a revision topic.

In general, you should aim to cover as many of the topics within each module as you can manage within the revision period to ensure you are able to answer as many questions as possible on the exam paper, as this gives you the ability to choose which questions you feel that you can answer most effectively. This is a far more sensible strategy than focusing your revision on two topics if you know that the exam requires you to answer two questions. What will you do if one or, worse still, both of your chosen topics do not appear on the exam paper? If you have only revised two topics then you have nothing left to fall back upon and you will have to try and tackle questions on topics that you have not revised. Similarly, you will be putting yourself at a disadvantage if you have revised two topics and you find that your topics are on the exam paper but that you either do not like the questions or do not understand what they are asking you to do. The only way to guard against this is to revise more topics than there are questions.

Some students have a tendency to 'question spot' by scrutinizing past papers and making predictions about what topics will appear in their forthcoming exam. This is a dangerous strategy because there is no reason why a topic will (or will not) appear just because it has (or has not) appeared in previous years.

Once you have a list of topics to revise in each subject, you can start to slot these into your revision timetable. Bear in mind that you will need to be realistic in allocating time to any particular topic; it would be unrealistic to expect to cover all of negligence in a single half-day session. Setting unrealistic goals means that you will struggle to meet them, which can lead you to lose motivation and to feel overwhelmed by the whole revision and examination process. It is better to overestimate the amount of time that it will take to revise a particular topic and then give yourself a reward when you finish with time to spare.

16.3 REVISION ACTIVITIES

Once the structure and content of your revision is decided, it will be time to make a start. But the next question that needs to be addressed is what you actually do during each study session in order to revise effectively. Many students do not really have a clear idea about the most effective way to approach revision and simply read and reread their notes and/or text-book in the hope that the information that they read will stick in their minds. A slightly more effective variant on this involves writing and rewriting notes again as a means of memorizing information. These strategies do lead to greater familiarity with the subject matter but are not generally as effective as revision techniques that involve more active engagement with the material.

It seems likely that the main reason that students adopt these approaches to revision is because of the perception that the purpose of revision is to fix information in the memory so that it can be recalled in the exam room. This is the reason why many students reread and rewrite notes in preparation for unseen exams and multiple-choice tests and feel that no revision is necessary to prepare for take-home exams or open book unseen exams where materials can be consulted during the exam. A more useful way to think about revision is that it is a process that prepares you for a test and preparedness will vary according to the nature of the assessment:

- **Unseen exams** require the ability to recall relevant information and an ability to use it effectively to answer questions.

- **Take-home exams** do not require recall of information as materials are at hand for reference purposes but they do require a basis of knowledge so that the correct information can be located and then the focus is exclusively on how well that information is used to answer the questions.

- **Multiple-choice tests** require the ability to recall sufficient information to enable the correct answer to be identified.

All three methods of assessment involve some combination of recollecting information and using it effectively albeit it in different ways. Simply rereading or rewriting notes in isolation might take you some way towards being able to recollect information (although it would be more effective in conjunction with other techniques) and it does nothing whatsoever in preparing you to be able to use the information in the way that you will need to do in the exam. A more active approach to revision will be more effective in achieving both of these aims so you might find it helpful to try some of the activities set out in the following sections.

16.3.1 Consolidating notes

Although note-making alone is not an effective revision strategy, a good set of notes is the foundation of successful revision. Ideally, as discussed earlier, these will have been produced incrementally as the course has progressed; it is not useful to start the revision process with a blank sheet of paper and nothing to revise. You should aim to take the notes that you have made during lectures, in preparation for seminars and as part of your private study, and condense them into a more concise set of key points. These can be used to test your recall if preparing for an unseen exam or multiple-choice questions or as easy reference materials if you have a take-home exam.

Condensing your notes is an important part of the revision process. Not only does it produce a set of concise points that can be committed to memory or used for reference, the actual process of filtering and recording information will contribute to your understanding of the material as you make decisions about the significance of different points and the relationship between them.

16.3.2 Improving your memory

It is essential that you find a way to make the material memorable.

The first point to note is that it is much easier to recall things you have understood. This is why it is useful to review the syllabus and weed out topics that have never made any sense to you. If you have not grasped them by the time the revision period starts, it will probably require far too great an investment in time to get to grips with them now. In fact, you should only really try to incorporate topics that have always mystified you into your revision if it is absolutely necessary, for example the topic is the subject of a compulsory question or you have been puzzled by so much of the course that dealing with some difficult topics is essential.

Memory is triggered by association so it can really help the revision process if you vary your strategies so that each topic is somehow associated with something in particular. If you sit in the same place, doing the same thing for all the topics that you revise, there is nothing for your memory to latch onto in order to differentiate it from all the other legal information milling around inside your head. Try varying the following factors to create an association:

- **Activities.** If you vary the activities that you use for revision, you improve your ability to recall information by linking a particular topic with a particular activity. For example, if you use a mind map to revise theft, a quiz to revise murder, and flashcards to revise sexual offences, you will be able to retrieve relevant information by visualizing the activity, something that you will not be able to do if you revise all topics using the same techniques.

- **Locations.** Again, varying the place where you revise will create an association in your mind with the place. Maybe you revise negligence in the library, nuisance sitting at your desk, and remedies in the park. Visualizing the place will help you to remember the topic.

- **People.** Not only will collaborative revision be more engaging and enjoyable, it can also help with memory if you associate a particular person with a particular topic. For example, you could ask a family member to test you on offer and acceptance, revise exclusion clauses with a friend, and ask your partner to listen to you explain consideration.

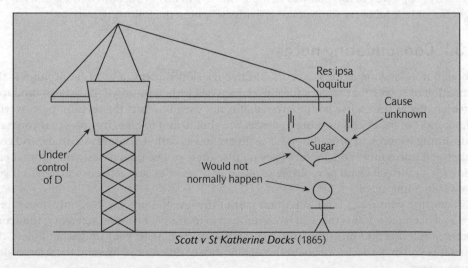

Figure 16.2 Using pictures to remember case law

- **Pictures.** Words can be hard to commit to memory but visual images can be more memorable. You could try to use diagrams, flow charts, and mind maps to make use of your visual memory or you could be really creative and draw pictures to help you remember the facts of case law (see Figure 16.2).

16.3.3 Testing your recall

Reading notes can become monotonous and even the best attempts at concentration can end with the eye gliding over the paper without taking in anything written on it, whilst copying out reams of notes can end up as a writing or typing exercise. In other words, reading and writing do not necessary involve the brain engaging with the words that are read or written and this could result in the information not being processed by the brain effectively so that it can be stored and retrieved. In essence, if you want to be able to recall information during an exam, it is important to adopt revision strategies that involve information retrieval so that the brain has practice at the task that you are asking it to do. This requires activities that involve more active engagement with the revision materials.

16.3.3.1 Revision flashcards

These are small cards that have a question, keyword, or other piece of information on the front and an answer, definition, or other response on the back. Preparing the flashcards requires you to identify key issues and using the flashcards tests recall. The cards are small which limits the amount of information that can be recorded which should help you to keep your points brief which will make them easier to remember (see Figure 16.3). They are portable so you can carry them with you so that you can revise in spare moments and they contain answers which makes it easier for others to help you with your revision by using them to test you even if they know nothing about the law. They are especially useful as a means of revising case law but remember to use them to revise both the facts and the legal principle from the case.

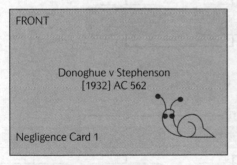

FRONT

Donoghue v Stephenson
[1932] AC 562

Negligence Card 1

BACK

Facts: D found remains of decomposed snail in bottle of ginger beer purchased for her by a friend. Suffered gastro-enteritis. Held that D could sue the manufacturer.

Principle: Established the 'neighbour principle' as basis for duty of care in negligence. See Card 2.

Figure 16.3 A revision flashcard

*There are some further examples of revision flashcards across a range of topics on the online resources at **www.oup.com/he/finch8e/**.*

16.3.3.2 Quizzes

You could create a series of questions on a topic to test your recall and understanding, perhaps working with other students to share the effort and swapping quizzes with each other. These might take the form of questions and answers or you could create a template which explains a particular case, principle, or concept but which leaves out key words and phrases (see Figure 16.4).

> JUDICIAL REVIEW is a process by which the...court exercises its...jurisdiction to review the decisions of...In order to bring an action for judicial review, an applicant must have..., meaning that he must have a...interest in the case, and bring the claim...and at least within...months. There are three grounds for judicial review which were identified by Lord...in the...case: these grounds are (1)...(2)...and (3)...

Figure 16.4 A template for judicial review revision

> *There are some further examples of revision templates on the online resources at www.oup. com/he/finch8e/.*

16.3.3.3 Diagrams and flow charts

Visual representations of information can be a great asset during revision in terms of enabling you to see the entirety of a large topic at a glance. This can be useful in helping you to understand and remember the relationships between the elements of an offence or a set of offences. The preparation of a flow chart or diagram will make you really think about these relationships and, once in the exam room, you should be able to visualize the diagram, which is an excellent way of jogging your memory as to its contents. You could scribble the diagram down from memory in the rough notes areas of your exam booklet (see Figure 16.5).

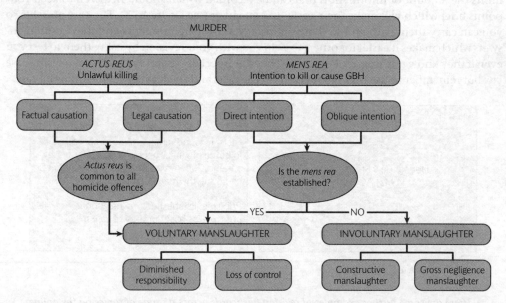

Figure 16.5 A murder flow chart

16.3.3.4 Recorded notes

Making a recording of your notes that you can play back can be a good way of adding variety to the way in which your mind receives information and can help you to make effective use of spare periods of time, such as when travelling by car or train, sitting in the bath, or lying in bed at night (although the merits of playing recordings through the night are hotly debated—do make sure that you have proper rest during the busy revision period). A variation upon this theme is to record a group of friends discussing a revision topic and listen to this, bearing in mind that you have less control over the accuracy of the content.

16.3.3.5 Free-flow writing

This is a fantastic way to generate ideas and you will often be surprised by how much you do actually know. You make a note of a word or phrase at the top of a blank sheet of paper or fresh document and allow yourself a set period of time in which to write absolutely everything that comes to mind about this topic without any concern for structure, order, or grammatical sense. Any period of time from one to five minutes will work well for revision and it might be an idea to start short and build up to longer periods of time as your knowledge increases. It can be a useful starting point for revision, so that you can identify what you know and, more importantly, what you do not know by comparing your free-flowing writing with your notes.

16.3.4 Practising for the exam

Although the revision period is often perceived as a time to commit material to memory, it is actually a time to prepare for the assessment. Some forms of assessment, such as unseen exams and multiple-choice tests, place an emphasis on the ability to recall relevant information but that is not all that they require—an exam answer that just sets out remembered information on a particular area of law will not receive very many marks at all. This is because the truth of the matter is that the ability to retrieve relevant information is just a necessary preliminary step to performing well in these sorts of assessments. What really matters is not how much law you can remember but what you do with that law once you have remembered it. And, of course, take-home exams place few demands on memory as the focus is primarily on the way that the law is used in the answers that are produced.

So even if the ability to remember information is part of the requirement of an assessment, it is not the whole picture and yet many students spend the entirety of the revision period doing nothing else but committing the law to memory in preparation for unseen exams and multiple-choice tests. Perhaps the assumption is that as long as they have the information, they will be able to create good answers from it but writing an essay or answering a problem question for coursework, when there is plenty of time available to think, plan, redraft, and look up the details of the law, is a very different task to writing an essay or answering a problem in exam conditions. Assimilating what a question requires, mustering the necessary information, creating a plan, and writing a clear and coherent answer within tight time constraints involves a specific set of skills. Like all skills, they will get better with practise and so it seems a risk strategy indeed to go into the exam room with a head full of memorized law and an assumption that you have the necessary skills to use that law to create really effective answers. Far better to devote some time during the revision period to practising those skills to ensure that they are as good as they can be by the time that you sit the first exam.

Writing practice answers is *the* most important part of revision.

What this means in practice is incorporating activities into the revision period which, as closely as possible, mirror the tasks that you will be completing in the exam period:

• **Unseen exams.** This means finding questions from past papers and writing an answer within the same constraints that will exist during the exam itself. This involves completing the answer within a strict time limit and usually writing the answer by hand rather than typing it. It is important to replicate the actual exam conditions as much as possible as it will give you a feel for how much you can write within the time and help you to manage your time in the exam itself. If the unseen exam is closed book then your practice answer should also be written without notes; this will also be a good way of testing how much information you have retained and can recall. If the exam is an open book format then the practice answer should involve using whatever materials will be available to you in the exam room. Again, you need to know how much time you will take up by consulting materials as this will impact on how long you have to write in the exam. It will also help you to be more familiar with the permitted materials so that you can navigate them more rapidly in the exam itself.

- **Take-home exams.** You may already feel that you are familiar with the task involved in take-home exams because they feel like a piece of coursework but with a very short time frame for completion. This is true to an extent but it is nonetheless also fair to say that there are some key differences that mean that practise is still a useful part of revision. The two key factors here are the ability to look up information and the limited time frame for completion. Whilst the ability to look up information may seem like a positive aspect of a take-home exam, it is something that could burn up a lot of time. Preparation is the key here. You should have a set of notes ready for each topic that you have revised, preferably organized in a way that is easy to navigate, and then you will only have to actually find additional literature relevant to the specific question that has been asked. In terms of the time frame for completion, if you have never written two, three, or however many essays and problem questions in a single day (or whatever the period is allowed for the completion of the take-home exam) then clearly this is something that you need to practise to get a feel for how long it will take you so that you can plan your time effectively in the actual exam period.

- **Multiple-choice test.** The biggest pitfall that students encounter in this type of assessment comes from the assumption that familiarity with the course materials is sufficient preparation and that there is no need to practise the questions themselves. This is not a good strategy. Multiple-choice questions come in many forms and it is essential that you are familiar with the style of questions that you will encounter and that you have a sense of how long it will take you to answer them. Sample questions should be available from your lecturer and you can use these to practise.

As you can see, one of the justifications for including practice questions in your revision is so that you have a clear understanding of how much work you can do in the time frame of the exam. This is a really important factor. You have to be able to complete the tasks set by the assessment in the time that is available. After all, the highest mark you could expect to achieve if you wrote two essays when you were supposed to answer four questions would be 50 per cent and then only if both essays were perfect in every way. Time management is a crucial factor in exam performance and it is a skill that you should practise during the revision period.

Despite their obvious value, students are often disinclined to write practice answers as part of their revision, partly because they do not understand just how valuable this can be and partly because there is no feedback available so they have no way of knowing whether the answer they produced was a good one. These points are addressed below:

- **The benefits of writing practice answers.** Some students say that there is no point in writing practice answers because different questions will come up in the exam. This is true but the value of the activity lies not in preparing in advance an answer to question that you hope will appear but in preparing you to answer any question that you encounter. Remember, exams do not just test *what* you know, they also test *how* you use that knowledge. Writing practice answers, in conditions that are as close as possible to those that you will encounter in the exam, enables you to test, review, and refine your technique and is the key to producing effective and successful answers in the exam room.

- **Finding feedback.** The absence of feedback is also a factor as students feel there is no means for ascertaining the quality of the answers that they produce. This may not be true. Many lecturers will give feedback on practice answers and, in the absence of this, the ability to evaluate your own work is a valuable skill that you should be striving to develop and there are a number of things that you can do to assess the quality of your work. For example, you can compare the answer with your notes, use the grade descriptors (see chapters 1 and 10) to check that you have demonstrated the necessary skills, and just read your answers through to see if you are pleased with the structure, flow, and use of language. You could also work with other students to evaluate each other's work: never underestimate the contribution to improving your own essay-writing or problem-solving skills that is made by engaging in constructive criticism of the work of others.

Overall, then, there are great benefits to writing practice answers or attempting practical multiple-choice tests as part of your revision. It gives you a sense of how much work you can do within the time frame, tests how much information you can recall, enables you to practise the skills involved in the assessment tasks, and provides an opportunity for you to enhance your knowledge and understanding of the topic by reviewing your own work and the work of others.

16.3.5 Revising with others

One of the best ways to make revision more effective and more enjoyable is to work with others. You could work with one other student or in a small group and share the work out between you. For example, if you are all taking the same module, you could agree to make a set of notes on one or two topics each and share them around the group to reduce the time spent on this activity. Alternatively, rather than just swapping paper notes, you could each agree to prepare one topic to teach the others by giving a mini lecture. This can be a really valuable exercise as having to explain the law to other people, especially if you allow them to ask questions, will really test whether you have understood the topic.

Another option for a revision group would be to all revise the same topic and then pool your understanding in a discussion session, perhaps recording this or nominating a note-taker so that you can all remember what was covered afterwards. This can be a really good way of ironing out areas of uncertainty as you all work together to fill in gaps in your understanding of the law.

You can work with other students to produce a bank of multiple-choice questions to practise together or work collaboratively on the creation of quizzes, templates, and flashcards. And do not be afraid to be creative. One group of students once spent a great deal of time making a version of Trivial Pursuit that replaced the usual categories with the six subjects that they were studying in their second year which they then played at every opportunity. It was so good that other students offered to pay to take part! This shows that you can make revision into an enjoyable activity but do be wary of devising activities that take too much time to set up and organize. These students came up with the idea at Christmas and spread the writing of questions across several months so that the game was ready by the start of the revision period.

Not only do these activities split the workload of revision, they also encourage you to talk to others about the law and this can be one of the more effective methods of gaining an understanding of the material.

Of course, you do not have to work with other law students during the revision period. Anyone else can be recruited to test you using flashcards that you have prepared or you can simply talk to people about the law. It is often said that you can only be sure that you have understood something if you can explain it in a way that enables someone else to understand it too, so you could explain legal concepts to family and friends to see how well you can communicate it to them. Give them an opportunity to ask questions to clarify any points that are unclear and then ask them to explain the concept back to you. If they are able to give you a relatively clear and detailed account, then your explanation to them was a good one.

16.3.6 Tailored revision

This chapter contains all sorts of tips and advice on tackling revision but the important thing is that you devise a strategy that is right for you. Everyone has a slightly different learning style and it is always a matter of trial and error to find an approach that works for you. This can cover the sorts of activities you undertake, whether you work alone or with others, and what sort of working patterns you adopt. For example, some people work well in the morning whilst others find it difficult to get started. Just before the exam is not the time to try and force new study habits upon yourself, so ensure that you devise a revision plan that fits within your usual working preferences provided, of course, that this gives you an appropriate time frame within which to work.

You should also tailor your revision to your preferences, as far as possible, when it comes to determining the sorts of questions you want to answer in the exam. If you had a free choice, would you prefer to write an essay or answer a problem question? This is an important consideration because your revision will need to be different if you are preparing for an essay than if you are planning to answer a problem question. Many students do not realize this and just tackle each topic of their revision in the same way. However, as essays and problem questions have different requirements, both in terms of the nature of the content and the type of skills involved in their production, it stands to reason that the approach to revision in preparation for each type of question would be qualitatively different.

- **Problem questions.** These assess your ability to disentangle a mass of interwoven facts in order to make a determination about the legal liability of the parties by applying the current law to the factual situation. As such, it requires knowledge of the current law and an awareness of the variety of ways in which it could be applied as demonstrated in case law.

- **Essays.** Essays involve a greater depth of knowledge about the topic which might include historical information about the evolution of the law and the ability to comment on future developments by way of evaluation of proposals for reform. The emphasis here is on the ability to consider the law in depth, to address policy considerations, and to engage in critical evaluation of the efficacy of the law. Figure 16.6 illustrates the differences between essays and problem questions in relation to oblique intention in homicide offences.

You will find a more detailed consideration of the requirements of essays and problem questions in chapter 14 and chapter 15. There will also be some discussion of factors that are important in tackling each of these types of question in the sections that follow.

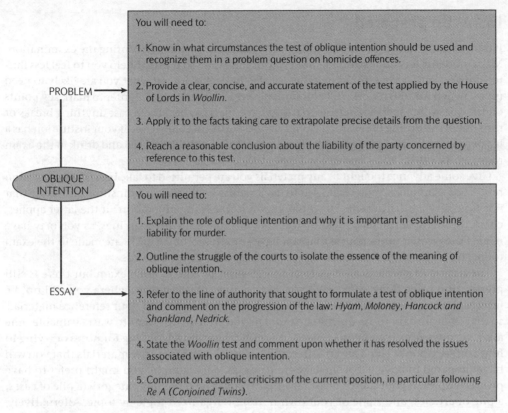

You will need to:

1. Know in what circumstances the test of oblique intention should be used and recognize them in a problem question on homicide offences.

2. Provide a clear, concise, and accurate statement of the test applied by the House of Lords in *Woollin*.

3. Apply it to the facts taking care to extrapolate precise details from the question.

4. Reach a reasonable conclusion about the liability of the party concerned by reference to this test.

PROBLEM

OBLIQUE INTENTION

ESSAY

You will need to:

1. Explain the role of oblique intention and why it is important in establishing liability for murder.

2. Outline the struggle of the courts to isolate the essence of the meaning of oblique intention.

3. Refer to the line of authority that sought to formulate a test of oblique intention and comment on the progression of the law: *Hyam, Moloney, Hancock and Shankland, Nedrick*.

4. State the *Woollin* test and comment upon whether it has resolved the issues associated with oblique intention.

5. Comment on academic criticism of the currrent position, in particular following *Re A (Conjoined Twins)*.

Figure 16.6 The different requirements of essays and problem questions

You should also be aware of your strengths and weaknesses, both in terms of the topics that you study and your preparation for essays and problem questions. Some students have a strong preference for essays whilst others favour problem questions but all students will need to answer a mix of both in the exams, so do give thought to strengthening your technique if you are weak in one or other answer style. Honing the quality of your answers should be an integral part of the revision process; remember, success in exams is not attributable exclusively to what you know/can remember but also to how you use it.

16.4 THE EXAM

It is probably true to say that however much revision you have done and however diligently you have followed the advice in the earlier section of this chapter, you will probably still quail at the thought of the exam itself, whatever format it takes. Most people dislike exams and suffer from varying degrees of nerves. The following sections are designed to address a range of issues related to the exam with a view to ensuring that you are able to put in a good performance that makes the most of your hard work during the revision period and throughout the year.

16.4.1 Be prepared

It is important that you have everything with you that you will need during the examination. Many students feel quite stressed on the day of the exam, so it might help you to feel less flustered if you gather your things together the day before. Work out what you are likely to need (pens, pencil for rough work, ruler for underlining case names, highlighter to mark key points on the question paper) and ensure that you have spares as backup in case anything breaks or runs out of ink during the exam. It would also be worth checking to see if your institution has a list of prohibited items: for example, some universities prohibit all food and drink in the exam room whilst others allow students to take bottles of water.

Give some advance thought to any materials you are permitted to take into the examination room. For example, if you are allowed to use a statute book, does your institution specify that it is from any particular series or require that it is free from annotation? If the latter applies, check through your statute book to make sure it is free from any markings, as you may have made notes earlier in the course that you have since forgotten. Checks are made in the exam room and materials that do not comply with the rules will be removed.

The nature of preparation is different in relation to a take-home exam but there is still preparation to be done. Make sure you have a quiet place to work where you will not be interrupted and give some careful thought to the organization of your reference materials so that they are easy to use during the exam period. You do not want to waste valuable time after the questions have been released in rummaging around looking for notes or trying to find your textbook. Think about different systems of organizing the materials that you will have prepared in advance of the take-home exam. For example, you might prefer to have printed copies of your source material and this could be set out by category (a pile of cases, a pile of articles, and a pile of your own notes) or organized topic by topic. Alternatively, perhaps your reference materials are on your laptop in which case you could establish a series of separate folders. There is no single right way to organize your materials but some system that enables you to find things quickly and easily is a good idea. You will also want to make sure that you have bookmarked any legal databases that you plan to use for ease of access.

16.4.2 Follow the rubric

The rubric is the explanatory notes or instructions that accompany the exam and are generally found on the front of the paper giving instructions about the format of the paper, the number of questions that must be answered, and the timing of the exam. The rubric may well be available in advance of a take-home exam so be sure to take the time to familiarize yourself with it so that you are clear about your task on the day. You should check the rubric of an unseen exam once you are in the exam room to make sure that you know how many questions to answer and whether there are any compulsory questions or requirements to answer questions from different parts of the paper. This is especially important if there is a different format for exams in different modules: it would be a terrible shame to answer the wrong number of questions because you assume that today's paper has the same requirements as the one you sat last week or to miss out on a compulsory question because there was not one on the last paper.

The rubric for a take-home exam will also include the requirements for its submission so make sure that you take note of these and follow them. For example, do you have to upload the completed paper to the virtual learning environment or do you have to submit it to the module convenor by email? Are there any stipulations about file format? For instance, some universities will stipulate submission as a PDF due to the file size whereas others will not accept PDF submissions because the markers want to annotate the answers with comments. Find out what the rules are and follow them. The rubric will also emphasize that it is your responsibility to save your work frequently and to upload it well in advance of the submission deadline.

16.4.3 Read the paper

Whatever the type of assessment, it makes sense to take a few moments to read through the paper in its entirety at the beginning so that you have a clear idea of the range of questions. Some universities build a short period of reading time into the beginning of an unseen exam but it is a good idea to give yourself this time if there is no formal reading period in your exam arrangements even if everyone else seems to have started writing straight away. A few minutes spent analysing the paper and thinking about the requirements of each question and whether or not you would be able to answer it will save you time overall.

The decision as to how to use your time in a take-home exam is your own but it still makes sense to read the questions all the way through at least once to make sure you are clear about what they require.

It can be useful to make notes about the questions, either on the paper itself or on rough paper or at the back of your answer booklet, to ensure that you have a clear idea of the scope of the questions. This will enable you to make an informed decision about which question to answer. You may find this technique useful for analysing the paper:

1. Write the question numbers on a sheet of paper, leaving a gap of a few lines between each number and note the main topic of the question and whether it is an essay or problem question.

2. On the basis of this information, eliminate any questions that you feel you would prefer not to answer. For example, if there is an essay on misrepresentation and you have a preference for problem questions and did not revise misrepresentation, you can probably rule out the possibility of answering that question from the outset.

3. For the remaining possibilities, look at the questions again and note a few more details about them that might help you to appreciate what they require and whether you might want to tackle them. Bear in mind that it is not enough to know a lot about the topic, you have to be able to answer that particular question.

4. If you are not sure whether or not you would be able to answer a particular question, try making a quick list of the issues you think are raised by the question to see how much information you can generate.

5. Make a note of the questions you feel you could definitely answer. Hopefully this will be sufficient to tackle the paper. If you have ticked more questions than are needed, you will have to make a judgement about which of these to tackle based upon your preferences for the subject matter. If you have not ticked sufficient questions to complete the paper, you will have to revisit some of those that you have crossed off and reconsider whether you could attempt an answer (see Figure 16.7).

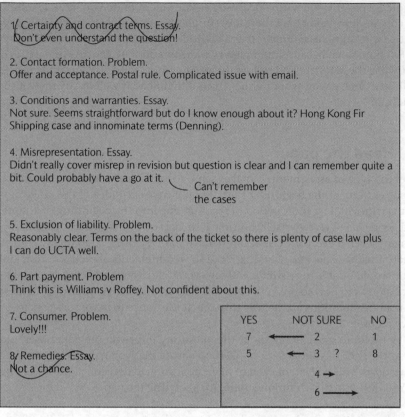

Figure 16.7 Analysing the question paper

It might not be feasible to read all the questions on a multiple-choice test before you start answering them as time tends to be quite tight but it is nonetheless a good idea to take a look through the questions to get a sense of the paper as a whole. If there are short questions at the beginning but longer questions towards the end, this might be an indication of complexity and, if nothing else, the longer questions will take longer to read. This sort of overview is only possible with written test papers. If you are sitting an online multiple-choice text, you may only be able to see one or a few questions at a time so you will just have to work steadily away.

16.4.4 Plan each answer

If you are writing an essay or answering a problem question in an unseen or take-home exam, it is a good idea to plan your answers. It does not take a great deal of time out of the overall time available to write an answer plan and this investment of time tends to pay immense dividends as it leads to a stronger and more focused answer. It is important that you realize it is not just knowledge that attracts marks in the exams, but the way this knowledge is deployed in response to the question. As with any form of assessment, exams assess not just what you know but what you do with that knowledge, so it is crucial to your success that your answers reflect a range of legal skills, including the construction of a structured essay and a methodical answer to a problem question, as well as your legal knowledge.

16.4.5 Structure

Students who start writing straight away without making a plan often produce a poorly structured essay that is peppered with asterisks and arrows denoting paragraphs that need to be inserted. Unplanned answers also tend to lack logical progression as the student raises different points as they come to mind and this impedes clarity of expression, limits the possibility for depth of analysis (in an essay), and carries a real risk that important material will be omitted (a particular issue with answers to problem questions).

Another major issue with answers to problem questions is that students tend to 'jump in' and deal with the most obvious issue raised by the question. This is usually something that reminds them of the facts of a case or they can remember the issue being discussed in a seminar. By tackling the obvious point first, this weakens the structure of the answer and carries a real possibility that the issues that were raised by earlier sections of the question are never addressed.

Of course, take-home exams are completed on a computer so you can make changes to the structure more readily than you can in a handwritten unseen exam but you will still save time overall if you take a little time to create a plan of your answer. It will also help you to identify any research that needs to be done if you are clear about what argument you plan to make.

16.4.6 Focus

It is imperative that you answer the question that you were asked and not the question that you hoped you would be asked. This is a common pitfall associated with 'question spotting' in which students predict that a particular question on a topic would be asked and prepare a model answer prior to the exam which they then memorize and reproduce. This is not a good strategy because it is incredibly rare for students to make accurate predictions and a good answer that was prepared in response to a different question will just not work well as a response to the exam question.

Another failure of focus comes when students do not tailor their knowledge to the question at all but instead respond to the topic of the question, writing everything they know about it and thereby including points that are relevant to the topic but have no bearing whatsoever on the specific question. Content that is only relevant to the topic is irrelevant to the question and will not gain any credit, plus it will be a missed opportunity to demonstrate essay-writing skills by selecting the relevant content and explaining it in a way that answers the question.

The production of prepared answers and the 'all I know about the topic' answers are both poor exam practice. Avoid both and instead respond to the specific question asked. Do this by finding your focus during the planning stage. Write the key words from the question in capitals at the top of your planning page or highlight them on the exam paper so that they are at the forefront of your mind and make a list of points for inclusion that are relevant only to this particular topic within the broader topic.

Focus is especially important in take-home exams. As you have the opportunity to use notes, books, and other materials in writing your answers, there is far less credit available than would be the case in an unseen exam for setting out the correct content unless it is also used skilfully to create an essay or answer to a problem question. In essence, there is a greater need to demonstrate understanding by the way that material is used.

16.5 TOP TIPS

This chapter concludes with three sections that outline some guidance for each of the three forms of assessment covered in this chapter.

16.5.1 Unseen exams

The key point to have understood about success in unseen exams is to remember that, contrary to popular belief, they are not tests of memory; they are tests of knowledge and understanding. You can survive an unseen exam by memorizing material and reproducing it in the exam but you will perform better if you move beyond the recitation of remembered facts and instead use the information to create tailored responses to the specific questions asked in a way that shows an understanding of the law.

- **Timing is important.** You have to use your time wisely. If the exam is three hours long and there are four questions to be answered, you have forty-five minutes per question. Take five minutes off for planning at the beginning and polish at the end. Write down the start time of each question on the exam paper and stick to it. There is no point in spending half the time writing the first question and trying to scribble the last answer in five minutes.

- **Answer the right number of questions.** If you have answered three questions and feel that you know nothing about the remaining questions left on the paper, you should still make an attempt at a fourth question as even some general points that you can remember about the topic will get you more marks than no attempt at all. You should also never answer an extra question in the hope that you will get marks for your best four answers. You will not. It is the first four answers that will be marked. If you have time to answer an extra question, that time would be better used going back over your other questions to see if you can add to them.

- **Incorporate authority.** The use of authority in the exam is an issue that tends to trouble students. It is true that your answer will appear more polished and knowledgeable if you are able to incorporate some reference to authority into your answer but it is important that the use of authority demonstrates understanding rather than appearing as if a random selection of case names have been sprinkled over your exam paper. It may seem as if there is an immense amount of case law to learn and remember but try to identify a few key cases in relation to each topic, with particular emphasis on those that demonstrate essential principles. Remember that it is more important that you know the legal principle from the case rather than the facts but that the facts might help you to demonstrate the operation of the law. Equally, do not trouble your memory with lists of case citations: the name and, if possible, the year will suffice. If you cannot call the case name to mind, draw reference to it by the use of key facts.

- **An essay requires an argument.** As discussed earlier in this chapter, there is always a temptation to focus on content in an unseen exam because there is a desire to make use of material that has been learned and memorized. But your essay needs to be more than a set of descriptive points about the main topic of the essay: there needs to be a line of argument that takes a position about the question asked which runs through the essay.

- **Problem questions require application.** Similar to the previous point, make sure you use the law to answer a problem question by setting out a methodical analysis of liability that makes use of the facts. The key to success in problem questions lies with a methodical approach to untangling the facts and identifying the issues that need to be resolved. Do not forget your problem-solving skills just because you are in the exam room.

You may like to consult the chapters on essays (chapter 14), problem questions (chapter 15), and writing skills (chapter 11) to remind yourself of the core characteristics that should be presented in a good answer.

16.5.2 Take-home exams

Take-home exams are relatively new types of assessment for many law students and the most common question asked is how they differ from unseen exams. The key difference here is the expectation of a greater level of skill in the execution of the answers as you have more time to plan and write and to reflect upon and refine what you have written. Answers are typed rather than handwritten so there is a greater expectation that they will have a clear and appropriate structure. Source material is readily available so there is greater emphasis on the use of supporting authorities.

- **Timing is important.** The need to use your time wisely is just as applicable to take-home exams even though they take place over a longer period of time. There is much to be done in order to create your answers: you need to read and understand the questions, create a plan for your answers, gather together your materials, identify any further materials that you might need, find those materials, read them and work out how to incorporate them into your answer plan, and then set about writing your answer. A day might sound like a long time but remember that in any twenty-four-hour period you will use about eight hours for sleeping and you cannot work non-stop for the remaining sixteen hours.

- **Preparation.** Much of the work involved in a take-home exam can be carried out in advance. You should revise your topics in the same way that you would for an unseen exam but with the objective of understanding the material and creating a good set of reference materials that you can use easily in the exam. This should include reading source materials, such as cases and articles, and highlighting and/or annotating them so that you can find the key information quickly.

- **Planning.** Have a plan of how you will spend your day. What time will you get up and when will you start to work? Are you going to work non-stop or will you work for an hour and then take a break? How much time do you think you will need to carry out research? Create a provisional running order for your day and practise it using questions from past exam papers. You will feel more confident about your ability to complete the task in the time if you have practised. Make sure you have a suitable place to work where you will be free from interruptions.

- **Focus on skills rather than content.** Now that you have the ability to consult materials, there is less credit available for accurate legal content because there is an expectation that this will be there because you can look it up. The same applies to supporting materials. Citing five articles in an essay written in an unseen exam is impressive but far less so in a take-home paper where you have time and resources to carry out research. This means that your essay-writing and problem-solving techniques become even more important. In essays, focus on analysis rather than description and make sure that there is frequent skilful application of the law to the facts in your answers to problem questions. It is your ideas, thinking, and creativity in the use of the law that will impress the examiners in this type of assessment.

16.5.3 Multiple-choice tests

This is an entirely different type of challenge to the requirement to write essays and answer problem questions. The trick here is to go into the test with a strong body of knowledge about the subject matter that is based upon thorough revision and then to read the questions and possible responses very carefully to enable you to select the correct answer.

- **Answer the question before reading the possible answers.** The most reliable way to identify the correct response from the selection available is to know what the answer to the question is before you read the responses. Read the question and answer it in your head then look at the list of responses to find one that matches your answer. Obviously, this strategy is only useful if you have an inkling of what the answer is when you read the question but it is the most sensible starting point because looking for the answer that you know is correct from amongst the responses is quicker and has less potential to confuse you than reading four or five possible answers, all of which might sound plausible.

- **Read the responses carefully.** If you do not know the answer to the question when you first read it, it is possible that you will recognize the correct answer in the range of responses. It is important to take a little time to do this, reading all the responses carefully and noting the differences between them. Remember that lecturers often write questions that focus on areas that are regularly misunderstood by students and include responses that are based on common student errors. The responses will have been worded so that they are close to each other in meaning so that they present an appropriate level of challenge to students so look for shades of meaning in the responses rather than fixing on a key word that you associate with the question and assuming that means that the answer is correct.

- **Use a process of elimination.** If you do not know the correct answer and cannot easily recognize it from the list of responses, see if you can reduce the number of options by eliminating those which are not plausible answers. It is sometimes easier to recognize the wrong answers than to identify the right one. Look at the responses that remain and think carefully and logically about them but try not to pause too long on any one question as the clock will be ticking. Try and jog your memory by thinking about other information that you know about the subject matter of the question as memory works by making links and associations. For example, if you are asked about the principle of a case but you can only remember the facts, think about them for a moment and see if it helps you to retrieve more about the case from your memory.

- **The answer is not (always) C!** The internet is full of advice about how to 'cheat' multiple-choice tests: in other words, how to work out the correct responses without knowing the answer to the questions. This advice is based upon common errors that people writing multiple-choice questions make such as making the correct response longer and more detailed or putting the correct response in the middle so that it is 'hidden' in amongst the incorrect responses (hence the myth that the correct answer is most often C). Avoid any temptation to use these techniques in the test as lecturers are very well aware of them and will have designed them out of the set of questions that you encounter and computer-generated tests will randomize the response order in any case.

- **Understand the rules.** It is important that you go into a test with an understanding of the rules. For example, is there only one right answer or are there multiple-response questions included in the test? Can you move backwards and forwards between questions in the test? If the test is taken on paper then this is always possible as you have control over the order in which you answer the questions but online tests may not offer this option. Many computerized tests offer no opportunity to revisit questions once they have been answered or to review your answers at the end of the test before it is submitted. If this is the system used at your university then it is essential that you know this because skipping a question that you do not immediately understand will mean that it cannot be answered later on. If you do have the ability to skip backwards and forwards between questions, you can use this to your advantage by tackling all the questions that you can answer first as quickly as possible and then taking more time on the questions where you need to puzzle the answer out.

- **Practise.** Familiarity with the types of question really will help with the speed at which you can work through the test. It will also ensure that you are not stumped by encountering unfamiliar styles of question on the day of the test. Questions will either text knowledge, understanding, or reasoning and they will be constructed differently in order to do this. For example, knowledge is tested by questions about what the law is whereas understanding may be tested by asking students to work out the best response to questions based upon a short extract from a case or one of the pieces of set reading for their module. Reasoning may be tested by setting out a short problem scenario and requiring students to answer questions about it that mirror the challenge of applying the law to the facts when answering a problem question. These types of question test different skills so practise will improve your ability to answer them quickly and accurately.

Practical exercise

 *Unlike the other chapters in this book, this chapter has not included any practical exercises or self-test questions. There are, however, practical activities online at **www.oup.com/he/ finch8e/** that are relevant to the material covered in this chapter, including an exercise in marking exam answers written by other students to help you to identify the good points and to learn from their mistakes! You will also find further examples of revision flashcards and revision templates that you may find useful in helping you put together your own revision materials.*

CHAPTER SUMMARY

Preparing to revise

- Take time to reflect on the requirements of the exams and the content of each subject to be examined in order to prepare an effective revision timetable
- Tailor your programme of revision to your own strengths and weaknesses as a student
- Gather all your revision materials together so that you can work effectively and without distraction in the revision period
- Revise for all your assessments with equal thoroughness. Avoid the misconceptions that take-home exams do not require revision because you can look up information once the questions have been released and that multiple-choice tests do not require revision because you will recognize the correct answer when you see it

Revision strategies

- Try to avoid exclusive reliance on reading and rewriting notes as a revision strategy as this is a passive approach which does not test your ability to use the material effectively
- Vary the activities that you use as part of your revision. This is to help you to remain engaged and interested in the process and it will aid recollection in the exam
- Tailor the activities to the type of assessment, remembering that unseen exams and take-home exams require different approaches to revision but that both require revision
- Consider using a range of methods to record information: written notes, diagrams, pictures, and voice-recordings all engage the brain in a different way.

- Involving others in your revision distributes the workload and enriches the revision process
- Writing sample answers is the most effective revision activity as it orientates you to the amount of writing that can be done in the time frame and enables you to make your mistakes prior to the exam and learn from them in order to strengthen your exam performance

Exam technique

- Make sure you are fully equipped for the exam with writing equipment, any materials that you are entitled to take into the exam room, and a clear knowledge of where and when the exam will take place if it is an unseen exam
- Ensure that you have a quiet place to work that is free from interruption with all the permitted materials set out in an organized fashion around you if you have a take-home exam.
- Read the question paper carefully, including the rubric, and analyse each question to determine its requirements so that you can make decisions about which questions to answer at the outset
- Allocate your time equally between the questions and remember to include time for planning at the start and time at the end to read through your answers, making any necessary amendments
- Do not forget that the ordinary requirements of structure, language, analysis, and application that are applicable to essays and problem questions are still needed in the exam. Answers that demonstrate legal skills as well as legal knowledge tend to be more successful
- Remember to include reference to authority to support your answer
- Answer the required number of questions—no more and no less—in legible handwriting using all of the time available. Pay particular attention to any instructions that accompany the question as there are no marks available for moving outside the requirements of the question

Dissertations

17

INTRODUCTION

The focus of this chapter is the range of different skills needed to produce a good quality and successful dissertation. Some of the skills involved will be familiar ones that are covered elsewhere in this book—research skills (chapter 3, chapter 6, and chapter 9), writing skills (chapter 11), and referencing (chapter 13)—so be sure to look back at these chapters as necessary. There are also some skills that are specific to the dissertation and those will be the ones that are covered in this chapter. Most universities allow you to choose your own topic so there will be a discussion of how to do this and the associated issue of how to formulate a research question. You will also find sections aimed at helping you to manage a large-scale research-based project and also at managing your relationship with your supervisor—something that can be surprisingly difficult. There is also a section at the end that addresses the common problems that students have when writing a dissertation.

Some students think of a dissertation as a long essay. Although it is true that dissertations do have some characteristics in common with an essay, to describe a dissertation as a long essay overlooks some of the key factors that set it apart from an essay. In particular, a dissertation gives control to the student: you select your own topic and decide how to approach it which allows you to determine the level of difficulty of the dissertation. The longer length of the dissertation makes it far more challenging to structure and there is much more emphasis on independent research. Due to the greater demands it makes, the dissertation is viewed as a real measure of the ability of the student, and the range of skills involved in its production means that the dissertation is a real showpiece of your aptitude for the law that can be used to impress potential employers.

 Learning outcomes

After studying this chapter, you will be able to:

- Make reasoned choices about whether to undertake a dissertation, how to select a topic, and how to convert this into a research question
- Construct a proposal that outlines the scope of your planned dissertation, its importance as a topic, and how you plan to carry out your research
- Break down the production of the dissertation into manageable stages and organize your time so that the work involved is spread over the time available

- Identify, locate, and keep track of relevant literature
- Structure the dissertation in an appropriate way and produce a piece of work that is well written, well presented, and thoroughly referenced

17.1 WHY WRITE A DISSERTATION?

Some universities have a compulsory dissertation module for final year students, but for most students the dissertation will be one of a selection of optional modules that you can take in the final year of your studies. So if the choice is yours, why might you choose to write a dissertation?

- **To pursue an interesting topic.** A dissertation module usually gives you the freedom to choose any subject matter whatsoever (provided that it is something to do with law and there is a lecturer who is willing to supervise it) so it is your opportunity to focus on an area of law that you find genuinely interesting. Perhaps it is something that captured your interest in one of your earlier modules and you would like to explore it in more detail or maybe you have seen something in the media that has sparked your interest. Some students like to use this as an opportunity to explore how the law affects something that they are interested in away from their studies or to research an issue that they encountered on a work placement.

- **To develop research skills.** Research is the foundation of a good dissertation. You will be exploring an area of law in far more depth and detail than is generally the case for a coursework essay and you may have to look behind the familiar sources of law that you are used to using, maybe looking at the literature of other disciplines or the law in a different jurisdiction. A dissertation will stretch your research skills and improve your ability to conduct independent research.

- **To work closely with an academic supervisor.** You will conduct your dissertation under the supervision of one of your lecturers and this means that you will have a series of one-to-one discussions about your research. For many students, this provides a really valuable opportunity to receive really tailored support and guidance from an academic about all aspects of the research and writing process.

- **To fit in with your future plans.** If you are thinking of studying law (or any other subject) at postgraduate level, it is likely that you will have to write a dissertation as this is more often a compulsory component of postgraduate study so it might be a good idea to build your skills now. If you intend to practise law, writing a dissertation will give you the opportunity to demonstrate a number of skills that will be important to potential employers including independent working and legal research. You could also tailor the subject matter of your dissertation to the area of law that you want to practise, especially if it is a particular specialist area or one that is not covered on your degree.

17.2 DISSERTATION TOPIC AND RESEARCH QUESTION

Once you have made the decision to write a dissertation, the next important question that needs to be answered concerns the choice of general topic, the isolation of a particular topic, and then, ultimately, the formulation of a research question; see Figure 17.1. This is a process

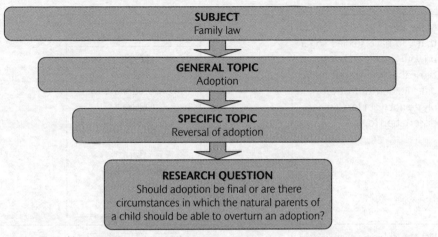

Figure 17.1 Moving from subject to research question

that involves incremental narrowing of focus until there is a single question that needs to be answered which is at the heart of the dissertation.

17.2.1 Choosing a topic

There are a number of factors to take into account when choosing a dissertation topic. Some of these are practical considerations: there must be enough relevant literature accessible to you to enable you to carry out your research, it must be a topic that someone in your department is willing and able to supervise, and the topic must be one that is capable of giving rise to a research question that can be explored in sufficient depth in the time available and within the constraints of the dissertation word limit.

In addition to these factors, it is important that the topic is one that invites analysis rather than merely description and that gives rise to a research question which raises sufficient complexities to allow you to present some 'clever' points in your dissertation.

A final factor which is often overlooked is that the topic must be one that you find interesting. Remember that it is a long-term project spanning the entirety of the academic year and you will find it easier to maintain your enthusiasm for your dissertation if the topic is one that you think is interesting. Students who select a topic that is of no interest to them but which they think will present an intellectual challenge and result in a good dissertation tend to struggle to maintain their interest far more than students who were motivated by interest.

Students often find the process of identifying a dissertation topic to be difficult. Have a look at the five stages suggested in Figure 17.2 to help to identify a topic for your dissertation.

You might also find it useful to think about the answers to some of the questions that students are often asked about the choice of dissertation topic.

- **Can my dissertation topic be something that has been covered in lectures and seminars?** There is no reason not to select a topic that was covered in lectures and/or seminars. Many students like to base their dissertations on such topics because they like

1. Make a list of all the subjects that you have studied so far on your degree and cross out those that you disliked, found difficult/dull, or that you simply do not want to revisit for a dissertation topic.	SUBJECTS STUDIED ~~English Legal Systems~~ ~~Land Law~~ ~~Constitutional Law~~ ~~Contract~~ Criminal Law Family Law Tort ~~European Law~~ Child Law ~~Land Law~~
2. List the subjects that remain in order of preference.	PREFERENCE 1. Family Law 2. Criminal Law 3. Child Law 4. Tort

3. Take the top three subjects and use them as headings. List up to four topics that you can remember enjoying from those subjects.	FAMILY	CRIMINAL	CHILD
	1 Domestic violence 2 Adoption 3 Cohabitants 4 Void marriages	1 Loss of control 2 Insanity 3 Necessity	1 Abortion 2 Right to know one's parents 3 Adoption

4. Create three columns: keep, consider, and discard. Allocate each of the topics that you have listed to one of these columns.	KEEP	CONSIDER	DISCARD
	1 Adoption 2 Right to know one's parents 3 Loss of control	1 Necessity 2 Abortion 3 Cohabitants	1 Void marriages 2 Insanity 3 Domestic violence

5. Take each of the topics listed under 'keep' and conduct some preliminary searches to identify issues that could be the focus for your dissertation.	POSSIBLE DISSERTATION TOPICS 1. Reversal of adoption: see current case in news. 2. Assessing suitability of adoptive parents: FLR article. 3. Children of rapists – too harmful to know? 4. Knowing parents after adoption – links with adoption case. 5. Battered women who kill. 6. Loss of control and sexual infidelity.

Figure 17.2 Stages in selecting a dissertation topic

the fact that they have already got a grasp of the subject matter which gives them a foundation of knowledge upon which to build. The other advantages of choosing topics that have been taught are that there will be at least one lecturer, and more if the topic was taught as part of a core subject, who has sufficient expertise to supervise your dissertation and there is likely to be a good range of source materials available in the library. The disadvantage of choosing such a topic is that you will need to move quite a way beyond the points covered on the syllabus in order to demonstrate your research skills. The best way forward is to put some sort of slant on the topic that takes you beyond the issues that were covered on your course. For example, if you are interested in adoption, have a look at the literature on the topic to see if you can find an interesting issue about adoption that was not covered in the syllabus.

- **Several other students want to write their dissertations on my topic—does that mean that I can't do it?** There are certain topics that are so popular that several students each year want to focus upon them. This does not mean that you cannot be one of them but you have to be aware that you are in competition for resources and that there is a certain extent to which you will be measured to see which of you produces the best dissertation (wider research, more depth of analysis, better written style). Try to avoid a direct comparison by adapting your chosen topic in some way that will make it different to the other dissertations: for example, domestic violence is always a popular choice so try a variant of this such as (1) male victims of domestic violence, (2) domestic violence in same-sex relationships, or (3) the impact of domestic violence on children.

- **Can I research something that isn't covered on the law syllabus at my university?** There are always one or two students each year who have a really original idea for a dissertation topic. Some universities place restrictions on novel dissertation topics, recognizing that students can come to grief if there is no supervisor available who can provide guidance on the subject matter, whilst other universities take the view that the supervisor's role is to guide the process of the dissertation rather than to check the accuracy of its content so it is immaterial whether or not they have expertise in the topic. If you want to research something a bit different, try approaching a few lecturers to seek their views on whether it is a good idea and whether they would be able to supervise you. You might find that your topic is a different slant to one of their existing areas of expertise or that you have provoked their interest so much that they are prepared to supervise outside their immediate area of expertise. For example, one of the most interesting dissertations supervised by one of the authors was on the topic of the legal regulation of spiritualist mediums: an original topic that made a fascinating dissertation.

- **Is it a problem that my subject matter covers a lot of different areas of law?** No, it is not a problem at all; in fact, it can be a really good way to demonstrate that you understand the way that different areas of law work together. There are also sorts of legal issues that do not fall neatly into just one of the subject areas that are taught on the law degree. Perhaps you want to look at why conviction rates are so low in rape cases. This would involve looking at the definition of rape (criminal law), the trial process (criminal justice), and the use of previous sexual history evidence (criminal evidence). These are all part of the criminal 'family' of subjects, but perhaps you are looking at an issue that brings together more different areas of law such as family law and criminal law if you are looking at the way in which the law manages allegations of sexual abuse.

17.2.2 Formulating a research question

In chapter 14, it was suggested that you will produce an essay with a stronger focus if you concentrate on what the essay question *asks* rather than the broader issue of what the essay is *about* and that same distinction can be made in relation to dissertations. Your dissertation is *about* whatever the topic is that you have chosen but you should also *ask* a question that your dissertation sets out to answer. This will help you to work with a purpose because you will know that each chapter, each section, and each paragraph is contributing to enabling you to answer the research question that you have posed.

It might help you to appreciate the importance of the 'asks/about' distinction if you view your dissertation in the same way that it is viewed in the more science-based disciplines. Research in the sciences is very much a two-stage process: first there is an experience that tests a hypothesis and this is followed by writing up the findings of that experimental process. In other words, their research asks a question which they answer with an experiment and write up their findings in their dissertation. For law students, there is no experiment but you do carry out an investigation by researching what the literature says in order to answer your research question. In law, a great deal of research tends to answer a variant of one of the following questions:

- Does the law on a particular topic achieve its purpose?
- Should the law regulate a particular situation?
- Is the law in operation fair to all those to whom it applies?

If you ask a question, finding the answer to that question becomes the focus of your investigation (the research stage of the dissertation). It should also make the writing stage easier as your introduction will outline the question and your conclusion will answer the question. Most students find that it is much easier to select material for inclusion and to sift out irrelevant or peripheral material if they are answering a question rather than thinking of their dissertation in terms of its general topic.

Students often find it difficult to formulate a research question but it is really just a matter of rewording your topic into a question: for example, if you were interested in male victims of domestic violence, you might want to ask 'does the law protect male victims of domestic violence as effectively as it protects female victims?' or 'does the law on domestic violence offer equal protection to male and female victims?'.

Practical exercise

Imagine that the following statements have been made by students about their dissertation topics. How could they be reformulated as research questions?

1. I want to look at the spread of CCTV and relate that to the right to privacy.

2. I'm interested in the changes that were made in the law concerning the defendant's right to silence and how it impacts on his right to a fair trial.

3. My dissertation is about sexual infidelity and the defence of loss of control that came in with the Coroners and Justice Act 2009.

Look at www.oup.com/he/finch8e/ to find ways in which these statements could be rephrased as research questions.

17.3 WRITING A DISSERTATION PROPOSAL

Not all universities require that students submit a full dissertation proposal as part of the procedure of signing up to undertake a dissertation: some institutions require nothing more than students stating that they wish to write a dissertation and giving a broad indication of the proposed focus of the dissertation so that they can be allocated a supervisor. However, in some institutions, places to undertake a dissertation are limited and the selection process involves the students submitting a dissertation proposal.

A detailed proposal will require a fair amount of thought, planning, and research. It is possible that your university will have particular requirements in terms of the points to be covered in the dissertation proposal. Make sure you find out whether this is the case and, if so, ensure that you adhere to the requirements of your particular institution. However, if no guidance is provided on the content of the dissertation proposal, you might expect that it covers the following points:

- Identify the focus of the dissertation and state the research question.

- Explain why the topic selected is interesting or why it raises an important question that is worthy of research. This is your justification for wanting to write the dissertation so it is important that you provide some sound rationalization for your choice of topic. For example, perhaps there is some evidence that the law is not working effectively or there is a conflict in case law.

- Outline the literature that has been identified so far or the steps that will be taken to identify relevant literature. This should include reference to the law that governs the dissertation topic so any relevant statute or important case law should be identified. Provide details of any books that you have found, any authors who seem to be specialists on the topic, and any journals that are likely to carry relevant articles. State any steps that you have taken or will take to conduct searches of databases such as Westlaw Edge UK or LexisLibrary (see chapter 4, chapter 6, and chapter 9). Have you considered looking for literature produced by relevant interest groups or specialist Government departments? Are there any websites that seem particularly useful? Remember that you are being asked not just whether useful literature exists but whether you will be able to get hold of it because this will determine whether or not the research is viable. State whether the material is held in your own university library or, if not, whether you can travel to another university to access it or order it on inter-library loan. If you are planning to access electronic journals, make sure that they are ones to which your university subscribes otherwise you will only be able to access the abstract and not the full article.

- Provide a preliminary indication of how the dissertation might be organized in terms of the number and content of chapters. This is only an indication of a possible structure to establish that you have thought about how your material could be organized; you will not be expected to stick to this precise structure in the final version of your dissertation. It is usually the case that a planned structure changes once your research discovers points that you had not initially realized would be in your dissertation or once the writing is under way and you start to think about how the various strands of your argument fit together.

You will find an example of a dissertation proposal that deals with these points in Figure 17.3. This is only an illustration: remember, it is important to find out what points your own institution expects to be covered in the proposal and what its requirements are in terms of factors such as the length of the proposal and level of detail to be provided about source material.

DISSERTATION PROPOSAL

'A final decision? Should a child's biological parents be able to apply for the reversal of an adoption order?'

Research Question

It is a well-established principle of family law that an adoption order creates a new and final family relationship that places the adoptive parents in the same legal position as the biological parents of a child. This could cause problems if there was some flaw in the adoption process. This dissertation will consider whether there are, or should be, circumstances in which the biological parents of a child who has been made the subject of an adoption order can seek to reverse that order thus restoring the rights of the biological parents. The question that will be addressed at the heart of this dissertation is 'should an adoption order always be final?'.

The Importantance of the Research

This dissertation poses a question that, until recently, has not been one that has troubled the family courts as the answer has always been a resounding 'yes'. However, there is a current case that seeks to challenge the established position. The crux of the case is that the initial adoption orders were unsound as they were based on allegations against the biological parents which were without foundation. This dissertation will outline the current law on adoption, examining the procedures which have to be followed in order to assess the extent to which they offer scope for incorrect decisions to be made and for children to be adopted against the wishes of their biological parents. It will highlight the policy concerns in relation to the desirability of placing children in a safe, appropriate and permanent family setting but also of ensuring that children are not irretrievably removed from their biological parents without cause. In doing so, this research will address important issues that go to the heart of the law on adoption.

The Literature

The foundation of the law is to be found in statute (Adoption and Children Act 2002) but has been interpreted in case law. The leading case law governing adoption will be identified and examined to extrapolate key principles. Particular attention will be given to the case currently being heard in which the parents are seeking to reverse the adoption order that removed three of their children from their family. Recourse will be had to authoritative works on family law and adoption including *Child Care and Adoption Law* (2006) and *Children, Family Responsibilities and the State* (2008). A literature search will be made to identify articles of relevance. It is anticipated that these are likely to appear in journals such as the *Family Law Review* and the *Journal of Family and Child Law* which are available in the library.

Proposed Structure

Introduction
Chapter 1: the evolution of the law governing the adoption of children
Chapter 2: adoption procedures and the potential for problems to arise
Chapter 3: case study: the application for the reversal of an adoption order
Chapter 4: an evaluation of the law taking into account competing policy considerations
Conclusion

Figure 17.3 Example of a dissertation proposal

17.4 GETTING STARTED

It is likely that the dissertation will be the longest piece of work that you have ever written and that it also has the most distant submission date of any piece of work that you have had to produce. These two things combined can lead to a situation in which students do not feel that there is any rush to get started with their dissertation: the deadline is a long time in the future and it is hard to know where to start with a piece of work of this size. Nevertheless, you have to make a start at some point: if you do not start then you can never finish, and the longer you leave it to get started, the more pressure you will put upon yourself.

For many students, the first step on the dissertation journey is a meeting with your supervisor. Your university might tell you when this has to take place or they may leave it up to you to arrange meetings that are convenient for you both. Try to meet your supervisor as soon as possible as they will be able to help you to break the large task of researching and writing a dissertation down into smaller stages. They will talk to you about the scope of your project and give you advice about research strategies and breaking the dissertation down into chapters.

It is also your opportunity to ask all the questions that you have about the dissertation. Make sure that you ask them all, perhaps covering basic matters, such as the frequency of your meetings and how the supervisory relationship will work in terms of submission of written work and feedback on draft material, as well as more general questions you have about the dissertation itself and the research process. You should come away from the first meeting with a clear sense of what you are doing next and when you need to do it. It will help you to get started if you have specific goals and deadlines so be sure to ask your supervisor to agree these with you if they do not suggest it themselves.

In general, at the beginning of the dissertation process, you should aim to find and read relevant literature. This will help you to become familiar with the issues and arguments that are relevant to your subject matter.

17.5 KEEPING GOING

Think, for a moment, about what you do over the course of a term or a semester or an academic year. Your studies involve a series of activities with deadlines supported by private study (see chapter 10). You have some tasks to complete every week (attend lectures, review your notes, prepare for tutorials) and others a couple of times a term (formative and summative coursework submissions) with one event occurring a fair time after everything else has finished (exams). This gives you a working pattern of constant seminar preparation with intermittent bursts of activity when coursework is due and a final push at the end when exams are looming.

If you are going to write a dissertation, you will need to consider how the process of researching and writing your dissertation will fit into this pattern of work.

Some students decide that the distant deadline of the dissertation means that it can be put aside and not given any thought at all until a couple of weeks before the submission date. This is a very dangerous strategy because so much can go wrong at the last minute: you might be ill; your supervisor might be ill, unavailable, or simply unwilling to cram a year's supervision into a matter of weeks; you may not be able to obtain the source materials that you need; and, most importantly, you are likely to find that you have not left yourself enough time to think about the dissertation and develop your ideas. You should also be conscious that the later you leave your dissertation, the more likely it is that you will be writing it at a time when you should be starting to revise for your exams.

A far more effective approach is to work steadily at the dissertation throughout the time available. This research project is the largest task that you will have to complete during your studies so it makes sense to slice it up into smaller, more manageable chunks and to spread the workload across several months. There are various different ways that you can divide up the work of researching and writing the dissertation that are outlined in the sections that follow. You might also find it useful to revisit the section on managing your time in chapter 10.

17.5.1 Allocate time

One way to ensure that you work steadily is to incorporate your dissertation into your timetable by allocating a certain amount of time to work on it: this might be one hour a week, one day a fortnight, or one weekend a month depending on your other commitments and whether you prefer working in frequent short bursts or less frequent concerted chunks.

Try to be disciplined in sticking to the time that you have allocated. You will probably find that you are more likely to stick to your schedule if you write in your dissertation study periods on your study timetable and regard them as immovable obligations in the same way that you would view tutorials. Of course, you can build in some flexibility as there may be weeks when you find you are too ill to concentrate or that you are overburdened with coursework preparation so that your dissertation has to take a back seat. If this happens, try to make up the missed time so that you do not start to fall behind your schedule.

17.5.2 Establish milestones

Some people find it difficult to commit to a particular time slot on a regular basis and prefer to be more flexible in their working arrangements. If this sounds familiar, try to set yourself milestones to achieve at staged intervals so that you can be sure that you are making steady progress with your dissertation.

It can be useful to have a goal in mind that you plan to achieve each month. Think about the various stages of the dissertation and work out what it is reasonable for you to achieve in a month. This will allow you to take into account that some months will be busier with seminars and coursework than others so you can adjust your dissertation milestones accordingly. You should be specific when creating milestones so that you are clear about what it is that you are trying to achieve. Compare the two examples in Figure 17.4 to see how much more useful a detailed and specific list of milestones will be at helping you to keep on track with your dissertation.

Your university may have a structure of meetings and milestones that have to be met by certain dates; for example:

1. Attend dissertation lecture in Week 2
2. First meeting with supervisor to discuss purpose, aims, and time frame of dissertation (Week 3)
3. Second meeting with supervisor to review progress (Week 10)
4. Third meeting with supervisor to review detailed chapter outline and at least one completed draft chapter (Week 16)
5. Final meeting with supervisor (Week 20)
6. Submission deadline—3 May (Week 24)

DISSERTATION MILESTONES	DISSERTATION MILESTONES
October: research November: research December: research January: plan out chapters February: start writing March: finish writing	October: search databases, Internet and textbooks to create a list of literature. Locate and acquire the literature. Write a preliminary list of chapters. November: Create a plan for each chapter. Continue identifying and acquiring literature. Write a summary of the current law for Chapter 1. December: Two pieces of coursebook due but try to make progress with Chapter 1. Go to British Library to find any missing literature. January: Complete Chapter 1 and make a start on Chapter 2. February: Complete Chapter 2 and Chapter 3. March: Chapter 4 and Introduction and Conclusion. Check references and bibliography. Proofread. Submit by 30th March.

Figure 17.4 General and detailed dissertation milestones

You should make sure that your plan fits in with the specific requirements of your university's dissertation programme. Check your student handbook to see if there are particular milestones and deliverables that you are expected to meet.

17.5.3 Create a 'to-do' list

The problem with allocating time or creating milestones is that they give you things to do at or by a particular time so you might feel despondent if you fail to meet your target. Nothing is more dispiriting than feeling as if you are already falling behind because you missed your second allocated study slot for your dissertation or you failed to meet your first milestone. For this reason, some students prefer to create a 'to-do' list that details all the tasks that need to be done towards the completion of the dissertation.

It can be particularly useful to have a master list that details everything and then separate lists that break this down into smaller sections either task by task (so you would have a 'to-do' list for each chapter) or month by month (or week by week if you prefer; it would give you a shorter list that might feel less daunting). The advantage of having separate lists for each month or chapter is that you can be very specific about the tasks that need to be done which will ensure that you are very clear about what it is that you need to achieve: see Figure 17.5. It is also very satisfying to see tasks crossed off the list or to put a tick by the tasks that have been completed: this is a real visible measure of your progress.

The flexibility that the 'to-do' list gives you can be immensely valuable in ensuring steady progress. If your milestone for the month is 'write Chapter 1' then you put pressure on yourself to achieve this goal. This will make you feel as if you have failed if you find yourself sitting at your computer with a new document and a blank mind. It is also a big and rather daunting goal which can make it hard to get started (see chapter 10 for techniques on recognizing and dealing with procrastination). However, if you have a 'to-do' list that breaks down your

DISSERTATION: THINGS TO DO	THINGS TO DO: OCTOBER
~~Find the statute law on non-fatal offences~~	Find a copy of the Offences against the Person Act 1861 (online or in a statute book)
Identify case law that contains important legal principles in general	
Identify case law thats deals with (a) psychology injury (Chapter 2) and (b) transmission of HIV (Chapter 3)	Search on Westlaw and LexisLibrary for cases decided under section 47, section 20 and section 18
Find any proposals for reform of non-fatals offences: Law Commission, Home Office	Make a list of cases involving (a) psychology injury and (b) transmission of HIV
~~Read leading criminal law textbooks~~	
Search for relevant articles	Print the cases and file them according to section
Create a plan of each chapter with anticipated content	
Create a bibliography file and keep it up to date	Get the leading criminal law textbooks from the library and copy/make notes on their chapters on non-fatal offences
Look for newspaper articles on the issues	
Draft each chapter	
Write each chapter	Note any articles or other materials mentioned in the footnote references of the textbooks
Polish each chapter	
Write introduction	
Write conclusion	Write case summaries for the important cases
Check bibliography and references	
Check the chapters flow into each other	
Proofread	
Submit by 30th March	Email supervisor to arrange a meeting

Figure 17.5 Examples of 'to-do' lists

chapter into a series of smaller tasks or a list for the month then you will be able to see that you have a whole range of other things that you can do that contribute towards your dissertation. As you can see that you are achieving tasks on your list, you will feel that you are making progress. This is important as students who feel positive about their dissertation tend to enjoy working on it even during the tricky stages whereas students who feel that they are making no progress develop a negative view of their dissertation and start trying to avoid it which can lead to a real crisis situation.

Practical exercise

Consider the different approaches adopted by three students to organizing their time. Who do you think is most likely to complete their dissertation on time by following their planned approach? What problems might you expect each of them to encounter? What advice would you give each student?

1. Andrew wants to finish his dissertation in good time so he decides to work on it for two hours every week. He looks at his timetable and sees that Friday afternoon is always free so he decides that Friday between 1.00pm and 3.00pm will be his dissertation time. He sticks to this and feels that he is making steady progress.

2. Bettina decides that the best way to ensure that her dissertation is completed on time is to set herself a deadline each month:

   October: general research, identify and acquire source material

November: write chapter 1

December: write chapter 2

January: write chapter 3

February: write chapter 4

March: write introduction/conclusion, proofread ready for submission

3. Carole makes a 'to-do' list of everything involved in the completion of her dissertation with an estimate of how long it will take her to complete:

Literature search to identify source material: 3 days

Acquiring copies of all material: 2 days

Planning structure of each chapter: 1 day (total 4 days)

Reading material and making notes: 10 days

Writing each draft chapter: 7 days (total 28 days)

Redrafting and polishing each chapter: 2 days (total 8 days)

Writing introduction: 1 day

Writing conclusion: 2 days

Checking referencing and bibliography: 1 day

Proofreading and checking for coherence: 1 day

Go to **www.oup.com/he/finch8e/** *to find out whether the strategies outlined were successful for each of these students and to discover what, if anything, they would have done differently if they were starting a dissertation again.*

17.6 RESEARCHING FOR A DISSERTATION

One of the factors that will determine the success (or otherwise) of your dissertation is the quality of your research and your ability to identify and locate relevant source material. You will find information on searching in electronic databases in chapter 3, chapter 6, and chapter 9 so you might find it useful to refer back to these parts of the book.

The source material that you will want to find will vary according to the subject matter of your dissertation. For example, you would expect to find very different literature in a dissertation on international humanitarian aid than you would in a dissertation on practitioner views on the law relating to euthanasia. You will need to make sure you that you are aware of the type of source material that is appropriate to your subject matter, checking this with your supervisor if you are uncertain.

17.6.1 A wide range of source material

Whatever the focus of your dissertation is, it is essential that you find a wide range of source material to use in your dissertation because you are expected to demonstrate research skills. The person marking your dissertation is not going to be impressed by a 12,000-word dissertation that refers to three textbooks, an article, and two cases!

Remember that a dissertation is a test of your research skills. You will therefore need to find all the 'usual' literature of the law (statute and case law as well as secondary sources such as books and journal articles), but also try to think beyond these sources to find other forms of literature that could contribute to your dissertation:

- **Case commentary.** Many law journals have a commentary section in which experts in a particular field outline and analyse recent developments in case law. These can be really valuable in helping you to understand case law and its implications as well as providing inspiration that will allow you to engage in critical analysis of the case. If you are researching recent developments in the law, case commentaries may be particularly useful as they are published more quickly than articles and books.

- **Monographs and edited collections.** These are books about the law that are more specialist and often more complex than textbooks. Monographs are detailed explorations of a specialist subject whereas edited collections are books that deal with a particular area of law but which are composed of different contributions from a range of authors. Either of these provide a good source of material for a dissertation as they take a much closer look at a topic than a textbook. Be aware, though, that it can be difficult to find chapters in edited collections because catalogues tend to use the main title of the book rather than list the individual contributions, but footnotes in textbooks or articles might help you to find relevant chapters or you could try searching Google Books.

- **Newspaper articles.** Although they are not academic sources, newspapers can provide information that might be relevant to your dissertation that is not covered elsewhere, especially if you are researching a particularly newsworthy topic. News coverage can give you an insight into public perceptions of the law and it is sometimes a good source of information about first instance court decisions that are not reported anywhere else. For example, very few of the early decisions on corporate manslaughter were appealed so the only place you would find coverage of them is in the newspapers. You can also use newspaper coverage to show you how views on a particular issue have changed over the years by using one of the newspaper databases such as Nexis.

- **Interest group reports.** Specialist groups often carry out their own research and produce their own literature which can give detailed information about a topic, albeit from a particular perspective. It is important to remember that interest groups are advocating a particular position so their literature may not be objective but it may still play a valuable role in your dissertation; just remember to try and find other material that balances the argument. For example, if you were writing a dissertation about the fox-hunting ban, you would want to look at reports created by the Campaign for Rural England as well as the information on the League against Cruel Sports website.

- **Blog posts.** You will find a great deal of commentary about the law online and, although it can be of variable quality, the blogs written by practitioners on the pages of law firms or barristers chambers offer an excellent insight into developments in the law, sometimes written by the lawyers who were involved in the case themselves.

- *Hansard.* There are many circumstances in which you might want to know what Parliament discussed when they introduced a new Act of Parliament (or considered introducing it if the Bill did not make it into the statute books), and you will find all the Parliamentary debates from the House of Lords and the House of Commons in *Hansard*. It can be really useful in helping you to understand what Parliament intended a piece of legislation to achieve when it was introduced or to gain insight into the problems that they anticipated with the law. The real value of looking at Parliamentary debates is that you can find out the reasoning behind the legislation and also what was left out of the Act which can be really useful if you are criticizing the effectiveness of the law.

- **Podcasts.** It is interesting that the focus of legal research is almost exclusively on the written word when there is so much good information available in other formats. There are podcasts on a whole range of legal topics, especially those that are of current public interest, often in the form of debates or discussions so that you will hear more than one viewpoint on the subject matter.

- **Literature from other disciplines.** Lawyers are not the only academics who write about the law. Sociologists, criminologists, and political scientists often write about legal issues from their own disciplinary perspective and you could also consider who else would be writing about your topic. For example, if you are researching the legal position on donor organs, it would be reasonable to think that academics in the health-care sciences might be writing about this in their journals.

When you are using some of these less familiar sources, it is even more important to take a moment to check that you have found literature that you can rely upon to support the arguments in your dissertation. You will find information about carrying out a PROMPT analysis in chapter 14 and you should get into the habit of doing this as you conduct your research so that you can make an informed decision about how much weight to put on each piece of literature that you find.

17.6.2 Managing your literature

Your research for your dissertation will generate a lot of literature and it is important that you keep track of what you have read so that you can use it effectively and ensure that it is included in your bibliography. You can do this by recording three separate pieces of information:

- **Keep a list of your literature searches.** It can be easy to lose track of what key words you have used and what databases you have searched especially if it has been several months since you last looked for literature. Making a list of your searches will help you to avoid unnecessary repetition and give you an easy way to repeat searches after a few months to check for new literature. It can also be a way of reassuring yourself that your search has been comprehensive so that you feel that you have not missed any key literature.

- **Organize your notes by chapter or topic.** The dissertation is a big project that spans the whole academic year but most students tend to do a lot of their research and reading at the early stages. It is unrealistic to think that you will remember to come back to a particular point in an article several months down the line when you are writing your second or third chapter so it makes sense to create a system of recording information by chapter or topic. This need only be the name of the article, a page reference, and a quick note of the point that you want to remember. Make sure to differentiate between three different things— quotations from the source, a paraphrase of an idea from the source, and your own thoughts about the source—because this has implications for how you reference (see chapter 13).

- **Create the bibliography as you go.** Far too many students reach the end of the dissertation just before the deadline only to realize that compiling the bibliography takes far longer than they had thought, especially if they have not kept careful note of the full bibliographic details of each source. That frantic scramble to put together a list of everything you have read during the course of the dissertation can be avoided if you get yourself into the habit of adding every new piece of literature as soon as you read it. You will find guidance on how to compile a bibliography according to the OSCOLA referencing system in chapter 13.

17.7 THE WRITING PROCESS

You might find it useful to look at the chapters on writing skills (chapter 11), referencing (chapter 13), and essay writing (chapter 14) as these deal with many of the issues that are important to writing a dissertation.

There are some issues that are specific to dissertation writing and these are dealt with below by identifying some of the common problems experienced by students. You will find suggestions on how to overcome or, better still, prevent these problems arising in the first place.

- **I've done all my research but I haven't started writing yet.** Some students get really immersed in the research process and are determined to track down every piece of information on their topic before they start writing. Thorough research is important but it is counterproductive if you do not leave yourself sufficient time to dedicate to the writing process. Avoid this problem by starting to write at an early stage of your dissertation so that you combine the research and writing processes.

- **I don't know when to start writing.** Start writing as soon as possible: the longer you delay, the harder it is to start. You do not have to complete your research for the first chapter in order to start writing it. Select something that you know is going to appear in your dissertation at some point—a summary of the current law is always a good choice—and write it. You will feel better once you have made a start on writing and it is something that you can show to your supervisor so that they can check whether your written style and approach to referencing are appropriate.

- **I don't know how to break my dissertation down into chapters.** This is something that puzzles many students. They have a clear picture of the material that needs to be in their dissertation but find it difficult to divide this into chapters. This is often something that you need to discuss with your supervisor because each dissertation topic would break down in a different way so generic advice could be misleading. However, one technique that you can use is to look at your research question and try to break it down into three or four smaller questions. For example, if you look at Figure 17.5 you will see the 'to-do' lists for a dissertation that asks the question 'is the Offences against the Person Act 1861 able to deal with modern manifestations of harm or is the law in need of reform?'. This could be broken down by asking three questions: 'what is the law?', 'what situations have given rise to problems with the law?', and 'how could the law be reformed to overcome the problems?'. This then breaks down into chapters as follows: (1) an outline of the law and identification of three problem areas, (2) first problem area: consensual harm caused for the purposes of sexual gratification, (3) second problem area: psychological injury, (4) third problem area: transmission of HIV, and (5) proposals for reform.

- **I don't know what order the chapters should come in.** This is usually less of a problem once you have worked out what content goes in each chapter (as discussed in the previous bullet point). Once the content is decided, sum up the purpose of the chapter in one sentence and then look at these sentences to see what order you would put them in if you were putting together a paragraph to describe your dissertation.

- **I have to write an abstract but I don't know what it is or how to do it.** An abstract is a short summary of your dissertation that identifies the research question, why it is important, and how you set about addressing it. It is the part of the dissertation that somebody would read to see if your work was interesting or relevant to them. It is a good idea to make it sound interesting so start with an attention-grabbing sentence. For example, you could start by saying 'this dissertation will explore some of the problem areas that suggest that the Offences against the Person Act 1861 is not able to deal with modern instances of harm', but that is rather bland compared to 'Anthony Burstow harassed a female work colleague for seven years, causing her to develop a serious psychological disorder, before the House of Lords finally concluded his conduct was a contravention of the criminal law'.

- **I've found so much literature that I can't keep track of it.** This is a serious problem because you will be expected to provide references for all your literature and a comprehensive bibliography. The best way to deal with this is start a document called 'bibliography' on the very first day that you start your dissertation and make sure that you enter every book, article, website, and other source material into it (with full details including the date of access if you are referring to web materials) as soon as you find it. This will help you to keep track of your material and will mean that your bibliography is being constructed as you go which will save you the last-minute panic of trying to find all your references.

- **I don't know whether or not to use subheadings in my chapters.** With a piece of work of this length, it is permissible to use headings and subheadings *provided the rules relating to dissertations at your university do not prohibit this*. Remember, though, headings are no substitute for structure and do not relieve you of the need to signpost your argument so use headings with care.

- **I'm worried that there will be mistakes in my dissertation.** If there are mistakes regarding the law, this could be a serious problem that affects the mark that your dissertation receives. Avoid problems here by checking that your law is up to date and make sure that you puzzle out issues that are unclear rather than simply ignoring them and hoping that the marker will not notice. Mistakes in writing and referencing can also affect your mark. Make sure that you leave yourself time to proofread your dissertation, preferably a few days before the deadline so that you have time to correct any problems that you spot. It can be hard to notice your own errors so you might find it useful to offer to swap with another student and proofread for each other. Careless errors suggest lack of care so it is worth taking the time to make sure that your work is perfect before it is submitted.

17.8 WORKING WITH YOUR SUPERVISOR

One of the things that is different about the dissertation module compared to all the other modules that you will study is the way that you work with your supervisor. Each university will vary according to the timetable it sets for the frequency and timing of supervisory meetings and these may be interspersed with group sessions on research skills, but all dissertations will involve some one-to-one meetings where you discuss your plans and progress with your supervisor and receive feedback and guidance in return. It is generally the case, however, that supervisors do not have very much input into the decision-making process about the content and direction of the dissertation; making these decisions is part of the skills set that the dissertation aims to help students develop and so there is an expectation that students will make these decisions for themselves.

Sometimes students find this level of freedom worrying and want more specific guidance from their supervisor and problems can arise if the student does not feel able to ask for this or if they ask for it and find that it is still not available. In fact, one of the commonest problems that occurs within the dissertation module arises from a disparity between the help that students want and the help that the supervisor is prepared to provide. One of the ways to resolve this problem or, better still, to prevent it from occurring in the first place is to have a discussion with the supervisor in the first meeting about what you can expect from each other.

Understanding expectations is a key part of a successful relationship between student and supervisor so make sure that you check any guidance provided by the university, perhaps in the module handbook, about what specifications there are about what the supervisor can do. For example, some universities limit the number of meetings whilst others restrict how much draft material a supervisor can read. Knowing the rules and working within them will help you to understand what you can expect from your supervisor.

If your university leaves it down to the supervisor and student to agree how they will work together, then it would be worth having a discussion about how the supervision will work. This might include:

- How many meetings will there be and when will they take place?
- What sort of help will they be able to give you? And what can they not do?

- How much, if any, of your draft work will they read?
- Are there any periods when they will be unavailable?
- Do they want you to submit work in advance of every meeting so that they can track your progress?
- Can you contact them in between meetings if you get into difficulties?

It may be that your supervisor will set out these matters as part of your first meeting but be prepared to take the lead and ask them how the supervisory relationship will work if they do not mention it. The dissertation is designed to help you develop all the skills that you need to carry out independent research and that includes managing your relationships with the other people involved in the project so you should be prepared to take the lead in finding out what your supervisor expects from you and what you can expect from them.

One of the issues that sometimes arises, though, is that each supervisor has their own preferences when it comes to working with students on a dissertation and this may well mean that there is a lack of uniformity to how supervision works in your law school. Students tend to compare experiences with each other and it can be frustrating if it seems that other students are getting more support from their supervisor than you are getting from yours. Think for a minute about how you would handle this. Obviously, you would not want to miss out on any help that is available but would you be comfortable raising it with your supervisor? If so, how would you go about it? Here are some thoughts about that situation that might help you to decide:

- Do you need the help that you think has been given to another student? It might be, for example, that another student's supervisor reads and corrects all their work but maybe your supervisor is not doing that because there is no problem with the way that you are writing.
- If you do feel that you need or would like something that another student seems to have then the only way to get this is to ask your supervisor for it. A simple enquiry as to whether they will be able to help you in a particular way will suffice; there is no need to point out that other supervisors are doing it—'I wondered if you would read my chapter and give me some feedback on my written style' is probably a better approach than 'other supervisors are reading draft chapters and giving feedback so I'd like you to do that for me'. You can make your request in an email if this feels more comfortable for you than doing it face to face.
- If your supervisor does not agree to do something that other supervisors seem to be doing then your first step should be to check whether it is something that they are required to do. Most universities set out minimum standards for dissertation supervision—at least four meetings, feedback on at least one chapter, and so on—and if these minimum standards have been met and your supervisor is not happy to go beyond them then unfortunately there is little more to be done. If you are really unhappy then you could email your supervisor again and try to explain why you would value a particular sort of assistance and ask if they can suggest any other ways that you could get this help if they are unable to give it to you.

17.9 PUTTING IT ALL TOGETHER

You should aim to complete your dissertation at least a week before the deadline to make sure that you have time to do a thorough proofread and to check that all your references are complete and accurate. It is also a good idea to read it though from start to finish a few times to make sure that all the chapters link together well and you can see a clear line of logical argument running through the dissertation. You will also need to be sure that you have left enough time to get your dissertation printed and bound if this is a requirement at your university.

CHAPTER SUMMARY

Dissertation topic and research question

- Select several alternative topics that you would like to research and conduct some preliminary research to identify what could form the basis of your dissertation

- Make sure that you select a topic that you find interesting as you will be working on it for a significant period of time

- Once you have decided on a topic, formulate a question that needs to be answered that can form the basis of your dissertation

Writing a dissertation proposal

- If you have to write a dissertation proposal, find out if your university stipulates how long this must be, what level of detail is required, and whether there are any particular issues that need to be addressed within the proposal

- If there are no guidelines on writing a proposal, it would be sensible to cover (1) the research question, (2) the importance of the research, (3) what literature you have found or where you plan to look for literature, and (4) a preliminary indication of how the dissertation will break down into chapters

Planning and organization

- Plan to work on your dissertation steadily in the time available rather than leaving it until a few weeks before the submission deadline to make a start

- Consider different ways to divide up the work of researching and writing the dissertation and adopt one (or adapt one) to suit your own study preferences

- Try to combine researching and writing as much as possible rather than seeing them as two separate stages of the dissertation process

Research

- Thorough research is the backbone of your dissertation. Remember that you are trying to impress your marker with the breadth and depth of your research

- Treat the research process as an investigation and do not be afraid to move beyond the sources of information that you would normally use in an essay. The dissertation gives you the scope to take a broader view of your topic so ensure that you make the most of this by using a wide range of resources

- Make sure that you know how to reference the materials that you are finding and keep a complete and accurate record of all sources to ensure that you can compile a comprehensive bibliography

Writing

- Refer to the chapters on writing skills, referencing, and essay writing to ensure that you have a thorough understanding of the requirements of good academic writing

- Start writing as soon as you can; it gets harder to start the longer you leave it

- Do not panic if you cannot think of how to start a chapter. If writing a whole chapter at once seems daunting, carve a section out of it that you know will be there and write that instead. A summary of the current law or an important case is a good starting point

- Leave yourself time to proofread your dissertation to ensure that your work is free of errors

PART III
Practical legal skills

This final part of the book covers some practical legal skills: namely presentations, mooting, and negotiation. These will help you move beyond online and written study to give you a broader range of real-life legal skills. The first chapter in this part will give you the skills you need in order to prepare and deliver an effective oral presentation, covering the issues of content as well as those relating to timing, combating nerves, and engaging the interest of your audience. Chapter 19 moves on to discuss mooting, which offers unparalleled opportunities for the development of the skills associated with the delivery of a comprehensive and persuasive oral argument as well as providing an opportunity to develop your research skills and enhance your ability to construct and organize a coherent legal argument. Finally, this part will conclude with an introduction to negotiation in chapter 20, which will give you an opportunity to develop a feel for how the law operates in practice and how it affects the lives of real people.

Presentation skills

18

INTRODUCTION

In some respects, a presentation could be said to be the oral equivalent of an essay or a research report: it is a way of disseminating the findings of a piece of research into a particular topic. Of course, the crucial distinguishing factor is that a presentation is delivered to a larger audience and the oral nature of the communication requires a different skill set to a piece of written work. This chapter will discuss the stages of preparation for a presentation such as selecting a topic and making decisions about the use of supplementary materials, particularly slides. The chapter will then move on to consider issues relating to the actual delivery of the presentation including matters such as timing, combating nerves, and engaging the interest of the audience.

Many students are reluctant to give an oral presentation. This is entirely natural; an oral presentation focuses the attention of many people on a single person which makes it a very nerve-wracking situation even for otherwise confident students. However, the ability to present information orally is important in many professions so it is a valuable skill to develop. Like anything else, the prospect of giving a presentation is daunting only until you know that you can do it proficiently. Many people are not natural speakers and will quail at the thought of addressing even a small audience but the fear does recede with practise so the experience would be extremely valuable. This is particularly important given the growing tendency amongst prospective employers to require a presentation from job applicants. This chapter aims to equip you to prepare and deliver an easy-to-follow and engaging presentation.

Learning outcomes

After studying this chapter, you will be able to:

- Select an appropriate topic that fits within the constraints of your course
- Conduct effective research into your presentation topic
- Construct an organized and flowing presentation
- Prepare some appropriate visual aids and use them effectively
- Understand the importance of practising the presentation
- Deal with common problems associated with nerves
- Deliver a comprehensive and engaging presentation
- Take questions from the audience with confidence
- Reflect upon your performance in order to strengthen future presentations

18.1 THE PRESENTATION PROCESS

For most people faced with the need to give a presentation, the focus is on the actual delivery of the material. It is usual to think of 'the presentation' as the time-slot in which the material is communicated to the audience. Whilst this is clearly an important time, most of the work required for an effective presentation will be complete before you get to your feet in front of your audience. Planning and preparation are essential prerequisites of a good presentation and yet this 'behind the scenes' activity tends to receive very little attention.

Most students accept that they have to do *something* before standing up and speaking but there seems to be general uncertainty as to what form this preparation might take and how exactly it prepares you to speak for the required amount of time. The central problem seems to be that students omit an essential stage of presentation preparation treating it as a two-stage process as shown in Figure 18.1.

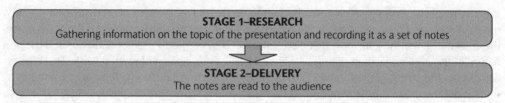

Figure 18.1 Two-stage presentation process

Although this approach does serve the purpose of transmitting the information to the audience, this is not necessarily packaged in a particularly palatable form. In fact, many student presentations are extremely boring because of the way in which the material is delivered: listening to someone read their notes for ten minutes is not in the least engaging for the audience and it can be very off-putting for the presenter to look around and see distracted and bored faces. To overcome these problems, it is valuable to insert a further stage in between research and delivery as shown in Figure 18.2.

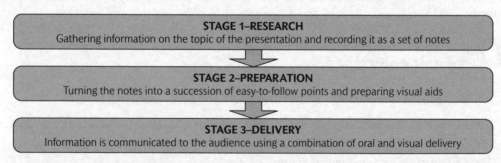

Figure 18.2 Three-stage presentation process

As you will see, by inserting a middle step in the process, the end stage is also different and the presentation is far more engaging for the audience as a result.

It is important to consider a fourth stage that takes place after the presentation is complete: see Figure 18.3.

| STAGE 4–REFLECTION |
| Critical evaluation of the performance in order to improve future presentations |

Figure 18.3 The reflection stage

This stage involves a period of review in which the presenter takes stock of the way in which the presentation was received and seeks to identify examples of good and bad practice. The reflection stage maximizes the learning impact of the presentation and should enable you to strengthen future performances.

Each of these stages will now be considered in turn to guide you through the process of preparing, constructing, and delivering a presentation as well as providing comment on the reflection stage.

18.2 THE RESEARCH STAGE

It is always tempting to see the delivery of the presentation—the end product—as being of primary importance. After all, it is the delivery of the presentation that seems to determine its success (or, if it does not go well, its lack of success), irrespective of whether success is measured in terms of the response of the audience or, in the case of an assessed presentation, the mark awarded. However, an effective end product is only possible if the groundwork has been done properly. We will start by addressing two of the important preliminary issues: topic choice and the research process.

18.2.1 Choosing a topic

In some instances, particularly if the presentation is part of assessed coursework or is a compulsory non-assessed part of a course, the topic of the presentation will be allocated to you. Although this gives you no scope to choose your subject matter, it does ensure that you have a workable presentation topic which gives you a clear direction for your research. This means the topic 'fits' within the time allocated (or is capable of fitting within it), that there is sufficient material available for you to research the topic, and that it is sufficiently linked to the relevant course material.

In the absence of a predetermined topic, you will have to choose an area of law upon which to base your presentation. This can be a tricky business as the success or otherwise of your presentation may depend upon the choice of subject matter, so give it some serious thought and take the following factors into account.

18.2.1.1 How long is the presentation?

Many presentations are spoilt by content overload as the presenter tries to cram too much material into the time available. The opposite problem arises if a topic is too narrow for the time available; here, the presenter ends up running out of things to say and having to fall back on repetition to fill the time available. Avoid these problems by selecting a topic that can be covered within the time available: obviously, more detail is expected in a forty-five-minute presentation than is the case in a ten-minute slot at the start of a tutorial.

18.2.1.2 What are the assessment criteria?

If the presentation is assessed, you should check the assessment criteria to discover what attributes are regarded as important to ensure that you select a topic that allows you to cover all the relevant skills. For example, it is usual for credit to be given for independent research so this might steer you away from topics that are covered in detail in textbooks. It may help to make a list of the desirable characteristics of a successful presentation from the assessment criteria and note how your topic will satisfy these characteristics.

18.2.1.3 What is your aim?

If you have been given a title, what does it suggest about the aim of your presentation? Is it to introduce the topic, to give an overview, or to deal with a particular issue in depth? If you are unclear, seek clarification from your course materials or by asking your lecturer. If you have free rein to select your own topic, it will add focus to your presentation and make the preparation process easier if you identify a clear aim to be achieved by your presentation. Are you going to pose a question and then answer it for your audience? Try to make sure that your presentation has a purpose and make sure that this is communicated to the audience at the outset.

18.2.1.4 Who are your audience?

It is likely that you will have your own aims in mind when delivering a presentation such as obtaining a good mark, not looking foolish in front of your friends, or impressing a prospective employer, but the predominant aim of any presentation is to communicate something of value to the audience. In order to achieve this, you need to have some idea of what the audience wants, needs, or expects from your presentation. In other words, in order to choose an appropriate topic and select content at a suitable level, you need to understand how much your audience already knows about the subject matter.

As the person organizing the presentation, what level of prior knowledge can you assume is possessed by your audience? If you are presenting to other students, are you supposed to treat them as law undergraduates or are you to treat them as some other audience who either has less or more advanced knowledge?

For example, some lecturers create hypothetical scenarios to encourage you to pitch your presentation at a particular level. You might be told that your presentation is to a group of GCSE students so you would need to ensure that you provided simple explanations of basic principles that you would not need to explain at all to fellow law students. Conversely, you might be told to imagine that you are trying to convince the Law Commission to adopt a particular change in the law in which case you would need to demonstrate how your proposals addressed a deficiency you identified in the existing legal framework.

18.2.1.5 What material is available?

The most brilliant presentation topic will only become a brilliant presentation if there is sufficient source material to enable you to research and prepare the topic thoroughly. You must be able to identify a range of source books, articles, cases, and reports on your chosen topic and be able to obtain them in good time to prepare for your presentation. The ever-increasing availability and depth of online resources may help here, but remember the importance of ensuring that material that you encounter online comes from a reputable academic or professional source.

You will find some valuable guidance on evaluating the source of online materials in chapter 8. Remember that anyone can post anything on the internet so you should not rely on material for academic purposes unless it comes from a reputable source.

18.2.1.6 Is the topic interesting?

If you have free choice, it is also useful to take into account any interests of your own within the subject as it is always easier to research something that interests you and your enthusiasm for the topic will communicate to the audience, making your presentation more engaging.

You should also consider whether the topic will be interesting for your audience. One important factor to take into account here is whether other students have also presented on the same topic. It will be more challenging for you to engage and hold the audience's interest if they have already heard ten presentations on the same subject matter. It is not impossible, of course, as you might find a different way of exploring the same topic but you should bear in mind that replicating a topic that has already been covered by others carries a risk that your presentation will seem uninteresting and uninspired to the audience even if it is actually the result of a great deal of hard work and independent research.

18.2.2 Researching the topic

Once you have an idea of a topic that could form the focus of your presentation, you can start to carry out your research. The process of identifying and locating books, articles, and other sources for a presentation is no different to that which is involved in any other piece of work in law so chapter 3, chapter 6, and chapter 9 of this book on finding legislation, case law, books, journals, and official publications will definitely be useful here.

There are some general points to consider:

- **Start early**. Students often leave insufficient time to carry out research for a presentation, perhaps because a presentation feels like a much smaller piece of work than a 2,000-word essay. However, even a ten-minute presentation can contain a lot of material and requires a great deal of detailed research so be sure that you give yourself enough time to research your topic thoroughly.

- **Be focused yet flexible**. Achieve a good balance between keeping your focus and being receptive to new material that may alter your presentation topic. Do not stick rigidly to your original topic (unless you have to) if you find a more interesting or original slant on it. Remember, your original choice of topic should be the starting point of your research but not necessarily your final destination.

- **Be effective in note-taking**. Remember that there is nothing to be gained from copying large reams of material word-for-word from books and journals unless you plan to use precise quotations in your presentation. Note key points and ensure that you know where to find them. You may find it useful to devise a note-taking strategy that allows you to differentiate between factual information that you find during the course of research and your ideas about how this could be useful in your research, perhaps by dividing your notes into two columns or by using different fonts or colours.

- **Keep a list of all your sources**. Although you are presenting material orally, you may still need to provide a bibliography to demonstrate the extent of your research to your lecturer or to detail further reading for your audience.

- **Consider how points will be presented**. Your presentation should be a combination of oral and visual communication. When you are carrying out your research, bear this in mind and think about the best way to present information. Can you use a graph to depict complex information that you then supplement with an oral explanation? Can you use video or sound clips? Will a picture help to demonstrate your point? Make sure that you cast your net widely when carrying out your research to ensure that you have access to all the possible types of sources that you need to create an engaging presentation.

- **Stop researching in good time.** Remember that you are engaged in a three-stage process: research, preparation, and presentation. You need to leave sufficient time to take the material that you have found and prepare a presentation with it. This takes time and it will need refinement. Moreover, you may find, once you start to put your presentation together, that you need to come back and do a little more research.

18.3 THE PREPARATION STAGE

Once you have conducted your research into your presentation topic, you will probably feel somewhat overwhelmed (a) by the volume of material that you have gathered and (b) by the prospect of turning it into a presentation. This is not unusual. However, this situation can result in two of the key limitations on the effectiveness of student presentations:

- Trying to cover too much information in the time available
- Reading from a set of notes that are not suited to oral delivery.

Both of these problems can be avoided by judicious selection of material and by planning a structured presentation that is not exclusively reliant on oral delivery but which makes effective use of visual aids.

18.3.1 Creating a presentation

If you think about the best and worst presentations that you have attended, you should realize that a good presentation tells a story and the worst are dull and rambling. Your presentation should tell a story from start to finish and keep focused on that story throughout. You have to present complex information to your audience so it is essential that it flows in a logical order and does not divert off into tributaries of interesting yet irrelevant detail. You can do this by taking care with the selection and organization of your material.

18.3.1.1 Selection of material

It is always tempting, having devoted time and effort to conducting research, to try to make use of all the interesting facts that you have discovered. However, it is important to ensure that you do not exceed the time allocated for your presentation: in fact, if the presentation is assessed, you may actually lose marks for failing to work within the time frame stipulated. Equally, a hurried presentation that skims over a great deal of material is very difficult for the audience to follow and is likely to be a negative factor if your presentation is assessed.

Formulating a question that you will answer in your presentation is a good way to identify your focus and select relevant material as it tends to identify the 'job' that the presentation is trying to do. Once you are clear about what you are trying to achieve, you can sift through all the material that you have gathered to eliminate that which is not relevant. As with essay writing, remember to judge the relevance of material in relation to the issue not the topic:

in other words, try not to think 'is this about the partial defence of loss of control?' or even 'is this about the characteristics of the defendant in the partial defence of loss of control?' but rather 'does this help me to explain the policy of the law in formulating the characteristics attributable to the person to whom the defendant is compared in the partial defence of loss of control?'. The more specific you are in framing your issue, the easier you will find it to decide whether material is relevant.

Practical exercise

Try the following technique to help you to determine the relevance of material to your presentation.

1. Write the title of your presentation at the top of a blank piece of paper (or at the start of a new document if you are typing).

2. Make a list of all the points that you found during the course of your research that you could include in your presentation.

3. Once it is complete, review the list. Group similar points together and eliminate any repetition or overlap.

4. Draw three columns headed 'essential', 'peripheral', and 'irrelevant' and allocate each of your points to one of these three columns, remembering that relevance is determined by reference to the specific title of your presentation and not to the general topic.

5. Dealing only with the points in the essential column, try to organize them so that they tell a story (there is more on this in section 18.3.1.2). Do you need any of the peripheral points to link the essential points together or to elaborate on them? If you have too much material, repeat the exercise again but this time divide only your essential points into the three columns.

This can be a really effective way of filtering out material that is interesting but which is not really needed in your presentation.

*You will find a worked example of this technique at **www.oup.com/he/finch8e/**. You might find it useful to look at this example and read the accompanying notes to ensure that you have a good understanding of how to select material for your presentation.*

18.3.1.2 Organization of material

Once you have made a preliminary selection of the material to include in the presentation, you need to consider the order in which your points will be made. Bear in mind that your presentation should follow a logical progression; as we keep emphasizing, it should 'tell a story' and, like all good essays, it should have a beginning (introduction), middle (the bulk of the presentation, divided into a series of issues), and end (conclusion), as illustrated in Figure 18.4.

18.3.1.3 Introduction

The introduction should be succinct, clear, and straightforward. It should outline the topic to be discussed, explain the structure and duration of the presentation (including any time at the end for questions), and it should tell the audience why the topic is important and/or interesting. In essence, the introduction should give the audience

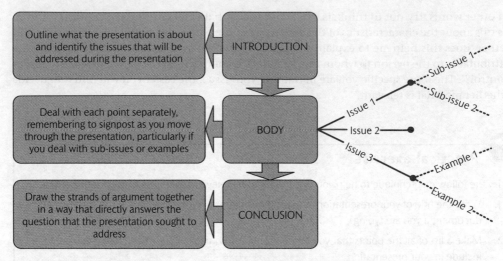

Figure 18.4 Organizing the material

an understanding of what is to follow and give them a clear and concise account of the issue that the presentation will address and the reason that this is important.

🌐 *You will find some further guidance on creating an effective introduction on the online resources at* **www.oup.com/he/finch8e/** *along with some examples of how you would introduce a presentation on a range of different topics.*

18.3.1.4 Main body

The body of the presentation can be more complicated to organize so keep in mind the argument that you are going to advance and break this down into a series of issues and sub-issues. Bear in mind that one point leads into another and that you should take care to select examples that demonstrate the point that you are making and do not distract from the flow of your presentation.

You might want to experiment with more than one potential structure to ensure that you find the most effective way to organize your material. Try making a list of all the points that you want to make and varying this to see which order seems to flow most smoothly. Remember that it is your words that create the flow between points so give some thought to what you will say as well as looking at the order of the points on paper. You could jot down some notes about this but do try to avoid the temptation to write a script. If you write a script, you will read it and that tends to lead to very stilted delivery.

For the audience listening to the presentation, there are two tasks that need to be carried out simultaneously. First, they have to digest the point that you are making and, secondly, they have to slot this into the bigger picture of the topic as a whole. This can be difficult so it is essential that you help your audience to follow the structure of the presentation with clear signposting: phrases that indicate to the listener how each point fits into the overall structure of the presentation, such as:

- The starting point for this discussion is …

- There are three important points here and I shall discuss each in turn. First …

- This is a strong argument but there is a powerful counter-argument that we must now consider.

- In conclusion …

18.3.1.5 Conclusion

The conclusion should provide a brief summary of the material covered and a direct answer to the question addressed in the presentation. Try to think of a way to make the central message of the presentation stick in the mind of the audience by identifying a maximum of three points that you want them to remember and highlighting these.

⊙ *You will find some examples of how you would create a memorable and effective conclusion on the online resources at www.oup.com/he/finch8e/.*

18.3.2 Using visual aids

Research into the psychology of effective communication has indicated that people take in more information from visual images than they do from listening. Therefore, it is a good idea to ensure that your presentation engages the eyes as well as the ears of the audience by using visual aids whether this is in the form of slides, or by writing/drawing on a whiteboard or flip-chart as the presentation progresses.

Effective use of visual aids can achieve the four objectives shown in Figure 18.5.

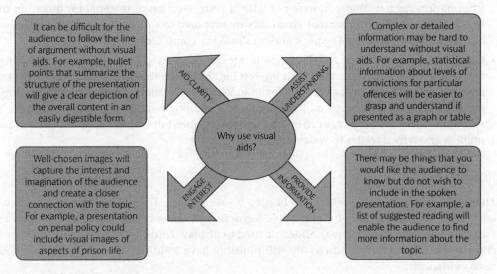

It can be difficult for the audience to follow the line of argument without visual aids. For example, bullet points that summarize the structure of the presentation will give a clear depiction of the overall content in an easily digestible form.

Complex or detailed information may be hard to understand without visual aids. For example, statistical information about levels of convictions for particular offences will be easier to grasp and understand if presented as a graph or table.

Well-chosen images will capture the interest and imagination of the audience and create a closer connection with the topic. For example, a presentation on penal policy could include visual images of aspects of prison life.

There may be things that you would like the audience to know but do not wish to include in the spoken presentation. For example, a list of suggested reading will enable the audience to find more information about the topic.

AID CLARITY • ASSIST UNDERSTANDING • ENGAGE INTEREST • PROVIDE INFORMATION

Why use visual aids?

Figure 18.5 Effective use of visual aids

Although there are clear benefits to using visual aids, there are some pitfalls associated with their use that can cause difficulties and may distract or disengage the audience. Follow these tips to help you to avoid these problems when producing visual aids:

• **Take care with their production.** Shoddy and ill-prepared visual aids give a negative impression to the audience so make sure that your visual aids look like they are the product of care and effort rather than something that was thrown together at the last minute.

• **Make sure you can use the technology.** If you are going to use slides, you must make sure you know how to use the technology in the room during your presentation. The overall effect of your presentation will be spoilt if you are constantly having to fiddle with your device to make your slides work.

- **Do not overload visual aids**. A lot of text in a small font is very hard to read. With slides in particular, the audience will be annoyed and feel that they are missing something important if they cannot read them.

- **Be selective in your use of colour**. Just because it is possible to use many different fonts and colours of text does not mean that this is a good idea. Visual aids that are too busy or colourful are not easy for the audience to use. Aim for simple use of colour to enhance the appearance of your visual aids and to assist the audience by perhaps using an accent colour to highlight points of particular importance.

- **Do not read from your visual aids**. If material is provided in written form, the audience can read it for themselves. Reading during your presentation will interfere with the manner of delivery and the audience will wonder why you are bothering to present at all if all the information is written down for them. If you have provided a quotation on a slide do not read it verbatim to the audience: draw their attention to it so that they can read it and then talk about it, perhaps drawing out the important message in it or highlighting part of it that is especially relevant to the part of your story you are telling at that particular time.

- **Do not use visual aids as a dumping ground**. As time is limited, there is a temptation to add all the information that you would like to cover on visual aids. A few additional points or suggestions for follow-up reading is fine but the inclusion of a vast amount of additional information suggests that you were not wise in your selection of material for inclusion in the presentation. Remember that visual aids are supposed to supplement, not replace, your oral presentation and that the presentation should be complete in itself.

- **Choose images with care**. A well-chosen image can be an effective way of communicating with the audience and engaging their interest but make sure that the relationship between any images is either clear or explained to the audience. You want the audience to be listening to you, not wondering why you have displayed a seemingly random picture. Of course, a seemingly incongruous image can be an attention-grabber, but you will need to be very clear on how and why it relates to your story.

18.3.2.1 Slides

There are a number of apps which can be used to create slides. The most commonly encountered are Microsoft PowerPoint and Apple Keynote, but many others are available (such as Prezi, Google Slides, and Canva). Slides are used to display words, images, graphs, and video clips to the audience. Your university will probably have training sessions available if you need guidance.

You should construct a set of slides that reflects the structure of your presentation. In doing so, the following types of slide are likely to feature:

- **Title slide.** This tells the audience who you are and the title of your presentation.

- **Presentation outline.** This should be used during your introduction as you tell the audience what points you are going to cover and in what order.

- **Content slides.** These slides will form the bulk of your presentation. The general rule is that there should be one slide for each major concept or idea that you introduce to the audience. Remember to be relatively sparing with the amount of words used on each slide and keep the font size large: visual aids are not useful if they cannot be read by the audience.

- **Summary slides.** This is the conclusion to your presentation and it should pick out the key points as you explain how they fit together. This can be a single slide or spread over several slides as necessary. Remember that there was a purpose to your presentation—an issue to be explained or a question to be answered—so make sure that your summary deals with this head on.

- **Any questions?** However much you might hope that nobody asks any questions, it is usual to allow the audience an opportunity to do so. In an assessed presentation, it is likely that the lecturer will ask a question even if nobody else does. Of course, you could just invite questions without having an accompanying slide.

When it comes to deciding on the content of your slides, there are a huge numbers of different template offerings with a range of layouts allowing you to incorporate content in a variety of different configurations. Take time to look at what options are available and experiment with different ways of setting out your material to decide on the most appropriate template. You can also create your own template if you wish.

A combination of text and image as illustrated in Figure 18.6 is a commonly used and engaging design for the audience. Notice that the text is limited to key phrases that encapsulate each of the points that you will discuss rather than setting out the point in full. Remember, the purpose of using slides is to make the presentation easier to follow for the audience so cramming on too much text will not achieve this.

Figure 18.6 Slide with text and image

If you have time within your presentation, adding a video or two can break up your slides in a smooth and effective way that will keep your audience more focused and engaged with the overall content. Videos are useful since:

- They engage the audience's attention.
- They allow for a lot of information to be shown in a very short time.
- They are relatively simple to make (or find on YouTube).

However, do not use video as a substitute for doing your job. As a presenter, it is up to you to carry the talk: you should be the main attraction. Remember that playing a video with sound in the middle of your presentation means that you lose the audience and, indeed, become part of it yourself. You need to think carefully about how you will get the audience's attention back to you after the video has played.

Carefully crafted slides should avoid the risk that you will subject your audience to what has become known as 'Death by PowerPoint'. This is a phrase used to describe the boredom and weariness experienced by an audience as a result of information overload during a presentation arising from these common faults:

- Too much detail, especially text, contained on each slide
- Too many slides which are passed through too quickly
- Overuse of distracting features, transitions, motion effects, and animations
- The presenter looking at and talking to the slideshow rather than the audience
- The presenter reading the text of the slides to the audience.

18.3.2.2 Handouts

Handouts used to be an essential accompaniment to every presentation, but their popularity has decreased enormously since the use of slides became widespread. However, you may wish to consider providing a handout to supplement your slides. The advantage that a handout has over a slide is that it is available for constant reference by the audience throughout the presentation whereas information on slides will change as the presentation progresses and one slide replaces another. As such, a handout can be a useful reference guide for the audience as it can help them to understand the structure of the presentation and to see how different points made fit into the overall picture of the presentation. It is more than just a copy of the slideshow.

A further advantage of the handout is that it can be taken away by the audience at the end of the presentation; therefore, it can be a means of ensuring that they are provided with core pieces of information relevant to the presentation, particularly in relation to material where accuracy of wording is important such as definitions, quotations, and statutory provisions. For example, if your presentation topic was corporate crime, you might want to discuss the implications of the Corporate Manslaughter and Corporate Homicide Act 2007, in which case giving the audience the wording of the statute might be useful. If you put this on a slide, it cannot be referred to throughout the presentation or taken away afterwards and if you read it to the audience, they will have to write very quickly to note it all down. The other advantage of a handout, of course, is that the audience can add their own notes during the presentation.

A handout is a guide for the audience and a source of essential information. It should not be overloaded with detail and it should never be a word-for-word copy of your presentation: why would the audience bother to listen to you if you are providing them with a transcript of your presentation? An audience who is paying no attention when you speak is very off-putting for a presenter, so make sure that you use your visual aids to increase engagement with the audience rather than to distract them or give them an excuse not to listen. Remember, visual aids supplement, rather than replace, the spoken word.

18.3.3 Practise

The most important element of the preparation stage is practise. Most people are not used to speaking in public so it is inevitably something that is going to need a little bit of practise.

18.3.3.1 Why practise?

You must practise your presentation several times over to ensure that:

- The presentation fits within the time allocated to it
- The order of the material is appropriate and one point runs smoothly into another

- There are no tricky words or phrases that trip up your tongue
- You familiarize yourself with the appropriate pace at which to speak
- You become accustomed to hearing your own voice
- You know how and when to use any visual aids
- You identify and eliminate any distracting habits.

Many of these points will be more readily addressed if you practise in front of an audience. For example, you may think that your pace of delivery is appropriate but only someone who is listening can tell you whether that is the case. Equally, if you have any odd habits, such as fiddling with a pen or flicking your hair, you are likely to be unaware of this unless it is pointed out to you. Finally, a third party can give you feedback on the most important element of all: whether your presentation makes sense to the audience. If you cannot persuade anyone to watch you practise, find out whether your university has a video suite that you can use to record your practice session so that you can observe yourself in action.

18.3.3.2 What to practise?

Although the obvious answer to this question would seem to be 'the presentation', it is not necessarily useful to devote too much practice time to the actual presentation. There are two separate facets to a good presentation: (1) the subject matter and (2) the presentation style.

Although you will want to practise the actual presentation for the reasons noted in section 18.3.3.1, you should not neglect to practise in order to strengthen your presentation style. Until you are a seasoned public speaker, it might be an idea to practise the two separately, particularly if you are asking an audience of your peers to comment on your presentation as they may get tied up with commenting on the content rather than style.

Practical exercise

The following exercise can be used to help you to practise your presentation style. You will find that it will also help you to work on issues such as the organization of the content of the presentation and incorporating signposting.

1. Choose something that you know extremely well as the topic for a ten-minute presentation. There is no need for it to have any academic merit as the essence of a good presentation is the communication of information irrespective of the nature of that information. Suitable topics could be (1) good places to eat in your home town, (2) favourite sporting activities, or (3) your first term as an undergraduate student.

2. Prepare a presentation on the topic. The idea of the exercise is to evaluate your presentation style but this will not work if you treat it as a free-flow speaking activity in which you spill forth thoughts without structure. Use some of the techniques suggested in this chapter to help you to structure and organize your presentation.

3. Ask a couple of friends to observe your presentation and comment upon your style. Try to emphasize to them that you want honest and constructive feedback: it is much easier for your friends to say 'that was great' as they do not want to upset you so you may need to convince them that you want to hear an objective review of the strengths and weaknesses of your technique. It can help to give them a feedback table and ask them to write comments as they may find this easier than voicing any negative views to you in person.

4.   Make a list of the strengths and weaknesses that your audience noted. Ask them for suggestions as to what they think would improve on areas of weakness. Reflect upon your own experience as a presenter: how did it feel when you were delivering the material? What things would you change in future presentations?

5.   Rework the presentation taking these observations on board and ask your friends to watch it again or present to a different group of friends. The aim is to determine whether you have improved on your previous performance.

You will find some additional tips on signposting at **www.oup.com/he/finch8e/**.

Once you have some general insight into your presentation style, it would be useful to practise the actual presentation to work on issues associated with the content. Remember to practise with the visual aids that you plan to use to make sure that you can use these without interrupting the flow of your presentation.

Having considered the mechanics of putting together a presentation, all that remains is to consider how to deliver it to the audience with clarity and confidence.

18.4 THE DELIVERY STAGE

This is the stage of the process that you probably think of as *the* presentation. Having followed the steps outlined in relation to preparation, you should have a presentation in a clear and accessible form which is supplemented by carefully constructed visual aids. This section will go through some of the factors which will influence the success of the actual delivery of the presentation.

18.4.1 Delivery style

Your main objective in giving a presentation is to communicate an idea to the audience. This means that they need to be able to understand you. It is your job to make sure that you deliver your presentation in such a way that it is capable of being understood and, more than that, that it is packaged so that the audience want to listen. As such, there are a number of points to take into account:

- **Do not read from a script.** People who read from a script tend to speak too quickly and in too flat a tone without making eye contact with the audience. This is not engaging. It can also create problems because good written language and good spoken language are very different so reading from a script tends to feel very stilted and unnatural for the audience.

- **Take care with timing, pace, and volume.** Presentation speech tends to be slightly slower than normal speech and to involve more pauses and more repetition. It is important to speak clearly and to use a slightly louder volume than usual to ensure that the audience do not have to strain to hear you.

- **Remember to face the audience.** This may sound silly, but it is particularly important when using visual aids: even experienced speakers sometimes look round at their slides rather than facing the audience. Not only do you lose engagement with your audience if you do this, but you also run the risk of not being heard. If you have a screen in front of you that is also showing your slides, this minimizes the risk of instinctively turning round.

- **Use plenty of signposting.** Telling the audience what you are doing makes it easier for them to follow the development of your argument. Your audience should always be clear whether the point you are making is an elaboration of something you have already mentioned, one in a line of examples, or an entirely new part of the discussion. You can do this in conjunction with your visual aids: for example, you could say 'this slide sets out the three theories that I will be discussing' or 'you can find these four points listed at the top of the second page of the handout'.

In essence, you should aim to adapt your natural style of speech to suit the task of making a presentation. If you know that you are going to give a presentation, start to really listen to the way that lecturers speak when they give lectures: focus on their style rather than content for a short period of time. You should notice the differences between this and their ordinary speech.

🕑 *You will find examples of students giving presentations with different delivery styles at* **www.oup.com/he/finch8e/.**

18.4.2 Combating nerves

Nerves are a problem for many students who are faced with the prospect of making a presentation. Even students who are confident at speaking out during group discussion in tutorials tend to find the prospect of standing in front of the group and speaking somewhat daunting. One of the best ways of overcoming nerves is to try and isolate what it is that is causing anxiety—knowing what the problem is takes you halfway towards overcoming it. The remainder of this section will identify some common fears and make suggestions as to how they can be combated.

18.4.2.1 Presenting inaccurate material

This is a common worry but it should not be an issue provided you have carried out your research thoroughly. Even if you do make some inaccurate points, it is unlikely that other students will notice. Your lecturer will notice but certainly should not interrupt the presentation to correct you or comment on any inaccuracy in front of other students. As such, it is a matter for the lecturer to raise with you in the feedback that you receive for your presentation so it will be no different to finding out that you made a mistake in a piece of written coursework.

If you find that you are very concerned about a particular point in your presentation that you are struggling to understand, it might be worth approaching your lecturer about this. If the presentation is assessed, there may be a limit to how much the lecturer will help you with the content but you can at least make them aware of the problem so that they can hopefully reassure you that they will not draw attention to any errors in front of other students. Some lecturers may be prepared to give you a little assistance if you are struggling with the material, perhaps pointing you towards some source material that will be easier for you to understand.

18.4.2.2 Forgetting what to say

Students who express this concern generally mean one of two things: either they will be so nervous that they cannot speak at all or they will forget the particular forms of words that they want to use in their presentation.

The first of these would be an exceptionally rare occurrence. You may feel nervous about speaking and your mouth will feel dry but it is highly unlikely that you will open your mouth and no words will come out. The trick to overcoming this fear is to make sure that you have some water to sip to deal with your dry mouth and to practise your first sentence over and over again. This is because students who experience presentation nerves report that the first sentence—actually starting to speak—is the most nerve-wracking part and that once the first sentence is out of their mouths, the rest follows on without difficulty.

As to problems with remembering a particular form of words, this should not be an issue because, provided your presentation is clear and people can understand you, it does not matter what words you actually use. Students often like to have particular phrases incorporated into their presentation because they look impressive on paper but remember that none of us speak in the same style that we write: written and spoken language are entirely different.

Practical exercise

The following exercise should demonstrate the difference between spoken and written words and persuade you that you do not need any particular form of words to communicate your ideas to the audience.

Select one point that you want to make in your presentation and write a script for it in your usual written style. Put this to one side. Now find a method of recording yourself speaking and explain the same point without planning and using ordinary language. Transcribe the recording and compare it with your script. Hopefully, you will find that you have made the same points but in different language.

You can take this a step further by recording yourself explaining an idea in ordinary language and then reading your script and listening to the difference between the two versions. This may convince you that your less formal, natural spoken language is actually a better way to communicate in your presentation.

18.4.2.3 Being visible and feeling judged

A presentation focuses uninterrupted attention on one person for a protracted period of time. This visibility and focus renders the speaker vulnerable to the criticisms of their peers and it is this that is the most commonly expressed fear associated with giving a presentation. In fact, you could say that all feelings of nervousness stem from a common concern about looking foolish in front of others.

There are a couple of points that you should note here. First, not every member of the audience will be paying attention to your presentation. The only person that you can guarantee is listening is the lecturer. Secondly, if people are paying attention then this is because they are interested in what you are saying, not because they want to criticize you. In fact, most people will be willing you on to succeed, knowing that they have either survived the experience or still have their own presentation to deliver, so it is really a mistake to assume that there is any negative judgement being directed towards you.

Ultimately, most students undertaking a presentation will not have much experience of speaking in front of others so it is only natural for them to feel nervous about it. Try to minimize this prior to the presentation by talking more in tutorial discussions to get more and more used to sharing your opinions with other students. There are all sorts of techniques to help people overcome nerves. Some students find that the best way to feel confident is to pretend to be confident; they watch those who they consider to be confident when giving presentations and emulate their behaviour. For others, a more forthright approach is useful and they start their presentation by confessing to the audience that they feel nervous. Overall, though, try to remember that it is unlikely that anything will go wrong during your presentation and, even if it does, there is no need to feel foolish. It will soon be over and major presentation disasters are rare and soon forgotten.

Practical exercise

The following exercise might help you to overcome any nerves that you are experiencing as the day of your presentation approaches.

1. Think about what aspect of the presentation makes you feel nervous. What is it that you think might go wrong? Try to be as specific as possible and write a numbered list.

2. Take each point in turn and ask yourself (a) why you think this will happen and (b) what the consequence will be if it does happen. For example, you might be worried that you will run out of time and not be able to finish your presentation. If the presentation is assessed, this could lead to a deduction of marks.

3. Think of at least two ways that you could prevent the problem from arising. For example, you could practise your presentation several times to make sure it fits within the time allocation and you could review your content to identify any points that could be omitted or condensed if you find you are short of time on the day.

4. Consider how you will deal with the outcome of your feared situation; in other words, address not just the consequence but the consequence of the consequence! For example, if you run out of time then you will lose marks as a consequence but this is unlikely to make a difference between a pass and a fail as it is only one factor that the marker will take into account. Moreover, if the presentation is only part of the assessment for the course, you can work hard to make up for the lost marks in the other pieces of coursework or the examination.

By identifying your fears, you should be able to reduce the possibility that they will occur and devise ways to cope if they do happen. Hopefully, this will help you to realize that there is very little that could go wrong in your presentation and, even if the worst happens, it will be something that you can survive.

18.4.3 Dealing with questions

Most presentations conclude with a period of time for the audience to ask questions. It is probably fair to say that even the most confident presenter has some qualms about dealing with questions. This is because it is actually the only part of the presentation that you cannot control. If the presentation is assessed, the ability to deal with questions assumes a particular importance because it gives the marker an indication of the depth of the speaker's background knowledge. Try to take into account the following points to help you deal with questions:

- **Listen to the question.** Concentrate on what the person asking the question is saying rather than worrying that you will not know the answer. Ask them to repeat the question if you did not follow it.

- **Take time to think about an answer.** Try not to be afraid of silence. It is better to take a few moments to ponder so that you can say something sensible rather than saying the first thing that pops into your head just to fill the silence. If you do not know the answer, say so rather than trying to bluff.

- **Do not talk for too long.** Think about your answer and make a couple of succinct points. Long rambling answers will detract from the overall impression of your presentation skills.

18.5 THE REFLECTION STAGE

You may think that your task is complete as soon as the final question has been answered and you have taken your seat with a sense of relief and achievement but there is another stage of the process which is frequently overlooked in its importance and that is the post-presentation reflection.

18.5.1 Why reflect?

You should reflect upon your performance to ensure that you gain something from the experience that will make you a more effective and confident presenter in the future. Try to formalize the reflection process by making notes so that you have a record of your thoughts while they are still fresh in your mind. Make a note of things that went well and what, if anything, you would do differently if you were giving a presentation next week.

Presentation skills are important and it may impress an employer if you can demonstrate that you reflected upon your performance and made changes to your approach to preparation or delivery as a result. It may also help you to fulfil any personal development planning (PDP) requirements at your institution (see chapter 10 on study skills).

18.5.2 Seek feedback

The process of reflection need not take long and you can make use of any feedback that you have been given by your lecturer and by the audience. If the presentation was assessed, you may have a written feedback form. If not, and you are struggling to remember any comments that the lecturer made at the time, drop them an email asking for more feedback. Remember that a specific answer often requires a specific question so rather than asking for feedback in general terms, perhaps you could ask the lecturer to list three things that were good about your presentation and three areas where improvement was needed.

You could also ask for feedback from the audience. If you are really keen to find out what people think, you could create a feedback form to distribute to the audience, asking them to note positive and negative features of the presentation. Make sure you do not ask for too much feedback from the audience; they are there to listen to your presentation not to provide you with a detailed commentary on your presentation technique.

 CHAPTER SUMMARY

The research stage

- Take care to formulate a presentation topic that takes account of the time frame within which the presentation must be delivered, the availability of material, the aim of the presentation, and the requirements of the assessment criteria

- Start your research as early as possible to ensure you have time to identify and obtain relevant material and make sure that your note-taking is effective

- Strive to find an original or interesting slant on the material to ensure that the presentation is engaging, particularly if you are aware that other students are covering the same topic

Preparing the presentation

- Content overload is a major problem for many presentations. Select your topic and the content of the presentation carefully to ensure that you do not try to cram too much material into the time available

- If you are having difficulties in making a decision about the content, try ranking each point on the basis of its relevance to the question that your presentation is seeking to answer

- Make sure that your presentation tells a story by giving it a clear introduction, a series of interrelated points within the body of the presentation, and a conclusion that draws together the issues raised and provides a succinct answer to the question posed by the presentation

- Give careful thought to the selection and presentation of visual aids to ensure that they complement, rather than replace or distract from, the presentation

- Practise, preferably in front of an audience. Present on everyday topics to practise your delivery style and then practise the actual presentation to ensure that it fits within the time frame and that everything flows smoothly

Delivering the presentation

- Try to adopt a style of delivery that is engaging for the audience to listen to and follow. Take particular care with the timing, pace, and volume of your presentation and remember that good spoken English differs enormously from good written English

- Signposting is essential to enable your audience to follow the line of your argument and to understand how each point relates to others in the presentation. Use a signposting phrase in relation to each new point raised

- Anticipate issues that will cause you to feel nervous and try to formulate a means of pre-empting any problems that you fear may arise. Remember that most people suffer from presentation nerves

- Be prepared to answer questions from the audience. Listen carefully to what is being asked and take a moment to think about the answer before launching into a response

Review and reflection

- Presentations are increasingly required as part of the job application process so take advantage of this opportunity to become a more accomplished presenter by reflecting upon your performance. Try to be honest with yourself about your limitations as a presenter and find ways to strengthen areas in which there is room from improvement

- Be active and precise in seeking feedback from others about your qualities as a presenter and remember that asking precise questions tends to elicit precise answers. Consider circulating a short feedback sheet to the audience

Mooting skills

INTRODUCTION

The focus of this chapter is mooting. It will provide a step-by-step guide to assist students through the process of preparation and delivery of a moot argument with reference made to associated issues such as conducting legal research and production of a skeleton argument. Attention will be drawn, in particular, to aspects of mooting that students tend to find worrying or difficult, such as formulating a flowing argument, developing a confident oral presentation style, and dealing with judicial interventions. This chapter is a general guide that will be invaluable for preparation of any moot but a sample moot is used throughout as a source of specific explanation and illustration.

Participation in a moot will provide an insight into the way that the law is used in practice and also acts as an invaluable introduction to the skills that are required to present a case on appeal. Mooting offers unparalleled opportunities for the development of the skills associated with the delivery of a comprehensive and persuasive oral argument as well as providing an opportunity to develop your research skills and enhance your ability to construct and organize a coherent legal argument. It is this 'skills-richness' that makes mooting an excellent activity for demonstrating a commitment to a career in the legal profession; thus, your level of involvement with these activities should be emphasized on your CV and in applications for a pupillage or training contract. Despite the clear benefits of taking part in these activities, many students are reluctant to do so. Although the explanation for this reluctance is usually said to be fear of standing up and presenting an argument, this fear often arises from a lack of understanding of what is required. This chapter seeks to demystify the mooting process and encourage more students to take part in this valuable and ultimately enjoyable activity.

 Learning outcomes

After studying this chapter, you will be able to:

- Analyse a moot problem and understand its requirements from the perspective of each of the mooters
- Appreciate the role of each of the mooters and be aware of the mechanics of mooting in terms of the timing and delivery of submission

- Engage in detailed and meticulous research and preparation including the production of a skeleton argument and a bundle
- Evaluate the strength of the opponent's argument and check to determine that the authorities relied upon are current and relevant
- Deliver a logical and organized moot speech with confidence and deal with judicial interventions
- Adhere to mooting conventions and the requirements of mooting etiquette including the use of appropriate terminology

19.1 THE MOOT PROBLEM

Just as a moot point is one that could be argued either way, a moot revolves around an unsettled legal argument that could go either way depending on the skill of the mooter. It involves a fictitious factual scenario set in one of the appellate courts, generally the Court of Appeal or the Supreme Court. Two teams of two mooters present submissions for each party and seek to persuade the judge that theirs is the correct interpretation of the law. The example provided is a typical moot problem that demonstrates its characteristics. It is always worth devoting time to the analysis of the moot problem as it has a great deal of essential information to convey to the mooters, as you will see in the sections that follow (see Figure 19.1).

19.1.1 Level of the court

There will always be an indication of the level of the court in which the moot will be heard. Take note of this and ensure that you keep it in mind when researching and constructing your legal argument. It will be influential in the way in which you use authorities and formulate your submissions owing to the doctrine of precedent.

Issues of precedent and the hierarchy of the courts are detailed in chapter 7, so you may like to revisit this and refresh your memory on the 1966 Practice Statement concerning the ability of the Supreme Court to depart from its own decisions and the rule in Young v Bristol Aeroplane *in relation to the status of Court of Appeal authority.*

19.1.2 The case name

You will have been told by the organizer of the moot whether your team represents the appellant or the defendant. Armed with this information, you need to work out which of the parties that means you are representing. In this example, this is straightforward as the first-named party (Montes) is the appellant and the second-named party (Watson) is the respondent. The case name does not necessarily indicate which party is the appellant and which is the respondent. It is essential to use the past history of the case and the way in which the grounds of appeal are stated to ascertain the roles of appellant and respondent. It is always painful when mistakes are made and a judge is confronted with two opposing teams who think they are representing the same party. Not only is this embarrassing for the team who made the mistake, it means elimination from the moot and a waste of all the time devoted to preparation.

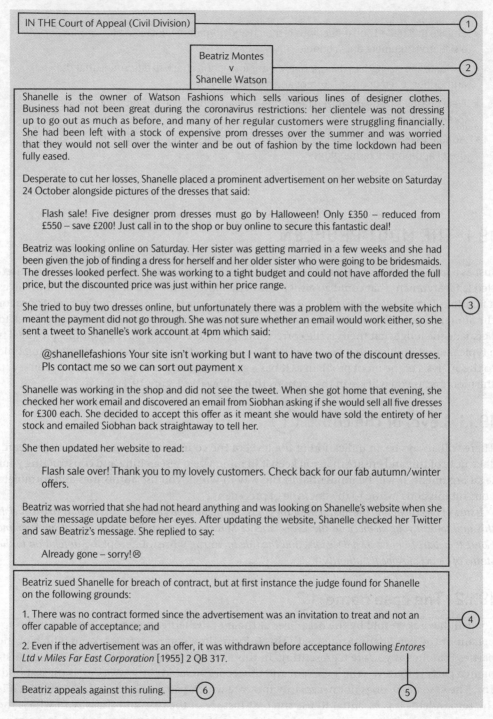

IN THE Court of Appeal (Civil Division) — ①

Beatriz Montes
v
Shanelle Watson — ②

Shanelle is the owner of Watson Fashions which sells various lines of designer clothes. Business had not been great during the coronavirus restrictions: her clientele was not dressing up to go out as much as before, and many of her regular customers were struggling financially. She had been left with a stock of expensive prom dresses over the summer and was worried that they would not sell over the winter and be out of fashion by the time lockdown had been fully eased.

Desperate to cut her losses, Shanelle placed a prominent advertisement on her website on Saturday 24 October alongside pictures of the dresses that said:

Flash sale! Five designer prom dresses must go by Halloween! Only £350 – reduced from £550 – save £200! Just call in to the shop or buy online to secure this fantastic deal!

Beatriz was looking online on Saturday. Her sister was getting married in a few weeks and she had been given the job of finding a dress for herself and her older sister who were going to be bridesmaids. The dresses looked perfect. She was working to a tight budget and could not have afforded the full price, but the discounted price was just within her price range.

She tried to buy two dresses online, but unfortunately there was a problem with the website which meant the payment did not go through. She was not sure whether an email would work either, so she sent a tweet to Shanelle's work account at 4pm which said: — ③

@shanellefashions Your site isn't working but I want to have two of the discount dresses. Pls contact me so we can sort out payment x

Shanelle was working in the shop and did not see the tweet. When she got home that evening, she checked her work email and discovered an email from Siobhan asking if she would sell all five dresses for £300 each. She decided to accept this offer as it meant she would have sold the entirety of her stock and emailed Siobhan back straightaway to tell her.

She then updated her website to read:

Flash sale over! Thank you to my lovely customers. Check back for our fab autumn/winter offers.

Beatriz was worried that she had not heard anything and was looking on Shanelle's website when she saw the message update before her eyes. After updating the website, Shanelle checked her Twitter and saw Beatriz's message. She replied to say:

Already gone – sorry! ☹

Beatriz sued Shanelle for breach of contract, but at first instance the judge found for Shanelle on the following grounds:

1. There was no contract formed since the advertisement was an invitation to treat and not an offer capable of acceptance; and — ④

2. Even if the advertisement was an offer, it was withdrawn before acceptance following *Entores Ltd v Miles Far East Corporation* [1955] 2 QB 317. — ⑤

Beatriz appeals against this ruling. — ⑥

Figure 19.1 Moot problem *Montes v Watson*

19.1.2.1 Civil cases

In civil cases, the name of the case usually remains the same from inception to completion; a case that is listed as *Montes v Watson* at first instance would be listed in the same way on appeal, irrespective of which party initiated the appeal. There are exceptions to this general rule. For example, *Nattrass v Tesco Supermarket* became *Tesco Supermarket v Nattrass*[1] upon appeal so it is advisable always to check carefully to ensure you are clear about which party you are representing in the moot.

19.1.2.2 Criminal cases

Criminal cases always list the Crown as the first party followed by the name of the defendant: *R v Smith*. If the defendant appeals against conviction, this will be listed as *R v Smith*. If the defendant is successful in the Court of Appeal and the prosecution appeal against this decision, the case will remain listed as *R v Smith*. The only exception to this occurs if the first appeal is initiated by the prosecution, that is, the appeal is by the Crown against the defendant's acquittal, as this is listed as *DPP v Smith* (with DPP standing for 'Director of Public Prosecutions').

19.1.2.3 Judicial review

Judicial review cases involve a different style of case citation, appearing as either *R v Secretary of State for the Environment, ex p Smith* or, if the case took place after 2001, as *R (Smith) v Secretary of State for the Environment*. Irrespective of the method of citation, the parties in a judicial review case are the aggrieved individual or group (Smith) and a public body (Secretary of State for the Environment); the Crown is never an actual party to the proceedings but is named in the citation as judicial review cases are public law matters in which the Crown is notionally representing the interests of the individual or group against the public body.

19.1.2.4 Unrepresented parties

The final style of citation that you might encounter is *Re Smith*. This indicates that the proceedings involve a party who is incapable of representing themselves. This is common in probate cases (dead person), family proceedings (child), or cases involving mental incapacity.

Self-test questions

 *Have a look at the sample moots online at **www.oup.com/he/finch8e/** and work out which party is the appellant and the respondent in each case. Compare your answers with those provided online and make sure that you understand the explanations that are also provided.*

19.1.3 The facts ③

The bulk of the information provided in a moot problem is the factual background that led to the dispute.

---

1. [1972] 1 AC 153 (HL).

19.1.3.1 Issues of fact and law

It is important that you remember that these facts were (hypothetically) established at first instance so cannot be changed, reinterpreted, or supplemented in any way. A moot is an argument on a point of law, so there is no scope whatsoever for a re-evaluation of the facts; you must work with the information that is provided. This means that you cannot research (or, worse still, invent) supplementary facts that support your argument. For example, in *Montes v Watson*, the respondent may want to argue that her website was, in fact, able to take online orders at 4pm on Saturday 24 October, but this is a question of fact and not a question of law.

19.1.3.2 Make use of the facts

Pay careful attention to the facts. Some mooters present an abstract legal argument on their ground of appeal that is too detached from the particular facts of the appeal. Remember that your job is not only to argue the niceties of the distinction between an offer and an invitation to treat but to *use* this to persuade the judge that the notice on the website was an offer (if you are representing Montes) or an invitation to treat (for Watson). Reference to the particular facts of the moot will help you to ground your argument and, because abstraction from the facts is a common weakness, your ability to relate the law to the facts will impress the judge if it is done effectively.

19.1.4 Case history

The past history of the case, that is, how it was decided at first instance and in any previous appeals, can be useful, particularly if the problem includes details of the reasoning of the judge.

19.1.4.1 Respondent's perspective

For the respondent (who won at the earlier stage of the proceedings), it can be a powerful argument that the decision of the judge at first instance, who had all the facts before him and had the advantage of hearing oral evidence from the parties, should not be disturbed (or the jury decision if the issue involves criminal law). The respondent should pick up on the reasoning given by the judge as the starting point for their submissions.

19.1.4.2 Appellant's perspective

The reasoning of the judge can also assist the appellant as it provides insight into the sort of argument that the respondent is likely to advance, so a fair amount of effort should be devoted to refuting this argument.

Neither party should limit their submissions to the issues raised in the reasoning of the judge but should include this as only one factor to be taken into account when dealing with their point of appeal.

Practical exercise

Montes v Watson does not give detailed reasoning for the judge's decision at first instance other than to state that reliance was placed upon *Entores Ltd v Miles Far East Corporation*. Have a look at the other sample moots listed that include more detailed reasoning for the earlier decisions and try to determine:

1. How the arguments raised could be used to assist the respondent.
2. How the arguments raised could be used to assist the appellant.
3. What dangers exist if either party fails to take these reasons into account?

 You will find the sample moots and some commentary on these questions at **www.oup.com/he/finch8e/**.

19.1.5 Court authorities

If a moot problem includes reference to a particular case within the facts, this acts as a court authority. This means that it can be used by both the appellants and the respondents without counting towards their allowed number of authorities. Therefore, if *Montes v Watson* was mooted and the rules stated that each mooter could rely on four cases, this means that each person may use four cases in addition to *Entores Ltd v Miles Far East Corporation*.

19.1.6 Grounds of appeal

In *Montes v Watson*, the grounds of appeal are not specifically stated but can be taken from the two findings of the trial judge. Other moots will phrase this differently and will state 'Beatriz appeals on the following grounds'.

 There are some examples that are differently worded in the sample moots listed at **www.oup.com/he/finch8e/**.

Self-test questions

It is essential to mooting success that you can identify which 'way round' the arguments go—in other words, what are the appellant and respondent respectively arguing? Have a look at *Montes v Watson*. Senior counsel for the appellant is arguing that the advertisement is an offer but what are the other parties arguing?

1. Junior counsel for the appellant.
2. Senior counsel for the respondent.
3. Junior counsel for the respondent.

 Answers to the self-test questions can be found at **www.oup.com/he/finch8e/** *where you will also find other sample moot problems. Make sure that you can identify the argument for each of the mooters in a couple of these and check your conclusions with the answers.*

It is worth noting that it is only a convention that the senior counsel deals with the first ground of appeal and that the junior counsel deals with the second. However, as it is such a well-established convention, if you intend to depart from this, it must be made clear to the judge in the opening submission of the senior counsel.

19.2 PARTICIPANTS

Mooting involves a simulation of an appellate hearing where the focus of the activity is the presentation of arguments on a particular point of law. This can be distinguished from a mock trial which is an enactment of a first instance trial where the focus is on the presentation of evidence and the examination of witnesses. Both activities are excellent vehicles for the development of advocacy skills but the latter is little used, largely owing to the complexities of its organization. Mooting, by contrast, is far easier to organize and can go ahead with just five people—four mooters and a judge—although it is relatively commonplace for the judge to be assisted by a clerk.

19.2.1 Layout and roles

This typical layout shows the relative positioning of the parties in the moot room. It is important to ensure that the judge can see each of the mooters clearly and that the clerk is positioned so that they can communicate easily with both the judge and the mooters (see Figure 19.2).

Each participant in the moot has a particular job to do (see Table 19.1).

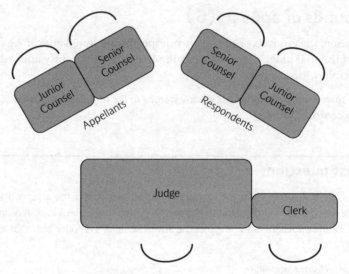

Figure 19.2 A typical moot room layout

In addition to the participants, the *Master of Moot*[2] also has a key role to play in organizing the moot, setting up the room, and overseeing the exchange of skeleton arguments and authorities as well as organizing any refreshments after the moot is complete (usually only if the moot is an internal final or part of a national competition involving teams from visiting institutions). As such, it is important that the role is held by someone reliable who is not averse to putting time into doing the spadework without getting any of the glory attached to winning a moot.

----

2. The title 'Master' in this context is gender-neutral, although the alternative 'Mistress of Moot' is also used.

Table 19.1 Moot participants and their roles

Participant	Role
Judge	Presides over the moot, hears arguments from counsel, asks questions during the moot, delivers a judgment on the law, and determines which team has won the moot
Clerk	Assists the judge by passing authorities and finding page references, keeps time and indicates how much time is remaining to the mooters
Senior counsel (appellant)	Opens the moot and introduces all the parties to the judge, presents the submissions concerning the first point of appeal on behalf of the appellant. In some instances, exercises a right to reply on behalf of himself and his junior
Junior counsel (appellant)	Addresses the second point of appeal on behalf of the appellant, ensures that the closing of his speech summarizes both points of appeal, and invites the judge to overturn the ruling of the lower court and uphold the appeal
Senior counsel (respondent)	Opens the moot for the respondents, presents submissions on the first point of appeal on behalf of the respondent, taking care to address the points raised by senior counsel for the appellant
Junior counsel (respondent)	Deals with the second point of appeal, responds to and counters the arguments advanced by the junior counsel for the appellant and closes the submissions for the respondent

19.2.2 Appellants and respondents

The two opposing teams are called the appellants and the respondents. Although the job of all the mooters has a strong common theme in terms of presentation of legal arguments with a view to persuading the judge that a particular outcome should be reached, there are distinctions between the job of appellant and respondent.

19.2.2.1 Appellants

The appellants are the team allocated the task of presenting the appeal, so will represent the party who was unsuccessful at the previous hearing. As the side that initiates the appeal, the appellants will set out the reasons why the previous ruling should be overturned. This means that the appellants set the agenda for the moot.

19.2.2.2 Respondents

The respondents, as the name suggests, must *respond* to the points raised by the appellants; in other words, they must tackle each of the submissions made by the appellants as to why the previous ruling should be set aside. Failure to address a submission advanced by the appellants is taken as conceding that point, that is, accepting that the appellants are correct. Therefore, the respondents must negate the arguments of the appellants before advancing their own submissions.

19.2.2.3 How do the roles differ?

It seems from this that the respondents have a harder task before them than the appellants as they have to tackle the arguments raised by the appellants before they can present their own submissions.

This seeming advantage to the appellants is actually less beneficial than it appears at first glance. An appellant who sets out their own argument without a thought for what opposing counsel will say in response is demonstrating a narrower range of mooting skills than the respondent who has to take note of what the appellant is saying and tailor the response to address the points raised.

Stronger mooters will incorporate an anticipated response into their submissions when acting for the appellant. As Figure 19.3 illustrates, this involves the appellant speculating about the way in which the respondent will seek to counter the appellant's submission and then explaining why the respondent's argument is unsatisfactory. By doing this, the appellant makes the work of the respondent much harder as they now not only have to get around the appellant's submission, they also have to find a way to overcome the appellant's anticipated rebuttal of their submission that has not yet been made!

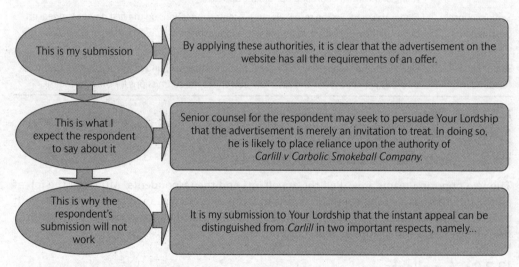

Figure 19.3 Anticipating responses

This approach can be extremely effective for the appellant. Of course, it is only speculation about what the respondent *might* argue and it is always galling when the respondent actually advances a wholly different line of argument, particularly if the respondent presents this with an air of incredulity. For example, the respondent may say:

> Senior counsel for the appellant has seen fit to entertain Your Lordship with fanciful arguments based upon a strange interpretation of *Carlill*. My Lord, I would not seek to waste Your Lordship's time with such frivolous arguments based upon a manifest misunderstanding of the law.

It would, of course, take a courageous respondent to make such a statement as the judge might respond by saying 'But I was quite convinced by senior counsel for the appellant's use of the authorities. Perhaps you could explain to me why you see them as erroneous.' In general, unless you are feeling exceptionally brave *and* very sure of your own interpretation of the law, it is preferable to take a less scathing approach to the submissions advanced by your opponent.

19.2.3 Senior and junior counsel

Just as it is a well-established mooting myth that it is easier to act as appellant than it is to take the role of respondent, it is also often said that it is easier to act as junior counsel.

So, how true is this?

The main advantage attached to the role of junior counsel is that senior counsel speaks first, so there is never any requirement to be the first person to stand up and speak. For this reason, it is usual that the most experienced of the pair of mooters should act as senior counsel. The allocation of the role of senior counsel to the more experienced (or less nervous) mooter is particularly advantageous to the appellants as senior counsel for the appellant utters the first words of the moot and a confident start has obvious advantages. Equally, it is senior counsel for the appellant who will exercise the right to reply if this is available and it makes sense for this role to be given to someone who is not too uncomfortable at voicing less practised submissions.

Having the more experienced mooter as senior counsel is less compelling for the respondents. Indeed, some teams of respondents allocate the role of junior counsel to their more experienced mooter for a number of reasons. First, the second ground of appeal is often (but not inevitably) more complex than the first, thus requiring a more adept presentation. Secondly, there is no particular need for experience attached to the role of senior counsel for the respondent. Finally, as junior counsel for the appellant will often be a less experienced or less skilful mooter than senior counsel for the appellant, it can be advantageous if the stronger respondent is pitched against the weaker appellant, particularly as junior counsel for the respondent is (in the absence of a right to reply) the last person that the judge will hear speak, leaving the judge with a favourable opinion of the advocacy skills of the respondents.

19.2.4 Timing and order of submissions

Each moot will have its own rules concerning the amount of time given to each of the parties to present their submissions, including rules relating to the way that this period of time is calculated. Some moots may also stipulate the order in which each of the parties must present their submissions.

19.2.4.1 How much time is available to each mooter?

Each of the mooters will have a particular amount of time allocated to them in which to present their submissions. This varies according to the rules of the particular moot, so it is essential that you check carefully to see how long you have to speak and what is included in this period of time.

For example, some moots may specify that each mooter has fifteen minutes to speak but that this does not include time taken in responding to judicial interventions. This approach makes life easier for the mooters because the amount of time available to deliver their submissions is clearly defined. It is much harder to prepare a speech when the rules state that the clock will not be stopped during questioning as it is impossible to predict how many or how few questions the judge will ask and how much of the allocated time will be taken up with judicial questioning.

19.2.4.2 Who speaks when?

The two main options are depicted in Figure 19.4. The first approach allows the judge to hear the entirety of the appeal case before hearing from the respondents whereas the second approach ensures that the first point of appeal is dealt with before the second is raised. The first option is more usual but some judges prefer the second approach, particularly if the points of appeal are complex, so it is worth checking before the moot starts. If neither the rules nor the judge

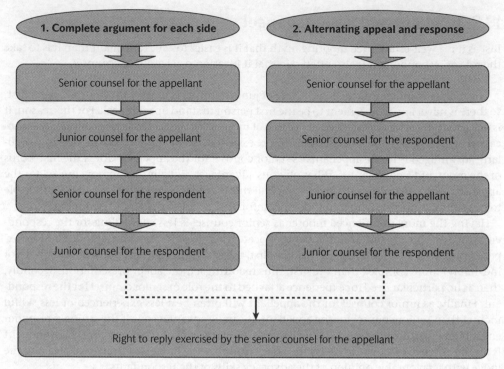

Figure 19.4 Who speaks when?

specify an order of play, it is courteous for the opposing teams to reach agreement prior to the commencement of the moot and to ensure that this is communicated to the judge and the clerk.

19.2.4.3 Right to reply

The right to reply gives the appellants one final opportunity to rebut the submissions made by the respondents. This is a right given solely to the appellants (and generally exercised by senior counsel for the appellant on behalf of both senior and junior counsel) because the respondents have already had an opportunity to rebut the appellant's submissions.

Not all moots include a right to reply. This is because the aim is to ensure that each of the mooters have a task of equivalent difficulty before them, hence they all speak for the same amount of time (although some moots allocate more time to senior counsel than junior). As the right to reply is only an issue for senior counsel for the appellant, some competitions take the view that this imposes a greater burden on senior counsel for the appellant.

If there is an option to reply, senior counsel is well advised to exercise it. Judges are aware that it is one of the more difficult tasks in the moot, particularly as it requires the senior to deal with the junior's grounds, plus it means that the appellants have the last word and their submissions are fresh in the judge's mind as he retires to make a decision.

19.3 RESEARCHING THE MOOT

Although mooting is associated with advocacy skills and the ability to 'think on one's feet', the contribution of detailed research and preparation to the quality of the speech that is delivered should not be underestimated. It is true that the best mooters may be able to bluff their way past any gaps in their knowledge but the thought of being lost for words during the moot is one of the greatest concerns expressed by prospective (and more experienced) mooters and the best way to avoid it is to engage in thorough and meticulous preparation.

19.3.1 Analyse the facts

The starting point for preparation should be an analysis of the moot problem itself. It is a good idea to familiarize yourself with the facts and issues before researching the law. It is true that some mooters prefer to start by researching the legal issues on the basis that a moot concerns a point of law. However, it seems preferable to know what the problem is (the facts) before investigating the answer (the law). By familiarizing yourself with the point of appeal and the relevant facts, you will be able to undertake more purposeful and effective legal research.

19.3.2 Keep focused

Make sure that your point of appeal is at the forefront of your mind at all times to focus your research and your thinking. In the sample moot, the point of appeal for senior counsel for the appellant is simple: the advertisement is an offer.

> 🌐 As you will see from the other examples at **www.oup.com/he/finch8e/** this is not always the case and some points of appeal can be several sentences long.

If this is the case, then try to reword your point of appeal in the simplest terms (without losing the meaning) to avoid confusion. Some mooters like to write their issue at the top of each page of their notes to help them retain their focus whilst others note it prominently at the top of their copy of the moot problem.

19.3.3 Construct a timeline

It is usually useful to construct a timeline of events that led to the appeal. Some moot problems span months or even years whilst others, like the sample moot used in this chapter, involve events that occur over much more condensed periods of time. Irrespective of the time frame involved, sifting through the facts of the moot and forming a chronology of significant events will help you to form a clear picture of how the situation developed and can be crucial in helping you to identify key issues (see Figure 19.5).

19.3.4 Search for relevance

Do not forget that each sentence holds information of relevance. You may not be able to work out why a particular fact is relevant at first reading. It may not become apparent until you have researched the law and given the facts further thought. If the relevance of a particular fact remains elusive, it can sometimes be illuminating to consider how the problem would be different if that fact was either altered or entirely absent.

For example, unless you had studied contract law recently, you would probably not grasp the significance of the fact that Shanelle has only five dresses available at the discounted price. Nonetheless, you should note it as a point that you do not understand and search for its relevance when researching the law. Never ignore facts merely because you do not understand them as they may be crucial to your opponent's argument.

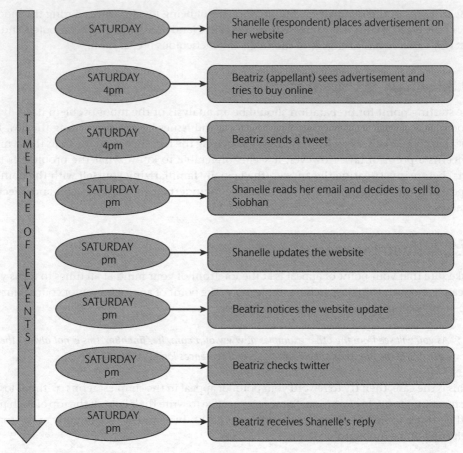

Figure 19.5 Constructing a timeline

19.3.5 Two sides to the argument

Remember that the point of appeal has been chosen because it can be argued either way, so there are probably as many facts in the problem that support your opponent's argument as there are that support your own.

Never blind yourself to your opponent's argument. A good mooter knows the opposing argument as well as they know their own, as only if you have considered how your opponent will attack your submissions can you attempt to defend them against this. Scrutinize the facts carefully for information that supports your own stance and for facts which favour your opponent and make a note of these. For example, a preliminary evaluation of the sample moot from the stance of senior counsel for the appellant might elicit the information shown in Figure 19.6.

19.3.6 Identify questions to be answered

Once you have a clear idea of the facts surrounding your point of appeal, you will probably find it relatively straightforward to make a list of questions that need to be answered. Of course, as you have not yet made a start with your research, your list of questions will probably be quite

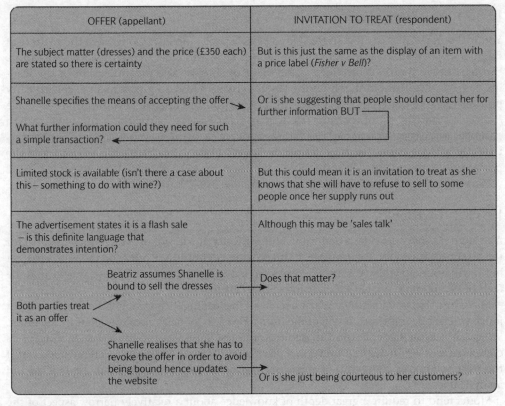

OFFER (appellant)	INVITATION TO TREAT (respondent)
The subject matter (dresses) and the price (£350 each) are stated so there is certainty	But is this just the same as the display of an item with a price label (*Fisher v Bell*)?
Shanelle specifies the means of accepting the offer What further information could they need for such a simple transaction?	Or is she suggesting that people should contact her for further information BUT
Limited stock is available (isn't there a case about this – something to do with wine?)	But this could mean it is an invitation to treat as she knows that she will have to refuse to sell to some people once her supply runs out
The advertisement states it is a flash sale – is this definite language that demonstrates intention?	Although this may be 'sales talk'
Both parties treat it as an offer → Beatriz assumes Shanelle is bound to sell the dresses →	Does that matter?
Shanelle realises that she has to revoke the offer in order to avoid being bound hence updates the website →	Or is she just being courteous to her customers?

Figure 19.6 Evaluating both sides

broad and general but it is still worth making a list, as this should identify the core issues and it is always much easier to research if you have a series of questions that need to be answered.

In relation to the sample moot, the following questions would probably appear on the list at this stage of the preparation process:

- What is the definition of an offer and what are its essential characteristics?
- What is the definition of an invitation to treat and what are its essential characteristics?
- Is there case law on advertisements on websites?
- What is the relevance of the finite quantity of items?
- If both parties behave as if the advertisement was an offer, does that help my argument?

Having analysed the facts and formulated some questions that need to be addressed, it is time to move on to consider the research process.

19.3.7 Research the law

As a starting point for your moot research, there are two key things that you should seek to find:

1. A concise and accurate statement of the current law, including relevant statutory provisions and case law.
2. A clear and relatively detailed summary of the law that provides some indication of the scope of the topic and insight into problem areas.

19.3.7.1 *Halsbury's Laws*

You will find the first of these in *Halsbury's Laws*, which is an encyclopedia of the entirety of English law organized alphabetically by subject area, and most frequently accessed online through LexisLibrary. It provides a statement of the law and an indication of the leading cases and statutes from which the law is derived. This can give you an excellent early pointer towards material that is relevant to your point of appeal. It is important to make *Halsbury* a starting point for your research as many judges, particularly those who are in practice, will expect you to cite *Halsbury* as a source of any definition of key concepts, particularly if there is no statutory definition, for example offer, invitation to treat, and the postal rule.

You will find a more detailed guide to locating material using Halsbury's Laws *in chapter 8.*

19.3.7.2 Textbooks

Although *Halsbury* provides a definition and authority, it will not provide sufficient detail for the totality of the moot. For example, it will provide a definition of offer and invitation to treat but it will not help you to resolve the dilemma that these definitions disclose, that is, that the facts of the moot do not fall squarely into either category.

Make sure that you identify and use a range of the leading 'heavyweight' textbooks; a moot judge will not be impressed if you quote from a revision guide as a source of law in the moot. Select a text which goes beyond straightforward description of the law to tackle some of its complexities—you may even find some discussion of the moot point but remember that if the textbook makes your point of appeal seem simple, you need to find a more detailed and analytical text.

Moots tend to require a great depth of knowledge about a relatively narrow aspect of the law, so it will not take you long to grasp the basics from textbooks and be ready to move on to deal with more detailed sources of information. You would also expect to find references to other pertinent materials in your textbook so you should ensure that you look at those texts that offer plentiful footnotes and references to articles and specialist works that deal with the more complex points.

You will find guidance on how to identify and locate books, journals, and official publications in chapter 9.

19.3.8 Using cases

Case law should form the bulk of your research for a moot. Starting with the core cases identified by *Halsbury* and your textbook research, you should read each case carefully, noting the points that support your point of appeal and the points that go against you. It is essential that you do not simply ignore the points that do not fit your argument, as it is likely that the judge will tackle you about this even if your opponent does not. It can be useful to use a two-column approach to organizing your notes that matches the points that favour your argument and the opposing points that favour your opponent.

There are a range of issues to take into account when dealing with case law.

19.3.8.1 Which court heard the case?

Remember the importance of the doctrine of precedent and the hierarchy of the courts. If you are in the Court of Appeal, you are likely to be bound by decisions of the Supreme Court or the House of Lords unless you are able to establish that the facts of the appeal are materially different to the case law. A decision of a lower court is of less assistance unless it is the only case that tackles the precise legal issue that is at the heart of your point of appeal.

19.3.8.2 What is the legal issue?

The legal issue is that question that needs to be resolved by application of the law. For example, in the sample moot, the legal issue is whether the advertisement is an offer or an invitation to treat. If you can find a case that deals with the same legal issue as your point of appeal, it is likely that it will be of some assistance to you in preparing your submissions, irrespective of whether the case supports or undermines your argument.

19.3.8.3 What was the *ratio* and what was merely *obiter*?

You should ensure that you have extrapolated the *ratio* from every case on which you seek to rely and on which your opponent places reliance as a routine part of your moot preparation. Remember that only the *ratio* of the case is binding whilst the remainder of the judgment—the *obiter dicta*—is merely persuasive. You should ensure that you can distinguish between the *ratio* and *obiter* statements. Part of your task as a mooter is to convince the judge that your submissions have more legal force than those of your opponent, so do not be afraid to draw the judge's attention to the fact that you are presenting a binding authority to the court (but do so respectfully).

This is something that students tend to find difficult. You will find more discussion on the distinction and tips on identifying the ratio *of a case in chapter 7, which should help you to deal with this issue.*

19.3.8.4 In what jurisdiction was the case heard?

This is important as only cases heard within your own jurisdiction can be binding upon the court. Cases heard in other jurisdictions, such as Scotland, Ireland, Commonwealth jurisdictions, and the EU (after the Brexit implementation period has passed) may be persuasive authority. Privy Council decisions are also strongly persuasive as the Judicial Committee of the Privy Council is comprised of Justices of the Supreme Court.

Never overlook the value of persuasive authority in mooting. If the law in this jurisdiction seems to go against you, there is much to be gained by finding overseas authority that deals with the issue in a different way; you may be able to persuade the judge to rule in your favour, particularly if you are mooting in the Supreme Court. Be sure to draw the fact that you are relying on a persuasive authority to the attention of the judge rather than hoping that they will not notice and explain why it is useful to the appeal in hand. This will be addressed in more detail in section 19.4.2 on constructing a moot speech.

You will find a more detailed discussion of the nature of persuasive authorities in chapter 7.

19.3.8.5 Has the case been used in subsequent cases?

Not only can awareness of this alert you to additional authorities but the way in which a case is used in the future can affect its status as an authority.

You should make it a habit to check the status of each case that you encounter; it is very embarrassing (and ultimately fatal to your prospects of success in the moot) to present an argument based upon a case that has been overruled. You should, of course, extend this practice of checking to your opponent's authorities when these are revealed to you upon exchange of skeleton arguments (discussed in section 19.4.3).

This is a key part of your moot preparation so make sure that you are able to check the status of your cases effectively rather than leaving it to chance. The means by which you can find out how a case has been used since it was decided and the effect of this on its status as an authority are detailed in chapter 7.

Practical exercise

1.   Use one of the methods outlined in chapter 7 to find out how *Entores* has been used in subsequent cases, for example has it been applied, distinguished, or overruled?

2.   Look at the summaries of any cases that you have identified to determine whether any of those cases would be of assistance in resolving the issue at the heart of the second point of appeal in the sample moot—whether a tweet should be treated like a letter or a telex.[3] It is worthwhile to get practice at checking cases in this way as it is a relatively quick and easy way of locating potentially useful resources to support your moot argument.

Compare your findings to the answers provided at www.oup.com/he/finch8e/.

19.3.8.6 Are the facts of the case similar to the facts of the moot?

The closer the factual match between the case and the moot, the more likely it is that you will be able to convince the judge that the case should be followed.

Even if the facts are not identical (and it is very unlikely that you will find an identical set of facts), look for parallels. Conversely, if the case is one that you want to avoid (because it favours your opponent's argument), you will need to point to how the cases differ in order to distinguish the case from the issue before the court.

In the sample moot, the issue is whether a message left by Twitter is more closely analogous to a letter (in which case the postal rule applies) or a telex (the rule relating to instantaneous electronic communications displaces the postal rule). As such, you would need to think what characteristics a tweet shares with each of the other forms of communication.

19.3.8.7 Which series of reports should be used?

Remember to use the correct version of a case that is reported in more than one set of reports. You will find details of the hierarchy of law reports and the Practice Direction (in chapter 6) but you may find Figure 19.7 useful for ease of reference.

It is frequently the case that mooters become so focused on the actual delivery of their speech that they forget that a whole range of other factors contribute to a thoroughly prepared and well-polished moot. Little details such as ensuring that you select the most appropriate series of reports for a particular case can go a long way to communicating an impression of professionalism and attention to detail to the judge. In the final decision as to who has won

---

3. The mode of communication used in *Entores*. The telex network is a switched network of printers similar to a telephone network, for the purposes of sending text-based messages. It was common at the time of *Entores* but has now mostly been superseded except in some maritime communications.

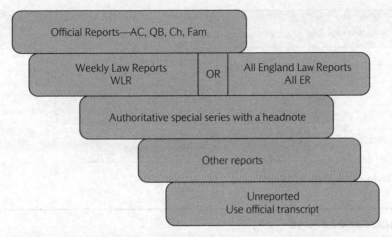

Figure 19.7 Hierarchy of law reports

the moot, the judge can be swayed by small details like this if the parties are otherwise evenly matched: a moot can be won by a quarter of a point, so even the smallest detail can be crucial.

Practical exercise

Make sure that you are familiar with the hierarchy of law reports. It is a good idea to practise selecting the most appropriate authority so that it becomes second nature to do so.

For now, can you put these (fictitious) case citations in the correct order?

- *R v Jones* [1999] 2 Cr App R 345
- *R v Jones* [1999] Ch 345
- *R v Jones* [1998] 3 WLR 1234
- *R v Jones* [1999] 1 All ER 98
- *R v Jones* [1998] Crim LR 42

 You will find the answer and additional exercises at **www.oup.com/he/finch8e/** *which will give you further guidance on choosing the appropriate reports to use.*

19.3.9 Articles

It can be useful to think of engaging in research for a moot as a staged process whereby you take a progressively deeper look at an increasingly narrow issue (see Figure 19.8).

Articles can provide a fantastic insight into the intricacies surrounding the interpretation of a particular issue or speculating on the implications of a particular case, so, in a way, can carry some of the weight of formulating your submissions for you. Articles may also provide a means to expand a particular legal principle into a new area in the absence of any case law that considers the issue. For example, the second point of appeal in the sample moot concerns whether a voicemail message should be likened to a letter or some other form of communication. It may be that you are able to find an article that looks at the law and considers how it applies to different forms of communication.

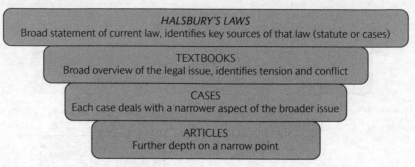

Figure 19.8 Researching a moot problem

 Practical exercise

Review the methods outlined in chapter 9 for finding articles. Note that the first stage of searching concerns the selection of key words and phrases to use as search terms. What words and phrases would you use to locate articles that might provide insight into the second point of appeal in the sample moot? Using search techniques effectively is a skill that will improve with practice so have a go at finding articles on the following issues:

1. Offer and acceptance by voicemail.

2. The *cy près* doctrine for charitable purposes concerning animals.

3. Circumstances that render the recipient of a gift liable for theft.

4. Liability for psychiatric injury caused to rescuers.

Compare your findings with the answers given online at **www.oup.com/he/finch8e/**. *You will find an explanation of the search terms and methods used to locate the material. There are further practical exercises online that will help you to become faster and more effective in locating relevant material.*

19.3.9.1 Choosing an article

When relying on articles to support your submissions in a moot, you should bear in mind that the receptiveness of the judge to the article may depend either on the status of the journal in which it was published or the reputation of the author that wrote it. Obviously, you cannot predict the preferences of the judge with regard to articles and it is a sweeping generalization to say that practitioner judges (solicitors, barristers, judges) prefer practitioner publications such as the *New Law Journal* whilst academic judges (lecturers) favour 'heavyweight' publications such as the *Modern Law Review* or the *Criminal Law Review*. Therefore, the best approach to take when choosing articles as authority is to use the one which best supports your argument. If the judge criticizes your choice of authority or asks if you are aware of a different article, try to have a reasoned explanation for your choice:

I am aware of the shorter piece in the *New Law Journal* but the article to which I have referred Your Lordship is a more detailed analysis of the law.

OR

I have read the piece to which Your Lordship refers but the article on which I rely is a more recent consideration of the law that takes into account new case law.

Of course, it may be that there is only one publication on that particular issue, in which case you could advise the judge of this to circumvent any criticisms regarding your choice of authority:

> This is the only academic commentary on this issue, My Lord, and is therefore the only guidance on the interpretation of this case that is available.

Do try to find out something about the author of an article if you want to rely upon it to support your interpretation of the law. Clearly, an article written by a leading expert with twenty years' experience will be better received than a case note written by a PhD student (not that the latter has no value, far from it, but the former is more likely to carry weight with the judge). Nobody will expect you to have a detailed knowledge of the background of the author, but a general awareness of the level of expertise of the writer will help your case:

> This article was written by so-and-so who is a Professor in contract law at the University of x who specializes in y and is the author of the leading work in this area.

This is preferable to either of the following (both of which are real answers given by mooters in response to a question from the judge about the author of an article they had relied upon):

> I don't know, my lecturer told me to use it.
> She's my criminal law lecturer. She's sitting over there. Do you want a word with her?

19.4 PREPARING TO MOOT

Once you have conducted your research and made a note of material pertinent to your point of appeal, you will be ready to move onto the next stage of preparation which takes you from the research stage to the moment that you enter the moot room. Do not keep these stages too firmly delineated in your mind; it may be that you do not realize that there is a gap in your research until you are putting your submissions together, in which case you will have to do more investigation of the law. Equally, once you receive the skeleton argument from your opponents, you will need to conduct research to find out exactly what it is that you plan to argue.

19.4.1 Constructing submissions

A submission is a strand of argument used to advance your point of appeal. In essence, your moot speech will be comprised of a series of submissions, each one dealing with a separate legal issue. There is no 'right' number of submissions and the same point of appeal could be broken up in several different ways, all of which would be perfectly acceptable. The following examples use the first point of appeal from the sample moot by way of illustration.

19.4.1.1 A single submission

In essence, this approach takes the entirety of the point of appeal and presents it as a single point:

1. The advertisement on the website was an offer

This has the merit of simplicity but it is not a particularly imaginative way to approach this point of appeal. It would be preferable if at least some information was added to substantiate this view and to make it read a little less like a straightforward 'cut' from the moot problem:

1.   There is binding authority upon this court which provides that the advertisement on the website must amount to an offer.

This is a brave approach as it leaves the mooter with little space to manoeuvre if the judge does not accept that the authority to which he is directed is binding. A less cut-and-dried alternative might be preferable:

1.   The preponderance of authority favours the construction of the advertisement on the website as an offer.

There is nothing wrong with making a single submission but it is worth considering whether your argument could be broken into more digestible chunks for the judge, particularly considering that the average time allocated to each mooter is around fifteen to twenty minutes.

19.4.1.2 Alternative submissions

This approach breaks your speech into chunks and avoids putting all your mooting eggs into a single basket as you are giving the judge two different ways of finding in your favour:

1.   The preponderance of authority favours the construction of the advertisement on the website as an offer.

2.   Alternatively, if this interpretation is not accepted by the courts, there are compelling policy arguments to support the treatment of the advertisement as an offer.

A policy argument is one which is not supported by authority (and which may actually go against authority) but which is nonetheless compelling on, for example, common-sense or moral grounds. It may be the case that strict application of case law would lead to a result which seems absurd in the context of the particular facts of the moot, for example, in which case policy grounds may dictate that the letter of the law should not be followed. Policy arguments can be supported by reference to overseas authorities or academic writings as well as case law and statute.

19.4.1.3 Cumulative submissions

This approach also breaks the speech into chunks but by dividing the overall point of appeal into smaller and more manageable segments:

1.   The advertisement on the website was sufficiently certain in its terms to amount to an offer.

2.   The inclusion of a specified quantity of goods in the advertisement removed any possibility of the vendor being contracted to supply goods that were no longer in existence.

3.   The respondent's subsequent actions in placing notification on the same website that the goods were no longer available demonstrated that she intended the advertisement to be an offer which would be binding upon acceptance.

It is important to remember that each submission should be a self-contained legal argument that is supported by authority as well as part of a larger legal question. For example, it is true to say that the 'big' legal question in the sample moot is whether the advertisement is an offer but this does break down into a series of sub-questions that form the basis of the three submissions above, each of which has been judicially considered in its own right.

19.4.1.4 Combined submissions

As the heading suggests, this approach combines cumulative and alternative submissions:

1. The advertisement on the website was sufficiently certain to amount to an offer.

2. The conduct of the respondent indicated that she intended the advertisement to amount to an offer.

3. Alternatively, even if the authorities do not support these submissions, there are compelling policy arguments that favour the treatment of the advertisement as an offer.

This approach is sometimes popular as a means of dividing the submissions that have some basis in legal authority into segments and then adding an alternative argument based upon policy as a 'back stop' if the earlier arguments are unsuccessful. This can be particularly useful if you feel that your arguments based upon legal principle are quite weak.

19.4.2 Preparing a speech

You will now be ready to turn your research and planning into a speech that can be delivered to the judge. Note from the outset that this section refers to the preparation of a speech rather than writing a speech. This is because writing out every word that you intend to address to the judge is one of the most counterproductive activities that you can do when preparing to moot.

There are several reasons for this:

1. **Good written English and good spoken English are not the same.** If you write a speech, you will probably use the same sort of words and phrases that you do when writing an essay, but this is not the sort of language that is best used in oral presentation. Oral communication tends to make use of more straightforward words and you may find that much of a written speech does not flow easily off the tongue when spoken out loud. Take heed of the experience from the early mooting career of one of the authors[4] who wrote a speech that included the phrase 'these cases are clearly of distinguishable material facticity' to which the judge responded 'do you mean that the cases can be distinguished on the facts, counsel? If so, say so. And stop reading your essay and speak to me, preferably in words that I can understand.'

2. **If you write a speech, you will read it.** If you read your speech, it is highly likely that it will sound flat, stilted, and expressionless plus you will not be able to make eye-contact with the judge if you are reading from a sheet of paper. Moreover, if you read, you are likely to lose your place if you take your eyes away from your paper and this is likely to make you flustered and waste valuable time as you shuffle through your papers to find your place (plus, rustling papers tends to annoy most moot judges).

3. **Your speed of delivery will be too fast.** Mooters who read from a prepared speech almost inevitably tend to do so far too quickly for their argument to be comprehensible to the listener. Remember that it takes more time to listen and to digest what you have heard, than it does to speak. Think about your lecturers. You would probably be really infuriated if any of them delivered their material at too fast a pace because it is difficult to take in what they are saying, let alone make a note of it. If you speak rather than read, you will have to think about your words and this is likely to slow your pace of delivery.

---

4. Emily.

4. **Reading does not demonstrate oral presentation skills.** Reading a prepared speech precludes the mooter from exhibiting a whole section of skills that are being evaluated by the judge. Not only does reading reduce your marks in this particular moot, it deprives you of an opportunity to improve upon your oral presentation skills.

5. **A scripted presentation is inflexible.** The judge may ask you a question that raises an issue that you had planned to address later in your speech. If you are tied to your script, you will need to find that point of your speech (more paper rustling) or, if you answer the question without reference to your script, you may find that you actually repeat the same point when you encounter it later in your speech.

That is not to say that you should not take any written material into the moot. Nobody expects you to deliver a twenty-minute speech without any written notes whatsoever and you will find that most practitioners have some notes to aid their recollection of the points that they wish to make and the order in which they are to be made. The form of your notes is a matter of personal preference. Many mooters use a series of cards (always numbered in case you drop them) each of which has a key point whilst others work from a plan that contains a list of numbered points. Others use a tablet, but make sure that it has sufficient charge before you begin.

19.4.2.1 Remember the housekeeping

Your speech must include various issues of housekeeping such as:

- Introductions: senior counsel for the appellant introduces everyone, senior counsel for the respondent introduces himself and his junior, junior counsel introduce themselves

- Summary of the facts: senior counsel for the appellant summarizes the facts of the appeal and senior counsel for the respondent may do so if there is a discrepancy between the team's view of the facts

- Summary of submissions: all mooters must summarize their submissions at the end of their speech

- Handover to the next mooter: all mooters should pass over to the next mooter properly rather than merely stopping and sitting down

- Reminder of the desired outcome: both junior counsel should close by reminding the judge of what they would like them to do, for example 'I would invite Your Lordship to uphold the appeal and confirm the finding of the court at first instance'.

19.4.2.2 Practise

It is always advisable to practise your moot speech out loud, preferably to an audience of at least one person, prior to the moot itself and to time your presentation. In the absence of an audience, you may have the means to record yourself delivering your speech; there is much to be learned from listening to an audio recording or watching a video recording of your performance. Try to overcome the natural reluctance to see yourself from a third-party perspective and instead take note of practical features: make sure that you are audible, that your pace of delivery is appropriate, and that you do not fidget or wave your arms about, for example. Try really to evaluate your performance objectively. You could make a two-column list of good and bad points and then try and think of practical ways in which you could improve on the weaknesses; for example, pausing at the end of key points or looking up towards the judge more often. Then record your performance again and see if it has improved. Even if you have no means of recording yourself, practising will help you become accustomed to the sound of your own voice and make the whole experience of standing up alone and speaking a more familiar one.

19.4.2.3 What do I call the judge?

Judges in the Supreme Court, Court of Appeal, and High Court (which is where most moots are situated) are addressed as 'My Lord' or 'My Lady' as appropriate.

In making oral submissions, mooters sometimes get confused over when to use 'Your Lordship' or 'Your Ladyship'. The distinction is quite straightforward:

- 'My Lord' or 'My Lady' is used where you are effectively calling upon the judge by name, and
- 'Your Lordship' or 'Your Ladyship' is used in place of 'you'.

So, for example, 'Do you have a copy of the bundle?' (which is informal and disrespectful) becomes 'Does Your Ladyship have a copy of the bundle?'. It is not 'Does My Lady have a copy of the bundle?', which would be analogous to saying, 'Does Lady Justice whoever have a copy of the bundle?' (this would just be an odd thing to say when addressing Lady Justice whoever directly). You can (and should) use both in the same sentence if the context requires it: 'My Lady, Your Ladyship has raised an interesting point, but …'

With enough practise and experience, using the correct form of address will become second nature.

Never call the judge 'Judge', 'Your Honour', 'Your Worship', 'Sir', or 'Madam'. These are the correct terms of address in less senior courts and you do not want to run the risk of annoying the judge by using the incorrect form of address as the very first thing you say.

19.4.3 Skeleton arguments

A skeleton argument is an outline of the submissions to be made in furtherance of the grounds of appeal that give the opposing team and the judge an indication of the nature of your case and the authorities that you intend to rely upon.

> You will find further examples of skeleton arguments at **www.oup.com/he/finch8e/**.

19.4.3.1 Exchange of skeletons

The rules of most competition moots require the exchange of skeleton arguments at least twenty-four hours prior to the moot whilst some national competitions will require exchange up to three days in advance. This means that you must construct a skeleton argument that outlines your submissions and authorities and provide a copy for the opposing team, usually via the Master of Moots (who will generally send a copy to the judge at this time). Even in internal competitions, an exchange of skeleton arguments or at least an exchange of authorities is usual the day before the moot.

IN THE Court of Appeal (Civil Division)

Beatriz Montes

-v-

Shanelle Watson

Senior counsel for the appellant:
The advertisement on the website was an offer capable of immediate acceptance and not an invitation to treat as contended by the respondents.

1. The advertisement on the website was sufficiently certain in its terms to amount to an offer capable of immediate acceptance.

Fisher v Bell [1961] 1 QB 394 (DC)

Partridge v Crittenden [1968] 1 WLR 1204 (DC)

2. The inclusion of a specified quantity of goods in the advertisement on the website removed any possibility that vendor could be contracted to supply goods that were no longer in existence.

Grainger v Gough (Surveyor of Taxes) [1896] AC 325 (HL)

Junior counsel for the appellant:

The offer contained in the advertisement on the website had been accepted thus a binding contract was formed prior to the purported revocation by the respondent.

1. A unilateral contract is capable of acceptance by performance. The appellant followed the stipulations of the advertisement on the website thus a binding contract was formed between the parties.

Carlill v Carbolic Smoke Ball Company [1893] 1 QB 256 (CA)

2. Even if the contract was not formed by performance, the respondent's revocation was not effective as the principle in *Entores Ltd v Miles Far East Corporation* [1955] 2 QB 327 (CA) is not applicable to these facts.

Entores Ltd v Miles Far East Corporation [1955] 2 QB 327 (CA)

LJ Korbetis v Transgrain Shipping BV (The 'Alexia M') [2005] EWHC 1345 (QB)

Senior Counsel: Ms Kalbir Khan
Junior Counsel: Mr Matthew Smith

Extract 19.1 Sample skeleton argument

19.4.3.2 Dealing with the opponent's skeleton

Ideally, once you have received your opponent's skeleton argument, you will be able to spend time studying their submissions and reading their authorities in order to ensure familiarity with their argument. It is a grave mistake to neglect this stage of preparation but some mooters take the view that they will still present their own arguments irrespective of the plans of the opposition team. This is an extremely unfortunate attitude and one that can lead to difficulties. In mooting, you should aim to know the opposing arguments as well as you know your own as only then are you in a position to counter them, and studying the opposing team's skeleton should provide a real insight into their approach to the moot.

• Obtain a copy of the authorities upon which the opposing team intends to rely.

• Read them carefully, noting the points that have the potential to support their argument and, more importantly, any points that are useful to your submissions.

• Are the cases that they have selected good law or have they been doubted or overruled?

• Can the cases they have chosen be distinguished on their facts from the facts of the appeal?

Remember, you cannot alter the wording of your submissions as they appear on the skeleton that you have sent to your opponents, but you can modify the content of your submission to take into account any points that have arisen as a result of the exchange.

19.4.3.3 Ethical considerations

Finally, a word about ethical considerations in the preparation of the skeleton argument: ideally, it should contain:

1. A clear statement of the submissions that will be made.
2. A corresponding list of the authorities that will be used to support these submissions.

Some mooters are reluctant to 'give away' their arguments to the opposing team in advance and try to formulate opaque or, worse still, misleading submissions. The ultimate in unethical behaviour is to include a case, usually a long and complicated one, which the mooters have no intention of using but which is listed on the skeleton to distract and confuse the opposing team. These practices are unacceptable and will be noted by the moot judge. Remember, moots are won by meticulous preparation and persuasive delivery, not by springing surprises on the opposing team.

19.4.4 Bundles

The final point to consider in preparation to moot is the construction of a bundle. A bundle is a collection of material upon which you will be placing reliance during your submissions. In practice, this is generally:

- A copy of the moot problem
- A copy of the skeleton argument
- Copies of each of the cases used by you (if you have individual bundles) or yourself and your partner (if you have a team bundle) in the order that they appear on your skeleton argument for the first time. It is good practice to use the copies of the bound law reports that you will find in the library rather than online transcripts (this is largely because of the pagination).

19.4.4.1 Bundle or no bundle?

In most moots, the preparation of a bundle is left to the discretion of the mooters. Bear in mind that it can be quite costly to prepare a bundle as it requires a fair amount of additional photocopying, so it is only worthwhile doing this if it is going to be an advantage to you.

A good bundle that is used effectively by the mooters can be a real plus but a poorly prepared or ill-used bundle is worse than no bundle at all, so it is not advisable to prepare one unless you do it properly and remember to guide the judge around it.

19.4.4.2 Preparing the bundle

If you decide to produce a bundle, you must be prepared to make full copies of each authority that you intend to use. It is poor practice to include only segments of a case. There is no need to include copies of cases that your opponent intends to use unless you plan to refer to the case in detail yourself, for example by quoting from it, in which case it should be included in the bundle. Make sure that you remember to signpost your use of your opponent's authorities, otherwise the judge may think that you have exceeded the number of cases permitted by the rules of the moot.

You should number each page of the bundle and some mooters use numbered dividers to separate the cases so that negotiation of the bundle is easier for the judge. Although you should have the relevant passages of the authorities marked (see Practice Direction 52 as amended by the Practice Direction: Citation of Authorities (2012)) you are still expected to be able to guide the judge there, using appropriate words:

> I refer Your Lordship to the case of Fisher and Bell which was reported in the first volume of the Queen's Bench Reports in 1961 at page three hundred and ninety-five. Your Lordship will find this case at Tab 3 of the bundle. I would like to direct Your Lordship to the words of Lord Chief Justice Parker on page three hundred and ninety-seven of the judgment, which is at page 17 of the bundle, halfway down the page, paragraph C, sentence commencing 'In my opinion'.

Bundles should not include authorities for propositions that are not in dispute.

In *Keystone Healthcare Ltd v Parr* [2019] EWCA Civ 1246; [2019] WLR(D) 406, Lewison LJ issued the following reminder on the importance of getting things right:

> 26. Finally, by way of postscript, it is a matter of considerable regret that the practice direction on the citation of authorities at [2012] 1 WLR 780 (referred to in PD 52C paragraph 29(2)) has been almost wholly ignored. We were supplied with print outs and handed down transcripts of authorities that have been reported in the official law reports (e.g. *Bristol & West BS v Mothew* [1998] Ch 1; *A-G v Blake* [2001] 1 AC 268; *Stein v Blake (No 2)* [1998] 1 All ER 724). Unreported cases were cited for propositions that could be found in reported ones. The whole of my gargantuan judgment in *Ultraframe (UK) Ltd v Fielding* [2005] EWHC 1638 (Ch); [2007] WTLR 835 (which runs to 494 pages) was copied, even though only a few pages were of any conceivable relevance to the issues on the appeal. Contrary to PD 52C paragraph 29 (2) many of the authorities were supplied without marking the relevant passages.
>
> 27. Judges of this court have limited time for pre-reading in advance of an appeal. Adherence to the practice directions means that that limited time can be more productively spent. Parties can expect that the cost of preparing a non-compliant bundle of authorities is at risk of being disallowed.

19.5 DELIVERING A MOOT SPEECH

Although this can seem like the most daunting aspect of mooting, remember that you have a solid background of research and preparation to rely on. Moreover, the majority of students who do participate in mooting will tell you that their nerves disappear as soon as they rise to their feet and start speaking to the judge. It can help to concentrate on the first words that you will say to the judge, as you will usually find that the words flow relatively easily once you are started.

19.5.1 Introductions, submissions, and conclusion

The starting point and conclusion of your speech will differ slightly according to the role that you have taken or been allocated in the moot (see Table 19.2).

Table 19.2 Structuring the speech

Senior Counsel	Junior Counsel
Introductions	Introductions
Senior counsel address the judge first on behalf of the appellant or respondent so are responsible for introducing the mooters and the issues to the judge.	As junior counsel follow on from their senior counsel, the main introduction will already have been made thus all that is needed is to remind the judge of your name.
Senior counsel for the appellant should introduce the appellants and the respondents whereas senior counsel for the respondents should simply introduce themselves and their junior.	Facts
Facts	Whilst there is no need to outline the entirety of the facts of the appeal, it is always useful to remind the judge of the key issues that comprise the second point of appeal.
Senior counsel for the appellant should also offer the judge a summary of the facts of the appeal. Senior counsel for the respondent should only deal with the facts of the appeal if he feels that the senior counsel for the appellant has misrepresented them in some significant way.	Conclusion
Conclusion	As the last person that the judge will hear speak for either the appellant or the respondent, junior counsel must summarize the submissions of both senior and junior counsel to pull the two strands of the appeal or response together. Junior counsel should invite the judge to grant the appeal and reserve the finding of the trial judge or Court of Appeal (appellant) or dismiss the appeal and uphold the decision of the trial judge or Court of Appeal (respondent).
Although the main responsibility for concluding for the appellant and respondent lies with junior counsel, senior counsel should summarize their submissions as they pass over to their junior.	

It is also good practice for each mooter to outline their submissions to the judge at the start in order to give a clear overview of the structure and content of the speech that will follow. The following is suggested wording for the opening and closing of senior and junior counsel arguments. Remember, there is no magic to any particular form of words; these are merely examples of the approach that could be taken.

Senior counsel for the appellant has the most information to include in the opening:

> If it pleases Your Lordship, my name is Ms Khan and I am senior counsel for Ms Beatriz Montes who is the appellant in this case. I am assisted by my junior counsel Mr Smith who will be addressing Your Lordship on the second point of appeal. My learned friends opposite Mr Simpson and Ms Narin appear for the respondent Ms Watson. Would Your Lordship benefit from hearing a summary of the facts of the case? [Pause to await a response, provide a brief summary if required and move on] My Lord, I shall be addressing the first point of appeal, namely that the advertisement on the website was an offer and not an invitation to treat as contended by the respondents. I shall be making three submissions in furtherance of this point of appeal, namely: [list them concisely—do not provide the same level of detail that is on the skeleton argument]. My Lord, might I proceed with my first submission?

Senior counsel's closing should be brief:

> In conclusion My Lord, it is the submission of the appellant that the advertisement on the website is sufficiently certain that it can amount to an offer which is capable of immediate acceptance. My learned junior will now address Your Lordship on the question as to the point in time at which the offer was accepted and a binding contract was formed. Unless I can be of further assistance to Your Lordship that concludes my submissions on the first point of appeal.

Junior counsel's opening may be equally concise:

> My Lord, as you have heard, my name is Mr Smith and I shall be addressing the second point of appeal on behalf of the appellant, Ms Montes, namely, that the offer was accepted and a binding contract formed prior to any purported revocation of the offer by Ms Watson. I have two submissions to make in furtherance of this argument: firstly [concise list]. May I proceed with my first submission?

The closing will be more detailed:

> My Lord, you have heard from my learned senior that the authorities favour the construction of the advertisement on the website as an offer and that reliance has been placed in particular on the attitude of the parties themselves towards the situation to support this conclusion. Your Lordship has also heard my submissions concerning the point in time at which the offer was accepted by Ms Montes and irrespective of whether this is to be taken as the time that the email was sent, when it arrived or at the resumption of trading hours, all these events preceded the notification of revocation to Ms Montes. Accordingly, I would invite Your Lordship to find in favour of the appellant by upholding the appeal and overturning the decision of the trial judge. Unless Your Lordship has any further questions, that concludes the case for the appellant.

19.5.2 Dealing with judicial interventions

It is almost inevitable that the judge will interrupt the delivery of your submissions to ask questions. This does not mean that your submissions are inaccurate or unclear; it is just part of the practice of mooting that enables the judge to test some of the core skills involved. For example, the judge will be able to ascertain how well you understand the issue at the heart of your point of appeal and the law that relates to it by asking questions and he will also be able to assess how you are able to depart from what you planned to say and then regain the flow of your argument after addressing the question. Keep in mind the following points.

19.5.2.1 Listen to the question

Too many mooters fail to listen to what the judge is asking as their mind is filled with thoughts along the lines of 'oh no, he's asking a question, I won't know the answer and then I'm going to look so stupid'. It is perfectly understandable that the prospect of answering questions might cause you to panic, particularly in the early days of your mooting career, but you cannot hope to give a good answer if you have not listened to the question.

19.5.2.2 Think before answering the question

Even if you have listened to and understood the question and know what to say, it is a good idea not to 'grab' at the question but to think carefully about how to present the answer to its best effect. Remember that it is better to pause and give a reasoned and coherent answer to the question rather than to gabble away with the first words that come into your head.

19.5.2.3 Ask for clarification

There is absolutely no point in trying to answer a question that you do not understand. Ask respectfully: 'I'm afraid that I didn't grasp Your Ladyship's meaning' or 'My Lady, I would be obliged if Your Ladyship could rephrase the question'. Alternatively, you could rephrase what you understand the question to be to check that this is correct before attempting to answer: 'Am I right in thinking that Your Ladyship is asking whether …'.

19.5.2.4 Deal with the question when it is asked

The judge will sometimes ask a question about an issue or case that you are going to address at a later point in your submissions. It is not good practice to tell the judge that you will deal with this 'later' for several reasons:

- It is impolite to make the judge wait for an answer
- The question must be relevant at this point of your submission or the judge would not have asked it
- It suggests to the judge that you are wedded to a script and cannot depart from it to answer a question

If you are really convinced that answering the question now would ruin the structure of your argument, it is acceptable to seek permission to deal with the question later: 'My Lord, I was planning to address this issue at a later point of my submission but, of course, if Your Lordship prefers I will deal with it now'.

19.5.2.5 Provide a clear, concise, and confident answer

Your response to questions should have the same ring of confidence as your submissions and should be relatively concise—it is poor form to keep rambling on in the hope that you will eventually hit on the answer to the question. Check that you have answered the question to the judge's satisfaction; 'Does that address Your Ladyship's question?' (never 'Is that alright?'). If you are keen to avoid the possibility that the judge might ask more questions, try asking instead: 'My Lady, might I continue with my submissions?'.

19.5.2.6 Ask for assistance

Ask the judge if you need some time/assistance to answer the question. The judge may say 'no' but there is no harm in asking: 'My Lord, might I take a moment to consult my notes/ the authorities so that I am able to address your question fully?' or 'My Lord, may I consult my learned junior?' (as you may not speak to others in the moot room without seeking the permission of the judge).

19.5.2.7 Know when to give up

If you really cannot answer the question, communicate this politely to the judge, stating 'My Lady, with apologies I find that I am unable to assist you on the point, might I return to my submissions'. The judge will usually allow you to do so and will only keep you with the question if he feels that he can guide you to the answer.

🌐 Visit **www.oup.com/he/finch8e** to watch a video of students participating in mooting and demonstrating these and other useful strategies and phrases. The video has accompanying commentary from the authors.

19.5.3 Using cases

It is usual for a great deal of time to be spent during the moot on the use of cases. The general idea is that the mooter presents principles of law taken from cases and seeks to persuade the judge that they should be applied to the facts of the moot in a particular way. As such, the effective use of cases is an essential part of a polished moot performance.

19.5.3.1 Which cases can I use?

To a certain extent, this depends upon the way that the moot rules are worded. If the rules state that each team can use eight cases, then each mooter within that team can use all eight cases if they wish to do so. If, however, the rules state that each mooter may use four cases each, then you cannot rely upon the four cases used by your mooting partner. Remember that a case which is cited in the facts of the moot is a court authority which can be used in addition to the allocated number of cases. In addition to this, you may use any of the cases relied upon by your opposite number (so senior counsel for the respondent if you are senior counsel for the appellant). In addition to this, you may refer to any material whatsoever, irrespective of whether it has been included on the skeleton argument of any mooter, in response to a judicial question.

19.5.3.2 Correct citation

Just as it is important to use the appropriate series of case reports during the moot, it is also essential that you follow mooting convention when referring to a case. This is best demonstrated by way of example. You will be familiar with the way that a case citation looks on paper:

> *Fisher v Bell* [1961] 1 QB 394

If you read that citation out loud, you might say that it is Fisher versus Bell nineteen sixty-one one queue-bee three nine four. This is *not* the correct way to cite a case orally. The following rules apply:

- The '*v*' in the case name should be read as 'and' (in a civil case) or 'against' (in a criminal case) and never as 'versus' or 'vee.'
- The name of the reports is said in full; they are never called by their abbreviation.
- Page and volume numbers must be spoken as words and not as numbers, for example, two hundred and fifty-five rather than two five five.

Following these conventions, you will be able to read the citation for *Fisher v Bell* correctly:

> I refer Your Lordship to the case of Fisher and Bell which is reported in the first volume of the Queen's Bench Reports for nineteen sixty-one at page three hundred and ninety-four.

You would only provide a citation for the case the first time that it is mentioned. On subsequent occasions, it is entirely proper to refer to the case as '*Fisher* and *Bell*'. If you are the respondent and the case has already been cited to the judge, you may refer to it as '*Fisher* and *Bell* as cited by my learned friend opposite'.

Just as the '*v*' in a case name is read as 'and' or 'against', the '*R*' in a criminal case is read as 'the Crown'. Therefore, a criminal case, such as *R v Caldwell* [1982] AC 341 would be read as 'the Crown against Caldwell which is reported in the Appeal Cases reports for nineteen eighty-two at page three hundred and forty-one'.

19.5.3.3 Summarize the facts

You should always offer the judge a summary of the facts of the case that you seek to rely upon after you have cited it to the court:

- Is Your Ladyship familiar with the facts of this case?
- Would Your Ladyship like to be reminded of the facts of this case?
- Would Your Ladyship like a summary of the facts?

You should prepare a summary of the facts of each case that you intend to present to the court—your own authorities, any court authorities, and, if you are the appellant, your opponent's authorities if it is possible that you will refer to them during your submissions as this will be the first time that they are presented to the court.

When you offer a summary of the facts to the judge, they may ask whether the facts are relevant. You need to know the answer to this question as it will become obvious if you are wrong in your answer. The judge is asking you whether you intend to draw parallels between the case cited and the appeal in order to persuade the court to reach the same conclusion or whether you intend to distinguish the facts in order to persuade the court not to follow the case. If so, then the facts are relevant. Alternatively, the facts may have no bearing whatsoever on the issue at stake in the moot but you are merely using the case as authority for a general legal principle. For example, you would cite *Barton & Booth*[5] in a criminal law moot as authority for the test to be applied to establish dishonesty; you would have no interest in the facts of the case, only the legal principle.

19.5.3.4 Quoting from a case

It is usual to quote from sections of the case. In doing so, it is your job to ensure that the judge can find the passage from which you are quoting: 'I would like to draw Your Lordship's attention to the words of Lord Diplock at page 324 of the judgment [pause for the judge to find that page; watch him, he will look up or nod when he has it] at paragraph B, halfway through the paragraph, sentence beginning "there is no doubt" [again look at the judge and wait until he indicates that he has found that right place and then begin to quote]'. You would pause at the end of the quotation to denote to the judge that you have finished and then recommence your submissions, preferably by explaining how that quotation applies to the facts of the moot.

Never quote from the headnote (anything said in the headnote will also be in the main body of the judgment) or from the speeches of counsel.

 CHAPTER SUMMARY

Getting started

- Make sure that you understand the roles of the different parties involved in a moot. It is a good idea to watch a moot or look at the clips online at www.oup.com/uk/finch8e/ to ensure you are clear about what happens when and how
- Analyse the moot problem carefully to ensure that you know what party you are representing, what ground of appeal you are addressing, and what the relevant facts are that make up the issue in hand

---

5. [2020] EWCA Crim 575, [2020] 2 Cr App R 7.

- Take care to ensure that you are familiar with the rules of the moot in relation to such matters as the number of cases that can be used and the time available for each mooter to present their submissions

Researching the moot

- Remember that you need to start with an accurate and authoritative statement of law so *Halsbury* might be a useful port of call
- Add depth to your understanding by reference to leading textbooks, articles, and cases
- Keep a strong focus on the central issue of the point of appeal and ensure that you take a balanced approach that notes rather than ignores opposing authority
- Be thoughtful in your selection of authorities and supporting material. Be prepared to justify your choice of cases to the judge if questioned

Preparing to moot

- Experiment with different structures and vary the content of your submissions until you find an approach that feels right. Your final choice of submissions should be the result of careful planning rather than being based on the first submissions that came to mind
- Prepare your submissions and note the main points on numbered cue cards. Never write a complete script or you will be tempted to read it and this is a cardinal mooting sin
- Leave yourself sufficient time to practise on several occasions before the moot, preferably in front of an audience of at least one person who will give you honest and constructive feedback on your performance. Alternatively, watching a recording of yourself can be a good way to gain insight into your performance
- Construct a clear and concise yet open and honest skeleton argument and ensure you meet the deadline for exchange
- If you decide to use a bundle, make sure that it is meticulously presented and that you are able to use it effectively, otherwise it will do you more harm than good
- Check each authority upon which you intend to place reliance to ensure that it is still good law and that you have the correct and appropriate series of law reports

Delivering the moot speech

- Try and make a confident start however nervous you may be feeling. Most people find that they forget about the presence of anyone else other than the judge once they have started to speak so it is effectively a two-person dialogue
- Take heed of courtroom etiquette at all times. In particular, make sure you address the judge appropriately for the court you are in. This will almost inevitably be My Lord/My Lady or Your Lordship/Your Ladyship and never Judge, Your Honour Your Worship
- Do not stray too far from the facts of the moot. Abstract statements of law are all very well and good but your key task is to use that law to persuade the judge to find in your favour in the moot. The judge will not do this unless you explain how the law applies to the set of facts before them
- Deal with judicial interventions when asked to do so and in a confident manner. Do not be afraid to ask for clarification or time to think
- Make sure you give the judge time to find the right place in a case or in your bundle. Pause frequently and watch the judge to see if they are keeping pace with you. Do not carry on regardless and hope they catch up. There is nothing to fear in silence so stand quietly and wait until the judge looks at you as this is a sign that they are ready for you to speak

Negotiation skills

20

INTRODUCTION

The focus of this chapter is negotiation. This is often predominantly seen as a method of alternative dispute resolution—that is, as a means of dealing with a legal dispute without the need for litigation—but it is also widely used to create legally binding relationships. Negotiation plays a role in the working life of most legal professionals and the ability to conduct an effective negotiation is an important legal skill. It is common for negotiation to feature in the lives of undergraduate law students, as well as students undertaking the LPC, SQE, or BPTC, either as an extra-curricular activity, as part of a skills programme embedded in the curriculum, or as a method of assessment. Participation in negotiation will give you a feel of how the law operates in practice as opposed to limiting your experience to 'law on paper' and it demonstrates a commitment to the development of legal skills that should strengthen your CV.

So negotiation is important in legal practice and it is important in the life of a law student. This chapter will help you to get started with negotiation by providing an introduction to the skills needed to prepare for and conduct an effective negotiation. It will cover all aspects of preparation and research as well as highlighting the problems that can arise once the negotiation is underway and the strategies that can be used to overcome them. In essence, it is a step-by-step introduction for those with no previous negotiation experience as well as a source of advice for the more experienced negotiator.

Learning outcomes

After studying this chapter, you will be able to:

- Recognize the role of negotiation in professional practice and have an insight into the skills necessary to conduct an effective negotiation

- Analyse a negotiation scenario and extrapolate information that provides an insight into the aims and interests of the client

- Engage in planning and preparation for negotiation which includes research into the factual and legal issues

- Open the negotiation in a professional manner that creates an effective working relationship between the parties and establish a workable agenda of issues to be addressed during the negotiation

- Work through each of the issues in an effective and ethical manner, eliciting necessary information from the other parties and managing concessions in a way appropriate to achieving the client's objectives
- Engage in a critical evaluation of the success of the negotiation and your performance as a negotiator in a way that enables you to use the experience as an opportunity to further develop your negotiation skills

20.1 ABOUT NEGOTIATION

Negotiation is essentially a mechanism for reaching an agreement between two or more parties. This agreement might be a way to resolve a legal dispute without going to court, in which case negotiation is a form of alternative dispute resolution, or it might be a means by which a legal relationship is created such as agreeing terms for the creation of a contract. Whether it involves making or breaking relationships, negotiation is a process where at least two parties with a common interest seek to reach an agreement that is acceptable to all the parties. This may be done by the parties directly but it is frequently done by lawyers on behalf of the parties especially in complex situations.

A negotiation can be conducted by telephone, in writing, by email, by video conferencing, or face to face. Distance negotiations offer fewer opportunities to interpret and respond to visual cues but that distance may be preferable when dealing with complex or emotional issues. Many negotiations will use a combination of methods of communication; for example, there may be an initial meeting at which the issues are established and explored followed by an exchange of emails to clarify points of contention and a final face-to-face negotiation to finalize the details of the agreement.

As a method of alternative dispute resolution, the objective of negotiation is to find a way for a dispute to be settled without litigation thus keeping parties out of the courts. In this, it shares an objective with other forms of alternative dispute resolution such as mediation and arbitration. These types of alternative dispute resolution differ in the way that they are conducted. Agreement is at the heart of negotiation. If the parties fail to reach an agreement, there is no settlement. This need for the parties to find consensus distinguishes negotiation from arbitration as the latter involves the imposition of an outcome on the parties by an objective third party making arbitration more akin to litigation. Mediation has more in common with negotiation as it involves a search for agreement between the parties but, rather than the oppositional process that characterizes negotiation, the proceedings are controlled by a mediator who facilitates discussion and seeks to help the parties to reach an agreed outcome. Although meditators are objective, they are able to introduce issues for discussion whereas the parties in a negotiation have direct control over which issues are addressed.

Negotiations can occur at any stage in the proceedings and can feature in most types of disputes; indeed, in most civil disputes, there is an expectation that there will be some attempt at alternative dispute resolution before the case reaches the courtroom. Even in criminal law, there is some scope for a degree of negotiation prior to court proceedings as representatives of the defendant can explore the possibilities of withdrawing or altering charges with the Crown Prosecution Service.

In recognition of the importance of negotiation as a legal skill, many universities run negotiation skills courses and negotiation competitions for their students. Many law schools enter teams in the National Student Negotiation Competition which takes place every year and is open to undergraduate and postgraduate students. It is organized by the Centre for Effective Dispute Resolution (CEDR) (www.cedr.com).

20.1.1 Types of negotiation

Although there are a number of different theories and models of negotiation, it is generally accepted that there are two main types of negotiation (although the terminology used to describe these categories varies) (see Figure 20.1).

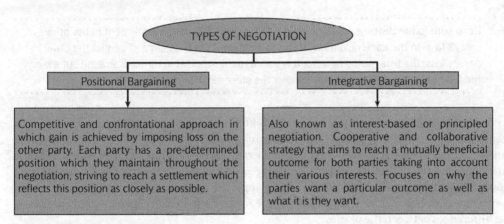

Figure 20.1 Positional and integrative bargaining

20.1.1.1 Positional bargaining

Positional bargaining is a term used to describe an approach to negotiation in which one of the parties takes up a particular position and argues for it irrespective of other issues. It is an approach that is best deployed where the issue is purely financial and there are no other issues to take into account. It is also best reserved for situations in which there is no need to preserve amicable relations between the parties.

Positional bargaining

Carter damaged two panels of his neighbour's fence beyond repair and agrees to pay for replacements. Oz, his neighbour, maintains that Carter should pay for the entire fence (ten panels) to be replaced as two new panels would stand out and spoil the look of the garden. She also demands top quality panels (£50 each) whilst Carter proposes to provide average quality panels (£30 each). Oz can fit the panels herself and there are no delivery costs.

The sum payable could be calculated four different ways:

- Two panels of average quality £60
- Two panels of high quality £100
- Ten panels of average quality £300
- Ten panels of high quality £1,000.

This gives a range of possible negotiated outcomes as shown in Figure 20.2. From a positional bargaining perspective, every pound gained for Oz leaves Carter one pound worse off. This is described as a zero-sum game.

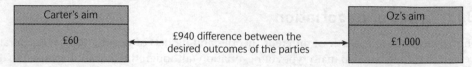

Carter's aim		Oz's aim
£60	← £940 difference between the desired outcomes of the parties →	£1,000

Figure 20.2 Positional bargaining

Zero-sum game describes a situation in which one party's gain is equivalent to the other party's loss. In the earlier example, if you calculate one party's gain and deduct the other party's loss, the total would be zero. It is useful to think of this in terms of sharing out a pie: the larger the slice taken by A, the smaller the piece remaining for B.

Positional bargaining is criticized for its inability to deal with non-pecuniary issues and its ineffectiveness in tackling complex negotiations involving multiple issues. Not everything can be reduced to monetary value: imagine, for example, how inappropriate it would be to use financial incentives to settle a dispute about access to children following marital breakdown. However, it can be useful in negotiations involving a strong financial element or one in which there is a narrow issue to be resolved and where reference to broader issues would emphasize the differences between the parties.

20.1.1.2 Integrative bargaining

This approach to negotiation focuses on the interests of the parties. It focuses on the needs, fears, desires, and emotions of the client in order to reach a negotiated outcome that is compatible with their goals. In essence, it looks at why the client wants particular things. If you focus exclusively on *what* the client wants without understanding *why* they want it, you could reach a settlement that seems objectively reasonable but which actually fails to satisfy your client's subjective interests. Have a look at this simple example that involves a disagreement over an orange.

Integrative bargaining

Sashi and Priya are arguing over one remaining orange. Their mother, Anjula, cuts the orange in half and gives half to each child, seeing this as a perfect compromise. However, if she had asked *why* each child wanted the orange, Anjula would have discovered that each had a different assignment at school the following day that involved part of an orange: Sashi needed the juice for a cookery class whilst Priya needed the peel for an art project. As such, Anjula's objectively fair solution failed to meet the subjective needs of either child whereas asking *why* they wanted the orange would have led to a different basis for division that would have given each child exactly what they wanted.

Self-test questions

Make a note of the sorts of interests that could be at stake in the following situations for each party. Remember, you need to move beyond an identification of *what* each party might want in order to discover *why* they want it.

1. A husband and wife engaged in negotiations for his access to their children following the breakdown of the marriage.

2. Negotiations for the sale of a house between the vendor and purchaser.

3. Contract negotiations undertaken on behalf of a professional golfer and a new sponsor.

4. The owner of a hotel and a carpet fitter concerning the supply and installation of new carpets.

🕐 *Answers to the self-test questions can be found at* **www.oup.com/he/finch8e/**.

As this example shows, it is not useful to make assumptions about a client's goals or to impose your interpretation of a good outcome on the client. By asking the client why they want something, you gain knowledge of their goals and this knowledge will enable you to negotiate more flexibly to achieve these goals in the face of unexpected offers from the other side.

Even in negotiations which appear to be limited to issues of a financial nature, integrative bargaining can be a more effective approach to adopt than positional bargaining. A client who has instructed you to obtain the highest financial settlement possible may have a particular reason to want or need money. Asking *why* should provide insight into the issues motivating the client and therefore give you greater flexibility in achieving a favourable settlement. Think about this example:

> David agreed to renovate Lydia's classic car by the end of March but fell behind schedule and is in breach of contract. David has completed most of the work and has purchased some expensive parts but Lydia wants her money refunded in full.

This seems straightforward at first glance. The work is not complete on Lydia's car and she wants her money back but further insight can be gained by enquiring into Lydia's goals. She needs the money to pay Shane who has agreed to fix the car within a week. Lydia needs the car within this time frame so that it can be used at her sister's wedding. So her goal is not a financial one at all. She needs the car by a particular date. Awareness of this goal gives more flexibility to negotiate with David on non-financial terms as David is able to offer Lydia a choice of three classic cars to use for her sister's wedding if she agrees to allow him to complete work on her car and keep the payment that has been made.

This should go some way to demonstrating the benefits of looking beyond the seemingly straightforward financial aspects of a dispute in order to find a more creative solution.

20.2 NEGOTIATION SKILLS

The good news is that it is likely that you already have a great many of the skills needed to conduct an effective negotiation. Most people have a solid bank of negotiation skills as we all learn to make bargains from a very early age. Think of the sorts of deal that are struck between parents and children such as those set out in Figure 20.3.

If you think about these situations, there are a number of factors that might influence the success of the negotiation. For example, the child may think that the trip to the park does not justify the effort of tidying their room whilst the parent may feel that the responsibility of feeding and entertaining another child is too onerous to be repaid by an offer of washing-up. In other words, the inducements on offer from one party may not be of sufficient value to the other party to tempt them into an agreement.

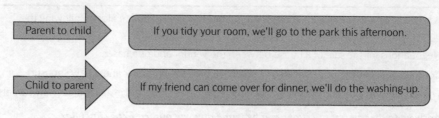

Figure 20.3 Deals between parent and child

Experience teaches us to be more proficient at negotiation. We become able to deal with more complex negotiations in which more accurate predictions are made about the factors that are likely to act as an incentive to the other party in order to obtain their agreement (see Figure 20.4).

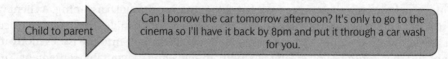

Figure 20.4 A more complex deal between parent and child

In this example, we can see that the child tries to predict the factors that might deter the parent from accepting the bargain and to pre-emptively negate them in order to gain agreement (a venue not associated with alcohol consumption and an early return time). This is supported by the offer of an incentive (washing the car) that involves little effort or loss to the child but which is consistent with the notion of taking care of another person's property that might help to persuade the parent to agree to the child's suggestion.

This example also shows us the importance of allowing room for manoeuvre within the negotiation strategy and it highlights the value of asking questions to find out more about the concerns of the other party (see Figure 20.5).

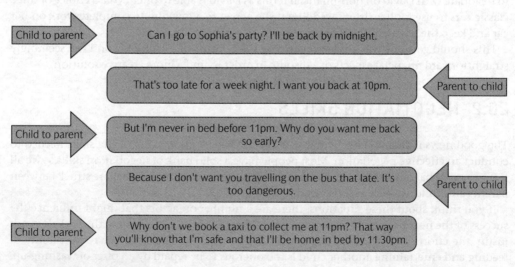

Figure 20.5 Room to manoeuvre

The child builds in room for manoeuvre by suggestion a later return time so that they can be seen to be making concessions to the parent whilst still staying out until the desired time of 11pm. By asking questions about the parent's concerns (remember the importance of finding out *why* as discussed earlier), the child is able to make a suggestion that overcomes these fears and contributes towards them achieving their objective.

From these simple examples of negotiation that have resonance with the everyday experiences of many people, we can identify some key negotiation strategies:

- The deal needs to be attractive to the other party so you need to offer them something of value.

- Find out (by asking questions) or predict (on the basis of your knowledge of the other party) what will hold value for them.

- Enhance your offer by 'throwing in' things of little value to you (this illustrates the variable nature of 'value': what holds value for one person may be of little significance to another).

- Keep the tone of negotiation amicable by making reasonable offers that leave you room to manoeuvre.

You may be wondering why you need to read a chapter on negotiation skills if these are learned naturally in childhood. The answer is that you need to be able to use the principles of negotiation in a structured and methodical way in relation to multifaceted and complex issues, so those basic skills will need some development. Everyday negotiations, such as those between parents and children, give you the basic skills but they are not enough on their own to prepare you for a complex negotiation in a legal setting. So you have the basic tools but these need to be strengthened and developed in order to prepare you to conduct a complex negotiation on behalf of a client, either in the real world of legal practice or in the setting of a university negotiation competition.

20.3 PREPARING TO NEGOTIATE

In the real world of legal practice, a negotiation will take place after a series of discussions with the client in which the solicitor will gain a clear and detailed insight into the nature of the client's problem and their objectives in terms of finding a resolution. A simulated negotiation is a replication of this process but usually one that involves written instructions from a fictitious client, although a few universities do opt to increase the reality of the experience by incorporating either face-to-face or email interaction with the 'client'. The most usual format for a negotiation competition is a two-way negotiation. This means that there are two parties in dispute and each party is represented by a team of (usually) two students. However, it is entirely possible for a dispute to involve more than two parties so you may encounter a multi-party negotiation in which there are three or more clients to be represented in the negotiation. This is a complicating factor to the negotiation as it is no longer a matter of finding compromise between two parties but a more complex exercise in balancing interests. The example used in this chapter is a two-way negotiation which is based upon a dispute between two members of a band. You will see the common facts that set out the background to the dispute and which are provided to both teams set out below along with the confidential information provided to the team representing one of the band members.

Sample negotiation: band dispute

Common facts

Persimmon for Gaia (often referred to as P4G) were the superstar band of the 1980s who are enjoying a surge of fresh popularity due to their appearances at various 1980s festivals in recent years. In fact, they are making more money now than they did at the height of their popularity in the 1980s and the four band members—Jonny, Kurt, Davis, and Jo-Jo—also gain a great deal of income from television appearances and participation in reality shows. So everything was going well for the four men who have always been good friends. But recently, an argument occurred which led to a split in the band. It came about when P4G were booked to play at the Nostalgia festival in Somerset. This was a new festival and the band were keen to play as they were all from Taunton originally so it was a chance to support a local festival. But problems arose when Jonny got into an online argument with one of the other acts booked at the festival, a singer called Omnoo, that jeopardized their appearance at the festival and, worse than that, tarnished their 'nice guys' image in the media. This caused tension between the members of the band, particularly Jo-Jo who feared that he would lose his new role on the judging panel of the *X Factor* as a result. In the arguments that ensued, Jo-Jo suggested that Jonny should 'do the decent thing' and leave the band so that they others would not suffer as a result of his stupidity. This sparked an argument about the division of the band's royalties that has escalated to include other points of contention. The matter is on the verge of court proceedings but the parties have agreed to attempt to resolve their issues through negotiation. The dispute is essentially between Jonny and Jo-Jo as Kurt and Davis have said that they will go along with whatever is agreed.

Confidential facts: Jonny

Jonny (John Grey) is the founder member of Persimmon for Gaia that enjoyed global success in the 1980s. He started the band in his garage in Taunton and recruited the other band members: Kurt (his cousin on bass), Davis (his best friend on drums), and Simon (a friend from his fencing club on guitar). Jonny also played guitar and was the lead vocalist for the band. He named the band, wrote most of the early music, and found the band gigs in local pubs around the Taunton area. They enjoyed moderate success and were content to be local celebrities. Simon decided to give up the band to focus on his career and suggested that his flatmate, Jo-Jo (John Parsons) might be a good replacement. Jo-Jo was an excellent guitarist but he was also a very talented songwriter and was soon writing most of their music. The band continued to play in local pubs but Jo-Jo had ambitions for them to go on to greater things and arranged for an agent to watch them perform, and it was this that set them on the path to global stardom. Although Jonny accepts that Jo-Jo's ambition and talent was a key factor in their success, Jonny has always thought of P4G as his band: he started it and worked away at it for years before Jo-Jo came along—it was his vision but Jo-Jo sharpened it and made it more marketable. There has never been any tension between the two men until now as Jo-Jo has suggested that Jonny should leave the band so that they can distance themselves from his public falling out with Omnoo and continue to enjoy their 'nice guys' reputation. Jonny cannot see why he should leave the band that he created. In his eyes, he is the band. He is its founder member, he named it, he is the lead singer, and he wrote the early music that created its distinctive sound. He has no objection to the other three leaving but Jonny would continue to be Persimmon for Gaia and would recruit new band members to replace the others just as he replaced Simon with Jo-Jo in the original line up. However, Jonny hopes that it will not come to this. Ideally, he would like to find an agreement that allows the band to continue as it has been all these years.

The problem is that Jo-Jo is now saying that, irrespective of whether Jonny leaves the band or they continue to perform together, he wants to revisit their agreement to split the royalties from their music equally on the basis that he believes that he is the creative force behind the band who wrote most of the music. Jonny accepts that Jo-Jo wrote all but ten of their songs (they have more than two hundred) which he wrote in the early days before Jo-Jo joined the band but he feels that it was a more collaborative venture than Jo-Jo seems to be suggesting. Jo-Jo would sit at the piano and play bits of a tune and the others would join in with their instruments, a tune would emerge, and they would then all suggest lyrics to go with the music, although it was Jo-Jo who took their ideas and fitted it together into the final version of the song. Jonny feels that their original agreement of a four-way split of royalties should continue. However, if Jo-Jo insists on altering this arrangement, he will have to give up all rights to royalties earned from the first ten songs which were written by Jonny. Moreover, Jonny will not permit the band to play these songs if he has to leave the band. He knows that this will be a problem as one of those songs 'Owl' is their ultimate best-seller and by far the most requested of all their songs: they have never had a booking where the organizer has not requested 'Owl' as one of their songs and it is always the song that they play as an encore at the end of a performance.

Jonny is worried that there would be a way for the other three members to force him out of the band and to continue to perform without him. He wants to resist this but, if the worst came to the worst, then he would expect a large lump sum to compensate him for loss of his right to perform plus a percentage of the fee, say 10 per cent, for every appearance the band makes without him. However, that is very much a measure of last resort. Jonny has instructed you to represent him in negotiations with Jo-Jo with a view to finding an amicable resolution to their problems that will allow them all to continue to work together.

🕑 *You will also find the confidential facts that would be given to the other side (the team representing Jo-Jo) on the online resources at www.oup.com/he/finch8e/ along with some video resources that demonstrate some useful techniques and negotiation skills.*

As the confidential facts set out all the information available about the dispute, it is important to ensure that you make effective use of them to prepare for the negotiation. Just reading through the instructions a couple of times is not enough. Unfortunately, this is all that some students do and it tends to lead to a weak performance as much more is required by way of preparation and planning to be able to negotiate effectively. Rather than thinking of 'the negotiation' as being the face-to-face discussion between the teams, it is preferable to think of it as a two-stage process (see Figure 20.6).

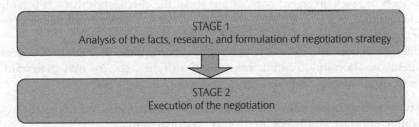

Figure 20.6 Negotiation as a two-stage process

Although settlement is reached at the second stage, the preparatory process is an essential foundation to conducing the negotiation and it should be undertaken with diligence. The second stage simply cannot be completed with success if insufficient preparation has been done at the first stage.

There are three elements to preparation for a negotiation: analysis of the scenario, research into the law and the facts raised, and planning a strategy for the negotiation. This is an iterative process which means that it should not be seen as three separate stages to be a carried out one after another but repeated as necessary in light of each other. In other words, you might start by analysing the scenario to work out what the issues are and then carry out research into the law which might cause you to return to your analysis to check whether your view of the issues has changed or whether any new issues can be identified. Similarly, once you start to plan your strategy, you may realize that there are gaps in your knowledge of the law that necessitate further research. So to prepare effectively, try to think of the three stages as a cycle that you repeat as many times as necessary rather than as separate stages (see Figure 20.7).

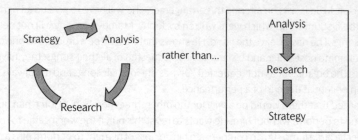

Figure 20.7 The cycle of preparation

Each of the stages will be explained in more detail in the sections that follow.

20.3.1 Analysis of the scenario

Analysing the scenario is the starting point of negotiation preparation as it contains all the information that is available to you about the facts of the dispute and the client's interests and priorities. You should pay particular attention to the client's instructions in terms of what they want from the negotiation as it is this that you need to achieve rather than an agreement that seems to you to be appropriate on the facts.

Working as a team has advantages both during the negotiation itself and during the preparatory stages as it reduces the risk that something important will be overlooked. It can also be a good way of highlighting ambiguities in the client's instructions as it will sometimes be the case that two different students reading the same scenario will draw different inferences from the same facts or reach divergent conclusions about the client's priorities. It is far better to spot these ambiguities and address them during the planning stages rather than to notice them for the first time during the negotiation.

It is generally a good idea to read the instructions several times through to get a general feel for the client's position and to familiarize yourself with the facts. You may then want to start to engage in closer analysis that takes into account the following points:

- **What is the general area of law involved?** In other words, identify the relevant area of law, for example, contract, family law, negligence, personal injury.

- **What does the client want?** Make a list of things that you need to achieve for your client during the negotiation, taking note of implied as well as express aims such as a quick resolution, a desire for an amicable resolution, or reluctance to litigate.

- **What are the client's interests?** Again, these might be stated explicitly in the scenario or you may need to read between the lines. Exercise caution in doing this; remember the pitfalls of making false assumptions about the client's interest noted earlier. Identify the client's interests by working down the list of 'wants' and asking the question 'why'. For example, the client may want to avoid court action but do you know why? It may be because it is expensive or in order to avoid any negative publicity and maintain an undamaged reputation. The underlying issue is likely to have an impact on the way in which the negotiation is handled.

- **What, if any, limitations are there?** For example, are you instructed to prioritize a particular aspect of the negotiation? Are you told that a particular outcome is unacceptable?

You need to be clear about what you can and cannot agree on behalf of the client. There is no point in agreeing something that the client will not accept.

- **What matters to the other party?** Are there any clues that provide insight into their priorities? Again, this may be explicit or implicit.

- **What are your strengths and weaknesses** and how do you plan to deal with them in the negotiation? This can be a key part of developing your negotiation strategy.

Self-test questions

Have a look back at the sample negotiation earlier in this chapter and have a go at analysing the scenario, remembering to take account of these six key points:

1. What is the legal framework for the negotiation?
2. What does Jonny want?
3. What are Jonny's interests?
4. Are any boundaries placed on the negotiation?
5. What do you anticipate that Jo-Jo might want from the negotiation?
6. What are the strengths and weaknesses of Jonny's case?

⏱ *Answers to the self-test questions can be found at* **www.oup.com/he/finch8e/**.

20.3.2 Research

Once you have analysed the scenario to acquire a good grasp of the facts and have started to formulate the issues, you will be ready to engage in research. The research stage is an important part of your preparation as it will help you to ensure that you have a full understanding of the client's problem and the legal framework within which it is situated.

20.3.2.1 Researching the law

In relation to contentious negotiations, that is, those involving a legal dispute that has the potential to end up in court, the result is an all-or-nothing outcome based upon application of the law to the facts. In other words, the law is used to determine which party wins and which party loses. A negotiation is an alternative approach to dispute resolution that involves giving both of the parties something of what they want and thus keeping the case out of court. As such, it is important that you do not try to turn your negotiation into a court case by presenting legal arguments in order to 'win' the case for your client. Instead, you should concentrate on finding persuasive arguments that achieve an outcome that is acceptable to your client but that also offers something attractive to the other party. The role of the law here is to inform the way that you use the facts and to help you to formulate a strategy for your negotiation. In essence, you need to be able to answer two questions:

1. **If the case were heard in court, would my client win?** The answer to this question is often a good indication of how much bargaining power you will have in the negotiation. If your client's case is strong then it is logical to assume that the other party's case is weak and that they therefore have greater incentive to reach a negotiated settlement. However, you

need to remember that you only know one side of the story and your client may have omitted facts that show the case in a different light. Moreover, even if the case seems likely to succeed, there may still be good reasons why your client does not want to go to court. Litigation is slow and expensive plus its all-or-nothing nature tends to make it unsuitable in some cases where the parties want an ongoing relationship. Negotiation also offers greater flexibility for the client to determine the shape of the settlement and to achieve the things that are of most importance to them in a way that may not be possible with a court-imposed outcome. Finally, there are no certainties in litigation so there may be even more incentive to negotiate even if that means reaching an agreement that is somewhat less than your client hoped to receive: remember that part of something is better than all of nothing which is what the client may receive if the case goes to court and they lose.

2. **If the case succeeded in court, what would my client receive?** The answer to this question will help you to find your 'bottom line' as you would usually not want to negotiate a settlement that gives your client a worse outcome than they would receive if they went to court and were successful. Remember, though, that sometimes a quick settlement that guarantees your client something may be preferable for them to the delay and uncertainty of waiting for the case to be heard in court. You will need a grasp of the financial issues raised by the case. These may be straightforward—damage to a car that cost £2,000 to repair—but how much money would you ask for to compensate your client if they suffered a broken arm in a car crash? It would help here to consult the tables that exist for calculating damages as part of your legal research or to look at decided case law to see if it offers a useful basis for comparison.[1]

The ability to answer both of these questions and to consider them in conjunction with each other is a key factor in determining how to tackle the issues in a negotiation and will be important in helping you to evaluate whether an offer made by the other team is an attractive one for your client.

Is it a good offer? Let's imagine that your client wants a settlement of three elephants but the other party offers one elephant. Is this a good or a bad deal? You can only answer this question by considering the strength of their case and what your client would be awarded if he was successful at court. In simple terms, if you think that you have a 90 per cent chance of winning and that a court would award your client three elephants then one elephant does not seem like a good offer. However, if you think that you have only a 10 per cent chance of winning at court then perhaps accepting one elephant is a good deal for your client. These factors can also help to alert you to anomalous offers from the other team: if you know that a court would award your client three elephants, an offer of five elephants from the other team should lead you to question why they are offering such a seemingly good deal.

Your evaluation of the desirability of offers made by the other team will depend upon your assessment of the boundaries of an acceptable agreement. You will find an explanation of how to determine these boundaries in section 20.3.3 on strategy.

These two questions are relevant to negotiations aimed at resolving disputes but have less (or no) bearing on negotiations where the objective is to create a new relationship between the parties. You will see an example of this type of negotiation in the multi-party scenario discussed later in this chapter. It involves a festival organizer negotiating with two bands to agree

---

1. W Norris and others, *Kemp & Kemp: Quantum of Damages* (Sweet & Maxwell). Updated quarterly; also available online via Lawtel.

the terms upon which they will perform. In such a case, the legal background will concern contract formation and may also involve intellectual property issues such as copyright and performance rights.

Do bear in mind the iterative nature of the analysis–research–strategy stages of negotiation preparation. It is a good idea to revisit your analysis and formulation of the issues once you have done some research into the legal framework in case this knowledge changes the issues that need to be addressed.

It is also important to remember that a negotiation is an agreed settlement and it is not binding. This is the case irrespective of whether the negotiation is aimed at dispute resolution or the creation of a new relationship. In both instances, therefore, it may be relevant to consider a further question:

3. **What will happen if the terms of the negotiation are breached?** If the negotiation was aimed at dispute resolution and its terms are breached, it is likely that the case will end up in court after all. This means that there is a real need to ensure that any negotiated settlement is genuinely acceptable to both parties as this reduces the risk that there will be a breach of the agreement. If the objective of the negotiation is the creation of a new relationship, then contemplating what will happen if the terms of the contract are breached could be an important part of negotiation terms. Think about all the things that could go wrong and try to ensure that you include some remedial measures in your agreement. For example, what will happen if one of the bands does not turn up to perform at the festival? Will it be enough that they do not receive their fee or would the organizer expect further compensation to reflect the disruption to the festival?

It may be that your scenario raises legal issues that you have not covered on your law degree in which case you will need to be creative in your research. You might want to revisit the guidance provided on legal research in chapter 3 and chapter 6.

20.3.2.2 Researching the facts

The scenario might involve factual issues that are unfamiliar to you and which you feel that you need to understand in order to be better able to deal with the issues raised in the negotiation. In the example involving a dispute between band members, you might want to know who usually owns the name of a band or how royalties are divided between band members. Now each of these questions might have an answer that can be found by applying the law (for instance, there could be a contract that deals with these issues) but remember that you are not concerned with the strict application of the law as you would be if the case reached court but in the wider possibilities that will enable you to reach a settlement. With this in mind, it might help you to understand how similar disputes have been resolved. So searching the internet might give you a sense of what your client can expect and whether what they want is realistic.

This is not dissimilar to the position in practice as clients will present a familiar legal issue (e.g. a contractual dispute) in a wide variety of factual settings. Of course, if you worked in a specialist area of law—take construction law as an example—then you would soon become familiar with the factual background of your specialism and, of course, you could always ask a client to explain things that you do not understand that seem material to the dispute. Even with subject expertise, it still makes sense to check factual information to ensure that you do not place too great a reliance on the client's perception of the facts, which may be inaccurate or distorted, to present their case in a favourable way. Imagine, for example, taking a client's assertion that a journey from Arborfield to Wokingham cost £400 in fuel without checking the distance between the towns (which is actually about five miles). In essence, then, you should always ensure that facts which are objectively determinable are objectively determined.

In other words, if it is possible for you to find something out for yourself, you should do so as only then will be you be confident that you are basing your negotiations on accurate and unbiased information.

> ### Practical exercise
>
> Think about the facts you might want to know in preparation for the negotiation between the band members.
>
> *You will find some suggestions online at* **www.oup.com/he/finch8e/** *along with explanations of the reasoning behind them.*

It may seem tempting to assume that all you need to know about the facts is provided in the scenario but researching the facts might help you to understand the issues in the negotiation in a different way. It may also disclose all manner of issues within the scenario that you would not otherwise have noticed. This can be particularly useful when you consider the flexibility that you have to negotiate a settlement that is in line with your client's interests. In other words, you may be able to find inspiration for an outcome that satisfies your client's objectives but which is not explicitly set out as something that they want in the facts. For example, perhaps both parties in the band negotiation want to ensure that there is a lot of good publicity for the band in the news media. You know that the festival takes place in Taunton so perhaps research into the area would disclose some local cause or charity that the band members could agree to promote together to restore their reputation and to attract media coverage. It is always important to look at the bigger picture in a negotiation and to try to find flexible and creative ways of achieving your client's goals without departing from the instructions given.

Once you have analysed the scenario and conducted research into the relevant law and any facts that needed exploration, you are ready to start planning your negotiation strategy. Remember though that it may still be necessary to reconsider your issues or conduct further research when you are formulating your strategy.

20.3.3 Strategy

This stage of preparation bridges the gap between planning to negotiate and the actual negotiation with the other team (or teams, in a multi-party negotiation) because it is here that you start to think about what points you will present and how and when you will present them. There is no single right answer here. In any negotiation, there are a number of different strategies that could be used to reach an agreement, all of which may be equally valid. You will, however, need to be sure that your strategy is realistic in terms of the strength of your case and the extent to which it achieves an outcome that is acceptable to your client in light of all the variables in the scenario.

20.3.3.1 Identifying potential outcomes

It should go without saying that you need to evolve a strategy that you believe will lead to an agreement that is in line with what your client has instructed you to obtain. However, this needs to be flexible because you will need to react to the points raised by the other team and take into account what they are trying to achieve for their client. You should, of course, try to anticipate what the other party is likely to want or how they are likely to respond to the things that your client wants as part of your preparation but it is still likely that they will offer something that is not what you have anticipated. You need to be able to evaluate the value of any offer to your client to determine whether it is a good one. In order to do this, you will need to work out (as best you can given that you only know one side of the story) the range of possible outcomes on each point and how they fit together as a negotiation settlement for your client. In doing so, you will be able to see the following positions:

- **Best negotiated outcome.** This is the 'best case scenario' outcome to the negotiation. It is what you will achieve for your client if you are successful in achieving the outcome that they want on all points.

- **Worst negotiated outcome.** As you would expect, this is the 'worst case scenario' that is still acceptable to the client. So it is an agreement that the client will accept but is at the bottom end of what they consider to be acceptable.

So a calculation of the best and worst negotiated outcomes will give you the parameters of your negotiation. This means that you know what your client ideally would like (best) and what they would reluctantly accept (worst) on every issue. The parameters of your negotiation fall within these two points. It would not be sensible to agree something that falls below your client's 'bottom line' on any of the points as the client is unlikely to accept this and the negotiation will have failed.

There are two further positions that you have to keep in mind so that you can assess whether you are achieving a good deal for your client. Essentially, this involves predicting the two possible outcomes for your client if the negotiation fails:

- **Best alternative to negotiated agreement (BATNA).** Essentially, this position represents the most advantageous outcome that your client could expect if the negotiation fails or if there is no negotiation. In many cases, this BATNA will be that the case goes to court and the judge finds in favour of your client. Other BATNAs are possible though: perhaps the most favourable outcome if the negotiation fails is that nothing at all happens so that the status quo is maintained.

- **Worst alternative to negotiated agreement (WATNA).** Conversely, the WATNA is the worst possible outcome for your client if the negotiation is not successful and, as you might expect, this is often that the case is heard by a court that rules against your client. Remember that the losing party at court usually has to cover the legal costs of the successful party so that will need to be factored into the calculation of the WATNA as well as other negative factors such as damage to reputation or loss of an existing business relationship.

Knowledge of the BATNA and WATNA is a crucial part of your negotiation strategy. You have to be conscious of the adverse consequences for your client if you fail to reach an agreement and how likely those consequences are to occur. In essence, the weaker your client's position would be at court, the greater the incentive to reach a negotiated settlement. It is important to bear in mind that sometimes a deal that offers little for your client but means that there is no risk of litigation will be a very good deal if there is a high likelihood that a court would find against them.

Self-test questions

Use the band dispute negotiation to practise finding these four positions.

1. Best negotiated outcome
2. BATNA
3. Worst acceptable outcome
4. WATNA

Having done this, try to assess the strength of the client's bargaining power. Remember that this is linked to whether they would win if the case went to court and what they would receive if they won but considered in the context of what the client has instructed you that they want to achieve. Sometimes it is the case that the client wants something that the court would be unwilling or unable to award—usually something that is unrelated to the legal issues in the case—in which case even a case which has a strong likelihood of success at court is not preferable for the client to a negotiated settlement.

 Answers to the self-test questions can be found at **www.oup.com/he/finch8e/**.

20.3.3.2 Formulating the issues

Once you have identified the most beneficial negotiated outcome for your client, you can break this down into a series of issues that can be dealt with individually within the negotiation. These are points that need to be resolved in the negotiation and your client will have a preference as to the outcome on each point. Using the band negotiation as an example, you can see that there are the following issues set out in the confidential facts for the team representing Jonny:

- Who will perform as Persimmon for Gaia and who owns the right to the use of the band's name?

- How are the royalties to be shared amongst the band members (a) if they stay together and (b) if they split up, taking into account that different songs were written by different band members?

- If the band no longer performs together, how much money will Jonny receive from their performances?

Once you have identified the issues, you may like to think about which order you would like to address them in during the negotiation. In this example, you have alternatives to consider. So Jonny's preference is for the band to continue to perform together and for the current arrangement for a four-way division of the royalties to continue. However, he seems to have accepted that this may not be possible and has offered alternative objectives if he cannot achieve his preferred outcome.

This can be helpful in suggesting an order in which the issues could be discussed: there is no point in considering how the royalties will be divided until you know whether there is an option for the band to stay together as this will affect what Jonny wants to happen with regards to royalties. In essence, you need to consider the way that the issues relate to each other to determine whether there is a critical pathway through the negotiation—in other words, a particular order in which the issues need to be determined—or whether the order in which the issues are considered is more of a matter of preference than necessity.

If there does not seem to be any logical requirement to discuss a particular issue before others, you might still want to give some thought to the order in which you would like to address the issues.

- **Hardest to settle first.** This ensures that there will be sufficient time to thrash out the issues on the trickiest point but you need to keep an eye on the clock to ensure that you have time to consider the other issues too. It may be the issue that involves the most argument which may get the negotiation off to an acrimonious start so be sure to manage the tone of the discussions carefully.

- **Easiest to settle first.** This can be quite a good strategy because it establishes a mood of agreement and cooperation and this can be useful in keeping the discussion calm when the more controversial issues are discussed thereafter.

- **Most important issue first.** Prioritizing the issue that matters the most to your client can be sensible as you may be willing to make concessions on the points that follow once the most important issue is agreed.

- **Least important issue first.** You may be more willing to make concessions on an issue which is of little concern to your client and this can be used to strategic advantage when trying to secure a better deal on the more significant issues that follow: 'well we moved a long way towards you on issue x so we'd hope to see similar flexibility from you on issue y'.

20.3.3.3 Balancing the issues

It would be unusual for a negotiation to involve a single issue. Multiple issues add complexity to a negotiation because you are not just agreeing each point in isolation but considering them collectively to see whether they fit together into a good settlement for your client. There is also an element of strategy here. You can make concessions on an issue that is of little importance to your client in order to strengthen your position when seeking concessions from the other team in relation to an issue that holds more significance for your client. So you are not just agreeing each point in isolation; you are balancing them against each other. In essence, you are saying 'I'm prepared to give away a lot on issue x in order to gain a lot on issue y'.

In order to carry out this balancing exercise, you need to take into account two factors:

- Your client's top and bottom line on each of the issues
- How important each of the issues is to your client.

When you can see the boundaries of each issue and their relative importance to your client, you will start to gain an understanding of how they can be offset against each other. This will allow you to make concessions on one issue in order to gain ground on another issue. This is an effective negotiation strategy and it helps you to keep your focus on the 'big picture'—the client's ultimate objective in the negotiation—rather than placing too great an emphasis on each separate point.

For example, you may feel that the most important objective from Jonny's point of view in the band negotiation is to ensure that he continues to perform as part of Persimmon for Gaia. In order to achieve this, he may be prepared to make concessions about the division of royalties even though his preference is to maintain the four-way equal split between the band members.

20.3.3.4 Generating more options

The negotiation scenario will not provide detailed instructions of all the potential outcomes that are agreeable to your client. You are provided with some indication of their aims and also of their broader interests and you should have tried to anticipate what the other party will want from your client. Working within this framework, try to generate some creative ways in which the aims of both parties could be satisfied.

For example, if the issue of band membership becomes contentious, for instance if both parties are insistent that they want incompatible outcomes (Jonny wants to remain in the band but Jo-Jo wants him to leave), then it would be useful to prevent deadlock if you can come up with an innovative solution that gets around this seemingly irreconcilable position. Perhaps you could suggest that the band continues to perform together for a specified period of time to see whether they can continue to work together and overcome their problems.

This is just one example of a creative use of the facts which is within the spirit of your instructions but which is not an outcome that is stipulated within your client's instructions. Remember that you cannot make up facts that are not included in the scenario (and you will be penalized for doing so) but you can draw reasonable inferences from the facts, provided you remain within the spirit of your instructions.

20.3.3.5 Negotiation plan

Once all the analysis and planning is complete, you might find it useful to prepare yourself a schedule of negotiation that notes the issues that you need to discuss, the order in which you would like to address them, and your best and worst outcome on each issue so that you can see quite clearly how much scope for negotiation there is on each point. This can serve as a particularly useful reminder not to move outside your instructions. It will also help you to see how the points relate to each other. This need be no more than one side of A4 and should be used as a reminder of your key issues rather than a strict schedule (you will be expected to demonstrate flexibility, so must be prepared to depart from your plan) or a crib sheet (good negotiations involve personal contact, not paper shuffling). You can see an example of how part of such a plan might look in Figure 20.8.

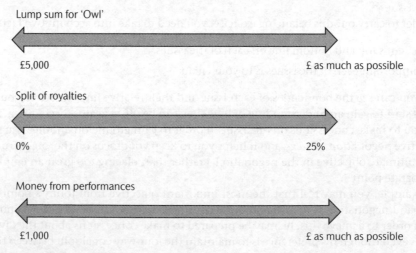

Figure 20.8 Issues and parameters for negotiation

20.4 CONDUCTING THE NEGOTIATION

This is the section of the chapter that you have been waiting for, isn't it? We've talked about the nature of negotiation and worked through all the stages of preparation and planning but this is the really important part: the bit where you find out what to actually do in the negotiation. Right? Sadly it is not that straightforward. That is because it is not really possible for one person (me) to tell another (you) how to negotiate. You and I would negotiate differently because we are different people with different personalities and different ways of seeing the world. The only real answer that can be given to 'how do I negotiate?' is that you have to speak in a way that puts your points across in the way that you have planned, listen to what the other team says, and respond appropriately to their points, modifying your own position where appropriate in order to work towards agreement. That is the best advice that anyone can give you. There is no magic formula of things that you should say or an order in which you should say them in order to negotiate 'properly' and any guide that purports to give you such a formula is misleading. It is never a good idea to go into a negotiation playing the role of a negotiator: you should go into the negotiation as you and set about negotiating in a way that feels natural and suitable to the situation that you are in.

20.4.1 Negotiation styles

You can, however, look at the work that exists on negotiation styles to determine where your natural style lies to determine whether you need to make any adjustments to maximize your chances of negotiating effectively. Figure 20.9 is often used to demonstrate negotiation styles that takes into account two scales: assertiveness and cooperativeness.

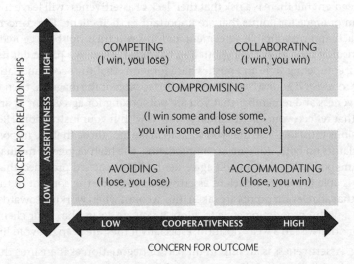

Figure 20.9 Different negotiation styles

Imagine a 1–10 scale for assertiveness and for cooperation and use this to plot your position on the diagram to see what this suggests about your natural negotiation style. For example, if you feel that you are 3 out of 10 for assertiveness but 8 out of 10 for cooperativeness then that would make you an *accommodating* negotiator. As the objective of negotiation is to reach agreement, you may feel that this is a good style to adopt but, as you will see from the diagram, being too cooperative without being sufficiently assertive may lead you to reach an agreement that is not sufficiently favourable for your client.

Take a moment to think about each style of negotiation. It is important to consider not only your own style but the style of the person who is negotiating on behalf of the other party. The dynamics of a negotiation and, ultimately, the agreement that is reached depends upon the interaction of the negotiators. This means that an *accommodating* negotiator will work differently and reach a different agreement with a *competing* negotiator than they would with an *avoiding* negotiator.

- **Avoiding.** It should be clear that very low scores on both scales is not a recipe for great success in a negotiation. Avoiding is characterized by an 'I don't care' attitude in which the negotiator is not able to present the client's interests with sufficient persuasiveness (low assertiveness) and is not very receptive to the proposals put forward by the other negotiator (low cooperativeness). This is a very passive negotiation style and can be a frustrating style to encounter. This style can be a result of lack of preparedness; here, the negotiator cannot engage with the issues as they are not sufficiently familiar with the facts so they are afraid to agree to anything in case it is inconsistent with their instructions. Alternatively, an avoiding negotiator can simply be someone who is very conflict-adverse so feels uncomfortable in asserting their client's claims. This leaves them feeling reluctant to enter into an agreement that is suggested as they are conscious that they have not contributed to it and, as a result, it may not be something to which their client wanted to agree. If you do encounter an avoiding negotiator, it may take a great deal of patience and skill to draw them into the negotiation and to ensure that they are fully engaged. This will be necessary as there is otherwise a risk that it will not be possible to reach an agreement. Try not to adopt this negotiation style!

- **Accommodating.** With a high level of cooperativeness, this type of negotiator is keen to work towards agreement but there is a risk that their lack of assertiveness will leave them struggling to stand firm or argue for points that are important to their client. The concern here is that they will reach an unfavourable agreement and this will then not be accepted by the client which means that ultimately the negotiation has failed. There is a particular risk if the other side adopts a competing style and pushes hard for terms that the accommodating negotiator feels unable to resist. If your scores put you in this section of the diagram, then try to develop your assertiveness and remember that you are not looking for agreement at any cost but an agreement that reflects your client's interests and is within your instructions. Remember that any concessions must be those that you want to make, not those that are imposed upon you. If the negotiators on both sides are accommodating, the high degree of mutual cooperativeness raises the possibility that a good agreement will be reached provided that one or both negotiators is able to muster sufficient assertiveness to shape the content of the negotiation and ensure that all relevant points are taken into account when working towards a settlement. This can be a useful negotiating style to adopt if you are aware that your client is at fault in some way or otherwise in a weak position, especially if they are keen to avoid litigation.

- **Competing.** Assertiveness is an important part of negotiation as it ensures that the client's interests are highlighted and given due consideration in any agreement that is reached. However, when combined with a lack cooperativeness this can lead the competing negotiator to push too hard towards terms that are favourable to their client at the expense of the other party's interests. This might feel like success but remember that an agreement that gives your client everything that they want is likely to give the other party nothing and so will not be accepted by them. The other danger is the risk of deadlock if both negotiators have a competing style.

- **Collaborating**. A high level of assertiveness combined with a high level of cooperativeness tends to result in a 'win-win' situation in which an agreement is reached that resolves all issues and reflects the key concerns of both parties. This approach can be particularly useful when there is a need for an ongoing relationship between the parties. Collaborating negotiators will work well together and generally their desire to work towards an agreement combined with a sound ability to lead and shape the negotiation means that they will work well with negotiators with different styles. The exception can be the competing negotiator whose lack of cooperativeness may thwart the best efforts of the collaborating negotiator to work towards an agreement.

- **Compromising**. This style is the result of moderate scores on both scales. This may seem like a desirable style: sometimes negotiation is described as 'the art of compromise'. However, this can be misleading. It is often the case that compromise involves a trade-off between the negotiators—'I will give you x if you will give me y'—which can be effective provided that this means that you have made a concession that you want to make in order to gain something more valuable for your client. It can also lead to a 'splitting the difference' approach in which one or both parties settle for less than they want or need in order to reach an agreement. So compromise can be tempting but remember that it is a 'some you win, some you lose' approach and be sure that the things that you 'lose' are not things that really matter to your client.

20.4.2 Conducting the negotiation

It can be tempting, particularly in a competition that has to be completed in a tight time frame, to jump straight into a discussion of the first issue, but this can end up getting quite muddled because each team will have their own issues to discuss. It makes sense to take a few moments at the start of the negotiation to clarify what issues are going to be discussed and in what order. You can then move on to dealing with these issues by a process of fact-finding, questioning, and clarification and then move into the delicate business of seeking an agreed position on each point. If you can create a clear structure and move methodically through the issues then there is every chance that you will complete the negotiation in time and with an agreement on at least some of the points that were important to your client. Each key stage in the negotiation will be explored in the sections that follow.

20.4.2.1 Introductions

It is a matter of good practice to start by introducing yourselves to the other negotiators. Try to make the introductions as natural and unhurried as possible. It can be quite chaotic if four people are all trying to introduce themselves and shake hands at once. It works quite well if one team member introduces themselves and their partner. There is no need to say very much: just your names and the name of the party that you represent will suffice with perhaps a brief indication of the issue.

20.4.2.2 Setting an agenda

As part of your preparation, you will have identified the issues that you want to address during the negotiation. You will need to communicate this to the other side at the outset and find out whether their issues are the same or whether they have some different points that need to be addressed. It will also be useful to decide on the order in which these points will be addressed so establishing an agenda for the negotiation.

It is possible to plan an agenda in advance, setting out the points that you wish to discuss and the order in which you wish to discuss them. This can be quite useful as a way of establishing a structure for the negotiation but this depends on the other side being agreeable to the order that you propose. If there is disagreement about this, it can lead to a 'negotiation within a negotiation' as the agenda itself becomes a contentious issue. This is not a good way to start the negotiation as it can create a tone of conflict rather than collaboration, and dispute at this early stage can lead one team to feel as if they have 'lost' before the discussions have been started.

If you do decide to propose an agenda, be sure to incorporate any additional points that the other team wish to include. If there is a disagreement about the order in which the points are to be discussed, be prepared either to be flexible or to justify your preferences if you wish to stand firm—'there would be no point in us discussing royalties first because our client's instructions on this hinge on whether or not he is able to continue performing in the band so we really do need to explore that first'—as this helps the other team to understand that there is a good reason to take the points in a particular order. This will dispel any concerns that they have that you are being stubborn for the sake of it.

20.4.2.3 Summarizing your position

Exchanging information with the other team is an important aspect of the negotiation. Remember that each team has a version of the same events from a different perspective so sharing information is useful to ensure that both teams have a more complete picture of the dispute.

One way to do this is for one person to summarize their client's position. Some students are reluctant to share information with the other team. They feel that they are 'giving away' their 'secrets' and that this will weaken their position. Try to remember that negotiation is most effective when it is based upon collaboration in which the teams work together to find an outcome that is beneficial for both parties. However that does not mean that you have to set out the entirety of your instructions, especially if there are particular facts that seem to weaken your client's position. Also be conscious that your instructions may stipulate that you should not disclose particular facts or only do so if it is strictly necessary to reach agreement. Any such facts must not be included in your opening summary.

A summary should be succinct. Select your facts carefully and do not overwhelm the other team with unnecessary detail. Can you sum up the gist of the situation and your client's objectives in two or three sentences? If you are listening to a member of the other team provide a summary, try to resist the urge to interrupt to 'correct' any facts that are inconsistent with your client's version. Remember, it is quite natural for two parties to a dispute to view the facts in different ways and, at this early stage, your objective should be to understand the other party's position so listen carefully and make notes if necessary (remembering not to scribble too much—it is important to stay engaged). You can always address any inconsistencies when the summary is complete.

Good negotiation involves interactive communication. This means that it is important that the summary is used as a springboard to establish common understanding and to start discussions. So each team should be given an opportunity to ask questions, to seek clarification, and to add information. It makes sense for the person who offers the summary to conclude with words that invite this type of interaction:

- Is there anything that you would like to add?
- Do you have any questions?
- How does that fit with your understanding of the dispute from your client's perspective?
- Is there anything that's important to your client that I haven't mentioned?

Setting out a summary of your position is a good way of starting the negotiation but it need not be confined to the beginning. There are other ways in which a summary can be a useful stage in negotiations. For example, it may be that discussions are becoming heated in which case taking a moment to summarize what has been agreed thus far can be a good way of emphasizing what progress has been made and seeking to build on it. It is also sometimes the case that discussions lose clarity and it seems as if the teams are talking at cross-purposes. A summary can be a useful way of bringing all the team members to a point of common understanding so that the negotiation can continue in a productive way.

20.4.2.4 Asking questions

The most effective method of eliciting information is to ask questions. If you are unclear about something or you feel that you are struggling to understand something about the other party's position then you should ask questions to gain a better understanding. These fall into two categories: open and closed questions (see Figure 20.10).

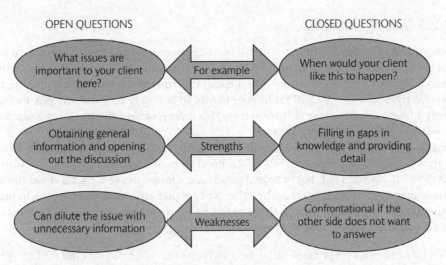

Figure 20.10 Open and closed questions

Remember, in particular, the importance of 'why' questions that provide insight into the motivation of the other team's client. Once you understand why the client wants to achieve a particular objective, you will be better placed to make creative suggestions that fit in with this objective and move the negotiation towards agreement. If the other team does not seem willing to answer 'why' questions then you can put forward possible explanations. For example, you might ask 'is your client refusing to allow my client to use the name of the band because he wants to use it himself?'. The other team will then either have to confirm that this is the case (in which case you can start to work towards resolving the problem) or deny it (at least then you can rule this out as the explanation).

It can be helpful if you identify things that you want to know as part of your preparation for the negotiation. You can think about the most effective way to phrase questions that will elicit this information if it is not volunteered by the other team and set this out in a grid to help you keep track of the information as it is provided. This will also help you to avoid missing anything.

Sometimes you may find that the other team is reluctant to answer questions. This may be because they want to hang on to their 'secrets' or it may be that they have been instructed not to disclose particular information. If you include the reason why you are seeking a particular piece of information as part of your question this will make it harder for the other team to withhold it from you:

- I don't really understand why your client is so determined not to allow my client to continue to perform in the band. Are there some other factors that are important to your client that I need to take into account?

- You don't seem receptive to my client's suggestion about division of future royalties. I thought that this was a very generous proposition so is there some reason that you feel that this would not be attractive to your client?

- I'm surprised that you don't seem to accept that my client is the one entitled to use the band's name. Can you explain your client's position to me to help me understand what the problem is because my client's instructions seem to take this point for granted.

20.4.2.5 Acting ethically

It is important to remember that negotiations are conducted within the parameters of professional practice and, as such, you must act in an ethical manner. This means that you must not misrepresent your position or in any way mislead the other team. Not only must you not do this explicitly, you must be cautious in your choice of language to avoid any possibility that you will mislead the other team inadvertently. This can become problematic if you are asked a question that you do not want to answer.

Imagine that you are representing Jonny in the band negotiation and that your instructions state that he would be prepared to allow the band to perform his song 'Owl' in return for a £1,000 one-off payment but that he would ideally like a far greater sum that is closer to £5,000. You have managed to establish that the other party is prepared to pay something in order to play the song and you are optimistic that you will be able to achieve a good deal for your client. But then you are asked the following question:

- What is the lowest sum of money that we could offer that your client would find acceptable?

How do you respond? The straightforward honest answer is that he would accept £1,000 but you may not wish to disclose that because it has the potential to limit your ability to achieve a better cash sum for him which, after all, is what he has instructed you to do. So it would be unethical to lie but it is also incumbent upon you to act in accordance with your client's instructions and obtain a good settlement for him. So you have to formulate a response that is honest and not in any way misleading otherwise you will be acting in an unethical manner. So you cannot say 'my client will not accept £1,000' but you can say 'I think that it is fair to say that my client was hoping for rather more than £1,000' (be careful, though, not to give the impression that you are saying that £1,000 is unacceptable). Another alternative would be to push the issue back to the other team: 'the question isn't really what the lowest sum is that my client would accept but what it is fair and reasonable for your client to pay him. So what sum did you have in mind as a fair and reasonable amount?'. You may also encounter an even more direct question:

- Would your client accept £1,000?

You know that the answer is 'yes' but you feel that this would prevent you from trying to achieve a greater sum. Perhaps something like 'well that's towards the lower end of what my client would consider. Would your client consider offering more? Let's not forget that 'Owl' is the band's most popular song so it would be beneficial for your client if the band were able to continue to play it. Surely that is worth more than £1,000 to your client?'.

20.4.2.6 Avoiding deadlock

Deadlock occurs if the parties want something that is incompatible and there is no scope to make movement towards each other. This may be that they both want the same thing (for example, if Jonny and Jo-Jo both want the right to exclusive use of the band name) or if one party wants something that the other is not prepared to provide (perhaps Jonny wants to receive a £10,000 payment to allow the band to perform the song 'Owl' but Jo-Jo is not prepared to make any payment whatsoever).

The most effective strategy to avoid deadlock is to steer clear of creating 'take it or leave it' positions. If you allow the other team no room for movement, there is no option other than deadlock if they are not willing or able to agree to your requirements. Moreover, backing the other team into a corner is quite an aggressive strategy that is likely to be viewed as bad negotiation practice: you are supposed to be reaching a mutually agreeable position, not imposing your will upon the other team. However, if a deadlock does arise, there are a number of ways that you can try to work around it:

- **Highlight concessions.** This is an assertive way to apply reasonable pressure to the other team to demonstrate flexibility. Negotiation should never be overtly aggressive but it should not be too passive either otherwise there is a risk that you will not achieve a sufficiently favourable settlement for your client. Emphasizing the concessions that you have already made is a way to highlight areas where you have been reasonable and accommodating in order to seek a reciprocal level of cooperation from the other team. For example: 'I understand that the issue of the band's name is important to your client but it will help us to reach agreement if you can be flexible here. After all, we moved from an original position of seeking 50 per cent of the royalties to accepting your suggestion of 25 per cent which is a considerable difference in favour of your client'.

- **Take a break.** It is often the case that the rules of a negotiation competition allow the teams to take a short break in which the negotiation stops and the teams step outside the room to converse in private. This can be useful in a number of situations including breaking deadlock especially if relations between the teams have become fraught and angry. It also gives the teams space for a private discussion in which to look for a way to break the deadlock. Remember to cast emotions aside during the break and come back to the negotiation in a calm and professional manner.

- **Find creative solutions.** Remember the importance of 'why' questions. When you understand why the other team's client wants something, you may be able to find an alternative way to help them to achieve it. For example: 'so both of our clients want to perform using the name "Persimmon for Gaia". Could we agree that neither of them uses it but that they both use something similar? Perhaps something as straightforward as "Jonny from Persimmon for Gaia" and "Jo-Jo from Persimmon for Gaia"'. Even if this does not work, at least you have demonstrated your commitment to working towards agreement and your creativity in doing so. Remember that any creative suggestions need to be within the spirit of your instructions. There is no point in finding a solution that would not be acceptable to your client.

If none of these strategies are effective in breaking the deadlock, try to keep the negotiation moving by parking it temporarily and moving on to a different issue. It can be the case that once other issues are agreed, the contentious issue becomes easier to resolve:

- It seems as if we're struggling to find common ground on this issue of the band's name. Can we leave this for now and look at some of the other issues—perhaps we could try and settle the division of royalties—and see if we can find agreement on those points?

- We seem to have reached stalemate on this point. I appreciate that use of the band's name is important to both our clients but we do have other points to consider. I'm going to suggest that we move on to consider the division of royalties—if we can sort out the financial issues perhaps that will help us to see how to resolve the matter of the band's name.

Even if you do not manage to break the deadlock after the other points have been agreed, at least you were able to move the negotiation on and reach agreement on some issues. Remember that it is important that you do not agree something that is incompatible with your instructions just for the sake of agreeing on all points. It is sometimes the case that the creators of negotiation scenarios put in issues that cannot be agreed to see how the teams deal with them. Keep your instructions in mind at all times to ensure that you stay within them and remember that it is better to walk away without reaching agreement than it is to agree something that is unacceptable to your client.

20.4.2.7 Closing the negotiation

It can be tempting, when the clock is ticking, to keep on discussing points and seeking agreement right to the last minute available but that creates a risk that the end of the negotiation will be hurried and the teams may lose sight of what has been agreed. It is important to build in time to spend a few minutes at the end clarifying the terms that have been agreed. The whole negotiation would become rather pointless if one or both teams were not clear about what proposed settlement they were taking back to their clients. It is important to have a firm and effective end to the negotiation in which everybody is clear about the terms of the agreement. It can be useful to work back through the agenda to ensure that all points have been addressed and to note what has been agreed on each issue. It may be that agreement was not possible on all points and further consultation with the clients is needed in which case this should also be highlighted at the close of the negotiation. Remember that the agreement that you have reached is subject to your client's agreement so be sure to reflect this in your closing comments.

20.5 DYNAMICS OF MULTI-PARTY NEGOTIATIONS

The final point to consider as this chapter draws to a close is the way in which the process of negotiation differs if it involves more than two parties. In many respects, the core skills involved in a negotiation remain constant irrespective of the number of parties involved: you still prepare to represent your client's interests with only a partial understanding of the dispute so the same process of preparation before and fact-finding during the negotiation is involved. There is, however, a critical difference when more than two parties are involved in a negotiation and that is the way that the presence of an additional interest changes the dynamics of the process of negotiation.

Imagine, for example, that a third band member, Kurt, is also a party to the band negotiations and is represented by a third team of negotiators. On each issue, there are a number of possibilities:

- Kurt will have no interest in the issue and the teams representing Jonny and Jo-Jo can agree the issue between them. For example, it may be that Kurt does not care who owns the rights to the use of the name Persimmon for Gaia. That does not mean that the team representing Kurt should play no role in the discussion on this issue. Perhaps listening will give you an insight into how other issues are likely to be argued or it may be possible to intervene to assist the parties to reach an agreement as a temporarily neutral party.

- Kurt will have an interest in common with your client that will strengthen Jonny's case. For instance, if Kurt and Jonny both want the band to continue to perform together then it may be harder for Jo-Jo to go against this so joining forces will help you to achieve Jonny's objective on this point. However, remember that you are still representing your own client so be alert for any points in any agreement suggested by the team representing Kurt to ensure that they are consistent with your client's interests.

- Kurt may have an interest that brings him into conflict with Jonny. Perhaps Jo-Jo has something that both Jonny and Kurt want—the profits from merchandising, for example—so each party will be vying to gain an agreement that favours their client.

- Kurt may be in disagreement with both Jonny and Jo-Jo so that there are three different interests in competition with each other. This makes it harder to find agreement as it is no longer the relatively straightforward matter that what one party concedes, the other party gains.

Negotiation management becomes even more important when there are more than two parties as there is the potential for alliances to be forged and that can alter the dynamics of the negotiation. It is also easy for a team that is not sufficiently assertive to lose their role in the negotiations as other more assertive negotiators take control of the discussions. In such situations, it is imperative to find a way back in otherwise your client's voice will not be heard and his interests will not be considered in any agreement that is reached.

 ## CHAPTER SUMMARY

Planning and preparation

- Analyse the negotiation scenario to ensure that you have a clear grasp of the issues that need to be resolved
- Use the strategies outlined in this chapter to assess the strength of your position. Work out the scope of movement in relation to each issue and consider how the issues can be used in conjunction to strengthen your bargaining power
- Research the relevant law and the facts to ensure that you have a thorough grasp of the key information
- Take a holistic view of your client's aims and think of creative ways to achieve these objectives within the spirit of your instructions

Conducting the negotiation

- Make a firm professional start with clear introductions, a summary of the factual situation, and a suggested agenda. Be prepared to amend your proposed agenda to reflect the requirements of the other team

- Remember that you only know half the story, so take time to find out about the issues that concern the other team and fill in the gaps of your factual knowledge

- Elicit information by asking questions. Remember that 'why' questions give insight into the aims of the other team's client and this may enable you to propose creative solutions that facilitate agreement

- A skilled negotiator will try and work around obstacles rather than stopping when confronted with them so try to use a range of different strategies to avoid or break deadlock

- It is important to evolve a strategy that enables you to work as a team and to form an effective working relationship with the other team so think about your own negotiation style and how it relates to other styles

- Ensure that you are always ethical in your dealings with the other team, taking care not to mislead them or misrepresent your position

- Conclude by outlining the proposed agreement to ensure that everyone is clear on its terms

INDEX